The Official® Price Guide to

OLD
BOOKS

The Official® Price Guide to

OLD
BOOKS

Marie Tedford
and
Pat Goudey

SECOND EDITION
House of Collectibles • *New York*

Important Notice. All of the information, including valuations, in this book has been compiled from the most reliable sources, and every effort has been made to eliminate errors and questionable data. Nevertheless, the possibility of error, in a work of such immense scope, always exists. The publisher will not be held responsible for losses that may occur in the purchase, sale, or other transaction of items because of information contained herein. Readers who feel they have discovered errors are invited to *write* and inform us, so the errors may be corrected in subsequent editions. Those seeking further information on the topics covered in this book are advised to refer to the complete line of *Official Price Guides* published by the House of Collectibles.

This is a registered trademark of Random House, Inc.

Published by: House of Collectibles
201 East 50th Street
New York, NY 10022

Distributed by Ballantine Books, a division of Random House, Inc., New York, and simultaneously in Canada by Random House of Canada Limited, Toronto.

Grateful acknowledgment is made to Peter Fraser & Dunlop Group Ltd. for permission to reprint an excerpt from THE BAD CHILD'S BOOK OF BEASTS by Hilaire Belloc, first published by Gerald Duckworth & Co. Copyright © The Estate of Hilaire Belloc.

Manufactured in the United States of America

ISSN: 1073-8614

ISBN: 0-676-60041-7

Text design by Holly Johnson
Cover design by Kristine V. Mills-Noble
Cover photo © George Kerrigan

Second Edition: June 1997

10   9   8   7   6   5   4   3   2   1

CONTENTS

Acknowledgments   ix
Introduction to the Second Edition   xi
Market Review   3
A Closer Look at the Book Trade   6
Children's Books   18
The Care and Repair of Old Books   24
How to Use This Book   31
Glossary   34
Abbreviations   72
Old Books Listing   75
Bibles Listing   360
Dealers   366
Recommended Periodicals and Research Sources   370

ACKNOWLEDGMENTS

Our thanks to the many booksellers who responded to our request for catalogs, and to Swann Galleries, Sotheby's, California Book Auction, Pacific Book Auction Galleries, and Kane Antiquarian Auction, who supplied us with information for the market review. Their invaluable assistance helped us make this book a useful tool to both bookseller and collector.

We thank the Vermont Antiquarian Booksellers, who allowed us to photograph booths at the Pomfret Book Show; and thanks to photographer Ilan Fisher of Sharon, Massachusetts, for taking those pictures. Our gratitude goes, also, to Alan and Mary Culpin, booksellers from Austin, Texas, and Boulder, Colorado; Stephen Smith of Fair Haven, Vermont; Cattermole Books of Newberry, Ohio; Monroe Street Books of Middlebury, Vermont; Roger and Joan Bassett, booksellers of Fullerton, Nebraska; Barbara B. Harris Books of Guilford, New Hampshire; and especially Donna Howard at The Eloquent Page in St. Albans, Vermont, whose expertise helped us put together the chapter on children's books.

Thanks to Lief Laudamus of Leyden, Massachusetts, who helped us put Bibles into perspective.

INTRODUCTION TO THE SECOND EDITION

Over the past twenty years or so, interest in antiquarian books has grown dramatically. The antiquarian book market has always been brisk and steady, but it was a somewhat esoteric interest—well known to those who participated, all but invisible to those who didn't. Not so now, as a new century nears.

Newcomers to the field have swelled the ranks of collectors and dealers alike. And the general public is becoming more aware of rare and collectible books as valuable items of trade and investment. Perhaps more people can afford to buy collectible books, or perhaps the mania for collecting everything from advertising posters to Disneyana has spilled over into books.

Whatever the reason, heightened interest is propelling ever greater numbers of dealers and collectors into the field to search out those unique volumes to round out a collection, or to present to the public for sale.

This book is designed to help in that search. No one research volume can contain all the information an antiquarian book dealer or collector will need. The literature available on the market includes many fine references for publication and price data. Cross-checking information on a book found in more than one reference will help you to be sure you've got the best price and accurate statistics. And searching through multiple references can net you information on a book that's hard to find, but valuable.

For this edition, we've combed our listings, updated prices, provided additional publication information, and added many new volumes. We've also written a chapter on children's books—especially series—and added a discussion on Bibles. We suggest you use the information we provide and also consult many other sources, the best of which we've listed at the back of this book.

We want this book to do more than tell you the going rate for a particular title. Books are much more than a commodity with a price tag. As always, our intention is to inform you, pique your interest, and even entertain you a bit, because we think the best reason for developing an interest in books is still the sheer fun of it.

The Official® Price Guide to

OLD
BOOKS

MARKET REVIEW

True to form, the collectible book market is enjoying a period of steady prosperity in the mid-1990s. Prices have fluctuated some as the shaky economy of the early part of the decade leveled off in 1996. A careful comparison of prices in this edition to those in the first edition will reveal more ups than downs. Most of the downturns, however, reflect increasing interest in certain genres or the passing of a fad (especially where modern first editions are concerned).

More than one dealer told us the customer base is growing in areas like women's issues and children's books, not to mention an upsurge in interest for science fiction and an unfailing market for maps and atlases.

Auctioneers, especially, report good customer response to sales over the past two years. Swann Galleries, Inc., in New York, held a sale devoted to modern literature in June 1995, including a first American edition of J.R.R. Tolkien's *The Hobbit* in a dust jacket (Bos. 1938) that realized $2,185. Raymond Chandler's *The Big Sleep* (NY. 1939) was sold for $2,300, and a first edition of Harper Lee's *To Kill a Mockingbird* (Phila. 1960) brought $977.

Swann was delighted with the results of an auction devoted entirely to African-Americana in March 1996 that included excellent attendance and coverage in the national media. Offered for sale was an original autobiographical manuscript written in Arabic in 1831 by slave author and scholar Omar Ibn Said. It sold for $21,850. Two autograph pages from a speech delivered by the controversial John Brown in 1857 sold for $12,650. A first printing of Harriet Beecher Stowe's *Uncle Tom's Cabin* (Bos. 1852) went for $2,990, and an 1802 letter from Napoleon issuing orders for the subjugation of Haiti realized $3,450.

Based on the success of that event, the gallery scheduled a second African-Americana auction for February of this year to coincide with Black History Month, and expects to make the sale an annual event.

"This is undoubtedly a growing field," writes Caroline Birenbaum, Director of Communications for Swann Galleries. Time to get in on the beginning of a growing specialty?

Another market on the rise, reported by Swann Galleries, is photographic literature. In an auction on February 29, 1996, the Steiglitz issue of *Camera Work*, New York, 1911, went for $10,350; the first Strand issue, New York, 1916, went for $4,600, among a host of other well sought-after items.

Sotheby's in New York reported excellent sales for the '95–'96 season, as well, including participation in the sale of the Jacqueline Kennedy Onassis estate in April 1996. The season sales total topped $21,000,000, the best year in this decade.

One notable item that realized an excellent price (a record breaker, actually) was the *Prague Haggadah*, printed in 1526, that sold for $277,500, nearly three times the highest pre-sale estimate. Sotheby's reports that they'd been advised their estimates were high, but apparently strong collector interest in fine and rare works is even higher. Sotheby's has the distinction of being the only house to have offered copies of this famous Hebrew printed book at auction since World War II. Sotheby's has auctioned three copies since 1970.

A sale in December 1995 devoted to the ever-strong and stable Americana market netted Sotheby's $2,655,000, with items like a first edition of *The Articles of Confederation*, Lancaster, 1777, and a copy of Henry Pelham's aquatint map, *Plan of Boston*, signed by the engraver, netting twice their pre-sale estimates.

Kurt Zimmerman at California Book Auction told us the house does well with Western Americana, and the ever-popular maps and atlases. He said interest in fine press books has slowed some, but modern literature remains strong.

Paul Jung of Kane Antiquarian Auctions in Pottstown, Pennsylvania, said illustrated books are a tried and true item, with artists like Maxfield Parrish, Rackham, and Wyeth remaining popular.

He said some members of the Brandywine school have fallen off lately, except for Lyendecker, who remains in demand. Lyendecker illustrated advertising, too, and perhaps the crossover collectors are maintaining his saleability, as Jung suggested. He said Marguerite DeAngeli, a Philadelphia illustrator of Amish and Germanic themes, is popular in his region. And series books like Zane Gray and the Baum books on Oz are constant strong sellers. Even reprints of some of these latter books move well, he said. People are paying $50 or $60 for the Grosset & Dunlap reprints, especially if they have good illustrations and clean dust jackets.

Other dealers report that interest is rising in the field of law, especially histories and bibliographies of law. Collectors of law materials are spurring dealers to search out and stock more of these books.

Science fiction and fantasy are on the rise, spurred again by marketplace demand. As the demand grows, research and cataloging by dealers is supplying information on the books, with scholarship in these genres beginning to grow, as well.

A CLOSER LOOK AT THE BOOK TRADE

Thou are the book, the library
Where I look.
—HENRY KING, BISHOP OF CHICHESTER

Whenever we mention that we're used and rare book dealers, we're met with a host of questions about books people have tucked away in an attic or closet. We suspect the world contains many would-be bookmen needing only a nudge to get them started. Below, we'll offer the nudge, try to dispel some of the mystery surrounding old books, and answer some questions we're often asked.

WHAT IS OLD IN OLD BOOKS?

This seems like a reasonable question, but instead of thinking in terms of "old," consider your books used, out of print, or rare. These descriptions apply to collectible books of all ages.

Instead of thinking in terms of age, think about content: What is the book about and who wrote it? If you must choose between two books in good condition, one printed in London in 1632 by an obscure British poet, and the other a nineteenth-century tome on the American Indian published in New York, choose the one on the

American Indian. There's a lively market for Native Americana, and you'll likely find a customer for the book. The poetry is merely fun to have on the shelf because it's old. It isn't automatically a collector's item.

We don't think anybody knows what the cut-off date is for "antiquarian" books. Is it the nineteenth century? Early twentieth? Unless you are a rare book dealer focusing on the earliest printed material—incunabula, for example, or the first printed books in the New World—put actual age out of your mind and learn which books are sought by dealers and other collectors. You'll discover a busy trade in books from past centuries and books from last year—from the antiquarian to the modern first editions.

WHERE WILL I FIND GOOD BOOKS?

The first source that comes to mind is the dealer in antiquarian and collectible books. For many genres, used book stores will yield exactly what you're after, often at bargain prices. Throw in a little conversation with the bookseller, and you've found your book and learned something about your subject, too. Bought from a reputable dealer, the book comes prescreened, and you won't have to do further research to verify your find.

Booksellers consider other dealers a prime source of good stock. You can buy direct from dealers through bookstores, dealer catalogs, advertisements, and industry periodicals, and at book fairs. As a beginner, attend the smaller regional fairs and shows that are popular all over the country. They're an education unto themselves.

Other excellent sources are flea markets, estate sales, auctions, the Salvation Army, antique stores, and garage sales. These are the places that professionals go to find books.

HOW GOOD ARE AUCTIONS FOR BUYING AND SELLING BOOKS?

Books at local auctions are plentiful and they're a fine source of collectibles, but you can't be sure of picking up a bargain any longer. In too many cases, except perhaps at the larger, more exclusive

At the Vermont Antiquarian Booksellers' Fair in Pomfret, Vermont. Photo by Ilan Fisher.

rare book and collectible houses, the popularity of auctions has brought with it a kind of recreational bidder. In the heat of competition for an item, bidding may drive the price much higher than a careful buyer would be willing to pay in a bookstore or in a private transaction.

Great books can still be had for excellent prices if buyers exercise caution, know how much they are willing to pay ahead of time, and sit on their hands when the bidding gets rowdy.

If you're selling books, auctions and dealers are on a par, each having their strong and weak points. On a particular day, if an auction attracts a spirited audience, you could do well. On an off day, you risk your books selling for less than you'd hoped. Selling through dealers requires more of your time and effort, but dealers have pipelines to collectors who may be looking for just the book you're selling.

In the final analysis, we can only tell you what is available. You must choose what's right for you.

A charming copy of Kate Greenaway's Almanack from 1888, *held in the Bailey-Howe Library Special Collections at the University of Vermont, was printed by George Routledge & Sons, Great Britain.*

WHAT BOOKS SHOULD I PICK UP?

There's no one answer to this question. Before you ask it, you have some decisions to make, and then the question will begin to answer itself. Are you buying books for investment or fun? Are you a collector? A dealer? Will you specialize or be a generalist?

Carefully bought collectible books hold their value well and grow in value at a steady rate of up to 10 percent per year. They're a safe investment, but with rare exceptions, they're not speculative and won't make you a killing.

As an example of the quality of investment, consider the sale of the Raymond Epstein collection, placed on the block at Swann Auction Galleries in April, 1992. Mr. Epstein had carefully recorded the purchase prices of his books, which were maintained in excellent condition, providing a fine opportunity to compare market price

Ever popular, The Compleat Angler *(sometimes spelled Complete Angler), by Izaac Walton (sometimes spelled Isaac Walton), in several incarnations, along with other books of the genre, are held in Special Collections at the University of Vermont's Bailey-Howe Library. Shown are (l. to r.) Izaak Walton and Charles Cotton,* The Complete Angler, *William Pickering, London, 1836; John Williamson,* The British Angler, *or a Pocket Companion for Gentlemen Fishers, 1740; Walton and Cotton,* The Complete Angler, *London, 1824; and Izaak Walton,* The Complete Angler, *illustrated by E. J. Sullivan, J. M. Dent Co., London, 1896.*

THE

PERSONAL NARRATIVE

John B. C. Wilson

OF *April 28th 1832.*

JAMES O. PATTIE,

OF

KENTUCKY,

DURING AN EXPEDITION FROM ST. LOUIS, THROUGH THE VAST REGIONS
BETWEEN THAT PLACE AND THE PACIFIC OCEAN, AND THENCE BACK
THROUGH THE CITY OF MEXICO TO VERA CRUZ, DURING JOURNEY-
INGS OF SIX YEARS; IN WHICH HE AND HIS FATHER, WHO
ACCOMPANIED HIM, SUFFERED UNHEARD OF HARDSHIPS
AND DANGERS, HAD VARIOUS CONFLICTS WITH THE IN-
DIANS, AND WERE MADE CAPTIVES, IN WHICH
CAPTIVITY HIS FATHER DIED; TOGETHER
WITH A DESCRIPTION OF THE COUNTRY,
AND THE VARIOUS NATIONS THROUGH
WHICH THEY PASSED.

EDITED BY TIMOTHY FLINT.

CINCINNATI:
PRINTED AND PUBLISHED BY JOHN H. WOOD,
1831.

Overland journey narratives (as this type of book is known to collectors) are always in demand, and the early ones—such as Pattie's—can go for really prodigious prices. In this case a well-preserved specimen would run about $10,000.

over an approximately thirty-year period. A copy of *Dracula* bought in 1965 for $46 was maintained in a specially made case costing $38. The book realized $11,000 at auction in 1992. A copy of *Ulysses* bought for $400 in 1965 and maintained in a $350 case sold for $19,800. Mr. Epstein acquired *Tom Sawyer* in 1966 for $1,250 and it sold for $9,350. An $885 *The Wizard of Oz* acquired in 1972 sold for $20,900.

Clear evidence that careful collecting is a solid investment. Still, often as not, even those who collect for investment become excited by the hunt and end up collecting for fun, too.

If you decide to specialize, whether as bookseller or collector, learn all you can about your subject. Don't neglect allied subjects that broaden and flesh out your knowledge. Visit bookstores, talk to dealers, read dealer catalogs to see what's being offered and what someone else wants. Visit libraries.

Michael Ginsberg, a bookseller from Massachusetts and past president of the Antiquarian Booksellers Association of America (ABAA), told us he likes to read the bibliographies in books related to his specialty to discover other books to read and some he might want to collect or resell.

CATEGORIES, OR ANA

When you get more involved as a dealer or collector, you'll become familiar with references to the common genres and specialties, sometimes called "ana" (see the glossary). These will include topics like the settling of the Americas, native peoples, black studies, maritime trades, foreign countries, children's books, medicine, science, sporting books, zoology, anthropology, magic, antiques, the military, cooking, poetry, railroads, billiards, the radical labor movement, and on and on. Add to that limited editions, fine presses, fine bindings, illustrated books—the list doesn't end. And each genre has subgenres, ad infinitum.

These categories help dealers and collectors communicate. Dealers use them to describe their specialties and collectors use them to define their areas of interest. But genres are not mutually exclusive; there's enormous overlapping, and they are just one tool for evaluating books.

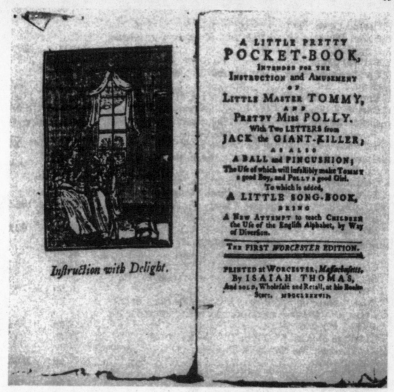

Instruction with Delight.

A LITTLE PRETTY
POCKET-BOOK,
INTENDED FOR THE
INSTRUCTION and AMUSEMENT
OF
LITTLE MASTER TOMMY,
AND
PRETTY MISS POLLY.
With Two LETTERS from
JACK the GIANT-KILLER;
AS ALSO
A BALL and PINCUSHION;
The Use of which will infallibly make TOMMY
a good Boy, and POLLY a good Girl.
To which is added,
A LITTLE SONG-BOOK,
BEING
A NEW ATTEMPT to teach CHILDREN
the Use of the English Alphabet, by Way
of Diversion.

THE FIRST *WORCESTER* EDITION.

PRINTED at WORCESTER, *Massachusetts*,
By ISAIAH THOMAS,
And SOLD, Wholesale and Retail, at his Book
Store. MDCCLXXXVII.

This charming little children's book would be a highly desirable collector's item even if it carried a foreign imprint. But as it was printed in Worcester, Massachusetts, by the very celebrated Isaiah Thomas, it carries far greater impact. Thomas was not only a printer/publisher but a pioneer antiquary who preserved many relics of the local New England history. No author is verified for this book.

AMERICANA VERSUS US-IANA

A very popular specialty is Americana, but what do bookmen mean by the term? Do they refer to books on the discovery, exploration, and political and cultural development of the United States alone? Or do they adopt the broader and truer meaning of the term and include all the Americas, from Canada to Argentina?

In modern vernacular, the meaning of Americana has narrowed to refer to the United States and its territories, though some dealers use it in the more inclusive form. To be technically correct when referring to the United States, the term US-iana was coined by bibliographer Wright Howes, author of *Howes USIANA*, issued in 1954, but that term is less widely used.

WHAT ABOUT CONDITION?

This is probably the most important judgment you will make about a book you're buying or selling. Depending on its condition, a book can be a collector's item or just a nice book to read. We often see the same look of perplexity on the faces of people not in the trade when we reject the old book in their hand. "But it's old!"

No matter.

Unless the book is an Eliot Bible, or another great rarity, it must be in good condition—bindings attached, pages all there, illustrations accounted for, no underlining, no tears, and clean covers. If the book was issued with a dust jacket, the jacket must be present and in good condition, especially for modern first editions. The absence of the jacket radically reduces the value.

Sounds cranky, doesn't it? Yet we can't stress enough the importance of condition in collectible books. But don't throw away that intact book in less than good condition. Scholars, researchers, and recreational readers are another market for inexpensive reading copies.

HOW IMPORTANT ARE FIRST EDITIONS?

Rare book collectors want first editions because they reflect the first time these particular words of an author appeared in print. They are perceived to be closest to the author's true intent. Also, as further editions are issued, the supply of books is increased, thereby diminishing the value of succeeding editions. But relative scarcity of firsts remains constant.

As often as not, collectors don't read their first editions, but buy them in order to enjoy the possession of something rare and special, something others don't have. Scholars and readers will pay a price for later editions, but it will be a mere shadow of the price paid for a first edition.

Now, after having said that, let us confuse you further. Popular titles are often reissued in limited editions. Printed on high-quality papers, with fine bindings and slipcases, these commonly include illustrations by noted artists. Limited editions may command higher prices than first editions, since most are numbered and signed by the author, the artist, or both.

WHAT'S THE STORY ON MODERN FIRST EDITIONS?

If any area of book collecting is in danger of falling victim to fads, this is it. Modern first editions attest to the fact that a book can be published in the past year or two and already have a collectible price affixed, which nullifies the idea that age determines price.

Sue Grafton's crime novels have been popular with collectors of modern first editions over the past few years. Her first book, *"A" Is for Alibi*, published in 1982, has been offered at prices ranging from $150 to $1000 depending on which catalog you're looking at. But auctioneers and dealers report that Grafton's books, especially those farther down the alphabet, haven't been leaving the bookshelves as quickly as they once did. Writers like John Galsworthy, once a popularly collected author, get scant attention from today's collectors. Whether Grafton and other currently popular writers like Tom Clancy, John Grisham, Anne Tyler, and Anne Rice will have staying power as collectibles remains to be seen.

Those authors who move into the literature category have the best chance, says Paul Jung, auctioneer and cataloger for Kane Antiquarian Auctions of Pottstown, Pennsylvania. Collectors buy literary modern firsts and put them aside, hoping the authors will be studied.

"The standbys are always there, Hemingway, Faulkner, Steinbeck," he says. "They're always collected. They're studied in school."

And then there are cases like the first edition of Raymond

Chandler's 1939 mystery, *The Big Sleep*. In a near-perfect dust jacket, it sold for $7,150 in 1992, more than twice what experts had estimated it would bring in. By 1996, experts were setting the price closer to $5,000. Even after all these years, the price fluctuates. Considered a classic in the genre for its era, *The Big Sleep* was dramatized in a movie starring Humphrey Bogart. Was it exposure that brought the price up and kept it there? What really sets the pace for what a book is worth? We suspect that whimsy has a lot to do with it.

This is the way it is with modern first editions. Either the books become classics, part of the popular culture—most notably, these days, through movies—or they are recognized as literature and are studied in the classroom, and their value remains high. Or they pass into oblivion and are relegated to the penny box.

Percy Muir has a wonderful discussion on the subject in his delightful publication *Book Collecting as a Hobby*. He says that when a contemporary author is "hot" the demand for first editions will drive up the price. When the demand is satisfied, prices decline. If the author's work has lasting substance, collectors will rediscover him or her and prices will rise again.

Muir cautions, "Never, never collect an author when he is in the height of fashion." He advises anticipating who will be the next to rise, if you can, or waiting until authors have weathered the test of time.

The bottom line is, take care in buying and pricing. Watch trends, understand them, plan for them, but don't be swept up in them.

HOW DO I PRICE A BOOK?

The plain truth is, there is no one right price for a used book. It's all subjective. The law of supply and demand is in play. During flush times, prices and sales soar, and in a lagging economy, they come back down. Market correction.

With a book in your hand, you'll do the research and then settle on a number. In the end, the value of a book is only what you or your customer is willing to pay. You will notice that for some books we've listed, the price range is narrow. According to our sources, including dealers' pricing and auction records, folks agree on the current value of those books. For others, the range is hundreds or even thousands of dollars. These are actual prices people have asked for and paid. They reflect differing opinions from one dealer to another, or from one part of the country to another. Such disparities are common.

We've listed some titles more than once to show the difference in price between, for instance, trade and limited editions, the first edition and a later edition, a first edition with dust jacket and one without, or a signed copy and an unsigned one. We've assigned our prices assuming very good to fine condition, with the rare exception noted. Where you don't find the actual title you're after, but we list other titles by the same author, you've verified the author as important if not collectible. You have more research to do, however, before you can price the book in your hand. Some authors have many titles to their credit, not all prized. The whole subject is fraught with cautions.

Talk to people in the business, consult price guides and dealer catalogs, visit antiquarian bookstores. Learn as much as you can and then learn some more.

Pricing stock for a shop begins when you buy the books. Will your initial investment be tied up for months or a year, or do you have a ready customer for the book? Do you have a shop with over- head costs or do you mail-order?

As dealers, when we know exactly what book we're looking for, the quickest way to find it is through other professionals. That means we dealers often buy from each other and the price goes up as a book passes from hand to hand before it ever reaches the public. How many times can that happen?

You must make these judgments based upon your growing knowledge of the business. In the end, you're bound to make some mistakes. It's that kind of business.

CHILDREN'S BOOKS

Child! do not throw this book about;
Refrain from the unholy pleasure
Of cutting all the pictures out!
Preserve it as your choicest treasure.
—HILAIRE BELLOC,
A BAD CHILD'S BOOK OF BEASTS.

In recent years, one category of old book collecting has attracted increasing interest from both the seasoned collector and the newcomer—children's books. Each year, prices rise, but they don't put a damper on collectors' appetites for their coveted treasures. Perhaps nostalgia motivates this interest, and a willingness to pay more, much as people's fondness for old toys is playing havoc with those collectibles' prices. Or maybe mothers and grandmothers are looking for the books that delighted them as children to pass on to their own kids.

Whatever the motivation for collecting, the desirable classic authors—Carroll, Milne, Potter, Wiggin, Burgess, and others too numerous to mention—take the lion's share of the market, but books in series like the Hardy Boys and Nancy Drew are back in circulation and enjoying a renaissance.

Unlike collectors who covet the first edition, collectors of series books don't always consider it important, says Stephen Smith of Fair Haven, Vermont. And, besides, determining a first edition series book isn't so easy. The copyright page tells you little about which edition you're holding. In the series milieu, content is king because most collectors are baby boomers who read these books as children and want to read them again. To the hard-core collector, however, all the points are important—dust jacket, first edition, very good condition, rarity—and that applies to the series books as well.

"Without a doubt, Nancy Drew, the Hardy Boys, and Tom Swift are the most popular and best known of the children's series," Joan Bassett of Antiquarian and Collector Books in Fullerton, Nebraska, told us. "Some of these series in dust jackets are extremely scarce and valued at hundreds of dollars. Often the last title in the series, with picture board covers, is the most valuable," she added, and this piqued our interest, since we are conditioned to think in terms of first editions.

We consulted Donna Howard at The Eloquent Page in St. Albans, Vermont, and she tried to explain. First, children's series books can be known by their titles and by their place in the series, which is their number. "In the children's series, often, though not always, the last number or the last few numbers are considerably more expensive than earlier numbers," Donna said. Taking the Cherry Ames books as an example, she said that the pictureboard book sells for $7.50, $12.50, or $15. The last title in the series, *Ski Nurse*, #27, sells for $100 to $150, if you can find it. This is because fewer books were published later in the series. As each new book in a series is produced, more copies of earlier titles are printed to meet a continuing demand. The result, she said, is that "the last numbers are usually printed once as the series goes out of print, therefore fewer copies are available to collectors and dealers." When publishers detect a slump in readership, too, they tend to publish smaller numbers of books or terminate publishing altogether. Donna commented, "You have the traditional mode of supply and demand working the marketplace."

The higher-number rule doesn't apply to all the series books, however. Those popular Hardy Boys and Nancy Drew books, most notably, have ongoing publication and follow the standard rule: the earlier the edition, the better.

Cattermole Books in Newberry, Ohio, doesn't deal in series books for children, but says the trade in classic children's books is great. Collectors are searching for illustrators whose drawings tickle their fancy or permit their imagination to re-create other worlds.

Valuable and collectible children's books are out there if you know what to look for, says Dick Chodkowski of Monroe Street Books in Middlebury, Vermont, and condition is most important. We know that children can read a book to death, but finding that well-loved book in very good condition is what renders it collectible. Dick cautions that some flaws are acceptable, such as cover wear or an owner's signature on a flyleaf; even a dust jacket can be missing, but a collector draws the line at books that are falling apart or have torn and scribbled pages.

Remember, too, the Middlebury bookseller advises, don't spurn a reprint, especially one in good condition. Unlike a reprint of a modern first edition, juvenile reprints hold a higher percentage of their value. Clean, crisp books with clean dust jackets sell fast and best. And prices can be considerable. Beginners in the children's category are amazed at how a dust jacket can add to the price of a book.

The mid-1930s through the 1950s were the true golden age of children's books in America. There's also strong interest in World War I air combat series like Al Avery, R. Sidney Bowen, and Eustace Adams. Older series like Ruth Fielding and Rover Boys, Motor Cycle Boys, and Boy Scouts seem to be increasing in interest and value.

The Bunny Brown, Bobbsey Twins, and Honey Bunch series are popular. Some of the less well known series like Six Little Bunkers and Curly Tops could be good items to pick up now, especially dust-jacketed copies.

Overall, booksellers give the children's market an A+. Old-favorite illustrators like Wyeth and Parrish still excite the buying public. In the series category, Tom Swift is right up there. The time-honored Oz books always command high figures.

Monroe Street Books offers these top post-1930s first edition titles:

1. *Little Black Sambo* by Helen Bannerman. This book is becoming scarce.

2. *Eloise* by Kay Thompson, illustrated by Hillary Knight. The 1955 first edition in a dust jacket is valued at over $100.

Children's books on display at the Vermont Antiquarian Booksellers Fair in Pomfret, Vermont, in the booth of Ray and Jean Kulp, of Hatfield, Pennsylvania. Photo by Ilan Fisher.

3. *Elves and Fairies* by Jane Werner, illustrated by Garth Williams. This Golden Book in nice condition can sell for $200.

4. *The Cat in the Hat* by Dr. Seuss. A word of caution: Dr. Seuss's first editions can be difficult to identify.

5. *Little House on the Prairie* by Laura Ingalls Wilder. A winner with many children, and now with their grandparents and parents, who grew up on the books and reruns of the television series.

6. *Where the Wild Things Are* and *In the Night Kitchen* by Maurice Sendak. Sendak's early illustrated books are hard to identify in first editions, but he is worth every bit of trouble it takes to ferret him out.

7. *Madeline* by Ludwig Bemelmans. This delightful book and the other Madeline books can cost between $100 and $200 each in dust jackets.

8. Newbery Medal titles. First editions of the books awarded this coveted prize are always desirable.

9. Caldecott Medal titles. Same as the Newbery titles. For further information, consult *Horn Book Magazine*.

10. And no list would be complete without the charm and language of *Charlotte's Web* by E. B. White.

Among the ten most requested authors from the 1930s to the present are Margaret Wise Brown, Lois Lenski, Roald Dahl, Eleanor Estes, Caroly Ryrie Brink, Jean De Brunhoff, Marguerite De Angeli, Robert Lawson, William Steig, and Maud Hart Lovelace.

The most-wanted series books are Nancy Drew, Hardy Boys, Tom Swift, Judy Bolton, Rick Brant, Ken Holt, Black Stallion Series, Thornton Burgess, Dr. Dolittle, Freddy the Pig, Landmark Books, and the Scribner's Illustrated Classics.

However, the Frank Baum Oz books, Uncle Wiggily, Mary Frances, Palmer Cox's Brownies, the Teenie Weenies, Joseph Altsheler's historical novels, Arthur Ransome, Rosemary Sutcliff, Volland Publishing, and Leo Edwards's series still have special appeal for collectors and nostalgia buffs.

If you are thinking into the future or you're making a list for your children to collect, keep these authors and illustrators in mind: Brian Jacques, James Marshall, Gary Paulsen, Arthur Yorinks (with Richard Egielski), Lisbeth Zwerger, Michael Hague, Susan Cooper, Ted Lewin, Jerry Pinkney, Daniel Pinkwater, Trina Schart Hyman, and the inimitable Chris Van Allsburg.

Alan Culpin at Abracadabra Booksearch International of Austin, Texas, and Boulder, Colorado, agrees the children's book market is doing very well. "It is one of the fastest-growing sectors in the out-of-print book world, and shows no sign of declining," he says. The Culpins list some classic authors and illustrators who still demand attention: Rackham, Dulac, Nielsen, Parrish, Pogany, and Tasha Tudor, as well as some new faces like Cicely Mary Barker, Margaret Tarrant, and E. H. Shepard.

"Fiction authors tend to be ephemeral, with names popping up only to disappear a year or so later," Alan says. Classic names from 1870 to the 1930s predominate—authors like Carroll, Milne, Potter, and Barker.

Oz-mania is still strong, and the later but still fairly early Oz books are holding up in value, Alan says. New Oz collectors show up regularly. He says authors Margaret Sutton, author of the Judy Bolton series, and Clair Bee, author of the Chip Hilton series, are particularly strong.

The world of children's books is wide and varied and contains many subdivisions—picture books, series, chapter, pop-up, toy, fiction, nonfiction, illustrated, and more. One of the best ways to learn more is to read catalogs offered by dealers who specialize in them. We have space only to skim the surface of this delightful collecting category. So, if your interest in collecting or selling leans toward the whimsical, but you find yourself in a tangled forest with lurking goblins and roads to nowhere, look for the sign of the bookseller and the proprietor will set you on the right path.

THE CARE AND REPAIR OF OLD BOOKS

A few strong instincts, and a few plain rules.
—WILLIAM WORDSWORTH,
ALAS! WHAT BOOTS THE LONG LABORIOUS QUEST?

AVOIDING DAMAGE

Though paper may be fragile, books are surprisingly durable if they are treated well. Proof of this is in the considerable number of incunabula that have survived from the Middle Ages in sturdy enough shape to delight collectors and continue serving as reference materials for serious scholars today.

Our own examination of a 300-year-old Natick Bible at the Boston Public Library revealed a book with pages solid enough to withstand the close attention of readers and researchers for many more years.

Even ignored and uncared for, an ancient tome left undisturbed and dry may survive without serious damage. A leather binding will certainly dry out and crack without proper dressing, but the pages of old books are stubbornly durable.

Unfortunately, newer books may not last so long. Modern paper manufacture produces a lot of paper fast, but the paper is inferior in quality, and it has a far shorter life span. The common product today has a high acid content that causes it to degrade, discolor, become brittle, and fall apart over a few decades. Pulp paper used in newspapers and cheap magazines shows this defect in the extreme, as newspapers yellow and become brittle after a mere few days. Unless the industry corrects this problem, older books will be in better shape a hundred years from now than books printed last year.

Some chief enemies of books are:

FIRE. Fire has totally or partially destroyed many important libraries, often during war (for example, the burning of the Alexandrian Library by Caesar's troops, and the destruction of the Library of Congress in Washington by the British in the War of 1812), and sometimes by accident. The Jenkins Company of Austin, Texas, lost an extensive inventory to fire in December 1985. Fortunately some of the more valuable items—many acquired from dispersal sales of other collections through the years—were stored in a large walk-in vault and survived the blaze.

Light or moderate fire damage to a book may be repaired. The binding can be replaced, and page ends, if scorched, may be trimmed. If a badly scorched book is still worth the trouble, the leaves may be unbound and mounted by a professional bookbinder.

Some precautions can be taken to minimize the threat of fire damage to a collection. A book room should have fire retardant carpets; draperies and curtains should be kept to a minimum; upholstered and overstuffed furniture should be avoided. Glass-enclosed bookshelves are safer than open shelves where fire is a risk. A fire extinguisher should be kept handy and the door kept shut when the room is not in use.

WATER. Books can be damaged by floods, fire fighting efforts, plumbing problems, storms, or any occasion when water comes into contact with covers and leaves.

Whether or not a soaked book can be salvaged depends on the paper quality. Vellum can often take a soaking and be reconditioned. A good rag paper has the best chance, but the book must be dismantled and each leaf dried separately. Modern books on coated paper, such as art books, however, are a total loss. The coating disintegrates and you're left with sticky goo and incomplete images on the pages.

Newspapers, too, cannot take moisture. They absorb water and return to the pulp they started from.

Drying out a book properly is a delicate process and should be done by a professional. Restoration is expensive, so a book should be evaluated carefully to determine whether it is worth the cost.

Steps to take to guard against water damage include avoiding rooms with overhead water pipes for book rooms. (Be aware of kitchens and bathrooms on the floor above. Those pipes are not always visible, but they can still leak down onto your books if they burst.) Avoid basement rooms that may leak or be damp at best. Cover books carefully when transporting them.

Excessive Humidity or Excessive Dryness. Dry air damages leather bindings. Humid air breeds mold and mildew, curls paper, and loosens bindings. The ideal humidity for books is around 50 percent, give or take 10 points. In a humid environment, without a dehumidifier, it's best to store books on open shelves rather than in glass cases where moisture can build up inside.

To help leather remain supple in all environments, but especially in dry air, treat it regularly with a leather dressing. This will be taken up at greater length when we discuss leather care.

Rough Handling. Books that are improperly handled do not remain long in collectible condition. Be gentle when handling all books, not just those that appear fragile. Even a big, brawny folio can be easily damaged sometimes by the weight of its own pages pulling on the spine, if it's not handled well.

Don't open any book too wide or press it flat on a table to copy from it; this cracks the hinges.

Older books with metal clasps require special handling. If the clasps are tight, don't tug at them to open them. Instead, gently squeeze the outer edges of the book until the clasps pop open easily. To close them, squeeze again and gently fit the clasps in place. If they won't close, don't force them. Over time these books, especially vellum, may have swelled and the clasps may no longer fit. Leave them open or risk damaging the binding with too much squeezing.

Improper Storage. A book can be damaged by improper shelving, though the harm is often done over time, almost imperceptibly, so you may not notice it's happening until it's too late. Common mistakes are wedging books too tightly on a shelf or letting books flop about on unfilled shelves; stacking books flat on their sides, one atop another; or shelving books on their fore-edge.

Most spine problems of books folio size and larger are caused by shelving on the fore-edge, causing the books to develop loose sections or covers, bent edges and corners, and possibly damaged pages. While it's tempting to place a book that's too large for the shelf on its edge, you should resist the impulse. The weight of the pages will pull them away from the spine and you'll end up with a broken book.

If you can, stand large books on top of the bookcase supported by bookends. If you can't do this, place them flat on the bookshelf, but don't put other books on top of them.

LIGHT. Especially sunlight. Direct sunlight, the ultraviolet component, degrades many kinds of paper and fades the color—or "mellows" the bindings—of books that stand for long periods in the sun. Nothing is more discouraging than to see a table full of books at a flea market warping and wilting, unprotected from a hot summer sun.

Bookcases shouldn't receive direct sunlight if this can be avoided, though indirect sunlight to brighten a room is okay. Interior lighting should be incandescent. Fluorescent light damages books.

INSECTS AND PESTS. A particularly nasty enemy of books is the bookworm. Not the bookish person devoted to reading, but any of the insect larvae that feast on the binding and paste of books. Bugs, too, can wreak havoc on books. Some bugs, like silverfish, love a meal of the sizing and starches used in the manufacture of paper. Some like the dyes and materials used in bindings like buckram.

The best recourse, if worms or insects are attacking your collection, is to call in a professional and have the entire house treated. But don't spray insecticide directly on your volumes. You may cause more damage than the bugs.

DISPLAYING YOUR BOOKS

BOOKSHELVES. You'd think it would be simple to figure out how to store and display your books. Put them on a bookshelf, of course. But, it's not as simple as it sounds. Many book enthusiasts think that old books belong in old bookcases, and they will go out to an antique shop or an auction and buy the first old bookcase they see. Wrong.

It's important to look past the brass trimming and the darling carved gargoyles to see how the bookcase is constructed. Are the shelves adjustable in height? Are they sagging, cracked, or splintered? Are all the shelf supports present? Are the shelves sturdy enough to carry the weight of heavy books?

Whether or not your bookcase should have glass doors depends on several factors. Do you want the books handled? Are there children in the house too young to appreciate the delicacy of your treasures? Do you have pets who like to sit on top of a shelf of books? (Cats do.)

Glass doors are a great protection from dust and they cut down on the work you must do—as well as wear and tear on your books—in keeping the books clean. But they are bulky and they stand between you and your collection in a way that open, inviting shelves don't.

BOOKENDS. Many bookends are collectible, particularly those from the Art Nouveau and the Arts and Crafts movements, stunning in brass, copper, and bronze. But do they do the job?

Bookends should keep your books from tumbling around and should support heavy volumes. If you find you're constantly repositioning and straightening or tightening them up, they aren't working and should be replaced. For the best service, and at a fraction of the cost of the fancy bookend, we recommend the metal L-shaped or T-shaped models in which the lower portion slides beneath the first several books. Be sure they are tall enough to support your books and that the edges are smooth and won't scuff the covers and pages.

BOOK REPAIR

We cannot emphasize too strongly leaving the repair of a rare book to a competent bookbinder. For those more common or moderately priced books, learning a few pointers on how to repair them yourself is worthwhile.

PROFESSIONAL BOOKBINDING. A good bookbinder is a valuable resource, and anyone interested in used and old books should know one. He's first aid for books, rescuing broken and defective volumes from oblivion, making suggestions, and offering alternatives you may not realize you had.

Do not order a complete new binding if the old, loose one is in fairly sound condition. A loose cover can be rehinged, and missing leather can be replaced. New bindings can be created in which usable portions of the old leather are inlaid into a leather of similar grain and color. The old spine—or what's left of it—can be reset into a new spine.

These procedures are expensive and probably not worth the cost unless your book has some special appeal or is particularly ancient or rare.

When pages or gatherings are loose, the book may need resewing. If the paper is too fragile to permit this, the book can be dismantled and the inner edges of the leaves can be attached to guards which are then sewn together. When guards are used, it is generally not possible to recase the volume—that is, return it to the original binding—because the page ends will protrude from the fore-edge. A new binding is necessary.

HOME REPAIR. You may try some home repair on mildly damaged books that are not so rare or expensive that a mistake would be a disaster. Some of the more common repairs are:

• *Loose bindings.* Loose cloth bindings can usually be repaired by opening the book midway, laying it face downward, and brushing glue along the inner side of the spine. Do not use cement-type glues; polyvinyl acetate, such as Elmer's Glue-All, does the job best. Use it sparingly. When the application is completed, place rubber bands around the book and allow it to dry for several hours.

• *Cracked inner hinges.* Inner hinges can be strengthened by folding a narrow strip of paper and pasting it along the hinge. The paper should be about as heavy as an index card for best results. Make sure it is neither too long nor too short.

• *Torn spines.* Spines are best treated by simply brushing a small quantity of glue on the torn sections, pressing them firmly into place, and allowing them to dry under the pressure of a rubber band.

• *Notations or underlinings.* Markings done in pencil can be easily—but gently!—erased. When the marks are in ink, nothing removes them satisfactorily, and it is probably wise not to make the effort. The paper could be damaged by using strong cleansers or by scraping. At times, the notations might be of interest and could even provide evidence on the book's previous ownership (called provenance).

• *Moisture.* Treat the book before the pages dry. Once stains are set by drying, they won't come out. Now, the treatment we recommend may seem a little strange, but if the book doesn't warrant professional attention, try this anyway.

First, mop up any surface water by patting gently with soft paper towels. Place an oversize sheet of wax paper between all leaves that have gotten wet. In a wooden box about twice the size of the book, place an inch-thick layer of pipe tobacco, and lay the book in it. Sprinkle a few more tobacco leaves over the book and seal the box tightly. Store the box in a dry place for several weeks. Some stains will probably remain, but they'll be less visible than if treatment had not been tried.

CARE OF LEATHER BOOKBINDINGS

Leather bindings, though more attractive than cloth, require more upkeep. Leather, an animal substance, has natural oils when new. As it grows old the oil dries out and the leather becomes brittle. Red dust on your bookshelves is a sure sign that your bindings are dry. At that point, emergency treatment is necessary. It won't cure damage that has already occurred but it will halt further deterioration.

Leather bindings must be dressed. This may not be the most pleasant chore, but it can be rewarding. Be sure to get a good leather-care preparation, and use it intelligently. Too much will leave the binding sticky.

For best results, use a dressing made expressly for bindings, such as the British Museum Leather Dressing. This old standby was once hard to get in America, and collectors sent to London for it and paid the price. Today, it can generally be purchased in the States. Abide by the directions and don't be disappointed if the leather doesn't look polished. The aim in dressing leather is to give it a drink, not a shine.

Most old leathers will not polish and should not be expected to.

Give your leather-bound books a dressing about every six months. With regular care, any leather binding bought in good condition should remain so. But don't buy a shabby binding in the belief that it can be easily refurbished, as this is impossible.

HOW TO USE THIS
BOOK

Books are part of man's prerogative.
—SIR THOMAS OVERBURY, *A WIFE*

The books in this listing are arranged alphabetically by author's last name, or, if no author, by the title.

Categories of books, such as Americana, travel, sporting, etc., have been dispensed with since most books can be assigned to more than one category. We believe our system is simpler and more "user friendly." We discuss genres and categories in the glossary, and again in our section on the book trade. A careful reader will soon be able to determine the proper categories for whatever book is in question.

In most listings, the author's name is followed by the title, the place of publication, and/or a date. Dates have been taken from the title page or the copyright page. In preferred bibliographic format, which we endorse and use in our own business, dates taken from the copyright page are bracketed. We have endeavored to adhere to this style as closely as possible and, where the information was known, we have included brackets for copyright page dates.

We have not limited ourselves to listing first editions, but we have identified first editions in the majority of cases. Where a question remains whether or not you have a first edition in hand, further research in reference bibliographies is called for. Several excellent research sources are listed at the back of this book.

In most cases, the number of pages in a volume is not given, but where we considered it helpful, or where identification of a work requires it, we have included the page count. Similarly, where illustrations include colored or engraved plates, we have included the number of plates in many cases, especially when identification of an important book is dependent on that information.

Note: When examining any volume, check the table of contents or list of illustrations against the plates present to be sure they are all accounted for, since some people remove plates from old books to frame and sell them separately.

Readers will notice that many books listed are not first editions. Some titles are rare and valuable in whatever edition they appear. Later editions may contain signatures, provenance, or other attributes of note or may be illustrated by artists of great renown; thus those editions may be more valuable than the first.

Unless otherwise stated, the prices given are for books in their original bindings except for those dating to the seventeenth century or earlier, in which case a good period binding is assumed.

Our prices reflect fair retail value based on a consensus of asking prices and realized prices of books on the open market over the past three years.

Dealers typically offer a 10 to 20 percent discount to other bookmen. A dealer may pay about 50 percent of retail for a book bought from a private individual if a customer is waiting in the wings for that book. For stock, a dealer will offer from 20 percent to 35 percent of a book's retail value.

If you should offer a dealer an extremely rare and sought-after item, the dealer may act as an agent to market the item and take only a commission on the sale. This happened to us recently when we discovered Professor Albert Einstein's signature on a dinner menu and program from a 1930s transatlantic ocean liner. Einstein was on the program to entertain that evening playing his violin. We informed the owner, who was not aware of the signature, and with her permission sent the program to Swann Galleries in New York. Not only are we thrilled to be the agents in this case, but discovering the signature was great fun.

Settling on prices for this guide, we used the tools available to us—auction records, dealer catalogs, conversations with book-sellers, and twenty years' experience in the trade—to give you the best estimates on the retail value of the books listed.

At times, the ranges in our price listings reflect slight differences in the condition of books offered by different dealers. At other times, they reflect the vicissitudes of the market, where a book may fetch a smart price in the mountains of New England and go far more cheaply in the deserts of Arizona. Or a dealer may offer a book at one price in his shop, while patrons of an auction house bought it at a far different price. We have not shied away from listing these broad ranges so the reader can see clearly the idiosyncrasies of the antiquarian book trade.

In all cases, books are assumed to be in at least very good condition, and, where modern first editions are concerned, excellent condition. To realize their best price, modern firsts must have their dust jackets intact. Some listings do not indicate a dust jacket. These books have been offered or sold for a lower price than they would have fetched with the jacket. Still, many modern firsts, even without their jackets, are worth more than the $.50 charged at library sales, so we've included them here.

At all times, remember that this is a guide and not a guarantee of prices. The marketplace, forever in flux, determines the real value of used and old books.

We have endeavored to verify statistics for each listing, but no book of this type can guarantee freedom from error. The serious bibliophile will not depend on any one source, but will use multiple research tools to verify data on important books.

GLOSSARY

A word fitly spoken is like apples of gold in pictures of silver.
—*PROVERBS*

ADDENDA (singular **ADDENDUM**). Supplemental material inserted at the end of a book.

ADVANCE COPY. Copies of a book issued ahead of schedule to gain final approval from the author or to send to reviewers before the edition is released. Sometimes the advance copies will be identical to the regular edition, but often they are not, at least to the extent that they are labeled advance copies. If the only difference is in style or color of binding, it may be difficult to determine later if the copies are an advance issue or simply a binding variant, which could be part of a normal trade run.

Collectors often value advance copies since they represent an early state of the text and, however rare the case, they may contain notations by the author.

ALL EDGES GILT. Indicates that all three edges of the leaves (top, bottom, and fore-edge) have been gilded. The term is abbreviated a.e.g. or, if only the top edge is gilded, t.e.g.

AMERICANA. In the strict sense, refers to material dealing with the American hemisphere. But today, the term more often refers narrowly and loosely to books, documents, pamphlets, and other printed material that shows why, how, when, and by whom the United States was developed.

ANA (or **IANA**). Suffix denoting items related to a particular subject, be it a person, a time or place in history, or some such. For instance, Joyceiana is material relating in some way to James Joyce, even if the connection is remote. The heading covers such things as pamphlets, books, newspaper accounts, artifacts, and letters by, about, or to the subject.

Collecting ana is widespread among those interested in a particular author or historical time or personality. Even those who have written only one book (or none) can be the subject of an extensive collection of written and artifact items. Institutions and libraries are notable collectors of ana.

ANTHOLOGY. A collection of short works, by one or more writers, in one book or set of volumes. Anthologies are most often collections of work that has appeared elsewhere.

ANTIQUARIAN BOOKSELLING. Sale of used, old, and rare books, printed fare, and related items; usually refers to trade in books that are out of print.

Until about the twelfth century, most books were handcrafted in monasteries and churches and remained their property. Except to those who owned them and valued the information they contained, books had no intrinsic value unless they contained gold gilt or were inlaid with precious stones. Not until sometime around the thirteenth century, when craftspeople in the secular world began to make and sell books, adding topics like philosophy and literature, did books take on a broader commercial value.

Michael Olmert, author of the *The Smithsonian Book of Books* (1992), remarks, "An intriguing question is when did books become valuable enough to steal?" Olmert says that thieves profited from stealing books once a commercial market for them was established. As proof that books were taking on value, he reports that book owners of the twelfth century began writing curses on their flyleaves to discourage theft, warning that whoever stole the books would be damned to hellfire.

Even as the first commercial markets were growing, bookmaking was done slowly by hand; comparatively few books were produced, and those were often custom-made for specific buyers. Bookselling was primarily a second-hand business but was not yet antiquarian bookselling. Since bound books were still in their infancy, you wouldn't term the trade in them antiquarian.

By the seventeenth century, enough time had elapsed, printing had become mechanized, and enough books were in circulation for true antiquarian bookselling to arise in England, France, and elsewhere.

Few catalogs were issued at first. Most early shops gathered in clusters, such as those that sprang up in St. Paul's Churchyard, London. Most shopkeepers located in large cities, primarily in stalls with much of their material displayed on the sidewalk and very little within. The **PENNY BOXES** that became such a favorite of the bargain hunters in later years were probably not present early on. Prints, engravings, maps, and such were sold by at least some dealers.

The emergence of the scholar-dealer—the collector at heart who studied his merchandise with interest—did not occur until the early part of the nineteenth century. By this time, bookselling was big business. The Bohn brothers of London are generally credited with giving birth to modern rare-book dealing. By 1900, at least a half-dozen English dealers boasted inventories in excess of half-a-million volumes. Several German booksellers by this time had stocks even larger.

APPRAISAL. Estimation of the value of a book or a collection. An appraisal should be made by a qualified professional in the antiquarian book trade with the tools and the experience to do the job right. Some appraisers will offer an opinion based on a mere list and description of volumes, but such an appraisal is not recommended. The value of a book depends on many factors, not the least of which is its condition. The best appraisals are done by experts who can hold the books in their hands and examine them in fine detail. This can't be done with a list.

AQUATINT. A method of etching that stresses soft tones and shades, resembling wash paintings. The French artist Le Prince is generally credited with perfecting the process during the late eighteenth century. The technique became popular in Britain during the eighteenth and nineteenth centuries.

Sometimes aquatint printing was done in color, and sometimes the coloring was added by hand later. When printing in colored aquatint, a separate plate for each color is necessary. A few famous artists such as Goya and Picasso experimented with the process.

ART PAPER. Shiny, coated stock on which most art books (or at least the illustrations) are printed. The paper ages badly and is easily damaged by moisture. Also, dirt stains cannot be removed without damaging the surface of the paper.

AS NEW. Showing no signs of wear; the book doesn't look used. Basically a British expression, Americans prefer **MINT**, which carries the same meaning.

ASSOCIATION COPY. A book that was part of the author's own library or was associated in one way or another with a famous person. It may be that the author inscribed the book to a friend; or the book may contain an inscription by another famous owner; perhaps a dedication or a presentation; or the book was merely included—without any inscriptions—in a famous person's library. But the point is, there must be proof that the book has been in the possession of someone famous.

The value of association copies to the collector derives from the book's connection to history or, in modern times, to people who are perceived as larger than life. If we were to learn that Abraham Lincoln had a favorite book of sonnets that he carried with him daily, we would love to have that book. It would be an association copy.

Association copies should be distinguished from signed copies, which proliferate these days with the popularity of book tours and autograph signings. And beware the forgeries! Experts in the trade can help you weed them out.

AUTHORIZED BIOGRAPHY. Usually refers to biographies written with the approval or even help of the subject. The term is intended to draw attention and interest, but a drawback to authorized editions is the public perception that if the subject of a biography authorized the work, it wouldn't tell tales of the subject's secret life.

B.A.L. The *Bibliography of American Literature*, authored by Jacob Nathaniel Blanck and published beginning in 1955 by Yale University Press for the Bibliographical Society of America. Virginia Smyers and Michael Winship edited the work and later added a final volume. The seven-volume work is a detailed bibliography of important American literature through much of the twentieth century and an indispensable research tool for the serious book person.

BASTARD TITLE. Another name for the **HALF-TITLE PAGE**, the leaf preceding the title page that carries the title in small print but no other information. Use of this page is a holdover from the incunabula days when the title page consisted of only this. It has no other real purpose and is retained in many volumes merely because old habits die hard. With a nod to decorum, many bibliographers referred to this as the "bas. title."

BAY PSALM BOOK. The first full-length American-printed book, issued at Cambridge, Massachusetts, in 1640 by Stephen Daye; the name derives from the Massachusetts Bay Colony. Only eleven volumes are known to remain, all but one in public or institutional collections. The total number of copies printed isn't known, but is guessed to be from 100 to 300. Though the usual press run at the time was considerably more, experts theorize that Daye would not have had a large market for books printed locally and would have printed less than the usual number. The book was collected as a rarity as early as the mid-1700s. The actual title of Daye's volume is *The Whole Booke of Psalmes Faithfully Translated into English Metre*, but printers in Europe had produced works with similar titles, and therefore *Bay Psalm Book* more clearly distinguishes Daye's work from the others.

BEVELED EDGES. Angle-cut edges on wooden boards once used in bookbindings. They're of little consequence when judging the value of an antiquarian book.

BIBLIOGRAPHY. Commonly, a list of books organized by subject or author. For instance, libraries consider an author bibliography to be a list, as complete as possible, of all specimens of an author's work that have appeared in print.

The term has taken on an alternate meaning coming into its own now as the study of books themselves, including their origins, history, development, physical appearance, construction, and value.

BIBLIOMANIA. A preoccupation with books; a compulsion to be around them, learn about them, and own them. Booksellers and collectors are prone to this disease. The malady can be observed at library sales, auctions, and house sales.

BIBLIOPHILE. An ardent and avid book collector. One who loves books. Indicates a mild, benign form of bibliomania.

Fine bindings on display at the Vermont Antiquarian Booksellers Fair in Pomfret, Vermont.

BIBLIOTHECA AMERICANA. A comprehensive directory of books on Americana, twenty-nine volumes in all, dating from the coming of the Europeans to the twentieth century. Begun by Joseph Sabin, who completed the first thirteen volumes, the work was continued by Wilberforce Eames and completed by R.W.G. Vail.

BINDING COPY. A book in need of a new binding. A British term.

BINDINGS. The permanent cover of a book, not to be confused with a dust jacket. As soon as books were made of folded leaves instead of scrolls, they needed a proper covering. The earliest bindings were probably uncovered wooden boards with a hide spine— comparable to what we call today a "half-leather" binding (see **HALF-BOUND**). This evolved into a full-leather binding. Early ornamentation on books consisted of painting and encrusting with jewels and bone carvings. In time, these gave way to **BLINDSTAMPING** and finally goldstamping.

Materials used over the centuries for binding books are numerous and even macabre. Most common were vellum, pigskin, calf,

On this VERY old binding—early seventeenth century—a bishop's hat and crozier adorn the coat of arms in the center. Research through heraldry books would tell you that these are the bearings of Antoine deSeve, the Abbot of Isle-le-Barrois, France. The book was printed in Venice in 1604 but bound in France. Later it popped up in an English collection and its location is presently unknown. $1,300–$1,500.

morocco, and various types of cloth or muslin. A practice arose during the Middle Ages of occasionally stripping the skin of slain enemy soldiers. One use of the leather made out of these skins: book bindings. (In some cathedrals in Europe one can still see doors covered in these human hides. Tour guides often hesitate to mention this fact.)

Collecting fine bindings is a major area of book collecting.

BLINDSTAMPING. Recessed or raised impressions on the bindings of books which are not inked or colored. Blindstamping did not originate with bookbinding but was long a popular means of hand-decorating leather. As a decoration for bindings, the process did not begin to be used until the twelfth century.

BOARDS. Uncovered hard cardboard, wooden boards, or boards covered with thin paper, linen, buckram, etc., used as front and back covers in bindings. The term is a holdover from the early days of printing, when books were bound with actual wooden boards held together by leather or buckram at the spine. In the bookselling trade today, "boards" refers to stiff bindings covered in paper instead of the more common cloth or even leather.

BOOK OF HOURS. Illuminated medieval prayer book. During the Middle Ages, wealthy patrons commissioned these stunning books for their personal use. The books were prized for their calendars, which frequently featured month-by-month pictures of activities—planting in spring, harvesting in fall, etc.—providing later historians with valuable insights into medieval society and habits. Small in size, handy to carry to church services, the books included psalms, litanies, and various offices of the church. The organization of these books was based on the church's prescribed daily schedule for devotions, hence the name "Book of Hours."

BOOK OF KELLS. An Irish manuscript of Christian scripture from the eighth century. The opening page of each Gospel is lavishly illustrated with brightly colored designs and images of saints and religious persons and events. Depictions of nature, such as animals, fish, and trees, abound throughout. The art of the monks and their use of color and whimsy shows the attainment of the Irish artists of the early Middle Ages. From the way figures are depicted in the hand illuminations, it is obvious artists of the day had not perfected the study of anatomy, but that deficiency was made up for in their exquisite concepts of color and design. The folio manuscript is housed in the Library of Trinity College, Dublin.

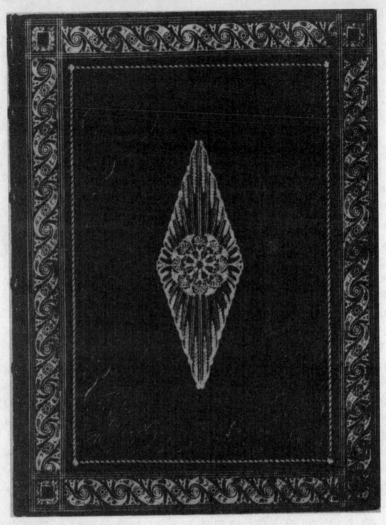

The above binding which features blindstamping and gilt tooling is French and dates from the second quarter of the nineteenth century. $325–$400.

BOOKPLATE. A label identifying ownership; usually pasted on the inside of a book cover. Older, intricately designed and executed bookplates are collector's items in their own right. Some are delightful examples of art. Their use dates from the fifteenth century. If a modern bookplate is inserted by a person of no particular renown, the plate does not detract from the book. When properly applied, plates do no harm, but they should not be affixed over existing plates or in such a way that they obscure important inscriptions or writings.

Plates of antiquity, either engraved by some famous craftsperson or showing possession by some notable person, are highly sought after by collectors of bookplates, but they really should not be removed from the books. Contrary to common belief, this practice damages the books and destroys evidence of a book's **PROVENANCE**, or history, an important aspect of bibliography.

BOOK SCOUT. A person who beats the bushes looking for salable books and who then markets these finds to booksellers. Since a bookseller is often tied down with a shop, scheduling time for a buying trip can be a problem. Enter the book scout. With no overhead and unfettered by the minutiae of a bookseller's store, scouts have time to ferret out books sitting on somebody's shelf in an attic or at the eternal Friends of the Library book sale.

A bookseller might have several scouts scattered in different parts of the country haunting the flea markets, Salvation Army stores, and garage sales. But for the most part, scouts work independently, seeking out the bookseller with the strongest interest in their finds.

Often a person starting out as a scout develops into a full-time bookseller. Scouts of the seedy, unsavory character described by John Dunning in his mystery novel *Booked to Die* (1992) may exist somewhere, but our experience of scouts in New England (Marie started out as a scout twenty years ago) reveals a type of person who loves books to begin with and is delighted to chase them for booksellers.

BOOK SIZES. Industry terms loosely implying the size of volumes. The terms describe books according to their **FORMAT** (the way they are printed and bound) rather than actual measurements, giving the practiced professional only an indication of how big the books really are.

The common book size formats are folio, quarto, octavo, and duodecimo, indicating the manner in which the printer folds the paper sheets on which a book is printed to create leaves (pages). Regardless of the planned format, all sheets are fed through a press

Miniature and micro books, displayed by Isaiah Thomas Booksellers of Massachusetts at the Vermont Antiquarian Booksellers' Fair in Pomfret, Vermont. Photo by Ilan Fisher.

in full size and folded later into "quires." These are collected and bound together; the closed edges of the folded sheets are slit, and, presto, you have a book.

If each printed sheet is folded once to create two leaves, the book becomes a folio, the largest format. If it is folded twice, we get four leaves, or a quarto, written "4to." Fold again and there are eight leaves, an octavo, or "8vo"; twelve leaves are duodecimo, "12mo." Keep going and you have progressively smaller sizes and larger numbers: 16mo, 24mo, 32mo, and 64mo. A 128mo format exists, but it's only seen in the very tiniest of miniature volumes.

You can't divine the actual dimensions of a book from the format, but it isn't a useless convention. What you can reliably ascertain from a statement of format is something about the shape of a volume. Octavos tend to be sleek, at least $1^1/_2$ times tall as they are wide. Quartos tend to be squarish and dumpy. Folios are tall and well-proportioned. The Gutenberg Bible is a folio. Most modern novels are 8vo's. Coffee-table art books are folios and large quartos.

BOOKWORMS. The larval stage of a beetle that likes to eat books—a pesty little worm that feeds upon the bindings and leaves. They've been preying on libraries since the very earliest times. These larvae were the scourge of monastic libraries in the Middle Ages. No area of Europe was free of the bookworm, and contrary to some beliefs, they did not seek out only filthy habitations but ate books in fine homes and libraries as well. Modern chemicals have virtually exterminated them.

BREAKER. Someone who takes books apart and then sells the parts separately, especially the illustrations. Breaking a book apart may bring a higher price for the parts than the book would fetch as a whole. When a book is so badly damaged that it cannot be repaired or recovered as a book, breaking is a way of preserving the plates and putting them into circulation.

Breaking books that are not otherwise damaged is looked down on by serious antiquarian booksellers and collectors as a horrendous practice.

BROADSIDE. A poster, announcement, or proclamation, usually printed on one side of a sheet and meant to be posted on a wall. Many a political statement was brought to the people's attention in this manner even after the advent of newspapers. Old auction posters, especially for horse auctions, might be adorned with an illustrated display of wares, adding to the value and desirability of the artifact.

Broadsides are popular with collectors today.

BUCKRAM. A modern binding material very much like cloth but tougher and somewhat more attractive. Libraries almost always have their books rebound in buckram. Inexpensive, buckram can be dyed all the colors of the rainbow, as well as goldstamped. The natural shade, which is rather like a cross between straw and wheat, is preferred by many.

Buckram bindings are often described in catalogs as cloth, and vice versa, a fact of life that collectors must endure.

CALF. Leather used for bookbindings.

CALLED FOR. Points mentioned in bibliographies that determine the edition of a book. For instance, if a handbook written by Smith says that a blank leaf follows the title in a certain edition of a certain book, then the blank leaf is "called for" for that edition and must be there for the book to be complete.

Two pages of The Boston Primer, *a popular chapbook (this one printed in 1811, with engravings to illustrate the alphabet for young learners), are typical examples of the style used on these popular little books.* (Courtesy of the Trustees of the Boston Public Library. Photographed by Marilyn Green.)

CAXTON, WILLIAM. The first English printer. Born in Kent, he started his business life as a mercer, or dealer in yard goods, a trade he followed for most of his life, showing no particular mechanical skills or flair for literature. Around 1441, Caxton went to Burgundy. He spent most of his adult life on the Continent. In 1471 he entered the service of the Duchess of Burgundy and, under her influence, performed his first effort with books, translating the *Recuyell of the Historyes of Troye.*

On a visit to Cologne that year, he was apparently introduced to the art of printing, which he brought back to Bruges, setting about to give the city a printing press. Together with a Flemish calligrapher, Colard Mansion, Caxton issued the first book printed in the English language, the same *Recuyell.* After printing two more books with Mansion, Caxton returned alone to England and founded a printing office in the parish of Westminster.

Compared to the best French and Italian printing of the time, Caxton's books come off a sorry second. His fame has led many to assume that his talent as a craftsman and type designer must have been extraordinary, but this was not the case. He did, however, exert much influence upon his contemporaries and followers. He began with types modeled on German Gothic and stuck with them to the end. This set the trend for English printers, and it was not until a century after his death that the types were replaced by the more graceful Roman.

A craze for Caxtons among collectors began in the early part of the nineteenth century and has gathered steam ever since. The finest collections are at the British Museum and John Rylands Library. In the United States, the Morgan and Huntington libraries are notable for their Caxtons.

CHAPBOOK. A small pamphlet or booklet usually associated with children's stories or rhymes. Most are diminutive in size and illustrated with woodcuts. In the eighteenth century, itinerant peddlers, or "chapmen," hawked the booklets door to door. Because they were cheaply made, many of the books have not survived in very good condition, but those that have are highly prized and collectible.

CHEAP COPY. A defective copy which is being offered at a discount. The dealer wants the prospective buyer to be aware of the poor condition.

Chapbooks were popular fare during the nineteenth century, often sold door-to-door by traveling salesmen commonly called chapmen. This collection is included in Special Collections at the Bailey-Howe Library at the University of Vermont. Shown are (top row) The Farm House, *Mahlon Day printer, early 1800s;* The Red Squirrel, *A. Phelps, Greenfield, 1846;* Cinderella or The Glass Slipper, *H & E Phinney, Cooperstown, 1834; (bottom row)* Stories for Children about Whales, *Rufus Merrill, Concord, NH, 1843;* Cock Robin's Courtship and Marriage, *Sidney's Press, New Haven, 1824;* The Young Sailor, or The Sea Life of Tom Bowline, *Kiggins & Kellogg, NY, 1840s.*

CLOTH BINDING. The ideal binding substance—cheap, durable, easy to apply, and comes in a variety of colors. For modern books, cloth has replaced leather as the binding of choice. True, the disappearance of leather is lamentable, but the cost of leather binding would prohibit ownership of books to all but a limited class of collectors.

In the first years of cloth binding, publishers let their imaginations run wild. Every effort was made to ornament the bindings lavishly. The books were gilded and blindstamped using patterns copied from notable bindings of earlier ages. But unlike the books of old, they were gilded with large panel stamps impressed by machine rather than with tools worked by hand. The purpose was to make the public forget leather. It succeeded: out of sight, out of mind. In time, only connoisseurs who kept fine libraries retained any affection for leather. That is not to say, however, that we have become so undiscriminating that we cannot still appreciate a book bound in fine, soft leather.

CODEX. Applies to leaves bound in book form—this book you are holding, for example—as opposed to scrolls or tablets. The invention is generally credited to Roman legal clerics who grew weary of cumbersome scrolls and cut them down to convenient size. The practice made sense at a time when the whole process of managing information was time-consuming and laborious.

COLLATED. Inspected from cover to cover to be sure all pages, plates, maps, and the like are present, intact, and in their proper place. In the case of earlier books, a perfect copy—or comprehensive knowledge of one—is necessary for comparison when collating.

A good practice when purchasing a book is to check out the list of illustrations numbered in the contents and confirm that they are all there. If maps should be present, check them out. Nothing is more frustrating when you get home than to discover pages missing from a book you were all excited about purchasing.

And never, never send out a book to a dealer or customer before collating it. Selling a book with missing pages could be cause for manslaughter—or, more seriously, labeling yourself unprofessional.

COLOPHON. The finishing touch. The tradition of medieval scribes when completing their manuscripts was to record, on the last page, their name and place of residence and, sometimes, the day on which the book was finished.

At times the addition of a colophon was done out of vanity, but, more often than not, such information was necessary. Without it, a printer or publisher could not identify an edition as his own, which might result in legal difficulties if the book were pirated or stolen by another printer.

The average colophon was a model of simplicity, one sentence or so, giving the essential facts. Colophons were replaced after the sixteenth century by information included on the title page. Some modern books, usually limited editions, still add a colophon, perhaps out of respect for tradition. You might find one that starts out: "This book was set on the monotype in Fournier. . . ."

CONDITION. The general state of a book. This singularly most important point cannot be overemphasized when considering whether to buy or sell a collectible book.

Like people, books are either in fine shape, very good shape, bad shape, or some state in between. As no hard-and-fast definitions exist, the terms used to designate a book's condition are subject to personal opinion. Having said that, we hasten to add that there is some agreement in the book trade as to what the terms mean.

Mint. As new. Right off the press.

Fine. Nearly new. Sometimes a dealer might overlap this with "mint."

Very Good. Definitely showing wear, but not damaged. Usually a clean, tight copy. Most collectible books fit this category.

Good. Obviously read. Perhaps the covers show moderate wear; a hinge is cracked in front or back; some minor spine fading might be present, the binding scuffed. Perhaps the book is even a little shaken, not quite as tight as it used to be. All in all, the condition shows the book has been around for a while and used. No really major defects.

Fair. Worn and used. Cover soiled, scuffed, evidence of repairs, shaken, perhaps a page torn here or there. The book has definitely been around the barn.

Reading copy. About all it is good for. Or, it may interest collectors of modern first editions who keep their pristine copies on a shelf safe from prying hands but who may still want to read Hemingway or Faulkner. Reading copies come in handy for research.

Now, when all is said and done, should a disheveled rare book come up at auction, you can bet your bottom dollar—and you might have to—that book will not lack for spirited bidding. So extenuating circumstances call for common sense. If a book is being purchased for investment, then by all means abide by the most rigid rules of condition.

COPPERPLATE ENGRAVING. A process for producing prints and book illustrations. Plates were prepared by a battery-hammer method, then smoothed by rubbing with pumice and oilstone. Though costly and time-consuming, this method gave the best possible surface for engraving. The majority of English illustrated books of the eighteenth century used copper plates.

COPYRIGHT. The equivalent of a patent on a work of literature. A copyright prohibits anyone from reproducing the work, either in whole or in part, without consent of the copyright holder.

CURIOSA. In today's market, books that deal with offbeat subjects—for example, a monograph on foot fetishes or the psychology of wearing hats. During the Victorian age, anything of a sexual nature was hidden under the heading of curiosa. Today's bookseller has no problem with such subjects and classifies erotic material where it belongs, under erotica.

C.W.O. Cash with order. Most booksellers append this to their ads to safeguard their interests, choosing not to send a book out to a customer before they have payment in hand. But through the years, we have never encountered a deadbeat customer or bookseller. We have sent out books before the check arrives—in particular, a $5,000 sporting book to a dealer with a fine reputation.

At times we need to have a little faith in our fellow human beings. Of course, in this case it was easy, as we knew the man's character.

DAMP STAINS. Damage caused by excessive humidity, but not by water, as is sometimes thought. Books damaged by damp are ragged and musty rather than crisp. Improper ventilation can cause as much damage as water. Humidity constantly above 70 percent can damage a book as it stands untouched in a bookcase. In a book with lovely plates, dampness can cause the pages to stick together. Pulling them apart damages the plates, thus greatly altering the value and esthetics of the book.

DAYE, STEPHEN. An important individual, the first man to print mechanically in America. Daye, a British locksmith, came to the Massachusetts Bay Colony in 1633. He and his son, Matthew, a printer's apprentice, set up a printing shop in Cambridge at Harvard College. The earliest surviving book of the Dayes' press is commonly known as the **BAY PSALM BOOK**, after the colony where it was printed.

DELUXE EDITION. Meant to imply extraordinary production qualities; those books which, by superior design, type, paper, binding, or other factors, are set above the pale.

DISBOUND. Refers to a pamphlet or other brief work that once was part of a larger work and has been separated. Purists look down on this practice of removing the piece from the larger collection, much as they look down on breaking a book.

DISCARD STAMP. A mark used by libraries when they are culling their collections to show that the books have been released for sale or distribution. This is a matter of procedure to guard against theft and to show that the book is legitimately no longer a part of the library collection. How nice when a librarian thinks like a book collector and carefully selects an unobtrusive place for the stamp.

DOG-EARED. Originally referred to the corners of pages that have become ragged or creased. Now, it applies to any pages that have the appearance of heavy use. One of the causes of dog-earing is the regrettable habit many readers have of turning down the corner of a page to mark their place. Thank goodness not all readers are guilty of this barbaric practice, choosing instead to use bookmarks.

DÜRER, ALBRECHT. A German artist, painter, and book illustrator at the turn of the sixteenth century, he was famous and in great demand for quality woodcuts used in book illustrations. Among his early works are the woodcuts for Sebastian Brant's famous *Ship of Fools*.

Most of Dürer's fame came after 1500, when he was prolific in his output not only in book illustration but working in oils, watercolor, silverpoint, and other artistic media.

DUST JACKET (or DUSTWRAPPER). The decorative paper cover that protects the binding from soil and wear. Jackets were sometimes used during the nineteenth century, and if you find a volume with a jacket of such antiquity, hooray for you. Jackets for books dating back to the early part of the twentieth century, too, are like icing on the cake. They're desirable, but hard to come by. For newer books, however—the **MODERN FIRST EDITIONS**—jackets are a must.

If a book such as William Faulkner's *Light in August* has no dust jacket, it can lose half or more of its value. Even reprints of Zane Grey or Edgar Rice Burroughs command higher prices when accompanied by dust jackets. A modern book with a jacket missing can be likened to an antique table without its legs.

EDGES. Refers to the three outer edges of the leaves. Style of edges is a very important part of a book's makeup, especially in fine or rare editions. New books are delivered to the binder in folded but uncut sheets, or gatherings, and the binder must separate the leaves

A page with a woodcut illustration from The History of Reynard the Fox, *printed in 1894 by David Nutt, London. It is included in Special Collections at the Bailey-Howe Library, University of Vermont.*

by cutting the folds. The edges are usually trimmed to make them perfectly even. Books bound without trimming the edges, showing the original state of the paper with all its irregularities, are valued by some collectors. But then, there is a collector for just about anything.

ELSE FINE. A term used after a recitation of a book's faults indicating that, otherwise, something is right with the book. The phrase "o/w very good" is more common.

ENGRAVING. Illustration printed from a metal plate or woodblock. Engravings on steel, developed in the fifteenth century, were an improvement over wood as they permitted more fine detail and delicate shading.

Collectors of engravings seek the early impressions in a print run, those among the first taken from a plate, as the fine lines of the engraved image sometimes wear down with repeated use.

EPHEMERA. Items that were meant to last a short time. Some booksellers abhor the myriad postcards, sheet music, and advertising paper that appear at book shows under this heading. But many of these items are extensions of book collecting that we accept as not only legitimate but desirable. Say you are putting together a collection of P. G. Wodehouse. Why would you reject the sheet music he wrote? Or the Christmas cards by Robert Frost to round out a collection of his books of poetry? Or the film scripts written by now-famous authors when they were down on their luck and needed to eat?

Ephemera are fun and exciting, and some very famous artists like Maxfield Parrish produced beautiful ads as well as book illustrations for some of the most sought-after children's books. Tucked into old volumes, many ephemera treasures have come to light. A Stevengraph, a hollow-cut silhouette, even a letter with historical information are some of the bonuses possible when turning the pages of an old book.

A Burlington, Vermont, bookseller was a little chagrined when she learned she'd sold a book on Calvin Coolidge with a holograph letter tucked unnoticed among the leaves. The next day the customer returned and asked, did she have any more of those books with letters of the presidents inside?

ERASURES. Removal of underlining or notations with an eraser, discussed further under Notations or Underlinings in the section "The Care and Repair of Old Books."

A bookseller may resort to erasing pencil or pen markings made by former owners of a book, generally by use of a wad of art gum or a pencil eraser. Collectors have mixed feelings about notations and whether or not they should be removed. The value and rarity of a book will influence whether a book is rejected due to the presence of notations or purchased and lived with as is. For the bibliophile, a notation might suggest some continuity with the former owners and be cherished.

The erasures themselves should be clean and not leave unsightly blotches or destroy the print.

ERRATA. Mistakes in printing. The "errata leaf" is still used in cases where a blooper was spotted too late to correct the print run but early enough to bind a note into the book stating the error and correction. More frequently seen is the "errata slip," a small strip of paper containing the correction which may be pasted in the book, or laid in loosely, after the book has been bound.

EX LIBRIS (EX LIB). Indicates the book belonged to a library or bears evidence of having been in a library collection, e.g., the library stamp, card pockets, or identifying marks on the spine. These books, unless they are exceedingly rare, are not often sought by collectors as they usually show considerable wear and damage due to use and library mutilation.

Ex-lib books are almost as difficult to sell as Book-of-the-Month Club or Reader's Digest editions, although many catalogs feature ex-lib books.

FINE PRINTING. Any book in which the quality of type and layout are a main consideration. Books printed by individuals or presses which design their own type may rate as fine printing if the type is well designed. Such books do not necessarily have to be limited editions or kept from public sale. All the products of early typographers were sold on the general market, yet some represent excellent presswork. Had these men bought their types from foundries rather than having a hand in their design, their books might not be so respected.

FIRST EDITION. The first appearance of a book in print. Collectors refer to the first impression (print run) of the book as a true first edition. Identification of true first editions can be an art, and even the most experienced booksellers and collectors run the risk of making an error.

The way printers specify the edition somewhere inside the book—or fail to give any indication at all of which edition it is—varies widely from printer to printer, era to era, and country to country. Best to go prepared with a pocket guide on the subject when browsing through bookstores, for you could not possibly keep in mind the vast number of codes that publishers have used or the legions of points that identify specific titles. Unfortunately, if a book does not readily admit in print to being a second or a third or a fifteen-thousandth edition, the uninformed public automatically assumes the book is a first. The collector or bookseller cannot afford this casual assumption, as most collectors acquire first editions for many reasons, not least among them investment.

FIRST IMPRESSION. The first time a set of plates has been used to print a book. Also called a **FIRST PRINTING**.

All impressions using the same set of plates constitute one edition, thus each edition can include more than one impression. Most sellers and collectors are speaking of the first impression of the first edition when discussing collectible **FIRST EDITIONS**.

FIRST THUS. Not the first edition, but you may see this used to describe an altered edition of an old book. Since the revised book is an edition unlike the original, perhaps issued by a different publishing house or illustrated by some other artist, the book can be presented as first thus. Like a distant cousin to the first edition.

FLYLEAF. Blank leaf after the front free endpaper, not always present. The term is often misapplied to the front endpaper.

FOLDING PLATES. Plates which fold out to a larger size than the book leaves. Volumes published by the Government Printing Office during the nineteenth century have many folding maps and color illustrations bound into the books. Guide books are designed with folding illustrations and maps, too. Through the years, unfortunately, folding plates begin to show wear and tear from handling.

FOLIO. A standard book size, measuring from about 12″ tall on up. An atlas folio is 24″, and an elephant folio is 20″ or more. Audubon's *Birds of America* is a most valued natural history book measuring 37″ tall.

FORE-EDGE. The outer edge of a book, opposite the spine.

FORE-EDGE PAINTING. Painting the edges of a book's leaves with a scene or other picture. The book must be held in a special press, and while the leaves are slightly fanned out the artist paints or decorates the exposed fore-edges of the leaves. When the book is fully closed, the edge is gilded to conceal traces of the painting. But lightly fan out the edges, and the fore-edge painting can be a lovely surprise. Because the painting is hidden, a book with a fore-edge painting can go undetected, even by a knowledgeable bookseller, until the book is opened.

FORMAT. The size of a book as determined by the specific number of times the original printed sheet of paper has been folded to form the leaves. For standard format sizes used in the book trade, see **BOOK SIZES**.

FOXED. Discolored with brown spots and blotches caused by microorganisms that find the paper in certain books appetizing. Dampness can encourage the problem. The spots are often dark and, when the foxing is heavy, can seriously detract from the value of an otherwise good book.

FRAKTUR. A German style of Gothic or black-letter type. Fraktur was most prevalent at Augsburg and Nuremburg in the post-incunabula period, when Gothic had been almost totally dropped by French and Italian printers. Popular with the Pennsylvania Dutch, early birth certificates decorated and embellished with fraktur are becoming harder to find and more expensive to buy.

FRONTISPIECE. An illustration appearing opposite the title page. More often than not, the frontis (as abbreviated) is a portrait of the author, but in many books, the frontis is a lovely color plate or a steel engraving.

GILT EDGES. Gold applied to all three edges of a book's leaves. In book parlance, t.e.g. means top edge gilt, and a.e.g. means all edges gilt.

HALF-BOUND. A book with leather extending over the spine and about an inch or so along the front and back covers. The rest of the binding is either cloth or paper. If the spine is leather and the four corners of the book are covered in leather triangles, you have a book which is called three-quarter leather. Thought to be an English custom, the practice goes back to the seventeenth century, but did not become popular until the eighteenth century.

HALF-TITLE. Usually the first appearance of print in a volume, the title printed on an otherwise blank sheet before the title page.

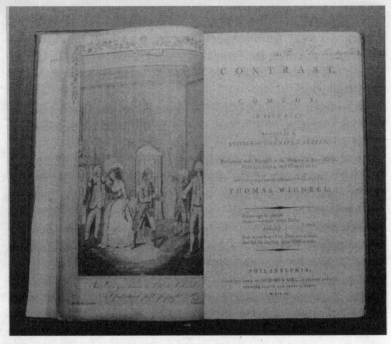

Frontis and title page of "Contrast, a Comedy, in Five Acts" from the private library of George Washington, containing Washington's signature in the upper right-hand corner of the title page. The play, written by the Vermont author of A Citizen of the United States, *Royal Tyler, was the first American play written by an American and produced on the American stage. This rare copy, bound in red leather with gold tooling, is in Special Collections at the Bailey-Howe Library of the University of Vermont.*

This is a holdover from the days of early printing when the title was the only information given on the title page.

The half-title is also known as **BASTARD TITLE**. Grant Uden, in his book *Understanding Book Collecting*, puts this appellation down to the insensitivity of Americans, who he says often adopt their own bibliographical terminology. But whosoever puts these terms together, all you have to remember is that the half-title is most often the first appearance of print in a volume.

In the past, when restoring a book, binders often discarded the half-title page. They may have considered it superfluous, and well it might be, unless you are a collector, and then that half-title page had better be there.

HEADBAND. A (usually) colorful band inside the spine, sewn across the top of the leaves. In modern bindery, it has no function and is primarily decorative, if it is present at all. Headbands are more often seen in older books. The term is used to include the tail-band (sewn across the bottom inside of the spine) as well.

HINGE. The ridge where the front or back cover meets the spine. When a book has a hinge crack, the cover is intact but loose. It definitely needs attention before worse can happen, which is separation of the covers from the book.

HOLOGRAPH. A document written wholly in the hand of the author. Although autograph collectors use the term more frequently, booksellers find it helpful to indicate more than mere inscription or presentation material on the flyleaf of a book; specifically, a laid-in letter or a **MANUSCRIPT**.

HORNBOOK. A sheet of paper, printed on one side with the alphabet or some other rudiments of schoolwork, pasted onto a handled piece of wood, then covered with transparent horn. In colonial America, these were a child's first schoolbooks. Used from the sixteenth to the eighteenth century, genuine hornbooks are rare, but imitations turn up now and then, no doubt prompted by the high price an original would command.

ILLUMINATED MANUSCRIPT. A work containing dazzling letters, initials, and sentence openings, hand decorated in bold colors and finished off with gold and silver. Spectacular and colorful, the art work did, in essence, brilliantly shed light upon the text. Manuscript illumination is known to have been practiced as early as the fifth century. Monks in the seventh and eighth centuries in Ireland produced specimens of great artistry, including the awe-inspiring **BOOK OF KELLS**.

Illuminating manuscripts remained the province of monastic scribes until the end of the fourteenth century, when the commercial manuscript industry came into its own and the secular world took a serious interest in book ownership. Unfortunately, the invention of printing, which literally set the book business on its head, also contributed to the demise of the manuscript trade. By 1470, the German manuscript industry had virtually ceased to function; those of Italy and Spain gave way soon after. France was the last stronghold of illuminated manuscripts, turning out specimens of quality even after the age of INCUNABULA. But in the end, the writing was on the wall and manuscripts were only hand illuminated by special request.

IMPRESSION. In the strictest sense, a run of copies, large or small, ordered by a publisher from the printer at one time. After the first impression, other runs may be printed from the same setting of type, and are usually so noted. Collectors of first editions are actually looking for the first impression of the first edition of a volume, as all impressions taken from one setting of type constitute an edition.

In days past, when type was set in metal and was ungainly and difficult to store for long periods, a book that remained in demand after its first edition sold out was likely to need resetting before it could be reissued. Printings from the new set of type then constituted impressions of a second edition.

IMPRINT. The information at the foot of the title page that refers to the publisher or the place of publication. The book trade includes collectors who specialize in imprints. Imprints of the Revolutionary period and the Confederacy are especially prized.

INCUNABULA (singular INCUNABULUM). Books printed on presses in the fifteenth century. The word is derived from the Latin root meaning "in the cradle," and indicates printing in its infancy. Incunabula are automatically valuable and collectible.

INDIAN BIBLE. The name commonly given to an edition of the Bible in a Native American language, an Algonquin dialect, translated and compiled by the Reverend John Eliot and published at Cambridge, Massachusetts, in 1663. This Bible is also known as the Natick Bible and the Eliot Bible.

INSCRIBED COPY. A book carrying a signed inscription, usually saying something like "with regards to" or "for a special friend." Should the author of the inscription be famous, the book's value is enhanced. However, an inscription by the former owner, who may be a nice person, does not constitute an inscribed copy.

ISSUE. A term applied to a second printing (impression) of an edition that includes a change or correction—but not a complete resetting of type—made after the first impression is printed. Adding to the confusion are "states," or printings in which changes have been made during the print run. The terms are technical but important to the identification of older first editions. Many booksellers use "issue" and "state" interchangeably.

LAID IN. Refers to a piece of paper, such as a letter or a photo, placed in the book but not attached.

LEAF. A single sheet of paper, with a **RECTO** (front) page and a **VERSO** (back) page. Many people confuse pages and leaves. A page is just one side of a leaf.

LIBRARY OF CONGRESS. America's largest library, located in Washington, D.C. Founded as a working library for members of Congress, the library now holds not only government documents, but one of the largest collections of incunabula in the United States.

LIMITED EDITION. Special printing of a limited number of books. Printing and binding is often of a higher quality than in the usual trade books or may be the product of a **PRIVATE PRESS**. The books are often numbered and signed by the author and illustrator, if there is one.

LIMP. Refers to bookbindings made of material that is not supported by boards. The cover is literally hanging limp. Limp vellum was used as a trade binding for printed books almost since the beginning of typography and remained popular in Italian, Spanish, and Portuguese bindery during the fifteenth to seventeenth centuries. Limp bindings were often fitted with leather thong ties in place of clasps.

In the nineteenth century, limp leather was often used as a binding for bibles, giving way to imitation leather in later years.

LITHOGRAPHY. A principal method of printing developed in the nineteenth and twentieth centuries, especially suited to reproducing drawings and illustrations. The process consists of printing from an impression drawn on smooth lithographic limestone using chemical inks. Many artists, including the renowned Currier and Ives, came to use the process to replace engraving. Lithography is now a prominent art form.

LOOSE. A book that is in danger of separating from its binding. No longer held tight by the spine, the joints cannot support the weight of the book.

MANUSCRIPT. In the book world, refers to a handwritten document. Technically, a work written by hand; but in the modern world, a manuscript can be typewritten and still be considered a manuscript. The distinction is that it was not typeset or printed. If the

*The English were the masters of panel binding. It is very
symmetrical and orderly. The material is black morocco, the
tooling is in gold, and the spine has extra embellishing, c. 1690.
$1,200–$1,500.*

writing is in the author's hand, it's termed a **HOLOGRAPH** manuscript. In the Middle Ages, monks copying sacred texts created
ILLUMINATED (illustrated) manuscripts of great beauty, but with
the invention and proliferation of mechanical printing, the practice
died out.

MARBLING. A technique of decorating paper to create the effect
of marble; mostly used for endpapers. Some examples of marbled
paper have intriguing patterns that craftspeople today are dupli-
cating to frame or to use as book covers.

MEZZOTINT. The process of engraving on copper plates.

MINIATURE. Actually not what you'd think; derived from *miniatus*,
which means painted with vermilion. The ancient artists who used this
red paint were called miniators. Originally, miniatures referred to the
colored drawings in early manuscripts.

MINT CONDITION. Like new. Right off the press.

MISPRINT. An error in printing, very important when identifying
first editions. For instance, in the first American edition of Mark
Twain's *Adventures of Huckleberry Finn* the word "saw" was
printed incorrectly as "was" on line 23, page 57. Misprints are often
among the important **POINTS** which must be present if a book is a
true first edition.

MODERN FIRST EDITIONS. Includes books published since the
turn of the twentieth century. Here again in book parlance phrases
are evolving with time, and most people use the term in reference to
books from the 1920s on.

MOROCCO. Leather made from goatskin.

ND. No date of publication is given.

NP. No place of publication is given.

OCTAVO. The most common size/format of books. Usually seen
expressed as "8vo," the most common octavos measure approximately 8″ high.

OUT OF PRINT. No longer obtainable from the publisher.

PAMPHLET. A small work, issued unbound or in wraps, and usually sewn or stapled together.

PAPERBACK. Softcovered book, primarily a book bound in heavy
paper, published from the 1930s on. Today, early paperbacks are
collectible and sought after, especially the horror and science fiction
genres.

A

THANKSGIVING SERMON,

PREACHED JANUARY 1, 1808,

In St. Thomas's, or the African Episcopal, Church.
Philadelphia:

ON ACCOUNT OF

THE ABOLITION

OF THE

AFRICAN SLAVE TRADE,

ON THAT DAY,

BY THE CONGRESS OF THE UNITED STATES

BY ABSALOM JONES,
RECTOR OF THE SAID CHURCH.

PHILADELPHIA:
PRINTED FOR THE USE OF THE CONGREGATION.
FRY AND KAMMERER, PRINTERS.
1808.

This tract, laying out the position of abolitionists decades before the Civil War made their arguments moot, has survived in excellent shape for a pamphlet in wraps. (Courtesy of the Trustees of the Boston Public Library. Photographed by Marilyn Green.)

The term is not to be confused with **WRAPS**, a thin paper cover.

PARTS. Books released in serial form or in installments. Many books started out this way and were only later published in book form. The works of Dickens followed this pattern; his *Dombey and Son* was printed in parts—nineteen of the twenty parts in green pictorial wrappers—as were several of his other works. Amassing all the parts can be a daunting task since unprotected paper is fragile, and many did not survive.

PENNY BOXES. Trays or boxes outside antiquarian bookshops where the bookseller puts cheap, miscellaneous stock to attract browsers.

PLATE. A full page devoted to an illustration, separate from the text pages of the book. The verso is blank.

POINTS. Characteristics which determine whether or not a book is a first edition. For instance, the first edition of a book may contain a specific spelling or other publishing mistake on a certain page that was corrected in later editions. The presence of the mistake is a point.

PRESENTATION COPY. Inscribed by the author as a gift. Not to be confused with a signature acquired by a total stranger who asked for the author's autograph in the book.

PRESS BOOK. A finely produced book, published by a private press, an individual, or an established publisher for the sake of excellence in printing and binding and not necessarily for the book's literary value. Prices run high on these specialties—from the outset, not just as collectibles—again for the high manufacturing standard, not because the book is wonderful literature, though it might be.

PRINT RUN. The number of copies of a book run off the press at one time.

PRIVATELY PRINTED. Not produced by a publisher. The author pays for the publication out of his own pocket. Quite often the privately printed book was compiled for a select group of people, family or friends. Some very collectible books have been privately published, not the least of which was Edgar Allan Poe's *Tamerlane*, a copy of which recently sold at auction for a quarter of a million dollars.

PRIVATE PRESS. Publishers of limited editions or, simply, a single person producing (publishing) books.

PROVENANCE. The history of a book's ownership. Provenance may add to value if it shows prized associations. Many bibliophiles like information on the provenance of a book for its own sake. A love of old books and of their history seem to go hand in hand.

QUARTER BOUND. Only the spine of a book is leather. The rest is boards or cloth.

QUOTES. The backbone of the bookseller's trade, a written description of a book with the asking price of the book stated. When quoting, use a 3″ × 5″ index card for each book quoted. Print the title, author, publisher, date, edition, number of pages, whether or not illustrations or maps are present, and the type of binding. Then carefully describe the condition. It is here a bookseller appreciates full disclosure of the defects. Even if you are as accurate as you know how to be, sometimes a dealer will envision something different and find the quote wanting. Include your name, address, and sale requirements and state whether the transaction is C.W.O. (cash with order) or future billing.

READING COPY. A book that has seen better days, worn from use and in less than good condition. Such copies are appreciated by scholars for research, but not by collectors unless the volume is exceedingly rare.

REBACKED. Fitted with a new spine and hinges. When considering such repairs, be prepared to pay well for a competent job. Unless you have a personal affinity for the book, before ordering any restoration by a professional bookbinder, have your volume appraised to see if it is worth the preservation cost.

REBOUND. Fitted with a new binding. Here again, as in the rebacked book, we are talking restoration and expensive repairs. Whenever this route is undertaken, opt for reattaching the original covers, if that is possible. Again, if you are selling the book, value should be there to justify the expense.

RECTO. In a book, the right-hand page, the front of the leaf.

REMAINDER. Selling book stock to a distributor at a considerable discount when the publisher believes the title has sold as many copies as it is likely to sell at full price in bookstores.

REPRINT. A reissue of a book previously published. A. L. Burt and Grosset & Dunlap reissued and made available many famous works to those who could not afford the first editions. In an elderly farm woman's house we visited in Vermont, the shelves in an upstairs bedroom were lined with books, reprints by Zane Grey,

E. R. Burroughs, Dixon, Henty, Horatio Alger, and more. And proud she was that she had read them all.

REVIEW COPY. Refers to complimentary copies of books sent to editors, journalists, and institutions in hopes of a review or at least a mention in their publications or programs.

RUBBED. A word used to describe leather bindings with scratches or wear spots.

SABIN, JOSEPH. An English bookseller who emigrated to the United States and became one of the foremost authorities on Americana, setting about to publish a comprehensive bibliography of the genre (**BIBLIOTHECA AMERICANA**). Unfortunately, Sabin lived to see only the first thirteen volumes realized. Wilberforce Eames and R.W.G. Vail completed the monumental work, finishing with a total of twenty-nine volumes.

SCUFFED. Worn, scratched, nicked.

SEARCH SERVICE. Precisely what the term implies, initiating a search for a title through dealership and trade channels. Let's say you want a particular book, and you cannot find it in a used book store. If you know the title and author, a bookseller will print an inquiry in the trade journals welcoming quotes from other dealers. Since these journals have wide exposure among booksellers, the likelihood of finding your book is strong.

Most booksellers now charge a basic fee for the service whether or not the book is found. Back in the good old days, Wright Howes noted in his fall 1933 catalog: "out of print and scarce books sought for and reported free of charge." The times, they are a-changing.

SPINE. The backstrip of a book.

STATE. Refers to changes or corrections made during a print run. Sometimes used interchangeably with "issue," which indicates changes or corrections, but not a full resetting of the type, made between impressions.

SUNNED. Faded. The original color of the book loses brightness and freshness when exposed to direct bright light, especially sunlight.

THREE-QUARTER LEATHER. Leather on the spine and about an inch beyond, along with triangles of leather at the corners of the book. The rest of the binding could be cloth or boards.

TIPPED-IN. Glued in, as when illustrations are not bound into a book but glued in after binding. The technique is most often used to

TAMERLANE

AND

OTHER POEMS

BY A BOSTONIAN

Young heads are giddy and young hearts are warm
and make mistakes for manhood to reform.

Cowper

BOSTON:

CALVIN F. S. THOMAS . . PRINTER

1827

Facsimile Title Page

FANSHAWE,

A TALE.

"Wilt thou go on with me?"-- Southey.

BOSTON:
MARSH & CAPEN, 362 WASHINGTON STREET.

PRESS OF PUTNAM AND HUNT.

1828.

Facsimile Title Page

add glossy pictures or maps, with glue applied to the back of the illustration at the top only. Tipping-in was used to incorporate illustrations that would have been too expensive to print and bind into the book.

TISSUE GUARDS. Tissue paper bound into the book to protect the plates.

TITLE PAGE. The page at the front of each book that gives the title, author, publisher, and sometimes the printing date. In most books, this information is on a recto page. Always consult the title page for pertinent information about a book; never depend upon what is printed on the spine or cover.

TOOLING. Impressing a design by hand in leather.

UNCUT. Untrimmed leaves. When sheets are printed, folded, and bound, the trimming process to open the leaves can miss some folds, leaving the pages uncut and unopened.

UNOPENED. Uncut leaves. Tearing can open them, but they remain uncut, though opened.

VELLUM. Calfskin binding. Also sometimes called parchment. Vellum and other leather bindings should be carefully cared for to keep them from drying and cracking (see "The Care and Repair of Old Books").

VERSO. Left-hand page of a book, the back of a leaf.

WANT LIST. A listing of books needed either to fill a dealer's bookshelves or to accommodate customers looking for particular works. Booksellers periodically send out want lists to other dealers. Often the bookseller will include a "permanent want list," in which case there is no cut-off date for acquiring those books, and duplicates may even be welcome.

WESTERN AMERICANA. The genre covering the settling of the American West and American western culture, including indigenous peoples. Everyone seems to want this category, and the prices are high for the really good stuff. The collector, of course, is looking for pioneer imprints, broadsides, handbills, documents, handwritten journey narratives, or ledgers. Books on Indians, explorations, outlaws, mining, and whatever else attested to the westward push are collectible.

WRAPPERS. Paper binding. This does not refer to modern paperbacks, which are bound in stiff paper with illustrations. The term refers to simple paper covering, sometimes plain paper serving also as a title page. Before modern bindings, books were often published with plain paper covers. Customers brought the works to their own binderies to have custom leather or cloth covers put on. Older pamphlets were often published with thin paper covers, or wrappers.

WRAPS. Same as wrappers.

ABBREVIATIONS

Albany	Alb
All edges gilded	aeg
American	Amer
American Museum of Natural History	AMNH
Association book	asso copy
Atlanta	Atl
Backed	bkd
Baltimore	Balt
Boards	bds
Boston	Bos
Black-and-white	b/w
British	Brit
Cambridge	Camb
Catalog	cat
Chicago	Chi
Cincinnati	Cinc
Cleveland	Cleve
Color, colored	clr

Copies	cc
Cover	cvr
Dust jacket/dust wrapper	dj
Edinburgh	Edin
Edition, edited	ed
Editor	(ed)
English	Eng
Engravings	engr
Ex libris	ex lib
Facsimile	facs
First edition	1st ed
Folding	fldg
Frontispiece	frontis
Government Printing Office	GPO
Hardcover	hc
Illustrated	illus
Impression	imp
Indianapolis	Ind
Inscribed	inscrb
Leather	lea
Limited edition	ltd
Lithograph	litho
London	Lon
Marbled	mar
Milwaukee	Milw
Minneapolis	Minn
Morocco	mor
Museum of Modern Art	MOMA
National Geographic Society	NGS
No date	nd
No place	np
Numbered	nbr
Oxford	Ox
Pages	pp
Philadelphia	Phila
Pittsburgh	Pitts
Photographs	photos
Printing	ptg
Providence	Prov

Rebacked	rbkd
Rebound	rbnd
Reprint	rprnt
Reproduction	repro
Revised	rev
Richmond	Rich
Sacramento	Sac
Salt Lake City	SLC
San Francisco	SF
Signed (by author)	sgn
Top edge gilded	teg
Tipped-in	tip-in
Title has been abbreviated	. . .
Toronto	Tor
United Kingdom	UK
Volumes	vols
Wrappers, soft covers	wrps

OLD BOOKS LISTING

*The University of these days
is a Collection of Books*
—THOMAS CARLYLE

1902 Models: Victor Talking Machines. Phila. Victor Talking Machine Co. 1902. printed wrps, illus, 24 pp. . . . .*$50–$75*

5th Reader. Cinc/NY. 1885. . . . .*$25–$40*

Abbot, W. J. *Panama and the Canal.* Syndicate Pub. Co. 1913. illus. 414 pp. . . . .*$12–$20*

A'Beckett, Gilbert Abbott. *The Comic History of England.* Lon. Routledge. [c 1880]. 200 b/w illus by John Leech. . . . .*$35–$45*

Abel, Clarke. *Narrative of a Journey in the Interior of China . . . Containing an Account of Lord Amherst's Embassy.* Lon. Longman, Hurst. 1818. 1st ed. maps, plates (8 hand-clr). . . . .*$1,200–$1,575*

Abelow, Samuel P. *History of Brooklyn Jewry.* Brooklyn. 1937. 1st ed. . . . .*$115–$175*

Abercrombie, John. *Pathological and Practical Researches on Diseases of . . . Abdomen.* Edin. 1828. . . . .*$35–$50*

Abernethy, John. *Surgical Observations . . . Treatment of Local Diseases. . . .* Lon. 1825. bds. . . . .*$50–$100*

Abernethy, John. *The Surgical Works.* Lon. 1816. 2 vols. new ed. 1 plate, calf. . . . .*$100–$200*

Abrahams, I. *By-paths in Hebraic Bookland.* Phila. Jewish Pub. Society of America 1943. illus. 371 pp. *$38*

Abrahams, Israel. *Jewish Life in the Middle Ages.* Phila. 1896. 1st ed. ...
....*$18–$30*

Ackerman, Irving C. *The Wire-haired Fox Terrier.* NY. 1928. illus. ....
....*$15–$18*

Ackley, Edith F. *Marionettes.* NY. Stokes. 1929. dj. ....*$25–$45*

Act for the Making of Bread. Lon. 1758. ....*$50–$75*

Adair, J. *Navajo and Pueblo Silversmiths.* Norman, OK. 1944. 1st ed. maps, charts, plates, dj. ....*$45–$95*

Adams, Andy. *The Log of a Cowboy.* Bos. 1903. 1st ed. illus by E. Boyd Smith, 2nd issue, maps, 6 plates. ....*$70–$125*

Adams, Andy. *A Texas Matchmaker.* Bos. 1904. 1st ed. ....*$20–$30*

Adams, Ansel. *An Autobiography.* Bos. 1985. wrps. dj. ....*$50–$85*

Adams, Ansel. *Born Free and Equal.* U.S. 1944. wrps. ....*$95–$150*

Adams, Ansel. *Camera and Lens Studio.* Morgan & Lester. 1948. 1st ed. .
....*$25–$40*

Adams, Ansel. *My Camera in the National Parks.* Yosemite National Park. Virginia Adams. 1950. illus. 97 pp, spiral bound bds. *$275*

Adams, Ansel. *The Negative.* 1964. sgn, dj. ....*$30–$60*

Adams, Ansel. *Yosemite and the Range of Light.* Bos. 1979. illus. sgn, dj.
....*$80–$125*

Adams, Ansel. *Yosemite Valley.* SF. 1959. 1st ed. pictorial wrps. *$75*

Adams, Ansel, and Nancy Newhall. *The Tetons and The Yellowstone.* Redwood City, CA. 1970. wrps. ....*$25–$35*

Adams, Ansel, and Nancy Newhall. *This Is the American Earth.* SF. Sierra Club. 1960. 1st ed. 89 pp, illus, dj. ....*$65–$80*

Adams, D. *The Hitchhiker's Guide to the Galaxy.* NY. 1979. 1st ed. dj. ..
....*$25–$35*

Adams, Emma H. *To and Fro, Up and Down in Southern California.* Cinc. 1888. 1st ed. 288 pp. ....*$50–$135*

Adams, George. *A Treatise Describing the Construction ... and Use of New Celestial and Terrestrial Globes.* Lon. the author. 1769. 2nd ed. plates. ....*$300–$425*

Adams, John. *The Adams-Jefferson Letters.* Univ. of North Carolina Press. 1959. 2 vols. 1st ed. boxed ....*$35–$65*

Adams, John D. *Arts-Crafts Lamps: How to Make Them.* Chi. 1911. illus.
....*$65–$85*

Adams, Joseph. *Observations on Morbid Poisons.* ... Lon. 1795. bds. ....
....*$130*

Adams, Joseph. *Salmon and Trout Angling.* NY. Dutton. 1923. 1st Amer ed. 288 pp. ....$40–$50

Adams, Paul M. *When Wagon Trails Were Dim.* . . . Montana. 1957. . . . .$12–$15

Adams, Ramon F. *More Burrs under the Saddle: Books and Histories of the West.* Norman, OK. (1979). 1st ed. dj. ....$35–$65

Adams, Richard. *Watership Down.* Macmillan. 1974. sgn, dj. . . .$60–$75

Adams, Richard. *Watership Down.* Lon. 1972. 1st ed. author's first book, dj. ....$600–$1,000

Adams, Richard C. *A Delaware Indian Legend and the Story of Their Troubles.* DC. private ptg. 1899. 1st ed. $125

Adams, W. H. Davenport. *Famous Caves and Catacombs Described and Illustrated.* Lon. 1886. pictorial cloth. ....$40–$60

Adanson, Michel. *A Voyage to Senegal, the Isle of Goree, and the River Gambia.* Lon. Nourse & Johnston. 1759. 1st English ed. fldg map. ....$300–$385

Adcock, Thomas. *Drown All the Dogs.* NY. Pocket Books. 1994. 1st ed. dj. ....$25–$35

Addams, Charles. *Black Maria.* NY. 1960. 1st ed. dj. ....$20–$30

Addams, Jane. *The Spirit of Youth and the City Streets.* NY. 1909. 1st ed. inscrb. ....$18–$25

[Addison, Joseph]. *The Free-holder.* Lon. Midwinter & Tonson. 1716. 1st collected ed. 400 pp, rbkd. $350

Adler, Felix. *An Ethical Philosophy of Life.* NY. 1925. ....$30–$45

Adney, Edwin Tappan. *The Bark Canoes and Skin Boats of North America.* DC. 1964. 1st ed. illus. ....$30–$45

Aesop's Fables. Lon. 1933. illus by Arthur Rackham, new translation by Vernon Jones. $75

Agassiz, L. *Geological Sketches.* Bos. 1873. ....$80–$100

Agassiz, L. *Lake Superior.* Bos. 1850. 15 plates, map. ....$175–$250

Agassiz, Louis. *The Structure of Animal Life: Six Lectures.* Scribner's, Armstrong. 1874. 3rd ed. ....$20–$35

Agassiz, Louis, and A. A. Gould. *Outlines of Comparative Physiology.* Lon. 1855. illus. ....$35–$40

Agee, James. *A Death in the Family.* Lon. Victor Gollancz. 1958. 1st ed. dj. $90

Agricultural Implements and Machines. Bos. Ames Plow Co. 1901. illus. pictorial wrps. $25

Aguilar, Grace. *The Vale of Cedars and Other Tales.* Lon. 1902. illus. . . .
. . . .*$50–$75*

Aguilar, Grace. *The Vale of Cedars and Other Tales.* Lon. 1902. Jewish
Pub. Society of America, teg. *$75*

Aguilar, Grace. *Women of Israel.* NY. 1870. 2 vols. illus. . . . . . .*$35–$50*

Ahlstrom, L. J. *Eighty Years of Swedish Baptist Work in Iowa, 1835–1933.*
Des Moines. 1933. 1st ed. illus. . . . .*$45–$75*

Aiken, Conrad. *The Jig of Forslin.* Bos. The Four Seas Co. 1916 1st ed. .
. . . .*$65*

Aiken, Conrad. *Senlin: A Biography.* Lon. Hogarth Press. 1925. 1st ed. . .
. . . .*$75*

Aiken, Conrad. *The Short Stories.* NY. (1950). dj. . . . .*$35–$45*

Ainsworth, Ed. *The Cowboy Art.* NY. World Publishing Co. [1968]. 1st
ed. illus. #222/1000 cc, slipcase. *$180*

The Aircraft Yearbook for 1944. NY. Lanciar Publishers. [1944]. annual
ed. ed by Howard Mingos, photos, dj. . . . .*$45–$60*

Akers, Floyd. *The Boy Fortune Hunters in Yucatan.* Reilly & Britton.
(1910). 1st ed. *$250*

Akin, Otis F. *A Reminiscences of the Klondike Rush of 1898.* 1st ed. wrps.
. . . .*$75–$100*

Albee, Edward. *Malcolm.* NY. 1966. 1st ed. dj. . . . .*$25–$40*

Albee, Edward. *Who's Afraid of Virginia Woolf?* NY. 1962. 1st ed. dj. . .
. . . .*$25–$40*

Albert, Lillian Smith, and Jane Ford Adams. *The Button Sampler.* NY.
illus. dj. . . . .*$18–$25*

Albion, Robert Greenhalgh, and Robert Howe Connery. *Forrestal and
the Navy.* NY. 1962. illus. dj. . . . .*$16–$25*

Albrecht, Arthur Amil. *International Seaman's Union of America.* . . .
GPO. 1923. wrps. . . . .*$18–$25*

Alcoholics Anonymous. 1st ed. 14th ptg, dj. . . . .*$350–$600*

Alcoholics Anonymous. 1948. 1st ed. 12th ptg. *$125*

Alcott, Louisa May. *Little Men.* Bos. Roberts. 1871. 1st ed. 1st issue,
green cloth. *$350*

Alcott, Louisa May. *An Old Fashioned Girl.* Bos. 1870. 1st ed. *$65–$100*

Alcott, William Tyler. *The Book of the Stars for Young People.* NY. 1929.
5th ptg, plates, 411 pp. . . . .*$30–$45*

Aldrich, Herbert L. *Arctic Alaska and Siberia.* Chi/NY. Rand McNally.
small 8vo, photos, maps. . . . .*$56–$70*

Aldrich, L. C. *History of Ontario County.* Syracuse. 1893. . . . .
. . . .*$85–$120*

Aldrich, Thomas Bailey. *Marjorie Daw.* Bos. 1908. 1st ed. illus. dj. . . . .
. . . .*$75–$150*

Alexander, E. P. *Military Memoirs of a Confederate.* NY. 1907. 1st ed.
illus. fldg map. . . . .*$100–$275*

Alexander, William. *The History of Women.* Lon. Strahan & Cadell. 1779.
2 vols bound in 1. 1st ed, scarce. *$600*

Alexie, Sherman. *The First Indian on the Moon.* NY. Hanging Loose
Press. 1993. 1st ed. without dj as issued, 1/500 cc, sgn. . . . .*$60–$75*

Alexie, Sherman. *The Lone Ranger and Tonto Fistfight in Heaven.* NY.
Atlantic Monthly Press. 1993. wrps. illus. special reader's ed, sgn. . . . . . .
. . . .*$30–$45*

Alger, Horatio. *Silas Snobden's Office Boy.* Garden City. 1973. dj. . . . . . .
. . . .*$14–$25*

Alger, Horatio. *Strive and Succeed.* Bos. 1872. . . . .*$75–$95*

Alger, William Rounseville. *Life of Edwin Forrest.* Phila. Lippincott.
1877. 2 vols. large 8vo, pictorial cloth, 864 pp, plates. . . . .*$85–$100*

Algren, Nelson. *The Man with the Golden Arm.* NY. 1949. 1st ed. dj. . . . .
. . . .*$15–$20*

Algren, Nelson. *A Walk on the Wild Side.* Farrar, Straus & Cudahy.
(1956). 1st ed. dj. . . . .*$25–$45*

Ali Baba and the Forty Thieves. Houghton Mifflin. 1950. 6 pop-ups. *$100*

Alken, Henry. *Scraps from the Sketch Book.* Lon. 1823. illus. hand-clr
plates, folio. . . . .*$500–$650*

All About Hawaii: Standard Tourist Guide. Honolulu. 1928. 1st ed. wrps.
illus. maps. . . . .*$60–$85*

Allen, Miss A. J. *Ten Years in Oregon.* Ithaca. 1848. 2nd issue. . . . .
. . . .*$100–$150*

Allen, Charles Dexter. *American Book-plates.* NY. 1905. illus. rprnt. . . .
. . . .*$18–$35*

Allen, Edward H. *Violin Making as It Was and Is.* 1885. illus. 2nd ed. dj.
. . . .*$40–$50*

Allen, Gardner Weld. *Our Navy and the Barbary Corsairs.* Bos/NY/Chi.
1905. 1st ed. illus. 16 plates . . . .*$30–$50*

Allen, Lewis. *American Herd Book, Containing Pedigrees of Short Horn
Cattle.* . . . Buffalo. 1846. 240 pp. . . . .*$90–$145*

Allen, R. P. *Birds of the Caribbean.* NY. 1961. plates. . . . .*$18–$27*

Allen, Woody. *Side Effects.* Random House. 1980. 1st ed. dj. . . .*$50–$75*

Allingham, Margery. *The Gyrth Chalice Mystery.* Garden City. Doubleday Crime Club. 1931. 1st ed. dj. . . . .*$30–$45*

Allsop, F. C. *Practical Electrical Light Fitting.* 1923. illus. 9th ed. . . . . . .
. . . .*$18–$25*

Alpatov. M. W. *Art Treasuries in Russia.* NY. (1967). illus. clr plates, dj.
. . . .*$50–$75*

Alsop, Gulielma. *History of the Woman's Medical College, Philadelphia, Pennsylvania, 1850–1950.* Lippincott. 1950. 1st ed. . . . . :*$10–$25*

Alvarez, A. *Biggest Game in Town.* Bos. 1983. dj. . . . .*$12–$15*

Alvarez, Julia. *How the Garcia Girls Lost Their Accents.* Algonquin Books, 1991. 1st ed. dj. . . . .*$28–$35*

Alvarez, Julia. *In the Time of the Butterfly.* Chapel Hill. Algonquin Books. 1994. 1st ed. sgn, dj. . . . .*$35–$45*

Ambler, Charles H. *Washington and the West.* 1936. dj. . . . .*$25–$33*

Ambler, Eric. *Passage of Arms.* NY. 1960. 1st U.S. ed. dj. . . . . .*$35–$45*

Ambler, Henry Lovejoy. *Facts, Fads and Fancies about Teeth.* Cleve. 1900. illus by W. L. Evans. . . . .*$16–$45*

The American Boy's Book of Sports and Games. . . . NY. (1864). illus. . .
. . . .*$40–$50*

The American Car and Foundry Company in Khaki: Its Production Achievements in the Great War. NY. 1919. 95 pp. *$75*

American Line Type. Jersey City. American Type Founders. 1903. large 4to, 292 pp. *$75*

American Pioneer in Science: William James Beal. Amherst, MA. 1925. 1st ed. illus. . . . .*$50–$75*

Amory, Thomas C. *The Life of Admiral Sir Isaac Coffin, Baronet.* . . . Bos. 1886. 1st ed. illus. . . . .*$50–$75*

Amsden, Charles Avery. *Navaho Weaving: Its Technique and History.* Albuquerque. 1949. 2nd ed. clr repro laid in. . . . .*$50–$150*

Amsden, Charles Avery. *Navaho Weaving.* . . . Glorietta, NM. 1974. illus. rprnt of 1934 ed. . . . .*$15–$25*

Amsden, Charles Avery. *Prehistoric Southwesterners, from Basketmaker to Pueblo.* Los Angeles. 1949. wrps. illus. . . . .*$25–$35*

Amundsen, Roald. *The South Pole.* NY. 1925. 2 vols in 1. . . . .*$95–$135*

Andersen, Hans Christian. *Fairy Tales.* L:1872. clr illus by Eleanor Vere Boyle *$450*

Andersen, Hans Christian. *The Nightingale and Other Stories.* NY/Lon. nd. 1st ed illus by Edmund Dulac, tip-in clr plates. . . . .*$150–$200*

Andersen, Hans Christian. *A Picture Book without Pictures.* NY. 1848. 1st U.S. ed. . . . .*$50–$60*

Andersen, Hans Christian, and Charles Perrault. *The Fairy Tales.* Illus. Ed. Co. illus by H. Clarke. . . . .*$150–$250*

Anderson, Andrew A. *Twenty-five Years in a Waggon: Sport and Travel in South Africa.* Lon. Chapman & Hall. 1888. new 1-vol ed. fldg map. . . . .
. . . .*$125–$195*

Anderson, Charles C. *Fighting by Southern Federals.* NY. 1912. 1st ed. blue cloth. . . . .*$85–$175*

Anderson, E. W. *The Machinery Used in the Manufacture of Cordite.* 1898. half-lea, mar bds. . . . .*$18–$25*

Anderson, Eva Greenslit. *Chief Seattle.* Caldwell, IN. 1943. 1st ed. map. . . . .*$75–$115*

Anderson, Isabel. *The Great Sea Horse.* Bos. 1909. . . . .*$55–$80*

Anderson, John. *Last Survivors in Sail.* Lon. nd. wrps. illus. . . . .*$18–$28*

Anderson, K. *Man-eaters and Jungle Killers.* Lon. 1957. 1st ed. illus. dj. . . . .*$30–$40*

Anderson, Lawrence. *The Art of the Silversmith in Mexico.* NY. 1975. 2 vols in 1 rprnt. . . . .*$30–$45*

Anderson, Marian. *My Lord, What a Morning.* NY. 1941. 1st ed. dj. . . . .
. . . .*$35–$45*

Anderson, Martha Jane. *Social Life and Vegetarianism.* Mt. Lebanon. [Chicago: Guilding Star Printing House]. 1893. 27 pp. . . . .*$50–$80*

Anderson, Poul. *Flandry of Terra.* Phila. 1965. 1st ed. dj. . . . . . .*$25–$35*

Anderson Poul. *The High Crusade.* Garden City. Doubleday. 1960. 1st ed. scarce. *$600*

Anderson, Poul. *Perish the Sword.* NY. Macmillan. 1959. 1st ed. dj. . . . .
. . . .*$75–$100*

Anderson, R. C. *The Rigging of the Ships in the Days of the Spritsail Topmast.* . . . Salem. 1927. illus. plates, dj. . . . .*$65–$110*

Anderson, Rufus. *The Hawaiian Islands: Their Progress and Condition under Missionary Labors.* Bos. Gould & Lincoln. 1864. 1st ed. fldg map. . . . .*$325–$375*

Anderson, Sherwood. *Puzzled America.* NY/Lon. Scribner's, 1935. 1st ed. dj. *$75*

Anderson, Sherwood. *Tar.* NY. 1926. 1st ed. dj. . . . .*$75–$150*

Anderson, Sherwood. *Tar: A Midwest Childhood.* (NY). Boni & Liveright. 1926. 1st ed. 1/350 cc, sgn. *$150*

Andrade, E. N. *The Structure of the Atom.* Lon. 1924. illus. 2nd ptg. . . . .
. . . .*$15–$20*

Andre, E. *Species Hymnopteres D'Europe et D'Algerie.* 1891. . . . . . .*$80*

Andrews, Allen. *The Pig Plantagenet.* Viking. 1981. 1st ed. illus by Michael Forema, dj. . . . .*$50–$95*

Andrews, Clarence L. *The Story of Alaska.* Caxton, Caldwell. 1938. 1st ed. dj. . . . .*$30–$40*

Andrews, Eliza Frances. *The War-time Journal of a Georgia Girl, 1864–1865.* NY. 1908. 1st ed. . . . .*$55–$85*

Andrews, Matthew Page (comp). *The Women of the South in War Times.* Balt. Norman Remington. 1920. 1st ed. . . . .*$30–$45*

Andrews, Roy Chapman. *Camps and Trails in China.* NY. 1920. pictorial cvr. . . . .*$100–$175*

Andrews, Wayne. *Architecture in New York.* NY. 1969. wrps. . . . .
. . . .*$35–$45*

Angelou, Maya. *Gather Together in My Name.* Random House. 1974. 1st Amer ed. sgn, dj. . . . .*$50–$65*

Angelou, Maya. *Heart of a Woman.* NY. (1981). 1st ed. dj. . . . . .*$35–$45*

Angelou, Maya. *I Shall Not Be Moved.* NY. Random House. 1990. 1st ed. dj. . . . .*$25–$30*

Angelou, Maya. *Just Give Me a Cool Drink of Water 'fore I Die.* NY. Random House. 1971. 1st ed. sgn, dj. . . . .*$50–$65*

Angelou, Maya. *Now Sheba Sings the Song.* Dutton. 1987. 1st ed. illus. dj. *$25*

Angelou, Maya. *On the Pulse of Morning.* Random House. 1993. 1st ed. wrps. inaugural. *$20*

Angelou, Maya. *Singin' and Swingin' and Gettin' Merry Like Christmas.* NY. Random House. (1976). 1st ed. dj, sgn. *$85*

Angolia, John R. *For Fuhrer and Fatherland.* San Jose. 1976. vol. 1. . . . .
. . . .*$35–$45*

Anno, Mitsumasa. *Anno's Flea Market.* Philomel Books. 1984. 1st U.S. ed. dj. . . . .*$15–$20*

Annual Report of Major Gen. Nelson A. Miles, War Dept., for the Year Ending June 30, 1898. DC. GPO. 1899. illus. 720 pp. fldg maps. *$35–$50*

Antarctic Bibliography, Vol. I. GPO. 1965. . . . .*$30–$40*

Anthony, Edgar Waterman. *A History of Mosaics.* Bos. 1935. #21/50 cc, sgn, vellum. . . . .*$95–$125*

Appender, Grace. *The Women of Israel.* NY. 1853. 2 vols. 1st ed. . . . . . .
. . . .*$50–$75*

Apperly, Charles J. *Memoirs of the Life of the Late John Mytton.* Lon. 1837. 2nd ed. 18 hand-clr plates by Alken. . . . .*$900–$1,050*

Appleton, John. *Beginners' Book of Chemistry.* Chautauqua Press. 1888. 254 pp, clr lithos. . . . .*$50–$75*

Appleton, L. H. *Indian Art of the Americas.* NY. (1950). illus. .*$75–$150*

Appleton, Victor. *Don Sturdy in the Port of Lost Ships.* Grosset & Dunlap. 1926. Sturdy #6, dj. *$42*

Appleton, Victor. *Don Sturdy on the Desert of Mystery.* Grosset & Dunlap. 1957. #1, dj. *$25*

Appleton, Victor. *The Moving Picture Boys.* Grosset & Dunlap. 1913. #1, dj. *$32*

Appleton, Victor. *Tom Swift among the Fire Fighters.* Grosset & Dunlap. 1921. #24, dj. *$57*

Appleton, Victor. *Tom Swift and His Air Scout.* Grosset & Dunlap. 1910. #51
. . . .*$8*

Appleton, Victor. *Tom Swift and His Electric Runabout.* Grosset & Dunlap. 1910. #34 . . . .*$20*

Appleton, Victor. *Tom Swift and His Ocean Airport.* Whitman. 1934. #9, dj. *$25*

Appleton, Victor. *Tom Swift and His Ocean Airport.* Whitman. 1934, #9, no dj. *$10*

Appleton, Victor. *Tom Swift and His Television Detector.* 1933. 1st ed. . .
. . . .*$12–$18*

Appleton, Victor, II. *Tom Swift Jr. and His G-force Inverter.* Grosset & Dunlap. 1968. #30. . . . .*$52*

Appleton, Victor, II. *Tom Swift Jr., His Repelatron Skyway.* Grosset & Dunlap. 1963. #22. . . . .*$12*

Appleton, Victor, II. *Tom Swift Jr., His Spectromarine Selector.* Grosset & Dunlap. 1960. #15. . . . .*$20*

Appleton, Victor, II. *Tom Swift Jr., The Asteroid Pirates.* Collins. 1969. #6. . . . .*$15*

Appleton, Victor, II. *Tom Swift Jr., The Race to the Moon.* Grosset & Dunlap. 1958. #12. . . . .*$7*

Appleton, Victor, II. *Tom Swift Jr. and His Electronic Retroscope.* Grosset & Dunlap. 1959.1st ed. dj. #14 ....$22

Appleton, Victor, II. *Tom Swift Jr., His Flying Lab.* Grosset & Dunlap. 1956. #1 ....$7

Appleton, Victor, II. *Tom Swift Jr., His Giant Robot.* Grosset & Dunlap. 1954. dj. #4 ....$15

Appleton, Victor, II. *Tom Swift Jr., His Jetmarine.* Grosset & Dunlap. 1954. dj. #2 ....$7

Appleton, Victor, II. *Tom Swift, Jr., His Rocket Ship.* Grosset & Dunlap. 1954. dj. #3 ....$5

Appleton, Victor, II. *Tom Swift Jr., His Ultrasonic Cycloplane.* Grosset & Dunlap. 1957. dj. $20

Aptheker, Herbert. *The Labor Movement in the South during Slavery.* NY. International Publishers. wrps. ....$25–$40

The Arabian Stud Book. Arabian Horse Club. 1918. ....$225

Arbona, Fred. *Mayflies, the Angler and the Trout.* NY. 1980. 1st ed. illus. dj, photos, charts. $45

Arbus, Diane. *Diane Arbus.* Millerton, NY. 1972. wrps. 4th ptg, 15 pp. ... .$20–$35

Archdeacon, W. *Archdeacon's Kitchen Cabinet.* Chi. 1876. ....$18–$25

Archer, Gleason. *Big Business and Radio.* 1939. 1st ed. illus. dj. $45–$65

Architectural Review Congress Number. Lon. 1906. illus.......$40–$55

Arctander, J. *Apostle of Alaska.* NY. 1909. illus. ....$25–$35

Arendt, Hannah. *Eichman in Jerusalem.* .... NY. 1963. 1st ed. dj. ....$15–$22

Armes, Ethel. *The Story of Coal and Iron in Alabama.* AL. 1910. 1st ed. illus. ....$45–$60

Armour, J. Ogden. *The Packers, the Private Car Lines, and the People.* Phila. 1906. 1st ed. illus. ....$65–$125

Armstrong, Benjamin G. *Early Life Among the Indians.* Ashland, WI. 1892. 1st ed. illus. 15 plates. ....$100–$300

Armstrong, Harry G. *Principles and Practice of Aviation Medicine.* Balt. 1939. illus. charts, dj. ....$100–$125

Armstrong, John. *The Young Woman's Guide to Virtue, Economy and Happiness.* .... Newcastle. nd. illus. ....$100–$140

Armstrong, Thomas R. *My First and Last Buffalo Hunt.* np. 1918. wrps. illus. ....$60–$75

Army Regulations Adopted for the Use of the Army of the Confederate States. New Orleans. 1861. 198 pp. ....*$400–$600*

Arnold, Augustus C. L. *Rationale and Ethics of Freemasonry.* . . . NY. 1858. 1st ed. ....*$60–$80*

Arnold, Isaac N. *History of the Life of Abraham Lincoln and the Overthrow of Slavery.* Chi. 1866. 1st ed. illus. ....*$75–$95*

Arnold, Isaac N. *Sketch of the Life of Abraham Lincoln.* NY. 1869. ....*$35–$40*

Arnold. W. H. *Ventures in Book-collecting.* NY. 1923. 1st ed. ....*$45–$65*

The Arthur Rackham Fairy Book. Lon. 1933. illus. ltd #59/450, sgn. *$1,000*

Art of Cookery Made Plain and Easy . . . by a Lady. Lon. 1774. calf, rbkd. ....*$275–$395*

Art Work of the Mohawk River and Valley, Its Cities and Towns. Chi. 1902. 9 vols. ....*$75–$90*

Asbury, Herbert. *A Methodist Saint: The Life of Bishop Asbury.* NY. 1927. ....*$15–$25*

Asch, Sholem. *The Nazarene.* Putnam. (1939). ltd 500 cc, presentation. .. ..*$45–$65*

Ashby, Thomas. *The Valley Campaigns.* NY. 1914. 1st ed. ....*$50–$100*

Ashley, George T. *Reminiscences of a Circuit Rider.* Hollywood. 1941. 1st ed. ....*$18–$20*

Ashton, James. *The Book of Nature, Containing Information for Young People.* . . . NY. 1870. flexible cloth. ....*$95–$130*

Ashton, John. *Chap-books of the Eighteenth Century.* Lon. 1882. ....*$48–$55*

Asimov, Isaac. *Asimov's Biographical Encyclopedia of Science and Technology.* Doubleday. 1964. 662 pp, dj. ....*$25–$35*

Asimov, Isaac. *A Choice of Catastrophes.* NY. Simon & Schuster. (1979). 1st ed. dj. ....*$37–$45*

Asimov, Isaac. *The Currents of Space.* NY. Doubleday. 1952. 1st ed. 217 pp, sgn, dj. *$135*

Asimov, Isaac. *The Death Dealers.* NY. Avon. 1958. 1st ed. wrps. paperback original. *$75*

Asimov, Isaac. *The End of Eternity.* Garden City. 1955. 1st ed. dj. ....*$85–$200*

Asimov, Isaac. *Foundation.* NY. Gnome Press. 1951. 1st ed. 1st binding, dj.
....*$350–$450*

Asimov, Isaac. *The Intelligent Man's Guide to Science.* NY. 1960. 2 vols.
1st ed. ....*$25–$35*

Asimov, Isaac. *In Memory Yet Green.* 1979. inscrb. ....*$25–$35*

Asimov, Isaac. *Murder at the ABA.* Garden City. Doubleday. 1976. 1st ed.
dj. *$45*

Asimov, Isaac. *Nemesis.* NY. Doubleday. [1989]. 1st ed. ltd 500 cc, numbered and sgn, slipcase (this state not issued with dust jacket). *$250*

Asimov, Isaac. *Robots and Empire.* Phantasia Press. 1985. 1st ed. 1/35 cc,
sgn, black lea. *$450*

Asimov, Isaac. *The Winds of Change and Other Stories.* Doubleday. 1983.
1st ed. dj. ....*$25–$35*

Asimov, Issac (ed). *The Hugo Winners.* 1985. dj. ....*$30–$50*

Askins, Charles. *Game Bird Shooting.* NY. 1931. 1st ed. dj. ....*$37–$55*

Assoc. of Edison Illuminating Co. *Edisonia.* 1904. 1st ed. illus. ....
....*$55–$75*

Astaire, Fred. *Steps in Time.* NY. (1959). 1st ed. wrps. sgn, dj. ....
....*$150–$225*

Atherton, Gertrude. *California: An Intimate History.* NY. 1927. ....
....*$10–$15*

Atherton, Gertrude. *The Foghorn.* Bos. 1934. 1st ed. dj. ......*$70–$85*

Atkinson, Joseph. *History of Newark, New Jersey.* Newark. 1878. 1st ed.
334 pp, plates. *$40*

Atwater, Caleb. *A History of the State of Ohio.* Cinc. 1838. 2nd ed. lea. ...
....*$48–$65*

Atwood, Margaret. *Bodily Harm.* Tor. McClelland & Stewart. (1981). 1st
ed. inscrb, dj. *$95*

Atwood, Margaret. *The Handmaid's Tale.* Lon. 1986. dj. ......*$28–$35*

Atwood, Margaret. *Lady Oracle.* Tor. McClelland & Stewart. (1976). 1st
Canadian ed. dj. *$45*

Atwood, Margaret. *Power Politics.* NY. 1973. 1st ed. dj. ......*$28–$37*

Atwood, Margaret. *Wilderness Tips.* NY. Doubleday. 1991. 1st ed. dj. ..
....*$25–$30*

Atwood, Margaret. *Wilderness Tips.* NY. Doubleday. 1991. 1st ed. sgn,
dj. ....*$40–$50*

Auchincloss, Louis. *The Injustice Collectors.* Bos. 1950. 1st ed. dj. .....
....*$75–$100*

Auchincloss, Louis. *The Injustice Collectors.* Lon. Victor Gollancz. 1951. 1st Brit ed. dj. $50

Auden, W. H. *The Age of Anxiety: A Baroque Eclogue.* Lon. Faber & Faber. (1948). 1st Brit ed. dj. $85

Auden, W. H. *The Age of Anxiety.* NY. (1947). 1st U.S. ed. dj. ..$60–$85

Auden, W. H. *The Collected Poetry of W. H. Auden.* Random House. 1945. 1st ed. dj. $100

Auden, W. H. *The Dance of Death.* (Lon). Faber & Faber. (1933). 1st ed. dj. $350

Auden. W. H. *On This Island.* NY. (1937). 1st U.S. ed. dj. ....$65–$100

Auden, W. H. *Poems.* Lon. Faber & Faber. (1930). 1st ed. blue wrps. ....
....$400

Audsley, George A. *Artistic and Decorative Stencilling.* Lon. 1911. illus.
....$95–$145

Audsley. W. and G. Audsley. *Guide to Art of Illumination and Missal Painting.* 1862. ....$93–$125

Audubon, John J. *Audubon's Western Journal 1849–1850.* Cleve. 1906. 1st ed. fldg map, rprnt. ....$125–$200

Audubon, John James. *The Birds of America.* NY. 1937. illus. clr plates.
....$35–$50

Audubon, John James. *The Birds of America.* NY/Amsterdam. 1971–72. 435 clr lithos, facs, ltd 1/250 cc in wooden flat files. $14,950

Audubon, John James. *The Birds of America.* NY/Phila. J. J. Audubon and J. B. Chevalier. 1840–44. 7 vols. 1st 8vo ed. 500 litho plates printed and clr by J. T. Bowen, half green mor, mar bds. $28,750

Letters of John James Audubon, 1826–1840. 1930. 2 vols. ltd 225 cc, slipcase. ....$250–$275

Audubon, John James. *The Quadrupeds of North America.* NY. 1849–51–54. 3 vols. 1st 8vo ed. 155 hand clr plates, calf over mar bds. ...
....$6,900

Audubon, Maria. *Audubon and His Journals.* NY. 1897. 2 vols. ....
....$125–$150

Auel, Jean. *Clan of the Cave Bear.* NY. 1980. 1st ed. sgn, dj. ...$50–$80

Auel, Jean. *Mammoth Hunters.* NY. (1985). 1st ed. dj. $25

Aurthur, R. A. *Third Marine Division.* DC. 1948. 1st ed. ......$50–$75

Austen, Jane. *Emma.* Lon. 1816. 3 vols. 1st ed. full brown mor....$4,312

Austen, Jane. *Lady Susan.* ... Oxford. 1925. 3 vols. 1st ed. now reprinted from the manuscript. ....$45–$50

Austen, Jane. *Mansfield Park.* Lon. 1814. 3 vols. 1st ed. full brown mor. *$4,025*

Auster, Paul. *Ghosts.* Los Angeles. Sun & Moon Press. 1986. 1st ed. dj. . . . .*$40–$55*

Austin, Mary. *The American Rhythm.* NY. Harcourt. (1923). 1st ed. 155 pp, dj. *$150*

Austin, Mary. *The Land of Little Rain.* Bos/NY. Houghton Mifflin. 1903. 1st ed. author's first book. . . . .*$125–$350*

Austin, Mary. *The Land of Little Rain.* Bos. Houghton Mifflin. 1950. 1st ed thus, photos by Ansel Adams, dj. *$150*

Avery, Al. *A Yankee Flyer in Normandy.* Grosset & Dunlap. 1945. #19, dj. *$27*

Avery, Al. *A Yankee Flyer with the RAF.* Grosset & Dunlap. 1941. Air Combat Stories #8, dj. *$24*

Ayers, James T. *The Diary of James T. Ayers, Civil War Recruiter.* Springfield, IL. 1947. 138 pp. . . . .*$30–$45*

Ayling, Augustus D. *Revised Register of the Soldiers and Sailors of New Hampshire in the War of the Rebellion, 1861–1866.* Concord. 1895. rev ed. folio, half-lea. . . . .*$100–$150*

Babbitt, Bruce. *Grand Canyon.* 1st ed. sgn. *$80*

Babington, S. H. *Navajo Gods and Tom-Toms.* NY. (1950). illus. dj. . . . .*$30–$45*

Bacom, G. *New Large Scale Ordnance Atlas of the British Isles.* 1884. hand-clr maps, full lea. *$250*

Bacon, Edgar Mayhew. *Narragansett Bay: Its Historic and Romantic Associations and Picturesque Setting.* Putnam. 1904. 1st ed. illus. by author, map. . . . .*$50–$65*

Badeau, Adam. *Grant in Peace . . . A Personal Memoir.* Phila. 1888. 1st ed. . . . .*$45–$65*

Baden-Powell, Lord. *Birds and Beasts in Africa.* Lon. 1938. clr plates. . . . .*$40–$80*

Baden-Powell, Lord. *Indian Memories.* Lon. 1915. 1st ed. . . . . .*$50–$85*

Baden-Powell, Lord. *Scouting for Boys.* np. 1913 6th ed. wrps. . . . .*$95–$120*

Baden-Powell, Robert. *Pigsticking or Hog Hunting.* Lon. 1924. dj. . . . .*$30–$40*

Baedeker, Karl. *Baedeker's Switzerland.* Leipzig. 1913. maps. . .*$18–$25*

Baedeker, Karl. *Belgium and Holland.* Leipzig. 1905. 14th ed. . .*$15–$20*

Baedeker, Karl. *Berlin and Its Environs.* 1923. 6th ed. dj. . . . . . .*$14–$18*

Baedeker, Karl. *Central Italy.* 1914. 14th ed. . . . .*$15–$25*

Baedeker, Karl. *The Dominion of Canada.* Leipsic. 1894. 254 pp. . . . . . .
. . . .*$95–$150*

Baedeker, Karl. *Egypt.* 1914. 7th ed. . . . .*$47–$95*

Baedeker, Karl. *Etats-Unis.* 1894. . . . .*$35–$50*

Baedeker. Karl. *Great Britain.* 1901. . . . .*$25*

Baedeker, Karl. *Italy.* 1909. . . . .*$20–$30*

Baedeker, Karl. *London and Its Environs.* Leipzig. 1908. 1st ed. *$25*

Baedeker, Karl. *The Mediterranean.* 1911. . . . .*$70*

Baedeker, Karl. *Northern France.* 1889. 1st ed. dj. . . . .*$35–$75*

Baedeker, Karl. *Rhine.* Leipzig. 1906. 16th ed. . . . .*$25–$35*

Baedeker, Karl. *The Rhine from Rotterdam to Constance.* Leipsic. 1882.
387 pp. . . . .*$30–$45*

Baedeker, Karl. *Die Rheinlande von der Schweizer bis zur Hollandischen
Grenze.* Coblenz. 1864. 358 pp. . . . .*$150–$250*

Baedeker, Karl. *Southern Germany.* Leipzig. 1907. 10th ed. . . . .*$15–$25*

Baedeker, Karl. *Spain and Portugal.* 1912. in German. . . . .*$25–$35*

Baedeker, Karl. *Switzerland.* 1907. . . . .*$22–$45*

Baedeker, Karl. *United States.* 1909. 4th ed. . . . .*$40–$75*

Bailey, F. M. *Birds of New Mexico.* DC. 1928. illus. . . . .*$100–$150*

Bailey, H. H. *The Birds of Florida.* Balt. 1925. illus. private prntg, ltd ed. . .
. . . .*$115–$150*

Bailey, L. H. *Cyclopedia of American Horticulture.* NY. 1900–02. 4 vols.
. . . .*$100–$195*

Bailey, L. H. *The Gardener: A Book of Brief Directions.* . . . NY. Book
League. 1929. illus. 260 pp. . . . .*$20–$30*

Bain, John, Jr. *Tobacco in Song and Story.* NY. 1896. suede, teg. . . . . . .
. . . .*$35–$60*

Bainbridge, Henry Charles. *Peter Carl Faberge: Goldsmith and Jewel-
ler.* . . . Lon. (1949). 1st ed. illus. 1/850 cc. . . . .*$70–$150*

Bainbridge, Oliver. *The Devil's Notebook.* NY. Cochrane Pub. Co. 1908.
1st ed. illus. 154 pp. . . . .*$60–$75*

Baird, Bill. *The Art of the Puppet.* NY. Macmillan. 1965. 1st ed. photos,
dj. . . . .*$70–$100*

Baird, P. D. *Expeditions to the Canadian Arctic.* 1949. 1st ed. wrps. . . . . . .
. . . .*$24–$32*

Baker, C. Alice. *A Summer in the Azores with a Glimpse of Madeira.* Bos. Lee & Shepard. 1882. 1st ed. ....*$30–$45*

Baker, J. C. *Baptist History of the North Pacific Coast.* . . . Phila. 1912. 1st ed. ....*$30–$60*

Baker, Gen. L. C. *History of the U.S. Secret Service.* Phila. 1867. 1st ed. . ...*$40–$75*

Baker, Marcus. *Geographic Dictionary of Alaska.* GPO. 1906. 2nd ed. .. ..*$85–$100*

Baker, Samuel W. *The Nile Tributaries of Abyssinia.* Lon. Macmillan. 1894. maps. ....*$50–$60*

Baker, Sir Samuel W. *Ismailia: Narrative of Expedition to Central Africa.* NY. 1875. 1st Amer ed. 542 pp, illus, maps. *$75*

Bakst, Leon. *The Designs of Leon Bakst for the Sleeping Princess.* Lon. 1923. ltd ed. *$550*

Balcom, Mary G. *Ketchikan Alaska's Totemland.* Chi. 1961. illus. softcover, sgn. ....*$25–$45*

Baldwin, Frederick W. *Biography of the Bar of Orleans County, Vermont.* Montpelier. 1886. illus. 303 pp. ....*$30–$40*

Baldwin, James. *The Fire Next Time.* 1963. 1st ed. dj. *$50*

Baldwin, James. *Going to Meet the Man.* Dial. 1965. 1st ed. dj. ....*$35–$50*

Baldwin, James. *If Beale Street Could Talk.* NY. 1974. 1st ed. dj. ....*$35–$45*

Baldwin, James. *Just Above My Head.* NY. (1979). sgn, dj, slipcase. ....*$100–$150*

Baldwin, James. *Nobody Knows My Name: More Notes of a Native Son.* NY. Dial Press. 1961, 1st ed. dj. *$150*

Baldwin, James. *Tell Me How Long the Train's Been Gone.* NY. Dial Press. 1968, 1st ed. dj. *$125*

Baldwin, Leland. *Pittsburgh: The Story of a City.* Pitts. 1937. 1st ed. ....*$30–$45*

Baldwin, William C. *African Hunting from Natal to the Zambesi.* NY. 1863. illus. fldg map. ....*$75–$125*

Ballantine, Stuart. *Radio Telephony for Amateurs.* Mckay. 1923. 2nd ed. ....*$15–$25*

Ballard, Michael. *Pemberton: A Biography.* Jackson. 1991. maps, photos, dj. ....*$20–$25*

Balzac, Honoré de. *Droll Stories.* Boni & Liveright. 1928. 2 vols. illus. . .
. . . .*$20–$45*

Bamford, Georgia Loring. *The Mystery of Jack London.* Oakland. 1931.
1st ed. dj. . . . .*$95–$125*

Bancroft, Hubert Howe. *History of Alaska, 1730–1886.* SF. 1886. map. .
. . . .*$150–$225*

Bancroft, Hubert Howe. *History of the Northwest Coast.* SF. 1886. 2
vols. . . . .*$150–$175*

Bancroft, Hubert Howe. *History of Utah.* SF. 1890. . . . .*$50–$120*

Bancroft, Hubert Howe. *The New Pacific.* NY. 1900. teg, frontis, map. . .
. . . .*$35–$50*

Banergi, P. *Snake-bite, with a System of Treatment and Reported Cases
and Notes.* Calcutta. 1956. illus. . . . .*$40–$50*

Bangay, R. D. *Wireless Telephony.* 1923. 1st ed. illus. . . . .*$18–$25*

Bangs, John Kendrick. *The Dreamers.* NY/Lon. 1899. 1st ed. . . . .
. . . .*$25–$45*

Bangs, John Kendrick. *The Enchanted Typewriter.* NY. 1899. 1st ed. illus
by Peter Newell. . . . .*$45–$55*

Bangs, John Kendrick. *Ghosts I Have Met.* 1898. 1st ed. . . . . . .*$25–$45*

Bangs, John Kendrick. *A House-boat on the Styx.* NY. 1896. 1st ed. . . . .
. . . .*$40–$55*

Bangs, John Kendrick. *Mr. Munchausen.* Bos. 1901. 1st ed. 4th state. . . .
. . . .*$18–$25*

Bangs, John Kendrick. *Mrs. Raffles.* 1905. 1st ed. . . . .*$60–$75*

Bangs, John Kendrick. *Olympian Nights.* 1902. 1st ed. . . . .*$25–$35*

Bangs, John Kendrick. *Peeps at People.* NY. 1899. illus by Penfield. . . .
. . . .*$25–$30*

Bangs, John Kendrick. *The Pursuit of the House-boat.* NY. Harper &
Bros. 1897. 1st ed. no dj. *$100*

Bangs, John Kendrick. *Songs of Cheer.* Bos. 1910. 1st ed. dj. *$95*

Bangs, John Kendrick. *The Water Ghost and Athens.* NY. 1894. 1st ed.
illus. . . . .*$65–$85*

Banks, Mike. *Rakaposhi.* Lon. Secker & Warburg. 1959. 1st ed. photos,
maps, dj. . . . .*$18–$30*

Banks, Nathaniel P. *Purchase of Alaska.* DC. 1868. 1st ed. . . . . .*$50–$75*

Banks, Russell. *Affliction.* NY. Harper & Row. 1989. 1st ed. dj. . . . .
. . . .*$18–$25*

Banks, Russell. *The Relation of My Imprisonment.* DC. Sun & Moon Press. 1983. 1st trade ed. dj. $30

Banks, Russell. *Searching for Survivors.* NY. Fiction Collective. 1975. 1st ed. author's first collection of short stories, dj. ....$100–$300

Bannerman, Helen. *Histoire du Petit Nègre Sambo.* Stokes. (1921). 1st ed. in French, dj. ....$55–$125

Bannerman, Helen. *Little Black Sambo.* NY. Little Golden Book. 1948. . ...$40–$55

Bannerman, Helen. *Little Black Sambo.* 1931. illus by Fern Bisel Peat. .. ..$50–$80

Bannerman, Helen. *Little Black Sambo.* Platt & Munk. 1928. dj. *$45–$60*

Bannerman, Helen. *Little Black Sambo.* Whitman. illus by Cobb and Shinn, 64 pp, dark brown cloth bds. ....$75–$100

Bannerman, Helen. *Sambo and the Twins.* Phila. 1946. illus by Helen Bannerman. ....$45–$60

Barbeau, M. *Alaska Beckons.* Caxton. 1947. 1st ed. dj. ....$25–$35

Barbeau, M. *Haida Myths Illustrated in Argillite Carvings.* Ottawa. 1953. 1st ed. wrps. ....$55–$65

Barbeau, M. *Totem Poles.* National Museum Canada. 1950. illus........ ....$150–$250

Barbeau, Marius. *Ancient France Lingers.* 1936. illus. softcover.*$20–$30*

Barbeau, Marius. *Jongleur Songs of Old Quebec.* NJ. 1962. ....*$15–$20*

Barbeau, Marius. *The Downfall of Temlaham.* Tor. 1928. 1st ed. illus. dj. ....$97–$125

Barber, Edwin A. *Lead Glazed Pottery.* Phila. 1907. 1st ed. illus........ ....$25–$35

Barber, Edwin A. *Majolica of Mexico.* Phila. 1908. ....$40–$60

Barber, Joel. *Wild Fowl Decoys.* NY. 1934. illus. dj. ....$50–$120

Barber, John (ed). *A History of the Amistad Captives.* New Haven. E. L. & J. W. Barber. 1840. 1st ed. 32 pp, pamphlet, fldg plate. .....$150–$250

Barker, Clive. *The Damnation Game.* Ace Putnam. (1987). 1st Amer ed. sgn. ....$25–$45

Barker, Clive. *The Great and Secret Show.* Lon. 1989. 1st ed. dj. ....$35–$65

Barker, Clive. *The Great and Secret Show.* NY. Harper & Row. 1989. 1st U.S. ed. dj, sgn. ....$25–$35

Barker, Clive. *Weaveworld.* Poseidon Press. 1987. 1st U.S. ed. dj. ...$30

Barker, Ralph. *The Last Blue Mountain.* NY. Doubleday. 1960. 1st ed. dj.
. . . .*$20–$25*

Barlow, Hilario (ed). *Clinical Memoirs of Abdominal Tumors and Intumescence of the Late Dr. Bright.* Lon. The New Sydenham Society. 1860. 326 pp. . . . .*$50–$60*

Barn Plans and Outbuildings. NY. 1883. illus. . . . .*$40–$65*

Barnard, Charles. *First Steps in Electricity.* NY. 1888. 1st ed. illus. . . . .
. . . .*$40–$60*

Barnard, Frederick A. P. *The Metric System of Weights and Measures.* Bos. 1879. 3d ed. . . . .*$40–$55*

Barneby, Henry W. *Life and Labour in the Far, Far West.* . . . Lon. 1884. 1st ed. map. . . . .*$150–$250*

Barnes, A. R. *The South African Household Guide.* Capetown. 1907. 4th ed. . . . .*$25–$55*

Barnes, Linda. *Bitter Finish.* NY. St. Martin's. 1983. 1st ed. dj. *$85*

Barnes, R. M. *Military Uniforms of Britain and the Empire.* Lon. 1972. wrps. . . . .*$18–$25*

Barnes, Robert. *United States Submarines.* New Haven, 1944. .*$75–$112*

Barnes, Will C. *Western Grazing Grounds . . . A History of the Live-stock Industry as Conducted on Open Ranges.* . . . Chi. Breeder's Gazette. 1913. 1st ed. illus. 390 pp. . . . .*$150–$300*

Barnhart, John D. *The Impact of the Civil War on Indiana.* Ind. 1962. 1st ed. wrps. . . . .*$18–$25*

Barnum, P. T. *Struggles and Triumphs.* Hartford. 1869. . . . .*$35–$45*

Baron, Salo. *A Social and Religious History of the Jews.* Columbia Univ. Press. 1939. 3 vols. . . . .*$30–$40*

Baroni, George (ed). *The Pyramiders.* np. nd. 300 pp, photos. *$75*

Barrett, Edwin S. *What I Saw at Bull Run.* Bos. Beacon Press. 1886. 48 pp. . . . .*$72–$95*

Barrie, J. M. *The Little White Bird.* NY. 1902. 1st Amer ed. . . . .*$50–$65*

Barrie, J. M. *Peter Pan in Kensington Gardens.* Lon. 1906. 1st ed. illus by Arthur Rackham. . . . .*$350–$400*

Barrie, James Matthew. *Quality Street: A Comedy in Four Acts.* Lon. 1912. 23 clr plates. . . . .*$85–$100*

Barron, Archibald F. *Vines and Vine Culture.* Lon. 1900. 4th ed. . . . .
. . . .*$25–$45*

Barrows, W. B. *Michigan Bird Life.* Lansing. 1912. illus. . . . . . .*$50–$85*

Barth, Henry. *Travels and Discoveries in the North and Central Africa ... 1849–1856.* Phila. J. W. Bradley. 1859. 1-vol ed. 1st Amer ed. illus map. . . . .$65–$75

Barth, John. *Chimera.* Lon. Andre Deutsch. (1974). 1st ed. dj. $65

Barth, John. *The End of the Road.* Doubleday. 1958. 1st ed. dj. $200

Barth, John. *The Floating Opera.* Garden City. (1956). 1st ed. sgn, dj. . . . .$200–$250

Barth, John. *Giles Goat-boy.* Doubleday. 1966. sgn, dj. . . . .$75–$85

Barth, John. *Lost in the Funhouse.* Garden City. 1968. 1st ed. dj. . . . .$30–$45

Barth, John. *The Sot-weed Factor.* Garden City. 1960. 1st ed. dj. . . . .$100–$300

Barthelme, Donald. *Great Days.* NY. Farrar, Straus & Giroux. (1979). 1st ed. dj. . . . .$18–$25

Barthelme, Donald. *Guilty Pleasures.* NY. (1974). 1st ed. dj. . . .$25–$35

Barthelme, Donald. *Sixty Stories.* NY. Putnam's. (1979). 1st ed. sgn, dj. . . . .$50–$75

Barthelme, Donald. *Unspeakable Practices, Unnatural Acts.* NY. (1968). 1st ed. dj. . . . .$45–$75

Bartholomew, Ed. *Wild Bill Longley, a Texas Hard-case.* Houston. 1953. illus. . . . .$30–$40

Bartholow, Roberts. *A Practical Treatise on Materia Medica and Thera-peutics.* NY. 1884. 5th ed. . . . .$25–$35

Bartlett, W. *An Elementary Treatise on Optics.* NY. 1839. 1st ed. illus. fldg plates. . . . .$30–$40

Barton, Clara. *The Red Cross in Peace and War.* 1899. 1st ed. .$85–$100

Barton, Lucy. *Historic Costume for the Stage.* Bos. 1935. 1st ed. illus. . . . .$25–$35

Barton, William E. *Hero in Homespun.* Bos. 1897. 1st ed. illus by Dan Beard. . . . .$18–$25

Bashline, James. *Night Fishing for Trout.* Rockville Center. 1972. 1st ed. dj. $35

Baskerville, Rosetta. *Flame Tree and Other Folk-lore Stories from Uganda.* Lon. nd. illus. . . . .$10–$15

Baskin, Esther. *The Poppy and Other Deadly Plants.* NY. 1967. 1st ed. illus by Leonard Baskin, dj. . . . .$22–$35

Bass, W. W. *Adventures in the Canyons of Colorado ... Grand Canyon.* 1920. wrps. 38 pp. . . . .$95–$250

Batchelder, Marjorie. *The Puppet Theatre Handbook.* NY. 1947. 1st ed. dj. ....*$15–$25*

Batchelor, D. *Jack Johnson and His Times.* Lon. 1957. illus. 190 pp, dj. *$45*

Bates, H. W. *The Naturalist on the River Amazon.* Lon. 1873. illus. 3rd ed. ....*$75–$150*

Bates, Joseph D. *Trout Waters and How to Fish Them.* Bos. 1949. 1st ed. *$27.50*

Bates, Joseph D., Jr. *Atlantic Salmon Flies and Fishing.* Stackpole. 1979. 1st ed. dj. *$95*

Bates, Joseph D., Jr. *Spinning for Game Fish.* Little Brown. (1947). dj. ... .*$14–$18*

Bates, Joseph D., Jr. *Streamers and Bucktails.* Knopf. 1950. dj. *$50*

Bates, Robert H., et al. *Five Miles High.* NY. Dodd Mead. 1939. 1st ed. . ...*$125–$165*

Battersby, Martin. *The World of Art Nouveau.* NY. 1968. .....*$24–$35*

Battleground Korea: The Story of the 25th Infantry Division. Arlington. 1951. 1st ed. dj. ....*$50–$85*

Batty, J. H. *Practical Taxidermy and Home Decoration.* NY. 1883. illus. . ...*$27–$65*

Bauer, Paul. *Himalayan Quest.* Lon. Nicholson & Watson. 1938. 1st ed. photos, maps. ....*$35–$40*

Baughman, A. J. *History of Huron County, Ohio.* Chi. 1909. 2 vols. 1st ed. illus. ....*$80–$100*

Baum, L. Frank. *Dorothy and the Wizard.* 1950s. *$30*

Baum, Frank. *Dot and Tot.* 1st ed. *$700*

Baum, L. Frank. *Glinda of Oz.* Tor. 1920. 1st ed. illus by John R. Neill. . ...*$175–$400*

Baum, L. Frank. *The Land of Oz.* illus by J. Neill. ....*$45–$60*

Baum, L. Frank. *The Lost Princess of Oz.* Chi. 1939. illus by J. Neill, junior ed. ....*$18–$27*

Baum, Frank. *Magic of Oz.* 1st ed. 1st state. *$375*

Baum, L. Frank. *The Magical Monarch of Mo.* 1947. illus. dj. ....*$18–$25*

Baum, L. Frank. *The Marvelous Land of Oz.* Reilly & Britton. 1904. 1st ed. illus by J. Neill, 2nd state. ....*$245–$275*

Baum, L. Frank. *The New Wizard of Oz.* Ind. 1903. illus by Denslow, 2nd ed. 2nd state. ....*$75–$110*

Baum, L. Frank. *Ozma of Oz.* Chi. Reilly & Britain. 1907. 1st ed. illus. . .
....*$100–$200*

Baum, L. Frank. *The Patchwork Girl of Oz.* Reilly & Britton. (1913). 1st ed. illus by Neill, 1st state. ....*$300–$375*

Baum, L. Frank. *Rinkitink in Oz.* Reilly & Britain. (1916). 1st ed. illus by J. Neill, clr plates. ....*$600–$675*

Baum, L. Frank. *Rinkitink in Oz.* 1939. 1st junior ed. *$22*

Baum, L. Frank. *Tik-Tok of Oz.* Reilly & Lee. illus by J. Neill, clr plates.
....*$65–$75*

Baum, L. Frank. *The Tin Woodsman of Oz.* Reilly & Lee. illus by J. Neill, clr plates. ....*$65–$75*

Baum, L. Frank. *The Wizard of Oz.* 1982. ltd 500 cc, slipcase. . .*$50–$65*

Baum, L. Frank. *The Wonderful Wizard of Oz.* West Hatfield, MA. 1985. illus by Barry Moser, deluxe copy, sgn, #9/50 cc, boxed. *$2,185*

Baumbach, Werner. *The Life and Death of the Luftwaffe.* NY. 1960. 1st Amer ed. photos. *$22.50*

Baxter, James P. *The Trelawny Papers.* Portland. 1884. fldg maps. ......
....*$30–$45*

Bayard, Samuel J. *A Sketch of the Life of Commodore Robert F. Stockton.* NY. 1856. ....*$35–$50*

Beach, S. A. *The Apples of New York.* Albany. 1905. 2 vols. illus. 130 clr plates. ....*$65–$195*

Beadle, Delos. *American Lawyer and Business-man's Form Book.* NY. Phelps & Fanning. 1851. 1st ptg. *$19.50*

Beadle, J. H. *Life in Utah.* Phila. 1870. map, plates. ....*$70–$85*

Beadle, J. H. *Polygamy, or the Mysteries and Crimes of Mormonism.* (1904). illus. ....*$22–$45*

Beale, George. *A Lieutenant of Cavalry in Lee's Army.* Balt. rprnt, dj. ...
....*$20–$30*

Beale, J. H. *Picturesque Sketches of American Progress.* NY. 1889. illus. 445 pp. *$15*

Beale, R.L.T. *History of the Ninth Virginia Cavalry in the War between the States.* Richmond. B. F. Johnson Publishing Co. 1899. 1st ed. 192 pp. .
....*$1,250–$1,500*

Bealer, Alex W. *The Art of Blacksmithing.* NY. 1969. dj. ....*$20–$25*

Beamish, Richard J. *The Boy's Story of Lindbergh, the Lone Eagle.* John Winston. 1928. illus. ....*$15–$20*

Bean, L. L. *Hunting, Fishing and Camping.* 1942. 3d ed. ....*$18–$25*

Beard, George M. *Stimulants and Narcotics: Medically, Philosophically, and Morally Considered.* NY. Putman. 1871. 1st ed. 155 pp. . . .*$80–$125*

Beard, James. *Delights and Prejudices.* NY. 1964. 1st ed. dj. . . .*$18–$25*

Beard, James A. *Fireside Cook Book.* NY. Simon & Schuster. 1949. 1st ed. illus. dj. . . . .*$20–$30*

Beard, James Melville. *K.K.K. Sketches, Humorous and Didactic.* . . . Phila. 1877. 1st ed. . . . .*$95–$175*

Beard, Mary R. (ed). *America through Women's Eyes.* NY. 1933. 1st ed. 558 pp. . . . .*$30–$45*

Beaton, Cecil. *The Face of the World.* NY. John Day Co. (1957). 1st Amer ed. illus. . . . .*$40–$55*

Beaton, Cecil, and Gail Buckland. *The Magic Image.* NY. 1975. illus. 1st U.S. ed. dj. . . . .*$22–$35*

Beattie, Ann. *Alex Katz.* Abrams. 1987. 1st ed. dj. . . . .*$30–$40*

Beattie, Ann. *The Burning House.* NY. Random House. (1982). review copy, dj. *$35*

Beattie, Ann. *Falling in Place.* 1980. 1st ed. . . . .*$10–$22*

Beattie, Ann. *Love Always.* Random House. 1985. 1st ed. dj. . . . .*$18–$20*

Beattie, Ann. *What Was Mine.* NY. (1991). 1st ed. dj. . . . .*$18–$30*

Beatty, Clyde, and Earl Wilson. *Jungle Performers.* NY. 1941. 1st ed. sgn, dj. . . . .*$25–$90*

Beaumont, Charles. *The Magic Man and Other Science Fantasy Stories.* Greenwich, CT. (1965). 1st ed. pictorial wrps. . . . .*$20–$35*

Beaumont, Robert. *Carpets and Rugs.* Lon. 1924. illus. dj. . . . . .*$60–$75*

Beaver, C. Masten. *Fort Yukon Trader—Three Years in an Alaskan Wilderness.* NY. 1955. 1st ed. illus. dj. . . . .*$25–$40*

Bechstein, J. M. *The Natural History of Cage Birds.* Lon. 1885. illus. engr. . . . .*$30–$45*

Bechtold, Fritz. *Nanga Parbat Adventure.* NY. (1936). 1st ed. illus. dj. . . . .*$30–$40*

Beck, Henry. *Bridge Busters: The 39th Bomb Group (M).* Cleve. 1946. photos, map. *$175*

Beddie, M. K. (ed). *Bibliography of Captain James Cook.* Sydney. 1970. 2nd ed. . . . .*$40–$60*

Bedford-Jones, H. B. *D'Artagnan's Letter.* Covici Friede. 1931. 1st ed. dj. . . . .*$20–$40*

Bedford-Jones, H. B. *The Mardi Gras Mystery.* NY. 1921. 1st ed. . . . .*$18–$25*

Bedford-Jones, H. B. *Saint Michael's Gold.* NY. 1926. 1st ed. . .*$14–$17*

Beebe, Lucius. *American West.* 1955. 1st ed. . . . .*$30–$35*

Beebe, William. *The Arcturus Adventure.* NY. Putnam. 1926. 1st ed. illus. clr and b/w. . . . .*$50–$70*

Beebe, William. *The Arcturus Adventure.* NY. Putnam. 1926. 3rd ptg. . . . .*$40–$50*

Beebe, William. *Beneath Tropic Seas.* NY. 1928. 1st ed. . . . .*$20–$30*

Beebe, William. *Book of Bays.* 1942. 1st ed. . . . .*$10–$18*

Beebe, William. *Half Mile Down.* NY. 1934. 1st ed. illus. dj. . . .*$25–$45*

Beebe, William. *Nonsuch Land of Water.* 1st ed. sgn, dj. . . . .*$45–$60*

Beebe, William. *Pheasants—Their Lives and Homes.* Garden City. 1936. illus. clr and b/w. . . . .*$75–$100*

Beecher, Catherine E. *Miss Beecher's Domestic Receipt Book.* NY. 1849. 3rd ed. . . . .*$60–$85*

Beecher, Catherine E. *A Treatise on Domestic Economy.* NY. 1850. illus. rev ed. . . . .*$35–$65*

Beecher, Catherine E., and Harriet Beecher Stowe. *The American Woman's Home.* NY. 1869. 1st ed. . . . .*$125–$200*

Beecher, Henry Ward. *Norwood, or Village Life in New England.* NY. 1868. . . . .*$25–$35*

Beecher, Lyman. *A Plea for Colleges.* Cinc/NY. Truman & Smith/Leavitt, Lord. 1836. 2nd ed. *$65*

Beede, A. McG. *Sitting Bull–Custer.* Bismarck, ND. 1913. 1st ed. illus. . . . .*$125–$150*

Beehler, W. H. *The Cruise of the Brooklyn.* Phila. 1885. illus. . . . .*$50–$95*

Beer, George Louis. *The Origins of the British Colonial System 1578–1660.* NY. 1908. . . . .*$32–$47*

Beerbohm, Max. *Fifty Caricatures.* NY. 1913. 1st ed. . . . .*$50–$65*

Beerbohm, Max. *Mainly on the Air.* NY. 1947. 1st ed. dj. . . . . . .*$30–$45*

Beerbohm, Max. *Observations.* Lon. 1923. 1st ed. dj. . . . .*$125–$200*

Beerbohm, Max. *A Survey.* Lon. William Heinemann. 1921. 1st ed. 51 tip-in plates. *$100*

Beerbohm, Max. *Things New and Old.* Lon. 1923. 1st ed. dj. . . .*$60–$85*

Beerbohm, Max. *Zuleika Dobson: An Oxford Love Story.* Lon. William Heinemann. 1911. 1st ed. *$225*

Beers. D. B. *Atlas of Luzerne County, Pennsylvania.* Phila. 1873. illus. hand-clr maps. . . . .'. . . . .*$210–$300*

Beers, F. W. *Atlas of Delaware County, New York.* NY. 1869. *$150–$200*

Beeton, Isabella. *The Book of Household Management.* Lon. 1861. 1st ed. half-lea. . . . .*$400–$600*

Begin, Menachem. *White Nights: The Story of a Prisoner in Russia.* NY. 1977. 1st U.S. ed. dj. . . . .*$35–$45*

Behan, Brendan. *Confessions of an Irish Rebel.* NY. 1965. dj. . .*$10–$15*

Behan, Brendan. *Hold Your Hour and Have Another.* Little Brown. 1954. 1st Amer ed. dj. . . . .*$25–$30*

Behan, Brendan. *Richard's Cork Leg.* Grove Press. 1974. 1st U.S. ed. dj. . . . .*$15–$25*

Behan, Brendan. *The Scarperer.* NY. 1964. 1st ed. dj. . . . .*$25–$35*

Beilis, Mendel. *The Story of My Sufferings.* Beilis Pub. 1926. 264 pp. .*$55*

Beirne, F. *The War of 1812.* NY. 1949. 1st ed. maps. . . . .*$20–$28*

Belasco, David. *Plays Produced under the Stage Direction of David Belasco.* NY. 1925. . . . .*$35–$45*

Belasco, David. *The Return of Peter Grimm.* 1912. illus by John Rae. . . . .*$20–$25*

Belknap, Jeremy. *A Sermon Preached at the Installation of Rev. Jedidiah Morse.* Bos. 1789. 1st ed. wrps. sewn. . . . .*$75–$100*

Bell Telephone Laboratories. *A History of Engineering and Science in the Bell System.* 1975. 1st ed. illus. dj. . . . .*$20–$30*

Bell, Maj. *Reminiscences of a Ranger . . . in Southern California.* 1927. . . . .*$18–$25*

Bell, Sir Charles. *Tibet Past and Present.* Oxford. nd. (c 1913). .*$45–$65*

Bell, Edward I. *The Political Shame of Mexico.* NY. 1914. 1st ed. . . . .*$22–$28*

Bell, Ernest A. *Fighting the Traffic in Young Girls.* np. nd. illus. .*$20–$24*

Bell, Helen G. *Winning the King's Cup.* NY. 1928. illus. fldg charts and plans. . . . .*$24–$30*

Bell, Louis. *The Telescope.* NY/Lon. 1922. 1st ed. illus. . . . .*$35–$50*

Bell, T. *A History of British Reptiles.* Lon. 1839. illus. . . . .*$25–$37*

Bell, W.O.M. *Karamojo Safari.* NY. 1949. 1st ed. . . . .*$30–$65*

Bell, Walter D. M. *Bell of Africa.* Bos. 1961. 1st Amer ed. dj. . . .*$18–$40*

Bellamy, Edward. *The Blindman's World.* Bos/NY. Houghton, Mifflin. 1898. 1st ed. $125

Belle, Francis P. *Life and Adventures of Bandit Joaquin Murrieta....* Chi. 1925 1st ed. ltd 975 cc. ....$50–$75

Bellow, Saul. *The Adventures of Augie March.* Viking. 1953. 1st ed. dj. .. ..$90–$120

Bellow, Saul. *The Dean's December.* NY. 1982. 1st ed. wrps. dj. $25–$35

Bellow, Saul. *The Dean's December.* NY. Harper & Row. (1982). 1/500 cc, nbr, sgn, slipcase. ....$100–$135

Bellow, Saul. *Henderson the Rain King.* NY. 1959. 1st ed. dj. ..$80–$110

Bellow, Saul. *Herzog.* NY. 1964. 1st ed. dj. ....$30–$40

Bellow, Saul. *Humbolt's Gift.* NY. Viking. (1975). 1st ed. dj. $45

Bellow, Saul. *The Last Analysis.* NY. 1965. 1st ed. dj. ....$40–$54

Bellow, Saul. *Great Jewish Short Stories.* Dell. 1963. 1st ed. wrps. ....$18–$25

Bemelmans, L. *The Donkey Inside.* NY. Viking. 1st ed. illus by the author. ....$25–$35

Bemelmans, Ludwig. *The Eye of God.* Viking. 1949. 1st ed. dj. $40

Bemelmans, Ludwig. *The Eye of God.* NY. 1949. dj. ....$12.50–$30

Bemelmans, Ludwig. *Hansi.* NY. 1934. 1st ed. ....$75–$175

Bemelmans, Ludwig. *Madeline and the Gypsies.* Viking. 1959. ....$20–$35

Bemelmans, Ludwig. *Now I Lay Me Down to Sleep.* NY. Viking. 1945. 1/500 cc, sgn (review copy), illus, slipcase. ....$90–$100

Benchley, Nathaniel. *Robert Benchley.* NY. 1955. dj. ....$12.50–$15

Benchley, Nathaniel. *A Winter's Tale.* NY. 1964. 1st ed. dj. ....$25–$35

Benchley, Robert. *Benchley or Else.* NY. 1947. 1st ed. ....$18–$25

Benedict, George Grenville. *Vermont in the Civil War....* Burlington, VT. 1886–88. 2 vols. 1st ed. ....$75–$125

Benét, Stephen Vincent. *Burning City.* Farrar & Rinehart. 1936. 1st ed. dj. ....$40–$50

Benét, Stephen Vincent. *John Brown's Body.* Garden City. 1928. 1st ed. . ...$20–$50

Benét, Stephen Vincent. *John Brown's Body.* 1930. illus by J. Daugherty, dj. ....$15–$20

Benét, Stephen Vincent. *Thirteen O'Clock.* NY. 1937. 1st ed. dj. ....$25–$35

Benjamin, Marcus. *Washington during War Time.* DC. nd. . . . . .$25–$30

Bennett, Arnold. *Our Women.* NY. Doran. (1920). 1st U.S. ed. $45

Bennett, Colin N. *The Guide to Kinematrography.* 1917. 1st ed. illus. . . .
. . . .$75–$85

Bennett, Frank M. *The Monitor and the Navy under Steam.* NY. 1900. . .
. . . .$14–$18

Bennett, Ira C. *History of the Panama Canal.* . . . DC. 1915. illus. plates.
. . . .$18–$24

Bennett, James. *Overland Journey to California.* . . . NY. 1932. ltd 200
cc, dj. . . . .$45–$50

Bennett, Russell H. *The Complete Rancher.* NY. 1946. 1st ed. illus by
Ross Santee, dj. . . . .$120–$150

Bennett, W. P. *The First Baby in Camp.* SLC. 1893. softbound. .$50–$75

Benson E. F. *Colin.* NY. Doran. (1923). 1st Amer ed. 334 pp. .$115–$150

Benson, Joseph. *The Life of the Rev. John W. Flechere.* NY. 1820. lea. . .
. . . .$27–$45

Benson, William S. *The Merchant Marine.* NY. 1923. . . . .$14–$20

Bent, Arthur Cleveland. *Life Histories of North American Thrushes.* DC.
1949. wrps. plates. . . . .$28–$35

Bent, J. Theodore. *The Ruined Cities of Mashonaland.* Lon. Longmans,
Green. 1893. fldg map, illus. . . . .$175–$225

Benton, Frank. *Cowboy Life on the Sidetrack.* Denver. (1903). 1st ed. . . .
. . . .$60–$90

Benton, Jesse J. *Cow by the Tail.* Bos. 1943. . . . .$18–$25

Benton, Josiah Hart. *Voting in the Field.* ltd 100 cc. . . . .$75–$100

Benton, Thomas Hart. *Artist in America.* NY. 1937. 1st ed. illus. . . . .
. . . .$18–$24

Beny, Roloff. *To Everything There Is a Season.* Lon. 1969. illus. photos,
dj. . . . .$45–$50

Berger, John A. *The Franciscan Missions of California.* Garden City.
1948. dj. . . . .$16–$20

Berkeley, Edmund Callis. *Giant Brains, or Machines That Think.* NY.
(1949). 1st ed. 270 pp. . . . .$100–$135

Berman, Bruce D. *Encyclopedia of American Shipwrecks.* Bos. 1973. dj. .
. . . .$22–$38

Berndt, R. M. (ed). *Australian Aboriginal Art.* NY/Lon. 1964. photos. . . .
. . . .$70–$90

Berners, Dame Juliana. *The Treatyse of Fysshynge wyth an Angle.* Lon. for William Pickering. 1827. 1st Pickering ed, frontis, woodcuts, three-quarter calf, reprinted from *The Book of St. Albans.* $300

Berrigan, Daniel. *The Bride.* Macmillan. 1959. 1st ed. dj. $30

Berrigan, Daniel. *Prison Poems.* Greensboro, NC. 1973. dj. .... .$10–$14

Berry, A. J. *Henry Cavendish—His Life and Scientific Work.* Lon. 1960. . ...$28–$40

Berry, F. A., Jr., et al. (eds). *Handbook of Meteorology.* NY. 1945. 1st ed. dj. ....$35–$60

Berry, Robert Elton. *Yankee Stargazer: The Life of Nathaniel Bowditch.* NY. 1941. 1st ed. ....$16–$20

Berry, Wendell. *Clearing.* NY. Harcourt. (1977). 1st ed. dj. $75

Berson, L. *The Negroes and The Jews.* 1971. ....$10–$15

Bertram, James M. *Crisis in China.* Lon. 1937. illus. ....$10–$15

The Best American Short Stories, 1951. Houghton. 1951. 1st ed. dj. $35

Best, F. *The Maori as He Was . . . in Pre-European Days.* New Zealand. 1934. 2nd issue. ....$15–$20

The Best Short Stories of 1923. Bos. 1924. ....$45–$60

Bester, Alfred. *The Demolished Man.* 1953. dj. ....$40–$50

Beston, Henry. *Fairy Tales.* 1952. 1st ed. illus. ....$18–$25

Bethe, H. A. *Elementary Nuclear Theory.* NY. 1947. dj. ....$18–$25

Betten, H. L. *Upland Game Shooting.* Phila. 1940. 1st ed. illus by Lynn Bogue Hunt. ....$40–$60

Betts, Doris, *The Gentle Insurrection.* NY. Putnam's. 1954. 1st ed. author's first book, dj. ....$60–$150

Beveridge, Albert J. *The Life of John Marshall.* Bos. 4 vols. .... .$50–$85

Bhushan, Jamila Brij. *Indian Jewelry, Ornaments and Decorative Designs.* Bombay. nd. 1st ed. illus. ....$75–$140

Bible Atlas. . . . Phila. American Sunday School Union. 1827. wrps. illus. clr maps, 9 leaves, 135 × 11 cm. $115

Biblia cum Postillis Nicolai de Lyra. Nuremberg. 1497. 4 vols. Dutch vellum, blind stamped. $7,425

Bick, Edgar. *History and Source Book of Orthopaedic Surgery.* 1933. ... .$14–$25

Biddle, Maj. Charles. *The Way of the Eagle.* NY. 1919. photos. *$25*

Biddle, Ellen. *Reminiscences of a Soldier's Wife.* Phila. 1907. . . .*$32–$40*

Biden, C. L. *Sea-angling Fishes of the Cape (South Africa).* Lon. 1930. illus. . . . .*$30–$40*

Bidwell, John. *Echoes of the Past.* Chico, CA. nd. softbound. . . .*$35–$50*

Bierce, Ambrose. *Ten Tales.* Lon. 1925. . . . .*$28–$35*

Bierce, Ambrose. *The Shadow on the Dial.* SF. 1909. . . . .*$34–$40*

Bierce, Ambrose. *Write It Right: A Little Blacklist of Literary Faults.* NY. 1909. dj. . . . .*$20–$35*

Bierhorst, John. *Songs of the Chippewa.* NY. 1974. illus. . . . . . .*$10–$15*

Bigelow. *Borderland of Czar and Kaiser.* NY. 1895. illus by F. Remington. . . . .*$20–$40*

Bigelow, Jacob. *The Useful Arts . . . with the Applications of Science.* Bos. Webb & Co. 1842. 396 pp, illus. . . . .*$60–$75*

Bigelow, John. *Memoir of the Life and Public Services of John Charles Fremont.* NY. 1856. . . . .*$40–$60*

Bigelow, John. *The Peach Orchard.* Minn. 1910. 1st ed. illus. fldg maps. . . . .*$55–$75*

Bigelow, Poultney. *White Man's Africa.* Harper. 1898. . . . .*$20–$25*

Biggers, Earl Derr. *The Chinese Parrot.* NY. 1926. rprnt, dj. . . .*$25–$35*

Biggers, Earl Derr. *Earl Derr Biggers Tells Ten Stories.* IN, Bobbs Merrill. (1933). 1st ed. . . . .*$20–$25*

Biggers, Earl Derr. *Keeper of the Keys.* Bobbs Merrill. 1932. 1st ed. . . . .*$60–$75*

Biggers, Earl Derr. *Love Insurance.* Bobbs Merrill. 1914. 1st ed. *$35–$75*

Billings, John D. *Hardtack and Coffee, or The Unwritten Story of Army Life.* Bos. 1887. 1st ed. illus. plates. . . . .*$200–$275*

Billings, John D. *Hardtack and Coffee, or The Unwritten Story of Army Life.* Alexandria. 1982. illus. . . . .*$25–$30*

Billington, Elizabeth. *The Randolph Caldecott Treasury.* NY. Frederick Warne. 1978. 1st ed. dj. *$35*

Bingham, Capt. *The Bastille.* NY. 1901. 2 vols. illus. ltd 150 cc, plates, djs. . . . .*$75–$90*

Bingham, Caleb. *The Columbian Orator.* Bos. 1817. . . . .*$10–$15*

Bingham, Hiram. *A Residence of Twenty-one Years in the Sandwich Islands.* Hartford. 1847. half-lea. . . . .*$100–$325*

Bingham, Hiram. *A Residence of Twenty-one Years in the Sandwich*

Islands. Hartford. Hezekiah Hunting. 1848. 2nd ed, illus, fldg maps. . . . . .
. . . .*$100–$165*

Bingham, John. *Trial of Conspirators . . . Assassination of President Lincoln.* DC. GPO. 1865. wrps. . . . .*$65–$75*

Binkerd, Adam D. *The Mammoth Cave and Its Denizens.* Cinc. 1869. 1st ed. wrps. . . . .*$65–$90*

Binkley, William C. *The Texas Revolution.* Baton Rouge. 1952. 1st ed. dj.
. . . .*$25–$50*

Binns, R. *The Loch Ness Mystery Solved.* Buffalo. 1984. . . . .*$18–$24*

Bird, Annie Laurie. *Boise, the Peace Valley.* Idaho. 1934. . . . . .*$32–$40*

Bird, H. E. *Chess: A Manual for Beginners.* Lon. nd. illus. . . . . .*$14–$20*

Bird, Isabella. *The Hawaiian Archipelago.* (NY. 1882). 5th ed. . .*$60–$75*

Bird, Isabella. *A Lady's Life in the Rocky Mountains.* Lon. 1910. 7th ed. . .
. . . .*$55–$65*

Bird, Isabella. *A Lady's Life in the Rocky Mountains.* 1885. illus. 5th ed. . .
. . . .*$65–$75*

Bird, William. *A Practical Guide to French Wines.* Paris. nd. wrps. maps.
. . . .*$14–$19*

Birds of New York. The State of New York. 1916. clr plates. . . . .*$40–$60*

Birdsong, James C. *Brief Sketch of the North Carolina State Troops.* . . .
Raleigh. 1894. . . . .*$42–$60*

Birkett, John. *The Diseases of the Breast and Their Treatment.* Lon. 1850.
11 plates. . . . .*$250–$450*

Bishop, Ebenezer. *Farewell Address of Elder Ebenezer Bishop of New Lebanon.* Canterbury. 1850. wrps. 15 pp. . . . .*$100–$170*

Bishop, Harriet E. *Floral Home.* NY. Sheldon, Blakeman. 1857. 1st ed. illus. 10 plates, 342 pp. *$225*

Bishop, Mrs. J. F. [Isabella L. Bird]. *The Yangtse Valley and Beyond.* NY. Putnam. 1900. 2 vols. illus, fldg map, pictorial cloth, teg. . .*$75–$135*

Bishop, Mrs. J. E. *The Yangtse Valley and Beyond.* Putnam. 1900. 2 vols. wrps. illus. . . . .*$195–$250*

Bishop, Nathaniel. *A 1,000 Miles Walk across South America.* Bos. 1869.
. . . .*$40–$65*

Bishop, Richard E. *Bishop's Wildfowl.* St. Paul. 1948. 1st ed. lea. . . . . . .
. . . .*$125–$200*

Bishop, Richard E. *The Ways of Wildfowl.* Chi. 1971. deluxe ed. leather. . .
. . . .*$75–$200*

Biss, Gerald. *The Door of the Unreal.* NY. Putnam. 1920. 1st Amer ed. . .
. . . .*$125–$150*

Bissell, Richard. *The Monongahela.* Rinehart & Co. 1952. illus. dj. *$5–$10*

Bixby, William. *South Street.* NY. 1972. illus. dj. . . . .*$15–$25*

Black Arrow. Scribner's. 1916. illus by N. C. Wyeth, 14 clr plates. . . . . . .
. . . .*$40–$55*

Black Book: The Nazi Crime against the Jewish People. NY. 1946. 1st
ed. dj. . . . .*$25–$40*

Black, Jeremiah S. *Eulogy on the Life and Character of General Andrew
Jackson.* Chambersburg. 1845 1st ed. . . . .*$45–$75*

Blackburn, I. *Illus. of Gross Morbid Anatomy of the Brain in the Insane.*
GPO. 1908. 1st ed. . . . .*$45–$65*

Blacker, J. F. *Chats on Oriental China.* Lon. 1919. illus. 4th imp. . . . . . .
. . . .*$12–$20*

Blackford, William Willis. *War Years with Jeb Stuart.* NY. 1945. 1st ed.
dj. . . . .*$35–$50*

Blackmore, Howard L. *British Military Firearms, 1650–1850.* Lon. 1961.
illus. . . . .*$20–$30*

Blackwell, Sarah Ellen. *A Military Genius . . . Life of Anna Ella Carroll
of Maryland.* DC. 1891. 1st ed. . . . .*$40–$50*

Blackwood, Algernon. *The Centaur.* Lon. 1911. 1st ed. . . . .*$45–$50*

Blackwood, Algernon. *Day and Night Stories.* NY. Dutton. (1917). 1st
Amer ed. 228 pp. *$75*

Blackwood, Algernon. *The Doll and One Other.* Arkham House. 1946. 1st
ed. dj. . . . .*$40–$70*

Blades, William F. *Fishing Flies and Fly Tying.* Harrisburg. 1962. 2nd ed.
dj. . . . .*$35–$60*

Blaikie, William. *How to Get Strong and How to Stay So.* NY. Harper &
Bros. 1879. wrps. . . . .*$35–$48*

Blaikie, Wm. G. *The Personal Life of David Livingstone.* NY. Harper &
Bros. 1881. fldg map. . . . .*$35–$45*

Blaine, John. *The Rocket's Shadow.* Grosset & Dunlap. 1947. Rick Brant
#1, dj. *$20*

Blaine, John. *The Rocket's Shadow.* Grosset & Dunlap. 1947. Rick Brant
#1. . . . .*$15*

Blair, Walter A. *A Raft Pilot's Log.* Cleve. 1930. . . . .*$33–$45*

Blake, John L. *Farmer's Every Day Book.* Auburn, NY. 1850. .*$75–$135*

Blake, John L. *A Geographical, Chronological and Historical Atlas.* NY. 1826. illus. charts, engr. ....$75–$80

Blake, Sallie E. *Tallahassee of Yesterday.* Tallahassee. 1924. 1st ed. ....$37–$45

Blake, W. O. *History of Slavery and the Slave Trade.* Columbus. 1858. .. ..$55–$75

Blakebrough, K. *The Fireball Outfit.* np. 1968. wrps. illus. maps. .$28.50

Blanch, H. J. *A Century of Guns.* ... Lon. 1909. illus. index. ...$35–$40

Blanchan, Neltje. *Bird Neighbors.* Doubleday & McClure. 1899. $20–$35

Blanchan, Neltje. *Birds That Hunt and Are Hunted.* Doubleday & McClure. 1898. 1st ed. illus. ....$30–$40

Blanchan, Neltje. *Nature's Garden.* NY. Doubleday Page. 1900. 1st ptg, photos. ....$25–$32

Blanchan, Neltje. *The Nature Library.* NY. 1926. 5 vols. illus. ..$32–$45

Blanchard, Leola H. *Conquest of Southwest Kansas.* Wichita. 1931. ....$30–$45

Blanchard, Rufus. *The Discovery and Conquests of the Northwest.* Chi. 1880. ....$65–$125

Blanchard, Rufus. *History of Illinois to Accompany an Historical Map of the State.* Chi. National School. 1883. 1st ed. 128 pp, fldg map mounted on linen. $125

Blanck, J. *Peter Parley to Penrod.* (Cambridge. 1961). 3rd ptg 25. ....$25–$35

Bland, J. O., and E. Backhouse. *China under the Empress Dowager.* Phila/Lon. 1912. ....$25–$65

Bland, W. *Hints on the Principles ... of Ships and Boats.* ... Lon. 1856. 2nd ed. ....$65–$85

Bland-Sutton, J. *Tumors, Innocent and Malignant.* Chi. nd. ....$15–$25

Blandford, G. F. *Insanity and Its Treatment.* Phila. 1871. 1st ed. $36–$45

Blavatsky, Helena Petrovna. *From the Caves and Jungles of Hindostan.* Lon. Theosophical Society. 1892. 1st ed. $125

Bledsoe, Albert T. *An Essay on Liberty and Slavery.* Phila. 1856. $65–$75

Bledsoe, Marvin. *Thunderbolt: Memoirs of a World War II Fighter Pilot.* NY. 1982. 1st ed. photos, dj. $38.50

Bleeker, S. *The Delaware Indians.* NY. 1953. dj. ....$25–$35

Bleeker, Sylvester. *Gen. Tom Thumb's Three Years' Tour around the World.* NY. c 1872. 144 pp, printed wrps. slipcase. ....$75–$100

Blindloss, Harold. *In the Niger Country.* Edin. Wm. Blackwood. 1898. maps (1 clr fldg). . . . .*$40–$50*

Blinn, Henry Clay. *The Life and Gospel Experience of Mother Ann Lee.* Canterbury. Shakers. 1842. wrps. 15 pp, 170. . . . .*$70–$90*

Blish, James. *Earthman, Come Home.* NY. Putnam. [1955]. 1st ed. dj. *$150*

Bliss, Percy. *A History of Wood Engraving.* Lon. 1928. . . . . . .*$125–$195*

Bloch, Robert. *Cold Chills.* 1977. wrps. . . . .*$18–$30*

Bloch, Robert. *Terror.* NY. 1962. 1st ed. paperback. . . . .*$15–$20*

Block, Herbert. *Special Report.* 1st ed. sgn. . . . .*$16–$20*

Block, Lawrence. *The Burglar Who Liked to Quote Kipling.* NY. Random House. 1979. 1st ed. dj. *$125*

Block, Lawrence. *Like a Lamb to Slaughter.* Arbor House. 1984. 1st ed. sgn, dj. . . . .*$30–$45*

Block, Lawrence. *The Sins of the Father.* Arlington Heights. Dark Harvest. 1992. 1st hardcover ed. intro by Stephen King, dj. *$65*

Block, Lawrence. *Sometimes They Bite.* NY. Arbor House. 1983. 1st ed. dj. *$65*

Block, Lawrence. *When the Sacred Ginmill Closes.* NY. Arbor House. 1986. 1st ed. dj. *$40*

Block, Robert. *The Dead Beat.* NY. 1960. 1st ed. dj. *$75*

Blond, Georges. *The Great Whale Game.* Lon. 1954. illus. 1st Eng. . . . .*$15–$20*

Blot, Pierre. *Hand-book of Practical Cookery.* NY. 1868. . . . . . .*$18–$25*

Blum, Arlene. *Annapurna: A Woman's Place.* Sierra Club. 1980. 2nd ed. inscrb. . . . .*$24–$30*

Bly, Robert. *Angels of Pompeii.* Ballantine. 1992. 1st ed. photos. dj. . . .*$20*

Bly, Robert. *Jumping out of Bed.* Barre Publishers. 1973. 1st ed. wrps. sgn. . . . .*$30–$45*

Bly, Robert. *The Loon.* Minnesota. Ox Head Press (1977). 1/500 cc, wrps. . . . .*$30–$40*

Bly, Robert. *The Man in the Black Coat Turns.* Dial. 1981. 1st ed. dj. . . . .*$20–$28*

Bly, Robert. *Morning Gloria.* SF. 1969. wrps. illus by Tommie De Paloa, 1/800 cc. . . . .*$25–$30*

Blyth, R. *Zen in English Literature and Oriental Classics.* Tokyo. 1942. illus. 446 pp. *$65*

Bochner, Salomon. *The Role of Mathematics in the Rise of Science.* Princeton Univ. Press. (1969). 1st ed. dj. . . . .*$30–$35*

Boddy, Alexander. *By Ocean, Prairie and Peak.* Lon. 1896. illus. . . . . . .
. . . .*$25–$35*

Bodfish, Capt. Hartson. *Chasing the Bowhead.* Harvard Univ. Press. 1936. 1st ed. dj. . . . .*$28–$37*

Bodine, A. Aubrey. *Chesapeake Bay and Tidewater.* NY. 1979. rprnt, dj.
. . . .*$16–$20*

Bodine, Aubrey. *Chesapeake Bay and Tidewater.* 1954. 1st ed. . . . .
. . . .*$24–$35*

Boerhaave, Hermann. *De Viribus Medicamentorum: The Virtue and Energy of Medicines.* Lon. 1720. illus. calf. . . . .*$150–$275*

Bohr, Neils. *The Theory of Spectra and Atomic Constitution.* Lon. 1922. .
. . . .*$35–$45*

Book of Baseball. NY. 1911. . . . .*$150–$300*

Book of Birds. NGS 1932–39. vols 1 & 2. dj. . . . .*$30–$40*

Book of Kalushin. Tel Aviv. 1961. 570 pp. Yiddish, photos. *$80*

Bolles, Albert S. *The Financial History of the U.S. from 1774 to 1789.* NY. 1879. . . . .*$48–$65*

Bond, James H. *From out of the Yukon.* Portland, OR. 1948. illus. dj. . . . . .
. . . .*$35–$50*

Bond, James H. *From out of the Yukon.* Portland, OR, 1948. illus. sgn, dj.
. . . .*$50–$75*

Boni, M. B. *Fireside Book of Folk Songs.* NY. 1947. . . . .*$35–$55*

Bonney, Edward. *The Banditti of the Prairies.* . . . Chi. 1856. wrps. illus. 3rd ed. woodcuts. . . . .*$3,500–$4,500*

Bonnin, Gertrude. *Oklahoma's Poor Rich Indians: An Orgy of Grafting and Exploitation.* Phila. 1924. softbound. . . . .*$65–$95*

Bontemps, Arna. *Free at Last.* Dodd Mead. 1971. illus. dj. . . . . . .*$5–$10*

Bonwick, James. *The Mormons and the Silver Mines.* Lon. 1872. . . . .
. . . .*$95–$125*

The Book of Fishes. NGS. 1924. illus. . . . .*$18–$25*

The Book of Kells. Lon/NY. 1933. illus. 4th ed. tip-in clr plate. . . . .
. . . .*$50–$65*

Boomer and Boschert. *Cider and Wine Presses.* Syracuse, NY. 1876. wrps. . . . .*$65–$90*

Booth, Mary. *History of the City of New York.* NY. 1867. 2 vols. lea. . . . .
. . . .*$50–$85*

Booth, Maud Ballington. *After Prison—What?* NY. 1903. rprnt, sgn. . . . .
. . . .*$28–$45*

Borden, Mrs. John. *The Cruise of the Northern Light.* . . . NY. 1928. 1st
ed. illus. . . . .*$28–$35*

Borges, Jorge Luis. *The Book of Imaginary Beings.* Dutton. 1969. 1st ed.
dj. *$75*

Borges, Jorge Luis. *A Personal Anthology.* NY. Grove Press. 1967. 1st ed.
dj. . . . .*$35–$50*

Born, Max. *Atomic Physics.* NY. 1946. 4th ed. . . . .*$28–$36*

Born, Max. *La Constitution de la Matiere.* Paris. 1922. wrps. illus. Nobel
Prize–winning author. . . . .*$37–$45*

Born, Max. *My Life: The Recollections of a Nobel Laureate.* Lon. 1978.
1st Eng ed. dj. . . . .*$30–$40*

Bosse, Sara, and Onoto Watanna. *Chinese–Japanese Cook Book.* Chi/NY.
1914. . . . .*$14–$20*

Bostock, Frank C. *The Training of Wild Animals.* NY. 1903. illus. . . . . . .
. . . .*$37–$45*

Boston Architectural Club Yearbook of 1917. Bos. . . . .*$35–$50*

Botkin, B. A. *A Civil War Treasury of Tales, Legends and Folklore.* NY.
Promontory Press. dj. . . . .*$20–$30*

Botkin, B. A. *Lay My Burden Down.* . . . Univ. of Chicago Press. 1957. 3rd
ed. dj. . . . .*$12–$20*

Botkin, B. A. *A Treasury of American Folklore.* 1944. . . . .*$15–$22*

Botkin. B. A. *A Treasury of Southern Folklore.* 1949. . . . .*$17–$22*

Botta, Charles. *History of the War of Independence of the U.S.A.* Phila.
1820. 2 vols. translated from Italian. . . . .*$100–$300*

Boucher, Jonathan. *Reminiscences of an American Loyalist, 1783–1789.*
Bos. 1925. bds, 575 cc, boxed. . . . .*$50–$100*

Bourke, J. G. *The Snake Dance of the Moquis of Arizona.* Tucson. 1984.
illus. rprnt. . . . .*$15–$22*

Bourke, John G. *An Apache Campaign.* Scribner's. (1958). dj. . . . .
. . . .*$18–$22*

Bourke-White, M. *Dear Fatherland, Rest Quietly.* NY. 1946. 1st ed. sgn.
. . . .*$200–$300*

Bourke-White, M. *Say, Is This the U.S.A.?* Duell, Sloan. 1941 1st ed. . . .
. . . .*$45–$65*

Bourke-White, M. *Shooting the Russian War.* NY. 1942. dj. . . . .*$22–$45*

Bourke-White, Margaret. *They Called It "Purple Heart Valley": A Combat Chronicle.* . . . NY. 1944. illus. 2nd ptg. . . . .*$20–$30*

Boutwell, George S. *Reminiscences of Sixty Years in Public Affairs.* NY. 1902. 2 vols. 1st ed. illus. . . . .*$30–$50*

Bouvier, Jacqueline, and Lee Bouvier. *One Special Summer.* NY. Delacorte Press. 1974. 1st ed. illus. . . . .*$80–$120*

Bovey, Martin. *The Saga of the Waterfowl.* DC. 1949. 1st ed. illus presentation copy, dj. . . . .*$40–$50*

Bowditch, Henry I. *Life and Correspondence of Henry I. Bowditch.* Bos. 1902. 2 vols. 1st ed. . . . .*$75–$100*

Bowen, Elizabeth. *The Death of the Heart.* Lon. Victor Gollancz. 1938. 1st ed. dj. . . . .*$85–$150*

Bowen, Elizabeth. *Ivy Gripped the Steps and Other Stories.* NY. Knopf. 1946. 1st ed. dj. . . . .*$31–$45*

Bowen, Elizabeth. *Look at All Those Roses.* NY. Knopf. 1941. 1st ed. tan wrps, advance copy. *$200*

Bowen, Frank C. *Men of the Wooden Walls.* Lon. Staple Press. (1952). 1st ed. clr frontis, dj. . . . .*$20–$30*

Bowen, Peter. *Imperial Kelly.* NY. Crown. 1992. 1st ed. dj. *$40*

Bowen, Peter. *Wolf, No Wolf.* NY. St. Martin's. 1996. 1st ed. sgn, dj. . . . .
. . . .*$35*

Bowles, Samuel. *Across the Continent: A Summer's Journey to the Rocky Mountains, the Mormons, and the Pacific States, with Speaker Colfax.* Springfield, MA. Samuel Bowles & Co. 1874. 2nd ed. fldg map. *$110*

Bowles, Samuel. *A Summer Vacation in the Parks and Mountains of Colorado.* MA. 1869. . . . .*$40–$60*

Bowles, Samuel. *The Switzerland of America: A Summer Vacation in the Parks and Mountains of Colorado.* Springfield, MA. Samuel Bowles. 1869. 1st ed. 166 pp. . . . .*$100–$150*

Boy Scouts of America: Handbook for Boys. 1928. wrps. Norman Rockwell cvr. . . . .*$20–$35*

Boyd, Brendan, and Fred Harris. *The Great American Baseball Card.* . . . 1973. 1st ed. dj. . . . .*$20–$28*

Boyd, James. *Drums.* NY. 1928. illus by N. C. Wyeth. . . . .*$35–$45*

Boyd, William. *An Ice Cream War.* Morrow. 1983. 1st ed. dj. . . .*$20–$45*

Boyington, Col. Gregory "Pappy." *Baa Baa Black Sheep.* NY. 1989. . . .
. . . .*$21.50*

Boyington, Col. Gregory "Pappy." *Baa Baa Black Sheep.* NY. 1958. photos, dj, sgn. *$125*

Boykin, Edward C. *Ghost Ship of the Confederacy.* NY. 1957. . . . .
. . . .*$25–$35*

Boyle, Frederick. *The Culture of Greenhouse Orchids.* Lon. 1902. . . . . . .
. . . .*$55–$65*

Boyle, Kay. *Nothing Ever Breaks except the Heart.* Garden City. Doubleday. 1966. 1st ed. dj. . . . .*$30–$40*

Boyle, Kay. *Year Before Last.* NY. Harrison Smith. 1932. 1st ed. dj. . . . . .
. . . .*$100*

Boyle, T. Coraghessan. *Descent of Man.* Bos. Atlantic Monthly Press. 1979. 1st ed. author's first book, sgn, dj. *$500*

Boyle, T. Coraghessan. *Greasy Lake and Other Stories.* NY. Viking. 1985. sgn and dated, dj. . . . .*$75–$100*

Boyle, T. Coraghessan. *Water Music.* Bos. Little Brown. (1981). 1st ed. sgn and dated, dj. . . . .*$60–$125*

Boy's Book of Shipwrecks and Ocean Stories. Phila. 1860. illus. rbkd. . . .
. . . .*$40–$75*

Boz [Charles Dickens]. *The Posthumous Papers of the Pickwick Club.* Lon. Piccadilly Fountain Press. 1931–32. 20 vols. wrps. illus. ed by "Boz," facs. *$150*

Bozman, John Leeds. *A Sketch of the History of Maryland.* Balt. 1811. 1st ed. lea. . . . .*$100–$250*

Brackenridge, Henry M. *History of the Late War between the U.S. and Great Britain.* Balt. 1817. illus. . . . .*$100–$250*

Bradbury, Ray. *Dark Carnival.* Hamish Hamilton. 1948. 1st ed. 1st Eng ed. dj. *$250*

Bradbury, Ray. *The Day It Rained Forever.* Lon. Rupert Hart-Davis. 1959. 1st U.K. ed. 254 pp, dj. . . . .*$60–$75*

Bradbury, Ray. *Death Has Lost Its Charm for Me.* Lord John Press. 1987. 1/150 cc, sgn. *$60*

Bradbury, Ray. *The Golden Apples of the Sun.* Garden City. 1953, dj. . . .
. . . .*$50–$75*

Bradbury, Ray. *The Halloween Tree.* NY. Knopf. (1972). 1st ed. dj. . . . .
. . . .*$75*

Bradbury, Ray. *The Illustrated Man.* Doubleday. 1951. 1st ed. dj, sgn. . .
. . . .*$350*

Bradbury, Ray. *Long After Midnight.* NY. 1976. 1st ed. dj. . . . . .*$30–$35*

Bradbury, Ray. *Martian Chronicles.* Ltd. Edition Club. 1974. illus. sgn, boxed. .... *$175–$200*

Bradbury, Ray. *Something Wicked This Way Comes.* Simon & Schuster. 1962. 1st ed. dj. .... *$90–$195*

Bradbury, Ray. *The Toynbee Convector.* NY. Knopf. (1988). 1st ed. sgn, dj. .... *$40–$50*

Bradbury, Ray. *The Toynbee Convector.* Knopf. 1988. 1st ed. dj. .... *$25–$40*

Bradbury, Ray. *Zen and the Art of Writing.* 1st ed. sgn. .... *$50–$60*

Bradford, E. *Four Centuries of European Jewelry.* Lon. 1967. illus. dj. .. .. *$25–$40*

Bradford, Roark. *John Henry.* NY. 1931. 1st ed. dj. .... *$22–$40*

Bradford's History "of Plimoth Plantation." Bos. 1899. 555 pp. .... *$50–$85*

Bradley, Marion Zimmer. *The House between the Worlds.* Garden City. 1980. 1st ed. sgn, dj. .... *$35–$45*

Bradley, Marion Zimmer. *The Mists of Avalon.* Knopf. 1982. 1st ed. dj. . ... *$45–$75*

Bradley, Will. *Peter Poodle, Toymaker to the King.* Dodd Mead. 1906. 1st ed. 4to, 166 pp. *$850*

Bradshaw, Gillian. *Hawk of May.* NY. (1980). 1st ed. dj. ..... *$20–$35*

Brady, Cyrus Townsend. *Recollections of a Missionary in the Great West.* NY. Scribner's. 1900. 1st ed. teg. *$55*

Brady, Edwin. *Australia Unlimited.* Melbourne. Geo. Robertson. c 1915. .... *$50*

Brady, Joseph P. *The Trial of Aaron Burr.* NY. 1913. 89 pp. ...*$28–$35*

Braga, Frederic. *A Dictionary of the Ojibway Language.* MN. Historical Society. 1992. wrps. rprnt. *$25*

Braid, James, and Harry Vardon. *How to Play Golf.* NY. nd. illus. .... *$45–$58*

Brain, Belle. *The Transformation of Hawaii.* (1898). illus. ...... *$25–$35*

Brain, R. *The Last Primitive Peoples.* NY. 1976. maps, photos. *$40*

Brake, Hezekiah. *On Two Continents.* KS. 1896. 1st ed. ...... *$85–$100*

Brand, Max. *Ambush at Torture Canyon.* NY. Dodd Mead. 1971. 1st ed. dj. *$45*

Brand, Max. *Drifter's Vengeance.* NY. Dodd Mead. 1973. 1st ed. dj. *$45*

Brand, Max. *The Gun Tamer.* Dodd Mead. (1929). 1st ed. dj. *$200*

Brand, Max. *Happy Jack.* Dodd Mead. 1936. 1st ed. dj. ......*$40–$65*

Brand, Max. *Lost Wolf.* Dodd Mead. (1953). dj. ....*$15–$20*

Brand, Max. *Mistral.* NY. Dodd Mead. 1929. 1st ed. dj. *$450*

Brand, Max. *Pillar Mountain.* NY. Dodd Mead. 1928. 1st ed. dj. ....
....*$450*

Brand, Max. *The Seventh Man.* NY. 1921. 1st ed. dj. ....*$25–$35*

Brandt, Herbert. *Arizona and Its Bird Life.* Cleve. 1951. illus. dj. ......
....*$150–$195*

Brant. *True Story of the Lindbergh Kidnapping.* NY. 1932. 1st ed. ......
....*$30–$35*

Brashear, John A. *John A. Brashear: The Autobiography of a Man Who Loved the Stars.* Bos. 1925. photos, 252 pp. ....*$50–$70*

Brazer, Esther Stevens. *Early American Decoration.* Springfield. Pond-Ekbert Cp. 1961. illus. 4th ed. dj. ....*$35–$50*

Brebner, John B. *North Atlantic Triangle.* New Haven. 1945. maps. ....
....*$28–$45*

Brehm, Alfred E. *From the North Pole to the Equator.* Lon. 1896. text illus..*$70–$85*

Brennan, Joseph Payne. *Nine Horrors and a Dream.* Arkham House. 1958. 1st ed. dj. ....*$100–$200*

Brewer, A. T. *History of the Sixty-first Regiment, Pennsylvania Volunteers, 1861–65.* Pitts. 1911.............................*$100–$150*

Brewer, Samuel Child. *Every Man His Own Brewer: A Small Treatise....* Lon. nd. 3rd ed. half calf. ....*$75–$115*

Brewster. *A Treatise on Magnetism.* Edin. 1838. 1st ed.........*$60–$85*

Brewster, Charles W. *Rambles about Portsmouth.* Portsmouth. 1859. 1st ed. ....*$75–$95*

Brewster, David. *The Stereoscope.* NY. (1971). facs, dj. ......*$35–$45*

Bricker, Charles. *Landmarks of Mapmaking.* NY. 1976. illus. maps, dj. ..
....*$55–$100*

Bridges, C. *Thin Air: A Himalayan Interlude.* 1930. 1st ed. .....*$15–$20*

A Brief Exposition of the Established Principles and Regulations of the United Society of Believers Called Shakers. NY. Dodge. 1879. 1st ed. illus. 32 pp. ....*$100–$150*

Briggs, Richard. *The English Art of Cookery....* Lon. 1794. illus. 3rd ed. engr plates. ....*$95–$150*

Bright, Charles. *The Story of the Atlantic Cable.* NY. 1903. 1st ed. illus. .
....$20–$30

Bright, John. *Speeches of John Bright, M.P.* Bos. 1865. 1st ed. ....
....$38–$45

Brickwork in Italy. Chi. 1925. illus. 298 pp. ....$45–$55

Brine, Vice-Admiral Lindesay. *Travels amongst American Indians, Their Ancient Earthworks and Temples.* . . . Lon. Sampson Low, Marston. 1894. 1st ed. illus. 429 pp, fldg map. ....$195–$225

Brininstool, E. A. *Fighting Red Cloud's Warriors: True Tales of Indian Days.* . . . Columbus, OH. 1926. 1st ed. illus. ....$55–$65

Brininstool, E. A. *Trooper with Custer and* . . . *Battle of the Little Bighorn.* Columbus, OH. 1925. 1st ed. illus. ....$60–$75

Brisbin, Gen. James. *Belden, the White Chief* . . . *among the Wild Indians of the Plains.* 1870. 1st issue, blue cloth. ....$125–$200

Bristol, Sherlock. *The Pioneer Preacher: An Autobiography.* Revell. (1887). 1st ed. ....$40–$50

The British Pharmacopoeia. Lon. 1885. ....$50

Brittain, Vera. *The Rebel Passion.* NY. Fellowship. (1964). 1st U.S. ed. 240 pp. $40

Brock, Alan St. H. *A History of Fireworks.* Lon. Harrap. 1949. 1st ed. illus. dj. ....$70–$100

Broder, Patricia Janis. *Bronzes of the American West.* NY (1974). illus. dj. ....$75–$125

Brogile, Louis. *Matter and Light.* NY. 1st. Amer ed. dj. ....$22–$35

Bromfield, Louis. *Mr. Smith.* NY. 1951. ltd 600 cc, sgn, dj. ....
....$20–$30

Brooke, Geoffrey. *The Way of a Man with a Horse.* Lon. 1929. illus. dj. .
....$20–$30.

Brooke, Henry K. *Book of Pirates.* . . . Phila. 1847. illus. ....
....$100–$175

Brooke, Rupert. *Democracy and the Arts.* Lon. Rupert Hart-Davis. 1946. 1st ed. dj. $50

Brooke, Rupert. *Letter from America.* Lon. Sidgwick & Jackson. 1916. 1st Brit ed. $75

Brooks, Charles E. *The Living River.* Nick Lyons Books. 1979. 1st ed. dj. $50

Brooks, E. S. *Under the Allied Flags: A Boy's Adventures* . . . *against the Boxers in China.* Bos. 1901. 1st ed. illus. $46

Brooks, Noah. *The Boy Emigrants.* NY. 1929. dj. ....$22–$30

Brooks, Van Wyck. *New England: Indian Summer, 1865–1915.* NY. 1940. 1st ed. slipcase, #151/997 cc, sgn. ....$50–$65

Brooks, Van Wyck. *The World of Washington Irving.* NY. 1944. ....
....$15–$20

Broomhall, Marshall (ed). *Martyred Missionaries of the China Inland Mission.* Lon. nd. illus. fldg maps, photos. ....$20–$30

Brown, Bernard. *Amateur Talking Pictures and Recording.* 1933. 1st ed. illus. ....$18–$22

Brown, D. W. *Salt Dishes.* MA. 1937. illus. ....$30–$45

Brown, Dee. *Bury My Heart at Wounded Knee.* (1970). dj. .....$18–$25

Brown, Dee. *The Gentle Tamers: Women of the Old West.* NY. 1958. 1st ed. illus. ....$18–$30

Brown, Dee. *Trail Driving Days: The Golden Days of the Old Trail Driving Cattlemen.* NY. 1952. 1st ed. 264 pp, folio, dj. $40

Brown, Frederic. *The Mind Thing.* NY. (1961). 1st ed. pictorial wrps. ...
....$20–$35

Brown, Frederick. *The Deep End.* NY. Dutton. 1952. 1st ed. dj. $200

Brown, G. S. *First Steps to Golf.* Bos. Small Maynard. nd. .....$60–$75

Brown, Helen E. *A Good Catch, or Mrs. Emerson's Whaling Cruise.* Phila. 1884. 1st ed. illus. ....$75–$125

Brown, Henry Collins. *The City of New York.* NY. Old Colony Press. 1915. 1st ed. illus. 3¼", limp lea. ....$35–$50

Brown, Hugh Victor. *A History of the Education of Negroes in North Carolina.* Raleigh. Irving Swain Press. 1961. 1st ed. sgn. ....$60–$90

Brown, Innis (ed). *How to Play Golf.* NY. Spalding's Athletic Library. 1930. illus. ....$45–$50

Brown, John. *Twenty Five Years a Parson in the Wild West.* Fall River, MA. published by author. 1896. ....$150–$175

Brown, John Henry. *History of Texas from 1685 to 1892.* St. Louis. (1892–93). 2 vols. $375

Brown, Lloyd A. *The Story of Maps.* Bos. Little Brown. 1949. 1st ed. illus. bibliography, dj. ....$20–$28

Brown, M. M. *Nature Underground: The Endless Caverns.* New Market. 1921. wrps. illus. ....$18–$25

Brown, Mark H. and W. R. Felton. *The Frontier Years.* NY. 1955. ....
....$40–$50

Brown, Riley. *Men, Wind and Sea.* NY. 1943. illus. rprnt. . . . .*$10–$20*

Brown, Susan A. *The Invalid's Tea Tray.* Bos. 1885. . . . .*$30–$45*

Brown, Thomas. *Lectures on the Philosophy of the Human Mind.* Bos. Armstrong. 1826. 2 vols. 1st Amer ed. *$285*

Brown, Capt. Thomas. *Taxidermist's Manual.* Lon. 1874. illus. 25th ed. . . . .*$25–$65*

Brown, Warren. *The Chicago Cubs.* NY. 1946. illus. . . . .*$30–$40*

Brown, William E. *How to Train Hunting Dogs.* NY. 1942. 1st ed. illus. dj. . . . .*$12–$20*

Brown, William Harvey. *On the South African Frontier.* NY. Scribner's. 1899. fldg maps. . . . .*$275–$325*

Brown, William Symington. *The Capability of Women to Practice the Healing Art.* Bos. Ripley. 1859. 1st ed. illus. 15 pp. *$85*

Browne, J. Ross. *Adventures in Apache Country.* NY. Harper & Co. 1869. illus. . . . .*$275–$3,325*

Browne, John Ross. *Crusoe's Island.* NY. 1864. 1st ed. 436 pp. . . . .*$130–$175*

Browne, Lewis. *Stranger Than Fiction.* NY. 1927. . . . .*$14–$18*

Browne, Lewis. *The Graphic Bible.* Macmillan. 1928. 1st ed. illus. . . . .*$16–$20*

Brownell, Clarence. *The Heart of Japan.* NY. 1903. 1st ed. illus. *$48*

Browning, E. B. *Sonnets from the Portuguese.* NY. Crowell. nd. wrps. illus. tip-in clr plates, dj. . . . .*$80–$125*

Browning, Robert. *The Pied Piper of Hamelin.* Lippincott. (1934). illus by Rackham, 1st Amer ed. . . . .*$140–$185*

Brownlow, W. G. *Sketches of the Rise, Progress and Decline of Secession.* Phila. 1862. 1st ed. illus. . . . .*$25–$35*

Bruccoli, M. *Raymond Chandler: A Bibliography.* Pitts. 1979. . . . .*$50–$60*

Bruce, George A. *The Capture and Occupation of Richmond.* np. nd. 1st ed. illus. presentation copy, sgn. . . . .*$60–$75*

Bruce, William C. *Benjamin Franklin, Self-revealed.* NY. 1917. 2 vols. . . . .*$60–$80*

Bruette, William. *American Duck, Goose and Brant Shooting.* NY. 1943. . . . .*$55–$125*

Bruette, William. *The Cocker Spaniel, Breeding, Breaking and Handling.* NY. 1937. 1st ed. .... *$25–$40*

Brummit, Stella W. *Brother Van.* NY. 1919. 1st ed. .... *$50–$75*

Bruno, Harry. *Wings Over America.* Garden City. 1944. illus. dj. *$23.50*

Bryan, Thomas Conn. *Confederate Georgia.* Athens. 1953. 1st ed. .... *$48–$65*

Bryant, William Cullen. *The Flood of Years.* NY. 1878. 1st ed. full mor, raised bands. .... *$100–$145*

Bryant, William Cullen. *Picturesque America.* NY. (1872–74). 6 vols. plates. *$150*

Bryant, William Cullen. *Picturesque America.* NY. 1872. 2 vols. steel plates. .... *$175–$350*

Bryce, Viscount. *Treatment of Armenians in the Ottoman Empire, 1915–16.* Lon. 1916. 1st ed. fldg map. .... *$50–$75*

Bryk, F. *Circumcision in Man and Woman.* 1934. ltd ed. .... *$30–$35*

Brynner, Irena. *Modern Jewelry—Design and Technique.* NY. 1968. illus. .... *$45–$60*

Buber, Martin. *Israel and Palestine.* Lon. 1952. dj. .... *$25–$45*

Buchan, John. *The Blanket of the Dark.* Lon. Hodder & Stoughton. 1931. 1st ed. dj. *$200*

Buchan, John. *Castle Gay.* Lon. Hodder & Stoughton. 1930. 1st ed. dj. *$200*

Buchan, John. *The Gap in the Curtain.* ... Bos/NY. 1932. 1st U.S. ed. .. .. *$25–$35*

Buchan, John. *The Island of Sheep.* Lon. Hodder & Stoughton. 1936. 1st ed. dj. *$85*

Buchanan, James. *Message of the Pres. of the U.S. ... Massacre at Mountain Meadows.* DC. 1860. softbound. .... *$75–$100*

Buchanan, Lamont. *Ships of Steam.* NY. 1956. illus. dj. .... *$22–$30*

Buck, Frank. *All in a Lifetime.* 1943. .... *$20–$24*

Buck, Frank. *Bring 'em Back Alive.* NY. 1930. 1st ed. illus. photos. .... *$30–$45*

Buck, Franklin. *A Yankee Trader in the Gold Rush.* Bos. 1930. dj. .... *$50–$65*

Buck, James. *The Modern Japanese Military System.* Lon. 1975. wrps. .. .. *$18–$25*

Buck, M. S. *Book Repair and Restoration.* 1918. illus. .... *$25–$30*

Buck, Pearl. *China in Black and White.* NY. 1944–45. 1st ed. illus. woodcuts, 95 pp, dj. *$45*

Buck, Pearl. *Death in the Castle.* NY. (1965). 1st ed. dj. . . . .*$30–$45*

Buck, Pearl. *Fighting Angel.* 1936. 1st ed. dj. . . . .*$24–$30*

Buck, Pearl S. *The Kennedy Women.* NY. 1970. 1st ed. illus. dj, sgn. . . . .
. . . .*$16–$20*

Buck, Pearl S. (trans). *All Men Are Brothers.* Grove Press (1937). 2 vols. 1st ed. dj, boxed. . . . .*$25–$45*

Buckingham. *The Slave States of America.* Lon. (1842). 2 vols. 1st ed. scarce. *$250*

Buckingham, J. E. *Reminiscences and Souvenirs of the Assassination of Abraham Lincoln.* DC. 1894. 1st ed. wrps. illus. . . . .*$85–$100*

Buckingham, Nash. *Game Bag.* NY. 1945. 1st ed. illus by Hoecker, dj. . .
. . . .*$22–$30*

Buckingham, Nash. *Mark Right!* Derrydale Press. (1936). ltd 1,250 cc, inscrb. . . . .*$175–$225*

Buckingham, Nash. *Tattered Coat.* Putnam. 1944. wrps. #279/995, sgn. . .
. . . .*$160–$300*

Buckley, James. *The Wrong and Peril of Woman Suffrage.* NY. Revell. 1909. . . . .*$35*

Budge, E. A. Wallis. *The Mummy.* Cambridge Univ. Press. 1894. 2nd ed. illus. . . . .*$75–$90*

Buechner, Thomas S. *Norman Rockwell, Artist and Illustrator.* NY. 1970.
. . . .*$50–$75*

Buhler, A. *Die Maske Gestalt und Sinn.* Basel. 1950. illus. soft cover. . . .
. . . .*$27*

Builders of Steam Fire Engines, Hose Carriages, Tenders, Etc. Hudson, NY. Clapp & Jones Mfg. Co. 1872. purple printed wrps, illus, 60 pp. . . . .
. . . .*$225–$300*

Buist, Robert. *The Family Kitchen Gardener.* . . . Judd. 1866. . . .*$35–$60*

Buist, Robert. *The Rose Manual.* Phila. 1847. 7th ed. . . . .*$47–$65*

Buley, R. Carlyle. *The Old Northwest.* Indiana Univ. Press. 1951. 2 vols. illus. maps, plates, slipcase. . . . .*$30–$45*

Bulfinch, Thomas. *Oregon and Eldorado.* Bos. 1866. . . . .*$57–$65*

Bull, J. *Birds of New York State.* NY. 1974. illus. . . . .*$45–$60*

Bull, Rice C. *Soldiering: The Civil War Diary of Rice C. Bull, 123rd Vol. Inf.* . . . CA. 1977. 1st ed. dj. . . . .*$30–$40*

Bullard, Robert L. *Personalities and Reminiscences of the War.* NY. 1925. 1st ed. . . . .*$45–$75*

Bullen, Frank T. *The Apostles of the Southeast.* NY. 1901. . . . . .*$22–$32*

Bullen, Frank T. *Cruise of the Cachalot.* NY. 1926. illus by Mead Schaeffer. . . . .*$25–$35*

Bullen, Frank T. *Deep-sea Plunderings.* NY. 1902. 8 illus. . . . . .*$20–$25*

Bullen, Frank T. *Denizens of the Deep.* NY. 1904. illus. . . . .*$30–$50*

Bullen, Frank T. *Idylls of the Sea.* NY. 1899. authorized ed. . . . .*$20–$25*

Bulley, Margaret H. *Ancient and Medieval Art: A Short History.* NY. 1914. illus. clr chart. . . . .*$18–$25*

Bullock, James D. *The Secret Service of the Confederate States in Europe, or How the Confederate Cruisers Were Equipped.* NY. Thomas Yoseloff. c. 1959. 2 vols.1st ed thus, illus. reprint of 1881 original, 1/50 cc in publisher's full lea binding. . . . .*$100–$275*

Bullock, Shan F. *A "Titantic" Hero: Thomas Andrews, Shipbuilder.* Riverside, CT. 1973. illus. rprnt, dj. . . . .*$18–$30*

Bulpin, T. V. *The Hunter Is Death.* Johannesburg. 1962. 1st ed. illus. . . . .*$22–$30*

Bumstead, John. *On the Wing.* Bos. 1869. illus. . . . .*$30–$50*

Bunyan, John. *The Pilgrim's Progress.* Century. 1898. 1st ed. folio, 184 pp. . . . .*$100–$105*

Bunyan, John. *The Pilgrim's Progress.* NY. 1928. . . . .*$25–$40*

Burack, Benjamin. *Ivory and Its Uses.* Rutland, VT. 1984. illus. dj. . . . .*$12–$18*

Burbank, Nelson L. *House Construction Details.* NY. 1942. 2nd ed. . . . .*$22–$30*

Burch, E. S., and W. Forman. *The Eskimos.* Norman. 1988. photos, maps. *$50*

Burch, John P., and Charles W. Burch. *Quantrell: A True History of His Guerrilla Warfare.* . . . Texas. published by author. (1923). 1st ed. illus. dj. . . . .*$45–$75*

Burckhardt, John Lewis. *Notes on the Bedouins and Wahabys.* Cinc. 1968. rprnt. . . . .*$20–$35*

Burder, George. *The Welch Indians.* NY. 1922. softbound. . . . . .*$24–$35*

Burdett, Charles. *The Life and Adventures of Christopher Carson.* Phila. 1861. . . . .*$28–$35*

Burdett, Charles. *The Life of Kit Carson.* 1902. . . . .*$25–$30*

Burdick, Usher. *The Last Battle of the Sioux Nation.* Fargo. 1929. 1st ed. dj. ....$35–$50

Burgess, Anthony. *A Clockwork Orange.* (1963). 1st Amer ed. dj. ......
....$75–$150

Burgess, Anthony. *The Devil of a State.* Lon. (1961). 1st ed. dj. ....
....$50–$125

Burgess, Anthony. *The End of the World News.* McGraw-Hill. 1983. 1st U.S. ed. dj...$25

Burgess, Anthony. *The Kingdom of the Wicked.* Franklin Library. 1985. 1st ed. illus. ....$48–$60

Burgess, Gelett. *Bayside Bohemia: Fin de Siecle San Francisco and Its Little Magazines.* SF. Book Club of California. 1954. 1st ed. ltd 375 cc. ..
....$65

Burgess, Gelett. *The Maxims of Methusaleh.* Stokes. (1907)............
....$25–$35

Burgess, Thornton. *Billy Mink.* Little Brown. 1924. 1st ed. illus by Cody, dj. ....$50–$105

Burgess, Thornton. *The Book of Nature Lore.* NY. 1965. dj. ....$25–$45

Burgess, Thornton W. *The Advent of Prickly Porky.* Little Brown. 1916. 1st ed. gray cloth, 116 pp, 6 plates........................$40–$50

Burgess, Thornton W. *Old Mother Westwind.* Little Brown. 1910. 1st ed. illus by Kerr, 169 pp, 7 plates. ....$100–$150

Burke, Emma Maxwell. *A Perfect Course in Millinery.* NY. 1925. illus. .
....$30–$40

Burke, James Lee. *Heaven's Prisoners.* NY. Henry Holt. 1988. 1st ed. dj, sgn. $150

Burke, James Lee. *A Morning for Flamingos.* Bos. Little Brown. 1990. 1st ed. illus. uncorrected proof copy. $250

Burke, James Lee. *The Neon Rain.* NY. Henry Holt. 1987. 1st ed. dj.....
....$250

Burness, Tad. *Cars of the Early Twenties.* NY. ....$10–$14

Burnet, J. A. *Treatise on Painting.* Lon. 1850. plates. ....$85–$100

Burnett, Frances Hodgson. *Editha's Burgler.* J. Marsh. 1888. blue cloth, 13 plates, 64 pp, illus by Sandham. ....$40–$50

Burnett, Frances Hodgson. *Giovanni and the Other.* Scribner's. 1892. 1st ed. ....$50–$60

Burnett, Frances Hodgson. *Sara Crewe, or What Happened at Miss Minchin's.* NY. 1888. illus................................$30–$45

Burnham, Maj. Frederick. *Scouting on Two Continents.* Garden City. 1926. 1st ed. sgn. . . . .*$25–$40*

Burns, Eugene. *Advanced Fly Fishing.* Harrisburg. 1953. illus. . . . .*$120–$150*

Burns, Robert. *The Songs.* Lon. 1903. 1st ed. 536 pp, 4 plates. . . . .*$50–$75*

Burns, Walter Noble. *The Saga of Billy the Kid.* Garden City. (1925–26). dj. . . . .*$22–$30*

Burns, Walter Noble. *Tombstone.* Grosset & Dunlap. (1929). illus. . . . .*$17–$25*

Burns, Walter Noble. *Tombstone: An Illiad of the Southwest.* NY. 1927. . . . .*$35–$50*

Burns, Walter Noble. *A Year with a Whaler.* NY. 1913. 1st ed. wrps. illus. . . . .*$50–$100*

Burpee, Lawrence J. *The Search for the Western Sea.* . . . Lon. 1908. 1st ed. illus. 6 maps, 51 plates. . . . .*$125–$200*

Burr, F. *The Life of General Philip Sheridan.* Prov. 1888. . . . . . .*$15–$20*

Burris-Meyer, Elizabeth. *Decorating Livable Houses.* NY. 1937. 1st ed. illus. . . . .*$20–$25*

Burritt, Elijah H. *The Geography of the Heavens and Class Book of Astronomy.* NY. 1860. 345 pp. . . . .*$75–$85*

Burritt, Elijah Hinsdale. *Logarithmick Arithmetick Containing a New . . . Table of Logarithms.* . . . Williamsburgh, MA. 1818. lea, fldg plates, 251 pp. . . . .*$100–$150*

Burroughs, Edgar Rice. *At the Earth's Core.* Grosset & Dunlap. 1923. . . . .*$10*

Burroughs, Edgar Rice. *At the Earth's Core.* McClurg. 1922. 1st ed. dj. . . . .*$275–$350*

Burroughs, Edgar Rice. *Beasts of Tarzan.* A. L. Burt. (1917). dj. . . . .*$50–$75*

Burroughs, Edgar Rice. *Beyond Thirty and The Man Eater.* NY. 1957. 1st ed. dj. *$65*

Burroughs, Edgar Rice. *Cave Girl.* Grosset & Dunlap. 1927. . . . .*$15*

Burroughs, Edgar Rice. *The Chessmen of Mars.* NY. Grosset & Dunlap. 1924. dj. . . . .*$60–$80*

Burroughs, Edgar Rice. *Escape on Venus.* Tarzana. (1946). 1st ed. dj. . . . .*$90–$150*

Burroughs, Edgar Rice. *The Gods of Mars.* NY. Grosset & Dunlap. (1919). dj. $65

Burroughs, Edgar Rice. *The Gods of Mars.* Tarzana. Edgar Rice Burroughs (publisher), (1940). ....$30–$50

Burroughs, Edgar Rice. *The Gods of Mars.* Chi. McClurg. 1918. 1st ed. red cloth, dj. ....$2,500–$4,000

Burroughs, Edgar Rice. *Jewels of Opar.* Grosset & Dunlap. 1927. dj. $40

Burroughs, Edgar Rice. *Jungle Tales of Tarzan.* McClurg. 1919. 1st ed. illus. green cloth, dj. ....$40–$60

Burroughs, Edgar Rice. *The Land That Time Forgot.* Grosset & Dunlap. 1925. dj. ....$25–$30

Burroughs, Edgar Rice. *The New Adventures of Tarzan "Pop-up."* Chi. Pleasure Books. (1935). illus. ....$300–$500

Burroughs, Edgar Rice. *The Return of Tarzan.* A. L. Burt. dj. ....$45–$65

Burroughs, Edgar Rice. *Tarzan and the Foreign Legion.* Tarzana. 1948. 1st ed. dj. ....$55–$110

Burroughs, Edgar Rice. *Tarzan of the Apes.* A. L. Burt. 1915. dj. ....$75–$150

Burroughs, Edgar Rice. *Tarzan the Terrible.* NY. Grosset & Dunlap. (c 1940). dj, later ed. ....$35–$50

Burroughs, Edgar Rice. *Tarzan the Untamed.* NY. Grosset & Dunlap. (c 1924). 4 illus, early ed. dj. ....$35–$50

Burroughs, Edgar Rice. *Tarzan's Quest.* Tarzana. (1936). 1st ed. dj. $45

Burroughs, Edgar Rice. *Thuria, Maid of Mars.* Burroughs, dj. $75

Burroughs, John. *Bird Stories.* Bos. 1911. 1st ed. illus by L. A. Fuertes. . ...$18–$25

Burroughs, John. *Camping and Tramping with Roosevelt.* Bos. 1907. 1st ed. illus. photos. ....$24–$35

Marie Burroughs Art Portfolio of Stage Celebrities. Chi. 1894. 14 parts, bound. ....$50–$75

Burroughs, William S. *Exterminator!* NY. Viking Press. 1973. 1st ed. dj. $100

Burroughs, William S. *The Naked Lunch.* Lon. 1964. ....$65–$85

Burroughs, William S. *Naked Lunch.* NY. (1959). dj. ....$75–$100

Burroughs, William S. *Soft Machine.* Lon. 1968. 1st U.K. ed. . . . .
. . . .*$45–$65*

Burroughs, William S. *Third Mind.* NY. 1978. dj. . . . .*$35–$40*

Burroughs, William S. *Tornado Alley.* Cherry Valley Editions. 1989. 1st
ed. 1/100cc. . . . .*$75–$150*

Burroughs, William S. *The Western Lands.* NY. Viking. (1987). 1st ed.
dj. . . . .*$20–$35*

Burton, Frederick R. *American Primitive Music . . . Songs of the Ojib-
ways.* NY. 1909. . . . .*$55–$65*

Burton, Richard. *Lake Regions of Central Africa.* NY. 1860. 1st Amer ed.
map. . . . .*$200–$450*

Burton, Richard F. *The City of Saints, and Across the Rocky Mts. to California.* NY. 1862. 1st Amer ed. maps, plates. . . . .*$125–$275*

Burton, Richard Francis. *Etruscan Bologna: A Study.* Lon. Smith, Elder.
1876. fldg frontis, illus. . . . .*$175–$225*

Burton, Richard Francis. *Wanderings in Three Continents.* Lon. Hutchinson & Co. 1901. 1st ed. ed by W. H. Wilkins, plates. . . . .*$125–$200*

Busch, W. *Das Goldene Wilhelm Busch Album.* Hanover. 1966. .*$45–$60*

Busch, Wilhelm. *Max und Moritz.* Munich. 1939. illus. . . . .*$25–$45*

Bush, Walter L. *A Saga of Duck and Goose Shooting.* Minn. 1979. illus.
2nd ptg. . . . .*$25–$35*

Bushnan, J. S. *The Naturalist's Library, Ichthyology, Vol II.* Edin. 1840.
illus. . . . .*$58–$75*

Bushnell, Charles I. *A Narrative of the Life and Adventures of Levi Han-
ford.* . . . NY. private ptg. (1863). 1st ed. illus. bds. . . . .*$95–$150*

Busk, Hans. *The Navies of the World.* Lon. 1859. . . . .*$55–$68*

Butler, Benjamin F. *Autobiography . . . of Major General Benjamin F.
Butler.* Bos. 1892. 1st ed. illus. . . . .*$27–$35*

Butler, Charles. *The American Lady.* Phila. Hogan & Thompson. 1849.
aeg. *$65*

Butler, Octavia. *Survivor.* Garden City. Doubleday. 1978. 1st ed. dj. . . . .
. . . .*$125*

Butler, Samuel. *An Atlas of Ancient Geography.* Phila. Carey, Lee &
Blanchard. 1838. hand clr maps. . . . .*$175–$200*

Butler, T. Harrison. *Cruising Yachts.* Southampton. 1958. 3rd ed. dj. . . .
. . . .*$22–$35*

Butterworth, Hezekiah. *Zig Zag Journeys in the Antipodes.* Estes & Lau-
riat. 320 pp. *$24*

Buttree, Julia M. *The Rhythm of the Redman.* NY. (1930) intro and illus by E. Thomson Seton. . . . .*$35–$45*

Butts, I. R. *The Merchant and Shipmaster's Manual.* . . . Bos. 1867. illus. 4th ed. plates. . . . .*$95–$135*

Butts, I. R. *The Tinman's Manual.* Bos. 1861. 205 pp. . . . .*$50–$85*

Buxton, Anthony. *Travelling Journalist.* Collins. 1948. 1st ed. dj. $30

Byington, Cyrus. *A Dictionary of the Choctaw Language.* DC. GPO. 1915. . . . .*$75–$85*

By-laws of the Chicago and Rock Island Rail Road Co. NY. 1858. wrps. 10 pp. . . . .*$85–$100*

By-laws of the Orphan House of Charleston, South Carolina, 4th April 1861. Charleston. Steam Power Press. 1861. 1st ed. wrps. 40 pp. $50

Byrd, Martha. *Chennault: Giving Wings to the Tiger.* Tuscaloosa. 1987. photos, dj. *$38.50*

Byrd, Admiral Richard E. *Alone.* Putnam. 1938. sgn, dj. . . . . . .*$30–$40*

Byrd, Admiral Richard E. (intro). *The Big Aviation Book for Boys.* Springfield, MA. [1929]. dj. $25

Byrd, Admiral Richard E. *Discovery: The Story of the Second Byrd Antarctic Expedition.* NY. Putnam. 1935. 1st ed. photos, dj. . . . .*$35.50–$65*

Byrd, Admiral Richard E. *Little America.* NY. 1930. 1st ed. maps, dj. . . . .*$30–$50*

Byrd, Admiral Richard E. *Little America.* NY. 1930. 1st ed. illus. sgn, dj. . . . .*$50–$90*

Cabell, James Branch. *Cream of the Jest: A Comedy of Evasions.* NY. 1927. . . . .*$35–$40*

Cable, George W. *The Creoles of Louisiana.* Lon. 1885. . . . . .*$145–$200*

Cable, George W. *Gideon's Band.* NY. 1914. 1st ed. . . . .*$30–$40*

Cable, George W. *Old Creole Days.* NY. 1879. 1st ed. without ads in rear. . . . .*$135–$175*

Cabot, W. B. *In Northern Labrador.* Bos. 1912. 1st ed. . . . .*$40–$80*

Cady, Daniel. *Rhymes of Vermont Rural Life.* Rutland. 1919. 1st ed. . . . .*$15–$25*

Caiger, G. *Dolls on Display.* Tokyo. nd. illus. silk brocade with silk ties, boxed. . . . .*$95–$150*

Cain, James M. *The Moth.* NY. 1948. 1st ed. dj. . . . .*$45–$60*

Calasanctius, M. J. *The Voice of Alaska: A Missioner's Memories.* Lachine. 1935. illus. 1st Eng ed. mar bds. . . . .*$40–$50*

Caldecott, Randolph. *"Graphic" Pictures.* Lon. 1891. ltd 1,250 cc, aeg. *$225*

Caldecott, Randolph. *Ride a Cock Horse to Banbury Cross.* Lon. 1884. illus. 6 clr plates. . . . .*$100–$150*

Caldecott, Randolph. *A Sketchbook of Randolph Caldecott.* Lon/NY. 1883. illus. . . . .*$70–$125*

Calderwood, W. L. *The Life of the Salmon.* Lon. 1907. illus. . . . .*$40–$50*

Caldwell, E. N. *Alaska Trail Dogs.* NY. 1950. photos, map. *$35*

Caldwell, Erskine. *The Bastard.* NY. Heron Press. (c 1929). 1st ed. illus by Ty Mahon,1/1100 cc, author's first book. *$200*

Caldwell, Erskine. *A Place Called Estherville.* NY. Duell Sloan Pearce. (1949). 1st ed. dj. . . . .*$30–$35*

Caldwell, Erskine. *Claudelle Inglish.* Bos. 1958. 1st ed. dj. . . . .*$20–$30*

Caldwell, Erskine. *Erskine Caldwell's Gulf Coast Stories.* Bos. Little Brown. 1956. 1st ed. dj. *$40*

Caldwell, Erskine. *God's Little Acre.* NY. 1933. 1st ed. . . . . .*$400–$800*

Caldwell, Erskine. *Southways.* NY. 1938. 1st ed. . . . .*$25–$35*

Caldwell, Erskine. *Tenant Farmer.* NY. Phalanx Pres. (c 1935). 1st ed. green wrps. *$150*

Caldwell, Erskine. *Tobacco Road.* NY. 1932. 1st ed. dj. . . . .*$650–$1,000*

Caldwell, Erskine. *Tobacco Road.* NY. 1940. wrps. illus by Fredenthal, boxed. . . . .*$25–$75*

Calendar of the American Fur Company's Papers. DC. 1945. 2 vols. 1st ed. . . . .*$50–$85*

California and the Far West. SF. Grabhorn Press. 1948. 1st ed. 217 pp, large folio, plates, ltd 500 cc. *$100*

Calisher, Hortense. *In the Absence of Angels.* Bos. 1951. 1st ed. dj. . . . .*$30–$75*

Calkins, Clinch. *Some Folks Won't Work.* NY. Harcourt. 1930. 1st ptg, dj. *$14.50*

Callaway, Nicholas (ed). *Georgia O'Keefe: 100 Flowers.* NY. 1987. 1st ed. clr plates, folio, dj. . . . .*$75–$100*

Calvert, Roy E. *The Death Penalty Enquiry.* Lon. 1931. softcover. . . . .*$14–$20*

Calvino, Italo. *The Silent Mr. Palomar.* Targ Editions. 1981. 1st ed. dj. *$100*

Camehl, A. W. *The Blue China Book.* NY. 1916 ....*$20–$30*

Camp, R. *Duck Boats: Blinds, Decoys.* NY. 1952. 1st ed. ......*$40–$50*

Camp, R. *Game Cookery.* NY. 1958. 1st ed. ....*$20–$30*

Camp, Samuel G. *The Fine Art of Fishing.* Macmillan. 1929 (1911). *$50*

Camp, Samuel G. *Fishing Kits and Equipment.* NY. Outing Publishing. 1910. 1st ed. ....*$30–$40*

Camp, Walter (ed). *Official Football Rules—1914.* NY. 1914. wrps. illus. ....*$18–$25*

Campbell, C. A. R. *Bats, Mosquitoes and Dollars.* Bos. 1925. illus. ....*$30–$47*

Campbell, Mary Emily. *The Attitude of Tennesseans toward the Union 1847–1861.* NY. 1961. 1st ed. ....*$30–$45*

Campbell, Patrick. *Travels in the Interior Inhabited Parts of North America.* Tor. 1937. ltd 550 cc. ....*$150–$300*

Campbell, Ruth. *Small Fry and Winged Horse.* Volland. [1927]. illus. ....*$55–$85*

Camus, Albert. *The Fall.* Kentfield, CA. The Allen Press. 1960. illus by Lewis Allen, folio, 1/140 cc, tan, grey and black bds, dj...........*$650*

Camus, Albert. *The Plague.* Knopf. 1948. 1st Amer ed. dj. .....*$30–$40*

Camus, Albert. *The Stranger.* NY. 1946. 1st U.S. ed. dj. ......*$75–$125*

Candee, Helen C. *The Tapestry Book.* NY. 1935. ....*$28–$40*

Candee, Helen C. *Weaves and Draperies.* NY. 1930. 1st ed. illus. ....*$40–$55*

Canfield, Dorothy. *Home Fires in France.* NY. 1918. 1st ed. ...*$20–$35*

Capa, Robert. *Death in the Making.* NY. (1938). 1st ed. ......*$75–$100*

Capa, Robert. *Images of War.* NY. (1964). 1st ed. dj. ....*$75–$95*

Capote, Truman. *A Christmas Memory.* NY. (1966). 1st ed. slipcase. ... .*$50–$75*

Capote, Truman. *The Grass Harp: A Play.* NY. (1952). 1st ed. dj. ....*$150–$200*

Capote, Truman. *In Cold Blood.* Lon. Hamish Hamilton. (1966). 1st ed. dj. ....*$40–$45*

Capote, Truman. *In Cold Blood.* NY. Random House. (1965). 1st ed. dj. *$45*

Capote, Truman. *The Muses Are Heard.* Random House. (1956). 1st ed. dj. ....$75–$95

Capote, Truman. *Other Voices, Other Rooms.* NY. (1948). 1st ed. dj. ... .$125–$250

Capote, Truman. *The Thanksgiving Visitor.* Random House. 1967. ....$24–$35

Capp, Al. *The Return of the Schmoo.* NY. 1959. 1st ed. wrps. ....$28–$35

Caras, Roger. *Monarch of Deadman Bay—The Life and Death of a Kodiak Bear.* Bos. 1969. 1st ed. dj. ....$15–$25

Carey, A. Merwin. *American Firearms Makers to the End of the 19th Century.* (NY. 1953). 1st ed. illus. dj. ....$15–$25

Carhart, Arthur H. *Fishing in the West.* NY. 1950. 1st ed. dj. $15

Carleton, Will. *Farm Ballads.* Harper. 1882. illus. ....$14–$25

Carleton, Will. *Farm Festivals.* NY. 1881. ....$20–$40

Carleton, Will. *Farm Legends.* NY. 1875. ....$20–$45

Carleton, William. *Traits and Stories of the Irish Peasantry.* Dublin. 1843–44. 2 vols. ....$115–$150

Carley, Kenneth. *Minnesota in the Civil War.* Minn. 1961. illus. maps, dj. ....$15–$22

Carlisle, D. *The Belvedere Hounds.* Derrydale Press. 1935. ltd. 1,250 cc, pictorial bds, glassine wrps. ....$75–$125

Carlisle, Lillian Baker. *Vermont Clock and Watch Makers.* VT. 1970. 1st ed. ltd 1000 cc, dj. ....$40–$50

Carmen, Carl. *French Town.* Pelican Pub. (1968). wrps. illus. presentation copy to Ralph Hill, Vermont writer. ....$20–$40

Carmer, Carl. *Deep South.* NY. 1930. 1st ed. sgn. ....$25–$50

Carmer, Carl. *Rivers of America: The Hudson.* NY. 1939. illus. sgn. ....$50–$100

Carnegie, Andrew. *The Empire of Business.* NY. Doubleday Page. 1912. ....$24.50

Carnegie, Andrew. *Round the World.* NY. 1884. 1st Amer trade ed. ....$35–$65

Caron, Pierre. *French Dishes for American Tables.* NY. 1886. 1st ed. ... .$25–$35

Carpenter, R. *Game Trails from Alaska to Africa, 1938.* private ptg. 1938. ltd 850 cc, sgn. ....$125–$150

Carpenter, W. *The Microscope and Its Revelations.* Lon. 1857. illus. 2nd ed. . . . .*$50–$100*

Carpenter, W. *The Microscope: and Its Revelations.* Phila. 1856. 1st Amer ed. . . . .*$100–$200*

Carpenter, W. *The Microscope and Its Revelations.* Wood. 1883. 2 vols. . . . .*$100–$150*

Carpenter, W. *Principles of Human Physiology.* Phila. 1853. 5th Amer ed. . . . .*$35–$45*

Carr, Harry. *The West Is Still Wild.* Bos. 1932. 1st ed. illus. . . . .*$25–$35*

Carr, John. *Pioneer Days in California: Historical and Personal Sketches.* Eureka. Times Publishing Co. 1891. 1st ed. *$150*

Carr, John Dickson. *Death Turns the Tables.* NY. Harper & Bros. 1941. 1st ed. dj. *$400*

Carrick, Alice Van Leer. *Collector's Luck in England.* Bos. 1926. illus. . . . .*$25–$30*

Carrick, Alice Van Leer. *A History of American Silhouettes . . . 1790–1840.* Rutland. (1968). dj. . . . .*$30–$50*

Carrington, Frances C. *Army Life on the Plains.* Phila. 1911. 2nd ed. . . . .*$45–$65*

Carrington, Henry B. *The Indian Question.* Bos. 1884. maps. . . . .*$225–$300*

Carroll, Lewis. *Alice's Adventures in Wonderland.* Doubleday. (1907). illus by Arthur Rackham. . . . .*$95–$165*

Carroll, Lewis. *Alice's Adventures in Wonderland.* Bos. Lee & Shepard. 1869. 1st ed. illus. printed in America, 192 pp, green cloth, scarce. . . . .*$300–$500*

Carroll, Lewis. *Alice's Adventures in Wonderland.* NY/Lon. 1901. illus by Peter Newell. . . . .*$75–$130*

Carroll, Lewis. *The Hunting of the Snark.* Lon. 1876. 1st ed. . . . .*$70–$100*

Carroll, Lewis. *Sylvie and Bruno.* Lon. 1893. 1st ed. illus by Harry Furnise. . . . .*$50–$70*

Carroll, Lewis. *Through the Looking Glass.* Stokes. 1915. illus by M. Kirk. . . . .*$50–$75*

Carroll, Lewis. *Through the Looking Glass.* Harper. 1902. illus by Newell, 40 plates. . . . .*$90–$120*

Carruth, Hayden. *The Adventures of Jones.* NY. Harper. 1895. 1st ed. illus. . . . .*$25–$35*

Carruth, Hayden. *Contra Mortem.* VT. (1967). 1st ed. wrps. 1/250 cc, sgn. . . . .*$85–$120*

Carruth, Hayden. *The Crow and the Heart.* Macmillan. 1959. 1st ed. dj. . . . .*$30–$45*

Carruth, Hayden. *The Mythology of Dark and Light.* NY. 1982. wrps. illus. . . . .*$20–$30*

Carruth, Hayden. *Tracks End.* NY. 1911. 1st ed. . . . .*$15–$25*

Carry, John. *The Life of George Washington.* NY. 1807. . . . .*$95–$250*

Carson, Rachel. *Silent Spring.* Houghton. 1962. 1st ed. dj. . . . .*$55–$75*

Carson, Rachel. *Under the Sea Wind.* NY. 1941. 1st ed. dj. . . . .*$100–$150*

Carter, Jimmy, and Rosalynn Carter. *Everything to Gain.* NY. (1987). 1st ed. 2nd ptg, sgn by both. . . . .*$50–$100*

Cartier-Bresson, Henri. *Photographs by Cartier-Bresson.* NY. Grossman. 1963. 1st ed. wrps. illus. . . . .*$22–$30*

Cartier-Bresson, Henri. *The People of Moscow.* NY. 1955. 1st ed. dj. . . . .*$50–$135*

Carvalho, S. N. *Incidents of Travel and Adventure in the Far West.* NY. 1857. . . . .*$95–$250*

Carver, Jonathan. *Travels through the Interior Parts of No. America . . . 1766, '67, '68.* Lon. 1781. 3rd ed. lea, mor bkd clamshell case, hand-clr maps and plates. . . . .*$900–$2,000*

Carver, Raymond. *Cathedral.* NY. 1983. 1st ed. dj. . . . .*$40–$50*

Carver, Raymond. *Early for the Dance.* Firefly Press. 1986. 1st ed. 1/100 cc, sgn. . . . .*$125–$150*

Carver, Raymond. *If It Pleases You.* Lord John Press. 1984. 1st ed. 1/200 cc, sgn. . . . .*$75–$125*

Carver, Raymond. *A New Path to the Waterfall.* NY. Atlantic Monthly Press. 1989. 1st ed. dj. . . . .*$30–$40*

Carver, Raymond. *This Water.* Ewert. 1985. wrps. 1/100 sgn cc of an ed of 136 cc. *$125*

Carver, Raymond. *The Toes.* Ewert. 1988. 1st ed. wrps. ltd 26 cc . . . .*$125–$175*

Carver, Raymond. *What We Talk about When We Talk about Love.* NY. 1981. 1st ed. dj. . . . .*$60–$100*

Carver, Raymond. *Where I'm Calling From.* PA. The Franklin Library. 1988. sgn, from the First Edition Society. . . . .*$200–$250*

Carver, Raymond. *Where I'm Calling From.* Franklin Library. 1988. 1st ed. sgn, dj. . . . .*$100–$200*

Carver, Raymond. *Where I'm Calling From.* NY. Atlantic Monthly Press. (1988). 1st ed. dj. . . . .*$45–$50*

Casey, Robert J. *The Black Hills and Their Incredible Characters.* Ind. (1949). . . . .*$20–$30*

Casey, Robert J. *The Texas Border.* Bobbs Merrill. (1950). 1st ed. illus. photos, ltd, sgn, dj. . . . .*$25–$40*

Cassidy, Carl (comp). *A History of the 755th Bombardment Squadron.* Iowa. 1982. illus. rprnt, 300 cc. sgn. *$125*

Cassill, R. V. *The Goss Women.* Doubleday. 1974. 1st ed. dj. . . . .*$22–$27*

Cassino, Samuel E. (ed). *The Naturalist's Directory.* Bos. 1884. . . . .*$20–$25*

Castaneda, Carlos. *The Teachings of Don Juan.* Berkeley. 1968. 1st ed. dj. . . . .*$90–$150*

Castle, Henry A. *The Army Mule and Other War Sketches.* Ind. 1898. illus. . . . .*$50–$75*

Castleman, Alfred. *Army of the Potomac.* Milw. 1863. . . . .*$100–$175*

Caswell, J. *Sporting Rifles and Rifle Shooting.* 1920. 1st ed. illus. photos. . . . .*$24–$35*

Catalogue and Price List for 1922 of Fireworks. . . . Bos. The Masten & Wells Fireworks Mfg. Co. 1922. red printed wrps. 32 pp. . . . .*$35–$50*

A Catalogue of Drugs, Chemicals, Dye Stuffs, Druggists' Sundries, Proprietary Medicines, Oils, Paints. . . . Burlington, VT. Wells, Richardon & Co. 1878. pebbled cloth, 200, ii pp. . . . .*$95–$125*

Catalogue of Hardy Fruit Trees and Plants. . . . Sioux Falls, Dakota Territory, E. DeBell. 1884. illus. self-printed wrps. 8 pp. . . . .*$75–$100*

Catalogue of Microscopes and Accessories, Microtomes, Bacteriological Apparatus, Laboratory Supplies . . . 5th ed. Phila. Charles Lentz & Sons. 1899. printed wrps, illus, 136 pp. . . . .*$125–$175*

Catalogue of Weathervanes, No. 9. Waltham, MA. L.W. Cushing & Sons. 1883. decorative wrps, illus, 20 pp. . . . .*$500–$750*

Cate, Wirt Armistead. *Lucius Q. C. Lamar: Secession and Reunion.* Chapel Hill. 1935. 1st ed. illus. . . . .*$30–$50*

Cather, Willa. *April Twilights.* Bos. Richard G. Badger/The Gorham Press. 1903. 1st ed. author's first book, paper covered bds, paper spine label, uncut, sgn. *$1,500*

Cather, Willa. *Death Comes for the Archbishop.* Knopf. 1927. 1st ed. dj. .
. . . .*$75–$200*

Cather, Willa. *Death Comes for the Archbishop.* NY. Knopf. 1927. 1st
trade, dj, inscrb. . . . .*$800–$1,000*

Cather, Willa. *A Lost Lady.* NY. Knopf. 1923. 1st ed. dj. *$125*

Cather, Willa. *The Old Beauty and Others.* NY. 1948. 1st ed. dj. . . . .
. . . .*$35–$65*

Cather, Willa. *The Professor's House.* NY. 1925. 1st ed. . . . .*$100–$200*

Cather, Willa. *Sapphira and the Slave Girl.* NY. 1940. 1st ed. dj. . . . .
. . . .*$75–125*

Cather, Willa. *Shadows on the Rock.* Knopf. 1931. 1st ed. dj. .*$100–$125*

Cather, Willa. *Youth and the Bright Medusa.* NY. Knopf. 1920. 1st ed. . .
. . . .*$50*

Catlin, George. *Illustrations of the Manners, Customs and Condition of
the North American Indians: In a Series of Letters and Notes.* . . . Lon.
Henry G. Bohn. 1845. illus. 5th ed. *$600*

Catlin, George. *Life Amongst the Indians.* Lon. 1861. 14 plates. . . . .
. . . .*$100–$250*

Catlin, George. *North American Indian Portfolio.* Lon. George Catlin.
1844. 1st ed. folio, 25 hand-clr lithos, half burgundy calf, hand-clr issue. .
. . . .*$79,500*

Catlin, George. *North American Indians: Being Letters and Notes on
Their Manners, Customs, and Conditions.* Phila. 1913. 2 vols. *$950*

Catton, Bruce. *Banners of Shenandoah.* Garden City. 1955. illus. dj. . . . .
. . . .*$30–$40*

Catton, Bruce. *Grant Moves South.* Bos/Tor. 1960. 1st ed. illus. presentation copy, sgn, dj. . . . .*$30–$40*

Catton, Bruce. *Terrible Swift Sword.* Garden City. 1963. 1st ed. dj. . . . . .
. . . .*$14.50*

Caverly. A. M. *History of the Town of Pittsford, Vermont.* Rutland. 1872.
illus. rbnd. . . . .*$80–$95*

Century Company War Book. *Battles and Leaders of the Civil War.* NY.
1884–87. 4 vols. . . . .*$75–$100*

Cervantes, Miguel de. *The History of Don Quixote.* Lon. illus by Gustave
Doré. lea bnd. . . . .*$100–$150*

Cescinsky, Herbert, and Ernest Gribble. *Early English Furniture and
Woodwork.* Lon. 1927. 2 vols. illus. folio, lea. . . . .*$135–$200*

Chadwick, Lee. *Lighthouses and Lightships.* Lon. 1971. illus. photos, dj. .
. . . .*$25–$33*

Chagall, Marc. *Drawings and Watercolors for the Ballet.* NY. (1969). 1st ed. 1 original litho, dj, slipcase. $200

Chagall, Marc. *The Jerusalem Windows.* George Braziller. (1962). 2 original lithos by Chagall, red cloth, gilt, dj. $1,380

Chagall, Marc. *Lithographs V.* NY. 1974–1979. 1st Amer ed. ....
....$40–$60

Chalfant, W. A. *Gold, Guns and Ghost Towns.* Stanford. 1947. ....
....$25–$35

Chamberlain, George A. *African Hunting among the Thongas.* NY. 1923. 1st ed. illus. ....$45–$65

Chamberlain, Jacob. *The Cobra's Den.* Revell. (1900). illus. ....$22–$35

Chamberlain, Samuel. *Open House in New England.* Brattleboro, NH. 1939. sgn. ....$18–$20

Chamberlain, Samuel. *Rockefeller Center.* 1947. photos, dj. ...$10–$18

Chamberlain, Samuel, and Narcissa Chamberlain. *Southern Interiors of Charleston, South Carolina.* NY. Hastings House. (1956). illus. 172 pp. ..
....$30–$40

Chambers, E. T. D. *The Ouananiche and Its Canadian Environment.* Harper & Bros. 1896. 1st ed. $85

Chandler, Raymond. *Backfire: Story for the Screen.* CA. 1984. 1st ed. 1/200 cc, softcover, sgn, presentation. $125

Chandler, Raymond. *The Big Sleep.* 1946. movie ed. ....$15–$25

Chandler, Raymond. *The Big Sleep.* NY. 1939. 1st ed. dj, slipcase. .....
....$2,500–$5,000

Chandler, Raymond. *Farewell, My Lovely.* NY. 1940. 1st ed. cloth, dj. ..
....$2,500–$4,000

Chandler, Raymond. *The High Window.* NY. Knopf. 1942. 1st ed. dj. ...
....$100

Chandler, Raymond. *Killer in the Rain.* Bos. Houghton Mifflin. 1964. 1st Amer ed. dj..$350

Chandler, Raymond. *The Little Sister.* Houghton Mifflin. 1949. 1st Amer ed. dj..$150–$350

Chandler, Raymond. *The Long Goodbye.* Bos. Houghton Mifflin. 1954. 1st ed. dj...$275

Channing, William Ellery. *Slavery.* Bos. 1835. 1st ed. ....$50–$68

Chapel, C. E. *Boy's Book of Rifles.* 1948. ....$18–$25

Chapelle, Howard I. *The History of American Sailing Ships.* NY. (1949). illus. photos, plates, dj. ....$45–$65

Chapelle, Howard I. *The History of American Sailing Ships.* NY. W. W. Norton. 1935. 1st trade ed. illus. plates, photos, ship drawings. . . . .
. . . .*$40–$55*

Chaplin, R. *Wobbly.* Chi. (1948). presentation copy, dj. . . . .*$30–$50*

Chapman, A. *On Safari.* Lon. 1908. illus. photos. . . . .*$150–$300*

Chapman, Allen. *The Radio Boys with the Iceberg Patrol.* Grosset & Dunlap. 1924. 1st ed. Radio Boys #7, dj. *$65*

Chapman, Charles E. *A History of California: the Spanish Period.* NY. 1921. illus. maps. . . . .*$40–$50*

Chapman, F. M. *The Distribution of Bird-life in Ecuador.* NY. 1926. 29 plates, fldg map (Bulletin of American Museum of Natural History, vol. 55). *$125*

Chapman, F. Spencer. *Northern Lights.* NY. 1933. illus. 1st Amer ed. fldg map. . . . .*$60–$75*

Chapman, Frank M. *Bird Life.* NY. 1900. 195 pp. . . . .*$75–$95*

Chapman, Frank M. *The Warblers of North America.* NY. 1907. 1st ed. clr plates. . . . .*$45–$85*

Chapman, Olive Murray. *Across Iceland, the Land of Frost and Fire.* Lon/NY. 1930. 1st ed. illus. . . . .*$40–$95*

Chapman, Priscilla. *Hindoo Female Education.* Lon. Seeley & Burnside. 1839. 1st ed. 4 engr illus. *$150*

Chappell, Fred. *Dagon.* NY. Harcourt Brace World. (1968). 1st ed. 177 pp, dj. . . . .*$35–$45*

Chapple, H. Barton. *Popular Television.* 1935. 1st ed. illus. dj. . . . .
. . . .*$45–$60*

Chaptal, M.F.A. *Elements of Chemistry.* Buckingham. 1806. 3 vols. 3rd Amer ed. 612 pp, calf. . . . .*$100–$135*

Chardin, Sir John. *Travels in Persia.* Lon. 1927. illus. ltd 975 cc. . . . . . .
. . . .*$125–$225*

Charteris, Leslie. *The Fantastic Saint.* Garden City. Doubleday. 1982. 1st ed. dj. *$45*

Charteris, Leslie. *The Saint Goes West.* Garden City. 1943. 1st ed. pictorial dj. . . . .*$60–$85*

Charteris, Leslie. *Senior Saint.* Lon. Hodder & Stoughton. 1959. 1st ed. dj. *$65*

Charteris, Leslie. *Thanks to the Saint.* Lon. Hodder & Stoughton. 1958. 1st ed. dj. *$65*

Charters, Ann. *Kerouac.* (1974). 1st Eng ed. wraps, dj. . . . .*$30–$50*

Chase, A. *Dr. Chase's Recipes.* Ann Arbor. 1866. . . . .*$30–$45*

Chase, Edward. *The Memorial Life of General William Tecumseh Sherman.* Chi. 1891. 1st ed. . . . .*$40–$85*

Chase, J. *California Desert Trails.* Bos. (1919). 1st ed. . . . .*$25–$40*

Chase, J. Smeaton. *Yosemite Trails: Camp and Pack-train in the Yosemite Region.* . . . Bos. Houghton Mifflin. 1911. 16 plates. . . . .*$50–$65*

Chase, Mary. *Benjamin Lee, 2d: A Record Gathered from Letters, Notebooks, and Narratives of Friends.* Bos. 1920. photos. *$65*

Chase, Mary Ellen. *The Fishing Fleets of New England.* Bos. 1961. illus. . . . .*$22–$35*

Chase, Peter S. *Reunion Greeting . . . Complete Description List of the Members of C1 2nd Regt. Vermont. Vols.* Brattleboro. 1891. . . . .*$45–$80*

Chatelain, Verne. *Defenses of Spanish Florida, 1565 to 1763.* DC. 1941. 1st ed. illus. fldg maps and plates. . . . .*$50–$75*

Chatham, Russell. *The Angler's Coast.* Doubleday. 1976. 1st ed. dj. *$40*

Chatterton, E. Keble. *Sailing Models Ancient and Modern.* Lon. 1934. 1st ed. . . . .*$75–$125*

Chatwin, Bruce. *On the Black Hills.* NY. Viking. 1983. 1st ed. dj. . . . .*$30–$35*

Chayefsky, Paddy. *Altered States.* NY. 1978. 1st ed. dj. . . . .*$28–$35*

Cheever, John. *Bullet Park.* NY. Knopf. 1969. 1st ed. sgn, dj. *$125*

Cheever, John. *The Brigadier and the Golf Widow.* NY. (1964). 1st ed. dj. . . . .*$35–$40*

Cheever, John. *The Enormous Radio.* NY. 1953. 1st ed. dj. . . . .*$75–$195*

Cheever, John. *The Housebreaker of Shady Hill and Other Stories.* Harper. 1958. 1st ed. dj. . . . .*$50–$75*

Cheever, John. *The Leaves, the Lion-fish and the Bear.* Sylvester & Orphanos. 1980. 1/300 cc sgn. *$90*

Cheever, John. *Oh What a Paradise It Seems.* NY. 1982. 1st ed. dj. . . . .*$20–$25*

Cheever, John. *The Wapshot Chronicle.* The Franklin Library. (1978). 1st ed. sgn. *$100*

Cheever, John. *The Wapshot Chronicle.* NY. (1957). 1st ed. dj. *$100*

Cheever, John. *The World of Apples.* NY. Knopf. 1973. 1st ed. sgn, dj. *$125*

Cheiro. *Palmistry for All.* NY. 1916. . . . .*$10–$18*

Chekov, Anton. *Two Plays: The Cherry Orchard, Three Sisters.* NY. Ltd. Ed. Club. 1966. illus. 1/1500 cc, sgn by Szalay, slipcase. . . . .*$40–$50*

Chennault, Anna. *Chennault and the Flying Tigers.* NY. 1963. photos, maps. *$35*

Chennault, Claire. *Way of a Fighter: Memoirs of Claire Lee Chennault.* NY. 1949. photos. *$40*

Chesterton, G. K. *The Ballad of the White Horse.* 1911. . . . .*$30–$37*

Chicago School of Architecture. Random House. 1964. dj. . . . . .*$60–$75*

Child, Hamilton. *Gazetteer and Business Directory of Rensselaer County, New York, 1870–71.* . . . .*$55–$85*

Child, Hamilton. *Gazetteer and Business Directory of Allegheny County, New York, for 1875.* Syracuse. Journal Office. 1875. fldg. map. . . . .
. . . .*$50–$60*

Child, Hamilton. *Gazetteer and Business Directory of Orange County, Vermont, 1762–1888.* Syracuse. 1888. illus. spine replaced. . . . . .*$75–$85*

Child, Hamilton. *Gazetteer and Business Directory of Windham County, Vt.* Syracuse. 1884. illus. 624 pp. . . . .*$75–$125*

Child, L. M. *An Appeal in Favor of That Class of Americans Called Africans.* NY. 1836. . . . .*$90–$115*

Child. L. Maria. *The American Frugal Housewife.* NY. Samuel & William Wood. 1838. 21st ed. 130 pp. *$200*

Child, L. Maria. *Letters from New York.* NY/Bos. Francis. 1843. 1st ed. 288 pp, 1/1500 cc. . . . .*$75–$125*

Child, L. Maria. *Letters from New York.* NY. 1849. 10th ed. . . . .*$20–$30*

Child, L. Maria. *The Right Way, the Safe Way.* . . . NY. 1860. wrps. . . . .
. . . .*$25–35*

Child, William. *A History of the Fifth Regiment, New Hampshire Vol., in American Civil War.* Bristol. 1893. . . . .*$100–$150*

Childress, Alice. *A Hero Ain't Nothin' but a Sandwich.* NY. 1973. sgn. . .
. . . .*$45–$50*

A Child's Garden of Verses. Saalfield. 1949. illus by Fern Bissel Peat. *$35*

Childs, Mary Fairfax. *De Namin' ob de Twins and Other Sketches from the Cotton Land.* NY. 1908. 1st ed. . . . .*$85–$125*

Chilton Automotive Directory. October 1918. clr ads, 770 pp. *$65*

Chiniquy, Father [Charles]. *The Priest, a Woman, and the Confessional.* Chi. Craig. 1888. 296 pp. *$35*

Chipman, Elizabeth. *Women on the Ice.* np. 1986. 1st ed. illus. map, dj. .
. . . .*$20–$30*

Chipman, N. P. *The Tragedy of Andersonville, Trial of Captain Henry Wirz.* . . . Sac. 1911. 2nd ed. . . . .*$50–$65*

Chittenden, Hiram M. *American Fur Trade of the Far West.* NY. Harper. 1902. 3 vols. map plates . . . .*$575–$900*

Chittenden, Hiram M. *History of Early Steamboat Navigation on the Missouri River.* . . . NY. 1903. 2 vols. ltd 950 cc. . . . .*$350–$500*

Chittenden, Hiram M. *A History of the American Fur Trade of the Far West.* Stanford. (1954). 2 vols. rprnt, maps, djs. . . . .*$75–$125*

Chittenden, Hiram M., and A. T. Richardson. *Life, Letters and Travels of Father Pierre-Jean De Smet.* NY. 1905. 4 vols. . . . .*$400–$850*

Chopin, Kate. *Bayou Folk.* Bos. Houghton Mifflin. 1894. 1st ed. scarce. *$300*

Christie, Agatha. *A Caribbean Mystery.* Lon. Collins Crime Club. 1964. 1st ed. dj. *$50*

Christie, Agatha. *And Then There Were None.* NY. 1940. 1st U.S. ed. . . . .*$24–$35*

Christie, Agatha. *At Bertram's Hotel.* Dodd Mead. 1966. 1st U.S. ed. dj. *$30*

Christie, Agatha. *Cards on the Table.* Lon. 1936. 1st ed. . . . .*$45–$60*

Christie, Agatha. *Cards on the Table.* Lon. 1936. 1st ed. dj. . . . .*$250–$300*

Christie, Agatha. *Cards on the Table.* NY. 1937. 1st Amer ed. dj. . . . .*$300–$375*

Christie, Agatha. *Easy to Kill.* NY. Dodd Mead. 1939. 1st ed. dj. *$250*

Christie, Agatha. *Miss Marple's Final Cases.* Lon. 1979. 1st ed. dj. . . . .*$35–$45*

Christie, Agatha. *N or M?* NY. 1941. 1st U.S. ed. dj. . . . .*$100–$150*

Christie, Agatha. *The Pale Horse.* NY. 1962. 1st ed. 1st U.S. ed. dj. . . . .*$20–$30*

Christie, Agatha. *Sleeping Murder.* Lon. 1976. dj. . . . .*$15–$20*

Christie, Agatha. *They Do It with Mirrors.* Lon. Collins Crime Club. 1952. 1st ed. dj. *$75*

Christie, Agatha. *Thirteen at Dinner.* NY. Dodd Mead. 1933. 1st ed. dj. *$350*

Christmas on Stage. Polygraphic Company of America. 1950. 5 pop-ups, spiral bound. . . . .*$35–$55*

Christy, Howard Chandler. *The Christy Girl.* Bobbs Merrill. (1906). illus. decorative binding, clr plates. .... *$50–$85*

Church, James R. *University Football.* NY. 1893. illus. ....
.... *$150–$175*

The Church Member's Book ... in Three Parts, by a Free-will Baptist. NH. 1847. .... *$28–$30*

Churchill, Winston. *Great Contemporaries.* NY. 1937. 1st U.S. ed. .....
.... *$50–$85*

Churchill, Winston. *A History of the English-Speaking Peoples.* Lon. 1956–58. 4 vols. 1st ed. djs. .... *$175–$200*

Churchill, Winston. *The Second World War.* Lon. 1948–54. 6 vols. 1st ed. djs. .... *$125–$275*

Churchill, Winston. *The Sinews of Peace.* Lon. 1948. 1st ed. dj. ....
.... *$75–$125*

Churchill, Winston. *While England Slept.* NY. 1938. 1st Amer ed. dj. ...
.... *$60–$75*

Chute, Carolyn. *The Beans of Egypt, Maine.* Lon. (1985). 1st U.K. ed. dj.
.... *$45–$80*

Chute, Carolyn. *Letourneau's Used Auto Parts.* Ticknor & Fields. 1988. 1st ed. dj. .... *$25–$35*

Clampitt, John W. *Echoes from the Rocky Mountains.* Chi. The National Book Concern. 1888. 1st ed. illus. 44 full-page woodcut plates, halftone plates, picture stamped in black and gilt on front and spine. *$150*

Clancy, P. A. *The Birds of Natal and Zululand.* Edin. 1964. illus. ....
.... *$85–$135*

Clancy, P. A. *Gamebirds of Southern Africa.* NY. 1967. illus. ....
.... *$45–$60*

Clancy, Tom. *Cardinal of the Kremlin.* Putnam. 1988. 1st ed. dj. ....
.... *$20–$30*

Clancy, Tom. *The Hunt for Red October.* Annapolis, Naval Institute Press. (1984). 1st ed. author's first book, 387 pp, sgn. dj. .... *$400–$750*

Clancy, Tom. *Patriot Games.* Putnam. (1987). 1st ed. dj. ....
.... *$25–$45*

Clancy, Tom. *Red Storm Rising.* Putnam. (1986). 1st ed. dj. ....
.... *$30–$50*

Clark, Emmons. *History of the Seventh Regiment of New York.* NY. 1890. 2 vols. 1st ed. .... *$75–$100*

Clark, Kenneth. *The Gothic Revival.* Lon. 1928. teg. .... *$50–$75*

Clark, Kenneth. *The Gothic Revival.* NY. 1929. 1st Amer ed. dj. . . . .
. . . .*$125–$200*

Clark, Susie C. *The Round Trip.* Bos. Lee & Shepard. 1890. 1st ed. 193
pp. *$75*

Clark, W. P. *Indian Sign Language.* Phila. 1885. 443 pp, map. . . . .
. . . .*$100–$150*

Clark, Walter van Tilburg. *The Track of the Cat.* NY. (1949). 1st ed. dj.
. . . .*$75–$100*

Clarke, Arthur C. *2001: A Space Odyssey.* Lon. 1968. dj. . . . .*$95–$115*

Clarke, Arthur C. *2001: A Space Odyssey.* NY. 1968. 1st ed. dj. . . . .
. . . .*$95–$150*

Clarke, Arthur C. *2061: Odyssey Three.* Del Rey. 1987. 1st U.S. ed. dj. .
. . . .*$25*

Clarke, Arthur C. *Childhood's End.* NY. (1953). 1st ed. pictorial wrps,
sgn. . . . .*$50–$75*

Clarke, Arthur C. *Expedition to Earth.* (1953). 1st ed. printed wrps. . . . .
. . . .*$30–$40*

Clarke, Arthur C. *The Foundations of Paradise.* Lon. Victor Gollancz,
Ltd. 1979. 1st ed. dj. *$175*

Clarke, Arthur C. *Sands of Mars.* NY. Gnome Press. (1952). 1st U.S. ed.
dj. . . . .*$90–$125*

Clarke, H. T. *The Chemistry of Penicillin.* Princeton. 1949. 1st ed. . . . . . .
. . . .*$75–$125*

Clarke, John A. *A Treatise on the Mulberry Tree and Silkworm.* Phila.
1839. 2nd ed. *$125*

Clarke, John Henry. *A Dictionary of Practical Materia Medica.* Sussex.
1962. 3 vols. *$100*

Clarke, Lewis. *Narr. of the Sufferings of Lewis and Milton Clarke.* . . .
Bos. 1846. wrps. . . . .*$85–$100*

Clarke, T. Wood. *The Bloody Mohawk.* NY. 1940. 1st ed. dj. . . .*$40–$65*

Clay, John. *My Life on the Range.* Chi. (1924). plates. . . . .*$100–$250*

Clay, John. *My Life on the Range.* NY. 1961. rprnt. . . . .*$45–$75*

Clay, R. S., and T. H. Court. *The History of the Microscope.* Lon. 1932. .
. . . .*$150–$200*

Clay, R. S., and T. H. Court. *History of the Microscope.* Lon. 1975. rprnt,
dj. . . . .*$60–$70*

Clayton, Victoria V. *White and Black under the Old Regime.* Milw.
(1899). 1st ed. . . . .*$125–$150*

Cleater, P. E. *Rockets through Space.* NY. 1936. illus. 1st Amer ed. . . . . .
. . . .$100–$150

Cleaver, Eldridge. *Eldridge Cleaver: Post Prison Writings and Speeches.*
NY. (1969). 1st ed. dj. . . . .$25–$35

Cleaver, Eldridge. *Soul on Ice.* NY. 1968. 1st ed. dj. . . . .$35–$75

Clebert, Jean-Paul. *The Gypsies.* NY. Dutton. (1963). 1st ed. illus. maps,
drawings, dj. . . . .$18–$25

Cleland, T. M. *The Decorative Work of.* . . . NY. 1929. 1st ed. ltd 1200 cc.
. . . .$225

Clement, Arthur W. *Our Pioneer Potters.* NY. 1947. illus. ltd. 500 cc,
slipcase. . . . .$45–$100

Clerk, Dugald. *The Gas Engine.* Lon. 1887. . . . .$35–$60

Cleveland, Grover. *Fishing and Shooting Sketches.* NY. 1906. illus. . . . .
. . . .$20–$30

Clifford, F. *Romance of Perfume Lands.* Bos. 1881. . . . .$32–$45

Clift, Virgil W. (ed). *Negro Education in America, Its Adequacy, Problems and Needs.* NY. 1962. 1st ed. . . . .$28–$37

Close, Etta. *A Woman Alone in Kenya, Uganda and the Belgian Congo.*
Lon. 1924. map. . . . .$30–$45

Clougher, T. R. (ed). *Golf Clubs of the Empire: The Golfing Annual.* Lon.
1931. 5th issue. . . . .$45–$50

Coan, T. *Life in Hawaii: An Autobiographic Sketch.* NY. 1882. . . . .
. . . .$30–$50

Coan, Titus. *Life In Hawaii (1835–1881).* NY. Anson D. F. Randolph.
1882. . . . .$100–$150

Coates, Robert. *The Outlaw Years.* NY. 1930. 1st ed. . . . .
. . . .$20–$30

Coatsworth, Elizabeth. *The Golden Horseshoe.* NY. 1935. 1st ed. illus by
Lawson. . . . .$25–$35

Cobb, Bert. *Hunting Dogs.* The Crafton Collection. ltd 990 cc. . . . .
. . . .$85

Cobb, Irvin S. *Roll Call.* Ind. (1942). 1st ed. dj. . . . .$17–$25

Cobb, Stanford. *The Story of the Palatines.* NY. 1897. . . . .$65

Cobb, Ty. *My Life in Baseball.* NY. 1962. 1st ed. dj. . . . .$30–$40

Cobb, W. Mantague. *The First Negro Medical Society . . . District of
Columbia, 1884–1939.* DC. 1939. . . . .$35–$45

Coblentz, Stanton A. *Into Plutonian Depths.* NY. (1950). 1st ed. pictorial
wrps. . . . .$50–$65

Coblentz, Stanton A. *Villains and Vigilantes.* NY. 1936. 1st ed. dj. . . . . .
. . . .*$35–$65*

Cochran, D. M. *Frogs of Southeastern Brazil.* DC. 1955. illus. . . . .
. . . .*$25–$45*

Cochran, D. M., and C. J. Goin. *Frogs of Columbia.* DC. 1970. illus. . . .
. . . .*$30–$45*

Cochran, Doris M. *Poisonous Reptiles of the World.* DC. 1943. wrps. . . .
. . . .*$40–$50*

Cody, William F. *Story of the Wild West and Camp Fire Chats by Buffalo Bill.* Phila. 1889. illus. . . . .*$35–$60*

Cody, William F. *True Tales of the Plains.* NY. 1908. . . . .*$50–$100*

Coffey, Leora S. *Wilds of Alaska Big-game Hunting.* NY. (1963). 1st ed. .
. . . .*$18–$30*

Coffin, Albert Isaiah. *A Treatise on Midwifery.* Manchester. Medico-Botanic Press. 1849. 184 pp. . . . .*$100–$165*

Coffin, Charles C. *Boys of 1861.* Bos. 1885. . . . .*$30–$65*

Coffin, Charles C. *Life of Abraham Lincoln.* NY. 1893. . . . .*$40–$50*

Coffin, Charles "Carleton." *Stories of Our Soldiers.* Bos. 1893. 1st ed. illus. . . . .*$22–$35*

Coffin, Joshua. *Sketch of the History of Newbury, Newburyport, and West Newbury.* Bos. 1845. . . . .*$40–$60*

Coffin, Robert Tristram. *Saltwater Farm.* NY. 1937. 1st ed. illus. dj. . . .
. . . .*$20–$30*

Cohen, I. B. *Introduction to Newton's "Principia."* Harvard Univ. Press. 1971. dj. . . . .*$35–$50*

Cohen, Octavus Roy. *Bigger and Blacker.* Bos. 1925. 1st ed. sgn. . . . . . .
. . . .*$50–$85*

Cohen, Octavus Roy. *The Townsend Murder Mystery.* Appleton Century. 1933. 1st ed. *$25*

Colbert, E. *Chicago and the Great Conflagration.* Cinc. 1872. 1st ed. illus. maps. . . . .*$28–$45*

Colcord, Joanna C. *Songs of American Sailormen.* NY. 1938. illus. . . . . .
. . . .*$35–$60*

Cole, George E. *Early Oregon. Jottings . . . of a Pioneer, 1850.* np. (1905). 1st ed. . . . .*$50–$60*

Cole, S. W. *The American Fruit Book.* . . . Bos. 1849. 1st ed. . . . .*$40–$50*

Colenso, John W. *Ten Weeks in Natal.* Cam. Macmillan. 1855. fldg map, plates. . . . .*$275–$325*

Coles, Robert. *The Last and First Eskimos.* Bos. 1978. 1st ed. illus. dj. . . .
. . . .*$40–$50*

Colkins Franklin Welles. *Two Wilderness Voyagers.* Revell. 1902. . . . . .
. . . .*$25–$35*

Collier, J. *The Indians of the Americas.* NY. 1947. photos, maps. . . . .
. . . .*$30–$40*

Collier's New Photographic History of the World's War. NY. 1918. 1st
ed. . . . .*$45–$90*

Collier's Photographic History of the European War. NY. Collier.
[1916]. oblong folio, 144 pp, photos. . . . .*$30–$40*

Collins, A. Frederick. *The Book of Wireless.* 1922. illus. 2nd ed. . . . .
. . . .*$18–$27*

Collins, A. Frederick. *Experimental Television.* 1932. 1st ed. illus. dj. . . .
. . . .*$95–$175*

Collins, Hubert E. *Warpath and Cattle Trail.* NY. 1928. 1st ed. . . . .
. . . .*$65–$95*

Collins, John S. *Across the Plains in '64.* Omaha. 1904. 1st ed. . . . .
. . . .*$50–$100*

Collins, Wilkie. *Armadale.* NY. 1866. 1st Amer ed. . . . .*$100–$300*

Collins, Wilkie. *The Moonstone.* NY. 1868. 1st Amer ed. . . . .
. . . .*$100–$225*

Collins, Wilkie. *No Name.* NY. 1863. 1st ed. illus. . . . .
. . . .*$85–$100*

Collis, Septima M. *A Woman's Trip to Alaska.* NY. (1890). illus. clr map.
. . . .*$55–$90*

Collodi, Carlo. *Pinocchio.* Garden City. 1932. illus. . . . .*$25–$45*

Collodi, Carlo. *Pinocchio.* (1940). illus by Tony Garg. . . . .*$45–$60*

Collodi, Carlo. *Pinocchio.* Donahue. nd. . . . .*$12–$18*

Colt, Mrs. S. S. *Tourist Guide through the Empire State.* . . . Albany.
1871. 1st ed. . . . .*$50–$60*

Colton, Calvin. *A Lecture on the Railroad to the Pacific.* NY. 1850. . . . . .
. . . .*$35–$45*

Colton, Harold S. *Hopi Kachina Dolls with a Key to the Identification.*
Albuquerque. 1949. 1st ed. dj. . . . .*$50–$80*

Colton, J. H. *Traveler and Tourist's Guide Book through the United
States.* NY. 1850. 2 maps. . . . .*$100–$250*

Colton, Walter. *Deck and Port.* . . . A. S. Barnes & Co. 1854. illus. clr
lithos. . . . .*$50–$75*

Colton, Walter. *Three Years in California.* NY. 1850. 1st ed. . . . .
. . . .*$95–$150*

Colum, Padraic. *Creatures.* NY. 1927. 1st ed. illus by Artzybashoff. . . . .
. . . .*$30–$50*

Colum, Padraic (ed). *Arabian Nights.* NY. 1923. illus. . . . .*$25–$30*

Colvin, F. and H. *The Aircraft Handbook.* McGraw-Hill. 1929. 4th ed.
690 pp. . . . .*$30–$50*

Colvin, Verplanck. *Narrative of a Bear Hunt in the Adirondacks.* Albany.
Joel Munsell. 1870. wrps. 16 pp. . . . .*$60–$85*

Combat Digest: 33rd Fighter Group. np. nd. 48 pp, photos, scarce. . . . . . .
. . . .*$195*

Combat History of 2nd Infantry Division. Baton Rouge. 1946. . . . .
. . . .*$55–$65*

Combe, Andrew. *The Principles of Physiology Applied to Preservation of
Health.* Edin. 1835. 3rd ed. . . . .*$25–$40*

Combe, George. *A System of Phrenology.* NY. 1897. . . . .*$18–$30*

Commager, Henry Steele. *The Blue and the Gray.* NY. (1950). 1st ed. of
1-vol. ed. . . . .*$18–$25*

Commager, Henry Steele. *The Blue and the Gray.* NY. (1950). 2 vols. 1st
ed. . . . .*$40–$90*

Comstock, John H. *The Spider Book.* Garden City. 1913. . . . . . .*$50–$65*

Conard, Howard L. *Uncle Dick Wootton, the Pioneer Frontiersman of the
Rocky Mountain Region.* Chi. 1890. 1st ed. . . . .*$150–$200*

Conder, Claude Reignier. *Syrian Stone-lore.* Lon. Palestine Exploration
Fund. 1896. illus. fldg maps. . . . .*$30–$45*

Condon, E. U., and G. H. Shortly. *The Theory of Atomic Spectra.*
Macmillan. 1935. 1st ed. . . . .*$45–$65*

Condon, Richard. *The Manchurian Candidate.* NY. (1959). 1st ed. dj. . . . .
. . . .*$75–$100*

Cone, Mary. *Two Years in California.* Chi. Griggs. 1876. 1st ed. illus. 238
pp. . . . .*$95–$125*

Conkey, W. B. *The Official Guide to the Klondyke Country.* . . . Chi. 1897.
softbound. . . . .*$200–$350*

Conklin, E. *Picturesque Arizona.* NY. 1878. . . . .*$250–$300*

Conn, Granville. *History of the New Hampshire Surgeons in the War of
Rebellion.* Concord. New Hampshire Assn. of Military Surgeons. 1906. 1st
ed. 558 pp. . . . .*$100–$150*

Connelley, William. *Wild Bill and His Era: The Life and Adventures of James Hickok.* NY. 1933. . . . .$125–$225

Connelley, William E. *Quantrill and the Border Wars.* Iowa. 1910. 1st ed. illus. maps. . . . .$125–$250

Connett, E. *Duck Decoys.* Vermont. 1953. clr and b/w illus. dj. . . . .
. . . .$14–$22

Connett, E. *Wildfowling in the Mississippi Flyway.* Van Nostrand. 1949. 1st ed. illus. . . . .$125–$195

Connett, E. (ed). *Duck Shooting along the Atlantic Tidewater.* NY. 1947. illus. dj. . . . .$55–$100

Connor, Ralph. *Black Rock.* NY. 1900. illus. . . . .$10–$15

Conrad, Joseph. *The Arrow of Gold: A Story between Two Notes.* Garden City. Doubleday. 1919. 1st Brit ed. pictorial wrps. $300

Conrad, Joseph. *A Conrad Argosy.* NY. 1942. illus. woodcuts, dj. . . . . . .
. . . .$35–$50

Conrad, Joseph. *Lord Jim: A Romance.* NY. 1900. 1st Amer ed. . . . .
. . . .$95–$135

Conrad, Joseph. *Lord Jim: A Romance.* NY. Doubleday & McClure. 1900. 1st ed. 2nd state. $300

Conrad, Joseph. *Lord Jim: A Tale.* Edin/Lon. William Blackwood. 1900. 1st ed. $600

Conrad, Joseph. *The Nigger of the Narcissus.* Lon. 1898. 1st ed. . . . .
. . . .$200–$450

Conrad, Joseph. *The Nigger of the Narcissus: A Tale of the Forecastle.* Garden City. Doubleday, Page. 1914. 1st ed. $200

Conrad, Joseph. *The Rover.* Doubleday. 1923. 1st ed. dj. $125

Conrad, Joseph. *Tales of Hearsay.* NY. (1925). 1st Amer ed. dj. . . . .
. . . .$50–$70

Conrad, Joseph. *Tales of Unrest.* NY. Scribner's. 1898. 1st ed. $450

Conrad, Joseph. *Typhoon and Other Stories.* Lon. Heinemann. 1903. 1st ed. $250

Conroy, Frank. *Stop-time.* NY. Viking. (1967). 1st ed. author's first book, dj. . . . .$40–$100

Conroy, Jack. *A World to Win.* Covici Friede. 1st Amer ed. dj. . . . .
. . . .$20–$35

Conroy, Pat. *Beach Music.* NY. Doubleday. 1995. 1st ed. sgn, dj. . . . .
. . . .$40–$50

Conroy, Pat. *The Great Santini.* Bos. 1976. 1st ed. sgn, dj. . . .*$125–$250*

Conroy, Pat. *The Lords of Discipline.* Houghton. 1980. 1st ed. sgn, dj. *$90*

Conroy, Pat. *Prince of Tides.* Bos. 1986. 1st ed. dj. . . . .*$35–$45*

Considine, Bob. *The Remarkable Life of Dr. Armand Hammer.* Harper & Row. 1975. 1st ed. wrps. . . . .*$20–$30*

Contributions to Medical and Biological Research. NY. 1919. 2 vols. illus. ltd #20/1,600 cc. . . . .*$75–$125*

Converse, Florence. *The Story of Wellesley.* Bos. 1915. 1st ed. . . . .*$25–$30*

Conway, Moncure D. *The Life of Thomas Paine.* NY. 1892. 2 vols. . . . .*$45–$85*

Conway, W. Martin. *The Alps.* Lon. Adam & Charles Black. 1904. 1st ed. illus by A. D. McCormick, 70 clr plates, pictorial blue cloth, teg. . . . .*$90–$110*

Conwell, R. H. *History of the Great Boston Fire, Nov. 9th and 10th, 1872.* Bos. 1873. 1st ed. illus. . . . .*$20–$30*

Cook, C. *Observations of Fox Hunting and Management of Hounds.* Lon. 1826. . . . .*$175–$250*

Cook, C. H. *Among the Pimos.* Albany. 1893. . . . .*$40–$50*

Cook, Frederick A. *My Attainment of the Pole.* NY. 1911. 1st ed. . . . .*$75–$225*

Cook, Frederick A. *To the Top of the Continent.* NY. 1908. 1st ed. . . . .*$75–$100*

Cook, Joel. *America Picturesque and Descriptive.* Phila. 1900. 3 vols. wrps. slipcase. . . . .*$25–$35*

Cook, Joel. *Switzerland Picturesque and Descriptive.* Henry Coates. 1904. 1st ed. illus. tissued photos, dj. . . . .*$30–$45*

Cook, John. *Study of the Mill Schools of North Carolina.* NY. 1925. 1st ptg. *$24.50*

Cook, Roy Bird. *The Family and Early Life of Stonewall Jackson.* VA. 1925. 1st ed. . . . .*$50–$75*

Cooke, Philip St. George. *Scenes and Adventures in the Army.* Phila. 1857. . . . .*$250–$500*

Cooke, Philip St. George. *Scenes and Adventures in the Army.* Phila. 1859. 2nd ed. . . . .*$100–$250*

Cooke, T. G. *Finger Prints, Secret Service, Crime Detection.* Chi. 1936. illus. . . . .*$20–$30*

Coon, Carleton S. *Riffian.* Bos. 1933. illus. sgn, dj. . . . .*$20–$30*

Cooper, A. *The Complete Distiller.* . . . Lon. 1757. . . . .*$225–$300*

Cooper, Lt. A. *In and Out of Rebel Prisons.* Oswego, NY. 1888. illus. . . .
. . . .*$75–$115*

Cooper. J. W. *The Experienced Botanist or Indian Physician.* PA. 1840. .
. . . .*$175–$215*

Cooper, James Fenimore. *The Deerslayer, or the First War-path.* Phila.
Lea & Blanchard. 1841. 2 vols. 1st ed. purple cloth, paper label, Fagan-
Ashmead imprint on copyright page of both volumes, scarce. . . . .
. . . .*$700*

Cooper, James Fenimore. *Deerslayer.* Lon. 1841. 3 vols. 1st U.K. ed. . . .
. . . .*$100–$150*

Cooper, James Fenimore. *Deerslayer.* Scribner's. 1929. illus by N. C.
Wyeth, 9 clr plates. . . . .*$35–$55*

Cooper, James Fenimore. *The Last of the Mohicans.* NY. 1919. 1st ed.
illus by Wyeth. . . . .*$75–$150*

Cooper, James Fenimore. *The Pathfinder.* Lon. 1840. 3 vols. 1st ed. . . . .
. . . .*$500–$850*

Cooper, James Fenimore. *The Pathfinder.* Phila. 1840. 2 vols. 1st Amer
ed. . . . .*$150–$250*

Cooper, James Fenimore. *The Prairie.* Phila. 1832. 2 vols. 5th ed. . . . . .
. . . .*$40–$60*

Cooper, John M. *Analytical and Critical Bibliography of Tribes of Tierra
del Fuego.* GPO. 1917. fldg map. . . . .*$35–$50*

Coover, Robert. *The Universal Baseball Association, Inc.* Lon. 1970. 1st
ed. dj. . . . .*$45–$65*

Coppard, A. E. *Fearful Pleasures.* Arkham House. 1946. 1st U.S. ed. dj. .
. . . .*$80–$100*

Coppinger, Joseph. *The American Practical Brewer and Tanner.* NY.
1815. 1st ed. plates. . . . .*$300–$450*

Copway, George. *The Life, History and Travels of Kah-Ge-Ga-Gak-Bowk
. . . Ojibway.* . . . PA. 1847. 2nd ed. presentation copy, sgn. . . . .
. . . .*$200–$225*

Corbett, Jim. *Man-eaters of Kumaon.* NY/Bombay. (1946). 1st U.S. ed.
dj. . . . .*$25–$35*

Corcoran, A. P. *Boy Scouts in Africa.* Barse & Hopkins. 1923. . . . . . .*$10*

Cornelius, Mrs. *The Young Housekeeper's Friend.* Bos/NY. 1846. . . . . . .
. . . .*$100–$175*

Corner, George W. *Doctor Kane of the Arctic Seas.* Phila. 1972. 1st ed. illus. dj, maps. . . . .*$28–$35*

Cornet, J. *Treasures from the Congo.* NY. 1971. 369 pp, clr and b/w photos. *$675*

Cornish, Dudley Taylor. *The Sable Arm: Negro Troops in the Union Army, 1861–1865.* NY. 1956. 1st ed. . . . .*$40–$65*

Correll and Gosden. *All about Amos 'n' Andy and Their Creators, Correll and Gosden.* NY. 1930. illus. 2nd ed. . . . .*$22–$35*

Corso, Gregory. *Bomb.* City Lights. 1958. . . . .*$85–$100*

Corso, Gregory. *The Happy Birthday of Death.* New Directions. (1960). 1st ed. wrps. . . . .*$35–$45*

Cotton, Bruce. *Reflections on the Civil War.* CT. 1981. . . . .*$35–$45*

Couch, Jonathan F. L. S. *A History of the Fishes of the British Isles.* Lon. George Bell & Sons. 1879. 4 vols. illus. with 252 tissue-guarded full-clr chromoliths, pictorial design of fish on front cvr. *$1,250*

Coues, Elliott. *Birds of the Northwest.* Bos. 1877. 791 pp. . . . . . .*$50–$65*

Coues, Elliott (ed). *New Light on the Early History of the Greater Northwest.* . . . NY. 1895. 3 vols. maps, 1/500 cc. . . . .*$250–$300*

Coulter, Ellis Merton. *Civil War and Readjustment in Kentucky.* Chapel Hill. 1926. 1st ed. . . . .*$65–$90*

Coulter, Ellis Merton. *William G. Brownlow, Fighting Parson of the Southern Highlands.* Chapel Hill. 1937. 1st ed. . . . .*$30–$60*

Courlander, Harold. *Negro Folk Music, U.S.A.* NY. 1963. dj. . . . .*$30–$45*

Covarrubias, Miguel. *Island of Bali.* NY. Knopf. 1937. 1st ed. illus by Covarrubias, photos, pictorial cloth, dj. . . . .*$75–$90*

Coward, Noel. *Bitter Sweet and Other Plays.* NY. 1929. 1st Amer ed. ltd 1000 cc, nbr, sgn. *$250*

Coward, Noel. *Private Lives.* Lon. 1930. dj. . . . .*$100–$150*

Coward, Noel. *Quadrille: A Play in Three Acts.* Lon. 1952. dj. . . . .*$25–$40*

Cowley, Charles. *Illustrated History of Lowell.* Bos/Lowell. Lee & Shepard/Sargeant & Merrill. 1868. illus. 235 pp, fold-out map, scarce. *$75*

Cox, Ernest Sevier. *Let My People Go.* Richmond. 1925. 1st ed. wrps. . . . .*$55–$75*

Cox, Ernest. *White America.* Richmond, VA. (special reprint for members of Congress. 1925). dj. . . . .*$40–$60*

Cox, Jacob D. *Military Reminiscences of the Civil War.* NY. 1900. 2 vols.
....*$195–$250*

Cox, James M. *Journey through My Years.* NY. 1946. 1st ed. sgn. ......
....*$22.50*

Cox, Palmer. *The Brownies: Their Book.* NY. (1887). 1st ed. illus bds. ...
....*$100–$175*

Cox, Warren. *Chinese Ivory Sculpture.* NY. 1946. 1st ed. folio. ....
....*$38–$50*

Cozzens, James Gould. *S. S. San Pedro.* NY. (1930). 1st ed. dj. ......
....*$25–$65*

The CP Book: A Comprehensive and Authoritative Guide to the Intelligent Selection and Use of Milady's Toilet Articles ... by Myron Leroy. NY. The California Perfume Co. 1906. illus. 466 pp. *$450*

Craig, Maurice. *Irish Book Bindings 1600–1800.* Lon. (1954). illus. dj. ...
....*$275–$350*

Craig, Maurice. *Psychological Medicine.* Lon. 1905. plates. ....
....*$20–$27*

Craik, Dinah Marie [*nee* Mulock] *Adventures of a Brownie, by Dinah M. Mulock-Craik.* Chi. 1923. illus by Milo Winter. ....*$35–$40*

Cram's Universal Atlas. Chi. 1889. three-quarter lea. ....*$95–$125*

Crane, Hart. *Seven Lyrics.* (Camb). The Ibex Press. (c 1966). 1st ed. 1/250 cc. *$75*

Crane, Stephen. *The Monster and Other Stories.* NY/Lon. Harper & Bros. 1899. 1st ed. *$150*

Crane, Stephen. *The Monster and Other Stories.* NY. 1899. 1st ed. illus. decorated cloth. ....*$40–$50*

Crane, Stephen. *The Open Boat and Other Stories.* NY. 1898. 1st ed. pictorial cvr. *$300*

Crane, Stephen. *The Red Badge of Courage.* NY. 1896. 2nd ed. ....
....*$95–$125*

Crane, Walter. *The Absurd ABC.* Lon. Routledge & Sons. 1st ed. red lea.
....*$350*

Crane, Walter. *Flora's Feast of Flowers.* Lon. 1889. 1st ed. illus. 40 pp, pictorial bds. ....*$90–$150*

Crane, Walter. *Walter Crane's Picture Book.* Lon. (1874). 1st ed. 64 clr plates, aeg. *$600*

Crapo, W. W. *New Bedford Centennial Address.* New Bedford. 1876. 1st ed. ....*$15–$20*

Crawdford, Capt. William. *Gore and Glory: A Story of American Heroism.* Phila. 1944. photos, dj. $35

Crawford, Marion. *Constantinople.* NY. 1895. decorated cloth. $35

Crawford, Samuel W. *The Genesis of the Civil War: The Story of Sumter, 1860–1861.* NY. 1887. ....$100–$125

The Creole Cookery Book. New Orleans. T. H. Thomason. 1885. 1st ed by Christian Woman's Exchange. ....$100–$150

Crews, Harry. *All We Need of Hell.* NY. Harper & Row. (1987). 1st ed. dj. $40

Crews, Harry. *Blood and Grits.* NY. (1979). 1st ed. dj. ....$40–$50

Crews, Harry. *The Gospel Singer.* NY. (1974). 1st ed. dj. ....
....$55–$150

Crews, Harry. *The Gospel Singer.* NY. 1968. 1st ed. author's first book, dj. ....$300–$400

Crews, Harry. *The Gypsie's Curse.* NY. (1974). 1st ed. dj. ....
....$40–$60

Crews, Harry. *Karate Is a Thing of the Spirit.* NY. 1971. 1st ed. dj. .....
....$100–$150

Crews, Harry. *The Knockout Artist.* NY. (1988). 1st ed. dj. ....
....$25–$40

Crews, Harry. *Madonna at Ringside.* Lord John. 1992. 1/275 cc, sgn. ...
....$75

Crichton, Michael. *The Andromeda Strain.* Knopf. 1969. 1st ed. dj. .....
....$40–$50

Crichton, Michael. *The Great Train Robbery.* Knopf. 1975. 1st ed. dj. ...
....$35–$60

Crichton, Michael. *Jurassic Park.* 1st ed. advance reader's ed. wrps. ....
....$150

Crichton, Michael. *Jurassic Park.* NY. 1990. 1st ed. dj. ....$50–$75

Crichton, Michael. *Rising Sun.* NY. 1992. sgn, dj. ....$25–$40

Crichton, Michael. *Sphere.* NY. Knopf. 1987. 1st ed. dj. $50

Crichton, Michael. *The Terminal Man.* NY. 1972. 1st ed. dj. ....
....$45–$60

Crockett, Walter Hill. *A History of Lake Champlain.* Burlington, VT. Hobart & Shanley. 1909. illus. $160

Croff, G. B. *Progressive American Architecture.* Wash. 1875. illus. folio, plates. ....$1,200–$1,450

Croffut, W. A., et al. *The Military and Civil History of Connecticut . . . during War of 1861–65.* NY. 1868. . . . .*$75–$150*

Croly, Mrs. J. C. *Jennie June's American Cookery Book.* NY. 1870. . . . .
. . . .*$45–$62*

Cromie, R. *Dillinger: A Short and Violent Life.* NY. 1962. 1st ed. sgn, dj.
. . . .*$22–$28*

Cronin, A. J. *Grand Canary.* Lon. 1933. dj. . . . .*$25–$40*

Crosby, Frances Jane. *The Blind Girl.* NY. Wiley & Putnam. 1844. 1st ed. *$150*

Cross, Wilbur. *The History of Henry Fielding.* Yale. 1918. 3 vols. 1st ed.
. . . .*$50–$75*

Crossman, E. C. *Military and Sporting Rifle Shooting.* NC. (1932). . . . . .
. . . .*$30–$40*

Crothers, Samuel McChord. *The Children of Dickens.* Scribner's. 1925. 1st ed. illus. . . . .*$50–$75*

Crowninshield, Mary Bradford. *All among the Lighthouses.* Bos. 1886. .
. . . .*$42–$50*

Cruise of the Revenue Steamer Corwin in Alaska. DC. GPO. 1883. illus. clr and b/w plates. . . . .*$95–$135*

Cullen, Countee. *The Black Christ.* NY. 1929. 1st ed. illus by Charles Cullen. . . . .*$100–$150*

Cullen, Countee. *Color.* NY. 1925. 1st ed. author's first book. . . . .
. . . .*$125–$200*

Cullen, Countee. *Copper Sun.* NY. 1927. 1st ed. mar bds, dj. *$300*

Cullen, William. *A Synopsis of Methodical Nosology . . . with the Synonimous of Those from Savages.* Phila. Parry Hall. 1793. enlarged, translated by Henry Wilkins, (8) pp, bds. . . . .*$350–$500*

Culver, Henry B. *The Book of Old Ships.* NY. 1928. illus. drawings, mor, mar bds. . . . .*$35–$55*

Culverwell, Robert J. *How to Live 100 Years.* Lon. 1847. stiff paper. . . .
. . . .*$30–$45*

cummings, e. e. *eimi.* NY. 1933. 1/1381 cc, sgn. . . . .*$175–$250*

Cuneo, John. *Winged Mars: Volume 1: The German Air Weapon, 1870–1914.* Harrisburg. 1942. illus. *$35*

Cunningham, Albert B. *Old Black Bass.* NY/Chi. (1922). illus. dj. . . . . .
. . . .*$22–$32*

Cunningham, Peter. *Hand-book of London.* Lon. 1850. . . . .*$45–$60*

Cunningham, Will M. *Cross Masonic Text-book.* Phila. 1864. illus. rev ed. $20

Curl, Peter. *Designing a Book Jacket.* Lon. Studio Publications. 1956. 1st ed. dj. $25

Curran and Kauffeld. *Snakes and Their Ways.* 1937. 1st ed. ....$20–$25

Currey, L. W. *Science Fiction and Fantasy Authors.* . . . Bos. (1979). 1st ed. dj. ....$100–$125

Currier & Ives Prints: The Red Indian. Lon/NY. 1931. intro by W. S. Hall, sgn by Hall, dj. ....$35–$45

Curry, Manfred. *Yacht Racing.* . . . NY. 1927................$25–$35

Curtis, Edward S. *Portraits from North American Indian Life.* NY. Promontory Press. [1972]. 1st ed thus, oblong folio, sepia portraits. ....$60–$100

Curtis, George William. *Howadji in Syria.* NY. 1856. 1st ed. maps. ....$30–$45

Curtis, John. *Harvey's Views on the Circulation of the Blood.* NY. 1915. ....$60–$75

Curtis, John H. *An Essay on the Deaf and Dumb.* Lon. 1834. 2nd ed. 2 plates. ....$40–$50

Curtis, Mattoon. *The Story of Snuff and Snuff Boxes.* NY. 1935. illus. dj. . ...$25–$35

Curtis, Natalie (ed and comp). *The Indians' Book.* NY. Harper & Bros. 1907. 1st ed. illus. $235

Curtis, Newton. *From Bull Run to Chancellorsville.* NY. 1906. ....$85–$95

Curtis, Paul A. *Sportsmen All.* Derrydale Press. (1938). 1/950 cc, illus. .. ..$80–$95

Curtis, Paul A., Jr. *American Game Shooting.* NY. 1927. dj. ...$48–$62

Curtis, W. H. *The Elements of Wood Ship Construction.* NY. 1919. 1st ed. illus. ....$65–$95

Curwood, James. *The Danger Trail.* Bobbs Merrill. (1910). 1st ed. ....$20–$30

Curwood, James. *The Plains of Abraham.* NY. 1928. 1st ed. dj. ....$20–$25

Cushing, Caleb. *Reminiscences of Spain.* Bos. 1833. 2 vols in 1......... ....$35–$45

[Cushing, Caleb]. *A Reply to the Letter of J. Fenimore Cooper.* . . . Bos. 1834. 1st ed. printed wrps, sewn, 76 pp, inscrb. ....$95–$125

Cushing, Harvey. *Consecratio Medici.* 1928. 1st ed. . . . .
. . . .*$40–$150*

Cushing, Harvey. *From a Surgeon's Journal 1915–1918.* Bos. 1936. 1st
ed. . . . .*$35–$75*

Cushing, Harvey. *Life of Sir William Osler.* Ox. 1940. . . . .
. . . .*$30–$40*

Cushing, Harvey. *The Life of William Osler.* Ox. 1925. 2 vols. 1st ed. 728
pp. . . . .*$150–$200*

Cushman, H. B. *History of the Choctaw, Chickasaw and Natchez Indians.*
Greenville. 1899. . . . .*$160–$250*

Cushman, Mary Floyd. *Missionary Doctor.* NY. 1944. map, dj. . . . .
. . . .*$15–$25*

Cussans, John E. *Handbook of Heraldry.* Lon. Chatto & Windus. 1893.
4th ed. *$45*

Custead, E. Rose, and Elza Custead. *Songs and Stories of Bygone Days
in Fayette County.* NY. 1882. 1st ed. . . . .*$20–$30*

Custer, Carl. *The Story of the American Clipper.* NY. (1930). illus. . . . . .
. . . .*$40–$55*

Custer, Elizabeth. *Boots and Saddles.* NY. 1885. 1st ed. 2nd issue, map
and portrait. . . . .*$75–$100*

Custer, Elizabeth. *Following the Guidon.* NY. 1890. 1st ed. . . . .
. . . .*$45–$110*

Custer, Elizabeth. *Tenting on the Plains.* NY. 1895. . . . .*$25–$35*

Custer, Elizabeth. *Tenting on the Plains.* Norman, OK. (1971). 3 vols.
new ed. boxed. . . . .*$35–$45*

Custer, Elizabeth B. *Following the Guidon.* NY. 1890. . . . .
. . . .*$125*

Custer, Gen. G. A. *Life on the Plains.* NY. 1874. 1st ed. illus. . . . .
. . . .*$100–$250*

Cutler, Carl C. *Greyhounds of the Sea.* NY. 1930. . . . .
. . . .*$50–$100*

Cutler, Carl C. *Queens of the Western Ocean.* U.S. Naval Institute. 1967.
illus. . . . .*$30–$40*

Cypress, J. *Sporting Scenes and Sundry Sketches.* Gould, Banks & Co.
1842. vols 1 & 2. . . . .*$275*

Dabney, R. L. *Life and Campaigns of Lieut.-Gen. T. J. Jackson.* NY. 1866.
1st ed. fldng map. . . . .*$75–$125*

Dabney, Wendell Phillips. *Cincinnati's Colored Citizens.* . . . Cinc. 1926.
1st ed. presentation copy. . . . .*$285–$300*

Dahl, Roald. *Ah, Sweet Mysteries of Life.* Knopf. 1989. illus. 1st U.S. ed. dj. . . . .*$30–$40*

Dahl, Roald. *Charlie and the Chocolate Factory.* NY. 1963. 1st ed. dj. . . . .*$45–$65*

Dahl, Roald. *Fantastic Mr. Fox.* NY. 1970. 1st ed. dj. . . . .*$16–$20*

Dahl, Roald. *The Gremlins.* Lon. (1943). 1st ed. author's first book. .*$400*

Dahl, Roald. *Kiss, Kiss.* NY. Knopf. 1960. 1st ed. dj. *$35*

Dahl, Roald. *Switch Bitch.* NY. 1974. 1st ed. dj. . . . .*$30–$50*

Dale, Harrison C. (ed). *The Ashley-Smith Explor. and Disc. of Route to Pacific 1822–1829.* Cleve. 1918. 1st ed. maps, plates. . . . .*$175–$250*

Dalgliesh, Alice. *Long Live the King.* NY. 1937. illus. 77 pp, pictorial endpapers. . . . .*$25–$35*

Dalgliesh, Alice. *The Enchanted Book.* 1947. 1st ed. dj. . . . .*$20–$35*

Dali, Salvador. *Hidden Faces.* 1944. illus. 1st U.S. ed. dj. . . . . . .*$65–$75*

Dali, Salvador. *The Secret Life of Salvador Dali.* NY. 1942. 1st Amer ed. dj. . . . .*$125–$250*

Dali, Salvador. *The Secret Life of Salvador Dali.* NY. Dial Press. 1942. water clr drawing and inscrb by Dali. *$2,587*

Dall, Wm. H. *Alaska and Its Resources.* 1870. 1st ed. map, scarce. *$275*

Dana, Charles. *Eastern Journeys.* NY. 1898. teg. . . . .*$30–$40*

Dana, Charles. *The Life of Ulysses S. Grant.* 1868. . . . .*$25–$40*

Dana, Charles L. *The Peaks of Medical History: Outline of Evolution of Medicine.* NY. 1926. 1st ed. illus. plates. . . . .*$75–$100*

Dana, E. S. *A Textbook of Mineralogy.* NY. 1926. 4th rev ed. . . . .*$25–$35*

Dana, James D. *Manual of Mineralogy and Lithology Containing the Elements of the Science of Minerals and Rocks.* Lon. 1882. 4th ed. . . . .*$40–$60*

Dana, Richard Henry. *To Cuba and Back.* Bos. 1859. 1st ed. 288 pp. . . . .*$100–$125*

Dana, Richard Henry, Jr. *Two Years before the Mast.* Chi. Lakeside. 1930. slipcase. . . . .*$60–$80*

Dance of the Hours. NY. Disney. (1940). 1st ed. stiff pictorial paper bds, illus, dj. *$125*

Dandridge, Dorothy. *Everything and Nothing.* NY. 1957. 1st ed. *$30*

Darby, Charles. *Bacchanalia, or A Description of a Drunken Club.* Lon. 1680. folio, calf. . . . .*$325–$425*

Darrow, Floyd L., and Clarence J. Hylander. *The Boy's Own Book of Great Inventions.* NY. 1941. rev ed. *$12*

Darwin, Charles. *The Descent of Man.* ... NY. 1871. 2 vols. 1st Amer ed. ....*$125–$185*

Darwin, Charles. *The Effects of Cross and Self Fertilization.* ... NY. 1889. ....*$38–$45*

Darwin, Charles. *Expression of the Emotions: Man and Animals.* Appleton. 1873. ....*$75–$125*

Darwin, Charles. *Insectivorous Plants.* NY. 1875. 1st U.S. ed. ....*$95–$125*

Darwin, Charles. *Journal of Researches ... Countries Visited by H.M.S. Beagle.* Hafner. (1901). 26 plates. ....*$40–$50*

Darwin, Charles. *A Naturalist's Voyage ... of H.M.S. Beagle.* Lon. John Murray. 1890. 500 pp. ....*$60–$75*

Darwin, Charles. *On the Origin of Species by Means of Natural Selection.* Lon. 1859. 3rd issue. ....*$8,000–$10,000*

Darwin, Charles. *On the Origin of Species by Means of Natural Selection.* Appleton. 1871. 5th ed. ....*$150–$180*

Darwin, Charles. *On the Origin of Species by Means of Natural Selection.* Lon. 1860. 2nd ed. ....*$300–$600*

Darwin, Charles. *The Power of Movement in Plants.* Da Capo Press. 1966. facs of 1881 ed. vinyl dj. ....*$25–$35*

Darwin, Charles. *The Various Contrivances by Which Orchids Are Fertilized.* Univ. of Chicago Press. 1984. wrps. facs of 1877 ed. ....*$25–$35*

Darwin. G. H. *The Evolution of Satellites.* GPO. 1898. pamphlet. ....*$20–$35*

Das Plakat. *Mitteilungen des Vereins der Plakat-Freunde.* Berlin. 1910–21. vols 1–12. wrps. clr and b/w illus. *$12,650*

Daumas, M. *Scientific Instruments of the 17th and 18th Centuries.* ... Lon. 1972. dj. ....*$30–$50*

Davenport, Alfred. *Camp and Field Life of the Fifth New York Volunteer Infantry.* NY. 1879. ....*$175–$250*

Davenport, Cyril. *Royal English Book Bindings.* Lon. 1896. 1st ed. illus. . ...*$45–$65*

Davenport, John. *Aphrodisiacs and Anti-aphrodisiacs.* Lon. 1869. 1st ed. illus. ....*$75–$125*

Davidson, Ellis. *A Practical Manual of House Painting.* ... Lon. 1884. .. ..*$45–$50*

Davidson, Gordon Charles. *The North West Company.* Berkeley. 1918. 1st ed. illus. maps, plates. . . . .*$95–$145*

Davidson, J. N. *Muh-he-ka-ne-ok: A History of the Stockbridge Nation.* Milw. 1893. . . . .*$45–$55*

Davies, Thomas. *The Preparation and Mounting of Microscopic Objects.* NY. 1876. 2nd ed, illus, 214 pp. . . . .*$30–$45*

Davies, Thomas. *The Preparation and Mounting of Microscopic Objects.* Lon. 1864. 1st ed. . . . .*$40–$50*

Davis. *Jamestown and Her Neighbors.* Richmond. 1929. 2nd ptg. . . . .*$15–$20*

Davis, Brian L. *German Army Uniforms and Insignia, 1933–1940.* NY. 1972. wrps. . . . .*$25–$35*

Davis, Burke. *Grey Fox: Robert E. Lee and the Civil War.* NY. 1956. illus. maps, dj. . . . .*$25–$35*

Davis, Rear-Admiral C. H. (ed). *Narrative of the North Polar Expedition, U.S. Ship Polaris.* DC. GPO. 1878. 2nd ptg, engr, lithos, maps, decorative red cloth. . . . .*$60–$75*

Davis, Daniel. *An Address to Inhabitants . . . Maine. . . .* Portland. 1791. . . . .*$50–$100*

Davis, Henry P. *Training Your Own Bird Dog.* Putnam's Sons. 1948. 1st ed. dj. *$30*

Davis, Jefferson. *The Purchase of Camels for Military Transportation.* DC. 1857. illus. . . . .*$150–$200*

Davis, Jefferson. *The Rise and Fall of the Confederate Government.* NY. 1881. 2 vols. 808 pp. . . . .*$150–$200*

Davis, M. L. *Memoirs of Aaron Burr.* NY. 1836. 2 vols. . . . . .*$100–$300*

Davis, Mary Lee. *Uncle Sam's Attic: the Intimate Story of Alaska.* Bos. 1930. 1st ed. . . . .*$35–$50*

Davis, Rebecca Harding. *Bits of Gossip.* Bos/NY. Houghton, Mifflin. 1904. 1st ed. *$45*

Davis, Reg. S. and Steiner. *Mona Lisa Philippine Orchids.* NY. 1952. . . . .*$50–$65*

Davis, Richard Harding. *The Bar Sinister.* NY. 1903. 1st ed. . . . .*$30–$50*

Davis, Richard Harding. *The Cuban and Porto Rican Campaigns.* NY. 1898. 1st ed. illus. . . . .*$30–$75*

Davis, Richard Harding. *Van Bibber and Others.* NY. 1892. 1st ed. . . . .*$35–$40*

Davis, Richard Harding. *Vera. . . .* NY. 1908. 1st ed. . . . .*$25–$35*

Davis, Richard Harding. *The West from a Car Window.* NY/Lon. 1892. 1st ed. illus by Frederick Remington. . . . .*$50–$65*

Davis, Susan Lawrence. *Authentic History of the Ku Klux Klan, 1865–1877.* NY. private ptg. 1924. . . . .*$140–$225*

Davis. W. *El Gringo, or New Mexico and Her People.* NY. 1857. . . . .
. . . .*$100–$300*

Davis. W. *The Spanish Conquest of New Mexico.* Doylestown, PA. 1869. 1st ed. map. . . . .*$575–$1,000*

Dawson, Mrs. Nelson [Edith B.]. *Enamels.* Chi. 1910. illus. . . . .
. . . .*$25–$35*

Dawson, Sarah M. *A Confederate Girl's Diary.* Bos. 1913. 1st ed. . . . . . .
. . . .*$125*

Day, Jeremiah. *Introduction to Algebra.* New Haven. 1814. 1st ed. . . . . .
. . . .*$45–$65*

Day, L. W. *Story of the One Hundred and First Ohio Infantry.* Cleve. 1894. 1st ed. illus. . . . .*$150–$250*

Day, Lal Behari. *Bengal Peasant Life.* Lon. 1892. . . . .*$22–$30*

Day, Lewis. *Art Nouveau Embroidery.* 1974. illus. . . . .
. . . .*$15–$25*

Dayan, Moshe. *The Story of My Life.* NY. 1976. 1st ed. illus. photos, sgn, dj. . . . .*$30–$45*

Dayton, Fred. *Steam Boat Days.* Stokes. 1925. 1st ed. . . . .
. . . .*$25–$40*

Dayton, Ruth Woods. *Pioneers and Their Homes on Upper Kanawha.* 1947. . . . .*$18–$32*

De Beauvoir, Simone. *Force of Circumstance.* NY. Putnam. [1965]. . . . .
. . . .*$45*

De Beauvoir, Simone. *The Long March.* Cleve/NY. 1958. 1st ed. dj. . . . .
. . . .*$47–$60*

De Beauvoir, Simone. *The Mandarins.* NY. 1956. 1st Amer ed. dj. . . . . . .
. . . .*$22–$30*

De Bothezat, George. *Back to Newton.* NY. 1936. 1st ed. 152 pp, dj. . . . .
. . . .*$30–$35*

De Brunhoff, Jean. *Babar and Father Christmas.* NY. (1940). 1st Amer ed in English, folio, illus, dj. . . . .*$200–$375*

De Brunhoff, Jean. *Babar and His Children.* NY. (1938). 1st Amer ed, illus, folio. . . . .*$100–$175*

De Brunhoff, Jean. *Babar the King.* Smith/Haas. 1935. 1st Amer ed, folio. . . . .*$140–$200*

De Brunhoff, Jean. *Histoire de Babar.* Paris. 1931. 1st ed. illus. . . . .
. . . .*$375–$900*

De Camp, Etta. *The Return of Frank Stockton.* NY. 1913. 1st ed. . . . .
. . . .*$75–$85*

De Camp, L. Sprague. *Scribblings.* Bos. 1972. 1st ed. 500 cc, sgn, dj. . . .
. . . .*$18–$25*

De Clifford, N. F. *Egypt, the Cradle of Ancient Masonry.* NY. 1907. 2
vols. . . . .*$65–$85*

Deering Ideals. Chi. Deering Harvester Co. 1902. illus. pictorial wrps. . . .
. . . .*$40–$50*

De Givry, Grillot. *Witchcraft, Magic and Alchemy.* Lon. 1931. 366 illus,
10 clr plates, dj. *$75*

De Groat, Robert W. *Totem Poles—A Happy Hobby for Boys.* NY. Boy
Scouts of America. 1930. 1st ed. wrps. illus. . . . .*$28–$35*

De la Mer, Walter. *Crossings.* NY. 1925. illus by Dorothy Lathrop. . . . . .
. . . .*$50–$70*

De la Mer, Walter. *Eight Tales.* Sauk City. 1971. 1st ed. 2,992 cc, dj. . . .
. . . .*$35–$45*

De la Mare, Walter. *Memoirs of a Midget.* Lon. (1921). 1st ed. dj. . . . . . .
. . . .*$35–$50*

De la Mare, Walter. *Peacock Pie: A Book of Rhymes.* NY. 1924. 1st Amer
ed. ltd #13/500 cc, embellishments by C. Lovat Taylor, sgn. *$145*

De la Mare, Walter. *The Riddle and Other Stories.* Lon. (1923). 1st ed.
blue cloth, dj. . . . .*$120–$150*

De Leon, T. C. (ed). *South Songs: From the Lays of Later Days.* NY.
1866. 1st ed. . . . .*$95–$125*

De Long, Sidney R. *The History of Arizona from the Earliest Times . . . to
1903.* SF. Whitaker & Ray Co. 1905. 1st ed. *$100*

De Marinis, Rick. *The Coming Triumph of the Free World.* NY. Viking.
1988. 1st ed. dj. . . . .*$15–$25*

De Maupassant, Guy. *The Odd Number.* Lon. 1891. 1st Eng ed. .*$50–$75*

De Morgan, John. *Marion and His Men.* McKay. 1892. dj. . . . .
. . . .*$22*

De Morgan, John. *The Hero of Ticonderoga.* McKay. 1896. dj. . . . .
. . . .*$22*

De Poncins, Gontran. *From a Chinese City.* Garden City. 1957. 1st ed. dj.
. . . .*$50–$65*

De Quille, Dan. *History of the Big Bonanza.* Hartford. 1876. . .*$100–$250*

De Quille, Dan. *History of the Comstock Silver Lode.* Nev. (1889). wrps. .
. . . .*$100–$250*

De Roos, Frederick. *Personal Narrative of Travels in the U.S. and Canada in 1826.* Lon. 1827. illus. 2nd ed. lithos, maps. . . . . . .*$165–$250*

Description of the New York Central Park. NY. 1869. . . . .*$50–$95*

Descriptive Catalogue of School Supplies. Chi. Central School Supply House. c 1897–98. illus. pictorial wrps, 88 pp. . . . .*$95–$125*

De Shields, James T. *Border Wars of Texas.* Tioga, TX. 1912. 1st ed. illus. . . . .*$175–$250*

De Smet, P. J. *Western Missions and Missionaries.* NY. 1859. 1st ed. . . . .
. . . .*$105–$195*

De Smet, Pierre-Jean. *Oregon Missions and Travels over the Rocky Mountains.* NY. 1847. 1st ed. wrps. plates, fldg map. . . . .*$350–$900*

De Voto, Bernard. *Across the Wide Missouri.* Bos. 1947. illus. . . . .
. . . .*$40–$90*

De Voto, Bernard. *Mark Twain at Work.* 1942. 1st ed. dj. . . . . . .*$22–$35*

De Voto, Bernard. *The Year of Decision, 1846.* Bos. 1943. 1st ed. dj. . . . .
. . . .*$24–$32*

De Vries, Hugo. *Species and Varieties: Their Origin by Mutation.* Chi. 1906. 2nd ed. . . . .*$75–$95*

De Vries, Peter. *I Hear America Singing.* Little Brown. 1976. 1st ed. dj. .
. . . .*$24–$30*

De Vries, Peter. *Into Your Tent I'll Creep.* Bos. 1971. 1st Amer ed. dj. . . .
. . . .*$20–$30*

De Vries, Peter. *Slouching towards Kalamazoo.* Bos. (1983). 1st ed. sgn, dj. . . . .*$20–$30*

De Vries, Peter. *The Tunnel of Love.* Bos. Little Brown. (1957). 1st ed. illus. the play. *$30*

De Vries, Peter. *The Vale of Laughter.* Bos. 1967. sgn, presentation copy, dj. . . . .*$35–$45*

Deane, Samuel. *History of Scituate, Massachusetts.* Bos. 1831. 1st ed. 406 pp. . . . .*$200–$225*

Dearborn, R. F. *Saratoga Illustrated.* Troy, NY. 1872. 1st ed. illus. fldg map, clr lithos. . . . .*$96–$125*

Debs, Eugene. *His Life, Writings and Speeches.* Girard. 1908. sgn. . . . . . .
. . . .*$100–$135*

Decker, Amelia Stickney. *That Ancient Trail.* published by author. (1942). illus. 3rd ed. . . . .*$20–$30*

Decker, John W. *Cheese Making.* WI. 1909. . . . .*$30–$45*

Decter, Midge. *The Liberated Woman and Other Americans.* NY. Coward McCann. (1971). 256 pp, dj. *$30*

Defoe, Daniel. *The Life and Surprising Adventures of Robinson Crusoe.* Lon. 1856. illus. one half calf, mar bds. . . . .*$75–$85*

Defoe, Daniel. *Moll Flanders.* Lane. 1929. illus. . . . .*$40–$75*

Deighton, Len. *Bomber.* NY. Harper & Row. 1970. 1st ed. dj. . . . .
. . . .*$44–$55*

Deighton, Len. *Funeral in Berlin.* Putnam. 1965. 1st U.S. ed. dj. . . . .
. . . .*$60*

Deighton, Len. *The Ipcress File.* NY. Simon & Schuster. 1963. 1st U.S. ed. dj. . . . .*$75–$140*

Deighton, Len. *Only When I Laugh.* NY. 1987. ltd 250 cc, sgn, slipcase. . .
. . . .*$95–$125*

Deignan, H. *The Birds of Northern Thailand.* DC. Smithsonian Institution. 1945. maps, 616 pp. *$115*

Deite, C. *Practical Treatise on Manufacture of Perfumery.* Phila. 1892. illus. 1st Amer ed. . . . .*$40–$55*

Del Rey, Lester. *Attack from Atlantis.* Phila. Winston. (1953). 207 pp, dj. . . . .*$50–$65*

Delany, Samuel R. *Dhalgren.* Bantam Books. (1975). 1st ed. pictorial wrps. . . . .*$20–$25*

Dempsey, Hugh. *History in Their Blood: The Indian Portraits of N. Grandmaison.* Hudson Hills, NY. 1982. 1st Amer ed. dj. . . . .*$40–$50*

Dempsey, Jack. *Dempsey: By the Man Himself.* 1960. 1st ed. sgn. . . . . . .
. . . .*$50–$65*

Dempsey, Jack. *Round by Round.* 1940. 1st ed. wrps. . . . .*$28–$35*

Dene, Shafto. *Trail Blazing in the Skies.* Akron. 1943. illus. photos. . . . . .
. . . .*$35*

Denham, Maj. Dixon. *Narrative of Travels and Discoveries in Northern and Central Africa.* 1826. . . . .*$650*

Denslow, W. W. *Denslow's Scarecrow and the Tin Man.* 1903. 1st ed. illus. linen. . . . .*$300–$600*

Denslow, W. W. *The Scarecrow and the Tin Man.* Dillingham. (1904). . . .
. . . .*$150–$300*

Derby, W. L. A. *The Tall Ships Pass.* Lon. 1937. illus. . . . .*$75–$110*

Derleth, August. *The Casebook of Solar Pons.* Sauk City. 1965. 1st ed. dj. . . . .*$35–$45*

Derleth, August. *Not Long for This World.* Sauk City. 1948. 1st ed. ltd, dj.
....*$150*

Derleth, August. *Over the Edge.* Arkham House. 1964. 1st ed. dj. ......
....*$30–$45*

Derleth, August. *Restless Is the River.* Scribner's. 1939. 1st ed. dj. ......
....*$50–$100*

Derleth, August. *Something Near.* Sauk City. Arkham House. 1945. 1st
ed. 274 pp, inscrb. ....*$75–$95*

Derleth, August. *Thirty Years of Arkham House.* Sauk City. 1970. 1st ed.
dj. ....*$50–$85*

Derry, Joseph. *Story of the Confederate States.* Richmond. 1895. 1st ed.
illus..*$50–$100*

Descharnes, Robert. *The World of Salvador Dali.* Atide Books. nd. dj. ..
....*$50–$80*

Desio, Ardito. *Ascent of K2.* Lon. 1955. 1st ed. photos, maps. ...*$45–$58*

Deutsch, Babette. *Take Them, Stranger.* NY. (1944). 1st ed. sgn. ....
....*$44–$60*

Dewees, F. P. *The Molly Maguires.* Phila. 1877. map. ....*$95–$150*

Dewees, William. *A Compendious System of Midwifery.* Phila. 1847. illus.
lea...*$75–$120*

Dewees, William, M.D. *A Compendious System of Midwifery.* Phila.
Carey & Lea. 1832. 5th ed. engr, 636 pp. ....*$75–$130*

Dewees, William. *A Treatise on the Diseases of Females.* Phila. 1840.
illus. 7th ed. calf, steel plates. ....*$75–$125*

D'Ewes, J. *Sporting in Both Hemispheres.* Lon. 1858. 2nd ed. ....
....*$95–$125*

Dewey, John. *Experience and Education.* 1938. 1st ed. sgn. ....*$55–$75*

Dewitt, David Miller. *The Judicial Murder of Mary E. Surratt.* Balt. 1895.
1st ed. ....*$185–$250*

Dick and Jane: Before We Read. 1962. paperback. *$75*

Dick and Jane: Fun Wherever We Are. 1962. paperback. *$40*

Dick and Jane: Fun with Dick and Jane. 1940. ....*$125*

Dick and Jane: Fun with Dick and Jane. 1946. ....*$50*

Dick and Jane: Now We Read. 1965. paperback. *$75*

Dick and Jane: Our New Friends. 1946. ....*$50*

Dick and Jane: We Look and See. 1946–47. paperback. *$120*

Dick and Jane: We Talk, Spell and Write. 1951. paperback. *$75*

Dick, Philip K. *The Broken Bubble.* NY. Arbor House. [1988]. 1st ed. dj. .
....$35

Dick, Philip K. *The Cosmic Puppets.* Severn House. (1986). 1st ed. dj. ...
....$35–$45

Dick, Philip K. *The Crack in Space.* [Wallington]. Severn House. (1989).
1st separate hardcover ed. dj. $45

Dick, Philip K. *The Golden Man.* Berkeley. (1980). 1st ed. paperback in
wrps, inscrb. ....$200–$350

Dick, Philip K. *I Hope I Shall Arrive Soon.* NY. 1985. dj. ......$25–$35

Dick, Philip K. *Our Friends from Frolix 8.* Lon. Kinnell. 1989. 1st hardcover ed. dj...$65

Dick, Philip K. *A Scanner Darkly.* Garden City. 1977. 1st ed. dj. ....
....$75–$100

Dick, William B. *Dick's Hand Book of Cribbage.* NY. 1885.....$18–$25

Dickens, Charles. *The Battle of Life: A Love Story.* Lon. Bradbury &
Evans. 1846. 1st ed. 4th issue. $75

Dickens, Charles. *The Chimes.* 1931. illus by Arthur Rackham, slipcase. .
....$400–$500

Dickens, Charles. *A Christmas Carol.* Lon. Chapman & Hall. 1843. 1st
ed. reddish-brown ribbed cloth. $5,750

Dickens, Charles. *Dombey and Son.* NY. 1847. wrps. ....$100–$210

Dickens, Charles. *The Haunted Man and the Ghost's Bargain.* Lon. 1848.
1st ed. $300

Dickens, Charles. *The Life and Adventures of Nicholas Nickelby.*
Chapman & Hall. 1839. 1st ed in book form...............$150–$200

Dickens, Charles. *Little Dorrit.* Lon. 1857. illus. 1st ed in book form,
engr, half calf, mar bds. ....$185–$285

Dickens, Charles. *Martin Chuzzlewit.* Ticknor & Fields. 1867. illus......
....$50–$85

Dickens, Charles. *Our Mutual Friend.* Lon. 1865. 2 vols. 1st ed in book
form. ....$150–$250

Dickens, Charles. *The Works of* ... NY. 1861–62. 24 vols. dark green
cloth. ....$200–$300

Dickens, Charles. *The Works of* ... Chi. M. A. Donohue. 14 vols. red
mor, mbl bds. ....$70–$100

Dickens, Charles. *The Works of* ... Lon. c 1880. 30 vols. gilt, half mor
binding by Riviere. ....$700–$900

Dickey, James. *Deliverance.* Bos. 1970. 1st ed. 1st ptg, dj. .....$20–$45

Dickey, James. *To the White Sea.* Houghton. 1993. 1st ed. sgn, dj. . . .*$45*

Dickey, James. *The Zodiac.* NY. Doubleday. 1976. 1st ed. sgn, dj. . . . . . .
. . . .*$35–$45*

Dickinson, Emily. *Bolts of Melody.* NY. 1945. ed by Todd and Bingham,
1st ed. . . . .*$25–$40*

Dickinson, Emily. *The Letters of Emily Dickinson.* Bos. 1894. 2 vols. ed
by M. L. Todd, 1st ed. . . . .*$200–$250*

Dickinson, Emily. *Poems.* Bos. Roberts. 1891. ed by T. W. Higginson and
Mabel Loomis Todd, 1st ed, second series, 8vo, 230 pp, teg, gray-green
cloth. *$850*

Dickson, Franklin W. *The Hidden Harbor Mystery.* Grosset & Dunlap.
1935. Hardy Boys #14. . . . .*$14*

Dickson, Franklin W. *The Mystery of Cabin Island.* Grosset & Dunlap.
1929. 1932B ed. Hardy Boys #8, dj. *$130*

Dickson, Franklin W. *The Secret Warning.* Grosset & Dunlap. 1938. 1941
ed. Hardy Boys #17, dj. *$77*

Dickson, Franklin W. *The Sign of the Crooked Arrow.* Grosset & Dunlap.
1949. Hardy Boys, #28, dj. *$12*

Didion, Joan. *Run River.* Obolensky. 1963. 1st ed. dj. . . . .*$75–$125*

Didion, Joan. *Slouching Towards Bethlehem.* NY. 1968. dj. . . . .
. . . .*$40–$60*

Dietz, August. *Postal Service of the Confederate States of America.* Richmond. 1929. 1st ed. sgn. . . . .*$200–$350*

Digges, Jeremiah. *Cape Cod Pilot.* Provincetown/NY. WPA. 1937. 2nd
ptg, dj. . . . .*$25–$35*

Dillard, Annie. *An American Childhood.* Harper. 1987. 1st ed. dj . . . .
. . . .*$25*

Dillin, Capt. John G. *The Kentucky Rifle.* Ludlum Beebe. 1946. 3rd ed.
slipcase. *$65*

Dillon, Richard H. *Hatchet Men.* NY. (1962). illus. . . . .*$10–$20*

Dimsdale, Thomas J. *The Vigilantes of Montana.* Univ. of Oklahoma
Press. (1968). 8th ptg, dj. *$10*

Dimsdale, Thomas J. *The Vigilantes of Montana.* Helena. nd. 4th ed. . . . . .
. . . .*$50–$75*

Dinesen, Isak. *Last Tales.* NY. 1959. 1st ed. dj. . . . .*$15–$25*

Dinesen, Isak. *Out of Africa.* NY. 1938. 1st ed. dj. . . . .*$100–$175*

Dinesen, Isak. *Seven Gothic Tales.* NY. 1934. 1st ed. dj. . . . .*$35–$85*

Dionne Quints. *Growing Up.* 1935. . . . .*$35–$55*

Directions for Cookery, by Miss Leslie. Phila. 1839. 468 pp, 7th ed. . . . . .
. . . .*$75–$100*

A Directory of the City of New Brunswick, 1855–56. J. Terhune. 1855. . .
. . . .*$100–$135*

*Dirigibles Captifs Spheriques; Parachutes; Treuils et Tenders D'Aero-
station.* Paris. Zodiac, Anciens Etablissements Aeronautiques. 1918. illus.
pictorial wrps, 32 pp. . . . .*$175–$250*

Disney, Walt. *Fantasia Program.* 1940. wrps. . . . .*$50–$100*

Disney, Walt. *Mickey Mouse Stories, Book #2.* Phila. David McKay. 1934.
wrps. illus. . . . .*$80–$100*

Disney, Walt. *Mickey Mouse Story Book.* Phila. (1931). orange pictorial
cloth. . . . .*$800–$950*

Disney, Walt. *Mickey Mouse Waddle Book.* NY. 1934. bds. . . . .
. . . .*$85–$110*

Disney, Walt. *Pop-up Mickey Mouse.* Blue Ribbon Books. 1933. illus. 3
pop-ups. . . . .*$200–$300*

Disney, Walt. *Pop-up Minnie Mouse.* 1933. illus. 3 pop-ups. . . . .
. . . .*$100–$200*

Disney, Walt. *Stories from Fantasia.* Random House. (1940). 1st ed. dj. . .
. . . .*$75–$100*

Disney, Walt. *Walt Disney's Pinocchio's Picture Book.* Whitman. 1940.
wrps. illus. . . . .*$125–$150*

Ditmars, R. *Reptiles of the World.* Lon. 1946. illus. rev ed. . . . . .*$25–$35*

Ditmars, R. L. *Snakes of the World.* NY. (1931). . . . .*$25–$35*

Dix, Dorothea. *A Memorial to the Legislature of Massachusetts.* Salem.
Gazette Office. 1843. 1st ed. wrps. unopened, 15 pp. . . . .*$200–$375*

Dixon, Franklin. *The Hooded Hawk Mystery.* Grosset & Dunlap. 1971.
Hardy Boys #34. . . . .*$7*

Dixon, Franklin. *The House on the Cliff.* Grosset & Dunlap. 1959. Hardy
Boys #2. . . . .*$7*

Dixon, Franklin. *The House on the Cliff.* Grosset & Dunlap. 1927. Hardy
Boys #2, dj. *$20*

Dixon, Franklin. *The Missing Chums.* Grosset & Dunlap. 1928. Hardy
Boys #4, dj. . . . .*$30–$40*

Dixon, Franklin. *The Missing Chums.* Grosset & Dunlap. (1957). Hardy
Boys, dj. *$12*

Dixon, Franklin. *The Mystery of Cabin Island.* Grosset & Dunlap. 1979.
Hardy Boys #8. . . . .*$7*

Dixon, Franklin. *The Secret of the Caves.* Grosset & Dunlap. 1929. Hardy Boys #7, dj. . . . .*$100–$150*

Dixon, Franklin. *The Short Wave Mystery.* Grosset & Dunlap. 1945. Hardy Boys #24, dj. *$18*

Dixon, Franklin. *The Sign of the Crooked Arrow.* Grosset & Dunlap. 1949. Hardy Boys #28. . . . .*$7–$12*

Dixon, Capt. Geo. *Voyage Around the World 1785 to 1788.* maps. *$600*

Dixon, H. *John Howard and the Prison World of Europe.* 1852. . . . .*$35–$50*

Dixon, Joseph K. *The Vanishing Race: The Last Great Indian Council.* . . . NY. 1914. illus. . . . .*$85–$125*

Dixon, Peter. *Bobby Benson in the Tunnel of Gold.* 1936. 1st ed. wrps. illus. . . . .*$24–$32*

Dixon, William Scarth. *Fox-hunting in the 20th Century.* 1925. . . . .*$25–$35*

Djilas, Milovan. *The Leper and Other Stories.* NY. Harcourt, Brace & World. 1964. 1st ed. dj. . . . .*$15–$25*

Dobell, Horace. *On the Nature, Cause, and Treatment of Tuberculosis.* Lon. 1866. . . . .*$20–$25*

Dobie, J. Frank. *Apache Gold and Yanqui Silver.* Little Brown. 1939. 1st ed. dj. . . . .*$30–$75*

Dobie, J. Frank. *As the Moving Finger Writ.* np. (1955). wrps. 12 pp. . . . .*$40–$70*

Dobie, J. Frank. *The Ben Lilly Legend.* 1950. 1st ed. dj. . . . .*$24–$35*

Dobie, J. Frank. *Life and Literature of the South West.* 1st ed. dj. *$65*

Dobie, J. Frank. *The Longhorns.* Bos. 1941. 1st ed. dj. . . . .*$40–$50*

Dobie, J. Frank. *The Mustangs.* Bos. (1952)1952. 1st ed. . . . .*$40–$60*

Dobie. J. Frank. *The Voice of the Coyote.* Little Brown. 1949. 1st ed. dj. . . . .*$50–$70*

Docstader, Frederick. *The Kachina and the White Man.* Cranbrook Inst. 1954. 1st ed. dj. . . . .*$30–$40*

Doctorow, E. L. *Billy Bathgate.* Random House. 1989. 1st ed. ltd 300 cc, sgn, slipcase. . . . .*$85–$125*

Doctorow. E. L. *Lives of the Poets.* NY. Random House. (1984). 1st ed. dj . . . .*$25–$30*

Doctorow, E. L. *Loon Lake.* NY. Random House. 1980. 1st ed. dj. . . . . . .
. . . .$20–$30

Doctorow, E. L. *Loon Lake.* NY. Random House. (1980). 1st ed. 1/350 cc,
sgn, slipcase. $100

Doctorow, E. L. *Ragtime.* NY. (1975). 1st ed. sgn, dj. . . . .$50–$60

Doctorow, E. L. *Welcome to Hard Times.* NY. 1960. 1st ed. dj. . . . .
. . . .$60–$75

Dodge, Grenville. *The Battle of Atlanta and Other Campaign Addresses,
Etc.* Monarch. 1910. 1st ed. illus. . . . .$65–$175

Dodge, Mary M. *Hans Brinker.* Scribner's. 1926. illus. clr plates.$22–$30

Dodge, Mary M. *When Life Is Young.* Century. 1894. 1st ed. illus. . . . . . .
. . . .$30–$40

Dodge, Col. Richard I. *Our Wild Indians.* Hartford. 1882. . . . .$50–$100

Dodge, Richard I. *The Plains of the Great West and Their Inhabitants.*
NY. 1877. 1st ed. illus. fldg map. . . . .$95–$125

Dolbear, A. E. *The Telephone.* 1877. 1st ed. illus. . . . .$60–$95

The Doll's House. Viking Press & Kestrel Books. 1981. oblong, facs of
antique pop-up book, illus by Meggendorfer. . . . .$30–$40

Domenech, Emmanuel. *Seven Years' Residence in the Great Deserts of
North America.* Lon. Longman, Green, Longman and Roberts. 1860. 2
vols. 1st ed. illus. fldg map, plates. . . . .$600–$850

Donaldson, Alfred L. *A History of the Adirondacks.* NY. 1921. 2 vols. 1st
ed. . . . .$140–$160

Donnelly, Ned. *Self-defense, or The Art of Boxing.* Lon. Weldon. 1879. 1st
ed. . . . .$150–$250

Doolittle, Hilda. *Collected Poems of.* . . . NY. Boni & Liveright. 1925. 1st
ed. 306 pp, inscrb. $450

The Dore Bible Gallery. Phila. 1883. illus. . . . .$45–$65

Dore, J. R. *Old Bibles, or An Account of the Various Versions of the
English Bible.* Lon. 1876. . . . .$45–$60

Dorsey, Sarah A. *Recollections of Henry Watkins Allen . . . Confederate
Army.* NY. 1866. 1st ed. lea. . . . .$125–$200

Dos Passos, John. *42nd Parallel.* NY/Lon. 1930. 1st ed. dj. . . .$150–$200

Doughty, Charles M. *Wanderings in Arabia.* Lon. Duckworth & Co.
(1923). 2 vols. maps. . . . .$60–$75

Douglas, Norman. *In the Beginning.* NY. 1928. 1st Amer ed. dj. $50–$80

Douglass, Frederick. *Frederick Douglass on Women's Rights.* Westport.
Greenwood Press. (1976). 190 pp. $35

Douglass, Frederick. *Life and Times.* Hartford. 1881. illus. . . . . .*$35–$75*

Douglass, Frederick. *My Bondage and My Freedom.* NY/Auburn. 1855. 1st ed. . . . .*$90–$130*

Dow, George Francis. *Whale Ships and Whaling: A Pictorial History.* . . . Salem. Marine Research Society. 1925. 1st ed. illus with b/w plates. . . . .*$100–$140*

Downing, A. G. *The Architectural Heritage of Newport, Rhode Island.* NY. 1967. 2nd ed. dj. . . . .*$50–$75*

Downing, A. J. *The Fruits and Fruit Trees of America.* . . . NY. 1858. illus. . . . .*$125–$200*

Downing, A. J. *The Fruits and Fruit Trees of America.* NY. 1859. rev. . . . .*$175–$225*

Downing, A. J. *Treatise on the Theory and Practice of Landscape Gardening.* NY. 1859. 6th ed. illus. . . . .*$200–$275*

Dowsett, H. M. *Wireless Telephony and Broadcasting.* 1924. 1st ed. illus. . . . .*$75–$100*

Doyle, Arthur Conan. *The Adventures of Gerard.* NY. 1903. 1st Amer ed. . . . .*$50–$65*

Doyle, Arthur Conan. *The Adventures of Sherlock Holmes.* NY. (1892). 1st Amer ed. 2nd issue. . . . .*$225–$300*

Doyle, Arthur Conan. *The Adventures of Sherlock Holmes.* Lon. 1892. 1st ed. illus. . . . .*$900–$1,000*

Doyle, Arthur Conan. *The Croxley Master.* NY. Doran. (1925). 1st Amer ed. dj. *$125*

Doyle, Arthur Conan. *Danger and Other Stories.* Doran. 1919. 1st ed. . . . .*$45–$55*

Doyle, Arthur Conan. *The Green Flag.* NY. 1900. 1st Amer ed. *$35–$65*

Doyle, Arthur Conan. *The Hound of the Baskervilles.* Lon. 1902. 1st ed. first issue, aeg, frontis, illus. . . . .*$750–$1,500*

Doyle, Arthur Conan. *The Hound of the Baskervilles.* NY. 1902. 1st Amer ed. . . . .*$100–$250*

Doyle, Arthur Conan. *The Lost World.* Lon. Hodder & Stoughton. (1912). 1st ed. illus. 319 pp. . . . .*$70–$85*

Doyle, Arthur Conan. *The Lost World.* NY. 1912. 1st Amer ed. .*$40–$75*

Doyle, Arthur Conan. *The New Revelation.* NY. (1918). . . . .*$25–$35*

Doyle, Arthur Conan. *The Sign of Four.* Lon. George Newnes. 1893. 3rd ed. red pictorial cvrs. *$375*

Doyle, Arthur Conan. *Sir Nigel.* NY. 1906. 1st Amer ed. . . . . . .*$30–$45*

Doyle, Arthur Conan. *Through the Magic Door.* Lon. 1907. illus. ......
....$65–135

Doyle, Arthur Conan. *The White Company.* NY. 1922. illus by N. C. Wyeth, dj. ....$60–$85

Drago, H. *Wild, Woolly and Wicked.* NY. 1960. 1st ed. dj. ......$30–$40

Dragoo, Don. *Mounds for the Dead.* Pitts. Carnegie Museum. 1963. illus. 315 pp. ....$30–$40

Drake, Benjamin. *Life of Tecumseh and of His Brother the Prophet.* ... Cinc. 1855. ....$90–$200

Drake, D. *Dr. Daniel Drake's Letters on Slavery.* NY. 1940. 1st ed. ltd 250 cc, dj. ....$65–$75

Drake, Ensg. Robert. *The Boy Allies under the Sea, or The Vanishing Submarine.* NY. 1916. illus. ....$25–$45

Drane, Maude Johnston. *History of Henry County, Kentucky.* 1948. 1st ed. ....$50–$60

Dreiser, Theodore. *A Gallery of Women.* NY. 1929. 2 vols. 1st ed. 560 cc, sgn. $150

Dreiser, Theodore. *Sister Carrie.* NY. 1900. 1st ed. $1,000

Driggs, Howard. *Westward America.* NY. (1942). dj. ....$30–$40

Driggs, Howard R. *The Pony Express Goes Through.* NY. 1935. ....
....$35–$45

Drinker, Frederick E., and James G. Lewis. *Radio—Miracle of the 20th Century.* 1922. 1st ed. illus. ....$20–$25

Drummond, H. *Tropical Africa.* NY. 1890. ....$50–$60

Du Bois, Theodora. *Murder Strikes an Atomic Unit.* NY. 1946. 1st ed. dj.
....$20–$30

Du Bois, W. E. B. *Darkwater.* Harcourt. 1920. 1st ed. ....$95–$130

Du Bois, W. E. B. *Mansart Builds a School.* NY. Mainstream Publishers. 1959. 1st ed. 367 pp, 2nd vol of trilogy, dj. $75

Du Bois, W. E. B. *The Souls of Black Folk.* Chi. 1903. 1st ed. .$300–$400

Du Bois, W. E. B. *The World and Africa.* NY. (1947). ....$35–$45

Du Chaillu, Paul. *Lost in the Jungle.* NY. 1869. 1st ed. ....$40–$50

Du Chaillu, Paul. *Midnight Sun.* NY. 1881. 2 vols. illus. fldg. map. ......
....$100–$200

Du Chaillu, Paul. *Stories of the Gorilla Country.* NY. 1868. 1st ed. illus. .
....$95–$125

Du Maurier, Daphne. *The Scapegoat.* NY. 1957. 1st ed. dj. ....$18–$25

Dubois, Abbe J. *Hindu Manners, Customs and Ceremonies.* Ox. Clarendon. 1899. 2nd rev, corrected, and enlarged ed. 732 pp. *$345*

Dubourg, George. *The Violin.* Lon. 1852. 4th ed. ....*$30–$40*

Dubus, Andre. *All the Time in the World.* NY. Knopf. 1996. 1st ed. ...*$35*

Dubus, Andre. *The Lieutenant.* NY. 1967. 1st ed. dj. ....*$40–$65*

Duchaussois, P. *Mid Snow and Ice: The Apostles of the North-west.* Lon. 1923. 1st ed. illus. ....*$60–$85*

Duffus, R. L. *The Santa Fe Trail.* NY. 1930. 1st ed. illus. sgn. ..*$30–$40*

Dufur, S. M. *Over the Deadline, or Tracked by Bloodline.* Burlington, VT. 1902. ....*$55–$75*

Dulac, Edmund. *Edmund Dulac's Fairy Book.* Doran. (1916). 1st ed. illus. ....*$160–$230*

Dulac, Edmund. *Edmund Dulac's Picture Book.* Hodder & Stoughton. 1st ed. wrps. illus. ....*$125–$150*

Dulac, Edmund. *Stories for the Arabian Nights.* Hodder & Stoughton. nd. illus by Dulac. ....*$100–$135*

Dulac, Edmund. *Stories from Hans Anderson.* Doran. nd. 1st ed. illus by Dulac, clr plates. ....*$100–$135*

Dumas, Lt. Gen. M. *Memoirs of His Own Time, Including the Revolution.* Phila. 1839. 2 vols. ....*$175–$250*

Dumont, Henrietta. *The Lady's Oracle.* Phila. Peck & Bliss. 1853. 270 pp, aeg. *$60*

Dunaway, W. F. *Reminiscences of a Rebel.* NY. 1913. ......*$175–$250*

Dunbar, Alice Moore. *Masterpieces of Negro Eloquence.* NY. 1914. ....*$140–$180*

Dunbar, Paul Laurence. *Candle-Lightin' Time.* NY. 1901. 1st ed. photos by Hampton Camera Club, 127 pp. ....*$150–$200*

Dunbar, Paul Laurence. *Li'l Gal.* NY. 1904. 1st ed. photos. ..*$100–$150*

Dunbar, Paul Laurence. *Lyrics of Love and Laughter.* Dodd Mead. 1903. 1st ed. ....*$50–$115*

Dunbar, Paul Laurence. *Poems of Cabin and Field.* NY. 1899. 1st ed. illus by Hampton Institute. ....*$125–$175*

Duncan Brothers. *The United States Homeopathic Pharmacopoeia.* Chi. 1878. 1st ed. 281 pp. ....*$50–$60*

Duncan, Isadora. *My Life.* NY. 1927. illus. ltd #105/650 cc. ....*$40–$50*

Dunlop, William. *History of the American Theatre.* NY. 1832. *$200–$350*

Dunne, Burt. *Play Ball!* NY. 1947. 1st ed. wrps. illus. ....*$25–$50*

Dunne, Peter M. *Early Jesuit Missions in Tarahumara.* Berkeley, CA. 1948. 1st ed. illus. fldg map. . . . .*$40–$75*

Dunning, John. *The Bookman's Wake.* NY. Scribner's. 1995. 1st ed. sgn, dj. . . . .*$45–$65*

Dunning, John. *Deadline.* Huntington Beach. James Cahill. 1995. 1st Amer ed. sgn, dj. *$35*

Dunsany, Lord. *The Blessing of Pan.* NY. Putnam. 1928. 1st Amer ed. 277 pp. . . . .*$30–$40*

Dunsany, Lord. *The Chronicles of Rodriquez.* Lon. Jarrolds. (1950). 1st ed. sgn, dj. *$185*

Dunsany, Lord. *His Fellow Man.* Lon. 1952. 1st ed. dj. . . . .*$65–$85*

Dunsany, Lord. *Selections from the Writings.* Churchtown, Dundrum. Cuala Press. 1912. 1st ed. 1/250 cc. *$200*

Dunsany, Lord. *The Sword of Welleran.* Lon. 1908. 1st ed. illus. *$70–$85*

Dunsany, Lord. *Time and the Gods.* Lon. Heinemann. 1906. 1st ed. 1st issue, 179 pp, illus. . . . .*$100–$150*

Dunsany, Lord. *Who Ate the Phoenix.* Lon. nd. 1st ed. dj. . . . . . .*$65–$75*

Durant, Will. *Philosophy and the Social Problem.* NY. 1917. . . . .
. . . .*$35–$45*

Durrell, Lawrence. *Clea.* Lon. 1960. 1st U.K. ed. dj. . . . .*$35–$45*

Durrell, Lawrence. *The Ikons and Other Poems.* Lon. 1966. 1st ed. dj. . .
. . . .*$25–$35*

Durrell, Lawrence. *Numquam.* Lon. Faber. (1970). 1st ed. dj. . . . .
. . . .*$25–$45*

Durrell, Lawrence. *Prospero's Cell and Reflections on a Marine Venus.* Dutton. 1960. 1st ed. dj. . . . .*$35–$45*

Durrell, Lawrence. *Sappho: A Play in Verse.* Lon. Faber & Faber. (1950). 1st ed. dj. *$75*

Durrell, Lawrence. *Sauve Qui Peut.* Lon. (1966). 1st ed. dj. . . . .*$30–$40*

Durrell, Lawrence. *Zero and Asylum in the Snow: Two Excursions into Reality.* Berkeley, CA. 1947. 1st ed. dj. . . . .*$30–$75*

Durso, Joseph. *Casey.* NJ. [1967]. 211 pp, photos, dj. *$14.50*

Dussauce, H. *A General Treatise on the Manufacture of Vinegar.* Phila. 1871. 1st ed. . . . .*$35–$45*

Dustin, Fred. *The Custer Tragedy.* Ann Arbor. 1939. 200 cc, maps. . . . . . .
. . . .*$150–$250*

Dustin, Fred. *The Saginaw Treaty of 1819.* Saginaw. 1919. 1st ed. sgn, present, wrps. *$100*

Dustin, Fred. *The Saginaw Treaty of 1819 between Gen. Louis Cass and Chippewa Indians.* Saginaw. 1919. illus. . . . .*$50–$75*

Dwight, N. *The Lives of the Signers of the Declaration of Independence.* NY. 1851. 1st ed. . . . .*$35–$60*

Dwight, S. E. *The Hebrew Wife.* Glasgow. Gallie. 1837. 1st Glasgow ed. 148 pp. *$150*

Dyke, A. L. *Dyke's Automobile and Gasoline Engine Encyclopedia.* Chi. 1924. illus. dj. . . . .*$45–$85*

Earhart, Amelia. *Last Flight.* NY. 1937. 1st ed. illus. dj. . . . .*$40–$65*

Earle, Alice Morse. *Stage Coach and Tavern Days.* NY. 1900. 1st ed. 449 pp. *$30*

Earle, Alice Morse. *Child Life in the Colonial Days.* NY. Macmillan. 1904. 1st ed. illus. *$15*

Earle, Alice Morse. *Customs and Fashions in Old New England.* Scribner's. 1893. sgn. . . . .*$35–$55*

Earle, Alice Morse. *Sun Dials and Roses of Yesterday.* NY. 1902. 1st ed. illus. . . . .*$45–$65*

Earle, Alice Morse. *Two Centuries of Costume in America.* NY. 1903. 2 vols. 1st ed. illus. . . . .*$100–$200*

Earle, Pliny. *Memoirs of Pliny Earle.* Bos. 1898. 1st ed. . . . .*$45–$80*

Early, Jubal. *Autobiographical Sketch and Narrative of the War Between the States.* Phila. Lippincott. 1912. 1st ed. illus. 496 pp. *$250*

East of the Sun and West of the Moon. NY. 1922. illus by Kay Nielsen, tip-in clr plates, dj. . . . .*$150–$300*

Eastlake, William. *A Child's Garden of Verses for the Revolution.* NY. Grove Press. 1970. 1st ed. dj. . . . .*$25–$40*

Eastlake, William. *Go in Beauty.* NY. (1956). 1st ed. author's first book, dj. . . . .*$100–$200*

Eastman, Charles A. *Indian Boyhood.* NY. 1902. illus. . . . .*$70–$85*

Eastman, Charles G. *Poems of. . . .* Montpelier. 1848. . . . .*$45–$55*

Eastman, F. *A History of the State of New York.* NY. 1830. lea. . . . .*$55–$65*

Eastman, M. E. *East of the White Hills.* North Conway, NH. (1900). 1st ed. illus. . . . .*$40–$60*

Easton, Mable. *Nyilac and Other African Sketches.* NY. 1923. photos, dj. . . . .*$20–$35*

Eaton, Allen H. *Handicrafts of the Southern Highlanders.* illus. 2nd ptg, dj. . . . .*$50–$65*

Eaton, Elon Howard. *Birds of New York.* Albany. 1910. 2 vols. illus. clr plates. ....*$100–$200*

Eaton, John H. *The Life of Andrew Jackson.* Phila. 1824. 2nd ed. ....*$50–$100*

Eaton, John P., and Charles A. Haas. *Titanic.* NY. 1986. illus. dj. ....*$30–$45*

Eaton, Seymour. *The Traveling Bears in Outdoor Sports.* Barse & Hopkins. 1915. illus. ....*$40–$55*

Eberlein, Harold D. *Manor Houses and Historic Homes of Long Island and Staten Island.* Phila. 1928. 1st ed. 318 pp, photogravure, illus. *$50*

The Economy Cream Separator. Chi. Sears, Roebuck & Co. 1907. illus, pictorial wrps. ....*$35–$45*

Eddington, A. S. *Space, Time, and Gravitation.* ... Camb. 1921. 1st ed. . ...*$40–$60*

Eddy, Daniel. *Lectures to Young Ladies on Subjects of Practical Importance.* Lowell, MA. Sargeant. 1848. 1st ed. 252 pp. *$75*

Edison Swan Co. *The Pageant of the Lamp.* 1948. 1st ed. illus. ....*$50–$65*

Edmonds, Walter R. *Drums along the Mohawk.* Bos. 1936. 1st ed. wrps. ....*$25–$50*

The Education of a French Model. NY. Boar's Head Books. 1950. 186 pp, illus, photos by Man Ray, rprnt, dj. ....*$75–$100*

Edwards, Amelia. *Pharaohs, Fellahs and Explorers.* NY. Harper & Bros. 1891. 1st Amer ed. illus. ....*$50–$70*

Edwards, Amelia. *A Thousand Miles Up the Nile.* NY. A. L. Burt. (1888). rev, aeg. ....*$30–$45*

Edwards, E., and J. Rattray. *Whale Off.* NY. 1932. 1st ed. illus. ....*$27–$40*

Edwards, John E. *Life of Rev. John Wesley Childs.* ... Early. 1852. 1st ed. ....*$90–$125*

Edwards, Jonathan. *A History of the Work of Redemption.* NY. 1786. ... .*$50–$80*

Edwards, William B. *Civil War Guns.* Harrisburg. 1962. illus. dj. ....*$35–$75*

Edwards, William B. *Story of Colts Revolver.* 1953. 1st ed. dj. ....*$75–$100*

Ehrlich, Sagan, Kennedy, and Roberts. *The Cold and the Dark: The World after Nuclear War.* NY. 1984. 1st ed. wrps. ....*$14–$20*

Eickemeyer, Carl. *Among the Pueblo Indians.* NY. 1895. . . . . . .*$50–$65*

Eidinoff, Maxwell Leigh, and Hyman Ruchlis. *Atomics for the Millions.* NY/Lon. 1947. 1st ed. illus by Maurice Sendak. . . . .*$100–$120*

Einstein, Albert. *Relativity: The Special and General Theory.* Lon. (1920). . . . .*$75–$150*

Einstein, Albert. *Über die spezielle und die allgemeine Relativitäts-theorie.* wrps. 4th ed. . . . .*$50–$65*

Einstein, Albert, and Leopold Infeld. *The New Physics.* Palestine. 1947. 1st Hebrew ed. sgn, dj. . . . .*$85–$125*

Eiseley, Loren. *The Invisible Pyramid.* NY. 1970. 1st ed. . . . . . .*$15–$25*

Eisenschiml, Otto. *The Story of Shiloh.* Chi. 1946. . . . .*$40–$50*

Eldridge, Eleanor. *Slave Narrative.* Prov. 1842. . . . .*$125–$150*

Electric Gas Lighting. Bos. Boston Electric Co. 1880. illus. 12 pp. . . . .*$40–$50*

Electric Railway Dictionary. McGraw. 1911. 1st ed. illus. . . . . .*$95–$125*

Electric Signals for Passenger and Freight Elevators. . . . NY. Elevator Supply & Repair Co. 1913. 48 pp. . . . .*$90–$100*

Eliot, George. *How Lisa Loved the King.* Bos. Fields, Osgood & Co. 1869. 1st ed. small 8vo, 48 pp, green cloth. *$200*

Eliot, George. *The Mill on the Floss.* Edin/Lon. William Blackwood. 1869. 3 vols. 1st ed. *$500*

Eliot, George. *Romola.* Lon. 1863. 3 vols. 1st ed. . . . .*$1,000–$2,000*

Eliot, George. *Romola.* NY. 1863. 1st Amer ed. . . . .*$95–$115*

Eliot, George. *Silas Marner.* Edin/Lon. 1861. 1st ed. 364 pp. . . . .*$300–$1,500*

Eliot, George. *Silas Marner, the Weaver of Raveloe.* Edin/Lon. 1861. 1st ed. terra cotta cloth. *$950*

Eliot, George. *The Works.* Edin. 1878–80. 20 vols. . . . .*$95–$125*

Eliot, T. S. *An Address to Members of the London Library.* (Lon, for the London Library by the Queen Anne Press. 1952). printed wrps, 1/500 cc. *$75*

Eliot, T. S. *Dante.* Lon. Faber & Faber. (1929). 1st ed. dj. . . . .*$100–$250*

Eliot, T. S. *The Confidential Clerk.* NY. (1954). 1st ed. dj. . . . . . .*$25–$50*

Eliot, T. S. *The Cultivation of Christmas Trees.* NY. Farrar, Straus & Cudahy. (1956). 1st ed. *$35*

Eliot, T. S. *The Elder Statesman.* NY. 1959. 1st Amer ed. dj. . . . . .*$55–$65*

Eliot, T. S. *Four Quartets.* Lon. Faber & Faber. (1944). 1st Brit ed. dj. *$200*

Eliot, T. S. *Old Possum's Book of Practical Cats.* Lon. 1939. 1st ed. dj. . .
. . . .*$400*

Ellet, Charles, Jr. *The Mississippi and the Ohio Rivers.* Phila. 1853.
inscrb, illus, 366 pp. . . . .*$125–$175*

Elliot, Prof. G. F. Scott. *Prehistoric Man and His Story.* Phila. 1915. illus.
398 pp. . . . .*$15–$22*

Elliot, George H. *Report on a Tour of Inspection of European Light-house
Establishments Made in 1873.* GPO. 1874. 1st ed. illus. . . . .
. . . .*$100–$150*

Elliot, George P. *Parktilden Village.* Bos. Beacon Press. 1958. 1st ed.
author's first book, dj. . . . .*$40–$50*

Elliott, Henry W. *Report upon the Condition of Affairs in the Territory of
Alaska.* DC. GPO. 1875. 277 pp. *$85*

Ellis, E. S. *The Story of the Red Feather.* NY. 1908. illus. *$80*

Ellis, Havelock. *Studies in the Psychology of Sex.* Phila. 1928. 7 vols. . . .
. . . .*$75–$125*

Ellis, Havelock. *The World of Dreams.* Bos. 1915. . . . .*$35–$85*

Ellis, R. A. *Spiderland.* Lon. 1912. illus. . . . .*$20–$35*

Ellison, Harlan. *Alone against Tomorrow.* NY. 1971. 1st ed. sgn, dj. . . . .
. . . .*$35–$60*

Ellison, Harlan. *Approaching Oblivion.* NY. 1974. 1st ed. sgn, dj. . . . . . .
. . . .*$40–$75*

Ellison, Harlan. *Demon with a Glass Hand.* (NY. 1986). 1st ed. pictorial
wrps. . . . .*$15–$25*

Ellison, Harlan. *Strange Wine.* Harper. 1978. 1st ed. dj. . . . .*$60–$70*

Ellison, Ralph. *Invisible Man.* NY. 1952. 1st ed. dj. . . . .*$650–$750*

Ellwanger, H. B. *The Rose.* Lon. William Heinemann. 1893. rev, 310 pp.
. . . .*$65–$85*

Elwes, H. J. *Memoirs of Travel, Sport and Natural History.* Lon. 1930.
317 pp. *$35*

Elzas, Barnett. *The Jews of South Carolina.* Phila. 1905. #104/175 cc. . . .
. . . .*$55–$65*

Emanuel, Walter. *A Dog's Day.* Lon. Heinemann. 1902. illus by Cecil
Aldin. *$250*

Embick, Milton. *Military History of the Third Division, 9th Corp. Army
Potomac.* np. 1913. 1st ed. illus. . . . .*$48–$60*

Emerson, Adaline E. *Ralph Emerson, Jr.: Life and Letters, Edited by His
Mother.* Rockford IL. 1891. 1st ed. illus. . . . .*$90–$125*

Emerson, Alice B. *Ruth Fielding at Snow Camp.* Cupples & Leon. 1913. Fielding #3, dj. *$15*

Emerson, Ralph Waldo. *The Complete Works of.* . . . Bos. Houghton Mifflin. 1903. 12 vols. illus. Concord ed. . . . .*$70–$100*

Emerson, Ralph Waldo. *The Essay on Friendship.* East Aurora. Roycroft. [1899]. ltd, illuminated and sgn by the illuminator. *$65*

Emerson, Ralph Waldo. *Essays.* . . . Bos. 1841, 1844. 2 vols. 1st ed. . . . .
. . . .*$950–$1,500*

Emerson, Ralph Waldo. *Society and Solitude.* Bos. 1870. 1st ed. small 8vo. . . . .*$50–$75*

The Encyclopaedia Britannica, 11th Edition. NY. 1910. 20 vols. . . . .
. . . .*$150–$200*

Endell, Fritz. *Old Tavern Signs: An Excursion in the History of Hospitality.* Houghton Mifflin. 1916. 1st ed. illus. ltd #327/500. . . . . .*$45–$55*

Endicott, William. *Wrecked among Cannibals in the Fijis.* Marine Research Soc. 1923. . . . .*$50–$95*

Engineers, Architects and Builders in Iron and Steel. East Berlin, CT. The Berlin Iron Bridge Co. c 1890–95. printed wrps, illus, 302 pp. . . . . . .
. . . .*$125–$250*

Ensko, Stephen. *American Silversmiths.* (1989). 1st ed. illus. dj. . . . .
. . . .*$35–$40*

Ephron, Nora. *Heartburn.* Knopf. 1983. 1st ed. dj. . . . .*$20–$28*

Epstein, Geo. J., M.D. *Strabismus: A Clinical Handbook.* Phila. 1948. illus. . . . .*$35–$48*

Ernst, C. B. *Venemous Reptiles of North America.* DC. 1992. illus. . . . . . .
. . . .*$25–$35*

EROS Magazine. vol 1, #1. . . . .*$30–$35*

Erskine, Laurie York. *Renfrew Rides North.* Grosset & Dunlap. 1931. Renfrew Books #3, dj. *$22*

Esquivel, Laura. *Like Water for Chocolate.* Doubleday. 1989. 1st ed. dj. . .
. . . .*$60*

Eustis, Celestine. *Cooking in Old Creole Days.* NY. 1903. 1st ed. . . . .
. . . .*$25–$40*

Evans, Augusta Inez. *A Tale of the Alamo.* NY. 1888. . . . .*$55–$68*

Evans, C. S. *The Sleeping Beauty.* Lon. (1920). illus by Arthur Rackham, 1 tip-in clr plate. . . . .*$70–$125*

Evans, Frederick William. *Egyptian Sphinx.* Mt. Lebanon. nd. wrps. . . . .
. . . .*$87–$110*

Evans, George Bird. *Grouse Along the Tramroad.* Old Hemlock. 1986. ltd 1,500 cc, sgn and nbr, slipcase. $200

Evans, George Bird. *Upland Gunner's Book.* Amwell. 1986. 1st trade ed. slipcase. $50

Evans, I. H. N. *Among Primitive Peoples in Borneo.* NY. 1978. rprnt. . . .
. . . .$60

Evans, Joan. *A History of Jewelry, 1100–1870.* NY. (1953). illus. dj. . . . .
. . . .$100–$125

Evans, John. *Ancient Bronze Implements, Weapons . . . Great Britain and Ireland.* NY. 1881. . . . .$65–$85

Evans, John. *The Ancient Stone Implements. . . .* NY. 1872. 1st ed. 640 pp.
. . . .$75–$100

Everett, Marshall. *The Book of the Fair.* 1904. illus. . . . .$27–$30

Ewart, John S. *The Kingdom of Canada; Imperial Federation; The Colonial Conferences; The Alaska Boundary; and Other Essays.* Tor. 1908. 1st ed. illus. 2 maps, sgn. $45

Examples of Church Furnishings. NY. J. & R. Lamb Co. 1886. stiff wrps, illus. 72 pp. . . . .$75–$100

Eyre, John. *The European Stranger in America.* NY. 1839. 1st ed. 84 pp.
. . . .$75–$100

Eyster, Nellie Blessing. *A Chinese Quaker.* NY. (1902). . . . .
. . . .$15–$22

Faber, Eduard. *Nobel Prize Winners in Chemistry, 1901–1961.* Abelard-Schuman. 1963. rev. . . . .$25–$35

Fabre, Jean-Henri. *Fabre's Book of Insects.* NY. 1935. . . . .$45

Fabre, Jean-Henri. *The Life of the Grasshopper.* NY. 1917. dj. . . . .
. . . .$35–$50

Fabre's Book of Insects. NY. 1927. clr plates. . . . .$15–$18

Fagg, William P. *Afro-Portuguese Ivories.* Lon. dj. . . . .$65–$90

Fahie, J. J. *Galileo.* Lon. 1903. illus. . . . .$40–$60

Fahnestock, W. P., MD. *Artificial Somnambulism, Called Mesmerism, or Animal Magnetism.* Phila. 1869. . . . .$95–$125

Fairbridge, Dorothea. *Historic Farms of South Africa.* Lon. 1931. 1st ed. illus. dj. . . . .$125–$150

Fairbridge, Dorothea. *The Pilgrim's Way in South Africa.* Lon. 1928. 1st ed. . . . .$35–$50

Fairchild, David. *The World Was My Garden.* Scribner's. 1938. 1st ed. illus. . . . .$35–$45

Fairchild, David and Marian. *Book of Monsters.* Wash. 1914. . . . .
. . . .*$100–$150*

Fairchild, T. B. *The History of the Town of Cuyahoga Falls, Summit County, Ohio.* Cleve. 1876. 1st ed. . . . .*$65–$75*

Fairfield, Richard. *Communes U.S.A.: A Personal Tour.* Balt. (1972). wrps. photos. *$8*

The Fairy Tales of Charles Perrault. Dodge. illus by Harry Clarke, intro by Bodkin. . . . .*$150–$250*

Faithfull, Emily. *Three Visits to America.* NY. Fowler & Wells. (1884). 1st U.S. ed. 400 pp. . . . .*$95–$125*

Fall, Bernard. *Hell in a Very Small Place.* Phila. 1966. 1st ed. dj. . . . .
. . . .*$40–$50*

Fall, Bernard B. *Street without Joy.* Harrisburg. 1961. 1st ed. dj. . . . .
. . . .*$425–$500*

Fall, Bernard B. *Vietnam in the Balance.* 1966. wrps. . . . .*$25–$35*

Family Cabinet Atlas. Phila. Carey & Lea. 1932. 1st Amer ed. rev, clr maps, bds. . . . .*$60–$100*

Family Circle's Guide to Trout Flies and How to Tie Them. (1954). illus. 48 pp, boxed. *$45*

Faris, John T. *Roaming the Rockies.* . . . Farrar & Rinehart. 1930. illus. . .
. . . .*$35–$45*

Farley, Walter. *Son of the Black Stallion.* 1947. 1st ed. dj. . . . .
. . . .*$25–$35*

Farmer, Fannie Merritt. *Chafing Dish Possibilities.* Bos. Little Brown. 1898. 1st ed. . . . .*$50–$80*

Farmer, Philip Jose. *Dare.* NY. (1965). 1st ed. pictorial wrps. . . . .
. . . .*$15–$25*

Farmer, Philip Jose. *Dayworld Breakup.* NY. (1990). 1st ed. dj. . . . .
. . . .*$20–$25*

Farmer, Philip Jose. *A Feast Unknown.* Essex House. (1969). 1st ed. . . . .
. . . .*$50–$100*

Farmer, Philip Jose. *Love Song.* Macmillan. 1983. 1st ed. ltd 500 cc, dj. . .
. . . .*$65–$75*

Farmer, Philip Jose. *The Magic Labyrinth.* Berkley Putnam. 1980. 1st ed. sgn, dj. . . . .*$20–$30*

Farmer, Philip Jose. *Tarzan Alive.* Garden City. 1972. 1st ed. dj. . . . .
. . . .*$65–$100*

Farnham, Eliza. *Life in Prairie Land.* NY. 1847. . . . .*$65–$85*

Farnham, Thomas J. *Travels in the Great Western Prairies: The Anahuac and Rocky Mountains in the Oregon Territory.* NY. published by author. 1843. 112 pp. *$175*

Farnol, Jeffrey. *The Money Moon.* NY. 1911. 1st ed. illus. . . . . .*$18–$25*

Farnol, Jeffrey. *The Shadow.* Bos. Little Brown. 1929. 1st Amer ed. 306 pp. . . . .*$25–$35*

Farquhar, Roger Brooke. *Historic Montgomery County Old Homes and History.* 1952. sgn. . . . .*$35–$50*

Farrell, James T. *Father and Son.* Vanguard. 1940. 1st ed. dj. *$125*

Farrell, James T. *My Baseball Diary.* NY. (1957). 1st ed. dj. . . . .
. . . .*$45–$55*

Farrell, James T. *My Days of Anger.* Vanguard. 1943. 1st ed. dj. . . .*$100*

Farrell, James T. *Yet Other Waters.* Vanguard. 1952. 1st ed. dj. *$50*

Farrington, S. Kip. *Atlantic Game Fishing.* 1939. . . . .*$28–$35*

Farrington, S. Kip. *Atlantic Game Fishing.* NY. 1937. illus. sgn. . . . .
. . . .*$145–$185*

Farrington, S. Kip, Jr. *The Ducks Came Back.* NY. Coward McCann. 1945. 1st ed. illus by Lynne Bogue Hunt, 138 pp. . . . .*$30–$40*

Fast, Howard. *The Naked God.* Praeger. 1957. 1st ed. dj. *$25*

Fast, Howard. *The Passion of Sacco and Vanzetti.* Lon. 1954. 1st Brit ed. dj. . . . .*$20–$30*

Faubion, Nina Lane. *Some Edible Mushrooms and How to Know Them.* OR. 1938. illus. . . . .*$14–$20*

Faulkner, William. *Absalom Absalom!* NY. 1936. 1st ed. fldg map at rear, dj. . . . .*$350–$450*

Faulkner, William. *As I Lay Dying.* Lon. 1935. 1st U.K. ed. dj. . . . .
. . . .*$360–$650*

Faulkner, William. *Big Woods.* Random House. 1955. 1st ed. *$95*

Faulkner, William. *Doctor Martino and Other Stories.* NY. Harrison Smith & Robert Haas. 1934. dj. *$350*

Faulkner, William. *A Fable.* Random House. 1954. 1st ed. dj. . .*$60–$80*

Faulkner, William. *The Faulkner Reader.* NY. 1959. . . . .*$30–$45*

Faulkner, William. *Go Down Moses and Other Stories.* NY. Random House. (c 1942). 1st ed. dj. *$350*

Faulkner, William. *Intruder in the Dust.* NY. (1948). 1st ed. dj. . . . .
. . . .*$125–$225*

Faulkner, William. *Light in August.* NY. Smith & Haas. (1932). 1st ed. dj. . . . .*$500–$850*

Faulkner, William. *The Mansion.* NY. Random House. (1959). 1st ed. dj.
....*$60–$75*

Faulkner, William. *Pylon.* Smith. 1935. 1st ed. dj..........*$350–$500*

Faulkner, William. *Requiem for a Nun.* Chatto & Windus. 1953. 1st U.K. ed. dj..*$35–$65*

Faulkner, William. *Requiem for a Nun.* Random House. (1951). 1st ed. dj.
....*$75–$125*

Faulkner, William. *Sartoris.* NY. (1929). 1st ed. dj. .....*$1,300–$2,600*

Faulkner, William. *The Town.* Random House. (1957). 1st ed. dj. ......
....*$65–$100*

Faulkner, William. *The Town.* Chatto & Windus. 1958. 1st Eng ed. dj. ..
....*$50–$75*

Faulkner, William. *The Wild Palms.* NY. (1939). 1st ed. dj. ....
....*$400–$550*

Fay, Bernhard. *Notes on the American Press at the End of the Eighteenth Century.* NY. The Grolier Club. 1927. 1st ed. 1/325 cc, folio, 29 pp, slipcase..*$225*

Fearing, Kenneth. *Loneliest Girl in the World.* NY. Harcourt Brace. 1951. 1st ed. dj. *$85*

Featherstonhaugh, G. W. *Geological Report of an Examination Made in 1834 of the Elevated Country Between the Missouri and Red Rivers.* DC. Gales & Seaton. 1835. 1st ed. 97 pp. *$275*

Feed My Sheep. Anchorage. nd. ....*$10–$14*

Feek, Andrew J. *Every Man His Own Trainer, or How to Develop ... Trotter or Pacer.* NY. 1889. 1st ed. ....*$68–$85*

Feiffer, Jules. *Little Murders.* NY. 1968. 1st ed. dj. ....*$50–$75*

Feldman, Leibl. *The Jews of Johannesburg.* 1956. illus. dj. .....*$20–$30*

Felix S. Cohen's Handbook of Federal Indian Law. Albuquerque. 1958.
....*$28–$35*

Fellows, M. H. *The Land of Little Rain.* Chi. 1946. illus. dj. .....*$45–$65*

Felt, E. P. *Insects Affecting Park and Woodland Trees.* Albany. 1905. illus.
....*$45–$60*

Ferber, Edna. *Giant.* Garden City. 1952. 1st ed. dj. ....*$35–$45*

Ferber, Edna. *Saratoga Trunk.* Garden City. 1941. 1st ed. dj. ...*$18–$25*

Ferlinghetti, Lawrence. *The Mexican Night.* New Directions. 1970. 1st ed. wrps. ....*$25–$45*

Ferlinghetti, Lawrence. *The Secret Meaning of Things.* 1968. dj. ....
....*$30–$40*

Ferlinghetti, Lawrence. *A Trip to Italy and France.* 1979. ltd 250 cc, sgn.
....$75–$100

Fermi, Enrico. *Thermodynamics.* Prentice-Hall. 1937. 1st ed. ....
....$300–$500

Ferree, B. *American Estates and Gardens.* NY. 1906. folio, 306 pp, photos. $150

Ferris, Benjamin G. *Utah and the Mormons.* NY. 1854. illus. ....
....$100–$250

Ferris, James Cody. *The X Bar X Boys on Big Bison Trail.* Grosset & Dunlap. 1927. X Bar X Boys #4, dj. $42

Ferris, Timothy. *Spaceshots.* Pantheon. 1984. 1st ed. dj. ....$20–$30

Ferris, W. A. *Life in the Rocky Mountains.* Salt Lake City. (1940). fldg maps, illus. ....$100–$150

Fessenden, T. *The New American Gardener.* NY. 1828. 1st ed. lea. .....
....$75–$100

Ficklen, John Rose. *History of Reconstruction in Louisiana.* Balt. 1910. 1st ed. wrps. ....$55–$100

Field, Eugene. *The Gingham Dog and the Calico Cat.* Newark. (1926). dj.
....$100–$150

Field, Eugene. *Lullaby-land.* NY/Lon. (1900). illus by Charles Robinson.
....$30–$50

Field, Eugene. *Winken, Blynken and Nod.* Saalfield. 1930. illus. ....
....$25–$45

Field, Henry M. *Bright Skies and Dark Shadows.* NY. 1890. 1st ed. maps, sgn. ....$20–$35

Field, Henry M. *History of the Atlantic Telegraph.* NY. 1866. 1st ed. illus.
....$55–$90

Field, M. *City Architecture, or Designs for Dwellings, Houses, Stores, Hotels, Etc.* NY. Putnam. 1853. 1st ed. illus. ....$80–$120

Field, Rachel. *Calico Bush.* NY. Macmillan. 1931. 1st ed. 213 pp, inscrb.
....$80

Fielde, Adele. *A Corner of Cathay.* NY. Macmillan. 1894. 11 clr plates, pictorial cloth, teg. ....$30–$45

The Fifth over the Southwest Pacific. L.A. AAF Publications [Fifth Air Force]. nd. wrps. illus. $125

Fifth Report of Senate Fact Finding Comm. on Un-Amer. Activities. Sac. 1949. wrps. illus. ....$20–$25

Figueira, L. *Racas e Tribos de Angola: Estudo.* Lisbon. 1938. inscrb. ....
....$50

Figuier. *Mammalia, Popularly Described by Typical Species.* Lon. 1870. illus. . . . .*$35–$45*

Findley, Palmer. *The Story of Childbirth.* NY. 1934. 1st ed. . . . .*$50–$75*

Findley, Palmer. *Priests of Lucina: Story of Obstetrics.* Bos. 1939. 1st ed. . . . .*$22–$35*

Finerty, John F. *War-path and Bivouac, or The Conquest of the Sioux.* Chi. private ptg. (1890). 1st ed. illus. fldg map. *$125*

Finger, Charles J. *Frontier Ballads Heard and Gathered by.* . . . NY. 1927. 1st ed. illus. woodcuts, #29/201 cc, sgn. . . . .*$25–$45*

Finley, Rev. James B. *History of the Wyandott Missions.* OH. 1840. 1st ed. 432 pp. . . . .*$200–$300*

Finley, Ruth. *Old Patchwork Quilts and the Women Who Made Them.* Phila. 1929. 1st ed. . . . .*$60–$75*

Finney, Ross. *Causes and Cures for the Social Unrest.* NY. Macmillan. 1922. 1st ptg. *$17.50*

Firebough, Ellen. *The Physician's Wife and the Things That Pertain to Her Life.* Phila. 1894. 1st ed. 186 pp. . . . .*$75–$125*

First Annual Report of the Bd. of Pharmacy of the St. of Washington. Olympia. 1892. 1st ed. wrps. . . . .*$40–$50*

First Annual Sports and Bicycle Races. PA. 1896. wrps. 8 pp. . . . .*$19–$30*

Fishbein, M., et al. *Bibliography of Infantile Paralysis, 1789–1944.* Phila. 1946. 1st ed. . . . .*$50–$65*

Fisher, A. K., and L. Steineger. *The Death Valley Expedition.* Wash. 1893. wrps. 5 maps. *$65*

Fisher, Dorothy Canfield. *Vermont Tradition.* Bos. 1953. 1st ed. . . . .*$18–$25*

Fisher, Harrison. *Dream of Fair Women.* NY. 1907. illus. . . . .*$140–$225*

Fisher, Harrison. *Harrison Fisher's American Girls in Miniature.* NY. 1912. illus. clr plates. . . . .*$75–$125*

Fisher, Harrison. *Hiawatha.* Ind. 1906. 1st ed. . . . .*$50–$95*

Fisher, M. F. K. *Here Let Us Feast.* NY. 1946. 1st ed. dj. . . . .*$18–$25*

Fisher, Rev. H. D. *The Gun and the Gospel.* Chi. 1896. 1st ed. . . . .*$50–$75*

Fisher, Vardis. *Darkness and the Deep.* NY. (1943). dj. . . . .*$40–$50*

Fiske, John. *The American Revolution.* Bos/NY. 1896. 2 vols. green cloth.
. . . .*$100–$125*

Fiske, John. *Dutch and Quaker Colonies in America.* Bos. 1899. 2 vols. .
. . . .*$30–$40*

Fiske, John. *John Fiske's Historical Writings.* Bos. 1902. 12 vols. . . . . . .
. . . .*$50–$65*

Fitch, Samuel S., A.M., M.D. *A Popular Treatise on the Diseases of the Heart.* . . . NY. 1860. illus. . . . .*$50–$75*

Fite, Emerson D. *A Book of Old Maps.* Camb. 1926. 1st ed. folio, maps. .
. . . .*$150–$195*

Fitzgerald, F. Scott. *Afternoon of an Author.* NY. Scribner's. (1957). 1st ed. dj. *$45*

Fitzgerald, F. Scott. *All the Sad Young Men.* NY. 1926. 1st ed. no dj. . . . .
. . . .*$50*

Fitzgerald, F. Scott. *All the Sad Young Men.* NY. Scribner's. 1926. 1st ed. dj. *$100*

Fitzgerald, F. Scott. *The Beautiful and Damned.* Scribner's. 1922. 1st ed.
. . . .*$65-$90*

Fitzgerald, F. Scott. *The Great Gatsby.* NY. Scribner's. 1925. 1st ed. 1st ptg. . . . .*$400–$675*

Fitzgerald, F. Scott. *Tales of the Jazz Age.* NY. 1922. no dj. *$75*

Fitzgerald, F. Scott. *Tales of the Jazz Age.* Tor. Copp Clark. 1922. 1st Canadian ed. *$350*

Fitzgerald, F. Scott. *Tender Is the Night.* NY. Scribner's. 1932. 1st ed. . .
. . . .*$200–$300*

Fitzgerald, Sybil. *In the Track of the Moors.* Dent & Co. 1905. illus. .*$75*

Fitzgerald, Zelda. *Save Me the Waltz.* Lon. Grey Walls. (1953). 1st U.K. ed, dj, scarce. *$125*

Five Thousand Miles . . . on the South African Railways. 1934. 1st ed. wrps. illus. . . . .*$32–$45*

Flagg, Fannie. *Fried Green Tomatoes at the Whistle Stop Cafe.* NY. Random House. 1987. 1st ed. dj. *$35*

Flagg, Fannie. *Fried Green Tomatoes at the Whistle Stop Cafe.* NY. Random House. 1987. 1st ed. sgn, dj. . . . .*$50–$60*

Flags of Army of U.S. During the War of Rebellion 1861–65. Phila. 1887. 1st ed. illus. clr lithos, folio. . . . .*$275–$450*

Flammarion, Camille. *Astronomy for Amateurs.* NY/Lon. 1921. . . . .
. . . .*$14–$20*

Flammarion, Camille. *The Atmosphere.* NY. 1873. illus. lithos, woodcuts.
....*$75–$90*

Flammarion, Camille. *The Unknown.* 1900. 1st ed. ....*$18–$25*

Flammarion, Camille. *Verdens Undergang.* 1894............*$18–$25*

Fleischer, Nat. *50 Years at Ringside.* NY. 1958. 1st ed. wrps. ....
....*$35–$50*

Fleming, Alexander (ed). *Penicillin: Its Practical Application.* Lon. Butterworth. 1946. 1st ed....................................*$55–$65*

Fleming, Ian. *Dr. No.* Macmillan. 1958. 1st Amer ed. dj.......*$95–$115*

Fleming, Ian. *Dr. No.* Lon. Jonathan Cape. 1958. 1st ed. dj. *$500*

Fleming, Ian. *From Russia With Love.* Lon. 1957. 1st U.K. ed. dj. ......
....*$75–$125*

Fleming, Ian. *Goldfinger.* Lon. 1959. 1st ed. dj. ....*$85–$300*

Fleming, Ian. *Goldfinger.* NY. Macmillan. 1959. 1st Amer ed. dj........
....*$200*

Fleming, Ian. *Live and Let Die.* Lon. Jonathan Cape. 1954. 1st ed. first state, dj. *$3,500*

Fleming, Ian. *Live and Let Die.* NY. Macmillan. 1955. 1st Amer ed. dj. ..
....*$450*

Fleming, Ian. *The Man with the Golden Gun.* Lon. Jonathan Cape. 1965. 1st ed. dj. *$100*

Fleming, Ian. *Octopussy and The Living Daylights.* Lon. Jonathan Cape. 1966. 1st ed. dj. *$45*

Fleming, John Ambrose. *Electrons, Electric Waves and Wireless Telephony.* 1923. 1st ed. illus. ....*$45–$65*

Fletcher, Archibald Lee. *Boy Scouts Test of Courage, or Winning the Merit Badge.* Donahue. 1913.................................*$5*

Flint, Austin. *Medical Ethics and Etiquette.* NY. Appleton. 1883. 1st ed. 97 pp..*$60–$95*

Flint, Austin. *Physical Exploration and Diagnosis of Diseases Affecting Respiratory Organs.* Phila. 1856. 1st ed. 636 pp. ....*$75–$100*

Flint, Timothy. *The Life and Adventures of Daniel Boone.* Cinc. 1868. maps, illus. ....*$100–$250*

Flint, Timothy. *Recollections of the Last Ten Years ... Journeys in the Valley of the Mississippi.* ... Bos. Cummings, Hilliard. 1826. 1st ed. .....
....*$125–$225*

Flower, F. A. *History of the Republican Party.* Springfield. 1884. 1st ed. .
....*$30–$45*

Flowers for a Juvenile Garland. New Haven. S. Babcock. 1840. wrps. pictorial wrps, 45 cm. $85

Foley, Edwin. *The Book of Decorative Furniture.* NY. 1911. 2 vols. 1st ed. 100 tip-in clr plates. ....$175–$250

Folig, Fred. *Lucy Boston on Women's Rights and Spiritualism.* NY. 1855. 1st ed. illus. ....$50–$65

Foner, Phillip S. *The Fur and Leather Workers Union.* NJ. 1950. ....$20–$30

Fontaine's Fables. Whitman Publishing. 1934. illus. ....$14–$20

Forbes, Alexander. *California, a History of Upper and Lower California.* Lon. 1839. 1st ed. illus. map. ....$925–$1,200

Forbes-Lindsay, C. H. *India Past and Present.* Phila. 1903. 2 vols. illus. fldg map. ....$50–$75

Forbush, Edward Howe. *Birds of Massachusetts and Other States.* Bos. 1925–29. 3 vols. 1st ed. ....$90–$125

Forbush, Edward Howe. *Game Birds, Wild Fowl and Shore Birds.* 1912. illus..$45–$60

Forbush, Edward Howe. *History of Game Birds ... of Massachusetts.* 1912. illus. plates. ....$45–$50

Forbush, Edward Howe. *Portraits of New England Birds.* MA. 1932. illus..$50–$75

Force, Manning Ferguson. *General Sherman.* NY. 1899. 1st ed. ....$50–$125

Ford, Ford Maddox. *Great Trade Routes.* Unwin. 1937. 1st ed. wrps. ... .$30–$45

Ford, Ford Maddox. *Women and Men.* Paris. Three Mountains Press. 1923. 1st ed. printed wrps, 1/300 cc. $375

Ford, Paul. *The Great K. & A. Train Robbery.* Dodd Mead. 1897. 1st ed. . ...$20–$30

Foreman, Grant. *Indian Justice: A Cherokee Murder Trial at Tahlequah in 1840.* Oklahoma City. 1934. ....$75–$85

Forester, C. S. *Admiral Hornblower in the West Indies.* Bos. Little Brown. (1958). 1st ed. dj. $45

Forester, C. S. *The African Queen.* Bos. 1935. 1st Amer ed, dj. ....$375–$500

Forester, C. S. *Captain Horatio Hornblower.* Bos. 1939. 1st Amer ed. illus by Wyeth, dj. ....$440–$500

Forester, C. S. *Commodore Hornblower.* Curtis Publishing Co. 1945. 1st ed. ....$16–$20

Forester, C. S. *Hornblower and the Hotspur.* Bos. Little Brown. (1962). 1st U.S. ed. 344 pp, dj. *$45*

Forester, C. S. *Lieutenant Hornblower.* Bos. Little Brown. 1952. 1st U.S. ed. 306 pp, dj. *$45*

Forester, C. S. *Lord Hornblower.* 1946. 1st ed. dj. *$40*

Forester, C. S. *Randall and the River of Time.* Little Brown. 1950. 1st ed. dj. . . . .*$30–$38*

Forester, Frank.*The Complete Manual for Young Sportsmen.* NY. 1856. 1st ed. 480 pp. *$75*

Forester, Frank. *Fishing with Hook and Line.* Hurst & Co. 1858. illus. . . . .*$50–$60*

Forester, Frank. *Hints to Horse-keepers.* NY. 1859. . . . .*$48–$75*,

Formby, John. *The American Civil War.* . . . NY. 1910. 2 vols. illus. maps. . . . .*$95–$125*

Forney, Hon. John A. *Life and Military Career of Winfield Scott Hancock.* . . . Phila. 1880. illus. . . . .*$35–$45*

Forster, E. M. *The Eternal Moment and Other Stories.* Lon. Sidgwick & Jackson. 1928. 1st ed. dj. *$375*

Forster, E. M. *A Passage to India.* Arnold. 1924. 1st ed. dj. . . . .*$600–$800*

Forster, E. M. *A Room with a View.* Lon. 1908. . . . .*$150–$250*

Forster, Frank J. *Country Houses.* NY. 1931. 1st ed. . . . .*$125–$175*

Forster, R. R. *The Spiders of New Zealand.* Dunedin. 1967–70. 3 vols. . . . .*$50–$60*

Forsyth, Frederick. *The Biafra Story.* Lon. Penguin. 1969. 1st ed. paperback original. *$85*

Forsythe, Frederick. *The Odessa File.* Viking. 1972. 1st U.S. ed. dj. *$30*

Fossett, Frank. *Colorado: Its Gold and Silver Mines.* NY. 1879. illus. maps, plates. . . . .*$100–$300*

Fossett, Frank. *Colorado: Its Gold and Silver Mines.* NY. 1880. illus. 2nd ed. fldg maps. . . . .*$50–$100*

Fowler, H. W. *A Dictionary of Modern English Usage.* Ox. 1926. 1st ed. . . . .*$50–$75*

Fowler, Harlan D. *Camels to California.* Stanford Univ. Pr. 1950. illus. dj. . . . .*$25–$35*

Fowler, L. N. *The Principles of Phrenology and Physiology.* . . . NY. 1842. 1st ed. . . . .*$55–$65*

Fowler, O. S. *Fowler's Practical Phrenology.* NY. 1853. . . . .*$35–$50*

Fowler, O. S. *A Home for All, or The Gravel Wall and Octagon Mode of Building.* NY. 1877. illus. . . . .*$45–$60*

Fowles, John. *The Collector.* 1963. 1st ed. 1st state, author's first book. *$450*

Fowles, John. *The French Lieutenant's Woman.* Little Brown. 1969. 1st U.S. ed. dj. *$70*

Fowles, John. *A Maggot.* Lon. Jonathan Cape. 1985. 1/500 cc, sgn. *$150*

Fox, Charles K. *This Wonderful World of Trout.* Carlisle, Pa. 1963. ltd ed. dj. . . . .*$30–$45*

Fox, Frances Margaret. *Adventures of Sonny Bear.* Rand McNally. 1935. illus by Warne Carr. *$35*

Fox, John. *The Little Shepherd of Kingdom Come.* NY. 1931. 1st ed. illus by Wyeth. . . . .*$150–$225*

Fox, John R. *In Happy Valley.* Scribner's. 1917. illus. . . . .*$20–$30*

Foxcraft, Thomas. *Observations, Historical and Practical, on the Rise and Primitive State of New-England. . .: A Sermon.* Bos. S. Kneeland & T. Green, for S. Gerrish. 1730. 1st ed. 46 pp. . . . .*$600–$1,500*

Frame, Janet. *Face in the Water.* NY. 1961. 1st ed. dj. . . . .*$30–$40*

France, Anatole. *The Gods Are Athirst.* Lon. (1927). dj. . . . .*$35–$45*

Franchere, Gabriel. *Narr. of a Voyage to the Northwest Coast of America 1811, 1812, 1813, 1814.* NY. 1854. 1st ed in Eng. . . . .*$250–$350*

Francis, Dick. *Blood Sport.* NY. Harper & Row. 1968. 1st Amer ed. sgn, dj. *$125*

Francis, Dick. *The Danger.* Lon. Michael Joseph. 1983. 1st ed. dj. *$45*

Francis, Dick. *High Stakes.* Lon. 1975. 1st ed. dj. . . . .*$75–$85*

Francis, Dick. *High Stakes.* NY. 1976. 1st Amer ed. dj. . . . .*$30–$40*

Francis, Dick. *In the Frame.* Lon. 1976. 1st ed. dj. . . . .*$50–$65*

Francis, Dick. *In the Frame.* NY. 1977. 1st Amer ed. dj. . . . .*$30–$40*

Francis, Dick. *Longshot.* Putnam. 1990. 1st U.S. ed. dj. . . . .*$18–$20*

Francis, Dick. *Odds Against.* NY. Harper & Row. 1966. 1st Amer ed. sgn, dj. *$150*

Francis, Dick. *Reflex.* Lon. Michael Joseph. 1980. 1st ed. sgn, dj. *$75*

Francis, Dick. *Risk.* wrps. . . . .*$18–$22*

Francis, Dick. *The Sport of Queens.* NY. 1st ed. . . . .*$100–$150*

Francis, Dick. *Wild Horses.* Lon. Michael Joseph. 1994. 1st ed. dj. . . .*$50*

Francis, John W. *Old New York, or Reminiscences of the Past Sixty Years.* NY. 1858. 1st ed. . . . .*$30–$50*

Francis, Lewis Cecile. *The Art and Craft of Leather Work.* Lon. 1928. 1st ed. illus. . . . .*$25–$35*

Frank, Larry. *Indian Silver Jewelry. 1868–1930.* Bos. 1978. 1st ed. . . . .*$45–$75*

Frank, Larry, and Francis H. Harlow. *Historic Pottery of the Pueblo Indians, 1600–1880.* Bos. New York Graphic Society. (1974). 1st ed. illus. dj. *$55*

Frank Leslie's Illustrated History of the Civil War. NY. 1895. 1st ed. small folio. . . . .*$85–$125*

Frankel, H. *Finger Print Expert.* Phila. 1932. 1st ed. . . . .*$20–$30*

Franklin, John. *Narrative of a Journey to the Shores of the Polar Sea, 1819–22.* Lon. 1823. 1st ed. illus. maps, plates. . . . .*$400–$885*

Fraser, C. Lovat. *Pirates.* NY/Lon. 1921–22. illus. woodcuts. . . . .*$35–$45*

Fraser, Chelsea. *Heroes of the Air.* Crowell. 1928. illus. rev, 550 pp. . . . .*$25–$35*

Fraser, J. Baillie. *Mesopotamia and Assyria, from the Earliest Ages to the Present.* NY. Harper. 1842. 1st Amer ed. fldg map frontis, 336 pp. . . . .*$30–$40*

Frederic Remington: The American West. Kent, OH. Volair, Ltd. 1978. ed by Philip St. Claire, plates, boxed. . . . .*$80–$120*

Freece, Hans P. *The Letters of an Apostate Mormon to His Son.* NY. private ptg, 1908. . . . .*$65–$85*

Freeman, Douglas Southall. *Robert E. Lee: A Biography.* NY. 1934–35. 4 vols. illus. . . . .*$95–$250*

Freeman, Harry C. *Brief History of Butte, Montana.* Shepard. 1900. 1st ed. . . . .*$75–$125*

Freeman, Joseph. *A Discourse of the Proper Training of Children.* Ludlow, VT. 1862. wrps. . . . .*$25–$40*

Freligh, Martin. *Homeopathic Practice of Medicine.* NY. Lamport, Blakeman & Law. 1854. 2nd ed. ....*$90–$150*

[Fremont, John]. *Life of Col. Freemont.* [NY]. 1856. 1st ed. 32 pp, sewn, portrait, two full-page illus. ....*$85–$100*

Fremont, John. *Report of the Exploring Expedition to the Rocky Mountains.* ... DC. 1842. maps. ....*$125–$250*

French, John C. *The Passenger Pigeon in Pennsylvania.* Altoona. Altoona Tribune. 1919. 1st ed. wrps. illus. ....*$100–$150*

Frere-Cook, Gervis. *The Decorative Arts of the Mariner.* 1966. 1st ed. ..
....*$32–$40*

Freud, Sigmund. *Interpretation of Dreams.* NY. 1937. dj. ......*$30–$40*

Freud, Sigmund. *Introductory Lectures on Psycho-analysis.* Lon. 1929. .
....*$50–$80*

Freud, Sigmund. *A Note on the Unconscious in Psycho-analysis.* Lon. 1912. wrps. ....*$25–$35*

Freud, Sigmund. *The Problem of Lay Analysis.* NY. 1927. 1st Amer ed. dj. ....*$65–$85*

Friedan, Betty. *The Feminine Mystique.* NY. 1963. 1st ed. dj. ....
....*$100–$150*

Friedan, Betty. *It Changed My Life.* NY. Random House. (1976). 2nd ed. dj. *$25*

Friede, Adele M. *Pagoda Shadows.* Bos. 1814. ....*$35–$45*

Friedman, Bruce Jay. *Black Angels and Other Stories.* NY. (1966). 1st ed. dj. ....*$30–$45*

Friedman, Bruce Jay. *Stern.* NY. 1962. 1st ed. dj. ....*$50–$60*

The Friend: A Monthly Journal. Honolulu. vols 18–25. 96 issues. ......
....*$1,842*

Frost, John. *American Naval Biography.* Phila. 1844. illus. three quarter mor. ....*$87–$185*

Frost, John. *The Book of the Colonies.* Appleton. 1846. 280 pp. ....
....*$35–$45*

Frost, John. *The Book of Travels in Africa.* NY/Phila. 1848. illus.*$20–$25*

Frost, John. *Pictorial History of Mexico and the Mexican War.* Phila. 1849. maps. ....*$35–$50*

Frost, Robert. *Complete Poems.* NY. Holt, Rinehart & Winston. (1962). 1st ed. dj. ....*$25–$45*

Frost, Robert. *The Complete Poems of Robert Frost.* Lon. (1951). dj. ....
....*$40–$50*

Frost, Robert. *A Further Range.* NY. 1936. ltd 803 cc, sgn. . .*$150–$275*

Frost, Robert. *In the Clearing.* NY. (1962). 1st ed. dj. . . . .*$35–$45*

Frost, Robert. *A Masque of Mercy.* NY. 1947. 1st ed. . . . .*$50–$85*

Frost, Robert. *A Masque of Reason.* NY. Henry Holt. (1945). 1st ed. dj. . .
. . . .*$50–$65*

Frost, Robert. *A Masque of Reason.* NY. Henry Holt. (1945). 1st ed.
inscrb, dj. *$450*

Frost, Robert. *New Hampshire.* NY. 1923. 1st ed. . . . .*$200–$300*

Frost, Robert. *A Witness Tree.* NY. (1942). 1st ed. dj. . . . .*$45–$60*

Frost, Stanley. *The Challenge of the Klan.* Ind. 1924. 1st ed. . . . .*$25–$40*

Fry, Benjamin St. James. *The Life of Rev. Willam M'Kendree.* NY. 1852.
. . . .*$12–$22*

Fry, Binyon, Siren, et al. *Chinese Art.* Lon. 1935. b/w and clr plates, dj. . .
. . . .*$42*

Fry, Christopher. *The Lady's Not for Burning.* Lon. 1949. dj. . . . .
. . . .*$30–$40*

Fry, J. Reese. *A Life of Gen. Zachary Taylor.* Phila. 1848. illus. . . . .
. . . .*$37–$45*

Fryer, Jane E. *The Mary Frances Cook Book.* Lon. 1912. 1st U.K. ed.
illus. . . . .*$35–$50*

Fryer, Jane E. *The Mary Frances Sewing Book.* Phila. 1913. 1st ed. illus.
patterns present. . . . .*$65–$100*

Fryer, Mary Ann. *John Fryer of the Bounty.* Lon. Golden Cockerel Press.
1939. illus. ltd #226/300 cc, sgn, colophon. . . . .*$325–$375*

Fuentes, Carlos. *Aura.* NY. 1965. 1st Eng ed. dj. . . . .*$75–$100*

Fuentes, Carlos. *The Old Gringo.* NY. 1985. 1st ed. 2nd ptg, dj. . . . .
. . . .*$20–$30*

Fugitives: The Story of Clyde Barrow and Bonnie Parker. Dallas. 1934.
1st ed. . . . .*$47–$65*

Fuhrer, Charles. *The Mysteries of Montreal.* . . . Montreal. 1881. 245 pp.
. . . .*$85–$100*

Fuller, Andrew. *The Grape Culturist.* NY. 1865. illus. . . . . . .*$100–$125*

Fuller, Andrew S. *The Grape Culturist.* NY. 1864. 1st ed. 262 pp. . . . . . .
. . . .*$75–$125*

Fuller, Buckminster. *Nine Chains to the Moon.* Phila. 1938. 1st ed.
author's first book, dj. . . . .*$75–$95*

Fuller, Buckminster. *Utopia or Oblivion.* Penguin Press. 1970. 1st U.K.
ed. dj. . . . .*$30–$50*

Fuller, Claude, and R. D. Steuart. *Firearms of the Confederacy.* Huntington, WV. 1944. . . . .*$135–$200*

Fuller, J. F. C. *The Generalship of Ulysses S. Grant.* NY. 1929. . . . .
. . . .*$37–$45*

Fulton, Frances I. Sims. *To and through Nebraska.* Lincoln. 1884. 1st ed. 273 pp. . . . .*$100–$145*

Fulton, James A. *Peach Culture.* NY. 1905. . . . .*$25–$50*

Furlong, Charles W. *Let 'er Buck.* NY. 1921. 1st ed. sgn. . . . . . .*$55–$65*

Furneaux, W. *British Butterflies and Moths.* Lon. 1911. plates. . . . .
. . . .*$45–$55*

Fuzzlebug, Fritz [John J. Dunkle]. *Prison Life During the Rebellion.* Singer's Glen, VA. 1869. 1st ed. wrps. . . . .*$95–$125*

Gade, John A. *Book Plates—Old and New.* NY. 1898. illus. . . . .*$25–$30*

Gaelic Fairy Tales. Glasgow. 1908. illus by Katherine Cameron. . . . .
. . . .*$30–$40*

Gag, Wanda. *Growing Pains.* Coward. 1940. 1st ed. illus. author's first book, 15 pp. dj. . . . .*$200–$300*

Gag, Wanda. *Millions of Cats.* Coward. 1928. 1st ed. illus by author, 15 pp, dj. . . . .*$200–$300*

Gage, S. H. *The Microscope.* Ithaca. Comstock Publishing. 1936. . . . .
. . . .*$40–$50*

Gage, W. L. *Palestine: Historical and Descriptive.* Bos. 1883. illus. . . . . . .
. . . .*$55–$95*

Gaines, G. T. *Fighting Tennesseans.* Kingsport. private ptg. 1931. . . .*$55*

Gallant, Mavis. *Across the Bridge.* NY. (1993). 1st ed. dj. . . . . . .*$18–$25*

Gallant, Mavis. *The Other Paris.* Bos. Houghton Mifflin. 1956. 1st ed. author's first book, dj. . . . .*$75–$85*

Gallaudet, Thomas. *Plan of a Seminary for the Education of Instructors of Youth.* Bos. Cummings, Hilliard & Co. 1825. 1st ed. illus. 39 pp. . . . . . .
. . . .*$75*

Gallico, Paul. *Ludmilla.* 1960. 4th impression, sgn and inscrb by Baron von Falz-Fein. *$75*

Gallico, Paul. *The Man Who Was Magic.* Garden City. Doubleday. 1966. 1st ed. dj. *$25*

Gallico, Paul. *Mrs. 'arris Goes to Paris.* NY. 1958. 1st ed. dj. . . . .
. . . .*$20–$40*

Gallico, Paul. *The Snow Goose.* 1941. 1st ed. dj. *$225*

Galsworthy, John. *Loyalties.* Scribner's. 1922. 1st U.S. ed. dj. *$60*

Galsworthy, John. *Maid in Waiting.* Lon. 1931. 1st ed. dj. . . . . .*$25–$50*

Galsworthy, John. *Memories.* NY. 1914. illus. . . . .*$30–$40*

Galsworthy, John. *A Modern Comedy.* Lon. Heinemann. 1930. 1st ed. ltd 1,030, sgn, inscrb, 1,039 pp, teg, full vellum, slipcase. *$125*

Galsworthy, John. *The Silver Spoon.* Lon. Heinemann. (1926). 1st ed. ltd 265 cc, sgn, 323 pp, dj. *$150*

Galsworthy, John. *Swan Song.* Lon. 1928. . . . .*$50–$75*

Gambling, Gaming Supplies. Chi. H. C. Evans Co. 1929. wrps. . . . .
. . . .*$85–$125*

Gambling World by Rouge et Noir. Dodd Mead. 1898. . . . .*$50–$65*

Gammon, Clive. *I Know a Good Place.* David R. Godine. dj. *$30*

Gammons, Rev. John G. *The Third Massachusetts Regiment Volunteer . . . 1861–1863.* Prov. 1906. 1st ed. illus. . . . .*$75–$100*

Gant, Richard. *Ian Fleming: The Fantastic 007 Man.* NY. Lancer. 1966. 1st ed. paperback original. *$65*

Gardi, R. *African Crafts and Craftsmen.* NY. 1969. 284 pp, clr and b/w photos. *$125*

Gardner, Erle Stanley. *The Case of the Grinning Gorilla.* Morrow. 1952. 1st ed. dj. . . . .*$25–$35*

Gardner, Erle Stanley. *The Case of the Lame Canary.* NY. William Morrow. 1937. 1st ed. dj. *$550*

Gardner, Erle Stanley. *The Case of the Screaming Woman.* NY. 1957. 1st ed. dj. . . . .*$35–$45*

Gardner, John. *In the Suicide Mountains.* NY. Knopf. 1977. 1st ed. dj. . . .
. . . .*$30–$35*

Gardner, John. *The King's Indian: Stories and Tales.* NY. Knopf. 1974. 1st ed. dj. . . . .*$35–$60*

Gardner, John. *The Life and Times of Chaucer.* NY. Knopf. 1977. 1st ed. dj. . . . .*$35–$45*

Gardner, John. *October Light.* Knopf. 1976. 1st ed. dj. . . . .*$45–$50*

Gardner, John. *The Sunlight Dialogues.* NY. 1972. 1st ed. dj. . .*$60–$70*

Garfield, V. E. *Meet the Totem.* Sitka. 1951. incrb. *$30*

Garland, H. *The Life of John Randolph of Roanoke.* NY. 1851. 2 vols. . . .
. . . .*$30–$40*

Garland, Hamlin. *Trail-makers of the Middle Border.* Macmillan. 1926. 1st ed. dj. . . . .*$25–$35*

Garner, T., and A. Stratton. *Domestic Architecture of England during the Tudor Period.* NY. (1929). 2 vols. 2nd ed. 210 plates. . . . . .*$150–$200*

Garnett, David. *First "Hippy" Revolution.* Cerrillos, NM. 1970. 1st ed. wrps. sgn. . . . .*$40–$50*

Garnett, Porter (ed). *Papers of San Francisco Vigilance Committee of 1851.* Berkeley. Univ. of California Press. 1910. wrps. . . . .*$40–$70*

Garrard, Lewis H. *Wah-To-Yah and the Taos Trail.* SF. Grabhorn Press. 1936. illus. ltd 550 cc. . . . .*$125–$140*

Garrison, Fielding H. *An Introduction to the History of Medicine.* Saunders. 1914. 763 pp. . . . .*$75–$100*

Garwood, Darrell. *Artist in Iowa: A Life of Grant Wood.* NY. W. W. Norton. 1944. 1st ed. illus. photos, dj. . . . .*$25–$30*

Gask, Norman. *Old Silver Spoons of England.* Lon. 1926. illus. rbnd, one quarter leather. . . . .*$75–$125*

Gass, William. *Omensetter's Luck.* (NY). New American Library. (1966). 1st ed. author's first novel, sgn, dj. . . . .*$225–$300*

Gass, William. *Omensetter's Luck.* (NY). New American Library. (1966). 1st ed. author's first novel, dj. . . . .*$150–$200*

Gass, William. *The Tunnel.* NY. Knopf. 1995. 1st ed. dj. . . . .*$30–$45*

Gass, William. *The World within the Word.* NY. Knopf. 1978. 1st ed. dj. . . . .*$34–$45*

Gaster, M. *Hebrew Illuminated Bibles of the 9th and 10th Centuries.* Lon. 1901. folio, plates. . . . .*$85–$125*

Gasthoff's Parade Floats and Decorations. Tampa, FL. Gasthoff's Display Service, Inc. 1937–38. pictorial wrps, illus, 24 pp. . . . .*$40–$50*

Gatty, Mrs. A. *The Book of Sun Dials.* Lon. 1872. 1st ed. illus. plates. . . . .*$100–$200*

Gay, John. *The Beggar's Opera.* Paris. 1937. illus. ltd #162/1,500 cc, slipcase. . . . .*$65–$75*

Gee, Ernest R. *Early American Sporting Books, 1734–1844.* NY. Derrydale Press. 1928. illus. 500 cc, sgn. . . . .*$85–$100*

Gee, Hugh, and Sally Gee. *Belinda and the Magic Journey.* NY. Chanticleer Press. 1948. dj. . . . .*$35–$45*

Geer, J. *Beyond the Lines, or A Yankee Prisoner Loose in Dixie.* Phila. 1863. 1st ed. illus. 285 pp. . . . .*$50–$75*

Geer, Walter. *Campaigns of the Civil War.* 1926. 1st ed. . . . .*$75–$130*

Genet, Jean. *The Book of the Dance.* Bos. 1920. dj. . . . .*$40–$55*

Genthe, Arnold. *Old Chinatown.* NY. 1908. 2nd ed. . . . .*$80–$100*

The German Pharmacopoeia. Phila. 1873. 1st Eng language trans. . . . . . .
. . . .*$75*

Georgia Scenes, by a Native Georgian. NY. 1840. illus. 2nd ed. . . . .
. . . .*$100–$195*

Gernsbach, Hugo. *Radio for All.* 1922. 1st ed. illus. . . . .*$30–$40*

Gernsbach, Hugo. *Ralph 124C41+ A Romance of the Year 2660.* 1925.
1st ed. . . . .*$175–$245*

Gerstaecker, Frederick. *Western Lands and Western Waters.* Lon. 1864.
1st ed. illus. 388 pp. *$45*

Gerstaecker, Frederick. *The Wanderings and Fortunes of Some German
Immigrants.* NY. 1948. . . . .*$95–$250*

Gerstaecker, Frederick. *Wild Sports in the Far West.* Bos. Crosby,
Nichols. 1859. . . . .*$55*

Gerstaecker, Frederick. *Wild Sports of the Far West.* NY. 1884. . . . .
. . . .*$35–$55*

Gertsch, W. J. *American Spiders.* NY. 1949. dj. . . . .*$15–$25*

Gharpurey, K. G. *The Snakes of India and Pakistan.* Bombay, 1954. . . . .
. . . .*$25–$35*

Gibran, Kahlil. *The Prophet.* 1966. illus. 10th ptg. . . . .*$24–$30*

Gibson, Charles Dana. *The Gibson Book.* NY. 1907. 2 vols. . . . .
. . . .*$125–$175*

Gibson. W. B. *The Book of Secrets.* 1927. 1st ed. dj. . . . .
. . . .*$175–$200*

Gibson, W. H. *Our Edible Toadstools and Mushrooms.* NY. 1895. illus. .
. . . .*$85–$125*

Gibson, William Hamilton. *Our Native Orchids.* NY. 1905. . . . .
. . . .*$50–$65*

The Gift: A Christmas, New Year and Birthday Present. Phila. Carey &
Hart. 1845. 1st ed. first issue, illus. . . . .*$200–$275*

Gilbert, William. *On the Magnet.* NY. (1958). rprnt, illus. . . . . .*$75–$95*

Gilder, Wm. H. *Schwatka's Search.* 1st ed. decorative cloth. *$75*

Giles, Herbert A. *A Chinese English Dictionary.* 1912. 2nd ed. rev. . . . . .
. . . .*$120–$160*

Giles, Rosean A. *Shasta County California.* CA. 1949. 1st ed. illus. map,
ltd 1000 cc. . . . .*$50–$60*

Gill, Emlyn M. *Practical Dry-fly Fishing.* Scribner's. *$95*

Gill, Sir William. *Pompeiana: The Topography, Edifices and Ornaments
of Pompeii.* Lon. 1835. 2 vols. illus. . . . .*$300–$400*

Gillespie, W. Bro. Nelson. *History of Apollo Lodge No. 13 . . . Troy, N.Y.* NY. 1886. illus. plates. .... *$30–$40*

Gillette, Mrs. F. L. *White House Cook Book.* Chi. 1889. .... *$65–$85*

Gilman, Arthur (ed). *The Cambridge of Eighteen Hundred and Ninety-six.* Camb. 1896. illus. 424 pp. .... *$25–$35*

Gilman, Caroline. *Recollections of a Southern Matron.* NY. Harper. 1838. 272 pp. .... *$125–$200*

Gilman, Charlotte Perkins [Stetson]. *Concerning Children.* Bos. Small, Maynard. 1901. 2nd ed. 298 pp. *$250*

Gilman, Charlotte Perkins. *The Home.* NY. McClure, Phillips. 1903. 1st ed. 290 pp. brown paper dj, rare. *$350*

Ginsberg, Allen. *Bixby Canyon, Ocean Path, Word Breeze.* Botham. 1972. sgn, ltd ed. 1/100 cc. .... *$100–$125*

Ginsberg, Allen. *The Fall of America.* SF. 1972. wrps. .... *$20–$30*

Ginsberg, Allen. *Planet News.* CA. City Lights. 1968. wrps. 1st U.S. ed. dj. *$35*

Ginsberg, Allen. *Reality Sandwiches.* 1963. 1st ed. wrps. ...... *$35–$45*

Ginsberg, Allen. *White Shroud: Poems 1980–1985.* NY. Harper & Row. (1986). 1st ed. dj. *$35*

Ginzburg, R. *An Unhurried View of Erotica.* NY. 1958. slipcase. .... *$25–$35*

Ginzburg, Ralph. *Castrated: My Eight Months in Prison.* Avant-Garde Books. 1973. 1st ed. dj. *$40*

Gissing, George. *The Crown of Life.* Lon. Methuen. 1899. 1st ed. . . . *$125*

Glackens, Ira. *William Glackens and the Ashcan Group.* NY. 1957. illus. .... *$20–$25*

Gladstone, J. H. *Michael Faraday.* Lon. 1874. 2nd ed. repairs. . . *$22–$35*

Glasgow, Ellen. *Phases of an Inferior Planet.* NY/Lon. Harper & Bros. 1898. 1st ed. *$100*

Glasser, Otto. *Dr. Wilhelm C. Roentgen.* 1934. 1st Eng. ed. dj. . . *$45–$60*

Glazier, Capt. Willard. *Down the Great River.* Phila. 1893. .... *$25–$35*

Glazier, Capt. Willard. *Headwaters of the Mississippi.* NY. 1893. .... *$35–$50*

Glenister, A. G. *Birds of the Malay Peninsula.* Oxford Univ. Press. 1951. illus. dj. .... *$35–$55*

Glidden Patent Two Point and Four Point Barb Wire Fencing. Worcester, MA. Washburn & Moen Manufacturing Co. 1880. illus. pictorial wrps. *$1,215*

Glob, P. V. *The Bog People.* Ithaca. Cornell Univ. Press. (1970). 2nd ptg. photos, maps, dj. . . . . *$18–$25*

The Gloucester Directory, 1899–1900. MA. 1899. bds. . . . .*$45–$55*

Goddard, Henry Herbert. *The Kallikak Family.* NY. 1916. . . . .*$25–$35*

Godwin, Gail. *Glass People.* NY. 1972. 1st ed. dj. . . . .*$45–$60*

Goebbels, Joseph. *Kampf um Berlin.* München. 1938. illus. . . . .*$24–$30*

Goerg, Alfred J. *Pacific and Northwest Hunting.* NY. 1952. 1st ed. dj. . . . .*$15–$22*

Gold, Herbert. *Fathers.* NY. 1966. 1st ed. dj. . . . .*$18–$28*

Gold, Herbert. *Love and Like.* NY. 1960. 1st ed. sgn, presentation copy, dj. . . . .*$40–$65*

Goldberg, R. *Rube Goldberg's Guide to Europe.* NY. 1954. 1st ed. presentation copy, sgn. . . . .*$30–$45*

Goldenberg, Samuel. *Lace: Its Origin and History.* NY. 1904. 1st ed. illus. presentation copy. . . . .*$50–$85*

Golding, Louis. *Luigi of Catanzaro.* Lon. E. Archer. 1926. 1st ed. 1/100cc, sgn, folder with gold-stamped titles. *$350*

Golding, William. *An Egyptian Journal.* Faber. 1985. 1st ed. dj. *$30*

Golding, William. *The Hot Gates and Other Occasional Pieces.* Lon. Faber & Faber. (1965). 1st ed. dj. *$60*

Golding, William. *The Pyramid.* Faber. 1967. 1st ed. dj. . . . .*$45–$60*

Golding, William. *The Pyramid.* Harcourt. 1967. 1st U.S. ed. dj. . . . .*$28–$35*

Goldman, Emma. *My Disillusionment in Russia.* Lon. 1925. 1st U.K. ed. 263 pp, red cloth, paper label, sgn. *$250*

Goldman, Emma. *The Place of the Individual in Society.* Chi. Free Society Forum. nd. wrps. . . . .*$35–$45*

Goldman, Emma. *The Social Significance of the Modern Drama.* Bos. 1914. . . . .*$30–$67*

Goldsmith, Alfred N. *Radio Telephony.* NY. Wireless Press. (1918). 1st ed. 247 pp, illus. . . . .*$50–$75*

Goldsmith, Oliver. *The Vicar of Wakefield.* Lon. J. M. Dent. (c 1910). illus. aeg, bound by Sangorski & Sutcliffe. . . . .*$100–$150*

Goldsmith, Oliver. *The Vicar of Wakefield.* McKay. 1929. illus by Arthur Rackham, clr plates. . . . .*$75–$125*

Goldstrom, John. *A Narrative History of Aviation.* NY. 1930. 1st ed. illus. . . . .*$65–$85*

Goldwater, Barry. *Arizona.* 1978. 1st ed. dj. ....$28–$35

Goldwater, Barry. *The Face of Arizona.* np. 1964. 1st ed. ltd #769/1,000 cc, sgn. ....$125–$180

Goldwater, Barry. *A Journey Down the Green and Colorado Rivers.* Tempe. 1970. illus. photos, dj. ....$35–$45

Gommez, R. *Cake Decoration: Flower and Classic Piping.* Lon. 1899. .. ..$65–$90

The Good Cook, by a Practical Housekeeper. NY. 1853. ....$55–$65

Goodison, N. *English Barometers 1680–1860....* Lon. 1969. illus. 1st U.K. ed. plates. ....$50–$60

Goodman, Paul. *The Breakup of Our Camp.* NY. 1949. dj. .....$25–$35

Goodman, Paul. *Compulsory Mis-education.* NY. 1964. dj. ....$20–$25

Goodman, Paul. *Hawkweed.* Random House. 1967. 1st ed. dj. ....$16–$20

Goodrich, Samuel Griswold. *History of the Indians of North and South America.* NY. 1844. 1st ed. illus. ....$45–$60

Goodrich, Samuel Griswold. *Recollections of a Lifetime.* NY. 1851. 2 vols. ....$95–$250

Goodrich, Ward L. *The Modern Clock.* Chi. 1905. 1st ed. illus. ....$40–$55

Goodrich-Freer, A. *Things Seen in Palestine.* NY. 1913. ......$45–$65

Goodwin, C. C. *The Wedge of Gold.* Salt Lake City. 1893. 1st ed. ....$50–$65

Goodwin, Grace A. *Anti-suffrage.* NY. Duffield. 1913. 1st ed. 143 pp, inscrb. $65

Goodwin, Grace Duffield. *Anti-suffrage: Ten Good Reasons.* NY. 1913. .. ..$25–$35

Goody, J. *Death, Property and the Ancestors.* Stanford. 1962. illus. ....$25–$35

Goodyear, W. A. *The Coal Mines of the Western Coast of the United States.* SF. 1877. 1st ed. 153 pp. ....$75–$125

Goor, A., and M. Nurock. *The Fruits of the Holy Land.* Jerusalem. 1968. dj. ....$25–$30

Gorbachev, Mikhail. *Perestroika Is the Concern of All Soviet Peoples.* Moscow. 1989. wrps. 1st English-language ed. ....$40–$50

Gordimer, Nadine. *Burger's Daughter.* Lon. 1979. ....$20–$28

Gordimer, Nadine. *July's People.* Lon. Jonathan Cape. (1981). 1st ed. $50

Gordimer, Nadine. *Occasion for Loving.* NY. (1963). 1st Amer ed. dj. ..
....*$25–$35*

Gordimer, Nadine. *The Soft Voice of the Serpent.* NY. 1952. 1st Amer ed.
dj. ....*$40–$55*

Gordimer, Nadine. *Something out There.* NY. Viking. 1984. 1st U.S. ed.
sgn, dj. ....*$50–$65*

Gordimer, Nadine. *Something out There.* NY. 1984. 1st U.S. ed. dj. ....
....*$35–$50*

Gordon, A. C., and Page Thomas Nelson. *Befo' de War—Echoes in Negro Dialect.* NY. 1888. ....*$40–$50*

Gordon, Armistead Churchill. *Jefferson Davis.* Scribner's. 1918. 1st ed.
....*$40–$50*

Gordon, Elizabeth. *Bird Children.* Volland. (1912). illus. ......*$85–$95*

Gordon, Elizabeth. *Flower Children.* Volland. (1910). illus. bds. ....
....*$75–$95*

Gordon, Elizabeth. *Really-so Stories.* Joliet. (1924). 1st ed. illus. ....
....*$40–$50*

Gordon, John B. *Reminiscences of the Civil War.* NY. 1904. ..*$80–$125*

Gordon, Mary. *The Company of Women.* NY. 1980. 1st ed. dj, sgn. .....
....*$30–$40*

Gordon, Mary. *Temporary Shelter.* NY. Random House. 1987. 1st ed. dj.
....*$18–$25*

Gordon, T. *A Gazetteer of the State of Pennsylvania.* Phila. 1832. 1st ed.
lea..*$65–$85*

Gordon, T. F. *Gazetteer of the State of New Jersey.* Trenton. 1834. 2 vols
in 1. map...*$175–$250*

Goren, Charles. *The Sports Illustrated Book of Bridge.* NY. 1961. illus. dj,
slipcase. ....*$50–$70*

Gorey, Edward. *The Black Doll.* NY. Gotham Book Mart. 1973. 1st ed.
black wrps. *$60*

Gorey, Edward. *The Blue Aspic.* Meredith Press. 1968. 1st ed. dj. ...*$85*

Gorey, Edward. *Dracula: A Toy Theatre.* Scribner's. 1979. folio, spiral
bound. ....*$50–$100*

Gorey, Edward. *The Unstrung Harp.* Duell. 1953. 1st ed. author's first
book, dj. ....*$150–$300*

Gorey, Edward. *Utter Zoo Alphabet.* NY. Meredith Press. (1967). 1st ed.
dj. *$40*

Gorey, Edward. *The Vinegar Works.* NY. 1963. 3 vols. 1st ed. .*$75–$125*

Gorey, Edward. *The Water Flowers.* NY. Congdon & Weed. (1982). 1st ed. sgn, dj. $45

Gorki, Maxim. *Bystander.* NY. Jonathan Cape & Harrison Smith. (c 1930). 1st Amer ed. dj. $75

Gorky, Maxim. *The Judge.* McBride. 1924. 1st ed. ....$30–$40

Gorrie, P. Douglas. *Black River and Northern New York Conference Memorial—2nd Ser.* Watertown. 1881. ....$35–$55

Gotham's Pageant of Games and Toys. NY. Gotham Pressed Steel Corp. illus. pictorial wrps, 36 pp. ....$75–$100

Gough, John B. *Sunlight and Shadow, or Gleanings from My Life Work.* Hartford. 1881. illus. 542 pp. $25

Goulart, Ron. *Skyrocket Steele Conquers the Universe and Other Media Tales.* Eugene, OR. (1990). 1st ed. 300 cc, sgn, dj. ....$20–$30

Gould, E. *The Housing of the Working People.* DC. GPO. 1895. illus. ... .$24–$35

Gould, Grace Margaret. *The Magic of Dress.* Garden City. 1911. 1st ed. presentation copy, illus, inscrb. $75

Gould, J. *The Birds of Great Britain.* Lon. 1873. 5 vols. illus. large folio, 367 clr plates. ....$50,000–$75,000

Gould, J. *A Century of Birds from the Himalaya Mountains.* Lon. 1832. 1st ed. illus. large folio, 80 hand-clr plates. ....$7,800–$10,000

Gould, J. *Handbook to the Birds of Australia.* Lon. 1865. 2 vols. ....$200–$300

Gould, J. *Toucans.* Lon. 1852–54. folio, 51 hand-clr plates. ....$25,000–$30,000

Gould, Marcus. *Report of the Trial of Friends.* Phila. 1829. one-fourth mor. ....$95–$150

Gould, R. T. *The Case for the Sea Serpent.* Lon. 1930. illus. ....$55–$95

Graebner, Theodore. *Church Bells in the Forest: A Story of Lutheran Pioneer Work on the Michigan Frontier, 1840–1850.* St. Louis. Concordia. 1944. wrps. illus. 98 pp. ....$28–$40

Graffagnino, J. K. *The Shaping of Vermont.* Rutland. 1983. illus. 147 pp, dj. ....$40–$50

Grafton, Sue. *"A" Is for Alibi.* NY. Holt. 1982. 1st ed. dj. ....$900–$1,000

Grafton, Sue. *"C" Is for Corpse.* NY. 1986. 1st ed. dj. ......$225–$300

Grafton, Sue. *"E" Is for Evidence.* NY. Holt. 1988. 1st ed. sgn, dj. .$225

Grafton, Sue. *"E" Is for Evidence.* NY. Holt. 1988. 1st ed. dj. . . . .
. . . .*$75–$150*

Grafton, Sue. *"F" Is for Fugitive.* NY. Holt. 1989. 1st ed. sgn, dj. . . . . . .
. . . .*$75*

Grafton, Sue. *"F" Is for Fugitive.* NY. Holt. 1989. 1st ed. dj. . . . .
. . . .*$45–$60*

Grafton, Sue. *"H" Is for Homicide.* NY. Holt. 1991. 1st ed. dj. . . . .
. . . .*$25–$30*

Grafton, Sue. *"I" Is for Innocent.* NY. Holt. 1993. 1st ed. sgn, dj. . . .*$45*

Grafton, Sue. *"J" Is for Judgment.* NY. Holt. (1993). 1st ed. dj. *$35*

Grafton, Sue. *"K" Is for Killer.* NY. Holt. (1994). 1st ed. 285 pp, dj. . . . .
. . . .*$35*

Grafton, Sue. *Keziah Dane.* NY. Macmillan. 1967. 1st ed dj. *$450*

Graham, Col. W. A. *The Custer Myth.* Harrisburg. (1953). 1st ed. illus. dj.
. . . .*$50–$65*

Graham, D. M. *The Life of Clement Phinney.* Dover. 1851. . . . .
. . . .*$20–$30*

Graham, Stephen. *Through Russian Central Asia.* Lon. 1916. illus. fldg
map, photos. . . . .*$30–$40*

Graham, W. A. *Custer's Battle Flags: The Colors of the Seventh at the
Little Big Horn.* np. private ptg. 1952. illus. 1st separate ed. #102/300 cc,
sgn. *$125*

Grahame, Kenneth. *Dream Days.* Lon. 1902. illus by Maxfield Parrish,
2,228 pp. . . . .*$95–$130*

Grahame, Kenneth. *The Golden Age.* Lon/NY. 1990. illus by Maxfield
Parrish. . . . .*$85–$100*

Grahame, Kenneth. *The Wind in the Willows.* Scribner's. 1908. 1st Amer
ed. . . . .*$150–$250*

Grainge, William. *Daemonologia: Discourse on Witchcraft.* Harrogate.
1882. . . . .*$30–$40*

Grand, Gordon. *Old Man and Other Colonel Weatherford Stories.* Derrydale. 1934. 1st Amer ed. . . . .*$45–$60*

Grand, Gordon. *The Silver Horn.* NY. 1932. illus. 1/950 cc. . . . .
. . . .*$75–$130*

Grand Union Grille Works. Chi. 1911. wrps. architectural cat. . . . .
. . . .*$38–$45*

Grant, Anne. *Memoirs of an American Lady.* NY. 1809. 2nd ed. 344 pp. .
. . . .*$125*

Grant, B. C. *Taos Today.* Taos. 1925. photos. ....$75–$150

Grant, Blanche C. (ed). *Kit Carson's Own Story of His Life.* Taos. 1926. softbound. ....$75–$125

Grant, Douglas. *The Fortunate Slave: An Illustration of African Slavery.* . . . Lon. 1968. 1st ed. dj. ....$33–$45

Grant, George Monro (ed). *Picturesque Canada: The Country as It Was and Is.* Tor. 1882. 1st ed. mor, engr. ....$125–$200

Grant, Madison. *The Passing of the Great Race, or The Racial Basis of European History.* Scribner's. 1923. 4th rev ed. 476 pp. ....$35–$50

Grant, Ulysses S. *Personal Memoirs of U.S. Grant.* NY. 1885. 2 vols. 1st ed. ....$50–$85

Grant, Ulysses S. *Report of Lt.-General U.S. Grant . . . 1864–65.* NY. 1865. wrps. ....$75–$90

Grass, Günter. *Local Anaesthetic.* (1970). 1st ed. dj. ....$26–$30

Grau, Shirley Ann. *The Black Prince.* NY. Knopf. 1955. 1st ed. author's first book, sgn, dj. ....$75–$100

Graves, A. P. *That Railroad Man.* Phila. 1900. 1st ed. $25

Graves, Jackson A. *My Seventy Years in California, 1857–1927.* Los Angeles, Times-Mirror. 1927. ....$60–$85

Graves, Robert. *Collected Poems.* Garden City. Doubleday. 1961. 1st ed. dj. ....$20–$30

Graves, Robert. *Poems.* Lon. Cassell & Co. (1953). 1st ed. dj. $50

Graves, Robert. *The Islands of Unwisdom.* Garden City. Doubleday. 1949. 1st ed. dj. ....$50–$75

Graves, Robert J. *Clinical Lectures on the Practice of Medicine.* Lon. 1884. 2 vols. ....$20–$35

Gray, Asa. *First Lessons in Botany and Vegetable Physiology.* Ivison & Phinney. 1857. 236 pp. ....$100–$135

Gray, Asa. *Gray's Botanical Text-book.* (6th ed). American Book Co. 1879. 2 vols. ....$60–$85

Gray, Asa. *Introduction to Structural and Systematic Botany.* NY. 1860. 5th ed. ....$25–$32

Gray, M. D. *How Plants Grow.* NY/Cinc. American Book Co. c 1858. illus. 500 wood engr. $145

Gray, W., et al. *The New Fun with Dick and Jane.* Scott. 1940. ....
....$38–$50

Gray, W., et al. *The New Fun with Dick and Jane.* Scott. 1946–47. ....
....$30–$45

Gray, W., et al. *The New Fun with Dick and Jane.* Scott. 1951. . . . .
. . . .*$28–$35*

Gray, W. H. *A History of Oregon, 1792–1849.* . . . Portland. 1870. 1st ed.
. . . .*$175–$225*

Great Northwest: A Guide Book and Itinerary. St. Paul. 1889. illus. fldg
map, engr. . . . .*$37–$45*

Greeley, Horace. *History of the Struggles for Slavery.* NY. 1856. 1st ed.
wrps. . . . .*$75–$100*

Greely, Adophus W. *Three Years of Arctic Service.* NY. Scribner's. 1886.
2 vols. 1st ed. illus. 428 pp, illus, pocket maps, frontis, full lea. . . . .
. . . .*$175–$250*

Green, Arthur R. *Sundials, Incised Dials, or Mass Clocks.* NY/Tor. 1926.
1st ed. illus. . . . .*$35–$45*

Green, Calvin, and Seth Y. Wells. *A Brief Exposition of . . . the Shakers.*
NY. 1851. . . . .*$115–$150*

Green, Edwin L. *The Indians of South Carolina.* Columbia, SC. (1904).
1st ed. . . . .*$55–$75*

Greenaway, Kate. *Kate Greenaway's Alphabet.* Lon. George Routledge
& Sons. 1885. . . . .*$100*

Greene, Graham. *19 Stories.* NY. Viking. 1949. 1st ed. dj. *$125*

Greene, Graham. *The Confidential Agent: An Entertainment.* Lon.
William Heinemann. (1939). 1st ed. *$75*

Greene, Graham. *The Human Factor.* Lon. 1978. 1st U.K. ed. . . . .
. . . .*$35–$65*

Greene, Graham. *The Man Within: A Play in Two Acts.* Lon. William
Heinemann. (1929). 1st ed. *$100*

Greene, Graham. *The Ministry of Fear: An Entertainment.* Lon. William
Heinemann. (1942). 1st ed. *$65*

Greene, Graham. *Our Man in Havana.* NY. 1958. 1st U.S. ed. dj. . . . . . .
. . . .*$45–$75*

Greene, Graham. *Our Man in Havana.* Lon. 1958. dj. . . . .*$85–$100*

Greene, Graham. *Travels with My Aunt.* 1969. 1st U.K. ed. dj. . . . .
. . . .*$20–$30*

Greene, Grahame. *This Gun Is for Hire.* NY. Doubleday Doran. 1936. 1st
Amer ed. no dj. . . . .*$100–$125*

Greenwood, Grace. *New Life in New Lands.* NY. 1873. 413 pp. . . . .
. . . .*$30–$45*

Gregg, E. C. *How to Tie Flies.* Barnes. 1940. 1st ed. dj. *$20*

Gregor, J. *Masks of the World.* NY. 1958. reissue. *$150*

Gremillion, Nelson. *Company G, 1st Regiment, Louisiana Cavalry, CSA.* np. private ptg. 1986. 1st ed. . . . .*$35–$65*

Grenfell, Wilfred. *Adrift on an Ice Pan.* Bos. (1909). 1st ed. 69 pp, sgn. *$50*

Grenfell, Wilfred. *Down North on Labrador.* Chi. 1911. 1st ed. illus. . . . .*$20–$30*

Grenfell, Wilfred. *Forty Years for Labrador.* NY. 1932. presentation copy, sgn, dj. . . . .*$45–$60*

Grenfell, Wilfred. *Labrador.* NY. 1922. . . . .*$35–$45*

Grenfell, Wilfred. *A Labrador Doctor.* NY. 1919. illus. original sketch on flyleaf by author. . . . .*$65–$95*

Grey, Zane. *Arizona Ames.* Grosset & Dunlap. 1932. rprnt, dj. . . . .*$7–$9*

Grey, Zane. *The Desert of Wheat.* Grosset & Dunlap. 1919. rprnt, dj. . . . .*$10–$15*

Grey, Zane. *Forlorn River.* Grosset & Dunlap. 1927. rprnt, dj. . . . .*$20–$35*

Grey, Zane. *Riders of the Purple Sage.* Grosset & Dunlap. 1940. rprnt, dj. . . . .*$10–$14*

Grey, Zane. *Tales of Fishing Virgin Seas.* Harper. (1925). 1st ed. illus. . . . .*$70–$95*

Grey, Zane. *Tales of Fresh-water Fishing.* NY. 1928. 1st ed. . . . .*$125–$200*

Grey, Zane. *Tales of Lonely Trails.* 1922. 1st ed. no dj. *$85*

Grey, Zane. *Tales of Southern Rivers.* Grosset & Dunlap. rprnt, dj. . . . .*$30–$50*

Grey, Zane. *Tales of the Angler's Eldorado.* NY. Grosset & Dunlap. 1926. illus. photos, dj. . . . .*$45–$75*

Grey, Zane. *The Red Headed Outfield.* NY. 1915. dj. . . . .*$14–$18*

Grey, Zane. *The Shepherd of Guadaloupe.* Grosset & Dunlap. 1930. rprnt, dj. . . . .*$45–$60*

Grey, Zane. *The Thundering Herd.* NY. 1925. 1st ed. dj. . . . . . .*$35–$100*

Gridley, A. D. *History of the Town of Kirkland.* NY. 1874. sgn. . . . .*$45–$55*

Griffin, J. H. *Church and the Black Man.* 1969. wrps. illus. . . . . .*$20–$25*

Griffin, S. G. *A History of the Town of Keene from 1732 to 1874.* Keene. 1904. half lea, 3 fldg maps, plates. . . . .*$50–$70*

Griffis, William Elliot. *Corea, the Hermit Nation.* NY. 1882. illus. map. .
....$75–$150

Grimm Bros. *Little Brother and Little Sister, and Other Tales.* Lon. (1917). illus by Arthur Rackham. ....$100–$200

Grinnel, J., H. C. Bryant, and T. I. Storer. *The Game Birds of California.* Berkeley. 1918. illus. dj. ....$175–$350

Grinnell, G. *American Duck Shooting.* NY. 1901. ....$45–$65

Grinnell, George Bird. *Blackfoot Lodge Tales.* NY. 1892. 1st ed.$50–$85

Grinnell, George Bird. *Blackfoot Lodge Tales.* NY. 1913. .....$30–$45

Grinnell, George Bird. *The Fighting Cheyennes.* NY. Scribner's. 1915. 1st ed. maps. $125

Grinnell, George Bird. *The Indians of Today.* NY. 1915. 3rd ptg, plates. .
....$45–$75

Grinnell, George Bird. *Two Great Scouts and the Pawnee Battalion.* Glendale. Arthur H. Clark Co. 1928. 1st ed. $200

Griscom, John H. *The Use of Tobacco and the Evils, Physical, Mental, Moral and Social, Resulting Therefrom.* NY. Putnam. 1868. 1st ed. wrps. 37 pp, scarce...$80–$100

Grisham, John. *The Chamber.* NY. Doubleday. (1994). 1/350 cc, sgn, nbr, slipcase. $150

Grisham, John. *The Firm.* NY. Doubleday. 1991. 1st ed. dj. $250

Grisham, John. *A Time to Kill.* Tarrytown. Wynwood Press. 1989. 1st ed. author's first book, dj. ....$1,200–$1,500

Griswold, Freeman C. *Canadian Excursion, Summer of 1885.* MA. 1885. wrps. ....$15–$25

Groot, Roy A. (ed). *The Hive and the Honey Bee.* Dadant. 1949. $25–$35

Gross, H. I. *Antique and Classic Cameras.* NY. 1965. 1st ed. illus. dj. ...
....$35–$50

Grover, Eulalie Osgood. *The Overall Boys.* Rand McNally. (1905). 1st ed. illus..$60–$80

Grover, Eulalie Osgood. *The Sunbonnet Babies Book.* NY. 1902. ......
....$50–$70.

Grover, Eulalie Osgood. *The Sunbonnet Babies Book.* Rand McNally. 1928. illus...$25–$35

Gruelle, Johnny. *Friendly Fairies.* Volland. (1919). illus. by author. ....
....$50–$75

Gruelle, Johnny. *Raggedy Ann Stories.* Volland. (1918). 1st ed. illus.....
....$50–$70

A Guide to the Birds of South America. Wynnewood. 1970. dj. . . . .
. . . .*$75–$100*

Guillemin, Amedee. *The Heavens: An Illustrated Handbook of Popular Astronomy.* Lon. Bentley. 1868. 3rd ed. 503 pp, clr litho. . . . .
. . . .*$60–$85*

Gump, Richard. *Jade, Stone of Heaven.* Garden City. 1962. 1st ed. illus. map, dj. *$48*

Gun Cotton and Its Uses. Lon. illus. . . . .*$25–$45*

Gunnison, J. W. *The Mormons.* Phila. 1852. 1st ed. . . . .
. . . .*$150–$200*

Gunther, R. T. *Historic Instruments for the Advancement of Science.* Humphrey Milford. 1925. glassine wrps. . . . .*$25–$45*

Gussow, H. T., and W. S. Odell. *Mushrooms and Toadstools.* Ottawa. 1927. 1st ed. illus. . . . .*$27–$38*

Guthrie, A. B. *The Big Sky.* NY. Sloane. (1947). 1st ed. dj. . . . .
. . . .*$135*

Guthrie, A. B. *The Blue Hen's Chick.* (1965). 1st ed. dj. . . . .
. . . .*$25–$35*

Haggard, H. Rider. *Ayesha.* NY. 1905. 1st Amer ed. . . . .*$50–$70*

Haggard, H. Rider. *Dr. Therne.* Lon. 1898. 1st ed. . . . .*$100–$145*

Haggard. H. Rider. *Lysbeth: A Tale of the Dutch.* NY/Lon/Bombay. 1901. illus. . . . .*$95–$100*

Haggard, H. Rider. *Maiwa's Revenge.* Lon. 1888. 1st ed. . . . .
. . . .*$50–$115*

Haggard, H. Rider. *Regeneration.* Lon. Longmans. 1910. 1st ed. . . . .
. . . .*$50–$75*

Haggard, H. Rider. *When the World Shook.* Longmans Green. 1919. 1st ed. . . . .*$50–$75*

Haggard, Howard W. *Mystery, Magic, and Medicine.* Garden City. 1933. 1st ed. illus. . . . .*$25–$35*

Haggard, Howard W. *The Lame, the Halt, and the Blind.* Lon. 1932. 1st ed. illus. . . . .*$25–$35*

Haig-Brown, Roderick. *The Western Angler.* Morrow. 1947. . . . .
. . . .*$25–$35*

Haines, Elijah M. *The American Indian (Uh-Nish-In-Na-Ba).* Chi. The Ma-sin-na'-gan Company. 1888. 1st ed. illus. . . . .*$75–$125*

Haines, Francis. *The Nez Percees.* Univ. of Oklahoma Press. (1955). 1st ed. dj. . . . .*$50–$75*

Hale, Edward E. *Stories of Invention.* Bos. 1885. . . . .*$14–$22*

Hale, Edwin M. *A Systematic Treatise on Abortion.* Chi. 1866. illus. clr plates. . . . .*$65–$95*

Hale, Lucretia. *Alone in Rome.* Rome. Gould Memorial Home. 1883. 27 pp, light orange wrps, tipped-in slip. *$60*

Haley, Alex. *Roots.* Doubleday. 1976. 1st ed. dj. . . . .*$40–$100*

Hall, Albert Neely. *The Wonderful Hill.* Chi. Rand McNally. (1914). 1st ed. illus. by Norman Hall. . . . .*$100–$135*

Hall, Capt. Charles Francis. *Narrative of the North Polar Expedition.* DC. GPO. 1876. 1st ed. illus. maps. . . . .*$120–$150*

Hall, Donald. *Exile.* Oxon. Fantasy Press. (1952). 1st ed. printed gray wrps. *$200*

Hall, Donald. *Life Work.* Bos. Beacon Press. (1993). 1st ed. dj. . . . .*$24–$30*

Hall, Donald. *The Yellow Room.* NY. Harper & Row. (1971). 1st ed. sgn, dj. . . . .*$40–$50*

Hall, Fred S. *Sympathetic Strikes and Sympathetic Lockouts.* NY. 1898. softbound. . . . .*$35–$45*

Hall, Henry. *Ethan Allen: The Robin Hood of Vermont.* NY. Appleton. 1897. . . . .*$22.50–$35*

Hall, Hiland. *History of Vermont.* Albany. 1868. 1st ed. inscr. . . . .*$100–$125*

Hall, James W. *Tropical Freeze.* NY. W. W. Norton. 1989. 1st ed. sgn, dj. *$45*

Hall, Radclyffe. *The Well of Loneliness.* NY. Covici Friede. 1929. 2 vols. Victory ed. #157/201 cc, sgn, publisher's box, rare. *$600*

Hall, Radclyffe. *The Well of Loneliness.* Lon. 1928. 1st ed. dj. . . . .*$250–$350*

Hall, Thomas F. *Has the North Pole Been Discovered?* Bos. Richard G. Badger. 1st ed. photos, charts, maps, dj. . . . .*$70–$90*

Halliday, Andrew. *Observations on Emphysema.* . . . Lon. 1807. bds. *$150*

Halliday, Samuel B. *The Lost and Found, or Life Among the Poor.* NY. Phinney, Blakeman & Mason. 1860. 1st ed. 356 pp. *$250*

Hallock, Charles. *Camp Life in Florida: A Handbook for Sportsmen and Settlers.* NY. 1876. . . . .*$35–$50*

Hallowell, A. Irving. *The Role of Conjuring in Saulteaux Society.* Univ. of Pennsylvania Pr. 1942. 1st ed. waxine dj. . . . .*$25–$35*

Halsey, E. W. *The Pioneers of Unadilla Village.* Unadilla, NY. 1902. ltd 650 cc. . . . .*$45–$55*

Halsey, Margaret. *Color Blind: A White Woman Looks at the Negro.* NY. 1946. . . . .*$20–$30*

Halstead, B. W. *Poisonous and Venemous Marine Animals of the World.* DC. 1965. 3 vols. illus. *$275*

Halstead, W. C. *Brain and Intelligence: A Quantitative Study of Frontal Lobes.* Chi. 1947. 1st ed dj. . . . .*$100–$125*

Haluck, Paul. *Harness Making.* Phila. 1904. . . . .*$35–$40*

Hamerton, Philip G. *The Saone: A Summer Voyage.* Lon. 1887. illus. maps. . . . .*$50–$65*

Hamilton, Robert. *The Gospel among the Redmen.* Nashville. 1930. wrps. . . . .*$50–$65*

Hamilton, William T. *My Sixty Years on the Plains. . . .* NY. 1905. 1st ed. illus. . . . .*$150–$175*

Hammerton, Philip. *The Etcher's Handbook.* Lon. 1875. illus. 2nd ed. . . . .*$50–$75*

Hammett, Dashiell. *The Big Knockover.* NY. Random House. (1966). 1st ed. dj. . . . .*$60–$75*

Hammett, Dashiell. *The Dashiell Hammett Omnibus.* Lon. Cassell. 1950. Omnibus ed, dj. *$200*

Hammett, Dashiell. *The Glass Key.* NY. 1931. 1st ed. . . . .*$150–$250*

Hammett, Dashiell. *The Novels of Dashiell Hammett.* NY. Knopf. 1965. dj. *$100*

Hammett, Dashiell. *The Thin Man.* NY. 1934. 1st ed. light green cloth. . . . .*$150–$200*

Hammett, Dashiell. *The Thin Man.* NY. Grosset & Dunlap. rprnt, dj. . . . .*$10–$20*

Hanaford, Mrs. P. A. *The Young Captain: A Memorial of Capt. Richard C. Berby. . . .* Bos. 1865. . . . .*$25–$35*

Hanaford, Phebe. *Daughters of America.* Augusta. True & Co. 1882. illus. . . . .*$20–$30*

Handbook for Scout Masters—Boy Scouts of America. NY. 1914. 1st ed. illus. . . . .*$25–$35*

Handbook for Travellers to Niagra Falls. . . . Buffalo/Rochester. Ontario & St. Lawrence Steamboat Co. 1854. 175 pp, fldg map. . . . .*$55–$70*

Handbook of Information for Passengers and Skippers. Nippon Yuse Kaisha. 1896. map in pocket. . . . .*$40–$65*

Handbook of Maintenance Instructions, USAF H-34 Helicopter (Sikorsky). USAF. 1955. rev. *$35*

Handbook of the Oneida Society. Oneida, NY. Office of Oneida circular. 1875. 48 pp. . . . . *$65–$85*

Handbook of Tobacco Culture for Planters in So. Rhodesia. Salisbury. 1913. 1st ed. illus. . . . . *$75–$115*

Hann, Julius. *Handbook of Climatology, Pt. I: General Climatology.* Macmillan. 1903. . . . . *$30–$65*

Hannah, Barry. *Airships.* Knopf. 1978. 1st ed. dj. sgn. *$75*

Hannah, Barry. *Geronimo Rex.* Viking. 1972. 1st ed. dj, sgn. *$150*

Hansard, George Agar. *The Book of Archery.* Lon. 1840. illus. rbnd. . . . . *$75–$125*

Hansberry, Lorraine. *A Raisin in the Sun.* NY. 1959. wrps. . . . . *$50–$85*

Hansen, Ron. *Desperadoes.* NY. Knofp. 1979. 1st ed. author's first book, dj. . . . . *$25–$35*

Hanson, F. A. L. *Counterpoint in Maori Culture.* Lon. 1983. illus. . . . . *$55–$70*

The Happy Hollisters and the Whistle-pig Mystery. Doubleday. 1964. dj. *$10*

Harbaugh, H. *The Birds of the Bible.* Phila. Lindsay & Blackston. 1854. 1st ed. illus. aeg. . . . . *$70–$100*

Hardee, W. *Rifle and Light Infantry Tactics.* NY. 1861. wrps. . . . . *$75–$125*

Harding, A. R. *Fox Trapping.* Columbus. 1906. illus. . . . . *$15–$30*

Harding, A. R. *Fur Farming.* OH. Harding Pub. 1916. 2nd ed. . . *$14–$20*

Harding, A. R. *Ginseng and Other Medicinal Plants.* Columbus. illus. photos, rev. . . . . *$25–$40*

Harding, A. R. *Mink Trapping.* Columbus. 1906. illus. . . . . *$20–$28*

Harding, A. R. *Wolf and Coyote Trapping.* OH. 1939. illus. . . . . *$50–$75*

Hardware. NY/New Haven, CT. Sargent & Co. 1888. 1,090 pp. . . . . *$195–$250*

Hardy, Jack. *The Clothing Workers.* NY. International Publishers. [1935]. 1st ed. 256 pp, dj. *$75*

Hardy, Thomas. *A Group of Noble Dames.* Lon. 1891. 1st ed. . . . . *$75–$115*

Hardy, Thomas. *Human Shows, Far Fantasies, Songs and Trifles.* Lon. 1925. 1st ed. dj. . . . .*$65–$100*

Hardy, Thomas. *Jude the Obscure.* NY. 1896. 1st Amer ed. . . . .*$50–$95*

Hardy, Thomas. *The Well-Beloved.* Harpers. 1897. 1st Amer ed. . . . .*$75–$95*

Hardy, Thomas. *Wessex Poems.* Lon/NY. (1898). illus by author, first one-vol ed. aeg, ltd 500 cc, 228 pp, white buckram, rare. *$750*

Hardy, Thomas. *The Woodlanders.* Lon. 1887. 3 vols. 1st ed. green cloth. *$1,380*

Harkness, Ruth. *The Lady and the Panda.* NY. Carrick & Evans. 1938. 1st ed. illus. 288 pp. *$54*

Harland, Marion. *Common Sense in the Household.* NY. Scribner's. (1871). rprnt, 556 pp. *$40*

Harlow, Alvin. *Old Waybills.* NY. 1934. dj. . . . .*$40–$60*

Harper, William Goodloe. *General Harper's Speech to the Citizens of Baltimore on the Expediency of Promoting a Connexion between the Ohio.* . . . Balt. Edward J. Coale. 1824. 1st ed. wrps. 78 pp, fldg map. *$750*

Harris, Gideon, and Assoc. *Audels Automobile Guide.* NY. (1918). photos, limp cl. *$20*

Harris, Joel Chandler. *Aaron in the Wildwood.* Bos. 1897. 1st ed. . . . .*$55–$95*

Harris, Joel Chandler. *Gabriel Tolliver.* NY. 1902. 1st ed. 448 pp. . . . .*$85–$225*

Harris, Joel Chandler. *A Little Union Scout.* NY. 1904. 1st ed. illus. . . . .*$75–$100*

Harris, Joel Chandler. *Nights with Uncle Remus: Myths and Legends of the Old Plantation.* Bos. 1883. 1st published ed. pictorial cloth, 416 pp. . . . .*$80–$120*

Harris, Joel Chandler. *On the Wings of Occasion.* NY. 1900. 1st ed. . . . .*$50–$75*

Harris, Joel Chandler. *The Tar Baby and Other Rhymes of Uncle Remus.* NY. Appleton. 1904. 1st ed. illus. portions of dj. . . . .*$100–$225*

Harris, Joel Chandler. *Uncle Remus: His Songs and His Sayings.* NY. Appleton. 1881. 1st ed. blue binding. . . . .*$300–$500*

Harris, Joel Chandler. *Wally Wanderoon and His Story Telling Machine.* NY. 1903. 1st ed. illus. 294 pp. . . . .*$85–$125*

Harris, M. H. *Hebraic Literature.* NY. 1936. 1st ed. *$46*

Harris, T. W. *Treatise on Insects Injurious to Vegetation.* Bos. 1862. illus. 640 pp, plates. . . . .*$125–$200*

Harris, Thomas. *Silence of the Lambs.* NY. 1988. 1st ed. dj. . . . .
. . . .*$45–$60*

Harris, Thomas L. *A Lyric of the Golden Age.* NY. 1856. 1st ed. 381 pp. . .
. . . .*$100–$150*

Harris, W. R. *The Catholic Church in Utah.* Salt Lake City. (1909). 1st ed. map. . . . .*$50–$75*

Harris, Walter. *Salmon Fishing in Alaska.* South Brunswick. 1967. 1st ed. illus. . . . .*$22–$30*

Harrison, Percival T. *Bungalow Residences: A Handbook.* Lon. Crosby, Lockwood. 1909. pictorial green cloth, plates, 79 pp. . . . .*$75–$135*

Hart and Tolleries. *Big-time Baseball.* NY. (1950). illus. by Sydney Weiss, 192 pp. *$20*

Hart, Albert Bushnell. *Slavery and Abolition, 1831–1841.* NY. 1906. 1st ed. 360 pp, frontis, maps. *$30*

Hart, George. *The Violin and Its Music.* Lon. 1875. illus. . . . .
. . . .*$50–$80*

Harte, Bret. *Clarence.* Lon. 1895. 1st ed. blue cloth. . . . .*$30–$40*

Harte, Bret. *East and West Poems.* Osgood. 1871. 1st ed. . . . .
. . . .*$35–$50*

Harte, Bret. *The Luck of Roaring Camp.* Grabhorn. 1948. 1/300 cc. . . . . .
. . . .*$45–$90*

Harte, Bret. *Three Partners, or The Big Strike on Heavy Tree Hill.* Bos/NY. 1897. 1st ed. . . . .*$35–$55*

Harte, Bret. *A Waif of the Plains.* Bos. 1890. 1st Amer ed. . . . .
. . . .*$50–$75*

Hartley, Florence. *Ladies' Handbook of Fancy and Ornamental Work.* Phila. 1859. . . . .*$75–$95*

Hartman, Joan. *Chinese Jade of Five Centuries.* Tuttle. 1969. 1st ed. 172 pp, 51 plates, dj. *$58*

Hartshorne, A. *Old English Drinking Glasses.* Lon. 1897. folio, plates, 499 pp. . . . .*$150–$250*

Harvey, Rev. M. *Newfoundland in 1897.* Lon. 1897. illus. . . . .
. . . .*$25–$40*

Harvey, William Fryer. *The Arm of Mrs. Egan.* NY. Dutton. 1952. 1st ed. 256 pp, dj. . . . .*$50–$65*

Haskell, Frank Aretas. *The Battle of Gettysburg.* WI. 1908. 1st ed. illus. . .
. . . .*$50–$75*

Haskett, William. *Shakerism Unmasked, or The History of the Shakers; Including a Form Politic of Their Government.* . . . Pittsfield. 1828. 300 pp.
. . . .*$275*

Haswell, Anthony (ed). *Memoirs and Adventures of Capt. Matthew Phelps.* Bennington. 1802. rare. *$50*

Hathaway, Ernest. *The Story of the Old Fort at Toronto.* Macmillan of Canada. 1934. wrps. . . . .*$25–$35*

Haupt, Herman. *General Theory of Bridge Construction.* NY. 1856. . . . .
. . . .*$45–$60*

Haviland, Laura S. *A Woman's Life Work.* Michigan. 1881. illus. . . . . . .
. . . .*$50–$75*

The Hawk Eye Camera. Bos. Blair Camera Co. 1889. illus, wrps. . . . .
. . . .*$50–$75*

Hawker, George. *An English Woman's 25 Years in Tropical Africa.* Lon. 1911. . . . .*$75–$90*

Hawker, P. *Instructions to Young Sportsmen . . . Guns and Shooting.* 1858. . . . .*$45–$50*

Hawley, Walter. *Oriental Rugs, Antique and Modern.* Tudor Publishing. 1937. 11 clr plates. . . . .*$60–$90*

Hawley, Walter A. *Early Days of Santa Barbara, California.* Santa Barbara. 1910. wrps. plates. . . . .*$100–$135*

Hawthorne, Nathaniel. *Doctor Grimshawe's Secret.* Osgood. 1883. 1st ed. . . . .*$50–$85*

Hawthorne, Nathaniel. *The House of the Seven Gables.* Bos. Tichnor, Reed, & Fields. 1851. 1st ed. 344 pp. *$750*

Hawthorne, Nathaniel. *The Marble Faun.* Bos. 1860. 2 vols. 1st Amer ed. 283 pp. . . . .*$190–$250*

Hawthorne, Nathaniel. *Our Old Home.* Ticknor & Fields. 1863. 1st ed. 1st state. . . . .*$100–$135*

Hawthorne, Nathaniel. *The Scarlet Letter.* Bos. 1850. 1st ed. . . . .
. . . .*$850–$1,000*

Hawthorne, Nathaniel. *Transformation.* Lon. Smith, Elder. 1860. 1st ed. 3 vols, 273 pp, 294 pp, 285 pp. *$750*

Hawthorne, Nathaniel. *A Wonder Book.* Doran. (1922). illus by Arthur Rackham. . . . .*$150–$200*

Hawthorne, Nathaniel. *A Wonder Book for Girls and Boys.* Houghton. 1893. 1st ed. illus by Walter Crane. . . . .*$100–$150*

Hawthorne, Nathaniel. *A Wonder Book for Girls and Boys.* Bos. 1885. illus by F. S. Church. *$40*

Hayden, A. *Spode and His Successors.* Lon. 1925. . . . .*$60–$75*

Hayden. A. S. *Early History of the Disciples in the Western Reserve, Ohio.* . . . Cinc. 1876. 1st ed. . . . .*$50–$125*

Hayden, F. V. *Report of the U.S. Geological Survey of the Territories.* DC. 1979. clr plates. . . . .*$65–$100*

Hayes, Albert H. *A Medical Treatise on Nervous Afflictions.* Bos. Peabody Medical Inst. (1870). 137 pp. . . . .*$50–$75*

Hayes, Dr. I. I. *The Open Polar Sea.* NY. Hurd & Houghton. 1867. 1st ed. 3 maps, 30 tail pieces, pictorial cloth. . . . .*$95–$130*

Hayes, Isaac. *An Arctic Boat Journey.* Bos. 1860. 1st ed. 375 pp, maps. . . . .*$40–$50*

Hayes, J. Gordon. *The Conquest of the South Pole.* NY. Macmillan. 1933. 1st Amer ed. illus, maps. . . . .*$60–$75*

Haynes, Warden G. *Pictures from Prison Life and Suggestions on Discipline.* 1869. . . . .*$50–$65*

Hayward, John. *A Gazetteer of Vermont.* . . . Bos. 1849. illus. 216 pp. . . . .*$65–$95*

Hazelton, William C. *Days among the Ducks.* Chi. 1938. illus. red cloth, duck and lettering on front, photos. *$245*

Head, Sir Francis B. *A Narrative.* Lon. 1839. 1st ed. 488 + 38 pp. *$95*

Headland, Isaac Taylor. *Court Life in China.* NY. (1909). illus. 2nd ed. photos. . . . .*$30–$40*

Headley, J. T. *The Adirondacks, or Life in the Woods.* NY. 1849. 1st ed. 288 pp. . . . .*$95–$115*

Heaney, Seamus. *Door into the Dark.* Faber. 1969. 1st ed. dj. . . . .*$100–$150*

Heaney, Seamus. *Poems, 1965–1975.* NY. Farrar, Straus & Giroux. (1980). 1st ed. dj. . . . .*$30–$40*

Heaney, Seamus. *Station Island.* Lon. 1984. 1st ed. dj. . . . .*$50–$75*

Hearn, Lafcadio. *The Boy Who Drew Cats.* Tokyo. 1898. printed and hand-clr in handmade crepe paper, 18 pp. *$120*

Hearn, Lafcadio. *Chita: A Memory of Last Island.* NY. 1889. 1st ed. 204 pp. . . . .*$200–$300*

Hearn, Lafcadio. *In Ghostly Japan.* Bos. 1899. 1st ed. illus. photos, teg, Hearn's last book. *$155*

Hearn, Lafcadio. *Japan.* NY. 1904. 1st ed. 1st issue, teg, dj. . . . .*$95–$325*

Hearn, Lafcadio. *Kokaro.* Bos. 1896. 1st ed. ....$50–$75

Hearn, Lafcadio. *Kwaidan.* Tokyo. 1932. illus. ltd 1,500 cc, sgn, silk case.
....$150–$225

Hearn, Lafcadio. *Out of the East.* Bos. (1895). 1st ed. ......$110–$125

Hearn, Lafcadio. *The Romance of the Milky Way.* Lon. 1905. 1st Eng ed.
....$45–$55

Hearn, Lafcadio. *The Romance of the Milky Way.* Bos/NY. Houghton Mifflin. 1905. 1st ed. 209 pp. $85

Heathcote, J. M. *Skating and Figure Skating.* Lon. 1892. illus. ....
....$60–$85

Hebert, Frank. *40 Years Prospecting and Mining in the Black Hills of So. Dakota.* Rapid City. 1921. 1st ed. sgn. ....$35–$45

Heckewelder, John. *A Narr. of United Brethren among Delaware and Mohegan Indians.* Cleve. 1907. large paper copy. ....$140–$275

Hedges, Isaac A. *Sugar Canes and Their Products, Culture and Manufacture.* St. Louis. 1881. illus. ....$28–$35

Hedin, Sven. *A Conquest of Tibet.* Garden City. Halcyon House. 1941. illus. dj. $25

Hedin, Sven. *Through Asia.* NY. Harper & Bros. 1899. 2 vols. 1st ed. 300 photos and sketches, fldg map at rear, decorative cloth, teg. ....
....$180–$200

Hedrick, U. P. *The Cherries of New York.* Albany. 1915. clr plates. .....
....$85–$100

Hedrick, U. P. *The Peaches of New York.* Albany. 1917. illus. clr plates. .
....$100–$200

Hedrick, U. P. *The Pears of New York.* Albany. 1921. illus. ..$100–$150

Hedrick, U. P. *The Plums of New York.* Albany. 1911. clr plates. ....
....$95–$125

Heilman, G. *The Origins of Birds.* NY. 1927. 2 clr plates, dj. ...$65–$75

Heilner, Van Campen. *Adventures in Angling.* (1922). 1st ed. illus. .....
....$25

Heilner, Van Campen. *Our American Game Birds.* Garden City. Doubleday Doran. 1941. 1st ed. illus. with clr paintings by Lynn Bogue Hunt, dj.
....$60–$85

Heilprin, Angelo. *Alaska and the Klondike.* NY. 1899. illus. incrb. ......
....$35–$45

Heilprin, Angelo. *Town Geology.* Phila. 1885. 1st ed. 142 pp, illus. .....
....$65–$75

Heindel, Max, and Augusta F. Heindel. *Astro-diagnosis....* Oceanside, CA/Lon. The Rosicrucian Fellowship. (1929). 2nd ed. illus. . . . .
. . . .*$60–$85*

Heiner, Dr. Henry. *Gesundheits Schatzkammer.* (Lancaster, PA. 1831). . .
. . . .*$30–$40*

Heinl, Lt. Col. Robert, Jr. *Marines of Midway.* DC. 1948. maps, soft covers. . . . .*$75–$95*

Heinlein, Robert A. *Assignment in Eternity.* Fantasy Press. (1953)1953. 1st ed. dj. . . . .*$100–$150*

Heinlein, Robert A. *Cat Who Walks through Walls.* NY. 1985. 1st ed. dj.
. . . .*$25–$30*

Heinlein, Robert A. *Farmer in the Sky.* Scribner's. 1950. 1st ed. dj. . . . . .
. . . .*$150–$225*

Heinlein, Robert A. *The Number of the Beast.* Lon. 1980. 1st ed. dj. . . . .
. . . .*$30–$40*

Heinlein, Robert A. *Orphans of the Sky.* NY. 1964. 1st Amer ed. dj. . . . .
. . . .*$225–$300*

Heinlein, Robert A. *Space Cadet.* NY. Scribner's. 1948. dj. *$85*

Heinlein, Robert A. *Stranger in a Strange Land.* NY. Putnam. (1961). 1st ed. dj. *$950*

Heinlein, Robert A. *Waldo and Magic, Inc.* Garden City. 1950. 1st ed. dj.
. . . .*$300*

Heisler Automotive Works. *Heisler Geared Locomotives.* Erie. Heisler Locomotive Works. 1908. wrps. illus. 47 pp, cat. . . . .*$60–$75*

Heitler, W. *The Quantum Theory of Radiation.* Oxford Univ. Press. 1950. 2nd ed. 272 pp, dj. . . . .*$50–$60*

Heller, Jospeh. *Catch-22.* NY. 1961. 1st ed. author's first book, dj. . . . . . .
. . . .*$400–$500*

Heller, Joseph. *God Knows.* NY. 1984. 1st ed. sgn, dj. . . . .
. . . .*$35–$40*

Heller, Joseph. *Good as Gold.* Simon. (1979). 1st ed. . . . .*$35–$45*

Hellman, Lillian. *The Children's Hour.* NY. 1934. 1st ed. dj. . . . .
. . . .*$250–$300*

Hellman, Lillian. *The Little Foxes.* NY. 1939. 1st ed. dj. . . . .*$30–$45*

Helper, Hinton Rowan. *The Impending Crisis of the South.* NY. 1857. . .
. . . .*$40–$60*

Helprin, Mark. *Ellis Island and Other Stories.* NY. Delacorte Press. (1981). 1st ed. dj. . . . .*$50–$60*

Hemenway, Abby M. *Clarke Papers: Mrs. Meech and Her Family....* Burlington. 1878. 312 pp. ....$42–$50

Hemenway, Abby Maria. *The Vermont Historical Gazetteer ... Vols. I & II.* Burlington. 1867, 1871. illus. $320

Hemenway, Abby Maria. *The Vermont Historical Gazetteer ... Vol. III.* NH. 1877. illus. hard to find. ....$300–$425

Hemenway, Abby Maria. *The Vermont Historical Gazetteer ... Vol IV.* Montpelier. 1882. illus. 1,200 pp. ....$130–$175

Hemenway, Abby Maria. *The Vermont Historical Gazetteer ... Vol. IV.* Montpelier. 1882. illus. rbnd. $165

Hemenway, Abby Maria. *The Vermont Historical Gazetteer ... Vol. V.* Brandon. 1891. illus. $475

Henenway, Abby Maria. *The Vermont Historical Gazetteer ... Vol. V.* Brandon. 1891. illus. rbnd. $425

Hemingway, Ernest. *Across the River and into the Trees.* NY. Scribner's. 1950. 1st ed. inscrb. $4,025

Hemingway, Ernest. *A Farewell to Arms.* Scribner's. 1929. 1st ed. dj. ... .$800–$1,400

Hemingway, Ernest. *For Whom the Bell Tolls.* NY. Scribner's. 1940. 1st ed. dj. ....$225–$500

Hemingway, Ernest. *For Whom the Bell Tolls.* NY. Scribner's. 1940. 1st ed. 2nd issue, dj. $165

Hemingway, Ernest. *Green Hills of Africa.* Scribner's. (1935). 1st ed. dj. ....$400–$500

Hemingway, Ernest. *Marlin, Big Fish.* 1992. ltd 1,000 cc of 1st hardcover appearance, dj. $60

Hemingway, Ernest. *Men without Women.* Scribner's. 1927. 1st ed. dj. .. ..$125–$150

Hemingway, Ernest. *A Moveable Feast.* NY. (1964). 1st ed. dj. ....$60–$100

Hemingway, Ernest. *A Moveable Feast.* Jonathan Cape. 1964. 1st U.K. ed. dj. ....$50–$75

Hemingway, Ernest. *The Old Man and the Sea.* Jonathan Cape. (1952). 1st Eng. ed. dj. ....$75–$100

Hemingway, Ernest. *The Old Man and the Sea.* NY. Scribner's. 1952. 1st ed. dj. ....$175–$350

Hemingway, Ernest. *Three Stories and Ten Poems.* Paris. Contact Publishing Co. 1923. 1st ed. author's first book, 1/300 cc printed, grayish-blue printed paper wrps, uncut, slipcase. $15,000

Hemingway, Ernest. *To Have and Have Not.* NY. Scribner's. 1937. 1st ed. *$200*

Hemingway, Ernest. *Winner Take Nothing.* NY. (1933). 1st ed. dj. . . . . .
. . . .*$600–$900*

Henderson, Alice P. *Rainbow's End: Alaska.* 1st ed. *$60*

Henderson, Mrs. Mary. *Diet for the Sick.* NY. 1885. illus. 234 pp, green decorated cloth. . . . .*$25–$35*

Henderson, Mrs. Mary F. *Practical Cooking and Dinner Giving.* NY. Harper. 1881. 1st ed. . . . .*$70–$100*

Henderson, Peter. *Henderson's Handbook of Plants and General Horti-culture.* NY. 1910. 2nd ed. illus. . . . .*$50–$65*

Henderson, W. A. *Modern Domestic Cookery and Useful Receipt Book.* Bos. 1844. . . . .*$135–$170*

Hendrick, Burton J. *The Lees of Virginia.* Bos. 1935. 1st ed. no dj. . . .*$25*

Hening, Mrs. E. F. *History of the African Mission of the Episcopal Church in the United States.* . . . NY. Stanford & Swords. 1850. 1st ed. fldg map, 300 pp. . . . .*$40–$50*

Henry, Alice. *Women and the Labor Movement.* NY. Doran. (1923). 1st ed. 241 pp. *$65*

Henry, O. [pseudonym of William Sydney Porter]. *Cabbages and Kings.* NY. 1904. 1st ed. . . . .*$100–$150*

Henry, O. *Heart of the West.* McClure. 1907. 1st ed. . . . .*$60–$85*

Henry, O. [pseudonym of William Sydney Porter]. *Whirlygigs.* NY. 1910. 1st Amer ed. . . . .*$60–$80*

Henry, Robert Mitchell. *The Evolution of Sinn Fein.* Dublin. 1920. 1st ed. sgn by Sean Cullen. . . . .*$35–$95*

Henry, Robert Selph. *The Story of the Confederacy.* Ind. (1931). *$30–$40*

Henry, Capt. W. S. *Campaign Sketches of the War with Mexico.* NY. 1847. 1st ed. illus. . . . .*$190–$250*

Henry, Will. *Alias Butch Cassidy.* NY. (1967). 1st ed. dj. . . . . . .*$50–$75*

Henry, Will. *Who Rides with Wyatt.* Random House. (1955). 1st ed. dj. . .
. . . .*$30–$40*

Henty, G. A. *Both Sides of the Border.* Lon. 1899. 1st ed. illus. . .*$50–$70*

Henty, G. A. *By Pike and Dyke.* Lon. (1890). . . . .*$25–$30*

Henty, G. A. *In the Irish Brigade.* Scribner's. 1900. 1st ed. . . . . .*$30–$35*

Henty, G. A. *Out with Garibaldi.* NY. 1900. 1st Amer ed. illus. . .*$40–$55*

Henty, G. A. *Redskins and Colonists.* NY. (1905). dj. . . . .*$25–$30*

Henty, G. A. *With Buller in Natal.* Lon. nd. 1st Eng ed. . . . .*$35–$55*

Henty, G. A. *With Cochrane the Dauntless.* NY. 1896. 1st Amer ed. . . . . .
. . . .*$30–$45*

Henty, G. A. *The Young Franc-tireurs.* NY. The Federal Book Company.
nd. illus. . . . .*$15–$20*

Herbert, Frank. *Charterhouse Dune.* NY. (1985). 1st ed. ltd 750 cc, sgn,
dj. . . . .*$50–$70*

Herbert, Frank. *Dune.* Chilton. 1965. 1st ed. dj. . . . .*$600–$700*

Herbert, Frank. *God Emperor of Dune.* Putnam. 1981. 1st ed. dj. . . .*$25*

Herbert, Frank. *God Emperor of Dune.* NY. 1981. 1st ed. sgn, dj. . . . . . .
. . . .*$50–$75*

Herbert, Frank. *Heretics of Dune.* NY. (1984). 1st Amer ed. 1,500 cc,
sgn, slipcase. . . . .*$50–$100*

Herbert, Frank. *The White Plague.* NY. (1982). 1st ed. 1/500 cc, sgn. . . .
. . . .*$40–$50*

Herbert, Henry William. *American Game in Its Season.* Scribner's. 1854.
2nd ed. *$85*

Herbert, Henry William. *Frank Forester's Field Sports.* Stringer &
Townshend. 1848. vols 1 & 2. 6th ed. rev. *$150*

Herbert, Henry William. *Frank Forester's Fish and Fishing.* Stringer &
Townshend. 1850. . . . .*$75*

Herford, Oliver. *An Alphabet of Celebrities.* Bos. 1899. 1st ed. . . . .
. . . .*$50–$75*

Heriot, George. *Travels through the Canadas.* Rutland. Chas. E. Tuttle
Co. (1971). rprnt, illus, fldg map, dj. . . . .*$60–$75*

Herrigel, Eugen. *Zen in the Art of Archery.* [NY]. Pantheon. (1953). 1st
ed. dj. . . . .*$30–$40*

Hersey, John. *Hiroshima.* NY. Knopf. 1946. 1st ed. dj. . . . .*$25–$45*

Hersey, John. *Key West Tales.* NY. 1994. 1st ed. dj. . . . .*$18–$25*

Hersey, John. *The Wall.* NY. 1950. 1st ed. dj. . . . .*$25–$35*

Hersey, John. *The War Lover.* Knopf. 1950. 1st ed. dj. *$30*

Hertz, Louis. *Handbook of Old American Toys.* Wetherfield. 1947. 1st ed.
. . . .*$30–$40*

Hesse, Hermann. *Siddhartha.* [NY. New Directions. 1951]. 1st Amer ed.
dj. . . . .*$85–$100*

Heuvelmans, B. *In the Wake of the Sea-serpents.* NY. 1968. maps. . . . . . .
. . . .*$30–$45*

Hewiit, Edward R. *A Trout and Salmon Fisherman for Seventy-five Years.*
Scribner's. 1948. . . . .*$75*

Hewitt, Abram S. *On the Statistics and Geography of the Production of Iron.* NY. 1856. wrps. . . . .*$45–$70*

Hewlett, John. *Harlem Story.* NY. 1948. 1st ed. dj. . . . .*$20–$25*

Heydecker, Joe J., and J. Leeb. *The Nuremberg Trial: A History of Nazi Germany.* Cleve. 1962. 1st ed. . . . .*$30–$40*

Heywood, DuBose. *The Half Pint Flask.* NY. 1929. 1st ed. . . . . .*$30–$40*

Hibben, Frank. *Prehistoric Man in Europe.* Univ. of Oklahoma Press. 1958. 1st ed. illus. . . . .*$22–$27*

Hibbert, Shirley. *Field Flowers.* Lon. 1878. illus. . . . .*$35–$45*

Hibbert, Shirley. *Wild Flower.* Lon. 1878. 2nd ed. illus. . . . .*$25–$40*

Higgins, Jack. *The Savage Day.* Lon. Collins. 1972. 1st ed. dj. . . . .
. . . .*$100*

Hildreth, Richard. *The White Slave.* Lon. 1852. 1st U.K. ed. . . .*$45–$65*

Hill, B. L. *An Epitome of the Homeopathic Healing Arts.* Detroit. 1869. . .
. . . .*$45–$55*

Hill, Grace Livingston. *Through These Fires.* Phila. 1943. 1st ed. dj. . . . .
. . . .*$35–$47*

Hill, L. *Meteorological and Chronological Register, 1806 to 1869.* Plymouth, MA. 1869. 1st ed. . . . .*$30–$45*

Hill, N. P. *The Birds of Cape Cod, Massachusetts.* NY. 1965. illus. . . . . . .
. . . .*$20–$27*

Hill, Ralph Nading. *Sidewheeler Saga.* Rinehart. 1953. 1st ed. illus. dj. . .
. . . .*$22–$35*

Hill, Robin. *Australian Birds.* NY. 1967. 1st ed. illus. clr plates, dj. . . . . .
. . . .*$35–$45*

Hill, W. Henry, et al. *Antonio Stradivari, His Life and Work (1644–1737).* Lon. Macmillan. 1909. illus. . . . .*$75–$150*

Hillary, Sir Edmund. *Schoolhouse in the Clouds.* Garden City. Doubleday. 1964. 1st ed. clr photos, dj. *$20*

Hillary, William. *Observations on the Changes of the Air . . . Yellow Fever.* Lon. 1766. 2nd ed. bds. *$235*

Hillerman, Tony. *Best of the West.* 1st ed. dj. *$50*

Hillerman, Tony. *The Blessing Way.* Lon. Macmillan. 1970. 1st ed. dj. . .
. . . .*$600*

Hillerman, Tony. *The Dark Wind.* Harper & Row. 1982. 1st ed. sgn, dj. . .
. . . .*$225*

Hillerman, Tony. *The Fly on the Wall.* NY. Harper & Row. 1971. 1st ed. dj. . . . .*$500–$1,000*

Hillerman, Tony. *The Great Taos Bank Robbery.* 1st ed. 1st issue, dj. ....
....$325

Hillerman, Tony. *People of Darkness.* 1st ed. dj. $60

Hillerman, Tony. *Skinwalkers.* NY. Harper & Row. 1986. 1st ed. sgn, dj.
....$100

Hillerman, Tony. *Talking God.* NY. Harper & Row. (1989). 1st ed. wrps.
advance review copy, 199 pp. $45

Hillerman, Tony. *Talking God.* Harper. (1989). 1st ed. dj .....$20–$35

Hillerman, Tony. *A Thief of Time.* Harper & Row. 1988. 1st ltd 1/250 cc,
sgn, num, slipcase. $325

Hillerman, Tony. *A Thief of Time.* Lon. 1989. 1st U.K. ed. dj...........
....$35–$45

Hindle, Brooke. *The Pursuit of Science in Revolutionary America,*
1735–1789. 1956. dj. ....$28–$38

Hinds, William. *American Communities....* Oneida. Office of the
American Socialist. 1878. 176 pp. ....$100–$150

Hinton, S. E. *The Outsiders.* NY. 1967. 1st ed. dj. ....$100–$250

Hinton, S. E. *That Was Then, This Is Now.* NY. (1971). 1st ed. dj. ......
....$60–$95

Hipkins, A. J. *Musical Instruments....* Lon. 1945. illus. ....$65–$75

Hiss Case: A Lesson for the American People. DC. GPO. 1950 (Nixon
speech). ....$35–$40

History of Beasts. Portland. Bailey & Noyes. nd. wrps. illus. 16 pp, 93 by
62 cm. $35

The History of Bluebeard. Windsor, VT. Cochran. nd. wrps. illus. 31 pp,
10 by 6 cm. $95

History of Flagellation among Different Nations. NY. 1903. illus. ......
....$25–$40

History of Iowa County, Wisconsin. Chi. 1881. one-quarter lea. ....
....$75–$110

History of Ireland from Earliest Times. NY. 1885. 2 vols. .....$22–$30

History of Medicine and Surgery and Physicians and Surgeons of
Chicago. Chi. 1922. 1st ed. ....$150–$200

History of Rock County, Wisconsin. Chi. 1879. three-quarter lea. ....
....$100–$125

History of the 2nd Infantry Division. 1953. ....$45–$75

History of the 14th Armored Division. Atlanta. nd. ....$55–$65

History of the 120th Infantry Regiment by Officers of the Regiment. DC. (1947). 1st ed. ....$50–$75

History of the 157th Infantry Regiment, 4 June, '43–8 May '45. Baton Rouge. 1946. 1st ed. illus. photos, fldg maps. ....$95–$130

History of the 413th Infantry. L.A. 1946. ....$57–$75

History of the Fire and Police Depts. of Patterson, NJ. Patterson. 1893. 1st ed. illus. plates. ....$48–$60

History of the Jews. Lon. 1829. 3 vols. maps, calf, mar bds. ...$150–$175

History of the Town of Johnson, VT. Burlington. 1907.........$20–$30

History of the Translations or Rather Versions of the English Bible, Anno Domini 1380 to 1611. Alhambra. Braun. 1948. 1st facs ed. $50–$80

Hitchcock, Edward. *Final Report on the Geology of Massachusetts.* Amherst. 1841. rbnd. ....$90–$125

Hitchcock, Edward, et al. *Report on the Geology of Vermont....* Claremont, NH. 1861. 2 vols. illus. fldg maps. ....$60–$100

Hitchens, Robert. *The Black Spaniel.* NY. F. A. Stokes. (1905). 1st Amer ed. 380 pp...$25–$35

Hitchens, Robert. *The Near East.* Century. 1913. 1st ed. 268 pp, plates...
....$75

Hitler, Adolph. *Mein Kampf.* 1939. 1st U.S. ed. dj. ....$150–$200

Hitt, Thomas. *A Treatise on Fruit Trees.* Dublin. 1758. 3rd ed. fldg copperplate engr, rbnd. ....$250–$325

Hoban, Russell. *Kleinzeit.* NY. 1974. 1st ed. dj. ....$25–$40

Hobbs, William H. *Exploring about the North Pole of the Winds.* NY. 1930. 1st ed. photos. ....$40–$60

Hobley, C. W. *Bantu Beliefs and Magic.* Lon. 1922. illus. .....$75–$125

Hobson, R. I. *The Wares of the Ming Dynasty.* Lon. 1923. 500 cc. ..$325

Hochbaum, H. Albert. *Travels and Traditions of Waterfowl.* MN. 1955. 1st ed. illus. dj. ....$18–$30

Hodge, Frederick Webb. *Handbook of American Indians North of Mexico.* GPO. 1907–10. 2 vols. illus. ....$95–$150

Hodge, Hirim. *Arizona....* NY. 1877. 1st ed. sgn. ....$175–$225

Hodgkin, A. E. *The Archers Craft.* NY. Barnes. nd. illus. dj. ....$30–$45

Hoegh, Leo A., and Howard Doyle. *Timberwolf Tracks.* DC. 1946. 1st ed. illus. photos, maps. ....$60–$80

Hoffman, Professor. *Modern Magic: A Practical Treatise on the Art of Conjuring.* Phila. nd. illus. 563 pp. $75

Hoffman, Professor. *More Magic.* Phila. McKay. nd. illus. dj, 457 pp. . . .
. . . .*$30–$50*

Hoffman, Professor. *Tricks with Cards.* NY. wrps. . . . .*$20–$30*

Hoffman, Abbie. *Square Dancing in the Ice Age.* NY. (1982). sgn, dj. . . .
. . . .*$100–$200*

Hoffman, Abbie. *Steal This Book.* NY. 1971. 1st ed. illus. sgn. . . . .
. . . .*$100–$150*

Hoffman, Abbie. *Woodstock Nation.* 1st ed. wrps. . . . .*$25–$40*

Hoffman, E. *The Nutcracker.* NY. 1984. 1st ed. dj. *$45*

Hoffman, Elisha. *Anti-saloon Campaign Songs.* Cabery, IL. the author.
1910. illus. . . . .*$14–$25*

Hoffman, Heinrich. *Slovenly Peter.* NY. 1935. #138/1,500 cc. . . . .
. . . .*$400–$600*

Hohman, Elmo P. *The American Whaleman.* NY. 1928. illus. rprnt. . . . . .
. . . .*$15–$25*

Holbrook, Florence. *Hiawatha Alphabet.* Chi. 1910. 1st ed. illus. . . . .
. . . .*$35–$50*

Holbrook, Stewart. *The Columbia.* NY. 1956. 1st ed. sgn, dj. . . . .
. . . .*$30–$50*

Holbrook, Stewart H. *The Story of American Railroads.* NY. 1947. 1st ed.
illus. dj. . . . .*$20–$25*

Holden, Dr. George Parker. *The Idyl of the Split-bamboo.* Appleton Cen-
tury. 1934. . . . .*$125*

Holder, C. *Life in the Open.* NY. 1906. 1st ed. . . . .*$40–$50*

Holder, Charles Frederick. *Big Game at Sea.* NY. 1908. presentation
copy, sgn. . . . .*$75–$100*

Hole, S. Reynolds. *A Book about Roses.* NY. Gottsberger. 1883. . . . .
. . . .*$45*

Holiday, Billie. *Lady Sings the Blues.* NY. Doubleday. 1956. 1st ed. 250
pp, dj. *$65*

Holland, Bob, Dan, and Ray. *Good Shot.* Knopf. 1946. 1st ed. . . . .
. . . .*$50*

Holland, Charles. *Spirited or Magnetic Forces.* NY. 1882. 2nd ed. 95 pp.
. . . .*$35–$45*

Holland, Mrs. Mary. *Economical Cook and Frugal Housewife.* . . . Lon.
1853. 16th ed. . . . .*$125–$155*

Holland, Ray P. *Shotgunning in the Lowlands.* NY. A. S. Barnes. 1945.
1st ed. illus by Lynne Bogue Hunt. *$75*

Holland, W. J. *The Moth Book.* NY. 1903. . . . .*$50–$75*

Hollander, Annette. *Decorative Papers and Fabrics.* NY. Van Nostrand Reinhold. 1971. 1st ed. dj. *$35*

Holley, Marietta. *Samantha at Saratoga.* Phila. 1887. illus. . . . .*$18–$25*

Holley, Marietta. *Samantha at the World's Fair.* NY. Funk & Wagnalls. 1893. 1st ed. illus by Baron C. DeGrimm, large 8vo, 694 pp, by Josiah Allen's Wife. *$65*

Holley, Marietta. *Samantha on the Race Problem.* Bos. 1892. illus. . . . .*$45–$75*

Holley, Marietta. *Samantha on the Woman Question.* NY. Revell. (1913). 1st ed. 192 pp, scarce. *$95*

Holliday, Carl. *A History of Southern Literature.* NY. 1906. . . . .*$30–$68*

Holling, H. C. *The Book of Indians.* NY. 1935. illus. *$28*

Holling, H. C. *Little Buffalo Boy.* Garden City. (1939). 1st ed. . . . .*$30–$40*

Hollon, W. Eugene. *Beyond the Cross Timbers.* Univ. of Oklahoma Press. 1955. 1st ed. dj. . . . .*$30–$40*

Holloway, J. N. *History of Kansas: From the First Exploration of the Mississippi Valley. . . .* Lafayette, IN. James, Emmons & Co. 1868. 1st ed. illus. 584 pp. . . . .*$100–$225*

Holme, C. G. *Children's Toys of Yesterday.* Lon. 1932. illus. dj. . . . .*$75–$100*

Holmes, Oliver Wendell. *The Autocrat of the Breakfast Table.* Bos. 1858. 1st ed. . . . .*$90–$125*

Holmes, Oliver Wendell. *Poems.* Bos. 1851. 1st ed. . . . .*$50–$60*

Holt, Rosa Belle. *Oriental and Occidental Rugs, Ancient and Modern.* Garden City. 1937. illus. . . . .*$50–$75*

Holzworth, John M. *The Wild Grizzlies of Alaska.* NY. 1930. 1st ed. illus. dj. . . . .*$37–$60*

Homans, James E. *Self-propelled Vehicles. . . .* NY. 1907. . . . .*$20–$35*

Homeopathic Domestic Medicine. NY. 1848. . . . .*$15–$25*

Honey, W. B. *Dresden China.* Lon. 1934. . . . .*$35–$50*

Honig, P., and F. Verdorn (eds). *Science and Scientists in the Netherlands Indies.* NY. 1945. dj. *$45*

Hood, Jennings, and Charles J. Young. *American Orders and Societies and Their Decorations.* Phila. 1917. illus. clr plates. . . . .*$30–$45*

Hood, Thomas. *The Epping Hunt.* NY. Derrydale Press. 1930. #229/490 cc, bds. . . . .*$50–$75*

Hook, Sidney. *Reason, Social Myths and Democracy.* NY. 1940. 1st ed. dj. . . . .*$25–$35*

Hooker, William F. *The Prairie Schooner.* Chi. 1918. 1st ed. illus. . . . .*$60–$100*

Hooper, Lucy. *The Lady's Book of Flowers and Poetry.* Phila. 1863. illus. clr plates. . . . .*$40–$95*

Hoover, Herbert. *A Boyhood in Iowa.* NY. 1931. ltd ed. sgn. . . . .*$125–$150*

Hope, Bob. *They Got Me Covered.* Hollywood. 1941. 1st ed. wrps. . . . .*$25–$45*

Hope, Laura Lee. *The Bobbsey Twins and Their Schoolmates.* Grosset & Dunlap. 1928. dj. #21 . . . .*$15–$20*

Hope, Laura Lee. *The Bobbsey Twins at Meadowbrook.* Grosset & Dunlap. 1915. Bobbsey Twins #7, dj. *$27*

Hope, Laura Lee. *The Bobbsey Twins in Cedar Camp.* Grosset & Dunlap. 1921. dj. #23 . . . .*$20–$25*

Hope, Laura Lee. *The Bobbsey Twins of Lakeport.* Grosset & Dunlap. 1961. #1. . . . .*$10*

Hope, Laura Lee. *The Bobbsey Twins on Blueberry Island.* Grosset & Dunlap. 1917. Bobbsey Twins #10, dj. *$37*

Hope, Laura Lee. *Bunny Brown and His Sister Sue Playing Circus.* Grosset & Dunlap. 1916. dj. . . . .*$12–$18*

Hope, Laura Lee. *In the Land of Cotton.* Grosset & Dunlap. 1942. #35. . . . .*$12*

Hope, Laura Lee. *The Outdoor Girls of Cape Cod.* Grosset & Dunlap. 1924. dj. #24 . . . .*$25–$35*

Hopkins, Gen. Frederick W. *Eulogy at Norwich, Vermont, Feb. 22, 1848* . . . *Truman R. Ransom.* . . . Hanover. 1848. 1st ed. wrps. . . . .*$45–$75*

Hopkins, Rev. Samuel. *Historical Memoirs Relating to the Housatonic Indians.* NY. 1911. rprnt. . . . .*$60–$85*

Hopkins, William F. *The Air-ship Dragon-fly.* NY. Doubleday. 1906. 1st ed. illus by Ruth M. Hallock. . . . .*$22–$27.50*

Hopkinson, E. *Records of Birds Bred in Captivity.* Lon. 1926. . . . .*$45–$60*

Hopkinson, F. *The Pathetic* . . . *Narrative of Miss Perrine.* Phila. 1841. . . . .*$900–$2,500*

Hoppe, Willie. *20 Years of Billiards.* NY. 1925. 1st ed. illus. *$45*

Horan, Jack. *Burnt Leather.* MT. 1937. wrps. . . . .*$30–$40*

Horan, James D. *Confederate Agent.* Crown. (1960). 3rd ptg, dj, illus. . . .
. . . .*$25–$35*

Horan, James D. *The McKenney-Hall Portrait Gallery of American Indians.* NY. Crown. (1972). 1st ed. illus. *$55*

Horgan, Paul. *Devil in the Desert.* NY. 1952. dj. . . . .*$40–$50*

Horgan, Paul. *Great River: The Rio Grande in North American History.* NY. Rinehart. 1954. 2 vols. 1st ed. illus. 1/1,000 cc, sgn. *$150*

Horgan, Paul. *The Peach Stone.* NY. (1967). 1st ed. dj. . . . .*$25–$45*

Horn, Stanley. *The Army of the Tennessee: A Military History.* Ind. Bobbs Merrill. (c 1941). 1st ed. illus. 1/1,000 cc, sgn. maps, dj. . . . . . .*$125–$200*

Horn, Stanley F. *Invisible Empire: The Story of the Ku Klux Klan.* Bos. 1939. 1st ed. illus. dj. . . . .*$45–$60*

Horn, Stanley Fitzgerald. *The Decisive Battle of Nashville.* Baton Rouge. 1956. 1st ed. presentation copy, dj. . . . .*$25–$35*

Hornaday, W. T. *Our Vanishing Wildlife.* NY. 1913. illus. . . . . .*$30–$45*

Hornaday, William T. *Campfires in the Canadian Rockies.* NY. Scribner's. 1906. 1st issue, maps. . . . .*$125–$175*

Hornbein, Thomas F. *Everest: The West Ridge.* SF. The Sierra Club. 1966. 201 pp, frontis, clr photos, map. . . . .*$60–$75*

Horne, George. *Pheasant Keeping for Amateurs.* Lon. illus. . . . .*$55–$95*

Horwood, A. R. *The Outdoor Botanist.* Lon. 1920. illus. photos. . . . .
. . . .*$40–$50*

Hough, Franklin B. *History of Jefferson County in the State of New York.* . . . Albany. 1854. 1st ed. 601 pp, illus. *$50*

Hough, Horatio Gates. *Diving . . . Attempt to Describe Method of Supplying Diver with Air.* Hartford. 1813. 1st ed. . . . .*$100–$170*

House, Edward J. *A Hunter's Camp-fires.* 1909. . . . .*$35–$55*

House, Homer D. *Wildflowers of New York.* Albany. 1923. 2 vols. illus. . . .
. . . .*$75–$100*

House, Homer D. *Wildflowers of New York.* Albany. 1918. 2 vols. illus. folio, plates. . . . .*$100–$150*

Houseman, A. E. *A Shropshire Lad.* Lon. (1907). 1st ed. sgn. . . . .
. . . .*$225–$600*

Houston, John W. *Address on the Hist. of the Boundaries of the State of Delaware.* Wilmington. 1879. 1st ed. wrps. . . . .*$35–$50*

Howard, F. E. *English Church Woodwork.* Lon. 1917. illus. . . . .*$50–$75*

Howard, Oliver O. *Nez Perce Joseph: An Account of.* . . . Bos. 1881. illus. plates, fldng maps. . . . .*$250–$500*

Howard, Robert. *Conan the Barbarian.* NY. Gnome Press. (1954). 1st ed. dj. . . . .*$95–$125*

Howard, Robert. *King Conan.* Gnome Press. (1953). 1st ed. dj. . . . .*$75–$100*

Howard, Robert. *The Sword of Conan.* Gnome Press. 1952. dj. . . . .*$40–$50*

Howe, Julia Ward. *A Trip to Cuba.* Bos. 1860. 1st ed. . . . .*$50–$60*

Howell, A. H. *Birds of Alabama.* Montgomery. 1924. illus. . . . . .*$30–$40*

Howells, W. D. *A Boy's Town.* Harper. 1890. 1st ed. illus. . . . .*$150–$200*

Howison, Robert R. *A History of Virginia, from Its Discovery . . . Present Time.* Phila/Richmond. 1846/1848. 2 vols. . . . .*$200–$400*

Howitt, William. *A Boy's Adventures in the Wilds of Australia.* Bos. 1855. 1st U.S. ed. illus. . . . .*$50–$65*

Hoyland, John. *A Historical Survey of the Customs, Habits and Present State of the Gypsies.* York. 1816. 1st ed. 265 pp. *$250*

Hrdlicka, Ales. *Alaska Diary 1926–1931.* PA. 1943. illus. . . . . . .*$65–$75*

Hubback, T. R. *To Far Western Alaska for Big Game.* Lon. Rowland Ward. 1929. 1st ed. decorated green cloth, photos. *$115*

Hubbard, Elbert. *Little Journeys to the Homes of Famous Women.* East Aurora. 1898. 470 cc, sgn. . . . .*$150–$200*

Hubbard, Henry V., and Theodora Kimball. *An Introduction to the Study of Landscape Design.* Bos. Hubbard Educational Trust. 1967. rev ed. dj. . . . .*$22–$35*

Hubbard, L. Ron. *Battlefield Earth: A Saga of the Year 3000.* St. Martin's Press. (1982). 1st ed. dj. . . . .*$35–$45*

Hubbard, L. Ron. *Dianetics: The Modern Science of Mental Health.* NY. Hermitage House. (1950). 1st ed. dj. *$95*

Hubbard, L. Ron. *Slaves of Sleep.* Chi. 1948. 1st ed. dj. *$400*

Hubbard, L. Ron. *Triton and Battle of Wizards.* Los Angeles. Fantasy Publishing Co. 1949. 1st ed. dj. *$200*

Hubbard, L. Ron. *Typewriter in the Sky/Fear.* Gnome. 1951. 1st ed. . . . .*$175–$275*

Hubbard, W. *A Narrative of the Troubles with the Indians in New England.* . . . Bos. 1677. illus. map. . . . .*$22,000–$45,000*

Huddle, David. *The High Spirits.* Bos. David R. Godine. 1989. 1st ed. dj. . . . .*$20–$25*

Huddle, David. *Intimates.* Bos. David R. Godine. 1993. 1st ed. dj. . . . . . .
. . . .*$20–$25*

Huddle, David. *Only the Little Bone.* Bos. David R. Godine. 1986. 1st ed.
dj. . . . .*$20–$25*

Hudson, W. H. *Afoot in England.* Lon. 1909. 1st ed. . . . .*$40–$60*

Hudson, W. H. *Far Away and Long Ago.* Lon. 1918. 1st ed. . . . .*$30–$45*

Hudson, W. H. *Green Mansions.* Phila. 1935. 1,500 cc, sgn by illustrator.
. . . .*$75–$100*

Hudson, W. H. *Green Mansions.* Lon. Duckworth. 1926. illus. aeg, bound
by Bayntun. . . . .*$100–$150*

Hudson, W. H. *Lost British Birds.* Lon. 1894. wrps. . . . .*$30–$50*

Huey, Pennock. *A True Hist. of Charge of 8th Pennsylvania Cavalry at
Chancelorsville.* Phila. 1885. 2nd ed. . . . .*$95–$115*

Hughes, Elizabeth, and Marion Lester. *The Big Book of Buttons.* MA.
1991. illus. rprnt. . . . .*$95–$125*

Hughes, Langston. *The First Book of Jazz.* NY. 1955. 1st ed. dj. . . . .
. . . .*$30–$50*

Hughes, Langston. *The Ways of White Folks.* NY. 1934. 1st ed. .*$50–$80*

Humphrey, F. *Humphrey's Homeopathic Medicine Company.* (1928).
wrps. 230 pp. . . . .*$25–$30*

Humphrey, Maude. *Treasury of Stories, Jingles and Rhymes.* Stokes.
1894. illus. clr plates. . . . .*$135–$160*

Humphreys, Frederick. *Manual of Specific Homeopathy.* . . . NY. (1869).
printed wrps, 16mo. . . . .*$75–$100*

Humphreys, G. R. *A List of Irish Birds.* Dublin. 1939. 5th ed. . . . .
. . . .*$30–$45*

Humphries, Sydney. *Oriental Carpets, Runners and Rugs.* Lon. 1910. . . .
. . . .*$150–$250*

Humphry, Maude. *Babes of the Year.* Stokes. 1888. illus. by author. . . . .
. . . .*$150–$250*

Hunt, Blanche Seale. *Little Brown Koko.* American Colortype. (1940). 1st
ed. . . . .*$50–$75*

Hunt, Maj. Elvid. *History of Fort Leavenworth, 1827–1927.* Ft. Leavenworth, Kansas. 1926. illus. sgn. . . . .*$25–$40*

Hunt, Frazier. *Custer, the Last of the Cavaliers.* NY. 1928. 1st ed. . . . . . .
. . . .*$40–$50*

Hunt, Ridgely, and George S. Chappell. *The Saloon in the Home.* NY.
1930. illus by John Held, Jr. . . . .*$15–$22*

Hunter, Dard. *Papermaker in Pioneer America.* Phila. 1952. 1st ed. . . . .
. . . .*$95*

Hunter, George L. *Decorative Furniture.* Phila. 1923. 1st ed. illus. . . . . .
. . . .*$75–$95*

Huntington, Dwight. *Our Big Game.* NY. 1904. 1st ed. illus. . . . .
. . . .*$40–$55*

Huntington, Dwight W. *Our Big Game.* NY. Scribner's. 1904. 1st ed. . . .
. . . .*$40–$50*

Huntington, Gen. R. *Grant's Arabian Horses.* Leopard & Linden Tree.
1885. plates. *$250*

Hurd, D. H. *Town and City Atlas of the State of New Hampshire.* Bos.
1892. Folio. . . . .*$150–$250*

Huse, Caleb. *The Supplies for the Confederate Army.* . . . Bos. 1904. 1st
ed. wrps. . . . .*$85–$125*

Hutchins, Samuel. *A Theory of the Universe.* NY. 1868. . . . .
. . . .*$60–$75*

Hutchinson, Francis. *An Historical Essay Concerning Witchcraft.* Lon.
1718. 1st ed. three-quarter calf. . . . .*$325–$400*

Hutchinson, H. G. *Golf.* Lon. 1898. illus. . . . .*$150–$250*

Hutchinson, Rev. H. N. *Prehistoric Man and Beast.* NY. 1897. illus by
Cecil Aldin, 298 pp. . . . .*$35–$55*

Huxley, Aldous. *Brave New World.* Lon. 1932. 1st ed. dj. . . . .
. . . .*$100–$300*

Huxley, Aldous. *Brave New World Revisited.* NY. 1958. 1st ed. dj. . . . . . .
. . . .*$50–$60*

Huxley, Aldous. *Brief Candles: Stories.* Lon. Chatto & Windus. 1930. 1st
ed. dj. *$75*

Huxley, Aldous. *The Defeat of Youth and Other Poems.* (Oxford. B. H.
Blackwell. 1918). 1st ed. stiff wrps. *$175*

Huxley, Aldous. *Leda.* Lon. Chatto & Windus. 1920. 1st trade ed. 80 pp. .
. . . .*$65*

Huxley, Aldous. *Point Counter Point.* Lon. 1928. 1st U.K. ed. dj. . . . .
. . . .*$175–$200*

Huxley, Aldous. *Time Must Have a Stop.* Harper. 1944. 1st U.S. ed. dj. . .
. . . .*$35*

Huxley, Elspeth. *On the Edge of the Rift: Memories of Kenya.* 1962. 1st
ed. dj. . . . .*$15–$25*

Huxley, Elspeth. *Scott of the Antarctic.* NY. 1978. illus. 1st Amer ed. dj. .
. . . .*$15–$22*

Huxley, Julian. *New Bottles for New Wines.* Lon. 1957. 1st ed. illus. . . . .
. . . .*$20–$30*

Huxley, Julian. *Science and Social Needs.* NY. Harper & Brothers. 1935.
inscrb. *$30*

Huxley, Leonard. *Life and Letters of Thomas Henry Huxley.* Lon. 1903. 3
vols. 2nd ed. . . . .*$40–$50*

Huxley, Thomas. *Yoga: Hindu Delusions with Its Explanations.* Lon.
1902. 1st ed. wrps. 43 pp. . . . .*$75–$100*

Huxley, Thomas H. *American Address with a Lecture on the Study of
Biology.* NY. 1877. 1st ed. illus. . . . .*$50–$75*

Huxley, Thomas H. *Evidence as to Man's Place in Nature.* NY. 1878. 1st
Amer ed. . . . .*$40–$75*

Huxley, Thomas H. *Lay Sermons, Addresses and Reviews.* Lon. 1870. . . .
. . . .*$30–$45*

Huxley, Thomas H. *A Manual of the Anatomy of Invertebrate Animals.*
Appleton. 1888. . . . .*$30–$50*

Hyatt, Rebecca Dougherty. *"Marthy Law's Kiverlid."* published by
author. (1937). . . . .*$25–$35*

Hyer, J. K., W. Starring, and A. Hann. *Dictionary of the Sioux Language.* New Haven. 1968. ltd 300 cc. . . . .*$75–$100*

Ibsen, Henrik. *A Doll's House.* Lon. T. Fisher Unwin. 1889. translated by
Wm. Archer, 1st ed. photos, 1/115 cc. *$150*

Ibsen, Henrik. *Hedda Gabler, Skuespil I Fire Akter.* Kobenhavn. Boghandels. 1890. 1st ed. wrps. 236 pp. *$300*

Ibsen, Henrik. *Pier Gint.* Garden City. 1929. 1st ed. . . . .*$50–$75*

Ickes, Anna Wilmarth. *Mesa Land: The History and Romance of the
American Southwest.* Bos. 1933. . . . .*$25–$35*

Illustrated Catalogue of Iron Toys. Fullerton, PA. Dent Hardware Co.
c 1900. pictorial wrps, 39 pp. . . . .*$75–$100*

Illustrated Catalogue of Lightning Conductors. Nottingham, England.
Blackburn, Starling & Co. Ltd. 1924. pictorial wrps, 8 pp. . . . . . .*$50–$75*

Illustrated Catalogue of Railway and Contractors Supplies. Buda
Foundry & Mfg. Co. 1902. illus. cat. . . . .*$75–$125*

Illustrated Catalogue of School Merchandise. Bos. J. L. Hammett Co.
1872–73. printed wrps, illus. . . . .*$150–$125*

***Illustrated Catalogue of U.S. Cartridge Company's Collection of
Firearms.*** MA. (c 1903). illus. 140 pp. . . . .*$50–$75*

Illustrated List of Bride Cakes. Chester, England. Bolland & Sons. c 1893.
beige wrps, 44 pp. . . . .*$50–$75*

In China Now. NY. 1941. dj. ....*$15–$22*

In Memoriam: John Booth ... Died in Austin, Nevada, 1884. Austin. 8 pp, softbound. ....*$22–$32*

Indian Narratives: Containing a Correct and Interesting History of the Indian Wars. Claremont. 1854. ....*$55–$75*

Inge, William. *The Dark at the Top of the Stairs.* NY. (1958). 1st ed. dj. . ...*$30–$40*

Ingersoll, C. J. *A Discourse Concerning the Influence of America on the Mind.* Phila. 1823. ....*$50–$75*

Ingersoll, Ernest. *Crest of the Continent.* Chi. 1885. 1st ed. frontis, engr. *$40*

Ingersoll, Ernest (ed). *Alaskan Bird Life.* NY. 1914. illus. ....*$35–$45*

Ingham, George Thomas. *Digging Gold among the Rockies.* Phila. 1888. illus. ....*$100–$250*

Ingham, J. Washington. *A Short History of Asylum, Pennsylvania.* Towanda, PA. 1916. wrps. illus. ....*$33–$42*

Ingraham, I. (ed). *Sunny South, or Southerner at Home.* 1860. 1st ed. ... .*$100–$250*

Inman, Henry. *The Great Salt Lake Trail.* NY. 1898. 1st ed. illus. 529 pp, plates. ....*$75–$100*

Inman, Col. Henry. *The Old Santa Fe Trail: The Story of a Great Highway.* Topeka. 1916. illus. ....*$25–$35*

Inn, Henry. *Chinese Houses and Gardens.* Honolulu. 1940. illus. ltd 2,000 cc, sgn. ....*$50–$85*

Instructions for Voluntary Observers of the Signal Service, United States Army. DC. GPO. 1882. illus. 108 pp. ....*$35–$55*

Iron Toys. PA. Dent Hardware. wrps. illus. cat. ....*$48–$55*

Irving, John. *The Cider House Rules.* The Franklin Library. 1985. true 1st ed. ltd, sgn. *$125*

Irving, John. *The Hotel New Hampshire.* 1981. 1st ed. dj. ....*$35–$45*

Irving, John. *The World According to Garp.* NY. (1978). 1st ed. dj. ....*$60–$75*

Irving, John Treat. *Indian Sketches Taken during an Expedition to the Pawnee.* ... Phila. 1835. 2 vols. half mor. ....*$150–$235*

Irving, Washington. *Astoria, or Anecdotes of an Enterprise beyond Rocky Mountains.* Phila. 1836. 2 vols. 1st Amer ed. ....*$350–$500*

Irving, Washington. *A History of New York by Diedrich Knickerbocker.* NY. 1812. 2 vols. 2nd ed. . . . .*$50–$100*

Irving, Washington. *Rip Van Winkle.* Phila. (1921). illus. by N. C. Wyeth, 8 clr plates, teg, pictorial cvrs. *$135*

Isadora Duncan: Twenty-four Studies by Arnold Genthe. NY. Mitchell Kennerly. 1929. 1st ed. teg. . . . .*$125–$175*

Isherwood, Christopher. *The Berlin Stories.* New Directions. (1945). 1st ed. dj. . . . .*$50–$100*

Isherwood, Christopher. *The Condor and the Cows.* NY. 1949. 1st Amer ed. . . . .*$40–$55*

Isherwood, Christopher. *Down There on a Visit.* NY. Simon & Schuster. 1962. 1st ed. dj. . . . .*$25–$30*

Isherwood, Christopher. *The Memorial.* NY. New Directions. 1946. 1st ed. dj. . . . .*$75–$100*

Isherwood, Christopher. *Prater Violet.* Lon. Methuen & Co. 1946. 1st ed. dj. . . . .*$50–$125*

J. S. Lothrop's Champaign County Directory 1870–71. . . . Chi. 1871. illus. fldg map. . . . .*$55–$75*

Jackson, C. *Foreign Bodies in the Air and Food Passages.* MA. 1924. . . . .*$50–$75*

Jackson, Daniel. *Religious Experience . . . of Rev. Daniel Jackson. . . .* Cinc. 1859. 1st ed. illus. . . . .*$60–$75*

Jackson, Frederick G. *A Thousand Days in the Arctic.* NY. 1899. 1st ed. illus. fldg maps. . . . .*$85–$140*

[Jackson, Helen Hunt]. *Ah-Wah-Ne Days: A Visit to the Yosemite Valley in 1872 by "H.H."* SF. Book Club of California. 1971. 1st separate ed. illus, 1/450 cc. *$100*

Jackson, Helen Hunt. *Glimpses of California and the Missions.* Bos. Little Brown. 1914. plates. *$35*

Jackson, Helen Hunt. *Ramona.* Roberts Bros. 1884. 1st ed. . . . .*$350–$500*

Jackson, Joseph H. *Gold Rush Album.* NY. 1949. 1st ed. . . . . . .*$30–$45*

Jackson, Sheldon. *Alaska and the Missions on the North Pacific Coast.* NY. 1880. engr, 400 pp, map. . . . .*$50–$100*

Jackson, Shirley. *The Bird's Nest.* NY. Farrar, Straus, Young. [1954]. 1st ed. 276 pp, dj. *$50*

Jackson, Shirley. *The Haunting of Hill House.* NY. 1959. 1st ed. dj. . . . .*$50–$60*

Jackson, Shirley. *The Lottery.* 1949. 1st ed. dj. . . . .*$150–$225*

Jackson, Shirley. *The Road through the Wall.* NY. Farrar, Straus. 1948. 1st ed. dj, author's scarce first book. *$375*

Jackson, Shirley. *The Sundial.* NY. Farrar, Straus & Cudahy. (1958). 1st ed. dj. . . . .*$50–$65*

Jacobs, Michael. *The Rebel Invasion of Maryland, Pennsylvania and Battle of Gettysburg.* Gettysburg. 1909. wrps. . . . .*$35–$40*

James, Edgar. *The Allen Outlaws and Their Career of Crime.* . . . Balt. 1912. 1st ed. wrps. illus. . . . .*$45–$55*

James, G. W. *Practical Basket Making.* Pasadena. nd. illus. . .*$100–$125*

James, George W. *Through Ramona's Country.* Bos. 1909. 1st ed. . . . .*$55–$65*

James, George Wharton. *California, Romantic and Beautiful.* Bos. 1914. 1st ed. illus. . . . .*$55–$75*

James, George Wharton. *Indian Blankets and Their Makers.* Chi. 1914. 1st ed. . . . .*$175–$225*

James, George Wharton. *Indian Blankets and Their Makers.* NY. 1937. new ed. . . . .*$75–$100*

James, Henry. *The American Scene.* NY. Harper. 1907. 1st Amer ed. *$125*

James, Henry. *The Bostonians.* Lon. 1886. 3 vols. boxed. . .*$900–$1,500*

James, Henry. *Daisy Miller.* NY/Lon. 1900. teg. . . . .*$35–$50*

James, Henry. *The Ivory Tower.* Lon. Collins. (c 1917). 1st ed. dj. . .*$600*

James, Henry. *Washington Square.* NY. Harper. 1881. 1st ed. illus. by George Du Maurier. *$275*

James, Henry. *What Maisie Knew.* Chi/NY. Herbert S. Stone. 1897. 1st Amer. ed. *$100*

James, Jesse, Jr. *Jesse James, My Father.* Missouri. 1899. wrps. . . . .*$100–$300*

James, P. D. *Death of an Expert Witness.* Lon. Faber & Faber. 1977. 1st ed. sgn, dj. *$150*

James, P. D. *Innocent Blood.* Lon. Faber & Faber. 1980. 1st ed. sgn, dj. *$125*

James, P. D. *Skull Beneath the Skin.* NY. 1982. 1st ed. dj. . . . . . .*$40–$50*

James, P. D. *A Taste for Death.* Lon. 1986. 1st ed. sgn, dj. . . . .*$75–$100*

James, Will. *Lone Cowboy: My Life Story.* NY. Scribner's. 1930. 1st ed. illus by author, dj. . . . .*$150–$250*

James, Will. *The Three Mustangeers.* NY. 1933. 1st ed. . . . .*$45–$65*

James, William. *The Will to Believe.* NY. 1897. 1st ed. ......*$200–$300*

Jane, Fred T. *The Imperial Russian Navy.* Lon. 1899. illus. . . .*$125–$200*

Jane's Fighting Ships. 1920. ....*$85–$100*

Jane's Fighting Ships. 1971. ....*$20–$30*

Jane's Weapons Systems. 1970. dj. ....*$20–$35*

Janney, Samuel. *Peace Principles Exemplified in the Early History of Pennsylvania.* Phila. 1876. ....*$30–$48*

Jansen, Mark. *Feebleness of Growth & Congenital Dwarfism.* . . . Lon. 1921. 1st ed. ....*$60–$80*

Janvier, T. A. *The Aztec Treasure-house.* NY. 1890. 1st ed. . . . .*$50–$75*

Janvier, Thomas A. *In the Sargasso Sea.* NY. Harper. 1898. 1st ed. ....*$30–$45*

Japan Imperial Government Railways Guide. Tokyo. 1915. 62 pp, maps, illus. ....*$40–$45*

Jarrell, Randall. *Pictures from an Institution.* NY. Knopf. 1954. 1st ed. dj. *$75*

Jay, Charles W. *My New Home in Northern Michigan.* Trenton. 1874. . . . .*$20–$25*

Jay, William. *Inquiry into Character and Tendency of American Anti-slavery Soc.* 1838. 6th ed. ....*$40–$50*

Jay, William. *A Review of the Causes and Consequences of the Mexican War.* Bos. Benjamin B. Murray & Co. 1849. 1st ed. inscrb. *$200*

Jay, William. *A View of the Action of the Federal Government in Behalf of Slavery.* NY. 1839. green cloth, 217 pp. ....*$75–$175*

Jeffers, Robinson. *Be Angry at the Sun.* NY. (1941). 1st ed. dj. . .*$35–$45*

Jeffers, Robinson. *Dear Judas and Other Poems.* NY. Horace Liveright. 1929. 1st ed. 1/375 cc, sgn, slipcase. *$300*

Jefferson, Joseph. *The Autobiography of Joseph Jefferson.* NY. 1890. . . . .*$20–$30*

Jefferson, Joseph. *The Life and Morals of Jesus of Nazareth.* DC. GPO. 1904. ....*$100–$150*

Jeffries, Richard. *The Gamekeeper at Home.* Bos. 1880. aeg, illus. ....*$40–$50*

Jehl, Francis. *Menlo Park—Reminiscences.* Dearborn, MI. Edison Institute. 1937. 3 vols. 2nd ed. ....*$120–$150*

Jehl, Francis. *Menlo Park: Reminiscences.* Edison Inst. 1936. 2 parts in 1 vol, 430 pp, dj. ....*$60–$85*

Jekyll, Gertrude. *Children and Gardens.* Lon. 1908..........*$35–$50*

Jekyll, Gertrude. *Lilys for English Gardens.* Covent Garden. 1901. 1st ed.
....*$60–$75*

Jekyll, Gertrude. *Old West Surrey.* Lon. 1904. 1st ed. photos. ....
....*$100–$150*

Jekyll, Gertrude. *Wood and Garden.* Lon. Longmans Green. 1899. illus.
4th impression. *$150*

Jellicoe, Viscount. *The Crisis of the Naval War.* NY/Lon. 1920. illus.
plates, pocket charts. ....*$40–$65*

Jenkins, C. Francis. *The Boyhood of an Inventor.* DC. 1931. inscrb. ....
....*$85–$110*

Jenkins, Dan. *Best 18 Golf Holes in America.* NY. 1966. 1st ed. dj. .....
....$22–$32

Jennings, N. A. *A Texas Ranger.* NY. Scribner's. 1899. 1st ed. 321 pp,
glassine dj. ....*$150–$500*

Jennings, Preston J. *A Book of Trout Flies.* Derrydale Press. 1935. ltd
850, numbered. *$250*

Jennings, Preston J. *A Book of Trout Flies.* Crown. 1935. 1st trade ed. ..
....*$45*

Jennings, Robert. *The Horse and His Diseases.* Phila. 1860. 1st ed. illus.
....*$25–$35*

Jewett, Charles. *Speeches, Poems and Miscellaneous Writings on ...
Temperance and Liquor Traffic.* Bos. Jewett. 1849. 1st ed. illus. 200 pp. ..
....*$75–$100*

Jewett, Sarah Orne. *Country By-ways.* Bos. Houghton, Mifflin. 1881. 1st
ed. 249 pp, green cloth, 2,000 cc printed. *$125*

Jewett, Sarah Orne. *The Life of Nancy.* Bos. Houghton Mifflin. 1895. 1st
ed. 322 pp, 2,500 cc printed. *$85*

Jillson, Willard. R. *The Coal Industry in Kentucky: An Historical Sketch.*
Frankfort. 1922. 1st ed. illus. ....*$35–$50*

Jobe, Joseph. *Great Tapestries.* Lausanne. 1965. large folio, dj, slipcase. ..
....*$50–$60*

Johns, Rowland. *Our Friend the Scottish Terrier.* NY. (1933). 1st ed. dj. ..
....*$15–$22*

Johnson, Burges. *The Lost Art of Profanity.* Bobbs Merrill. 1948. 1st ed.
dj. ....*$30–$40*

Johnson, Clifton. *The Picturesque Hudson.* NY. 1909. 1st ed. illus. .....
....*$25–$35*

Johnson, Edward, M. D. *Hydropathy.* Lon. 1843. illus. ....*$60–$80*

Johnson, G. *Ante-bellum North Carolina.* 1937. ....*$75*

Johnson, Harold. *Who's Who in the American League.* 1935. . . . .
. . . .*$27–$35*
Johnson, Harry H. *British Central Africa.* NY. Edward Arnold. 1897. fldg
maps, illus, pictorial cloth. . . . .*$150–$350*
Johnson, Helen Kendrick. *Woman and the Republic.* NY. 1897. 1st ed.
327 pp. . . . .*$65–$75*
Johnson, J. H. *Great Western Gun Works.* 1873. cat. . . . .*$95–$150*
Johnson, James R. *Treatise on the Medicinal Leech.* Lon. Longman,
Hurst, Rees, Orme & Brown. 1816. 1st ed. library stamps, 147 pp, scarce. .
. . . .*$225–$450*
Johnson, James Weldon. *God's Trombones.* NY. 1927. 1st ed. . . . .
. . . .*$50–$70*
Johnson, James Weldon (ed). *The Book of American Negro Spirituals.*
NY. 1925. . . . .*$50–$70*
Johnson, Martin. *Safari.* NY. 1928. illus. . . . .*$35–$40*
Johnson, Merle. *American First Editions.* NY. 1936. 3rd ed. . . . .
. . . .*$25–$30*
[Johnson, Richard M]. *A Biographical Sketch of Col. Richard M.
Johnson of Kentucky, by a Kentuckian.* NY. 1843. 1st ed. pictorial wrps,
sewn, 46 pp. . . . .*$150–$200*
Johnson, W. Fletcher. *Life of Sitting Bull and History of the Indian War
of 1890–91.* Edgewood Publishing Co. 1891. 1st ed. illus. . . . .
. . . .*$40–$50*
Johnson, W. Fletcher. *Life of Wm. Tecumseh Sherman.* Phila. 1891. 1st
ed. illus. *$20*
Johnson, Walter R. *A Report to the Navy Dept. of the U.S. on American
Coals.* . . . GPO. 1844. 1st ed. . . . .*$60–$75*
Johnson's Illustrated Family Atlas. NY. 1863. folio. . . . .*$385–$425*
Johnson's New Illustrated Family Atlas of the World. NY. 1865. folio,
mor, maps. . . . .*$600–$750*
Johnston, F. B., and T. T. Waterman. *The Early Architecture of North
Carolina.* Univ. of North Carolina Press. 1947. 2nd ptg, folio, plates. . . . .
. . . .*$150–$200*
Johnston, Mary. *The Witch.* Houghton. 1914. dj. . . . .*$30–$40*
Johnston, Sir Harry. *British Central Africa.* NY. 1897. illus. maps, deco-
rative cvrs, teg. *$125*
Johnstone, Annie Fellows. *Ole Mammy's Torment.* Bos. 1897. . .*$25–$45*
Jolly, Ellen Ryan. *Nuns of the Battlefield.* [Providence, RI]. Providence
Visitor Press. 1927. 1st ed. 336 pp. *$65*

The Jolly Jump-ups and Their New House. MA. McLoughlin Bros. 1939. 6 pop-ups. . . . . *$30–$40*

Jones, Bobby. *Golf Is My Game.* NY. 1960. 1st ed. dj. . . . .*$30–$40*

Jones, Charles C., Jr. *Negro Myths from the Georgia Coast, Told in the Vernacular.* Bos. Houghton Mifflin. 1888. 1st ed. 171 pp. . . . .*$150–$250*

Jones, Howard. *Key for the Identification of Nests and Eggs of Common Birds.* OH. 1927. wrps. . . . .*$25–$30*

Jones, James. *From Here to Eternity.* NY. 1951. 1st ed. author's first book, dj. . . . . *$130–$150*

Jones, James. *Some Came Running.* NY. Scribner's. (1957). 1st ed. dj. . . . .*$45–$85*

Jones, Laurence Clifton. *Piney Woods and Its Story.* Revell. 1922. 1st ed. illus. . . . .*$35–$50*

Jones, LeRoi. *Home: Social Essays.* Morrow. 1966. 1st ed. dj. . . . .*$30–$50*

Jones, LeRoi (aka Imamu Amiri Baraka). *Raise: Essays since 1965.* Random House. 1971. 1st ed. dj. . . . .*$25–$35*

Jones, N. E. *The Squirrel Hunters of Ohio.* . . . Cinc. 1898. 1st ed. illus. . . . .*$70–$85*

Jones, P. *Annals and Recollections of Oneida County.* Rome, NY. 1851. . . . .*$60–$80*

Jones, Robert Edmond. *Drawings for the Theatre.* NY. 1925. . . . .*$60–$80*

Jones, Thomas. *The Experience of Thomas Jones . . . a Slave for Forty-three Years.* Bos. 1850. wrps. 2nd ed. . . . .*$50–$85*

Jones, Virgil Carrington. *Ranger Mosby.* Chapel Hill. (1944). 1st ed. . . . .*$40–$85*

Jones, Winfield. *Story of the Ku Klux Klan.* DC. (1921). ex lib, 107 pp. *$150*

Jones, Winfield. *Story of the Ku Klux Klan.* DC. (1921). 107 pp. . . . .*$150–$175*

Jong, Erica. *Fear of Flying.* NY. 1973. dj. . . . .*$35–$45*

Jong, Erica. *Loveroot.* NY. 1975. 1st ed. dj. . . . .*$35–$45*

Jordan, Weymouth T. *Hugh Davis and His Alabama Plantation.* Univ. of Alabama Press. 1948. 1st ed. dj. . . . .*$30–$40*

Josephus, Ben Gorion. *The Wonderful and Most Deplorable Hist. of Latter Times of Jews.* Bellows Falls, VT. 1819. calf over bds. . . .*$45–$75*

Journal of a Prisoner of War in Richmond. NY. 1862. . . . .*$40–$50*

Journal of a Young Lady of Virginia, 1782. Balt. 1871. . . . .*$20–$25*

Joyce, James. *Chamber Music.* NY. 1923. . . . .*$45–$50*

Joyce, James. *Exiles: A Play.* NY. Huebsch. 1918. 1st U.S. ed. *$250*

Joyce, James. *Finnegans Wake.* Lon. (1939). 1st ed. 425 cc, dj. . . . .
. . . .*$1,400–$1,900*

Joyce, James. *Portrait of the Artist as a Young Man.* NY. (1948). wrps. . .
. . . .*$40–$50*

Joyce, James. *Portrait of the Artist as a Young Man.* Lon. The Egoist Ltd.
(c 1916). 1st Brit ed. *$600*

Joyce, James. *Stephen Hero.* np. New Directions. (c 1944). 1st Amer ed.
dj. *$125*

Joyce, James. *Ulysses.* Paris. Shakespeare & Company. 1922. 1st ed.
#443/750 cc on handmade paper. *$7,000*

Judd, Henry P. *The Hawaiian Language.* Honolulu. Honolulu Star Bulletin. 1944. . . . .*$25–$35*

Judd, Henry P., Pukui, and Stokes. *Introduction to the Hawaiian Language.* Honolulu. (1943). dj. *$30*

Jung, Carl G. *Contributions to Analytical Psychology.* Harcourt. 1928. 1st
Amer ed. . . . .*$50–$60*

Kafka, Franz. *Parables.* NY. (1947). 1st ed. dj. . . . .*$35–$45*

Kahn, Edgar. *Cable Car Days in San Francisco.* Stanford. 1946. sgn, presentation copy, 9th ptg. . . . .*$25–$35*

The Kalish Book. Tel Aviv. 1964. 630 pp. *$70*

Kane, Elisha Kent. *Arctic Explorations: . . . in Search of Sir John
Franklin.* Phila. 1856. 2 vols. maps. . . . .*$100–$175*

Kane, Elisha Kent. *The U.S. Grinnell Expedition in Search of Sir John
Franklin.* NY. 1854. 1st ed. 552 pp, maps, illus. . . . .*$75–$100*

Kantor, MacKinlay. *Andersonville.* NY. 1955. . . . .*$40–$50*

Kantor, MacKinlay. *Wicked Water.* NY. (1949). 1st ed. dj. . . . .
. . . .*$50–$60*

Karloff, Boris (ed). *And the Darkness Falls.* Cleve. 1946. 1st ed. . . . .
. . . .*$20–$25*

Katayev, Valentin. *A White Sail Gleams.* Moscow. 1954. illus. . . . .
. . . .*$22–$35*

Katzenbach, Lois and William. *The Practical Book of American Wallpaper.* Phila. (1951). inscrb, dj. . . . .*$45–$55*

Kay, S. *Travels and Researches in Caffaria.* NY. 1834. fldg map. . . . .
. . . .*$30–$45*

Keene, Carolyn. *The Clue of the Velvet Mask.* Grosset & Dunlap. 1953. Nancy Drew #30, dj. *$20*

Keene, Caroline. *The Haunted Bridge.* Grosset & Dunlap. 1937. 1938A ptg, Nancy Drew #15, dj. *$77*

Keene, Carolyn. *The Hidden Staircase.* Grosset & Dunlap. 1959. Nancy Drew #2. . . . .*$7*

Keene, Caroline. *The Message in the Hollow Oak.* Grosset & Dunlap. 1935–36. 1936B ed. Nancy Drew #12, dj. *$180*

Keene, Carolyn. *The Mystery at the Moss-covered Mansion.* Grosset & Dunlap. 1941. Nancy Drew #18, 215 pp, dj. . . . .*$60–$70*

Keene, Carolyn. *Nancy's Mysterious Letter.* Grosset & Dunlap. 1932. Nancy Drew #8, early copy, 209 pp, dj. . . . .*$200–$250*

Keene, Carolyn. *The Ringmaster's Secret.* Grosset & Dunlap. 1959. Cameo ed of Nancy Drew #31, dj. . . . .*$25–$35*

Keene, Caroline. *The Secret at the Hermitage.* Grosset & Dunlap. 1936. 1st ed. Dana Girls #5, dj. *$255*

Keene, Carolyn. *The Secret of the Old Clock.* Grosset & Dunlap. 1959. Nancy Drew #1, dj. *$15*

Keene, Carolyn. *A Three Cornered Mystery.* Grosset & Dunlap. 1935. Dana Girls, dj. #4 . . . .*$20–$27*

Keene, Carolyn. *The Witch Tree Symbol.* Grosset & Dunlap. 1955. Nancy Drew #33. . . . .*$10*

Keillor, Garrison. *Lake Wobegone Days.* Viking. 1985. 1st ed. dj. . . . .*$30–$50*

Keithahn, Edward. *Monuments in Cedar.* Ketchikan. 1945. 1st ed. illus. . . . .*$40–$95*

Kelemen, P. *Medieval American Art.* NY. 1943. 2 vols. 1st ed. . . . .*$75–$150*

Keller, Helen. *Our Duties to the Blind.* Bos. 1904. 1st ed. wrps. . . . .*$75–$125*

Keller, Helen. *The Story of My Life.* NY. Doubleday. 1903. 1st ed. 441 pp. . . . .*$35–$50*

Kelly, Emmet. *Clown.* NY. 1954. 1st ed. wrps. . . . .*$55–$100*

Kelly, Fanny. *Narrative of My Captivity among the Sioux Indians.* Hartford. 1871. illus. . . . .*$50–$100*

Kelly, H. *Medical Gynecology.* NY/Lon. 1908. 1st ed. illus. . . . .*$75–$120*

Kelly, H. A. *Snakes of Maryland.* Balt. 1936. wrps. illus. . . . .*$15–$25*

Kelly, L. V. *The Range of Men: The Story of the Ranchers and Indians of Alberta.* Tor. William Briggs. 1913. 1st ed. illus, teg. *$750*

Kelly, Walt. *The Incomplete Pogo.* NY. (1954). 1st ed. wrps. . . .*$18–$25*

Kelly, Walt. *Pogo.* 1961. wrps. . . . .*$65–$75*

Kelly, Walt. *The Pogo Peek-a-Book.* NY. 1955. 1st ed. wrps. illus. . . . .*$27–$30*

Kelly, Walt. *Positively Pogo.* NY. 1957. 1st ed. wrps. . . . .*$18–$25*

Kelly, Walt. *Song of the Pogo.* Simon & Schuster. 1956. 1st ed. illus. . . . .*$35–$60*

Kelly, Walt. *Uncle Pogo So-So Stories.* NY. 1953. 1st ed. wrps. . . . .*$18–$25*

Kelso, Isaac. *The Stars and Bars, or The Reign of Terror in Missouri.* Bos. 1863. 1st ed. . . . .*$50–$75*

Kemelman, Harry. *Sunday the Rabbi Stayed Home.* NY. 1969. 1st ed. dj. . . . .*$25–$30*

Kemp, John R. *New Orleans.* Preservation Resource Center. (1981). 1st ed. photos and maps. *$17.50*

Kendall, J. B. *A Treatise on the Horse and His Diseases.* VT. 1891. . . . .*$25–$40*

Kennan, George. *Siberia and the Exile System.* NY. Century. 1891. 2 vols. 1st ed. illus. maps, woodcuts, 409 pp, 575 pp. . . . .*$90–$125*

Kennan, George. *Tent Life in Siberia.* NY. Putnam. 1882. . . . . . .*$75–$90*

Kennedy, Edward. *Our Day and Generation.* 1979. sgn, dj. . . . .*$30–$40*

Kennedy, John. *The History of Steam Navigation.* Liverpool. 1903. illus. . . . .*$90–$110*

Kennedy, John F. *Profiles in Courage.* NY. 1956. 1st ed. dj. . .*$65–$100*

Kennedy, Sen. John F. *The Strategy of Peace.* NY. 1960. 1st ed. . . . .*$35–$40*

Kennedy, Joseph P. *I'm for Roosevelt.* NY. 1936. . . . .*$95–$125*

Kennedy, William. *Quinn's Book.* Lon. Jonathan Cape. 1988. 1st Brit ed. dj. sgn. *$20*

Kent, Rockwell. *N by E.* Brewer & Warren. 1930. 1st ed. illus. dj. . . . .*$25–$35*

Kent, Rockwell. *A Northern Christmas.* NY. (1941). dj. . . . .*$50–$70*

Kent, Rockwell. *Rockwell kentiana.* NY. 1933. 1st ed. . . . .*$40–$75*

Kent, Rockwell. *Salamina.* NY. 1935. 1st ed. dj. . . . .*$35–$50*

Kerouac, Jack. *The Dharma Bums.* NY. 1958. 1st ed. dj. . . .*$125–$200*

Kerouac, Jack. *Dr. Sax.* NY. (1959). 1st ed. dj. ....$500–$700

Kerouac, Jack. *Lonesome Traveler.* NY. (1960). 1st ed. dj. ....
....$75–$125

Kerouac, Jack. *On the Road.* Viking. 1957. 1st ed. dj. ....$1,000–$1,500

Kerouac, Jack. *Pull My Daisy.* Grove Press. (1961). 1st ed. dj. ....
....$95–$150

Kerouac, Jack. *The Town and the City.* NY. Harcourt. (1950). 1st ed. 499 pp, dj. $600

Kerouac, Jack. *Tristessa.* NY. 1960. 1st ed. wrps. ....$40–$60

Kerouac, Jack. *Satori in Paris.* NY. (1966). 1st ed. dj. ....$75–$150

Kerouac, Jack. *Visions of Cody.* McGraw Hill. (1972). 1st ed. dj. ....
....$65–$85

Kersh, Gerald. *The Song of the Flea.* Garden City. 1948. dj. ....$45–$55

Kesey, Ken. *Demon Box.* NY. Viking. 1986. 1st ed. dj, sgn. ....
....$45–$65

Kesey, Ken. *Kesey's Garage Sale.* NY. Viking. 1986. dj, sgn by Kesey and Ken Babbs. ....$100–$125

Kesey, Ken. *Kesey's Garage Sale.* NY. Viking. 1973. 1st ed. dj. ....
....$50–$100

Kesey, Ken. *Sometimes a Great Notion.* (1964). 1st ed. dj. ....
....$150–$200

Ketchum, Milo S. *Designs of Steel Mills Buildings and the Calculation of Stresses in Framed Structures.* NY. 1905. 1st ed. ....$40–$60

Keynes, J. M. *A Treatise on Money.* NY. (1930). 2 vols. 1st ed. dj. ......
....$100–$200

Kidder, Daniel P. *Mormonism and the Mormons.* NY. 1844. 2nd ed. 342 pp. ....$75–$125

Kieran, John W. *The American Sporting Scene.* NY. 1941. 1st ed. dj. ...
....$30–$45

Kiernan, Dr. P. F. *Hints on Horse-shoeing.* GPO. 1871. 1st ed. 11 pp. ...
....$75–$100

Killikelley, Sarah H. *History of Pittsburgh.* Pitts. 1906. 1st ed. illus. 568 pp. $45

Kincaid, Jamaica. *A Small Place.* NY. (1988). 1st ed. dj. ......$35–$45

King, Clarence. *Mountaineering in the Sierra Nevada.* Bos. 1872. 1st ed. ....$125–$200

King, Constance Eileen. *The Collector's History of Dolls.* Lon. (1983). dj. ....$40–$60

King, Coretta Scott. *My Life with Martin Luther King, Jr.* NY. 1969. 1st ed. dj. sgn. . . . .*$50–$75*

King, Martin Luther, Jr. *Where Do We Go from Here: Chaos or Community?* NY. (1967). 1st ed. dj. . . . .*$75–$125*

King, Stephen. *Cujo.* 1981. 1st ed. dj. *$30*

King, Stephen. *The Dark Half.* Viking. 1989. 1st ed. sgn, dj. . . . .
. . . .*$75–$100*

King, Stephen. *The Dark Tower: The Gunslinger.* Grant Pub. 1982. 1st ed. dj. . . . .*$300–$600*

King, Stephen. *The Shining.* Doubleday. 1977. 1st ed. dj. . . . .
. . . .*$100–$150*

King, Stephen, and Peter Straub. *The Talisman.* West Kingston. Donald M. Grant. 1984. 2 vols. 1st ed. slipcase. . . . .*$100–$125*

Kingsford, Anna Bonus. *The Ideal in Diet.* Lon. 1898. . . . .*$24–$35*

Kingsley, Charles. *The Water Babies.* NY. nd illus by G. Sopher. *$50*

Kingsley, Charles. *Westward Ho!* NY. (1920). illus. by N. C. Wyeth. . . . .
. . . .*$45–$65*

Kinietz, Vernon. *Chippewa Village.* Bloomfield Hills, MI. Cranbrook. 1947. 1st ed. illus. 259 pp, dj. *$150*

Kinnell, Galway. *Black Light.* Bos. 1966. 1st ed. dj, sgn. . . . .*$35–$45*

Kinnell, Galway. *What a Kingdom It Was.* Bos. 1960. 3rd ptg, sgn, dj. . . .
. . . .*$60–$75*

Kinney, Henry W. *Manchuria Today.* Darien. 1930. illus. 100 pp. . . . . . .
. . . .*$15*

Kinsey, A. C. *The Gall Wasp Genus Cynips.* Bloomington. 1929. . . . .*$35*

Kinsey, Alfred C., et al. *Sexual Behavior in the Human Female.* Phila/Lon. Saunders. 1953. 1st ed. *$125*

Kinsey, Alfred C., et al. *Sexual Behavior in the Human Male.* Phila/Lon. Saunders. 1948. 1st ed. *$125*

Kip, William I. *The Early Jesuit Missions in North America.* NY. 1846. 2 vols in 1, map. . . . .*$150–$225*

Kipling, Rudyard. *Barrack Room Ballads.* 1892. 1st ed. illus. . . . .
. . . .*$100–$130*

Kipling, Rudyard. *The Brushwood Bay.* NY. 1891. illus. . . . . .*$85–$100*

Kipling, Rudyard. *Captains Courageous.* NY. Century. 1897. 1st Amer ed. green cloth, teg. . . . .*$75–$100*

Kipling, Rudyard. *Collected Dog Stories.* Lon. 1934. lea, teg. . . . .
. . . .*$125–$200*

Kipling, Rudyard. *Just So Stories.* Lon. 1902. 1st ed. . . . .*$300–$500*

Kipling, Rudyard. *Kim.* Lon. 1901. 1st ed. lea. . . . .*$75–$125*

Kipling, Rudyard. *Kim.* NY. 1901. 1st Amer ed. . . . .*$75–$100*

Kipling, Rudyard. *Many Inventions.* NY. Appleton. 1893. 1st ed. . . .*$75*

Kipling, Rudyard. *Puck of Pook's Hill.* NY. 1906. illus by Arthur Rackham, 4 clr plates, teg. *$45*

Kipling, Rudyard. *Sea Warfare.* Lon. Macmillan. 1916. 1st ed. *$50*

Kipling, Rudyard. *The Second Jungle Book.* Lon. 1895. 1st ed. . . . .
. . . .*$75–$100*

Kipling, Rudyard. *Songs of the Sea.* NY. Doubleday. 1927. 1st ed. 99 pp, vellum, sgn. *$400*

Kipling, Rudyard. *With the Night Mail.* NY. Doubleday, Page. 1909. 1st ed. illus by Frank X. Leyendecker and H. Reuterdahl. . . . .*$75–$95*

Kipling, Rudyard. *The Works of Rudyard Kipling.* Doubleday & McClure. 1898. 14 vols. three-quarter lea, bds, teg. . . . .*$150–$175*

Kirby, Georgiana B. *Years of Experience: An Autobiographical Narrative.* NY. 1887. 1st ed. . . . .*$120–$200*

Kirkland, Mrs. [Caroline Matilda]. *The Evening Book, or Fireside Talk on Morals and Manners.* NY. Scribner. 1852. 1st ed. red cloth, stamped, aeg, 312 pp. *$150*

Kirkland, Thomas, and Robert Kennedy. *Historic Camden.* Columbia, SC. The State Co. 1905–26. 2 vols. 1st ed. 486 pp, illus, maps. . . . .
. . . .*$175–$250*

Kitto, John. *Palestine: Physical Geography, Natural History.* . . . Lon. 1841. illus. three-quarter calf. . . . .*$45–$75*

Kittredge, George Lyman. *Witchcraft in Old and New England.* NY. Russell & Russell. (1956). 641 pp. *$20*

Kittredge, George Lyman. *Witchcraft in Old and New England.* Harvard. 1929. wrps. . . . .*$45–$62*

Kittredge, Henry. *Shipmasters of Cape Cod.* 1935. 1st ed. dj. . . .*$25–$35*

Kitzmiller, Helen H. *One Hundred Years of Western Reserve.* OH. 1926. photos. . . . .*$20–$30*

Klansman's Manual. Atlanta. 1924. 1st ed. wrps. . . . .*$75–$125*

Klein, Frederic Shriver (ed). *Just South of Gettysburg: Carroll County, Maryland, in the Civil War.* MD. 1963. 1st ed. sgn, dj. . . . .*$42–$50*

Klein, H. *Mushrooms and Other Fungi.* Garden City. 1962. 1st Amer ed. photos, dj. . . . .*$30–$40*

Klingberg, Frank. *An Appraisal of the Negro in Colonial S.C.* DC. 1941. 1st ed. . . . . *$35–$45*

Kluckhohn, C. and K. Spencer. *A Bibliography of the Navaho Indians.* NY. 1940. . . . . *$100*

Knee, Ernest. *Santa Fe, New Mexico.* NY. Hastings House. 1942. 1st ed. photos. . . . . *$20–$35*

Knight, Damon. *In Search of Wonder: Essays on Modern Science Fiction.* Chi. 1956. 1st ed. dj. . . . . *$20–$25*

Knight, Mrs. Helen C. *Hannah More.* . . . NY. American Tract Society. (1862). rev ed. . . . . *$42–$55*

Knights of the Ku Klux Klan. . . . Atlanta. 1926. wrps. . . . . *$55–$75*

Knowles, James D. *Memoir of Mrs. Ann H. Judson.* Bos. 1829. fldg map, calf. . . . . *$50–$60*

Knox, Dudley W. *The Naval Genius of George Washington.* Bos. 1932. 1st ed. ltd 550 cc. . . . . *$65–$85*

Knox, Thomas. W. *Adventures of Two Youths in a Journey to Egypt and Holy Land.* NY. 1883. illus. . . . . *$20–$30*

Knox, Thomas. *The Travels of Marco Polo for Boys and Girls.* NY. 1885. . . . . *$50–$95*

Koch, Rudolph. *The Little ABC Book of.* . . . Bos. David R. Godine. 1976. 1st ed thus, ltd 2,500 cc. *$25*

Koontz, Dean R. *Coldfire.* Putnam. 1991. ltd 750 cc, dj, slipcase. . . . . *$75–$125*

Koontz, Dean R. *Night Chills.* NY. Atheneum. 1976. 334 pp, dj. . . . . *$185–$225*

Koontz, Dean R. *The Servants of Twilight.* Illinois. 1988. 1st U.S. ed. dj. . . . . *$35–$45*

Kopp, Marie. *Birth Control in Practice.* NY. 1934. 1st ed. dj. . . . *$40–$50*

Korn, Bertram Wallace. *American Jewry and the Civil War.* Phila. 1951. 1st ed. illus. . . . . *$50–$75*

Kornbluth, C. M. *A Mile Beyond the Moon.* Garden City. 1958. 1st ed. dj. . . . . *$75–$85*

Kornbluth, Jesse. *Pre-pop Warhol.* NY. 1988. 1st ed. . . . . *$58–$70*

Koros, Alexander Cosma de. *A Dictionary of Tibetan English.* New Delhi. Cosmo Publications. 1978. rprnt. *$45*

Korson, George (ed). *Pennsylvania Songs and Legends.* Phila. 1949. 1st ed. dj. *$25*

Kouwenhoven, John. *The Columbia Historical Portrait of New York.* NY. 1953. dj. ....$40–$60

Kovacs, Ernie. *Zoomar.* Doubleday. 1957. 1st ed. dj. $60

Krauss, Ruth. *A Hole Is to Dig.* NY. 1952. 1st ed. illus by Maurice Sendak, dj. ....$125–$200

Krider, John. *Forty Years Notes of a Field Ornithologist.* Phila. 1879. ....$30–$50

Krige, E. J. *The Social System of the Zulus.* Lon. 1957. illus. 3rd ed. ....$35–$45

Krug, J. A. *The Columbia River.* DC. 1947. illus. folio, pocket maps. ....$50–$75

Kunitz, Stanley. *Intellectual Things.* NY. Doubleday Doran. 1930. author's first book, 63 pp, dj. $150

Kunitz, Stanley. *Passport to the War.* NY. Holt. (1944). 1st ed. 60 pp, dj, sgn. $30

Kunz, George Frederick. *The Curious Lore of Precious Stones.* Phila. 1913. illus..$125–$150

Kuran, Aptullah. *The Mosque in Early Ottoman Architecture.* Chi. 1968. illus...$35–$50

Kurtz and Erlich. *The Art of the Toy Soldier.* NY. 1987. illus. folio. ....$40–$60

Kylie, Hieronymus and Hall. *CCC Forestry.* DC. GPO. 1937. 335 pp, photos..$18–$25

Lacroix, Paul. *The Arts in the Middle Ages.* NY. 1875. illus. ....$22–$30

La Farge, Oliver. *As Long as the Grass Shall Grow.* NY. Alliance Book Corp. 1940. 1st ed. sgn...................................$50–$65

La Farge, Oliver. *The Enemy Gods.* Bos. 1937. 1st ed. dj. $20

La Farge, Oliver. *The Higher Life in Art.* NY. 1908. 1st ed. ....$45–$50

La Farge, Oliver. *Laughing Boy.* Houghton. 1929. 1st ed. dj. ....$75–$125

La Fayette, Gen. *Memoirs of Embracing Details of Public and Private Life.* Hartford. 1825. 1st ed. lea. ....$50–$100

Lafever, Minard. *The Beauties of Modern Architecture.* NY. Appleton. 1855. illus. new edition. ....$80–$120

La Fontaine, Jean de. *Fables in Rhyme.* Volland. (1918). illus by Rae. .. ..$35–$50

Lahee, Henry C. *Famous Violinists of To-day and Yesterday.* Bos. 1906. illus. . . . .*$25–$35*

Lake, Simon. *The Submarine in War and Peace.* Phila. 1918. 1st ed. illus. photos, presentation copy, sgn. . . . .*$50–$75*

Lamb, Charles, and Mary Lamb. *Tales from Shakespeare.* Lon/NY. 1909. illus. with 12 clr plates by Arthur Rackham, red lea. . . . .*$100–$150*

Lamb, Frank W. *Indian Baskets of North America.* Riverside, CA. 1972. illus. dj. . . . .*$45–$75*

Lamb, M. *The Homes of America.* NY. 1879. illus. 256 pp, aeg. . . . .
. . . .*$100–$150*

Lamb, Mrs. Martha. *History of the City of New York: Its Origin, Rise and Progress.* NY. Barnes. 1877. 2 vols. illus. maps, plates. . . . .*$50–$65*

Lamb, Wallace E. *The Lake Champlain and Lake George Valleys.* NY. 1940. 3 vols. illus. maps. . . . .*$100–$165*

Lamon and Slocum. *The Mating and Breeding of Poultry.* NY. 1920. illus. . . . .*$40–$60*

La Monte, Francesca. *North American Games Fishes.* NY. 1945. 1st ed. illus. limp lea, clr plates. . . . .*$25–$35*

L'Amour, Louis. *Bendigo Shafter.* NY. (1979). 1st ed. dj. . . . . .*$75–$100*

L'Amour, Louis. *Frontier.* Bantam. (1984). 1st ed. photos, dj. . .*$40–$60*

L'Amour, Louis. *Last of the Breed.* sgn, dj. *$50*

L'Amour, Louis. *The Lonesome Gods.* 1st ed. sgn, dj. *$175*

L'Amour, Louis. *Over on the Dry Side.* NY. (1975). 1st ed. dj. . . . .
. . . .*$100–$150*

L'Amour, Louis. *Rivers West.* NY. 1975. 1st ed. dj. . . . .*$100–$150*

L'Amour, Louis. *Sackett's Land.* NY. 1974. 1st ed. dj. . . . . . .*$140–$165*

Lamson, David. *Two Years Experience among the Shakers; Being a Description of.* . . . West Boylston. 1848. 212 pp. *$185*

Lands in Alabama. . . . GPO. 1828. 1st ed. . . . .*$18–$25*

Landor, A. Henry Savage. *In the Forbidden Land.* NY. Harper & Bros. 1899. fldg map, clr plates. . . . .*$125–$200*

Lang, Andrew. *The Animal Story Book.* Lon. 1896. 1st ed. illus. . . . .
. . . .*$50–$75*

Lang, Andrew. *The Green Fairy Book.* Lon. 1924. illus. . . . .*$30–$40*

Lang, Andrew. *The True Story Book.* Lon. 1893. 1st ed. illus. . . . .
. . . .*$75–$125*

Lankes, J. J. *A Woodcut Manual.* NY. Crown. 1932. rprnt. *$25*

Lardner, Rev. Dionysius. *The Cabinet Cyclopaedia.* Phil. 1832. illus. . . .
. . . .*$50–$65*

Lardner, Ring W. *Bib Ballads.* Chi. Vollard. (1915). 1st ed. author's first
book, illus, 1/1500 cc. *$350*

Lardner, Ring. *The Big Town.* Ind. 1921. 1st ed. . . . .*$50–$65*

Lardner, Ring. *Gullible's Travels.* Ind. (1917). 1st ed. . . . .*$50–$70*

Lardner, Ring. *My Four Weeks in France.* Ind. (1918). 1st ed. illus. . . . . . .
. . . .*$60–$70*

Lardner, Ring. *You Know Me Al.* NY. (1916). 1st ed. . . . .*$30–$37*

Larned, Linda H. *The New Hostess To-day.* NY. 1917. . . . .*$14–$21*

Larsen, Kenneth. *Flying Saucer Designs.* LA. 1965. 1st ed. illus. three-
ring binder. . . . .*$50–$80*

Last Journals of David L. Livingstone. Hartford. 1875. illus. maps. . . . . . .
. . . .*$35–$40*

Lathrop, Elise. *Early American Inns and Taverns.* NY. 1926. 1st ed. . . . .
. . . .*$25–$30*

Lathrop, Elise. *Historic Houses of Early America.* NY. 1936. rprnt, 464
pp, photos, dj. *$25*

Lattimore, Owen. *Inner Asian Frontiers of China.* NY. 1940. illus. . . . . . .
. . . .*$25–$35*

Laurie, J., and R.S. Gutteridge. *The Homeopathic Domestic Medi-
cine.* . . . Lon. 1888. . . . .*$45–$55*

Laut, A. C. *Vikings of the Pacific.* NY. Macmillan. 1914 (1905). illus.
maps. . . . .*$18–$25*

Laut, Agnes C. *The Blazed Trail of the Old Frontier.* NY. 1926. 1st ed.
illus. 271 pp. . . . .*$60–$125*

Laut, Agnes C. *The Conquest of Our Western Empire.* NY. 1927. 1st ed.
dj. . . . .*$50–$80*

Laut, Agnes C. *The Conquest of the Great Northwest.* . . . NY. 1908. 2
vols. 1st ed. illus. . . . .*$65–$85*

Laut, Agnes C. *Pathfinders of the West.* NY. 1927. dj. . . . .*$25–$40*

Laut, Agnes C. *Pathfinders of the West.* NY. 1904. 1st ed. . . . .
. . . .*$40–$50*

Laut, Agnes C. *Story of the Trapper.* Tor. 1902. 1st ed. . . . .*$35–$50*

Lavin, Mary. *The House in Clewe Street.* Bos. 1945. 1st ed. dj. . . . .
. . . .*$50–$65*

LaWall, Charles H. *Four Thousand Years of Pharmacy.* Lippincott. 1927.
665 pp, presentation copy. . . . .*$65–$85*

Lawrence, D. H. *Amores.* NY. 1916. 1st Amer ed. . . . .*$80–$100*

Lawrence, D. H. *David.* Knopf. 1926. dj. . . . .*$35–$65*

Lawrence, D. H. *Lady Chatterly's Lover.* Knopf. 1932. 1st Amer ed. . . . .
. . . .*$75–$125*

Lawrence, D. H. *The Ladybird, The Fox, The Captain's Doll.* Lon. Martin
Secker. (1923). 1st ed. dj. *$125*

Lawrence, D. H. *The Lovely Lady.* Lon. Martin Secker. 1932. 1st ed. . . . .
. . . .*$60–$75*

Lawrence, D. H. *Mornings in Mexico.* Lon. Martin Secker. 1927. 1st ed.
dj. *$300*

Lawrence, D. H. *Pansies.* NY. 1929. 1st Amer ed. dj. . . . .
. . . .*$95–$115*

Lawrence, D. H. *Pansies: Poems.* np. (1929). pink wraps. . . . .
. . . .*$125*

Lawrence, D. H. *Pornography and Obscenity.* Faber & Faber. 1929. 1st
Eng ed. . . . .*$25–$50*

Lawrence, D. H. *Rawdon's Roof.* Lon. Elkin, Mathew & Marrot. 1928.
#83/530 cc, sgn, grey bds printed in blue, dj, slipcase. *$500*

Lawrence, D. H. *Touch and Go: A Play in Three Acts.* Lon. C. W. Daniel.
1920. 1st ed. wrps. illus. *$300*

Lawrence, D. H. *The Virgin and the Gypsy.* Lon. Martin Secker. (1930).
1st English ed. dj. *$100*

Lawrence, D. H. *Women in Love.* Lon. Martin Secker. 1921. 1st trade ed.
. . . .*$125*

Lawrence, Robert M. *Magic of the Horseshoe.* Bos/NY. 1898. 1st ed. . . .
. . . .*$50–$75*

Lawrence, T. E. *Revolt in the Desert.* NY. 1927. illus. 1st U.S. ed. fldg
map, dj. . . . .*$75–$100*

Lawrence, T. E. *Seven Pillars of Wisdom.* Doubleday Doran. 1935. 1st ed.
#3/750 cc, dj. . . . .*$300–$400*

Laws of the State of Vermont. Rutland. Josiah Fay. 1798. lea. . . . .
. . . .*$115–$135*

Lawson, Charles. *Lawson's Switcher Guide on the Game of Checkers.*
Worcester, MA. 1899. 1st ed. . . . .*$22–$35*

Lawson, John. *The History of North Carolina.* Raleigh. 1860. 1st ed. . . . .
. . . .*$115–$150*

Lawson, Robert. *Ben and Me.* Little Brown. 1944. dj. . . . .*$50–$60*

Lawson, Robert. *Rabbit Hill.* NY. 1944. 1st ed. dj. . . . .*$40–$60*

Layard, Austen Henry. *Discoveries in the Ruins of Nineveh and Babylon.* NY. 1853. 1st ed. illus. maps, lithos, 686 pp. . . . .*$75–$100*

Layard, Austen Henry. *Nineveh and Its Remains.* . . . NY. 1849. 2 vols. mor, aeg. . . . .*$95–$145*

Layard, Austen Henry. *Nineveh and Its Remains.* NY. Putnam. 1849. 2 vols. illus. 1st Amer ed. litho, map. . . . .*$195–$250*

Lazarus, Emma. *Songs of a Semite.* NY. 1882. 1st ed. . . . .*$65–$90*

Le Carré, John. *Call for the Dead.* 1962. 1st Amer ed. dj. . . . .*$600–$900*

Le Carré, John. *The Little Drummer Girl.* Knopf. 1983. 1st U.S. ed. dj. *$30*

Le Carré, John. *The Little Drummer Girl.* Lon. Hodder & Stoughton. 1983. 1st U.K. ed. dj. . . . .*$45–$60*

Le Carré, John. *The Russia House.* Lon. Hodder & Stoughton. 1989. 1st Eng ed. proof copy, wraps. *$125*

Le Carré, John. *The Russia House.* Lon. 1989. 1st ed. sgn. . . . . .*$50–$75*

Le Carré, John. *The Secret Pilgrim.* NY. 1991. 1st Amer ed. sgn, dj. . . . .*$85–$100*

Le Carré, John. *A Small Town in Germany.* Coward. (1968). 1st U.S. ed. dj. . . . .*$35–$50*

Le Carré, John. *Smiley's People.* Lon. Hodder & Stoughton. 1980. 1st ed. sgn, dj. *$200*

Le Carré, John. *Tinker, Tailor, Soldier, Spy.* Lon. 1974. 1st U.K. ed. sgn, dj. . . . .*$75–$100*

Le Gallienne, Eva. *At 33.* NY. Longmans. 1940. rprnt, 260 pp, inscr, dj. *$45*

Le Gallienne, Richard. *The Romance of Perfume.* NY. 1928. 1st ed. illus by George Barbier, clr plates, Richard Hudnut brochure in rear pocket, dj. . . . .*$100–$185*

Le Guin, Ursula K. *The Dispossessed.* NY. (1974). 1st ed. dj. . . . .*$50–$60*

Le Guin, Ursula. *The Lathe of Heaven.* Lon. 1972. 1st U.K. ed. dj. . . . .*$30–$85*

Le Guin, Ursula. *The Word for World Is Forest.* NY. Putnam. 1976. 1st Amer ed. dj. . . . .*$95–$125*

LeMay, Curtis. *Mission with LeMay: My Story.* NY. 1965. photos. *$25*

Le Moine, J. M. *Picturesque Quebec.* Montreal. 1882. softcover. . . . .*$24–$30*

Lea, Elizabeth E. *Domestic Cookery, Useful Receipts, Etc.* Balt. 1853. 5th ed. . . . .*$50–$85*

Lea, Isaac. *Descriptions of the Soft Parts . . . of Unionidae of the U.S.* Phila. 1863. 1st ed. wrps. illus. folio. . . . .*$75–$100*

Lea, Tom. *Bullfight Manual for Spectators.* Mexico. 1949. 1st ed. wrps. . . . .*$30–$40*

Lea, Tom. *The King Ranch.* Little Brown. (1957). 2 vols. 1st ed. . . . .*$75–$100*

Lea, Tom. *The Wonderful Country.* Bos. (1952). 1st ed. dj. . . . . .*$25–$35*

Leadbeater, C. W. *Some Glimpses of Occultism.* Lon. 1903. . . . .*$20–$30*

Leaf, Munro. *Wee Gillis.* NY. 1938. 1st ed. illus. dj. . . . .*$100–$150*

Leary, Timothy. *High Priest.* NY. 1968. 1st ed. . . . .*$35–$45*

Lederer, William, and Eugene Burdick. *The Ugly American.* 1958. 1st ed. dj. . . . .*$25–$35*

Lee, Art. *Fishing Dry Flies for Trout on Rivers and Streams.* NY. 1982. 1st ed. dj. . . . .*$30–$50*

Lee, Harper. *To Kill a Mockingbird.* Lon. 1960. 1st Brit ed. dj. . . . .*$200–$300*

Lee, Robert. *Clinical Midwifery.* Phila. 1849. 1st Amer ed. . . . .*$125–$150*

Leeson, F. *Identification of Snakes of the Gold Coast.* Lon. 1950. illus. . . . .*$65–$100*

Leffingwell, William Bruce. *The Art of Wing Shooting.* Rand McNally. 1895. 1st ed. slipcase. *$125*

Leffingwell, William Bruce. *Shooting on Upland, Marsh, and Stream.* Rand McNally. 1890. 1st ed. *$125*

Leffingwell, William Bruce. *Wild Fowl Shooting.* Rand McNally. 1890. 1st ed. *$75*

Leger, Jacques Nicolas. *Haiti: Her History and Her Detractors.* NY/DC. 1907. 1st ed. . . . .*$95–$150*

Leiber, Fritz. *Bazaar of the Bizarre.* Kingston. 1st ed. 1300 cc, dj. . . . .*$25–$35*

Leiber, Fritz. *Heroes and Horrors.* Whispers Press. 1978. 1st ed. dj. . . . .*$25–$35*

Leibovitch, J. *Ancient Egypt.* Cairo. 1938. 1st ed. wrps. illus. . . .*$25–$40*

Legend of the Shasta Spring of California. SF. nd. 1st ed. wrps. . . . .*$50–$75*

Leighton, Clare. *Four Hedges.* NY. 1935. illus. sgn, dj. ......*$75–$100*

Leighton, Clare. *Growing New Roots: An Essay with Fourteen Wood Engravings.* [SF]. Book Club of California. 1979. 1st ed thus, #264/500 cc, sgn. *$60*

Leighton, Clare. *Southern Harvest.* Macmillan. 1942. 1st ed. 1st ptg, sgn, dj. ....*$45–$60*

Leighton, Clare. *Where Land Meets Sea.* NY. (1954). illus by Leighton, dj. ....*$20–$30*

Leland, E. H. *Farm Homes.* NY. 1881. illus. ....*$30–$67*

L'Engle, Madeleine. *Ladder of Angels.* Seabury. 1979. 1st ed. illus. dj. .. ..*$25–$35*

L'Engle, Madeleine. *A Wrinkle in Time.* NY. 1962. 1st ed. dj. ....*$65–$75*

Lennon, John. *In His Own Write.* Lon. 1964. 1st ed. ....*$50–$60*

Lennon, John. *A Spaniard in the Works.* Lon. 1965. ....*$85–$125*

Lenski, Lois. *Jack Horner's Pie.* Harper. 1927. 1st ed. illus. ....*$20–$35*

Lenski, Lois. *The Little Fire Engine.* 1946. 1st ed. ....*$30–$50*

Lenski, Lois. *Strawberry Girl.* Lippincott. 1945. 1st ed. illus. ...*$25–$35*

Lentz, Harold. *The Pop-up Pinocchio.* NY. 1932. ....*$95–$125*

Leonard, Elmore. *City Primeval.* NY. Arbor House. 1980. 1st ed. dj. *$65*

Leonard, Elmore. *City Primeval.* Lon. W. H. Allen. 1981. 1st Eng ed. dj. *$85*

Leonard, Elmore. *Stick.* NY. Arbor House. 1983. 1st ed. dj. *$45*

Lesley, J. P. *Geological Hand Atlas of the Sixty-seven Counties of Pennsylvania ... 1874 to 1884.* Harrisburg. 1885. maps. ....*$65–$85*

Leslie, Miss. *75 Receipts for Pastry, Cakes, and Sweetmeats.* Bos. nd. ... .*$145–$185*

Leslie, Miss. *Directions for Cookery.* Phila. 1863. 59th ed. .....*$18–$25*

Leslie, Miss. *Miss Leslie's New Recipes for Cooking.* Phila. 1854........ ....*$120–$150*

Leslie, Frank. *Famous Leaders and Battle Scenes of the Civil War.* NY. 1896. 1st ed. folio.....................................*$135–$160*

Lessing, Doris. *African Stories.* Simon. 1965. 1st U.S. ed. dj. *$35*

Lessing, Doris. *The Fifth Child.* NY. 1988. 1st ed. dj. ....*$20–$25*

Lessing, Doris. *The Real Thing.* HarperCollins. [1992]. 1st ed. 214 pp, dj. *$25*

Lester, Chadwick. *Baseball Joe Around the World.* Cupples & Leon. 1918. Baseball Joe #8, dj. *$42*

Lester, J. C., and D. L. Wilson. *Ku Klux Klan.* Nashville. 1884. wrps. *$795*

Lever, John. *A Practical Treatise on Organic Diseases of the Uterus.* Newburgh, NY. Proudfit. 1845. 1st Amer ed. ....*$100–$175*

Levi, Wendell M. *The Pigeon.* Sumter, SC. 1963. illus. sgn. ....*$50–$65*

Levine, Philip. *A Walk with Tom Jefferson.* NY. 1988. 1st ed. sgn, dj. ....*$55–$72*

Lewis, Alfred Henry. *Wolfville.* Stokes, NY. 1902. 1st ed. .....*$70–$90*

Lewis, G. Griffin. *The Practical Book of Oriental Rugs.* Phila/Lon. 1920. illus. 5th ed. ....*$65–$100*

Lewis, G. G. *The Practical Book of Oriental Rugs.* Phila. 1920. map, illus. ....*$75–$95*

Lewis, James Otto. *The Aboriginal Portfolio.* Phila. 1835–36. folio, 72 hand-clr lithos. *$16,100*

Lewis, Sinclair. *Ann Vickers.* Lon. Cape. (1933). 460 pp, inscr. *$750*

Lewis, Sinclair. *Arrowsmith.* NY. 1925. ....*$45–$55*

Lewis, Sinclair. *Dodsworth.* NY. (1929). 1st ed. dj. ....*$100–$250*

Lewis, Sinclair. *Elmer Gantry.* NY. 1927. 1st ed. dj. ....*$25–$35*

Lewis, Sinclair. *Free Air.* NY. 1919. 1st ed. dj. ....*$45–$55*

Lewis, Sinclair. *The Prodigal Parents.* Doubleday. 1938. 1st ed. dj. ....*$45–$60*

Lichten, Frances. *Folk Art of Rural Pennsylvania.* NY. Scribner's. (1946). illus. ....*$35–$65*

Liddle Hart, B. H. *Sherman, the Genius of the Civil War.* Ernest Benn, Ltd. 1930. ....*$30–$45*

Lieber, Fritz. *A Specter Is Hauntin' Texas.* NY. Walker. (1968). 1st ed. 245 pp, dj. ....*$30–$45*

Liebetrau, Preben. *Oriental Rugs in Color.* NY. 1963. illus. dj. ....*$40–$50*

Liebig, Justus. *The Natural Laws of Husbandry.* Lon. Walton & Maberly. 1863. 416 pp. ....*$125–$175*

Life and Adventures of Sam Bass, the Notorious ... Train Robber. Dallas. 1878. wrps. ....*$75–$100*

Life of Fremont. NY. 1856. 1st ed. illus. . . . .*$32–$40*

Life of Miss Anne Catley: Celebrated Singing Performer. . . . Lon. 1888.
. . . .*$30–$40*

Lincoln, Almira. *Familiar Lectures on Botany . . . for the Use of Schools
and Academics.* Hartford. Huntington. 1832. 3rd ed. 440 pp. . . . .*$25–$40*

Lindbergh, Anne Morrow. *Dearly Beloved.* Harcourt. 1962. sgn, dj. . . . .
. . . .*$35–$45*

Lindbergh, Anne Morrow. *The Flower and the Nettle: Diaries and Letters of . . . 1936–39.* NY. Harcourt Brace. (1976). 1st ed. dj. *$25*

Lindbergh, Anne Morrow. *Gift from the Sea.* 1955. 1st ed. illus. slipcase.
. . . .*$35–$50*

Lindbergh, Anne Morrow. *North to the Orient.* Harcourt Brace. 1935. 1st
ed. dj. *$35*

Lindbergh, Charles A. *The Spirit of St. Louis.* NY. Scribner's. 1953. dj. .
. . . .*$50–$90*

Lindbergh, Charles A. *We.* NY. Putnam. 1927. 1st ed. illus. ltd 1,000 cc,
308 pp. large paper copy, vellum, sgn. *$900*

Lindley and Widney. *California of the South.* NY. 1888. 1st ed. illus. . . .
. . . .*$32–$45*

Lindsay, David Moore. *A Voyage to the Arctic in the Whaler "Aurora."*
Bos. 1911. 1st ed. illus. . . . .*$60–$75*

Lipton, Lawrence. *The Holy Barbarians.* NY. 1959. 1st ed. dj. . . . .
. . . .*$45–$65*

The Little Keepsake. New Haven. S. Babcock. nd. wrps. 16 pp, 91 by 55
cm. *$40*

Littlejohn, F. J. *Legends of Michigan and the Old Northwest.* MI. 1875. .
. . . .*$40–$60*

Livermore, Mary. *My Story of the War.* Hartford. 1889. illus. . . .*$50–$75*

Livermore, Mary. *My Story of the War.* Hartford. 1890. 700 pp. . . . .
. . . .*$35–$45*

Lives of Distinguished Shoemakers. Portland. 1849. 1st ed. brown cloth. .
. . . .*$50–$100*

*The Lives of the Holy Evangelists and Apostles, with Their Martyr-
doms.* . . . Barnard, VT. 1813. 120 pp. . . . .*$20–$25*

Livingston, John. *Birds of the Northern Forest.* Houghton Mifflin. 1956.
1st ed. dj. . . . .*$20–$35*

Livingstone, David L. *Missionary Travels and Researches in South
Africa.* Lon. John Murray. 1857. 1st ed. 687 pp, map. . . . .*$200–$350*

Livingstone, David L. *Missionary Travels and Researches in South Africa.* NY. 1858. illus. 1st Amer ed. maps. . . . .*$125–$200*

Livingstone, David and Charles. *Narrative of an Expedition to the Zambesi and Its Tributaries, 1858–1864.* NY. Harper & Bros. 1866. 1st Amer ed. illus, fldg map. . . . .*$110–$125*

Lloyd, Freeman. *All Spaniels.* NY. nd. illus. . . . .*$15–$25*

[Locke, David Ross]. *Ekkoes from Kentucky by Petroleum B. Nasby.* Bos. 1868. 1st ed. illus by Thomas Nast. . . . .*$100–$150*

Lockwood, Luke V. *Colonial Furniture in America.* NY. 1926. 2 vols. 3rd ed. . . . .*$95–$125*

Lockwood, Thomas D. *Electricity, Magnetism, and Electric Telegraphy.* 1883. 1st ed. illus. . . . .*$45–$65*

Lodge, Sir Oliver. *Electrons.* Lon. 1907. 2nd ed. . . . .*$40–$50*

Lodge, Sir Oliver. *Ether and Reality.* Lon. 1925. 1st ed. . . . .*$30–$40*

Lofting, Hugh. *Dr. Dolittle and the Secret Lake.* Lippincott. (1948). 1st ed. illus. dj. . . . .*$75–$100*

Lofting, Hugh. *Doctor Dolittle in the Moon.* Cape. 1929. 1st ed. illus. . . . .*$75–$100*

Lofting, Hugh. *Dr. Doolittle's Circus.* Lon. 1925. 1st ed. illus. . . . .*$30–$50*

Logan, H., and L. C. Cosper. *Orchids Are Easy to Grow.* Englewood Cliffs, NJ. 1949. dj. . . . .*$25–$35*

Logan, James, and R. R. McIan. *The Clans of the Scottish Highlands.* Lon. Ackerman & Co. 1845–47. 2 vols. 1st ed. illus. 72 hand-clr plates, folio, 2 clr armorial frontises. . . . .*$5,000–$7,000*

Logue, Roscoe. *Tumbleweeds and Barb Wire Fences.* Amarillo. 1936. 1st ed. illus. . . . .*$30–$45*

Logue, Roscoe. *Under Texas and Border Skies.* Amarillo. 1935. wrps. 2nd ptg. . . . .*$45–$65*

Lomax, A. *The Folk Songs of North America.* Garden City. (1960). . . . .*$25–$35*

Lomax, John. *Adventures of a Ballad Hunter.* NY. 1947. 1st ed. dj. . . . .*$30–$50*

Lomax, John. *American Ballads and Folk Songs.* NY. 1934. 1st ed. . . . .*$45–$50*

Lommel, A. *Masks: Their Meaning and Function.* Zurich. 1970. photos. . . . .*$100–$135*

London, Jack. *Burning Daylight.* Macmillan. 1910. 1st ed. . . .*$100–$125*

London, Jack. *The Cruise of the Snark.* NY. 1911. illus. . . . . .*$125–$200*

London, Jack. *Daughter of Snows.* NY. 1902. 2nd ed. . . . .*$22–$35*

London, Jack. *The Game.* Macmillan. 1905. 1st ed. . . . .*$150–$225*

London, Jack. *Jerry of the Islands.* Macmillan. 1917. 1st ed. . . . .
. . . .*$85–$100*

London, Jack. *John Barleycorn.* NY. Century. 1913. 1st ed. *$75*

London, Jack. *The Little Lady of the Big House.* Macmillan. 1916. 1st ed.
illus. . . . .*$85–$100*

London, Jack. *Love of Life.* 1st ed. . . . .*$100–$115*

London, Jack. *Scarlet Plague.* Macmillan. 1915. 1st ed. . . . . .*$150–$200*

London, Jack. *Smoke Bellew.* NY. Century. 1912. 1st ed. . . . .*$150–$250*

London, Jack. *The Turtles of Tasman.* Macmillan. 1916. 1st ed. . . . .
. . . .*$150–$250*

London, Jack. *The War of the Classes.* NY. 1905. 1st ed. . . . . . .*$55–$70*

Long, E. *History of Pathology.* Balt. 1928. 1st ed. . . . .*$40–$50*

Long, Huey. *My First Days in the White House.* Telegraph Press. 1935. 1st
ed. . . . .*$45–$50*

Long, William J. *Following the Deer.* Ginn & Co. 1903. 1st ed. *$40*

Longfellow, Henry Wadsworth. *The Courtship of Miles Standish and
Other Poems.* Bos. Ticknor & Fields. 1858. 1st ed. *$150*

Longfellow, Henry Wadsworth. *The Courtship of Miles Standish.* Ind.
1903. 1st thus. clr and b/w illus. . . . .*$50–$85*

Longfellow, Henry W. *The Divine Tragedy.* Bos. 1871. 1st ed. . . . .
. . . .*$25–$35*

Longfellow, Henry Wadsworth. *Tales of a Wayside Inn.* Bos. 1863. 1st
ed. . . . .*$145–$200*

Longfellow, Henry Wadsworth. *The Song of Hiawatha.* Bos. 1855. 1st
ed. . . . .*$95–$125*

Longstreet, Augustus B. *Georgia Scenes.* NY. 1860. 2nd ed. 214 pp, illus.
. . . .*$65–$85*

Longstreet, Helen D. *Lee and Longstreet at High Tide: Gettysburg.* . . .
Gainesville, GA. 1905. illus. 2nd ed. . . . .*$50–$100*

Longstreth, T. Morris. *Understanding the Weather.* NY. 1953. rev ed, dj,
illus, 118 pp. *$14*

Longus. *Les Amours Pastorales des Daphnis et Chloe.* Lon. Ashendene
Press. 1933. wood engr by Gwen Raverat, emerald green pigskin, 310 cc. . .
. . . .*$10,925*

Lonn, Ella. *Reconstruction in Louisiana after 1868.* NY/Lon. 1918. 1st ed maps. . . . .*$125–$150*

Lonn, Ella. *Salt as a Factor in the Confederacy.* NY. 1933. 1st ed. . . . . . .
. . . .*$125–$175*

Loomis, Frederic. *Hunting Extinct Animals in Patagonian Pampas.* NY. 1913. 141 pp, illus. . . . .*$65–$85*

Loos, Anita. *Gentlemen Prefer Blondes.* NY. 1925. 1st ed. dj. . . . .
. . . .*$65–$95*

Loque, Roscoe. *Tumbleweeds and Barb Wire Fences.* Amarillo. 1936. 1st ed. wrps. . . . .*$50–$85*

Lorentz, H. A. *The Theory of Electrons . . . Light and Radiant Heat.* Leipzig. 1969. 2nd ed. Nobel Prize–winning author. . . . .
. . . .*$35–$55*

Loss of the United States Steamer Oneida. U.S. Gov. Doc., HED #236. 1870. fldg map. . . . .*$25–$35*

Lossing, Benson J. *History of the Civil War, 1861–1865.* NY. 1912. illus. . . . .*$65–$90*

Lossing, Benson J. *The Pictorial Field Book of the American Revolution.* Freeport NY. 1969. 2 vols. rprnt. . . . .*$35–$55*

Lossing, Benson J. *Pictorial History of the Civil War in the United States. . . .* Phila. 1866. 3 vols. half lea. . . . .*$85–$100*

Lossing, J. G. *Biographical Sketches of Signers of the Declaration of American Independence.* 1848. . . . .*$45–$50*

Lothrop, Jason. *The Juvenile Philosopher, or Youth's Manual of Philosophy, Natural, Experimental and Analytical.* Bogert. 1823. 312 pp. . . . .
. . . .*$125–$150*

Love, Robertus. *Rise and Fall of Jesse James.* NY. (1939). . . . .
. . . .*$22–$33*

Lovecraft, H. P. *Dagon and Other Macabre Tales.* Sauk City. Arkham House. 1965. 1st ed. dj. *$150*

Lovecraft, H. P. *Dunwich Horror and Others.* Arkham House. 1963. 1st ed. dj. . . . .*$65–$75*

Lovecraft, H. P. *Something about Cats.* Arkham House. 1949. 1st ed. dj. . .
. . . .*$125–$200*

Lovecraft, H. P., and August Derleth. *The Watchers Out of Time.* Arkham House. 1974. 1st ed. dj. . . . .*$30–$45*

Lovell, Mrs. F. S., and L. C. Lovell. *History of the Town of Rockingham, Vermont.* Bellows Falls. 1958. illus. . . . .*$45–$55*

Lowel, G. *More Small Italian Villas and Farmhouses.* NY. 1920. folio. $85

Lowell, James Russell. *The Courtin'.* Bos. 1874. illus by Winslow Homer. . . . .$75–$125

Lowell, James Russell. *The Rose.* Bos. 1878. . . . .$20–$30

The Lowell Offering. Lowell, MA. Misses Curtis & Farley. May 1845. wrps. rare. . . . .$35–$50

Lowell, Robert. *The Dolphin.* NY. (1973). 1st ed. dj. . . . .$25–$35

Lowell, Robert. *For the Union Dead.* NY. Farrar, Straus & Giroux. (c 1964). 1st ed. dj. $50

Lowell, Robert. *Lord Weary's Castle.* NY. (1946). 1st ed. dj. .$175–$200

Lowell, Robert. *The Mills of the Kavanaughs.* NY. 1951. 1st ed. . . . .$100–$125

Lubbock, Basil. *The China Clippers.* Glasgow. 1946. . . . .$50–$80

Lubbock, Basil. *The Log of the Cutty Sark.* Charles Lauriat. 1924. 1st ed. illus. dj. . . . .$50–$80

Lubbock, Sir John. *Ants, Bees and Wasps.* NY. 1890. . . . .$37–$40

Lubbock, Sir John. *The Origin of Civilization and the Primitive Condition of Man.* NY. Appleton. 1875. 3rd ed. plates. $60

Ludlow, Fitz Hugh. *Heart of the Continent: A Record of Travel across the Plains.* . . . NY. 1870. . . . .$100–$150

Ludlum, Robert. *Osterman Weekend.* NY. 1972. 1st ed. dj. . . . .$40–$60

Ludlum, Robert. *The Road to Gandolfo.* Dial. 1975. 1st ed. 3 dj's. . . . .$60–$85

Ludlum, Robert. *The Scarlatti Inheritance.* NY. 1971. 1st ed. dj. . . . .$75–$100

Lumholtz, Carl. *Among Cannibals.* NY. 1889. portrait maps, chromoliths, decorative cloth, 395 pp. . . . .$175–$225

Lummis, Charles. *Mesa, Canon and Pueblo.* Century. (1925). illus. . . . .$22–$35

Lummis, Charles F. *The King of the Broncos and Other Stories of New Mexico.* NY. 1897. . . . .$40–$55

Lutz, Alma. *Created Equal.* John Day. (1940). 1st ed. sgn, dj. . . . .$40–$50

Lutz, Frank. *Fieldbook of Insects.* NY. 1921. illus. clr plates. . . . .$18–$25

Lydenberg, Harry. *The Care and Repair of Books.* NY. R. R. Bowker Co. 1931. 1st ed. $40

Lyell, Charles. *Elements of Geology.* Lon. 1839. 1st ed. 543 pp. . . . .
. . . . *$200–$300*

Lyell, Sir Charles. *Travels in North America, Canada, and Nova Scotia, with Geological Observations.* Lon. John Murray. 1855. 2nd ed. fldg map, plates. . . . . *$250–$325*

Lymon, Henry, and Frank Woolner. *The Complete Book of Striped Bass Fishing.* NY. (1954). dj. *$15*

Lynch, Bohun. *A History of Caricature.* Bos. 1927. ltd #22/53 cc, sgn. . . .
. . . .*$300*

Lynch, Jeremiah. *Egyptian Sketches.* Lon. 1890. illus. . . . .*$40–$75*

Lynch, W. F. *Narrative of the U.S. Expedition to the River Jordan and Dead Sea.* Phila. 1849. illus. . . . . *$50–$100*

Lynk, M. V. *The Black Troopers . . . in the Spanish American War.* Tenn. 1899. illus. 163 pp. . . . . *$75–$100*

Lyons, Nick. *Confessions of a Fly Fishing Addict.* Simon & Schuster. 1989. 1st ed. dj. *$40*

MacDiarmid, Hugh. *Sangshaw.* Blackwood. 1925. 1st ed. dj. . . . .
. . . . *$150–$300*

MacDonald, Alexander. *Design for Angling: The Dry Fly on Western Trout Streams.* Bos. 1947. . . . . *$65–$100*

MacDonald, John D. *Pale Gray for Guilt.* NY. 1968. paperback original.
. . . . *$40–$50*

MacFall, Haldane. *Aubrey Beardsley: The Man and His Work.* Lon. 1928. illus. . . . . *$75–$100*

MacGillivray, D. *A Mandarin-Romanized Dictionary of Chinese.* Shanghai. 1918. 4th ed. . . . . *$25–$35*

MacGillvray. *A History of British Quadrapeds.* Edin. 1838. 1st ed. 310 pp.
. . . .*$140*

Machen, Arthur. *Far Off Things.* Lon. (1922). 1st ed. . . . .*$20–$45*

Machen, Arthur. *The Great God Pan and the Inmost Light.* Lon. 1894. 1st ed. dj. . . . . *$25–$65*

Machen, Arthur. *The London Adventure.* Lon. Martin Secker. (1924). 1st trade ed. . . . .*$50–$65*

Machen, Arthur. *The Terror.* Lon. (1917). 1st ed. . . . .*$35–$45*

Machen, Arthur. *Things Near and Far.* Lon. Martin Secker. (1923). 1st ed. . . . . *$30–$45*

Mack, Connie. *My 66 Years in the Big Leagues.* Phila. 1950. 1st ed. . . . . . .
. . . . *$25–$35*

MacKay, Douglas. *The Honourable Company—A History of the Hudson's Bay Company.* Ind. (1936). 1st ed. dj. ....$25–$50

Mackenzie, Alexander. *Voyages from Montreal on River St. Lawrence . . . Preliminary Account of the Rise and Progress of the Present Fur Trade.* Lon. Caldwell & Davis. 1801. 1st ed. 412 pp, fldg maps. $950

Maclean, Alistair. *The Guns of Navarone.* Lon. Collins. 1857. 1st ed. dj. $75

Maclean, Alistair. *Ice Station Zebra.* Lon. Collins. 1963. 1st ed. dj. $45

Maclean, Alistair. *South by Java Head.* Lon. Collins. 1958. 1st ed. dj. $75

MacLean, Norman. *A River Runs through It.* Chi. 1976. 1st ed. illus. dj. . ...$35–$75

Macleish, Archibald. *Conquistador.* Lon. Victor Gollancz. 1933. 1st British ed. 1/1000 cc. $75

MacLeish, Archibald. *Herakles.* Bos. 1967. 1st ed. dj. ....$20–$25

MacLeish, Archibald. *The Irresponsibles.* Duell. 1944. 1st ed. dj. $65

MacManus, Seaumas. *The Red Poocher.* 1903. 1st U.S. ed. ....$25–$35

MacMillan, Donald B. *Four Years in the White North.* Bos. 1925. illus. . . ..$50–$65

MacPhail, Christian. *Kitchen Adventures . . . or Experiments in Diet Changes.* Edin. 1933. 1st ed. ....$15–$22

Maeterlinck, Maurice. *The Blue Bird.* NY. 1913. illus. ......$125–$145

Maeterlinck, Maurice. *Life of the White Ant.* 1939. illus. sgn by von Hagen. ....$20–$25

Magalever, Jacob. *Death to Traitors.* 1960. 1st ed. dj. ....$20–$25

Magician's Own Book. .... NY. 1857. 1st ed. ....$150–$200

Mahan, Captain A. T. *The Life of Nelson.* Bos. Little Brown. 1900. 2 vols. 2nd ed. rev, illus, 20 maps and plans, teg. $150

Mahan, Capt. A. T. *The Influence of Sea Power upon History.* Lon. 1890. illus. 1st Eng ed. 557 pp. ....$100–$125

Mahan, A. T. *Sea Power in Its Relation to the War of 1812.* Lon. 1905. 2 vols. dj. ....$78–$95

Mahan, A. T. *Types of Naval Officers.* Lon. 1902. illus. plates. ....$55–$74

Mahan, D. H. *An Elementary Course of Civil Engineering.* .... NY. 1838. 2nd ed. fldg plates. ....$75–$220

Mahan, D. H. *A Treatise on Field Fortification.* NY. 1861. 3rd rev ed. . . .
. . . .*$30–$50*

Maidment, James (ed). *Scottish Ballads and Songs.* Edin. 1868. 2 vols. . .
. . . .*$45*

Mailer, Norman. *Advertisements for Myself.* NY. Putnam. 1959. 1st ed.
dj. . . . .*$35–$45*

Mailer, Norman. *An American Dream.* Dial. 1971. 1st ed. dj. . . . .*$*
. . . .*28–$35*

Mailer, Norman. *The Last Night: A Story of Armageddon.* NY. 1984. ltd
250 cc, sgn. . . . .*$95–$130*

Mailer, Norman. *Marilyn: A Biography.* NY. 1973. 1st ed. dj. . . . .
. . . .*$35–$50*

Mailer, Norman. *The Naked and the Dead.* NY. Rinehart. (1948). 1st ed.
sgn, dj. . . . .*$200–$300*

Mailer, Norman. *The Prisoner of Sex.* NY. 1971. dj. . . . .*$20–$30*

Malamud, Bernard. *Dubin's Lives.* NY. 1979. 750 cc. . . . .*$45–$60*

Malamud, Bernard. *The Fixer.* NY. 1966. 1st ed. dj. *$100*

Malamud, Bernard. *The Magic Barrel.* Farrar Straus. 1958. 1st ed. dj. . .
. . . .*$40–$65*

Malamud, Bernard. *The Natural.* NY. (1952). 1st ed. author's first book.
. . . .*$125–$250*

Malamud, Bernard. *Pictures of Fidelman.* Farrar. 1969. 1st ed. dj. . . . . .
. . . .*$32–$40*

Malamud, Bernard. *The Tenants.* Farrar. (1971). 1st ed. dj. . . . .*$45–$65*

Malls, Thom. E. *The People Called Apache.* NJ. 1974. dj. *$125*

Malory, Sir Thomas. *The Romance of King Arthur and His Knights of the
Round Table.* Lon. 1917. illus by Rackham, ed by Pollard, red lea. . . . . . .
. . . .*$275–$350*

Manley, William Lew. *Death Valley in '49.* San Jose. 1894. 1st ed. illus.
498 pp. . . . .*$125–$200*

Mann, A. *History of the Forty-fifth Regiment (Massachusetts).* 1908. . . . .
. . . .*$100–$150*

Mann, F. W. *The Bullet's Flight from Powder to Target.* Huntington, WV.
1942. illus. photos, 2nd ed. . . . .*$50–$95*

Mann, H. *Historical Annals of Dedham, Massachusetts, to 1847.* Dedham,
MA. 1847. . . . .*$65–$85*

Mann, Horace. *Speech of Hon. Horace Mann of Massachusetts on Slavery
and the Slave Trade.* . . . Phila. 1849. 48 pp, unbound. . . . .*$60–$85*

Mann, Horace. *Twelve Sermons.* Bos. Ticknor & Fields. 1861. 1st ed. ex lib. *$45*

Mann, Mrs. Horace. *Christianity in the Kitchen.* . . . Bos. 1861. . . . .*$50–$72*

Mann, Kathleen. *Peasant Costume in Europe.* Lon. 1931. illus. clr plates. . . . .*$35–$60*

Mann, Thomas. *Joseph and His Brothers.* NY. 1938. 6th ptg of Amer ed. sgn. . . . .*$125–$150*

Mann, Thomas. *The Magic Mountain.* NY. 1962. 2 vols. 1st ed. 1500 cc. . . . .*$125–$150*

Mann, Thomas. *Tales of Jacob.* Lon. 1934. 1st ed. dj. . . . .*$75–$100*

Mann, Thomas. *This War.* NY. 1940. 1st Amer ed. 69 pp, dj. . . . .*$50–$65*

Mann, Thomas. *The Transposed Heads.* [Kentfield]. The Allen Press. 1977. 140 cc, folio, decorated. *$750*

The Manners, Customs, and Antiquities of the Indians of North and South America. Bos. 1844. 1st ed. . . . .*$125–$150*

Manni, Pietro. *Manuale Pratico per la Cura degli Apparentemente Morti.* Napoli. 1835. 4th ed. plates. . . . .*$200–$300*

Manning, Rev. Samuel. *Palestine.* NY. Hurst & Co. nd. illus. folio, 195 pp. *$20*

Mansfield, Katherine. *The Aloe.* Lon. Constable. 1930. 1st ed. dj, 1/750 cc. *$275*

Mansfield, Katherine. *The Dove's Nest and Other Stories.* Lon. Constable. (1923). 1st ed. . . . .*$40–$50*

Mansfield, Katherine. *Poems.* NY. Knopf. 1924. 1st ed. . . . .*$35–$45*

Mansfield, Katherine. *Novels and Novelists.* Lon. Constable. 1930. 1st ed. ed by J. Middleton Murray, dj. *$150*

Mansfield, Katherine. *Something Childish and Other Stories.* Lon. Constable. (1924). 1st ed. dj. *$250*

Manson, F. L. *Wright to 1910: The First Golden Age.* Reinhold. 1958. dj. . . . .*$120–$150*

Manufacturers of Bells and Toys Catalogue No. 40. East Hampton, CT. The N. N. Hill Brass Co. 1921. printed wrps, 31 pp. . . . .*$50–$75*

Manufacturers of Every Description of Aircraft, Balloons, Parachutes, Airships and Aeronautical Apparatus. . . . Lon. C. G. Spencer & Sons, Ltd. 1919. illus. pictorial wrps, 12 pp. . . . .*$125–$200*

Manufacturers of Horse Clothing, Harness and Saddlery. Phila. Blair & Letts. 1888–89. illus. printed wrps, 16 pp. . . . .*$50–$75*

Manufacturers of Military, Sporting, Hunting, and Target Breech-loading Rifles, Shotguns, and Pistols. NY. E. Remington & Sons. 1883. printed wrps, 48 pp. . . . .*$175–$250*

Manual of Homeopathic Veterinary Practice . . . Domestic Animals. NY. 1874. half-lea. . . . .*$45–$55*

Manwaring, Christopher. *Essays, Historical, Moral, Political and Agricultural.* New London, CT. 1829. 1st ed. bds. . . . .*$85–$125*

March, Joseph. *Mancure.* NY. 1928. 6th ptg. . . . .*$18–$22*

Marcy, Randolph. *The Prairie Traveler.* NY. Harper. 1859. 1st ed. illus. fldg map. . . . .*$500–$700*

Marquand, John P. *Stopover: Tokyo.* Bos. 1957. 1st ed. dj. . . . .*$27–$35*

Marquis, Don. *Archie's Life of Mehitabel.* 1933. 1st ed. dj. . . . .*$50–$85*

Marquis, Don. *Danny's Own Story.* Garden City. 1912. 1st ed. . . . .*$55–$65*

Marquis, Don. *Revolt of the Oyster.* NY. 1922. dj. . . . .*$30–$45*

Marriott, Alice. *Maria, the Potter of San Idelfonso.* Norman. 1948. 1st ed. dj. . . . .*$50–$100*

Marryat, Frank. *Mountains and Molehills, or Recollections of a Burnt Journal.* Lon. Longmans Green. 1855. 1st ed. illus. *$900*

Marryat, Frank. *Mountains and Molehills, or Recollections of a Burnt Journal.* NY. Harper & Bros. 1855. 1st Amer ed. illus. *$85*

Marryat, Capt. Frederick. *The Settlers in Canada.* Lon. 1844. 2 vols. 1st ed. mor, mar bds. . . . .*$100–$150*

Marsh, Ngaio. *Swing, Brother, Swing.* Lon. Collins Crime Club. 1949. 1st ed. dj. *$75*

Marsh, Othniel Charles. *Dinocerata: A Monograph of an Extinct Order of Gigantic Mammals.* DC. GPO. 1886. illus. plates. . . . .*$125–$175*

Marshall, J. *A History of the Colonies Planted by the English.* Phila. 1824. . . . .*$40–$55*

Marshall, John. *Life of George Washington.* . . . Phila. 1836. 2 vols. . . . .*$50–$90*

Marshall, Logan. *The Sinking of the Titanic and Great Sea Disasters.* Myers. 1912. illus. photos, rbnd. . . . .*$35–$45*

Martin and Martin. *Harness, Saddlery, Horse Clothing.* NY/Phila. 1890s catalog. . . . .*$45–$60*

Martin, L. C. *Optical Measuring Instruments.* Glasgow. 1924. illus. ex lib, 270 pp. . . . .*$30–$45*

Martin, Sadie E. *The Life and Professional Career of Emma Abbott.* Minn. 1891. illus. photos. . . . .*$25–$35*

Martineau, Harriet. *Retrospect of Western Travel.* NY. Harper. 1838. 1st U.S. ed. 276 pp, 239 pp. . . . .*$100–$250*

Martyn, Mrs. S. T. *Women of the Bible.* NY. American Tract Society. 1868. illus. . . . .*$20–$30*

Marx, Groucho. *Memoirs of a Lousy Lover.* NY. 1963. 1st ed. wrps. . . . .*$25–$35*

Mary Rose, Rev. Mother. *A Mission Tour in the Southwest Pacific.* (Bos. 1942). illus. . . . .*$15–$22*

Masefield, John. *John M. Synge.* Churchtown, Dundrum. Cuala Press. 1915. 1st ed. 1/350 cc. *$350*

Masefield, John. *The Midnight Folk.* Lon. 1927. 1st U.K. ed. dj. . . . .*$75–$95*

Masefield, John. *The Wanderer of Liverpool.* NY. 1930. 1st ed. 350 cc. . . . .*$100–$135*

Mason, Bobbie Ann. *In Country.* NY. Harper & Row. (1985). 1st ed. sgn, dj. *$65*

Mason, Bobbie Ann. *Shiloh.* NY. Harper & Row. 1982. 1st ed. dj. *$60*

Mason, Charles F. *Medical Electricity.* 1887. 1st ed. . . . .*$30–$45*

Mason, Michael H. *Where the River Runs Dry.* Lon. 1934, illus. dj. . . . .*$20–$30*

Mason, Otis Tufton. *Aboriginal American Harpoons.* DC. 1900. illus. . . . .*$35–$65*

Masters, Edgar Lee. *The Golden Fleece of California.* NY. (1936). 1st ed. . . . .*$25–$35*

Masters, Edgar Lee. *Spoon River Anthology.* NY. 1915. 1st ed. . . . .*$250–$350*

Maternal Physician . . . by an American Matron. Phila. 1818. 2nd ed. lea. . . . .*$175–$225*

Matheson, R. *Handbook of the Mosquitoes of North America.* Ithaca. 1944. . . . .*$25–$35*

Mathews. *The Writing Table of the 20th Century.* NY. 1900. illus. . . . .*$35–$40*

Mathews, John Joseph. *Wah'Kon-Tah: The Osage and the White Man's Road.* Univ. of Oklahoma Press. 1932. 1st ed. illus. fldg map. . . .*$25–$45*

Matthews, B. *Tales of Fantasy and Fact.* NY. 1896. 1st ed. . . . . .*$35–$50*

Maugham, W. Somerset. *Cakes and Ale.* Lon. (1930). 1st ed. dj. . . . .
. . . .*$200–$300*

Maugham, W. Somerset. *The Making of a Saint.* Lon. T. Fisher Unwin.
(1898). 1st ed. green bds. . . . .*$90–$125*

Maugham, W. Somerset. *Of Human Bondage.* Doran. 1915. 1st ed. dj. . .
. . . .*$175–$250*

Maugham, W. Somerset. *Then and Now.* Lon. (1946). 1st ed. dj. . . . .
. . . .*$30–$60*

Maugham, W. Somerset. *A Writer's Notebook.* Lon. (1949). 1st ed. dj. . .
. . . .*$40–$50*

Mauldin, Bill. *This Damn Tree Leaks: A Collection of War Cartoons.*
Stars & Stripes. 1945. 1st ed. wrps. . . . .*$20–$30*

Mauldin, Bill. *Up Front.* NY. 1945. 1st ed. . . . .*$10–$20*

Maunsell, Henry. *The Dublin Practice of Midwifery.* NY. William
LeBlanc. 1842. 1st Amer ed. 292 pp. . . . .*$200–$275*

Maurice, Sir Frederick. *Statesmen and Soldiers of the Civil War.* Bos.
1926. 1st ed. . . . .*$35–$50*

Mauriceau, Dr. A. M. *The Married Woman's Private Medical Com-
panion.* NY. 1852. . . . .*$100–$175*

Maury, M. F. *The Physical Geography of the Sea.* NY. 1856. illus. fldg
plates, 6th ed. . . . .*$65–$80*

Maxim, Sir Hiram. *Artificial and Natural Flight.* NY. 1908. 1st ed. illus.
. . . .*$50–$100*

Maxwell, Aymer. *Pheasants and Covert Shooting.* 1913. illus. clr plates. .
. . . .*$60–$85*

May, J. B. *The Hawks of North America.* NY. 1935. . . . .*$75–$85*

Mayer, John. *The Sportsman's Director.* Simkin Marshall. 1845. 7th ed. .
. . . .*$45*

McAdie, Alexander. *Fog.* Macmillan. 1934. 23 pp, plates. . . . .
. . . .*$30–$50*

McAllister, Agnes. *A Lone Woman in Africa.* NY. 1896. illus. . . . .
. . . .*$60–$85*

McBain, Ed. *Ax.* NY. Simon & Schuster. 1964. 1st ed. dj. *$175*

McBain, Ed. *Poison.* NY. Arbor House. 1987. 1st ed. dj. *$45*

McCaleb, Walters. *The Conquest of the West.* Prentice-Hall. (1947). 1st
ed. dj. . . . .*$14–$22*

McCarthy, Cormac. *All the Pretty Horses.* NY. Knopf. 1992. 1st ed. dj. .
. . . .*$75–$100*

McCarthy, John J. *The Science of Fighting Fire.* NY. 1943. 1st ed. illus.
....$45–$55

McCarthy, Mary. *Cannibals and Missionaries.* NY. 1970. 1st ed. dj. . . . .
....$10–$20

McCarthy, Mary. *The Group.* NY. 1963. 1st ed. dj. ....$25–$30

McCarthy, Mary. *Vietnam.* NY. 1967. wrps. ....$30–$45

McClane, A. J. *The Practical Fly Fisherman.* NY. 1953. dj. $25

McClellan, Elisabeth. *History of American Costume.* NY. 1937. ....
....$30–$45

McClellan, George B. *Report on the Organization and Campaigns . . .
Army of the Potomac.* NY. 1864. 1st ed. illus. maps. ....$35–$60

M'Clintock, Capt. *Narrative of the Discovery of the Fate of Sir John
Franklin.* . . . Lon. 1860. illus. maps. ....$50–$75

M'Clintock, Francis L. *The Voyage of the "Fox" in the Arctic Seas.* Bos.
Ticknor & Fields. 1860. author's ed. small 8vo, frontis, illus, fldg maps. . .
....$100–$130

McClintock, John S. *Pioneer Days in the Black Hills.* Deadwood. 1939.
1st ed. ....$100–$145

McClure, J. B. *Edison and His Inventions.* 1879. 1st ed. illus. ....
....$65–$100

McCormick, A. *The Tinker Gypsies of Galloway.* Dumfries. 1906. illus.
sgn. ....$25–$38

McCormick, John. *The Complete Aficionado.* 1967. 1st ed. dj. $25

McCracken, H. *Alaska Bear Trails.* NY. 1931. 1st ed. ....$40–$50

McCracken, H. *The Charles M. Russell Book.* Garden City. 1957. 1st ed.
dj. ....$45–$60

McCracken, Harold. *The Flaming Bear.* Phila/NY. 1951. 1st ed. presentation copy, sgn. ....$55–$75

McCracken, Harold. *The Frank Tenny Johnson Book.* NY. 1974. 1st ed.
folio, dj. ....$48–$65

McCracken, Harold. *George Catlin and the Old Frontier.* NY. 1959. 1st
ed. illus. sgn, dj. ....$50–$70

McCracken, Harold. *Portrait of the Old West.* NY. (1952). illus. dj. . . . .
....$25–$35

McCullagh, Rev. Joseph H. *The Sunday-school Man of the South.* . . .
Phila. 1889. 1st ed. illus. ....$55–$75

McCullers, Carson. *Clock without Hands.* Bos. Houghton Mifflin. 1961.
1st ed. dj. $85

McCullers, Carson. *The Member of the Wedding.* Bos. Houghton Mifflin. 1946. 1st ed. dj. . . . .*$50–$125*

McCullock, J. R. *A Dictionary, Practical, Theoretical, and Historical, of Commerce and Commercial Navigation.* Phila. Thomas Wardle. 1840. 2 vols. 1st Amer ed. *$275*

McCullough, Colleen. *A Creed for the Third Millennium.* Harper. 1985. 1st ed. sgn, dj. . . . .*$35–$45*

McCullough, Colleen. *The Square Root of Wonderful.* Lon. 1958. 1st Eng ed. dj. . . . .*$20–$35*

McCullough, David. *The Great Bridge.* NY. 1972. 1st ed. . . . . . .*$20–$30*

McDiarmid, Hugh. *The Fire of the Spirit.* Glasgow. 1965. wrps. . . . .*$30–$45*

McDougall, John. *Forest, Lake and Prairie: Twenty Years of Frontier Life in Western Canada 1842–62.* Tor. Briggs. 1895. 1st ed. 267 pp, plates and drawings. *$30*

McDuddie, Franklin. *History of the Town of Rochester, New Hampshire.* Manchester. 1892. 2 vols. 1st ed. illus. . . . .*$50–$65*

McEwan, Ian. *In between the Sheets.* Lon. 1978. 1st ed. dj. . . .*$175–$250*

McFee, William. *Pilgrims of Adversity.* Doubleday Doran. 1928. 1st ed. dj. . . . .*$45–$50*

McGahern, John. *The Collected Stories.* NY. 1993. 1st Amer ed. dj. . . . .*$18–$25*

McGlashan, C. F. *History of the Donner Party: A Tragedy of the Sierra.* SF. A. L. Bancroft & Co. 1881. 4th ed. inscrb by McGlashan. *$125*

McGlashan, C. F. *History of the Donner Party: A Tragedy of the Sierra.* SF. A. Carlisle & Co. 1929. 15th ed. inscrb by McGlashan. *$70*

McGowan, Archibald. *The Prisoners of War: A Reminiscence of the Rebellion.* NY. 1901. 1st ed. . . . .*$75–$125*

McGuire, J. *Diary of a Southern Refugee during the War.* NY. 1867. 1st ed. . . . .*$60–$75*

McKay, Claude. *Banjo.* NY. 1929. 1st ed. dj. . . . .*$110–$300*

McKay, G. L., and C. Larsen. *Principles and Practices of Butter-making.* NY. (1922). 3rd ed. 405 pp, illus. . . . .*$20–$35*

[McKenney and Hall]. *Ahyouwaighs, Chief of the Six Nations.* Phila. F. W. Greenough. 1838. Atlas folio, litho. *$500*

McKenney, Thomas L., and James Hall. *History of the Indian Tribes of North America, with Biographical Sketches and Anecdotes of the Principal Chiefs. . . .* Phila. D. Rice & A. N. Hart. 1855. 3 vols. 3rd octavo ed. illus,

120 hand-clr litho plates, royal octavo (10 ¹/₂ by 7 inches), aeg. . . . .
. . . .*$7,200*

McKenney, Thomas L., and Jason Hall. *The Indian Tribes of North America.* Edin. 1933. 3 vols. dj. . . . .*$500–$625*

McLean, John, M.A., Ph.D. *The Indians of Canada, Their Manners and Customs.* Lon. Kelly. 1892 (1899). illus. 3rd ed. *$95*

McMullen, Joseph V. *Islamic Carpets.* NY. 1965. . . . .*$150–$200*

McMullen, Thomas. *Handbook of Wines.* NY. 1852. 1st ed. . . . .
. . . .*$28–$40*

McMurtry, Larry. *Anything for Billy.* Simon & Schuster. (1988). 1st ed. dj. . . . .*$30–$45*

McMurtry, Larry. *The Desert Rose.* NY. Simon & Schuster. 1983. 1st ltd ed. 1/250 cc, sgn, slipcase. *$300*

McMurtry, Larry. *The Last Picture Show.* Dial Press. 1966. 1st ptg, dj. . .
. . . .*$300*

McMurtry, Larry. *Moving On.* NY. Simon & Schuster. 1970. 1st ed. dj. . .
. . . .*$100*

McMurtry, Larry. *Terms of Endearment.* NY. Simon & Schuster. 1975. 1st ed. dj, sgn. . . . .*$130–$175*

McNemar, Richard. *A Concise Answer . . . Who or What Are the Shakers.* Stockbridge. 1826. 1st ed. . . . .*$200–$250*

McPhee, John. *Coming into the Country.* Lon. 1978. 1st ed. dj. . . . .
. . . .*$30–$45*

McPhee, John. *The Deltoid Pumpkin Seed.* Farrar. 1973. 1st ed. dj. . .*$35*

McPhee, John. *Giving Good Weight.* NY. Farrar, Straus & Giroux. (1979). 1st ed. dj. *$40*

McPhee, John. *Looking for a Ship.* NY. Farrar, Straus & Giroux. (1990). 1st ed. sgn, dj. *$60*

McPhee, John. *The Pine Barrens.* Farrar, Straus & Giroux. 1968. dj. . . . .
. . . .*$75–$95*

McPhee, John. *A Roomful of Hovings.* NY. 1968. dj. . . . .*$85–$100*

McPherson, Edward. *A Handbook of Politics for 1878.* DC. 1878. large 8vo. . . . .*$40–$50*

McQuade, James. *The Cruise of the Montauk to Bermuda, the West Indies and Florida.* NY. Thos. R. Knox. 1885. 1st ed. illus. . . . .*$62–$75*

McRae, D. G. W. *The Arts and Crafts of Canada.* Tor. 1944. illus. dj. . . .
. . . .*$25–$35*

Mead, Margaret. *Male and Female.* NY. 1st ed. dj. . . . .*$45–$65*

Mead, Margaret. *Sex and Temperament in Three Primitive Societies.* NY. Morrow. 1935. 1st ed. 335 pp. *$35*

Mead, Margaret. *Twentieth Century Faith, Hope and Survival.* NY. 1972. 1st ed. dj. ....*$28–$45*

Mead, McKim, and White. *Monograph of . . . in Two Volumes.* NY. Architectural Book Publishing Co. 1925. folders with string ties, students' edition. ....*$200–$300*

Meade, Robert D. *Judah P. Benjamin, Confederate Statesman.* NY. 1943. illus. 4th ptg, presentation copy, dj. ....*$20–$35*

Meany, Tom. *Babe Ruth.* 1947. 1st ed. ....*$20–$25*

Meany, Tom. *The Boston Red Sox.* 1956. 1st ed. dj. ....*$22–$30*

Medical Society of Virginia. *Confederate Medicine 1861–1865.* np. 1961. wrps. ....*$54–$75*

Meignan, Victor. *From Paris to Peking over Siberian Snows.* Lon. 1889. illus. 2nd ed. ....*$125–$245*

Meigs, Charles D. *A Complete Treatise on Midwifery.* Phila. 1852. illus. 4th Amer ed. calf, steel plates. ....*$60–$75*

Meigs, Charles D. *Woman: Her Diseases and Remedies.* Phila. 1851..... ....*$25–$50*

Meigs, Cornelia. *Railroad West.* Little Brown. 1944. ....*$18–$20*

Mellon, James. *African Hunter.* NY. Harcourt Brace Jovanovich. [1975]. 1st ed. photos, dj. ....*$240–$300*

Melville, Herman. *Journal of a Visit to London and the Continent.* Lon. 1949. dj. ....*$20–$35*

Melville, Herman. *Journal up the Straits.* NY. The Colophon. 1935. 1st ed. 182 pp, paper bds with lea label, 650 copies printed. ....*$50–$100*

Melville, Herman. *Moby-Dick.* NY. Harper. 1851. 1st Amer ed. half mor, slipcase. *$11,500*

Melville, Herman. *Typee: A Peep at Polynesian.* NY. 1855. revised ed. black cloth. ....*$90–$125*

Mencken, H. L. *A Book of Burlesques.* Lon. 1923. 1st Eng ed. ..*$24–$32*

Mencken, H. L. *Happy Days.* NY. 1940. 1st ed. dj. ....*$25–$35*

Mencken, H. L. *Minority Report—Notebooks.* NY. 1956. 1st ed. dj. ....*$30–$40*

Mencken, H. L. *Notes on Democracy.* NY. Knopf. (1926). 1st ed. #77/235 cc, sgn. *$125*

Mencken, H. L. *The Philosophy of Friedrich Nietzsche.* Bos. 1913. 3rd ed. ....*$35–$50*

Mencken, H. L. *Treatise on Right and Wrong.* NY. 1934. 1st ed. dj. . . . . .
. . . .*$30–$50*

Menefee, Josephine T. *Virginia Housekeeper's Guide.* Roanoke. Stone
Printing. 1935. . . . .*$50–$80*

Menninger, Karl A. *Man against Himself.* NY. 1938. sgn. . . . . .*$65–$95*

Menocal, A. G. *Report of the U.S. Nicaragua Surveying Party, 1885.*
1886. 1st ed. illus. folio, fldg maps, drawings. . . . .*$150–$250*

Merril, George P. *Contributions to the History of Geology.* DC. GPO.
1906. illus. 780 pp. . . . .*$85–$100*

Merryman, Richard. *Andrew Wyeth.* Bos. 1968. 1st trade ed. clr plates,
oblong, dj. . . . .*$100–$200*

Merryweather, James C. *Fire Protection of Mansions.* Lon. 1899. 3rd ed.
. . . .*$60–$110*

Mertins, Louis and Esther. *The Intervals of Robert Frost.* Berkeley.
1947. wrps. . . . .*$50–$65*

Merton, H. W. *Descriptive Mentality from the Head, Face and Hand.*
Phila. 1899. 1st ed. illus. . . . .*$65–$75*

Merton, Thomas. *The Ascent to Truth.* NY. Harcourt Brace. (1951). 1st
ed. dj. *$50*

Merton, Thomas. *The Waters of Siloe.* Harcourt. 1949. 1st ed. dj. . . . .
. . . .*$50–$75*

Merwin, Samuel. *Silk.* Bos. 1923. 1st ed. illus. by N. C. Wyeth. . . . .
. . . .*$20–$30*

Meyrick, F. J. *Life in the Bush.* Lon. Thomas Nelson. (1939). 1st ed. illus.
dj. . . . .*$30–$40*

Michener, James. *The Drifters.* NY. Random House. (1971). 1st ed. dj. . . .
. . . .*$40*

Michener, James. *Floating World.* NY. 1954. 1st ed. dj. . . . .*$70–$85*

Michener, James. *Hawaii.* NY. 1959. 1st ed. dj. . . . .*$17–$24*

Michener, James. *Heirs of the Incas.* NY. 1924. 1st ed. dj. . . . . .*$10–$20*

Michener, James. *Sayonara.* NY. 1954. 1st ed. dj. *$125*

Michener, James. *The Source.* NY. 1965. 1st ed. dj. . . . .*$25–$40*

Michener, James. *Space.* 1982. wrps. uncorrected proof. . . . .*$75–$95*

Michener, James A. *The Unit in the Social Studies.* Camb. (1940). 1st ed.
wrps. author's first book. . . . .*$300–$500*

Michigan in Summer. Grand Rapids & Indiana Railroad. 1898. wrps. illus.
22 pp, brochure, fldg maps. . . . .*$30–$50*

Milburn, George. *The Hobo's Hornbook.* NY. 1930. dj. *$50*

Mill, John Stuart. *Autobiography.* NY. 1874. 1st Amer ed. . . . . .*$60–$85*

Mill, John Stuart. *The Subjection of Women.* Lon. Longmans Green. 1869. 1st ed. 188 pp, inscrb, scarce. *$1,500*

Mill, John Stuart. *The Subjection of Women.* NY. Appleton. 1870. 2nd U.S. ed. 188 pp. . . . . : *$150*

Mill, John Stuart. *The Subjection of Women.* Phila. 1869. 1st U.S. ed. 174 pp. *$200*

Millais, J. G., et al. *British Deer and Ground Game, Dogs, Guns and Rifles.* The London & Counties Press Association. 1913. ltd 950 cc, nbr, full lea. *$650*

Millay, Edna St. Vincent. *The Buck in the Snow.* 1928. 1st ed. dj. . . .*$60*

Millay, Edna St. Vincent. *Fatal Interview.* Harper. 1931. 1st ed. dj. . . . .*$25–$35*

Millay, Edna St. Vincent. *Mine the Harvest.* NY. 1954. 1st ed. dj. . . . .*$27–$35*

Millay, Edna St. Vincent. *The Princess Marries the Page.* Harper & Bros. 1932. 1st ed. dj. . . . .*$22–$35*

Millburn, William Henry. *The Rifle, Axe, and Saddlebags and Other Lectures.* NY. 1857. . . . .*$35–$75*

Miller. *The World in the Air: Story of Flying in Pictures.* NY. 1930. 2 vols. . . . .*$75–$95*

Miller, Arthur. *Collected Plays.* NY. 1957. 1st ed. dj. . . . .*$38–$50*

Miller, Arthur. *Death of a Salesman.* NY. 1949. 1st ed. dj. . . . .*$75–$125*

Miller, Arthur. *Focus.* Reynal & Hitchcock. 1945. 1st ed. dj. . . .*$38–$60*

Miller, Arthur. *The Price: A Play.* NY. Viking. (1968). 1st ed. dj. . . .*$45*

Miller, Francis Trevelyan. *Byrd's Great Adventure.* Phila. Winston. (1930). 1st ed. maps. . . . .*$18–$25*

Miller, Francis Trevelyan (ed). *The Photographic History of the Civil War.* NY. 1912. 10 vols. illus. lea & cloth. . . . .*$350–$400*

Miller, Henry. *Black Spring.* NY. Grove Press. 1963. 1st U.S. ed. dj. . . . .*$35–$50*

Miller, Henry. *Tropic of Cancer.* NY. Grove Press. 1961. 1st authorized Amer ed. dj. . . . .*$40–$65*

Miller, Henry. *Tropic of Capricorn.* Lon. (1964). 1st ed. dj. . . . .*$35–$60*

Miller, Henry. *The Wisdom of the Heart.* Lon. 1947. . . . .*$15–$25*

Miller, O. B. *Little Pictures of Japan.* (1925). . . . .*$25–$40*

Miller, Olive Beaupre. *My Book House.* Chi. The Bookhouse for Children. 1937. 12 vols. . . . .*$75–$100*

Miller, Olive Beaupre. *My Book House: The Latchkey.* Chi. 1921. . . . . . .
. . . .*$25–$30*

Miller, Olive Beaupre. *My Book House: The Treasure Chest.* Chi. 1920.
illus. . . . .*$20–$25*

Miller, Olive Beaupre. *Nursery Friends from France.* 1927. illus. . . . . . .
. . . .*$20–$35*

Miller, Olive Beaupre. *Tales Told in Holland.* 1926. . . . .*$25–$35*

Miller, W. *Structure of the Lung.* Bos. 1893. sgn. . . . .*$25–$32*

Milligan, Robert H. *The Jungle Folk of Africa.* Revell. (1908). 2nd ed.
decorative cvr. . . . .*$25–$35*

Milne, A. A. *By Way of Introduction.* NY. 1929. 1st Amer ed. ltd 166 cc,
sgn, slipcase. . . . .*$200–$300*

Milne, A. A. *Four Days' Wonder.* Lon. 1933. 1st ed. dj. . . . .*$35–$45*

Milne, A. A. *Gallery of Children.* McKay. (1925). 1st Amer ed. . . . .
. . . .*$75–$125*

Milne, A. A. *The House at Pooh Corner.* NY. Dutton. (1928). 1st Amer ed.
#134/250 cc, sgn by author and artist, 8vo, aeg. *$750*

Milne, A. A. *The King's Breakfast.* Lon. Methuen. (1925). 4to, cloth
backed bds, paper label, 1/100 cc, sgn. *$650*

Milne, A. A. *Michael and Mary.* Lon. 1930. 1st ed. dj. . . . .*$50–$80*

Milne, A. A. *Now We Are Six.* Dutton. (1927). 1st Amer ed. illus by
Shepard. . . . .*$100–$140*

Milne, A. A. *Now We Are Six.* Lon. 1927. 1st ed. illus. teg. . . . .
. . . .*$150–$275*

Milne, A. A. *Toad of Toad Hall.* Lon. 1929. 1st ed. dj. . . . .*$65–$115*

Milne, A. A. *When We Were Very Young.* Lon. 1924. 1st ed. dj. . . . .
. . . .*$800–$1,500*

Milne, A. A. *Winnie-the-Pooh.* Lon. (1926). 1st ed. red lea. . . . .
. . . .*$400–$600*

Milne, A. A. *Winnie-the-Pooh and Some Bees.* Dutton. 1952. 4 pop-ups,
spiral bound. . . . .*$40–$55*

Minarik, Else. *Little Bear.* Harper & Row. (1960). illus by Maurice
Sendak. . . . .*$15–$20*

**Miniatures from Paris, Showing the Leading Designs by the Great
Parisian Modistes.** . . . Bos. Wm. S. Butler & Co. 1898–99. pictorial wrps,
32 pp. . . . .*$50–$75*

Minkoff, George R. *Bibliography of the Black Sun Press.* Great Neck.
1970. . . . .*$50–$95*

Minogue, Anna C. *Loretto Annals of the Century.* NY. 1912. 1st ed. illus. 252 pp. . . . . *$18–$25*

Miscellany of Arms and Armor, Presented to Bashford Dean. np. 1927. illus. ltd # 127/150 cc, presentation copy from Hugh Smiley. . . . .
. . . .*$125–$200*

Miss Beecher's Domestic Receipt-Book. NY. 1867. 5th ed. . . . . *$30–$45*

Mitchell, Margaret. *Gone with the Wind.* NY. 1936. 1st ed. inscrb, sgn, gray cloth, "Published May 1936" appears on copyright page, pictorial dj. *$4,025*

Mitchell, S. A. *Mitchell's New Atlas of the United States.* Phila. 1874. illus. hand-clr maps. . . . .*$115–$135*

Mitchell, S. Weir. *The Autobiography of a Quack.* NY. 1900. 1st ed. illus by A. J. Keller. *$45*

Mitchell's Modern Geography of the World. Phila. 1856. illus. woodcuts. . . . .*$25–$35*

Mitchell's New General Atlas. Phila. 1864. folio, maps. . . . . . .*$300–$400*

Mitchener, C. H. (ed). *Historic Events in the Tuscarawas and Muskingham Valleys.* Dayton. 1876. . . . .*$40–$65*

Mitford, Mary Russell. *Our Village.* Lon. Macmillan. 1893. illus. by Hugh Thompson, 1/475 cc, printed December 1883. . . . .*$155*

Mitford, William. *The History of Greece.* Lon. Cadell. 1822. 10 vols. three-quarter calf, mar bds. . . . .*$125–$220*

Mivart, St. George. *On Genesis of Species.* NY. 1871. 1st ed. illus. 1st Amer ed. , ...*$26–$35*

Molyneux, Edwin. *Chrysanthemums and Their Culture.* Lon. 1881. 1st ed. . . . .*$30–$40*

Monroe, James. *Message from the President.* DC. 1821. 1st ed. wrps. sewn. . . . .*$75–$95*

Monroe, Marilyn. *My Story.* NY. 1974. 1st ed. dj. . . . .*$30–$35*

Montessori, Maria. *Dr. Montessori's Own Handbook.* NY. Stokes. (1914). 1st ed. *$35*

Montessori, Maria. *The Montessori Method.* NY. Stokes. 1912. illus. 1st U.S. ed. author's first book, 377 pp, scarce. . . . .*$125–$150*

Montgomery, Frances. *Billy Whiskers Tourist.* Saalfield. 1929. illus. . . . .*$20–$35*

Montgomery, L. M. *Anne of Avonlea.* L. C. Page. . . . .*$25–$35*

Montgomery, L. M. *Anne of the Island.* A. L. Burt. dj. . . . .*$25–$35*

Montgomery, L. M. *Anne's House of Dreams.* A. L. Burt. dj. . . .*$25–$37*

Montgomery, L. M. *Chronicles of Avonlea.* NY. 1912. dj. . . . . .*$12–$18*

Montgomery, L. M. *Golden Road.* 1913. 1st ed. . . . .*$25–$40*

Montgomery, L. M. *Jane of Lantern Hill.* Grosset. 1937. dj. . . . .
. . . .*$25–$35*

Montgomery, L. M. *Rainbow Valley.* NY. 1919. wrps. rprnt. . . . .
. . . .*$30–$40*

Moore, Brian. *Cold Heaven.* NY. Holt Rinehart Winston. (1983). 1st ed.
dj. . . . .*$20–$25*

Moore, Brian. *The Great Victorian Collection.* NY. Farrar, Straus &
Giroux. (1975). 1st ed. dj. *$50*

Moore, Brian. *Judith Hearne.* Lon. 1955. 1st ed. sgn, dj. . . . .
. . . .*$300–$650*

Moore, Clement C. *The Night before Christmas.* Chi. 1908. illus. by J. R.
Neill. . . . .*$40–$50*

Moore, Clement C. *Poems.* NY. 1844. 1st ed. . . . .*$800–$1,000*

Moore, Frank. *Rebel Rhymes and Rhapsodies.* NY. 1864. 1st ed. calf
spine, bds. . . . .*$55–$100*

Moore, Frank. *Women of the War.* Hartford. 1866. 1st ed. 9 steel engr,
illus. . . . .*$35–$45*

Moore, George Henry. *Notes on the History of Slavery in Massachusetts.*
NY. 1866. 1st ed. . . . .*$150–$175*

Moore, H. N. *Life and Services of Gen. Anthony Wayne.* Phila. 1845. illus.
. . . .*$45–$50*

Moore, John Hamilton. *The Seaman's Complete Daily Assistant and New
Mariner's Compass.* Lon. 1796. 5th ed. sailcloth over calf. . . . .
. . . .*$190–$235*

Moore, Joseph. *Penicillin in Syphilis.* Chas. Thomas. 1946. 1st ed. dj. . . .
. . . .*$22–$25*

Moore, Marianne. *Collected Poems.* Lon. Faber & Faber. 1951. 1st ed. dj.
. . . .*$55–$90*

Moore, Marianne. *The Complete Poems.* NY. Macmillan. (1967). 1st ed.
dj. . . . .*$55–$100*

Moore, Marianne. *A Marianne Moore Reader.* NY. Viking. 1961. 1st ed.
301 pp, inscrb, dj. *$225*

Moore, Marianne. *O to Be a Dragon.* NY. Viking. 1959. 1st ed. 37 pp,
inscrb, dj. *$250*

Moore, Marianne. *Poems.* Lon. Egoist Press. 1921. 1st ed. author's first
book, decorative wraps. . . . .*$500–$600*

Moore, Marianne. *Tell Me, Tell Me.* NY. Viking. 1966. 1st ed. dj. . . . . . .
. . . .*$45–$90*

Moore, William. *Indian Wars of the United States . . . with Accounts of the Origin, Manners, Superstitions, etc. of the Aborigines.* Phila. Leary. 1850. 1st ed. illus. rbnd. . . . .*$80–$120*

Moravian Tiles. Doylestown, PA. Moravian Pottery & Tile Works. early 20th century. printed wrps, illus, 16 pp. . . . .*$40–$50*

Morgan, Lewis H. *House and House-life of the American Aborigines.* DC. GPO. 1881. illus. litho and photo plates. . . . .*$95–$125*

Morley, Christopher. *The Old Mandarin.* NY. 1947. 1st ed. . . . .
. . . .*$22–$30*

Morley, Christopher. *Seacoast of Bohemia.* 1929. 1st ed. wrps. . . . .
. . . .*$15–$20*

Morley, Christopher. *Where the Blue Begins.* NY. 1922. 1st ed. illus by Rackham, dj. . . . .*$30–$75*

Morris, Frank, and E. A. Eames. *Our Wild Orchids.* NY. 1929. 1st ed. illus. dj. . . . .*$28–$35*

Morris, Gouverneur. *Diary and Letters. . . .* NY. 1888. 2 vols. 1st ed. illus. . . . .*$45–$75*

Morris, Robert. *Freemasonry in the Holy Land.* NY. Masonic Publishing. 1872. 1st ed. illus. . . . .*$60–$70*

Morrison, Toni. *Beloved.* NY. (1987). 1st ed. sgn, dj. . . . .*$60–$70*

Morrison, Toni. *The Bluest Eye.* Lon. 1979. 1st ed. dj. . . . .*$65–$75*

Morrison, Toni. *Tar Baby.* 1981. 1st ed. dj. . . . .*$30–$60*

Morse, A. H. *Radio: Beam and Broadcast.* 1925. 1st ed. illus. . . . .
. . . .*$70–$90*

Morse, Edward Lind. *Samuel F. B. Morse: His Letters and Journals.* 1914. 2 vols. 1st ed. illus. . . . .*$65–$115*

Morse, Frances. *Furniture of Olden Time.* Macmillan. (1941). illus. . . . . . .
. . . .*$35–$45*

Morse, J. *Geography Made Easy.* Utica, NY. 1819. . . . .*$30–$50*

Morse, J., and E. Parish. *A Compendious History of New England.* Charlestown. 1820. . . . .*$20–$30*

Morse, Jedidiah. *American Gazeteer.* Bos. 1797. 7 maps. . . . .*$100–$300*

Morse, Jedidiah. *American Gazetteer.* Bos. 1810. rev, 2 maps. . . . .
. . . .*$50–$100*

Morse, Jedidiah. *Annals of the American Revolution. . . .* Hartford. 1824. illus. . . . .*$85–$100*

Morse, Samuel (ed). *Confessions of a French Catholic Priest.* NY. 1873.
....$14–$20

Morse, Samuel F. B. *Examination of the Telegraphic Apparatus.* GPO.
1869. vol 4. ....$30–$40

Mortensen, William. *Mortensen on the Negative.* NY. 1940. 1st ed. illus.
....$25–$35

Mother Goose. Saalfield. 1933. illus by Fern Bissel Peat. $40

Moton, Robert Russa. *What the Negro Thinks.* Garden City. 1929. 1st ed.
sgn. ....$60–$95

Moxon, Joseph. *A Tutor to Astronomy and Geography.* Lon. S. Roycroft.
1686. 4th ed, enlarged, lea, drawings, diagrams, 271 pp. $700

Mrs. Putnam's Receipt Book. Bos. 1858. ....$33–$40

Muenscher, W. C. and M. A. *Rice, Garden Spice and Wild Pot Herbs.*
Ithaca. 1955. illus. ....$40–$50

Muir, John. *My First Summer in the Sierra.* Bos. 1911. 1st ed. ....
....$95–$125

Muir, John. *The Mountains of California.* NY. 1922. illus. .....$22–$40

Muir, John. *Notes on My Journeying California's Northern Mountains.*
Ashland, OR. 1975. wrps. illus. private ptg. $15

Muir, John. *Our National Parks.* Bos. 1902. 2nd ptg. ....$37–$45

Muir, John. *Travels in Alaska.* Bos. 1916. illus. ....$28–$35

Muir, John (ed). *Picturesque California....* NY. 1894. illus. folio. .....
....$140–$180

Muir, John. *Yosemite and the Sierra Nevada.* Bos. Houghton Mifflin.
(1948). 1st ed. later ptg, photos by Ansel Adams, dj. $65

Muir, Percy. *English Children's Books, 1600 to 1900.* Lon. 1954. 1st ed.
dj. $95

Mulford, Isaac S. *A Civil and Political History of New Jersey.* Phila.
1851. 500 pp. $60

Mulfurd, Clarence. *Hopalong Cassidy's Coloring Book.* NY. 1951. wrps.
....$15–$20

Mullins, Michael A. *The Fremont Rifles: A Hist. of 37th Ill. Vet. Vol.
Infantry.* NC. 1990. illus. sgn, dj. ....$35–$50

Mulock, Dinah Maria. *The Woman's Kingdom.* NY. 1869. 1st ed. illus. .
....$33–$40

Mulvaney, Charles Pelham. *The History of the Northwest Rebellion of
1885.* Tor. 1886. 440 pp, maps. $50

Mumford, John Kimberly. *Oriental Rugs.* NY. 1902.........$50–$75

Mumford, John Kimberly. *Oriental Rugs.* NY. 1923. illus. 4th ed. . . . . .
. . . .*$35–$50*

Munn, Robert F. *The Coal Industry in America.* Morgantown. West Virginia Univ. Library. 1977. 2nd ed. . . . .*$20–$30*

Munro, Alice. *Who Do You Think You Are?* Macmillan of Canada. 1978. 1st ed. dj. . . . .*$35–$45*

Munro, Hector Hugh ["Saki"]. *The Toys of Peace.* Lon. John Lane. 1919. 1st ed. 303 pp. . . . .*$60–$75*

Munson, John W. *Reminiscences of a Mosby Guerilla.* NY. 1906. 1st ed. illus. . . . .*$75–$100*

Munson, Loveland. *The Early History of Manchester, VT.* Manchester. 1876. . . . .*$35–$55*

Murdoch, Iris. *The Unicorn.* Lon. 1963. 1st ed. dj. . . . .*$35–$45*

Murphy, E. Jefferson. *Understanding Africa.* NY. (1969). illus by Louise Jefferson, sgn, dj. . . . .*$15–$20*

Murphy, Robert Cushman. *Oceanic Birds of So. America.* NY. 1936. 2 vols. illus. boxed. . . . .*$80–$125*

Murray, W. H. H. *Daylight Land.* 1888. illus. . . . .*$28–$37*

Murray, W. H. H. *How John Norton the Trapper Kept His Christmas.* private ptg. 1885. . . . .*$25–$30*

Murray, W. H. H. *Lake Champlain and Its Shores.* Bos. (1890). 1st ed. . . .
. . . .*$30*

Mursell, James L. *Music in American Schools.* NY. 1943. illus. . . . .
. . . .*$10–$12*

Mussolini, Benito. *The Cardinal's Mistress.* NY. 1928. 1st ed in English.
. . . .*$45–$65*

My Cave Life in Vicksburg. NY. Appleton. 1864. 1st ed. . . . .
. . . .*$150*

Myers, Frank. *Soldiering in Dakota among the Indians.* SD. 1936. wrps. .
. . . .*$20–$35*

Myrick, Herbert. *Cache La Poudre, the Romance of a Tenderfoot in the Days of Custer.* NY. 1915. 1st trade, illus, 202 pp. *$50*

Mytinger, Caroline. *Headhunting in the Solomon Islands.* Macmillan. 1942. 1st ed. illus. dj. . . . .*$18–$25*

Nabokov, Vladimir. *Invitation to a Beheading.* Putnam. 1959. 1st U.S. ed. dj. . . . .*$45–$75*

Nabokov, Vladimir. *King, Queen, Knave.* McGraw-Hill. 1968. 1st U.S. ed. dj. *$30*

Nabokov, Vladimir. *Lectures on Russian Literature.* 1981. 1st ed. . . . . . .
. . . .*$25–$30*

Nabokov, Vladimir. *Lolita.* Paris. 1955. 2 vols. 1st ed. wrps. 1st issue. . . .
. . . .*$275–$400*

Nabokov, Vladimir. *Look at the Harlequins!* McGraw-Hill. 1974. 1st ed.
dj. . . . .*$25–$30*

Nabokov, Vladimir. *Nabokov's Quartet.* NY. 1966. 1st ed. . . . . .*$35–$55*

Nabokov, Vladimir. *Notes on Prosody.* NY. 1964. dj. . . . .*$50–$75*

Nabokov, Vladimir. *Pale Fire.* Putnam. 1962. 1st U.S. ed. dj. . . . .
. . . .*$95–$125*

Nagel, Charles. *Boy's Civil War Story.* St. Louis. 1934. 1st ed. presentation copy, sgn. . . . .*$20–$30*

Naipaul, V. S. *The Loss of El Dorado.* Lon. Andre Deutsch. 1960. 1st ed.
dj. . . . .*$80–$100*

Naipaul, V. S. *A Turn in the South.* NY. Knopf. 1989. 1st trade ed. dj. . . .
. . . .*$14–$20*

Nansen, Fridtjof. *Eskimo Life.* Lon. Longmans Green. 1893. frontis, plates, woodcuts. . . . .*$130–$175*

Nansen, Fridtjof. *Farthest North . . . 1893–96.* NY. Harper & Bros. 1897.
2 vols. 1st Amer ed. 4 fldg maps, 16 clr plates, pictorial cloth, teg. . . . .
. . . .*$95–$120*

Nansen, Fridtjof. *The First Crossing of Greenland.* Lon. 1892. illus. fldg map. . . . .*$45–$65*

Nansen, Fridtjof. *Through Siberia, the Land of the Future.* NY. Stokes.
1914. 1st Amer ed. illus, maps. . . . .*$175–$250*

Napheys, Geo. H. *The Physical Life of a Woman.* Phila. George Maclean.
1870. . . . .*$28–$38*

Narrative of Capt. James Cook's Voyages Round the World. Lon. 1848. .
. . . .*$58–$70*

Narrative of Five Youths from the Sandwich Islands. . . . NY. 1816. wrps.
. . . .*$50–$100*

Nash, E. B. *Leaders in Homeopathic Therapeutics.* Phila. 1901. 2nd ed. . . .
. . . .*$35–$40*

Nash, Ogden. *The Moon Is Shining Bright as Day.* Lippincott. 1953. 1st
ed. . . . .*$25–$35*

Nash, Wallis. *Two Years in Oregon.* Appleton. 1882. 2nd ed. . . .*$60–$75*

Nasmyth, James, and James Carpenter. *The Moon: Considered as a Planet, a World, and a Satellite.* Lon. 1885. illus. 3rd ed. . . . . . .*$75–$150*

Nathan, George Jean. *Art of the Night.* NY. 1928. 1st ed. ltd #192/200 cc, sgn. . . . .*$45–$75*

Nation, Carry A. *The Use and Need of the Life of Carry A. Nation.* . . . Topeka. 1905. wrps. illus. . . . .*$85–$125*

The Natural History of the Whale. Concord, NH. Rufus Merrill. 1844. wrps. illus. 152 by 10 cm. *$250*

The Nature Library. Doubleday. 1904. 10 vols. . . . .*$200–$280*

The Nautical Almanac and Astronomical Ephemeris for the Year 1837. Lon. John Murray. 1835. 526 pp. . . . .*$35–$45*

Near, I. W. *A History of Steuben County, New York, and Its People.* Chi. 1911. 2 vols. . . . .*$100–$135*

Nearing, Scott. *The Conscience of a Radical.* MA. 1965. 1st ed. dj. . . . .*$22–$30*

Nearing, Scott. *Maple Sugar Book.* 2nd ed. dj. . . . .*$18–$25*

Neff, Jacob. *The Army and Navy of America from the French and Indian Wars.* . . . Phila. 1845. fldg plates. . . . .*$52–$60*

Neill, Miss E. *The Every-day Cook-book and Encyclopedia of Practical Recipes.* NY. 1888. . . . .*$25–$35*

Neill, Edward. *The History of Minnesota.* . . . Phila. 1858. 1st ed. fldg map. . . . .*$50–$95*

Nelson, E. W. *Report upon the Natural History of Collections . . . Alaska.* DC. 1887. illus. . . . .*$85–$125*

Nelson, Henry Loomis, and H. A. Ogden. *Uniforms of the United States Army.* NY. 1959. illus. . . . .*$40–$50*

Nevins, W. S. *Witchcraft in Salem Village.* Salem/Bos. 1892. illus. . . . .*$60–$85*

New, Egan. *Battersea Enamels.* Lon/Bos. 1926. illus. . . . .*$50–$95*

The New England Primer. Worcester. S. A. Howland. nd. wrps. 644 pp. *$45*

New Jersey: A Profile in Pictures. NY. Barrows & Co. 1939. 1st ed. American Guide Series, WPA, dj. . . . .*$15–$20*

New System of Domestic Cookery . . . by a Lady. Edin. 1843. illus. rbnd, three-quarter calf, mar bds. . . . .*$95–$110*

New Treatise on Surveying and Navigation. NY. 1864. . . . .*$18–$25*

Newcombe, Rexford. *Old Kentucky Architecture.* NY. 1940. 1st ed. plates. . . . .*$35–$45*

Newell, Peter. *The Hole Book.* NY. 1908. 1st ed. illus. . . . .*$70–$125*

Newhall, Walter S. *A Memoir.* Phila. 1864. 1st ed. regimental. . .*$60–$75*

Newhouse, S. *The Trapper's Guide: A Manual.* . . . NY. 1869. illus. 3rd ed. . . . .*$35–$47*

Newton, Helmut. *White Women.* 1976. 1st ed. presentation copy, dj. . . . .
. . . .*$75–$150*

Newton, Robert R. *Ancient Planetary Observations and the Validity of Ephemeris Time.* Balt. 1976. . . . .*$15–$25*

Nichols, Frederick. *The Early Architecture of Georgia.* Chapel Hill. Univ. of North Carolina Press. 1957. 1st ed. illus. 292 pp, slipcase. . . . .
. . . .*$150–$200*

Nightingale, Florence. *Notes on Nursing.* Bos. William Carter. 1860. 104 pp. *$250*

Nikoleyev, B. A. *Thermodynamic Assessment of Rocket Engines.* NY. 1963. translated by W. E. G. Jones, 150 pp. . . . .*$30–$40*

Nimoy, Leonard. *I Am Not Spock.* Millbrae. 1975. 1st ed. softbound, photos. . . . .*$30–$40*

Nin, Anaïs. *Children of the Albatross.* Dutton. 1947. 1st U.S. ed. dj. . . . . .
. . . .*$50–$95*

Nin, Anaïs. *The Four Chambered Heart.* 1950. 1st ed. dj. . . . . .*$75–$175*

Nin, Anaïs. *Ladders to Fire.* Dutton. 1946. 1st ed. dj. . . . .*$50–$110*

Nin, Anaïs. *A Spy in the House of Love.* NY. 1954. . . . .*$50–$60*

The Ninth Air Force Service Command in the European Theatre of Operations. NY. 1945. 1st ed. photos. . . . .*$75–$95*

Niven, Larry. *The Integral Trees.* NY. Ballantine. 1984. 1st ed. dj, presentation copy. *$35*

Nixon, Richard. *The Memoirs of Richard Nixon.* NY. Grosset. 1978. 1st ed. boxed, sgn. . . . .*$145–$175*

Nixon, Richard. *No More Vietnams.* sgn. . . . .*$45–$75*

Noah, Mordecai M. *Discourse . . . Consecration of the Synogogue of K.K. She'erith Yilra'el . . . on Friday, the 10th of Nisan, 5578.* NY. C. S. Van Winkle. 1818. 1st ed. . . . .*$125–$250*

Nobel, Alfred. *Les Explosifs Modernes.* Paris. 1876. 1st ed. . . .*$200–$230*

Nordhoff, Charles. *The Communistic Societies of the United States.* . . . NY. Harper & Brothers. 1875. 439 pp. . . . .*$100–$200*

Norman, Dorothy. *Alfred Stieglitz: An American Seer.* NY. 1973. 1st ed. illus. dj. . . . .*$75–$90*

Norris, Frank. *McTeague: A Story of San Francisco.* NY. 1899. 1st ed. . . .
. . . .*$100–$245*

Norris, Frank. *The Octopus: A Story of California.* NY. 1901. 1st ed. claret cloth, leaded, decorated in gilt. *$200*

Norris, Frank. *The Pit: A Story of Chicago.* NY. Doubleday. 1903. 1st ed. inscrb. *$125*

Norris, Frank. *The Pit.* NY. 1903. 1st ed. . . . .*$50–$80*

Norris, Frank. *The Works.* Garden City. Doubleday. 1928. 10 vols. .*$100*

Northrop, Solomon. *Narr. of a Citizen of N.Y. Kidnapped . . . in 1841, Rescued in 1853.* Derby & Miller. 1853. . . . .*$75–$100*

Northrup, H. D. *Chinese Horrors and Persecutions of Christians.* . . . Phila. 1900. 1st ed. illus. engr, photos. . . . .*$135–$225*

Norton, A. Tiffany. *History of Sullivan's Campaign against Iroquois.* Lima, NY. 1879. fldg map. . . . .*$65–$70*

Norton, Andre. *Catseye.* Harcourt. 1961. 1st ed. dj. . . . .*$30–$45*

Norton, Andre. *Moon Mirror.* NY. (1988). 1st ed. dj. . . . .*$15–$25*

Norton, Andre. *Night of Masks.* Harcourt. 1964. 1st ed. dj. . . . . .*$65–$85*

Norton, Andre. *Ordeal in Otherwhere.* World. 1964. 1st ed. dj. .*$20–$85*

Norton, Andre. *The Sword Is Drawn.* Bos. Houghton Mifflin. 1944. 1st ed. 180 pp. . . . .*$30–$45*

Norton, Andre. *Wraiths of Time.* NY. 1976. 1st ed. dj. . . . .*$50–$65*

Norton, Caroline T. *The Rocky Mountain Cook Book.* Denver. 1903. . . . .*$30–$40*

Norton, John P. *Elements of Scientific Agriculture.* Pease. 1859. 1st ed. 208 pp. . . . .*$60–$75*

Noyes, A. J. *In the Land of Chinook, or The Story of Blaine County.* Helena. 1917. 1st ed. illus. . . . .*$75–$145*

Noyes, Katherine M. *Jesse Macy: An Autobiography.* Springfield, IL. 1933. 1st ed. illus. . . . .*$50–$75*

Nutt, Frederick. *The Complete Confectioner.* . . . Lon. 1809. illus. plates, calf. . . . .*$150–$225*

Nuttall, T. *Manual of Ornithology.* Bos. 1834. . . . .*$45–$75*

Nutting, Wallace. *American Windsors.* Wallace Nutting. (1917). . . . .*$65–$75*

Nutting, Wallace. *Beautiful Maine.* . . . .*$15–$20*

Nutting, Wallace. *The Clock Book.* Old America. 1924. 1st ed. . .*$55–$67*

Nutting, Wallace. *England Beautiful.* NY. 1928. illus. . . . .*$15–$22*

Nutting, Wallace. *Furniture of the Pilgrim Century 1620–1720.* Bos. 1921. 1st ed. illus. . . . .*$50–$60*

Nutting, Wallace. *Ireland Beautiful.* NY. 1925. 1st ed. ....$14–$22

Nutting, Wallace. *New Hampshire Beautiful.* 1923. 1st ed. wrps. ....
....$25–$45

Nutting, Wallace. *Pennsylvania Beautiful.* 1924. 1st ed. illus. ....$18–$25

Nutting, Wallace. *Pennsylvania Beautiful.* 1935. illus..........$12–$20

Nutting, Wallace. *Photographic Art Secrets.* NY. 1927. 1st ed. illus. ....
....$60–$75

Nutting, Wallace. *Vermont Beautiful.* 1st ed. ....$20–$22

Oates, Joyce Carol. *Angel of Light.* Dutton. 1981. 1st ed. dj. ....$20–$25

Oates, Joyce Carol. *The Goddess and Other Women.* Vanguard. 1974. 1st
ed. dj..$30

Oates, Joyce Carol. *Marriages and Infidelities.* Vanguard. 1972. 1st ed.
dj. $30

Oates, Joyce Carol. *On Boxing.* NY. 1987. illus. sgn, dj. ....$45–$55

Oates, Joyce Carol. *Triumph of the Spider Monkey.* ltd 350 cc, presentation copy, sgn. ....$75–$85

O'Brien (ed). *Best Short Stories of 1923.* NY. 1924. ....$20–$30

O'Brien, F. *Atolls of the Sun.* NY. 1992. photos, map. ....$18–$27

O'Brien, Tim. *The Nuclear Age.* NY. Knopf. 1985. 1st ed. sgn, dj. ......
....$50

O'Brien, Tim. *The Things They Carried.* 1990. 1st ed. dj. $40

O'Cathasaigh, P. *The Story of the Irish Citizen Army.* Dublin. 1919. 1st
ed. wrps. ....$150–$225

O'Connor, Flannery. *A Good Man Is Hard to Find.* NY. Harcourt Brace.
(1955). 1st ed. 251 pp, dj. ....$400–$600

O'Connor, Flannery. *Mysteries and Manners.* NY. 1969. 1st ed. dj. ....
....$45–$60

O'Connor, Flannery. *Wise Blood.* NY. 1952. 1st ed. dj. .....$350–$725

O'Connor, Frank. *Lords and Commons: Translations from the Irish.*
Dublin. Cuala Press. 1938. 1st ed. 1/250 cc, dj. $300

O'Connor, Jack. *The Art of Hunting Big Game in North America.* NY.
1967. 1st ed. illus. dj. ....$35–$50

O'Connor, Jack. *The Big Game Animals of North America.* NY. 1961.
folio, dj. ....$45–$60

O'Connor, Jack. *The Big Game Rifle.* NY. 1952. 1st ed. dj. ...$60–$100

O'Connor, Jack. *Jack O'Connor's Big Game Hunts.* NY. 1963. illus. ...
....$60–$75

O'Connor, John. *The Adobe Book.* Santa Fe. Ancient City. 1973. 1st ed.
dj. *$45*

Odets, Clifford. *Clash by Night.* NY. Random House. (c 1942). 1st ed. dj.
. . . .*$50*

Odets, Clifford. *Golden Boy.* NY. 1937. 1st ed. sgn. . . . .
. . . .*$135–$150*

Odets, Clifford. *Paradise Lost: A Play in Three Acts.* NY. Random House.
(c 1936). 1st ed. dj. *$150*

Odets, Clifford. *Three Plays: Awake and Sing!; Waiting for Lefty; Till the
Day I Die.* NY. Covici Friede. (c 1935). 1st ed. dj. *$150*

Odum, Howard Washington. *The Negro and His Songs.* Chapel Hill.
1925. . . . .*$45–$75*

Odum, Howard Washington. *Rainbow round My Shoulder: The Blue
Trail of Black Ulysses.* Bobbs Merrill. 1928. 1st ed. dj. . . . .*$37–$65*

O'Faolain, Sean. *Come Back to Erin.* Viking. 1940. 1st U.S. ed. dj. . . . . .
. . . .*$45–$50*

O'Faolain, Sean. *The Life Story of Eamon De Valera.* Dublin. 1933. 1st
ed. . . . .*$60–$75*

Official Guide of the National Association of Pro. Baseball Leagues. NY.
Spalding. 1903. wrps. illus. photos. . . . .*$100–$125*

***The Official Railway and Steamboat Traveler's Guide ... Tourists in
Japan.*** Yokohama. 1889. map in pocket. . . . .*$40–$55*

Ogg, Frederick Austin. *The Opening of the Mississippi.* NY. 1904. 1st ed.
illus. maps. . . . .*$37–$50*

O'Hara, John. *And Other Stories.* 1968. 1st ed. dj. . . . .*$8–$18*

O'Hara, John. *The Farmers Hotel.* Random House. 1951. 1st ed. dj. . . . .
. . . .*$30–$40*

O'Hara, John. *From the Terrace.* NY. Random House. 1958. 1st ed. dj. . .
. . . .*$30–$40*

O'Hara, John. *Ten North Frederick.* NY. Random House. (1955). 1st ed.
dj. *$35*

O'Hara, John. *Waiting for Winter.* NY. 1966. 1st ed. dj. . . . .
. . . .*$30–$45*

Okaura, Kakuzo. *The Book of Tea.* NY. 1912. . . . .*$20–$45*

O'Keefe, Georgia. *Georgia O'Keefe.* NY. 1976. 1st ed. folio, dj. . . . .
. . . .*$75–$100*

Olcott, Charles S. *The Lure of the Camera.* Bos. 1914. 1st ed. 301 pp. . . . .
. . . .*$20–$35*

Old Dame Trot and Her Comical Cat. Lon. nd. illus. . . . .$350–$450

Oliver, W. R. B. *The Moaris of New Zealand and Australia.* Wellington. 1949. . . . .$50–$65

Oliver, W. R. B. *New Zealand Birds.* Wellington. 1955. 2nd ed. clr plates. . . . .$67–$75

Olympia 1936. Germany. 1936. 2 vols. illus. photos. $195

Omar Khayyám. *Rubaiyát.* NY. Grolier Club. 1935. 1st ed. Eng translation by Edward Fitzgerald, gilt floral wraps, 1/150 cc. $200

Rubaiyát of Omar Khayyam. NY. Doran. nd. illus by Edmund Dulac. . . . .$45–$65

O'Neill, Eugene. *Ah, Wilderness.* Random House. 1933. 1st ed. dj. $115

O'Neill, Eugene. *Anna Christie.* NY. 1930. illus. 775 cc, sgn. . . . .$95–$125

O'Neill, Eugene. *Dynamo.* NY. Horace Liveright. 1929. 1st ed. dj. . . .$100

O'Neill, Eugene. *The Iceman Cometh.* NY. 1982. illus. ltd 2,000 cc, sgn by Baskin, slipcase. . . . .$65–$95

O'Neill, Eugene. *Lazarus Laughed.* NY. 1927. 1st ed. dj. . . . . .$75–$125

O'Neill, Eugene. *Mourning Becomes Electra.* Boni & Liveright. 1925. 1st ed. dj. . . . .$45–$75

O'Neill, Eugene. *Strange Interlude.* NY. Boni & Liveright. 1928. 1st ed. dj. $75

Oppenheimer, J. Robert. *Science and the Common Understanding.* NY. 1954. 1st ed. . . . .$25–$30

Oration Delivered in Wallingford . . . before Republicans of Connecticut. New Haven, 1801. . . . .$32–$45

Orcutt, Samuel. *The Indians of the Housatonic and Naugatuck Valleys.* Hartford. 1882. illus. . . . .$90–$135

Orwell, George. *Animal Farm.* NY. Harcourt. 1946. 1st U.S. ed. dj. . . . .$65–$110

Orwell, George. *Animal Farm.* Lon. 1945. 1st ed. . . . .$75–$125

Orwell, George. *England Your England, and Other Essays.* Lon. Secker & Warburg. 1953. 1st ed. dj. $65

Orwell, George. *Nineteen Eighty Four.* NY. 1949. 1st Amer ed. red dj. . . . .$125–$250

Orwell Reader, George Orwell. NY. 1956 1st ed. wrps. . . . .$50–$75

Osborne, Russell. *Journal of a Trapper.* Boise. 1921. . . . .$37–$50

Osgood, C. *Ingalik Material Culture.* New Haven. 1940. illus. . .$60–$80

Osler, William. *Aeguanimitas.* Phila. 1906. 2nd ed. 475 pp. ....*$60–$75*

Osler, William. *An Alabama Student and Other Biographical Essays.* Oxford. 1908. ....*$75*

Osler, William. *Biblioteca Osleriana: A Catalogue of Books Illustrating the History of Medicine and Science.* McGill-Queens Univ. Pr. 1969. 2nd ed. 792 pp. ....*$250–$375*

Osler, William. *Lectures on the Diagnosis of Abdominal Tumors.* Lon. 1900. ....*$20–$25*

Osler, William. *The Old Humanities and the New Science.* Bos. 1920. dj. ....*$95–$125*

Osler, William. *Principles and Practice of Medicine.* NY. 1892. ....*$540–$900*

Osler, William. *Principles and Practice of Medicine.* NY. (1898). illus. 3rd ed. ....*$200–$250*

Osler, William. *Science and Immortality: Ingersoll Lecture.* Bos. 1904. 1st ed. ....*$45–$60*

Ossoli, Margaret Fuller. *Woman in the 19th Century.* Jewett. 1955. ....*$30–$40*

Oswald, John Clyde. *Printing in the Americas.* NY/Lon. 1937. 1st ed. illus. dj. ....*$45–$85*

Otis, James. *Toby Tyler, or Ten Weeks with a Circus.* NY. Harper & Bros. 1881. 1st ed. illus. ....*$135–$195*

Ottley, Roi. *New World A-Coming: Inside Black America.* Bos. [1943]. illus. 364 pp. ....*$9.50–$14*

Oudemans, A. C. *The Great Sea-serpent.* Lon. 1892. illus. ....*$55–$150*

Our New Friends: Dick and Jane Reader. *1946* ....*$25–$50*

Owen, Catherine. *Choice Cookery.* NY. 1889. ....*$30–$45*

Owen, Catherine. *Culture and Cooking.* NY. 1881. ....*$30–$45*

Owen, Sir R. *Memoir on the Gorilla.* Lon. 1865. ....*$500–$750*

Ozick, Cynthia. *The Messiah of Stockholm.* NY. Knopf. 1987. 1st ed. dj. *$30*

Paddock, Mrs. A. G. *The Fate of Madame La Tour: A Tale of Great Salt Lake.* NY. 1861. 1st ed. ....*$37–$45*

Page, Harry S. *Between the Flags: The Recollections of a Gentleman Rider.* NY. Derrydale Press. 1929. 1/850 cc, 8vo. ....*$60–$90*

Page, V. *Ford V-8 Cars and Trucks.* NY. 1940. ....*$30–$35*

Page, Victor W. *The Model T Ford Car.* NY. 1917. ....*$45–$65*

Paige, Satchel. *Maybe I'll Pitch Forever.* NY. 1962. 1st ed. ....*$35–$50*

Paine, A. B. *Mark Twain: A Biography.* NY. 1912. 3 vols. 1st ed. illus. ..
....$50–$95

Paine, Thomas. *The Rights of Man.* Lon. 1791. 6th ed. ......$200–$225

Paley, Grace. *Enormous Changes at the Last Minute.* NY. Farrar, Straus & Giroux. 1974. 1st ed. author's first book, sgn, dj. ....$75–$100.

Paley, Grace. *Later the Same Day.* NY. 1985. 1st ed. dj. ......$15–$25

Paley, Grace. *The Little Disturbances of Man.* Garden City. 1959. 1st ed. dj. sgn. ....$95–$140

Palmborg, Rilla. *The Private Life of Greta Garbo.* NY. 1931...........
....$40–$75

Palmer, C. H. *The Salmon Rivers of Newfoundland.* Bos. 1928. illus. fldg map. ....$75–$95

Palmer, Frederick. *With Kuroki in Manchuria.* NY. 1904. illus. ....
....$25–$35

Palmer, Howard and J. Monroe Thorington. *A Climber's Guide to the Rocky Mountains of Canada.* NY. Knickerbocker Press. 1921. 1st ed. 16mo, 183 pp, maps. ....$95–$120

Palmer, Peter S. *History of Lake Champlain.* NY. nd. 3rd ed. 250 pp, map. ....$50–$70

Pankhurst, Christabel. *The Great Scourge and How to End It.* Lon. 1913. 156 pp. ....$60–$75

Pankhurst, E. Sylvia. *The Life of Emmeline Pankhurst.* Bos/NY. Houghton Mifflin. 1936. 1st U.S. ed. $45

Pankhurst, E. Sylvia. *The Suffragette.* NY. 1911. 1st U.S. ed. 517 pp, illus. ....$65–$95

Pankhurst, E. Sylvia. *The Suffragette Movement.* Lon. Longmans. 1931. 1st ed. 631 pp, dj, scarce. $150

Pankhurst, Sylvia. *The Suffragette Movement.* Lon. 1932. 2nd ptg, illus, dj. $125

Parker, Dorothy. *After Such Pleasures.* NY. 1933. #189/250 cc, slipcase, sgn. ....$100–$125

Parker, Dorothy. *Sunset Gun.* NY. 1928. 1st ed. ....$40–$60

Parker, Robert B. *Pale Kings and Princes.* NY. Delacorte. (1987). 1st ed. dj. $35

Parker, Thomas V. *The Cherokee Indians ... Their Relations with the U.S. Govt.* NY. 1907. 1st ed. illus. ....$65–$75

Parkman, Francis. *History of the Conspiracy of Pontiac.* Bos. Little Brown. 1855. 4 maps. ....$70–$85

Parkman, Francis. *The Old Regime in Canada.* Bos. 1874. 1st ed. map. .
....$20–$35

Parkman, Francis. *The Oregon Trail.* Bos. 1925. illus by N. C. Wyeth
and F. Remington, ltd #907/975 cc. ....$100–$145

Parkman, Francis. *The Oregon Trail.* Bos. Little Brown. 1892. 1st ed.
illus by Frederick Remington............................$125–$550

Parloa, Maria. *First Principles of Household Management and Cookery.*
Bos. Houghton, Mifflin. 1888. 176 pp. $45

Parloa, Maria. *Miss Parloa's New Cook Book.* Bos. 1881. 1st ed. ....
....$45–$55

Parlour Magic. Phila. 1938. 1st U.S. ed. ....$50–$60

Parrish, Maxfield. *Knave of Hearts.* NY. 1925. 1st ed. hardbound. ......
....$950–$1,250

Parry, William Edward. *Journal of a Second Voyage for the Discovery of
a North-west Passage from the Atlantic to the Pacific.* Lon. John Murray.
1824. 1st ed. illus. 26 plates, 5 charts, fldg maps............$780–$925

Parsons, C. G. *Inside View of Slavery.* Bos. 1855. 1st ed. 318 pp. $25

Parton, J. *Life of Andrew Jackson.* NY. 1861. 3 vols. ....$45–$75

Pasley. *Al Capone: The Biography of a Self-made Man.* NY. 1930. 1st ed.
....$30–$40

Pasternak, Boris. *Doctor Zhivago.* Pantheon. 1959. 1st Amer ed. ....
....$45–$60

Pasteur, M. Louis. *Inoculation against Hydrophobia.* NY. 1886. wrps. ..
....$30–$45

Patchen, Kenneth. *Before the Brave.* Random House. 1936. 1st ed. dj,
author's first book. $200

Patchen, Kenneth. *Hurrah for Anything.* 1957. 1st ed. wrps. ....$37–$45

Paton, Alan. *Cry, the Beloved Country.* NY. 1948. sgn. ......$125–$150

Paton, Alan. *Oh, but Your Land Is Beautiful.* NY. 1982. sgn, dj. ....
....$30–$35

Paton, Alan. *Too Late the Phalarope.* Capetown. 1953. 1st ed. dj. ......
....$65–$100

Patrick, Rembert Wallace. *Jefferson Davis and His Cabinet.* Baton
Rouge. 1944. 1st ed. ....$35–$50

Patterson, A. *Notes on Pet Monkeys.* Lon. 1888. ....$60–$85

Patterson, Robert. *A Narrative of the Campaign in the Valley of the
Shenandoah.* Phila. 1865. map, sgn. ....$112–$120

Paulding, James K. *Slavery in the United States.* NY. 1836. wrps. 312 pp.
....$100–$275

Pauling, Linus. *No More War!* NY. 1958. sgn. . . . .*$40–$60*

Pauling, Linus, and E. Bright Wilson. *Introduction to Quantum Mechanics.* NY/Lon. 1935. dj. . . . .*$30–$40*

Pauling, Linus, and E. Bright Wilson. *Introduction to Quantum Mechanics, with Applications to Chemistry.* NY. 1935. . . . .*$25–$35*

Paullin, Chas. Oscar. *Commodore John Rodgers, Captain, Commodore and Senior Officer of American Navy.* Cleve. 1910. 1st ed. 434 pp. *$60*

Pavlov, Ivan Petrovich. *Lectures on Conditioned Reflexes.* . . . NY. 1928. illus. 1st ed in Eng. . . . .*$125–$150*

Payson, Howard. *The Boy Scouts on the Range.* Burt Reprint. dj. *$12*

Peabody, F. *Education for Life: The Story of Hampton Institute.* 1918. 1st ed. . . . .*$27–$38*

Peary, Robert Edwin. *The North Pole.* NY. Stokes. 1910. 1st ed. illus. fldg map. . . . .*$90–$125*

Peary, Robert Edwin. *The North Pole.* NY. Stokes. 1910. 2nd ed. 373 pp, frontis, clr and b/w photos, fldg map. *$70*

Peck, J. M. *A New Guide for Emigrants to the West.* Bos. 1836. 2nd ed. . . . .*$150–$225*

Peckham, G. W., and E. G. *On the Instincts and Habits of the Solitary Wasps.* Madison, WI. 1898. . . . .*$30–$45*

Pendergast, A. *Cigar Store Figures.* Chi. 1953. 1st ed. illus. . . . .*$35–$40*

Pendray, G. Edward. *The Coming Age of Rocket Power.* NY/Lon. Harper & Bros. 1945. 1st ed. illus. . . . .*$35–$60*

Pennell, Elizabeth Robins. *French Cathedrals.* NY. 1909. illus. teg, plans and diagrams. . . . .*$25–$45*

Penzer, N. M. *The Book of the Wine Label.* Lon. 1947. 1st ed. illus. . . . .*$38–$45*

Percival, A. S. *Optics: A Manual for Students.* Lon. 1899. 403 pp. . . . .*$20–$25*

Percy, Walker. *Lancelot.* NY. Farrar. 1977. 1st ed. dj. . . . .*$25–$50*

Percy, Walker. *The Last Gentleman.* Farrar. 1966. 1st ed. dj. . .*$60–$125*

Percy, Walker. *Lost in the Cosmos.* Farrar, Straus & Giroux. 1983. 1st ed. dj. *$30*

Percy, Walker. *Love in the Ruins.* 1971. dj. . . . .*$28–$35*

Percy, Walker. *The Second Coming.* NY. 1980. 1st ed. dj. . . . . . .*$8–$15*

Percy, William Alexander. *Lanterns on the Levee.* NY. 1941. 1st ed. sgn, dj. . . . .*$50–$75*

Perelman, S. J. *Chicken Inspector.* Simon. 1966. 1st ed. dj. *$50*

Perelman, S. J. *The Ill-Tempered Clavicord.* Simon. 1952. 1st ed. dj. . . . .
. . . .*$70*

Perelman, S. J. *Listen to the Mockingbird.* Simon. 1949. 1st ed. dj. . .*$75*

Perkings, Charles E. *The Pinto Horse.* CA. 1927. 1st ed. 76 pp, plates. . .
. . . .*$45*

Perkins, D. A. W. *History of O'Brien County, Iowa.* Sioux Falls. 1897. illus. . . . .*$45–$65*

Perkins, James. *Annals of the West.* Cinc. 1846. 1st ed. maps. . . . .
. . . .*$58–$70*

Perkins, Lucy Fitch. *The Indian Twins.* Houghton. 1930. illus. . . . .
. . . .*$18–$30*

Perkins, Lucy Fitch. *The Italian Twins.* Houghton. 1920. illus. . . . .
. . . .*$22–$40*

Perkins, Lucy Fitch. *The Japanese Twins.* Houghton. 1912. illus. . . . .
. . . .*$14–$25*

Perkins, P. D., and Ione Perkins. *Bibliography of Lafcadio Hearn.* NY. 1968. . . . .*$45–$60*

Perrault, Charles. *Cinderella.* Scribner's. 1954. 1st ed. illus. sgn by Brown. . . . .*$75–$85*

Perry, Robert E. *The Secrets of Polar Travel.* Century. 1917. 1st ed. . . . .
. . . .*$65–$85*

Peters, F. J. *Currier & Ives Railroad, Indian and Pioneer Prints.* NY. 1930. folio, dj. . . . .*$35–$45*

Petersen, Wm. J. *Steamboating on the Upper Mississippi.* Iowa City. 1937. 1st ed. 575 pp. *$85*

Petersham, Maud and Miska. *The Story Book of Aircraft.* Phila. John C. Winston Co. 1935. . . . .*$18–$35*

Peterson, Roger Tory. *A Field Guide to Birds.* . . . Bos. 1947. illus. 2nd ed. sgn. . . . .*$35–$45*

Peterson, S. *The Living Tradition of Maria Martinez.* NY/SF. 1977. Special Southwest Museum ed. ltd 500cc, sgn and nbr. *$275*

Peto, Florence. *Historic Quilts.* NY. 1939. 1st ed. illus. dj. . . . .
. . . .*$55–$125*

Pfeiffer, Ida. *The Last Travels of Ida Pfeiffer.* Harper & Bros. 1861. 1st U.S. ed. . . . .*$65–$75*

Phair, Charles. *Atlantic Salmon Fishing.* Derrydale Press. 1937. ltd, green cloth, foldout map, 193 pp. *$475*

The Pharmacopoeia of the United States. Phila. 1830. . . . .*$150–$225*

Phillippi, J. *Shakerism, or The Romance of Religion.* Dayton. The Otterbein Press. 1912. 133 pp. . . . .*$50–$65*

Phillips, John. *China Trade Porcelain.* Harvard Univ. Press. 1956. 1st ed. illus. clr and b/w. . . . .*$75–$185*

Phillips, Paul Chrisler. *The Fur Trade.* OK. (1961). 2 vols. 1st ed. illus. slipcase. . . . .*$50–$100*

Phillips, W. J. *Maori Carvings.* New Plymouth. 1941. photos. *$70*

Phillips, W. S. *Indian Tales for Little Folks.* NY. Platt & Munk. 1928. illus. clr plates. . . . .*$35–$50*

Phister, Harold Francis. *Facing the Light . . . Daguerreotypes.* DC. Smithsonian. 1978. 1st ed. wrps. . . . .*$40–$55*

Physician's and Dentist's Directory of the State of Pennsylvania. Phila. Galen Gonsier. 1902. 1st ptg, illus. 458 pp. . . . .*$35–$48*

Piaget, H. E. *The Watch.* 1860. illus. . . . .*$100–$200*

Picard, Mary Ann. *Official Star Trek Cooking Manual.* NY. 1978. 1st ed. paperback, sgn. . . . .*$12.50–$18*

Picasso, Pablo. *Desire: A Play.* NY. 1948. 1st ed. dj. . . . .*$25–$35*

Pictographic History of the Oglala Sioux. Lincoln. 1967. illus by Amos Bad Heart Bull, boxed. . . . .*$37–$45*

Pictorial History of the 69th Infantry Division . . . 15 May, 1943 to 15 May, 1945. np. 1945. 93 pp. . . . .*$70–$85*

Pictorial History of the Second World War. NY. 1944–65. 5 vols. illus. photos. . . . .*$45–$60*

Pictures of Old Chinatown. NY. Moffat Jard & Co. 1909. 2nd ptg, 57 pp, photos by Arnold Genthe. . . . .*$135–$150*

Pierce, Gerald S. *Texas under Arms . . . Rep. of Texas, 1836–1846.* Austin. 1969. dj. . . . .*$27–$35*

Pike, James. *The Scout and Ranger . . . in the Indian Wars.* Cinc. 1865. 1st issue, plates. . . . .*$1,000–$2,000*

Pike, James. *The Scout and Ranger . . . in the Indian Wars.* Cinc. 1865. 1st issue, plates, rebnd. *$450*

Pike, Nicholas. *A New and Complete System of Arithmetick.* Bos. 1808. 3rd ed. calf. . . . .*$22–$45*

Pike, Warburton. *The Barren Ground of Northern Canada.* Lon. 1892. 1st ed. fldg maps. . . . .*$85–$125*

Pike, Zebulon Montgomery. *Exploratory Travels through the Western Territories.* Denver. 1889. ....$100–$125

Pike, Zebulon Montgomery. *Exploratory Travels through the Western .Territories of North America. in the Years 1805, 1806, 1807.* Lon. Longman, Hurst, 1811. maps........................$1,900–$2,185

Pilling, James Constantine. *Bibliography of the Eskimo Language.* GPO. 1887. wrps. ....$55–$75

Pinkerton, Allan. *Claude Melmotte as a Detective and Other Stories.* Chi. 1875. 1st ed. ....$50–$65

Pinkerton, Allan. *Professional Thieves and the Detective.* NY. Dillingham. 1888. illus. not a 1st ed. $30

Pinkham, Lydia E. *Nature's Gift to Women.* Lynn, MA. Lydia Pinkham Medicine Co. (c 1917). wrps. 32 pp........................$20–$35

Pinkham, Lydia E. *Text Book upon Ailments Peculiar to Women.* Lynn, MA. Lydia Pinkham Medicine Co. (c 1875). printed wrps, frontis, 79 pp. . ...$60–$85

Pinter, Harold. *The French Lieutenant's Woman: A Screenplay with a Foreword by John Fowles.* Bos. Little Brown. 1981. 1st ed. dj. $50

Pinto, Edward H. *Treen or Small Woodware throughout the Ages.* Lon. (1949). 1st ed. illus. dj. ....$32–$40

Pitchford, R., and F. Combs. *The Projectionist's Handbook.* 1933. 1st ed. illus..$30–$40

Plath, Sylvia. *Ariel.* NY. Harper & Row. (1966). 1st ed. dj. ....$85–$100

Platt, Ward. *The Frontier.* NY. (1908). wrps.................$18–$22

Plowden, E. *The History of Ireland.* Lon. 1812. 2 vols. 2nd ed. one-quarter lea..$50–$75

Pocock, Roger. *Following the Frontier.* NY. 1903. ....$85–$115

Poe, Edgar Allan. *Eureka.* Paris. Levy. 1864. 1st ed. 248 pp, bds with original wrps tip-in, rare. $650

Poe, Edgar Allan. *Poetical Works of Edgar Poe.* Lon. 1858. 1st ed thus, full lea, aeg, 247 pp, illus. $225

Poe, Edgar Allan. *Tales of Mystery and Imagination.* Tudor. 1935. illus. by Harry Clarke. ....$50–$100

Poe, Edgar Allan. *The Works of Edgar A. Poe.* NY. 1902. 10 vols. library ed. ....$100–$135

Pohl, Frederick. *Man Plus.* NY. Random House. (1976). 1st ed. 215 pp, dj. ....$50–$65

Point, Fr. Nicolas. *Wilderness Kingdom: . . . Indian Life in the Rocky Mountains, 1840–1847.* NY. 1967. . . . .*$25–$35*

Poisonous Snakes of the World. DC. GPO. nd. illus. b/w and clr plates. . .
. . . .*$40–$55*

Pokagon, Chief. *O-Gi-Maw-Kwe Mit-I-Gwa-Ki (Queen of the Woods); also, A Brief Sketch of Algaic Language.* (1972). 220 pp, rprnt, originally printed in 1901. . . . .*$20*

Polkinghorne, R. K. and M. I. R. *Toymaking in School and Home.* NY. (1920). illus. 299 pp. *$35*

Pollard, Edward A. *The First Year of the War.* Richmond. 1862. 1st ed. Confederate imprint. . . . .*$225–$250*

Pollard, Edward A. *The Lost Cause Regained.* NY. 1868. 1st ed. . . . .
. . . .*$25–$30*

Pollard, Edward A. *The Lost Cause: A New Southern Hist. of War of the Confederates.* NY. 1866. . . . .*$25–$35*

Pollard, Edward A. *Southern History of the Great Civil War.* Tor. 1863. . .
. . . .*$75–$100*

Polo, Marco. *Book of Sir Marco Polo.* Lon. 1875. 2 vols. illus, plates, chromolith title pages. *$125*

The Pop-up Book of Magic Tricks. NY. Viking. 1983. . . . .*$20–$30*

The Popular History of the Civil War in America. NY. 1884. 1st ed. illus.
. . . .*$10–$15*

Porok, Byron Kuhn D. *Digging for Lost African Gods.* NY. Putnam. 1926. 1st ed. photos, fldg map, teg. . . . .*$60–$70*

Porter, Eliot. *Birds of North America.* E. P. Dutton. 1972. 1st ed. illus. dj.
. . . .*$40–$60*

Porter, Gene. *Music of the Wild.* Garden City. 1910. 1st ed. . . .*$95–$150*

Porter, Gene Stratton. *Birds of the Bible.* Cinc. 1909. 1st ed. . . . .
. . . .*$150–$200*

Porter, Gene Stratton. *The Firebird.* Garden City. 1922. 1st ed. illus. . . .
. . . .*$22–$35*

Porter, Gene Stratton. *The Magic Garden.* NY. 1927. 1st ed. . . .*$35–$48*

Porter, Gene Stratton. *Michael O'Halloran.* Doubleday. 1915. 1st ed. . .
. . . .*$32–$40*

Porter, Gene Stratton. *Moths of the Limberlost.* NY. 1926. . . . .
. . . .*$125–$140*

Porter, Gene Stratton. *The Song of the Cardinal.* Bobbs Merrill. 1903. illus. buckram. . . . .*$80–$90*

Porter, Gene Stratton. *What I Have Done with Birds.* Ind. 1907. 1st ed. .
....*$165–$220*

Porter, Gene Stratton. *The White Flag.* NY. 1923. 1st ed. dj. ....
....*$75–$100*

Porter, Gene Stratton. *The White Flag.* NY. 1923. 1st ed. ....
....*$22–$35*

Porter, Katherine. *My Chinese Marriage.* NY. 1921. ....*$50–$65*

Porter, Katherine Anne. *A Christmas Story.* NY. 1958. 1st ed. ....
....*$30–$40*

Porter, Katherine Anne. *The Leaning Tower.* NY. Harcourt Brace. (1944). 1st ed. dj. ....*$50–$100*

Porter, Katherine Anne. *Ship of Fools.* Bos. 1962. 1st ed. dj. ....
....*$20–$30*

Porter, Kenneth W. *The Jacksons and the Lees: ... Massachusetts Merchants, 1765–1844.* Camb. 1937. 2 vols. 1st ed. illus. dj. ......*$65–$100*

Potter, Beatrix. *The Peter Rabbit Pop-up Book.* Columbia. 1983. ....
....*$35–$45*

Potter, Beatrix. *The Pie and the Patty Man.* NY. 1905. ....*$45–$60*

Potter, Beatrix. *The Story of Peter Rabbit and Other Stories.* Whitman. 1928. ....*$14–$18*

Potter, Beatrix. *The Tale of Benjamin Bunny.* Lon. 1904. 1st ed. ....
....*$375–$495*

Potter, Beatrix. *The Tale of Mr. Toad.* 1939. illus. dj. ....*$20–$35*

Potter, Beatrix. *Wag-by-Wall.* Horn Book. 1944. 1st ed. illus. dj. ....
....*$45–$65*

Pound, Ezra. *70 Cantos.* Lon. 1950. 1st Eng ed. ltd 1,622 cc, dj. ....
....*$90–$120*

Pound, Ezra. *The Classic Anthology Defined by Confucius.* Harvard Univ. Press. 1954. 1st ed. dj...................................*$50–$125*

Pound, Ezra. *Personae: The Collected Poems.* NY. 1926. 1st ed. ....
....*$75–$100*

Pound, Ezra. *Section: Rock Drill 85–95 de los Cantares.* New Directions. (1956). 1st U.S., ed. 107 pp, dj, presentation copy. *$450*

Powall, Thomas. *A Topographical Description of the Dominions of the United States of America.* Pitts. Univ. of Pittsburgh Press. 1949. 1st ed thus, illus. ....*$100–$150*

Powell, Agnes Baden. *Handbook for Girl Scouts.* 1917. 1st ed. ....
....*$30–$45*

Powell, Anthony. *At Lady Molly's.* Lon. Heinemann. (c1957). 1st ed. dj. .
....$65

Powell, Anthony. *Venusberg and Agents and Patients: Two Novels.* NY.
Periscope-Holliday. (1952). 1st Amer ed. dj. $65

Powell, J. W. *14th Annual Report of the Bureau of Ethnology.* DC. GPO.
1896. illus. maps. ....$65–$95

Powys, T. F. *Mr. Weston's Good Wine.* NY. Viking. 1928. 1st Amer ed.
317 pp. ....$30–$40

Poyas, Mrs. Elizabeth A. *Carolina in Olden Time.* Charleston. 1855. 1st
ed. ....$50–$75

Practical Aeronautics. 1917. 1st ed. illus. ....$40–$65

Practical Guide to Homeopathy for Family and Private Use. Bos/Prov/Cinc.
Otis Clapp/A. F. Worthington. 1892. 180 pp. ....$60–$85

Prayerbook for the Camp. Richmond. Macfarlane & Fergusson. 1863. 1st
ed. 64 pp. $750

Prescott, W. H. *Conquest of Mexico.* NY. 1848. 3 vols. 1st ed. ..$85–$110

Prescott, W. H. *History of the Conquest of Peru.* Phila. 1874. 2 vols. ....
....$14–$18

Prescott, William H. *History of the Conquest of Peru.* 1865. 2 vols. ......
....$35–$45

Price, George. *The Modern Factory.* NY. Wiley. 1914. 1st ptg. ....
....$75

Price List; Manufacturers of and Dealers in Masonic Supplies. Cinc.
John D. Caldwell. 1883. wrps. illus, 40 pp. ....$50–$75

Price, Mary, and Vincent Price. *Treasury of Great Recipes.* NY. 1965.
lea. ....$50–$70

Price, Reynolds. *A Generous Man.* NY. Atheneum. 1966. 1st ed. dj. ......
....$35–$50

Price, Reynolds. *Permanent Errors.* NY. Atheneum. 1970. 1st ed. sgn, dj.
....$50–$75

Prideaux, Humphrey. *The Old and New Testament ... Hist. of Jews and
Neighbouring Nations.* Balt. 1833. illus. fldg maps, calf. ....$50–$65

Priest, Josiah. *American Antiquities and Discoveries in the West.* Albany.
1833. illus. fldg map, calf. ....$90–$135

Priestley, J. *Discourses Relating to the Evidences of Revealed Religion.*
Phila. 1796. 1st ed. lea. ....$95–$120

Priestley, J. B. *Angel Pavement.* Lon. 1930. ltd #842/1,025cc, sgn. ......
....$40–$50

Prieur, J. C. *Boyer's Royal Dictionary.* Dublin. 1796. full lea, 17th ed. . .
. . . .*$55–$85*

Prime, William C. *The Old House by the River.* NY. 1853. . . . .
. . . .*$25–$40*

Prime, William C. *Tent Life in the Holy Land.* NY. (1857). sgn. . . . .
. . . .*$22–$35*

Pritchett, V. S. *The Sailor, Sense of Humour, and Other Stories.* NY.
Knopf. 1956. 1st ed. dj. . . . .*$30–$40*

Probable Termination of Mormon Troubles in the Utah Territory. GPO.
1858. . . . .*$45–$55*

Proceedings of the Exec. of the U.S. Respecting . . . Insurgents. Phila.
1795. (Whiskey Rebellion). . . . .*$125–$175*

***Proceedings of the Fifth Imperial Konvokation Held in Chicago, Illinois,
August 18 and 19, 1930.*** wrps. 16 pp. . . . .*$40–$50*

Proctor, R. *Chance and Luck.* Lon. 1887. . . . .*$50–$90*

Prosch, Charles. *Reminiscences of Washington Territory.* . . . Seattle.
1904. sgn. . . . .*$95–$125*

Proulx, E. Annie. *The Complete Dairy Foods Cookbook.* PA. Rodale
Press. 1982. 1st ed. illus. bds, sgn. . . . .*$50–$100*

Proulx, E. Annie. *Heart Songs.* NY. Scribner's. 1988. 1st ed. dj. . . . .
. . . .*$100–$350*

Proulx, E. Annie. *Postcards.* NY. Scribner's. 1992. 1st ed. dj, sgn. . . . . . .
. . . .*$300–$450*

Pullen, John J. *20th Maine: A Volunteer Regiment in the Civil War.* Lippincott. 1957. 2nd imp, dj. . . . .*$28–$40*

Pusey, William Allen. *The Wilderness Road to Kentucky.* NY. 1921. dj. . .
. . . .*$58–$75*

Putnam, George Palmer. *In the Oregon Country.* NY. 1915. illus. . . . . . .
. . . .*$14–$22*

Putnam, George Palmer. *A Prisoner of War in Virginia.* NY. 1912. 1st
ed. . . . .*$35–$45*

Putnam, George R. *Lighthouses and Lightships of the United States.*
1933. illus. . . . .*$30–$45*

Pyle, Howard. *Men of Iron.* Harper. 1892. 1st ed. illus. . . . .*$55–$75*

Pynchon, Thomas. *The Crying of Lot 49.* Phila. 1966. 1st ed. dj. . . . .
. . . .*$150–$275*

Pyne, Henry R. *The History of the First New Jersey Cavalry.* Trenton.
1871. 1st ed. . . . .*$125–$175*

Quaife, Milo M. *Checagou: From Indian Wigwam to Modern City 1673–1835.* Chi. 1933. 1st ed. dj. . . . .*$20–$35*

Queen, Ellery. *Devil to Pay.* NY. 1938. 1st ed. dj. . . . .*$30–$55*

Queen, Ellery. *Double, Double.* Little Brown. 1950. 1st ed. dj. . . . .
. . . .*$45–$70*

Queen, Ellery. *Ellery Queen's Double Dozen.* NY. 1964. 1st ed. dj. . . . . .
. . . .*$32–$40*

Queen, Ellery. *The Murderer Is a Fox.* Bos. Little Brown. 1945. 1st ed. dj.
. . . .*$75*

Queen, Ellery. *Ten Days Wonder.* Bos. Little Brown. 1948. 1st ed. dj. . . .
. . . .*$100*

Queen, Ellery (ed). *To the Queen's Taste.* Bos. 1946. 1st ed. dj. . . . .
. . . .*$25–$40*

Queeny, Edgar. *Prairie Wings.* 1946. 1st ed. dj. . . . .*$125–$150*

Queeny, Edgar M. *Cheechako: The Story of an Alaskan Bear Hunt.* NY. 1941. photos. . . . .*$40–$60*

Question of Color. NY. 1895. . . . .*$33–$38*

Quick, Herbert, and Edward Quick. *Mississippi Steamboatin'.* 1st ed. . . .
. . . .*$30–$40*

Quick, Jim. *Trout Fishing and Trout Flies.* Castle Books. 1957. 1st ed. dj.
. . . .*$30*

Quiller-Couch, A. T. *Old Fires and Profitable Ghosts.* NY. Scribner's. 1900. 1st Amer ed. 384 pp. . . . .*$100–$135*

Quiller-Couch, A. T. *The Sleeping Beauty and Other Fairy Tales.* Lon. nd. illus by Edmund Dulac. . . . .*$125–$175*

Quiller-Couch, A. T. *The Twelve Dancing Princesses.* NY. nd. illus. tip-in plates, dj. . . . .*$90–$200*

Quiller-Couch, Arthur T. (ed). *The Oxford Book of English Verse, 1250–1900.* Ox. 1926. . . . .*$25–$85*

Quincy, John. *Pharmacopoeia Officinalis and Extemporanea: or A Complete English Dispensary.* . . . Lon. 1782. 15th ed. . . . .*$40–$60*

Quint, Alonzo. *Record of the Second Massachusetts Infantry 1861–65.* Bos. 1867. 528 pp. . . . .*$90–$150*

R. J. *The Gamekeeper at Home.* Smith, Elder & Co. 1878. 3rd ed. . . . .
. . . .*$65*

Radio Amateur's Handbook. 1927. 2nd ed. softcover. . . . .*$25–$35*

Radford. *Stores and Flat Buildings.* Chi/NY. 1909. . . . .*$58–$75*

Radin, P. *The Story of the American Indian.* NY. 1944. illus. enlarged ed.
....$20–$30

Radley, J. A. *Photography in Crime Detection.* Lon. 1948. illus. ....
....$28–$40

Raht, C. G. *The Romance of Davis Mountains and Big Bend Country.* El Paso. 1919. 1st ed. illus. fldg map, plates. ....$55–$100

Raine, William M. *Guns of the Frontier.* NY. 1940. 1st ed. dj. ....
....$35–$45

Ralph, Julian. *On Canada's Frontier.* Harper & Bros. 1892. 1st ed. illus by Remington. ....$75–$95

Ramsay, D. *The History of the American Revolution.* Trenton. 1811. 2 vols. 2nd ed. lea. ....$95–$125

Ramsdell, Charles W. *Laws and Joint Resolution of Last Session of Confederate Congress.* Durham. 1941. ....$45–$70

Rand, Ayn. *Atlas Shrugged.* Random House. 1957. 1st ed. dj. ....
....$100–$250

Rand, Ayn. *The Fountainhead.* Ind. 1943. 1st ed. dj. ....$125–$200

Rand, Ayn. *The Fountainhead.* Ind. 1943. ....$16–$20

Rand, Ayn. *We the Living.* NY. 1936. 1st ed. dj. ....$65–$75

Rand McNally & Co.'s New Dollar Atlas of the U.S. and Canada. Chi. 1884. cloth, bds. ....$40–$60

Randall, E. O. *History of the Zoar Society from Its Commencement to Its Conclusion.* Columbus. Press of Fred J. Heer. 1899. 100 pp. ...$95–$135

Randall, Henry. *Youatt on the Structure and Diseases of the Horse.* NY. Judd. 1865. ....$24–$32

Randolph, Mrs. Mary. *The Virginia Housewife.* Balt. Plaskitt. 1836. 180 pp. $350

Ransom, John L. *Andersonville Diary.* NY. private ptg. 1881. 1st ed. ...
....$95–$125

Ransome, Stafford. *Japan in Transition.* NY. 1899. illus. maps, 261 pp. .
....$45–$50

Raper, Charles. *North Carolina: A Study in English Colonial Government.* NY. 1904. 1st ed. ....$30–$35

Rarey, John Solomon. *The Modern Art of Taming Wild Horses.* Columbus. 1856. 1st ed. wrps. ....$900–$1,500

Raum, Green B. *The Existing Conflict between Republican Gov. and Southern Oligarchy.* Cleve. 1884. 1st ed. ....$48–$65

Raum, Joan O. *History of the City of Trenton.* NJ. 1871. 1st ed. illus. fldg map. *$35*

Rawling, Charles J. *History of the First Regiment, Virginia Infantry.* Phila. 1887. 1st ed. . . . .*$275–$350*

Rawlings, Marjorie Kinnan. *Cross Creek Cookery.* NY. Scribner's. 1942. 1st issue, illus, dj. *$125*

Rawlings, Marjorie Kinnan. *The Sojourner.* NY. 1953. 1st ed. dj. . . . . . .
. . . .*$30–$40*

Rawlings, Marjorie Kinnan. *The Yearling.* Scribner's. 1940. illus by Wyeth, 12 clr plates. . . . .*$50–$75*

Rawlings, Marjorie Kinnan. *The Yearling.* Scribner's. 1938. 1st ed. dj. . .
. . . .*$100*

Rawson, P. *The Art of Southeast Asia.* NY. 1967. photos, map. . . . .
. . . .*$35–$50*

Rawstorne, L. *Gammonia.* Lon. 1837. 15 clr plates. . . . .*$850–$1,000*

Ray, P. *Report of the Internat. Polar Expedition to Point Barrow, Alaska.* GPO. 1885. 1st ed. . . . .*$60–$85*

Rayner, B. L. *Sketches of Life, Writings and Opinions of Thomas Jefferson.* . . . NY. 1832. . . . .*$35–$50*

Reagan, R. *Speaking My Mind.* sgn. . . . .*$98–$125*

Rebold, E. *General History of Free-masonry in Europe.* Cinc. 1868. . . . .
. . . .*$35–$50*

Receipt Book of Melvina Poe. Augusta, GA. 1833. handwritten, lea, mar bds. . . . .*$275–$315*

Redmond, Pat. H. *History of Quincy and Its Men of Mark.* 1869. 1st ed. Howes, scarce. *$30*

Redpath, James. *The Public Life of Captain John Brown . . . with an Autobiography of His Childhood and Youth.* Bos. 1860. 1st ed. . . . .
. . . .*$45–$150*

Redpath, James. *The Roving Editor.* NY. 1859. 1st ed. blue cloth, plates.
. . . .*$100–$325*

Reed, Ishmael. *Flight to Canada.* NY. Random House. 1976. 1st ed. sgn, dj. . . . .*$65–$85*

Reed, Ishmael. *Flight to Canada.* NY. Random House. 1976. 1st ed. review copy, dj. . . . .*$22–$30*

Reed, Ishmael. *Mumbo Jumbo.* Garden City. 1972. 1st ed. dj. . . .*$35–$55*

Reed, John. *An Apology for the Rite of Infant Baptism . . . Modes of Baptism.* Prov. 1815. calf. . . . .*$25–$30*

Reed, John A. *History of the 101st Regiment Pennsylvania Volunteer Infantry.* Chi. 1910. . . . .*$40–$50*

Reed, William Howell. *Hospital Life in the Army of the Potomac.* Bos. William V. Spencer. 1866. 1st ed. . . . .*$95–$150*

Reese, A. M. *The Alligator and Its Allies.* NY. 1915. illus. . . . .*$55–$75*

Reeves, J. E. *A Hand-book of Medical Microscopy.* Phila. 1894. 1st ed. illus. . . . .*$37–$45*

Reeves, James J. *History of the 24th Regiment New Jersey Volunteers.* Camden, NJ. 1889. 1st ed. wrps. 45 pp. . . . .*$110–$135*

Regulations for the Care of Camels. Cairo. War Office Printing Press. 1896. wrps. . . . .*$55–$75*

Reichard, Gladys. *Spider Woman: A Story of Navajo Weavers and Chanters.* 1934. 1st ed. . . . .*$25–$48*

Reichenbach, W. *Six Guns and Bulls Eyes.* Sam Worth. 1936. 1st ed. dj. . . . .*$40–$50*

Reid, Mrs. Hugo. *Woman: Her Education and Influence.* NY. 1847. wrps. . . . .*$30–$45*

Reid, Capt. Mayne. *The White Chief: A Legend of North Mexico.* NY. 1875. . . . .*$22–$30*

Reinhardt, Col. G. C., and Lt. Col. W. R. Kintner. *Atomic Weapons in Land Combat.* Harrisburg. 1953. 1st ed. wrps. illus. . . . .*$20–$30*

Religious Folk Songs of the Negro. Hampton, VA. 1918. new ed. . . . .*$25–$40*

Remarque, Erich Maria. *All Quiet on the Western Front.* Bos. Little Brown. 1929. 1st Amer ed. dj. . . . .*$100–$125*

Remarque, Erich Maria. *Heaven Has No Favorites.* NY. 1961. 1st Amer ed. advance copy, dj. . . . .*$30–$35*

Remarque, Erich Maria. *The Road Back.* Bos. Little Brown. 1931. 1st ed. second book, dj. *$75*

Remington, Frederic. *Crooked Trails.* NY. Harper & Bros. 1898. illus by Remington. . . . .*$200–$275*

Remington, Frederic. *Done in the Open: Drawings by. . . .* NY. 1904. Folio. . . . .*$80–$120*

Remington, Frederic. *Pony Tracks.* NY. Harper. 1895. 1st ed. illus by Remington. . . . .*$300–$500*

Remington, Frederic. *The Way of an Indian.* NY. 1906. 1st ed. illus by Remington. . . . .*$350–$475*

Report of the Director of the Mint . . . during the Calendar Year 1888. DC. GPO. 1889. . . . .*$20–$30*

Report of the Regents of New York on Longitudes of Dudley Observatory. NY. 1862. wrps. . . . .*$30–$50*

Report of the Secretary of the Navy . . . Nov. 5, 1864. Richmond. 1864. 1st ed. wrps. 52 pp, Confederate imprint. . . . .*$250–$350*

Report of the Watering Committee of the Select and Common Councils of Philadelphia. Phila. 1830. 1st ed. wrps. 18 pp. . . . .*$45–$60*

Report on Indians Taxed and Not Taxed in the United States . . . Eleventh Census: 1890. DC. GPO. 1894. 683 pp, maps, plates. . . . .
. . . .*$700*

Report on Japanese Research on Radio Wave Propagation. U.S. Army. 1946. 1st ed. . . . .*$50–$65*

Report on the Census of Cuba, 1899. DC. GPO. 1900. illus. photos. . . . . .
. . . .*$48–$60*

Report on the Control of the Aborigines of Formosa. 1911. illus. maps. .
. . . .*$75–$100*

Report on U.S. Geographical Surveys West of 100th Meridian. . . . DC. GPO. 1877. illus. . . . .*$80–$120*

Reports of Explorations and Surveys to the Pacific Ocean. illus. plates. . .
. . . .*$150–$250*

Reports . . . Joint Palestine Survey Commission, October 1, 1928. Bos. 1928. illus. . . . .*$95–$125*

Reuter, Edward Byron. *The Mulatto in the United States.* NY. Negro Univ. Press. (1969). 417 pp. . . . .*$15–$22*

Revised Regulations for the Army of the United States. Phila. Lippincott. 1862. . . . .*$75–$95*

Rey, H. A. *Zebrology.* Lon. Chatto & Windus. c 1937. illus. clr. *$75*

Reynolds, E. W. *The True Story of the Barons of the South. . . .* Bos. 1862.
. . . .*$28–$35*

Reznikoff, Charles. *By the Waters of Manhattan.* Charles Boni. 1930. paperback. . . . .*$15–$25*

Reznikoff, Nathan and Charles. *Early History of a Sewing-machine Operator.* NY. (1936). 1st ed. . . . .*$55–$75*

Rhead, Louis. *American Trout-stream Insects.* Stokes. 1916. 1st ed. . . . . .
. . . .*$55*

Rheims, Maurice. *The Flowering of Art Nouveau.* NY. nd. dj. . . . .
. . . .*$85–$115*

Rhinegold and The Valkyrie. Lon/NY. 1914. illus. by Arthur Rackham, tip-in plates. . . . .*$60–$75*

Rhoades, J. *The Little Flowers of St. Francis of Assissi.* Lon. Oxford Univ. Press. 1934. rprnt, 319 pp, full lea, gold tooled, aeg. *$40*

Rice, Anne. *Cry to Heaven.* NY. 1982. 1st ed. dj. . . . .*$30–$45*

Rice, Anne. *Lasher.* Knopf. 1993. 1st ed. dj, sgn. *$50*

Rice, Anne. *Memnock the Devil.* NY. Knopf. 1995. 1st ed. sgn, dj. . . . . . .
. . . .*$45*

Rice, Anne. *The Mummy, or Ramses the Damned.* NY. Ballantine. (1989). 1st ed. illus. Harlan Ellison's copy with his sgn bookplate. *$35*

Rice, Anne. *The Queen of the Damned.* Knopf. 1988. sgn, dj. . . . .
. . . .*$45–$60*

Rice, Anne. *The Tale of the Body Thief.* 1992. 1st ed. dj. *$30*

Rice, Anne. *The Vampire Lestat.* NY. Knopf. 1985. 1st ed. dj. *$285*

Rice, Louise. *Dainty Dishes from Foreign Lands.* Chi. 1911. . . . .*$15–$22*

Rice, William Gorham. *Carillons of Belgium and Holland.* NY. 1914. illus. . . . .*$22–$35*

Rich, E. E. *Hudson's Bay Company, 1670–1870.* NY. Macmillan Co. (1961). 3 vols. 1st Amer ed. six plates, two fldg maps. *$150*

Rich, Prof. George. *Artistic Horse Shoeing.* NY. 1890. . . . .*$35–$45*

Richard Whittington and His Cat. New Haven. Sidney's Press. 1825. wrps. 23 pp, 103 by 85 cm. *$175*

Richards, Laura. *Captain January.* Bos. 1893. illus. . . . .*$35–$45*

Richards, Laura E. *The Golden Windows.* Little Brown. 1903. illus. . . . . .
. . . .*$30–$40*

Richards, Laura E. *The Hurdy-gurdy.* Bos. 1902. illus. . . . .*$65–$85*

Richards, Laura E. *The Silver Crown.* Little Brown. 1906. illus. . . . .
. . . .*$20–$40*

Richards, Laura E. *When I Was Your Age.* Bos. 1849. 1st ed. . . .*$20–$30*

Richardson, A. E. *The Old Inns of England.* Lon. 1942. . . . .*$25–$40*

Richardson, Albert D. *The Secret Service, the Field, the Dungeon and the Escape.* Hartford. 1865. 1st ed. illus. . . . .*$65–$145*

Richardson, Beulah. *A Black Woman Speaks . . . of White Womanhood, of White Supremacy, of Peace.* Chi. American Women for Peace. 1951. wrps. 12 pp. *$45*

Richardson, Frank. *From Sunrise to Sunset: Reminiscence.* Bristol, TN. 1910. 1st ed. illus. . . . .*$90–$125*

Richardson, Frank. *The Secret Kingdom.* Lon. (1911). 3rd ptg. ....
....*$50–$75*

Richardson, James D. *Messages of the Presidents.* Bureau of National Literature. 22 vols. ....*$75–$100*

Richardson, James (ed). *Wonders of the Yellowstone.* NY. Scribner, Armstrong. 1875. illus. fldg map............................*$50–$80*

Richardson, Sir John. *Arctic Searching Expedition for Sir John Franklin.* NY. 1852. ....*$60–$80*

Richmond, Mary. *A Day in the Life of a Spoiled Child.* New Haven. S. Babcock. nd. wrps. 24 pp, 15 by 85 cm. *$50*

Rickard, T. A. *The Copper Mines of Lake Superior.* NY. 1905. 1st ed. ...
....*$33–$45*

Rickett, H. *Wildflowers of the U.S.: The Southeastern States.* 1966. 2 vols. slipcase. ....*$85–$120*

Rickmers. *Skiing for Beginners and Mountaineers.* 1910. ......*$30–$50*

Riding, William H. *Overland Express (1837–1875).* Ashland. 1970. wrps. #441/650cc. ....*$35–$45*

Ridgely, Mabel L. *The Ridgelys of Delaware and Their Circle.* Portland, ME. (1949). 1st ed. 427 pp, plates, illus, small folio. *$40*

Ridgeway, Robert. *A Manual of North American Birds.* Phila. 1887. 1st ed. illus. ....*$65–$78*

Riggs and Carvie. *Modern Guns and Smokeless Powder.* Lon. 1892. ....
....*$48–$60*

Riggs, Stephen R. *A Dakota-English Dictionary.* St. Paul. Minnesota Historical Soc. 1992. wrps. rprnt. *$25*

Riggs, Stephen R. *Dakota Grammar, Texts and Ethnography.* DC. GPO. 1893. ....*$60–$95*

Riggs, Stephen R. *Mary and I: Forty Years with the Sioux.* Bos. (1887). 2nd ed. 437 pp. *$50*

Rights, Douglas LeTell. *The American Indian in North Carolina.* NC. 1947. 1st ed. ....*$50–$65*

Riis, Jacob. *The Battle with the Slum.* NY. 1902. ....*$25–$45*

Riis, Jacob A. *How the Other Half Lives ... the Tenements of New York.* NY. 1891. 1st ed. blue cloth, illus. ....*$125–$175*

Riker, James. *Revised History of Harlem.* NY. 1904. fldg map. ....
....*$60–$95*

Riley, James Whitcomb. *The Old Swimmin' Hole and 'leven More Poems.* ... Ind. 1891. 1st ed. 3rd state. ....*$50–$75*

Rinehart, Mary Roberts. *Tenting Tonight.* Bos/NY. 1918. illus. . . . .
. . . .*$45–$60*

Rinehart, Mary Roberts. *Through Glacier Park.* Bos. 1916. 1st ed. illus.
sgn. . . . .*$32–$40*

Rinehart, Mary Roberts. *When a Man Marries.* Tor. 1909. illus. 1st
Canadian ed. . . . .*$50–$65*

Ripley, Mary. *The Oriental Rug Book.* Stokes. (1904). clr illus. . . . .
. . . .*$30–$45*

Ritchie, George Thomas. *A List of Lincolniana in the Library of Congress.* GPO. 1903. . . . .*$35–$50*

Ritchie, Leitch. *Ireland, Picturesque and Romantic.* Lon. 1837. 1st ed.
illus. engr, aeg. . . . .*$85–$125*

Rivera, Diego. *Frescoes.* NY. (1929). . . . .*$100–$135*

Robbins, R. A. *The 91st Infantry Division in WWII.* DC. 1947. 1st ed.
illus. maps, photos. . . . .*$50–$60*

Roberts, John. *Modern Medicine and Homeopathy.* Phila. Edwards &
Docker. 1895. 1st ed. 69 pp. . . . .*$90–$125*

Roberts, Kenneth. *The Battle of Cowpens.* Doubleday. 1958. 1st ed. dj. . .
. . . .*$22.50*

Roberts, Kenneth. *It Must Be Your Tonsils.* NY. 1936. sgn. . . . .*$45–$55*

Roberts, Kenneth. *Lydia Bailey.* Garden City. 1947. 1st ed. dj. . . . .
. . . .*$20–$30*

Roberts, Kenneth. *Northwest Passage.* NY. 1937. 1st ed. wrps. inscr. . . .
. . . .*$60–$150*

Roberts, Kenneth. *Trending into Maine.* Bos. 1938. 1st ed. illus by N. C.
Wyeth. . . . .*$45–$75*

Roberts, Morley. *The Private Life of Henry Maitland: A Record Dictated
by J. H.* Lon. Eveleigh Nash. 1912. 1st ed. *$125*

Roberts, Thomas S. *The Birds of Minnesota.* Minn. 1932. 2 vols. 1st ed.
clr plates. . . . .*$100–$125*

Robeson, Eslanda Goode [Mrs. Paul Robeson]. *African Journey.* NY.
1945. 1st ed. dj. . . . .*$45–$65*

Robeson, Kenneth. *Quest of the Spider: A Doc Savage Novel.* NY. 1935.
. . . .*$95–$130*

Robie, Virginia. *Historic Styles in Furniture.* Chi. 1905. 1st ed. illus. . . . .
. . . .*$35–$40*

Robinson, Bert. *The Basket Weavers of Arizona.* Albuquerque. 1954. dj. .
. . . .*$50–$75*

Robinson, Charles. *The Kansas Conflict.* NY. 1892. 1st ed. . . . .
. . . .*$95–$150*

Robinson, Edward Arlington. *Cavender's House.* 1929. dj. . . . .
. . . .*$30–$35*

Robinson, Edward Arlington. *Dionysus in Doubt: A Book of Poems.* NY. Macmillan. 1925. 1st ed. 1/350 cc, sgn, dj, slipcase. *$75*

Robinson, G. *Travels in Palestine and Syria.* Paris. 1837. 2 vols. illus. half calf, maps, plates. . . . .*$150–$200*

Robinson, Leigh. *The South before and at the Battle of the Wilderness.* Richmond. 1878. wrps. . . . .*,$75–$100*

Robinson, Rowland E. *Sam Lovel's Camps.* NY. 1893. . . . .*$20–$35*

Robinson, Rowland E. *Uncle Lisha's Outing.* Bos/NY. 1897. 1st ed. . . . .
. . . .*$25–$35*

Robinson, S. *Kansas: Interior and Exterior Life.* Bos. 1856. . . . .*$35–$45*

Robinson, Samuel. *A Course of Fifteen Lectures on Medical Botany.* Columbus. Pike, Platt & Co. 1832. . . . .*$125–$165*

Robinson, Will. *The Story of Arizona.* Phoenix. 1919. . . . .*$30–$65*

Robison, Capt. S. S. *Robison's Manual of Radio Telegraphy and Telephony, 1919.* 1919. illus. 5th ed. . . . .*$30–$40*

Rockne, Knute. *Coaching.* NY. 1931. . . . .*$28–$35*

Rockwell, A. H. *Improved Practical System of Educating the Horse.* NY. 1971. illus. . . . .*$25–$35*

Rockwell, Carey. *Danger in Deep Space.* Grosset & Dunlap. (1954). dj. . .
. . . .*$20*

Rockwell, Carey. *The Robot Racket.* Grosset & Dunlap. (1956). dj. . . . . .
. . . .*$14*

Rockwell, Carey. *Stand by for Mars.* Grosset & Dunlap. (1953). Tom Corbett, Space Cadet, dj. *$25*

Rockwell, Carey. *Treachery in Outer Space.* Grosset & Dunlap. 1952. Tom Corbett #6, dj. *$25*

Rockwell, Norman. *My Adventures as an Illustrator.* NY. 1960. 1st ed. slipcase, dj. . . . .*$40–$45*

Rockwood, Roy. *Through the Air to the North Pole.* . . . NY. 1906. 1st ed. illus. . . . .*$32–$45*

Rocky Mountain Country Club. 1905. . . . .*$45–$60*

Rodgers, Otis, and Pat Mulkern (eds). *Hobo from Texas.* np. 1950. 1st ed. thus, illus, pictorial wrps. . . . .*$50–$80*

Roe, F. G. *The North American Buffalo.* Lon. 1972. 2nd ed. . . . .*$25–$35*

Roemer, Ferdinand. *Texas with Particular Reference to German Immigration.* San Antonio. 1935. 1st ed. wrps. ....$100–$150

Rogers, Alice Lang. *Poodles in Particular.* NY. 1951. illus. ....
....$14–$18

Rogers, Dale Evans. *Angel Unaware.* Revell. 1953. dj. ....$15–$22

Rogers, J. E. *The Shell Book.* NY. 1908. illus. ....$25–$50

Rohmer, Sax. *The Bat Flies Low.* NY. 1935. ....$20–$35

Rohmer, Sax. *The Book of Fu Manchu.* NY. 1929. ....$25–$35

Rohmer, Sax. *Dope.* NY. 1919. 2nd ptg. ....$22–$28

Rohmer, Sax. *The Green Eyes of Bast.* NY. 1920. 1st ed. ....
....$45–$75

Rohmer, Sax. *Hangover House.* NY. (1949). 1st ed. dj. $225

Rohmer, Sax. *Island of Fu Manchu.* Garden City. 1941. 1st ed. Crime Club, dj. ....$100–$450

Rohmer, Sax. *Moon of Madness.* Garden City. 1928. ....$20–$40

Rohmer, Sax. *President Fu Manchu.* Garden City. 1936. 1st ed. dj. .....
....$250–$350

Rohmer, Sax. *White Velvet.* Garden City. 1937. dj. ....$25–$35

Rolle, Andrew F. *The Lost Cause: The Confederate Exodus to Mexico.* Univ. of Oklahoma Press. 1965. 1st ed. ....$28–$35

Rollicking Rhymes for Youngsters. Fleming Revell Co. Pub. 1902. 1st ed. illus. ....$27–$55

Rolvaag, O. E. *Giants in the Earth.* Harper. 1927. dj. ....$65–$95

Romance of the Oriental Rug. Tor. Babylon's Ltd. (1925). 1st ed. clr plates. ....$35–$45

Ronalds, Alfred. *Fly-fisher's Entomology.* Lon. 1883. illus. 9th ed. plates.
....$125–$180

Roop, Guy. *Villas and Palaces of Andrea Palladio, 1508–1580.* Milano. Arti Grafiche Francesco Ghezzi. 1968. illus. 1st ed in English, slipcase. ..
....$70–$100

Roosevelt, Eleanor. *This Troubled World.* NY. Kinsey. 1938. 1st ed. 47 pp, dj. $65

Roosevelt, Eleanor [Anna]. *It's Up to Women.* NY. Stokes. 1933. 1st ed. 263 pp, dj, scarce. $200

Roosevelt, Franklin D. *The Happy Warrior: Alfred E. Smith.* Bos. 1928. 1st ed. ....$35–$50

Roosevelt, Theodore. *African Game Trails.* NY. 1910. 1st ed. illus. .....
....$45–$95

Roosevelt, Theodore. *Good Hunting.* Harper & Bros. 1907. 1st ed. .....
....$65

Roosevelt, Theodore. *Hunting Trips of a Ranchman.* Putnam's. 1886. 1st
ed. $135

Roosevelt, Theodore. *Outdoor Pastimes of American Hunter.* NY. 1905.
1st ed. illus. ....$60–$75

Roosevelt, Theodore. *Ranch Life and the Hunting Trail.* NY. Century.
1896. illus by Remington, 186 pp. ....$80–$120

Roosevelt, Theodore. *Rank and File.* NY. 1928. 1st ed. ....$30–$50

Roosevelt, Theodore. *Roosevelt in* The Kansas City Star: *War-time Edito-
rials.* ... Bos. 1921. 1st ed. illus. ltd 375 cc. ....$45–$75

Roosevelt, Theodore. *Through the Brazilian Wilderness.* NY. 1914. 1st
ed. ....$67–$75

Roosevelt, Theodore. *The Winning of the West.* NY. 1910. 4 vols. rprnt. .
....$30

Roosevelt, Theodore. *The Winning of the West.* NY. 1900. 4 vols. ......
....$70–$225

Roosevelt, Theodore and Kermit. *East of the Sun and West of the Moon.*
Scribner's. 1927. illus. photos by author, maps. ....$60–$80

Roosevelt, Theodore and Kermit. *Trailing the Giant Panda.* NY.
Scribner's. 1929. 1st ed. photos, fldg map. ....$50–$75

Root, Edward W., and Phillip Hooker. *A Contribution to the Study of the
Renaissance in America.* NY. Scribner's. 1929. 1st ed. 242 pp, 1/750 cc. ...
....$175–$225

Root, S. *Primary Bible Questions for Young Children.* Atlanta. 1864. 3rd
ed. ....$125–$150

Roper, Steve, and Allen Steck. *Fifty Classic Climbs of North America.*
SF. Sierra Club. 1979. 1st ed. photos, maps, dj. ....$40–$50

Rosendahl, Commander C. E. *What about the Airship?* NY. 1938. 1st ed.
dj. ....$65–$80

Rosengarten A. *A Handbook of Architectural Styles.* Lon. 1910. 509 pp,
new ed. $85

Ross, Alexander. *Adventures of First Settlers on the Oregon or Columbia
River.* Lakeside Press. 1928. ....$40–$45

Rossetti, Christina. *A Pageant.* Lon. Macmillan. 1881. 1st ed. 198 pp. ...
....$225

Roth, Cecil (ed). *The Haggadah.* Lon. Beaconsfield Press. 1939. illus by
Arthur Szyk, #39/125 cc on vellum, sgn by Szyk and Roth. $6,900

Roth, Philip. *The Great American Novel.* NY. 1973. 1st ed. dj. . . . .
. . . .*$25–$40*

Roth, Philip. *Letting Go.* Random House. 1962. 1st ed. dj. *$60*

Roth, Philip. *Our Gang.* Lon. Jonathan Cape. (1971). 1st ed. dj. *$40*

Roth, Philip. *Portnoy's Complaint.* Random House. 1969. 1st ed. dj. . . . .
. . . .*$65–$85*

Roth, Philip. *The Professor of Desire.* NY. 1977. 1st ed. sgn, dj. . . . .
. . . .*$55–$65*

Roth, Philip. *When She Was Good.* Random House. 1967. 1st ed. dj. . . . .
. . . .*$35–$50*

Rowe, Samuel. *A Perambulation of the Antient and Royal Forest of Dart-moor.* Lon/Exeter. 1896. 3rd ed. illus. . . . .*$50–$75*

Roy, I. *A Lecture Delivered before the Rhode Island Institute of Instruc-tion, Oct. 18, 1850.* Bos. 1851. 1st ed. 52 pp. . . . .

Royce, Sarah. *A Frontier Lady: Recollections of the Gold Rush and Early California.* New Haven. Yale Univ. Press. 1932. 1st ed. dj. *$70*

Royko, Mike. *I May Be Wrong, but I Doubt It.* Chi. 1968. 1st ed. . . . .
. . . .*$24–$37*

Ruark, Robert. *The Honey Badger.* NY. 1965. 1st ed. dj. . . . . . .*$30–$50*

Ruark, Robert. *Horn of the Hunter.* NY. 1953. 1st ed. illus. . . . .
. . . .*$70–$125*

Ruark, Robert. *The Old Man and the Boy.* NY. 1957. 1st ed. illus. . . . . . .
. . . .*$45–$100*

Ruark, Robert. *The Old Man's Boy Grows Older.* NY. 1961. 1st ed. dj. . .
. . . .*$50–$65*

Ruark, Robert. *Something of Value.* Garden City. 1955. 1st ed. dj. . . . . . .
. . . .*$30–$45*

Ruark, Robert. *Something of Value.* Garden City. 1955. 1st ed. illus. . . . .
. . . .*$40–$55*

Ruark, Robert. *Uhuru.* Lon. 1962. 1st Brit ed. dj. . . . .*$50–$65*

Ruark, Robert. *Use Enough Gun.* NY. 1966. 1st ed. illus. dj. . . . .
. . . .*$35–$75*

Ruark, Robert. *Women.* NY. 1967. dj. . . . .*$50–$60*

Rubin, Jerry. *We Are Everywhere.* 1971. 1st ed. dj. . . . .*$20–$25*

Rugg, H. W. *History of Freemasonry in Rhode Island.* Prov. 1895. . . . . . .
. . . .*$30–$45*

Rukeyser, Muriel. *The Green Wave.* NY. Doubleday. 1948. 1st ed. dj. . . . .
. . . .*$100*

Rukeyser, Muriel. *The Life of Poetry.* Current Books. 1949. 1st ed. dj. . . .
. . . .*$70*

Rundle, Maria Eliza. *A New System of Domestic Cookery.* . . . Lon. 1807.
illus. . . . .*$75–$125*

Rundle, Maria Eliza. *A New System of Domestic Cookery.* . . . Lon. 1849.
illus. enlarged. . . . .*$40–$50*

Rush, Benjamin. *An Account of the Bilious Remitting Yellow Fever.* . . .
Phila. Thomas Dobson. 1794. 2nd ed. lea, rbckd. . . . .*$150–$275*

Rush, Benjamin. *An Inquiry into the Various Sources of the Usual Forms
of Summer and Autumnal Disease in the United States and the Means of
Preventing Them.* Phila. J. Conrad [etc]. 1805. 1st separate ed. 113 pp. . . .
. . . .*$200–$350*

Rush, Benjamin. *Letters of the American Philosophical Society.* 1951. 2
vols. 1st ed. djs. . . . .*$45–$65*

Rush, Benjamin. *Medical Inquiries and Observations.* Phila. 1809. vol 1,
3rd ed. . . . .*$65–$100*

Rush, Richard. *Memoranda of a Residence at the Court of London.* Phila.
1833. 1st ed. . . . .*$50–$75*

Rushdie, Salman. *Is Nothing Sacred?* Granta. 1990. illus. 16 pp. *$35*

Rushdie, Salman. *The Jaguar Smile.* NY. Viking Press. (1987). 1st ed. dj.
. . . .*$35*

Rushdie, Salman. *Midnight's Children.* NY. Knopf. 1981. 1st ed. dj. . . . .
. . . .*$145–$225*

Rushdie, Salman. *The Moor's Last Sigh.* NY. Pantheon. 1996. 1st U.S. ed.
dj, sgn. . . . .*$40–$65*

Rushdie, Salman. *The Satanic Verses.* NY. 1989. 1st Amer ed. dj. . . . . . .
. . . .*$45–$60*

Rushdie, Salman. *Shame.* NY. Knopf. 1983. 1st U.S. ed. dj. . . . .*$20–$30*

Ruskin, John. *Letters and Advice to Young Girls and Young Ladies.* NY.
1879. . . . .*$35–$45*

Russell, Bertrand. *The ABC of Relativity.* NY/Lon. 1925. 1st ed. . . . .
. . . .*$75–$100*

Russell, Charles M. *Good Medicine.* Garden City. 1930. illus. . .*$50–$75*

Russell, George. *Tour through Sicily in the Year 1815.* Lon. 1819. plates,
clr fldg map. . . . .*$75–$100*

Russell, Keith. *The Duck-huntingest Gentlemen: Collection of Water-
fowling Stories.* 1977. ltd, slipcase, sgn. . . . .*$85–$125*

Russell, Prof. William. *Scientific Horse Shoeing.* 1901. illus. 6th ed. . . . .
. . . .*$30–$45*

Russell, William Howard. *My Diary North and South.* NY. 1954. rprnt, dj. . . . .*$18–$25*

Rutherford, Livingston. *John Peter Zenger: His Press, His Trial . . . Bibliog. of Imprints.* NY. 1904. 1st ed. illus. ltd 325 cc. . . . .*$150–$250*

Rutledge, Archibald. *An American Hunter.* NY. 1937. illus by Lynne Bogue Hunt, 2nd prntg. . . . .*$18–$45*

Rutledge, Archibald. *Brimming Chalice.* NY. 1936. 1st ed. sgn, dj. . . . . .
. . . .*$95–$150*

Rutledge, Archibald. *Etiquette among the Beasts.* np. 1981. . . . .
. . . .*$18–$22*

Rutledge, Archibald. *Hunters Choice.* NY. 1946. 1st ed. dj. . . . .
. . . .*$35–$50*

Rutledge, Archibald. *Plantation Game Trails.* 1921. 1st ed. dj. . . . .
. . . .*$60–$85*

Rutledge, Archibald H. *Home by the River.* Ind. 1941. plates, sgn, dj. . . .
. . . .*$25–$35*

Rynhart, Susie Carson. *With the Tibetans in Tent and Temple.* Revell. 1901. illus. decorative cvrs. *$25*

Sabin, Edwin L. *Building the Pacific Railway.* Lippincott. 1919. . . . .
. . . .*$25–$37*

Sabin, Joseph. *A Dictionary of Books Relating to America. . . .* Amsterdam. 1961. 15 vols. rprnt. . . . .*$950–$1,250*

Sachs, B., and L Hausman. *Nervous and Mental Disorders from Birth through Adolescence.* NY. 1926. 1st ed. illus. . . . .*$50–$85*

Sachs, Ernest, M. D. *Fifty Years of Neurosurgery.* Vantage. 1958. 1st ed. sgn. . . . .*$22–$30*

Sackville-West, Vita. *Daughter of France.* NY. Doubleday. 1959. 1st U.S. ed. 336 pp, dj. *$75*

Sackville-West, Vita. *Devil at Westease.* NY. 1947. 1st ed. dj. . . . .
. . . .*$20–$25*

Sackville-West, Vita. *The Garden.* Lon. Michael Joseph. (1946). 1st ed. 135 pp, dj. *$135*

Sadler, William S. *Race Decadence.* Chi. 1922. 1st ed. dj. . . . .
. . . .*$27–$35*

Sagan, Carl. *Broca's Brain.* NY. (1979). 1st ed. dj. . . . .*$25–$35*

Salinger, J. D. *The Catcher in the Rye.* Bos. 1951. 1st ed. dj. . . . .
. . . .*$200–$850*

Salinger, J. D. *Franny and Zooey.* Bos. 1961. 1st ed. dj. . . . .
. . . .*$45–$65*

Salinger, J. D. *Nine Stories.* Bos. 1953. 1st ed. dj. . . . .*$250–$425*

Salinger, J. D. *Raise High the Roof Beam, Carpenters.* Little Brown. 1963. 1st ed. 2nd state. . . . .*$50–$75*

Salinger, J. D. *Raise High the Roofbeam, Carpenters.* 1963. 1st ed. 3rd issue, dj. . . . .*$20–$30*

Salinger, J. D. *The Kitbook for Soldiers, Sailors and Marines.* 1943. 1st ed. . . . .*$50–$85*

Salk and Salk. *World Population and Human Values.* NY. 1981. sgn, dj. . . . .*$55–$70*

Salten, Felix. *Bambi's Children.* Bobbs Merrill. 1939. 1st ed. dj. . . . .*$30–$40*

Salten, Felix. *Bambi: A Life in the Woods.* Simon & Schuster. 1928. ltd 1,000 cc. . . . .*$50–$60*

Salten, Felix. *Bambi.* Simon & Schuster. 1928. 1st ed. . . . .*$40–$50*

Samuels, Edward. *Ornithology and Zoology of New England . . . with Illustrations of Many Species of Birds. . . .* Bos. Nichols & Noyes. 1867. illus. plates, 583 pp. . . . .*$75–$95*

Sanborn, F. B. (ed). *The Life and Letters of John Brown, Liberator of Kansas. . . .* Bos. 1891. 1st ed. . . . .*$45–$55*

Sanborn, Helen. *Winter in Central America and Mexico.* Bos. 1887. 1st ed. . . . .*$32–$45*

Sanborn, Kate. *Old Time Wallpapers.* 1905. illus. ltd 975 cc, sgn and dated. . . . .*$120–$200*

Sanborn, Kate. *Old Time Wallpapers.* NY. 1905. 1st ed. . . . .*$200–$300*

Sanborn, Kate. *A Truthful Woman in Southern California.* NY. 1893. 1st ed. . . . .*$15–$25*

Sandburg, Carl. *Abraham Lincoln: The Prairie Years.* NY. Harcourt Brace. 1926. 2 vols. 1st trade ed, sgn. . . . .*$75–$100*

Sandburg, Carl. *Abraham Lincoln: The War Years.* NY. Harcourt Brace. 1940. 4 vols. illus. slipcase. . . . .*$60–$90*

Sandburg, Carl. *Always the Young Strangers.* NY. 1953. 1st ed. sgn, dj. . . . .*$30–$50*

Sandburg, Carl. *The American Songbag.* NY. 1927. . . . .*$25–$75*

Sandburg, Carl. *Chicago Poems.* Holt. 1916. dj. . . . .*$20–$25*

Sandburg, Carl. *Good Morning America.* Harcourt. 1928. 1st ed. dj. . . . .*$45–$55*

Sandburg, Carl. *Honey and Salt.* Harcourt Brace & World. (1963). 1st ed. dj. *$45*

Sandburg, Carl. *Potato Face.* Harcourt. 1930. 1st ed. dj. . . . . . .*$50–$75*

Sandburg, Carl. *Remembrance Rock.* NY. 1948. 1st ed. dj. . . . .*$20–$30*

Sandburg, Carl. *Remembrance Rock.* NY. 1948. 1st ed. presentation copy to August Derleth, sgn, dj. . . . .*$150–$275*

Sandburg, Carl. *Rootabaga Pigeons.* NY. 1923. 1st ed. illus. . . . .*$75–$110*

Sandburg, Carl. *Steichen the Photographer.* NY. (1929). 1st ed. 975 cc, sgn by Steichen and Sandburg, slipcase. *$690*

Sanderson, G. P. *Thirteen Years among the Wild Beasts of India.* Lon. 1893. . . . .*$18–$25*

Sandoz, Mari. *The Cattlemen.* NY. 1958. dj. . . . .*$27–$35*

Sandoz, Mari. *The Horse Catcher.* 1957. sgn, dj. . . . .*$25–$30*

Sandoz, Maurice. *The Maze.* NY. 1945. 1st ed. illus by Salvador Dali. . . . .*$40–$75*

Sandoz, Mari. *Old Jules.* 1935. . . . .*$5–$10*

Sandoz, Mari. *Son of the Gamblin' Man.* 1st ed. dj. . . . .*$35–$40*

Sanger, Margaret. *An Autobiography.* NY. (1938). 1st ed. 504 pp, dj. . . . .*$75–$85*

Sanger, Margaret. *My Fight for Birth Control.* NY. (1931). 1st ed. 360 pp. . . . .*$65–$75*

Sanger, Margaret. *Woman and the New Race.* NY. Truth. (1921). 3rd ed. *$45*

Sanger, Margaret. *Woman and the New Race.* NY. 1920. 1st ed. . . . .*$75–$90*

Sanger, Margaret, and Hannah M. Stone, M.D. (eds). *The Practice of Contraception.* Balt. Williams & Wilkins. 1931. 1st ed. 316 pp. *$200*

Sanger, William W. *The History of Prostitution.* NY. 1859. 1st ed. . . . .*$35–$40*

Sangree, Allen. *The Jinx: Stories of the Diamond.* NY. 1911. illus. . . . .*$60–$90*

Sansom, Joseph. *Travels in Lower Canada.* . . . Lon. 1820. one-quarter calf. . . . .*$85–$125*

Santayana, George. *Sonnets and Other Verses.* Camb/Chi. 1894. 1st ed. ltd 450 cc. . . . .*$75–$100*

Sanz, Carlos. *Bibliografia General de la Carta de Colon.* Madrid. Libreria General. 1958. 1st ed. wrps. 305 pp. ....*$125–$150*

Sarg, Tony. *Tony Sarg's Book of Animals.* Greenberg Pub. 1925. 1st ed. . ...*$30–$40*

Saroyan, William. *The Daring Young Man on the Flying Trapeze.* Covello. Yolla Bolly Press. 1984. 15th anniversary ed. #23/175 cc, illus, slipcase. ....*$300–$400*

Saroyan, William. *Get Away Old Man.* NY. Harcourt Brace. (1944). 1st ed. a play, dj. *$45*

Saroyan, William. *The Laughing Matter.* Doubleday. 1953. 1st ed. dj. ... .*$30–$55*

Saroyan, William. *My Heart's in the Highlands.* NY. (1939). dj. ....*$75–$100*

Saroyan, William. *Rock Wagram.* NY. 1951. 1st ed. dj. ....*$20–$30*

Saroyan, William. *The Time of Your Life.* Harcourt Brace. 1939. 1st ed. . ...*$20–$30*

Sarre, Friedrich, and Hermann Trankwald. *Old Oriental Carpets.* Vienna. Anton Schroll & Co. 1926–1929. 2 vols. elephant folio, lea. *$2,500*

Sarton, May. *Anger.* NY. 1982. sgn, dj. ....*$25–$40*

Sarton, May. *Conversations with May Sarton.* Jackson. Univ. Press of Mississippi (1944). 1st ed. dj. *$40*

Sarton, May. *December Moon.* Ewert. 1988. 36 cc, sgn. ....*$40–$50*

Sarton, May. *Encounter in April.* Bos. Houghton Mifflin. 1937. 1st ed, author's first book, 85 pp. *$250*

Sarton, May. *Faithful Are the Wounds.* NY. Rinehart. (1955). 1st ed. 281 pp, dj. *$75*

Sarton, May. *In Time Like Air.* NY. (1958). 1st ed. 80 pp, dj. *$75*

Sarton, May. *Miss Pickthorn and Mr. Hare.* NY. 1st ed. sgn, dj. ....*$45–$50*

Sarton, May. *The Poet and the Donkey.* NY. 1969. 1st ed. dj. ....*$25–$30*

Sarton, May. *Shadow of a Man.* NY. Rinehart. (1950). 1st ed. no dj. *$40*

Sarton, May. *A Shower of Summer Days.* NY. Rinehart. (1952). 1st ed. 244 pp, dj, scarce. *$75*

Sartre, Jean-Paul. *The Devil and the Good Lord.* Knopf. 1960. 1st U.S. ed. dj. ....*$27–$35*

Sartre, Jean-Paul. *Existentialism....* Philosophical Library. 1947. 1st U.S. ed. dj. . . . .*$45–$55*

Sartre, Jean-Paul. *Nausea.* CT. 1949. 1st U.S. ed. dj. . . . .*$40–$55*

Sartre, Jean-Paul. *Situations.* 1965. 1st ed. dj. *$35*

Sartre, Jean-Paul. *Theatre: Les Mouches; Huis-clos; Morts san sepul-chre; La Putain Respectueuse.* (Paris). Gallimard. (c 1947). 1st ed thus, 1/2000 cc. *$100*

Sartre, Jean-Paul. *The Wall and Other Stories.* New Directions. 1948. ltd ed. slipcase. . . . .*$50–$60*

Sassoon, Siegfried. *Memoirs of an Infantry Officer.* NY. 1931. illus. 1st U.S. ed. dj. . . . .*$25–$35*

Sassoon, Siegfried. *Nativity.* Lon. nd. 1st ed. dj. . . . .*$25–$35*

Satterlee, L. *American Gun Makers.* NY. 1940. 1st ed. . . . .*$35–$40*

Saundby, R. *Lectures on Bright's Disease.* Bristol/Lon. 1889. . . . .
. . . .*$22–$25*

Saunders, Ann. *Narrative of the Shipwreck and Sufferings of....* Prov. 1827. 1st ed. wrps. . . . .*$75–$85*

Saunders, Charles Francis. *The Indians of the Terraced Houses.* NY. 1912. . . . .*$30–$45*

Saunders, Louise. *The Knave of Hearts.* Racine, Wisconsin. 1925. illus by Maxfield Parrish, folio, spiral bound. . . . .*$500–$750*

Saunders, Ruth. *The Book of Artists' Own Bookplates.* Claremont. Saunders Studio Press. 1933. 1st ed. ltd 360 cc, sgn and numbered. *$75*

Sawyer, Charles Winthrop. *Our Rifles.* The Cornhill Co. 1920. 1st ed. . .
. . . .*$65*

Sayler, Oliver M. *The Russian Theatre.* NY. Brentano. 1922. . . . .
. . . .*$50–$80*

Schabalie, John. *The Wandering Soul.* Woodstock, VA. 1849. 1st ed thus, first published in 1645. . . . .*$300*

Schaeffler, Casper. *Memoirs and Reminiscences, Together with Sketches of the Early History of Sussex County, New Jersey....* Hackensack, NJ. private ptg. 1907. illus. ltd 250 cc, 187 pp. *$50*

Schaff, Morris. *The Sunset of the Confederacy.* Bos. 1912. maps. . . . .
. . . .*$25–$37*

Schaldach, William J. *Coverts and Casts.* NY. 1943. 1st ed. illus. . . . . . .
. . . .*$35–$45*

Schaldach, William J. *Fish by Schaldach.* Phila. 1937. ltd 1,500 cc. . . . . .
. . . .*$80–$150*

Schaldach, William J. *Upland Gunning.* VT. 1946. illus. presentation copy, dj. . . . .*$100–$175*

Schell, William G. *Is the Negro a Beast?* Moundsville. 1901. 1st ed. . . . .*$40–$45*

Schenck, David. *North Carolina, 1780–81.* Raleigh. 1889. 1st ed. . . . .*$75–$100*

Schley, W. S. *Report of Greely Relief Exped. of 1884.* DC. 1887. 1st ed. . . . .*$85–$110*

Schmitt, Martin, and Dee Brown. *The Settlers' West.* NY. 1955. 1st ed. illus. dj. . . . .*$24–$30*

Schmookler, Paul. *The Salmon Flies of Major John P. Traherne.* 1993. ltd and only ed. 300 cc, photos, lea, French hand-dipped clr paper over bds, slipcase, aeg. *$350*

Schoenberger, J. *From Great Lakes to Pacific.* 1934. 1st ed. . . . .*$50–$65*

Schoener, Allan (ed). *Harlem on My Mind.* NY. Dell. 1979. 272 pp, illus, 2nd ed. wraps. . . . .*$40–$50*

School, Wm. M. *Dictionary of the Foot.* Foot Publishing Co. 1918. 89 pp. . . . .*$25–$40*

Schoolcraft, Henry. *The American Indians: Their History, Condition and Prospects.* . . . . Rochester. 1851. illus. rev ed. plates. *$150*

Schoolcraft, Henry R. *Journal of a Tour into the Interior of Missouri and Arkansaw . . . toward the Rocky Mountains . . . in the years 1818 and 1819.* Lon. Richard Phillips. 1821. fldg map. . . . .*$350–$425*

Schoolcraft, Henry R. *New York Historical Society.* NY. 1854. . . . .*$90–$120*

Schoolcraft, Henry R. *A Report of Schoolcraft's Expedition among the Northwestern Indians.* 1838. House document #125, lea wraps, 16 pp. . . . .*$50–$60*

Schoolcraft, Henry. *A View of the Lead Mines of Missouri.* . . . NY. Charles Wiley. 1819. 1st ed. illus. 299 pp, plates. . . . .*$300–$500*

Schooling, Sir William. *The Hudson Bay Company.* Lon. 1920. photos. *$150*

Schoonmaker, W. J. *The World of the Grizzly Bear.* Phila/NY. 1968. illus. . . . .*$30–$40*

Schoonover, T. *Life of General J. Sutter.* 1895. 1st ed. . . . .*$60–$75*

Schulberg, Budd. *The Harder They Fall.* Random House. 1947. 1st ptg, sgn, dj. *$75*

Schulberg, Budd. *Sanctuary V.* World. 1969. 1st ed. dj. . . . .*$20–$25*

Schulthess, Emil. *Antarctica.* NY. 1960. 1st Amer ed. plates. . . .*$60–$75*

Schultz, A. H. *The Life of Primates.* NY. 1969. illus. . . . .*$35–$45*

Schultz, J. W. *My Life As an Indian.* NY. 1907. photos. . . . . . .*$125–$150*

Schulz, Charles M. *Good Grief, More Peanuts.* NY. 1956. wrps. . . . .
. . . .*$30–$40*

Schulz, Charles M. *Snoopy and the Red Baron.* NY. 1966. 1st ed. dj. . . . .
. . . .*$28–$38*

Schuyler, George W. *Colonial New York.* NY. 1885. 2 vols. . . . .
. . . .*$150–$175*

Schuyler, Keith. *Lures.* Stackpole. (1955). dj. . . . .*$15–$22*

Schwatka, Frederick. *A Summer in Alaska.* St. Louis. 1893. illus. . . . . . .
. . . .*$45–$75*

Schweinfurth, Charles. *Orchids of Peru.* Chi. 1958. 2 vols. . . . .*$50–$60*

Schweizer, Charles H. *Billiard Hints.* La Crosse, WI. 1906. . . . .*$20–$28*

Schwiebert, E. *History of the U.S. Air Force Ballistic Missiles.* NY. 1965.
1st ed. dj. . . . .*$25–$30*

Scott, Emmett. *Scott's Official History of the American Negro in the
World War.* 1919. illus. . . . .*$20–$25*

Scott, Harold (ed). *English Songbook.* NY. 1926. dj. *$35*

Scott, Robert Falcon. *Scott's Last Expedition.* Lon. Smith, Elder. 1913. 2
vols. 3rd ed, teg. . . . .*$200–$260*

Scott, W. W. *History of Orange County, Virginia.* Richmond. 1907. 1st ed.
. . . .*$85–$90*

Scott, Winfield. *General Scott and His Staff. . . .* Phila. 1849. illus. . . . . . .
. . . .*$37–$45*

Scouting for Girls. NY. Girl Scouts. 1923. 5th ed. . . . .*$35–$50*

Scrivenor, Harry. *History of the Iron Trade.* Lon. 1854. 2nd ed. 321 pp. . .
. . . .*$60–$75*

Scudder, S. H. *The Tertiary Insects of North America.* DC. 1890. 4to, 734
pp, map frontis, 28 plates (U.S. Geological Survey, vol 13). . . .*$125–$250*

Sculpture from Africa in the Museum of Primitive Art. NY. 1963. 16 pp,
photos. *$17*

Seale, Bobby. *Seize the Time: The Story of the Black Panther Party.* NY.
(1970). 1st ed. dj. . . . .*$25–$35*

Seaman, Louis L. *From Tokio through Manchuria with the Japanese.* NY.
1905. . . . .*$22–$35*

Seawell, Molly. *The Ladies' Battle.* NY. 1911. 1st ed. 119 pp. . . . .
. . . .*$30–$45*

Sedgwick, Catherine Marie. *The Deformed Boy, by the Author of "Redwood."* Brookfield, MA. E & G Merriam, Printers. 1826. wrps. 36 pp, 135 by 82 cm. *$165*

Sedgwick, James. *The Law of Storms.* Lon. Partridge & Oakey. 1852. illus. . . . .*$45–$85*

Seeger, Alan. *Poems.* 1916. 1st ed. . . . .*$30–$45*

Sendak, Maurice. *Outside over There.* NY. 1981. illus by Sendak, dj. . . . .*$25–$40*

Sendak, Maurice. *Posters by.* . . . Harmony, NY. 1986. 1st ed. dj. . . . .*$28–$35*

Sendak, Maurice. *Works of Maurice Sendak, 1947–1994.* Portsmouth. Peter Randall. 1995. 1st ed. dj. *$35*

Senn, C. Herman. *Luncheons and Dinner Sweets . . . Ice Making.* Lon. 1st ed. illus. dj. . . . .*$15–$20*

Senn, Dr. Nicholas. *In the Heart of the Arctics.* Chi. 1907. 1st ed. illus. *$65*

Sergeant, F. L. *Wright's Usonian House.* 1978. dj. . . . .*$47–$60*

Serling, Rod. *The Season to Be Wary.* Bos. Little Brown. (1967). dj. . . . .*$30–$45*

Service, Robert. *Rhymes of a Rolling Stone.* Tor. 1912. 1st ed. . . . .*$60–$100*

Service, Robert W. *Ballads of a Cheechako.* NY. 1909. . . . .*$6–$12*

Seton, Ernest Thompson. *Animal Heroes.* 1st ed. *$100*

Seton, Ernest Thompson. *The Arctic Prairies.* NY. 1917. illus. rprnt, photos, maps, drawings. . . . .*$40–$55*

Seton, Ernest Thompson. *The Biography of a Grizzly.* NY. 1900. illus. presentation copy, sgn. . . . .*$42–$55*

Seton, Ernest Thompson. *The Biography of a Grizzly.* Lon. Hodder & Stoughton. 1914. illus by author, 11th impression. *$45*

Seton, Ernest Thompson. *The Birchbark Roll of Woodcraft.* NY. 1931. illus. softcover. . . . .*$20–$27*

Seton, Ernest Thompson. *The Book of Woodcraft.* Garden City. 1921. illus. . . . .*$30–$35*

Seton, Ernest Thompson. *Ernest Thompson Seton's America.* NY. 1954. 1st ed. 1st ptg, dj. . . . .*$20–$30*

Seton, Ernest Thompson. *Gospel of the Red Man.* 1st ed. dj. . . . .*$40–$55*

Seton, Ernest Thompson. *Lives of the Hunted.* 1901, 1st ed. *$60*

Seton, Ernest Thompson. *Monarch: The Big Bear of Tallac.* NY. 1904. 1st ed. illus. 1st imp. . . . .*$25–$50*

Seton, Ernest Thompson. *Rolf in the Woods.* Doubleday. 1911. illus. . . . .*$30–$45*

Seton, Ernest Thompson. *Rolf in the Woods.* NY. 1922. illus. . .*$25–$30*

Seton, Ernest Thompson. *Rolf in the Woods.* 1st U.K. ed. *$70*

Seton, Ernest Thompson. *Trail of an Artist-Naturalist.* NY. 1940. 1st ed. illus. . . . . : *$45*

Seton, Ernest Thompson. *Two Little Savages.* NY. 1903. 1st ed. illus. . . . .*$40–$55*

Seton, Ernest Thompson. *Wild Animals I Have Known.* NY. 1898. 1st ed. illus. . . . .*$40–$50*

Seton, Ernest Thompson. *Woodmyth and Fable.* 1st ed. *$45*

Seton, Grace. *A Woman Tenderfoot.* Lon. 1900. illus. . . . .*$18–$22*

Seton, Grace Thompson. *Yes, Lady Saheb.* NY/Lon. 1925. 1st ed. illus. photos. . . . .*$15–$25*

Seton, J. M. *The Indian Costume Book.* Santa Fe. 1938. ltd 500 cc, photos, buckram, three-quarter dec and wood cvr, hand bound. *$475*

Seton, Julia M. *The Pulse of the Pueblo.* NM. 1939. presentation copy, sgn. . . . .*$25–$30*

Seuss, Dr. *More Boners.* NY. 1931. . . . .*$15–$40*

Seuss, Dr. *Thidwick the Big-Hearted Moose.* NY. 1948. 1st ed. . . . .*$33–$40*

Sewell, William. *The History of the Rise, Increase and Progress of the Christian People Called Quakers.* Burlington, NJ. Isaac Collins. 1774. 812 pp. . . . .*$100–$125*

Sewell, Anna. *Black Beauty.* Bos. 1890. illus. 1st Amer ed. *$200*

Sewell, Anna. *Black Beauty: His Grooms and Companions.* Bos. 1890. 1st thus, American Humane Ed. Soc. . . . .*$150–$295*

Sextus, Carl. *Hypnotism.* Chi. 1893. 1st ed. illus. . . . .*$30–$45*

Seymour, C. *Intimate Papers of Colonel House.* 2 vols. 1st ed. . . . .*$40–$60*

Seymour, Prof. W. P. *Seymour's Key to Electro-therpeutics.* Newark. 1904. 2nd ed. *$30*

Shackleton, Ernest H. *Aurora Australis.* Aukland, New Zealand. SeTo Publishing. 1988. rprnt, dj. . . . .*$18–$25*

Shackleton, Ernest H. *The Heart of the Antarctic.* Phila. 1914. illus. fldg map, clr plates. . . . .*$50–$75*

Shackleton, Ernest H. *The Heart of the Antarctic.* Phila. Lippincott. 1909. 2 vols. 1st Amer ed. illus, maps. . . . .*$400–$500*

Shackleton, Ernest H. *South.* NY. Macmillan. 1920. 1st Amer ed. illus, map. *$165*

Shackleton, Ernest H. (ed). *Aurora Australis.* New Zealand. 1988. illus. rprnt, dj. . . . .*$25–$30*

Shahn, Ben. *Haggadah.* Bos. 1965. small folio. . . . .*$55–$65*

Shakespeare, William. *The Comedies, Histories and Tragedies of Wm. Shakespeare.* 1939. 37 vols. illus. Ltd. Ed. Club, 8 slipcases. . . . .*$850–$950*

Shakespeare, William. *Complete Works.* NY. 1856. 3 vols. illus. . . . .*$185–$225*

Shakespeare, William. *The Dramatic Works.* Bos. Hilliard Gray. 1839. 8 vols. . . . .*$75–$100*

Shakespeare, William. *Midsummer Night's Dream.* Lon/NY. 1908. 1st ed. illus by Arthur Rackham, clr plates. . . . .*$275–$325*

Shakespeare. *Passionate Pilgrim.* Clarendon. 1905. facs of 1st ed. vellum. . . . .*$115–$150*

Shakespeare, William. *Romeo and Juliet.* NY. 1936. illus. dj. . . . .*$50–$75*

Shakespeare, William. *Shakespeare's Comedy As You Like It.* Lon/NY. nd. 1st ed. illus. 39 tip-in clr pls. . . . .*$195–$250*

Shakespeare, William. *Shakespeare's Comedy of The Tempest.* Lon. 1915. illus by Edmund Dulac. . . . .*$250–$300*

Shakespeare, William. *A Winter's Tale.* Lon. 1856. 105 pp. . . . .*$85–$125*

Shakespeare, William. *Works.* Lon/NY. The Nonesuch Press/Random House. 1929–33. 7 vols. *$2,500*

Shakespeare, William. *Works.* Lon/NY. 1892. 12 vols. boxed. . . . .*$50–$75*

Shakespeare, William. *Works.* Phila. Porter. nd. 8 vols. limp lea. . . . .*$90–$125*

Shakespeare, William. *Works of Shakespeare.* NY. Defau. 1903. 12 vols. ltd 1,000 cc, mor, mar bds. . . . .*$275–$350*

Shakespeare, William. *Works of Shakespeare.* Lon. 1904. 10 vols. deluxe ed. ltd #197/500 cc. . . . .*$120–$135*

Shand, Alex Innes. *The Gun Room.* The Bodley Head. 1895. 1st ed. . .*$65*

Shapiro, Karl. *Essay on Rime.* Reynal & Hitchcock. 1945. 1st ed. dj. . . . .*$40–$45*

Shapiro, Karl. *White-haired Lover.* NY. 1968. 1st ed. sgn, dj. . . . .
. . . .*$30–$45*

Sharp, H. *Modern Sporting Gunnery Manual.* . . . Lon. 1906. small folio.
. . . .*$30–$40*

Shaw, Edward. *Shaw's Civil Architecture.* Bos. 1852. . . . .*$40–$50*

Shaw, Edward Richard. *The Pot of Gold: A Story of Fire Island Beach.*
Chi/NY. 1888. . . . .*$85–$125*

Shaw, George Bernard. *The Adventures of a Black Girl in Her Search for
God.* Dodd Mead. 1933. illus. 1st Amer ed. dj. . . . .*$30–$40*

Shaw, George Bernard. *The Intelligent Woman's Guide to Socialism and
Capitalism.* NY. 1928. 1st Amer ed. . . . .*$35–$45*

Shaw, George Bernard. *The Intelligent Woman's Guide to Socialism and
Capitalism.* NY. Brentano. 1928. 2nd U.S. ptg, 495 pp, dj. *$25*

Shaw, George Bernard. *The Intelligent Woman's Guide to Socialism and
Capitalism.* Lon. Constable. 1928. 1st ed. dj. *$75*

Shaw, George Bernard. *The Quintessence of Ibsenism.* Lon. Walter Scott.
1891. 1st ed. *$150*

Shaw, George Bernard (ed). *Fabianism and the Empire: A Manifesto.*
Lon. Grant Richards. 1900. 1st ed. wrps. *$100*

Shaw, Irwin. *Mixed Company.* Random House. 1950. 1st ed. dj. . . . .
. . . .*$40–$50*

Shaw, Irwin. *Sailor off the Bremen and Other Stories.* NY. Random
House. (c 1939). 1st ed. dj. *$65*

Shaw, Irwin. *The Troubled Air.* NY. 1951. 1st ed. dj. . . . .*$35–$40*

Shaw, Irwin. *The Young Lions.* NY. 1st ed. dj. . . . .*$35–$45*

Shaw, Robert. *Visits to High Tartary, Yarkand, and Kashgar.* Lon. John
Murray. 1871. 1st ed. 2 fldg maps, 7 tinted plates. . . . .*$300–$450*

Shaw, Thomas George. *The Wine Trade and Its History.* Lon. nd. . . . . . .
. . . .*$37–$75*

Sheckley, Robert. *Damocles.* NY. 1983. . . . .*$22–$25*

Sheckley, Robert. *Is That What People Do?* NY. 1984. sgn, dj. . . . .
. . . .*$15–$20*

Sheehan, Neil. *A Bright Shining Lie.* NY. 1988. 1st ed. dj. . . . .
. . . .*$30–$50*

Sheldon, Charles. *The Wilderness of the Upper Yukon.* NY. 1913. illus.
maps. . . . .*$50–$75*

Shelley, Mary. *Frankenstein.* Univ. of California Press. 1984. 1st ed thus,
dj. *$65*

Shelley, Mary. *Frankenstein.* Bos. Sever, Francis. 1869. 2nd Amer ed. 177 pp. *$450*

Shepherd, Sam. *Operation Sidewinder.* NY. 1970. . . . .*$35–$40*

Sheridan, Philip H. *Personal Memoirs.* NY. 1888. 2 vols. 1st ed. *$50–$75*

Sherman, John. *Recollections.* 1895. 2 vols. 1st ed. . . . .*$45–$65*

Sherman, S. M. *History of the 133rd Regiment, O.V.I.* Columbus. 1896. 1st ed. . . . . *$95–$125*

Sherman, William Tecumseh. *Home Letters of General Sherman.* NY. 1909. 1st ed. . . . . *$40–$50*

Sherman, William Tecumseh. *Memoirs of. . . .* 1891. 2 vols. 4th ed. . . . . *$40–$70*

Sherwood, Mary Martha. *The History of Little Henry and His Bearer.* Hartford. George Goodwin & Sons. 1822. 52 pp, 14 by 87 cm. *$95*

Sherwood, Robert Emmet. *The Queen's Husband.* NY. 1928. 1st ed. . . . .*$40–$45*

Shiel, M. P. *Children of the Wind.* NY. 1923. 1st U.S. ed. . . . . . .*$30–$40*

Shirts, Augustus F. *History of . . . Hamilton County, Indiana (1818 to Civil War).* 1901. 1st ed. illus. . . . .*$65–$100*

Shoemaker, Henry. *Black Forest Souvenirs.* Reading, PA. Bright-Faust Printing Co. 1914. illus. plates, inscrb. . . . .*$60–$75*

Shriner, C. H. *Birds of New Jersey.* 1896. . . . .*$25–$45*

Shuckers, J. W. *The Life and Public Services of Samuel Portland Chase.* NY. 1874. 1st ed. . . . .*$28–$35*

Shurtleff, Nathaniel. *A Topographical and Historical Description of Boston.* Bos. 1871. . . . .*$45–$75*

Shute, Nevil. *On the Beach.* NY. 1957. 1st ed. dj. . . . .*$30–$40*

Shute, Miss T. S. *The American Housewife Cook Book.* Phila. 1878. . . . .*$30–$40*

Sidney, M. *Five Little Peppers Grown Up.* Bos. 1892. 1st ed. . . .*$20–$30*

Siebert, Wilbury H. *Vermont's Anti-slavery and Underground Railroad Record. . . .* Columbus, OH. 1937. 1st ed. illus. map, plates. . . . . .*$50–$75*

Siegbahn, M. *Spectroscopy of X-Rays.* Lon. 1925. 1st Eng ed. . . .*$40–$50*

Sikorsky, Igor I. *The Story of the Winged-S, with New Material on . . . Helicopter.* NY. 1942. illus. photos, inscr, dj. . . . .*$40–$45*

Silverberg, Robert. *Lord Valentine's Castle.* Harper & Row. (1980). 1st ed. sgn, dj. . . . .*$20–$25*

Silverberg, Robert. *The New Springtime.* Warner Books. (1990). 1st U.S. ed. dj. . . . .*$14–$20*

Silverstein, Shel. *Different Dances.* 1978. 1st ed. dj. . . . .*$55–$100*

Simkins, Francis Butler, and James Welch Patton. *The Women of the Confederacy.* Rich/NY. 1936. 1st ed. dj. . . . .*$90–$125*

Simmons, Amelia. *American Cookery.* NY. 1958. ltd 800 cc, boxed. . . . .
. . . .*$35–$50*

Simmons, L. W. (ed). *Sun Chief: The Autobiography of a Hopi Indian.* New Haven. 1942. illus. . . . .*$30–$40*

Simms, W. Gilmore. *The Lily and the Totem.* NY. 1850. . . . .*$35–$45*

Sinclair, Upton. *The Flivver King: A Story of Ford-America.* Upton Sinclair. 1937. 1st ed. dj. . . . .*$45–$50*

Sinclair, Upton. *Our Lady.* NY/Pasadena. (1938). 1st ed. 162 pp, inscrb. .
. . . .*$150*

Sinclair, Upton. *Wide Is the Gate.* Viking. 1943. 1st ed. dj. *$30*

Singer, Isaac Bashevis. *The Estate.* NY. 1969. 1st ed. dj. . . . . . .*$25–$35*

Singer, Isaac Bashevis. *Nobel Lecture.* Farrar. 1979. 1st ed. dj. *$30*

Singer, Isaac Bashevis. *Old Love.* NY. 1979. 1st ed. dj. . . . .*$15–$30*

Singer, Isaac Bashevis. *Passions and Other Stories.* Lon. (1976). 1st U.K. ed. dj. . . . .*$25–$35*

Singer, Isaac Bashevis. *The Penitent.* PA. 1983. 1st ed. dj. . . . .*$75–$100*

Singer, Isaac Bashevis. *The Penitent.* Signed First Edition Society. 1983. sgn, no dj as issued. *$95*

Singer, Isaac Bashevis. *Short Friday.* NY. 1964. 1st ed. . . . .*$35–$40*

Singleton, Esther. *The Shakespeare Garden.* NY. 1931. . . . .*$20–$25*

Singleton, Esther. *Social New York under the Georges, 1714–1776.* NY. 1902. 1st ed. . . . .*$30–$40*

Sinnett, A. P. *The Occult World.* Bos. 1882. 1st ed. . . . .*$45–$85*

Siringo, Charles. *A Cowboy Detective.* Chi. 1912. 1st ed. photos. . . . .
. . . .*$200–$250*

Siringo, Charles. *Lone Star Cowboy.* Santa Fe. 1919. 1st ed. *$100*

Siringo, Charles. *Riata and Spurs.* Bos. 1927. 1st ed. . . . .*$95–$150*

Siringo, Charles. *Riata and Spurs.* Bos. 1931. . . . .*$25–$35*

Siringo, Charles. *A Texas Cowboy.* NY. Time-Life. 1980. facs of an 1885 original ed, 316 pp. . . . .*$25–$35*

Sitwell, Sacheverell. *Dance of the Quick and the Dead.* Lon. Faber & Faber. 1936. 1st ed. illus. dj. *$47.50*

Sitwell, Sacheverell. *The Gothick North.* Bos. Houghton Mifflin. 1929. plates. . . . .*$30–$40*

Sitwell, Sacheverell. *Great Palaces of Europe.* NY. illus. . . . . . .*$14–$25*

Sitwell, Sacheverell. *Monks, Nuns and Monasteries.* NY. Holt, Rinehart & Winston. (1965). 1st ed. illus. dj. ....*$18–$25*

Sizer, Nelson. *Forty Years in Phrenology.* NY. 1882. ....*$18–$27*

Sketch of the 126th Regiment Pennsylvania Volunteers. PA. 1869. 1st ed. ....*$95–$125*

Skinner, Charles M. *Myths and Legends of Our Own Land.* Phila/Lon. 1896. 2 vols. 1st ed. illus. ....*$25–$35*

Skinner, H. *The Theodores of the Bible.* np. 1877. 12 pp. ....*$20–$30*

Skinner, Otis. *Footlights and Spotlights.* Bobbs Merrill. 1924. ltd #27/500 cc, sgn. ....*$35–$45*

Slang Dictionary. Lon. 1864. 2nd ed. ....*$40–$60*

Sloane, T. O'Connor. *Electric Toy Making for Amateurs.* NY. Munn & Co. 1903. illus. 25. ....*$35–$85*

Slocum, Capt. Joshua. *Sailing Alone around the World.* Lon. Samson, Low, Marston & Co. (c 1900). 3rd ed. illus, pictorial cloth, aeg. ....*$38–$50*

Slocum, Joshua. *The Voyage of the Liberdade.* Bos. 1894. illus. ....*$125–$255*

Small Homes. Ithaca, NY. Driscoll Bros. & Co. c 1940s. pictorial wrps, for National Plan Service, 48 pp. ....*$35–$50*

Smalley. *A Brief History of the Republican Party.* .... NY. 1888. ....*$24–$32*

Smiles, LL. D., Samuel. *Josiah Wedgewood.* NY. Harper & Bros. 1895. illus. 330 pp. ....*$30–$60*

Smiley, Jane. *The Age of Grief.* NY. Knopf. 1987. 1st ed. dj. *$60*

Smith, Mrs. *The Female Economist ... for the Use of Families.* Lon. 1810. half calf. ....*$45–$65*

Smith, A. *Dental Microscopy.* Lon/Phila. 1895. plates. ....*$35–$45*

Smith, Adam. *An Inquiry into the Nature and Causes of the Wealth of Nations.* Lon. 1799. 3 vols. lea, bds. ....*$150–$210*

Smith, Adam. *The Wealth of Nations.* Oxford. 1880. ed by Thorold Rogers, 2nd ed. 2 vols. ....*$75–$100*

Smith, Amanda. *An Autobiography.* .... Chi. 1893. 1st ed. ....*$45–$175*

Smith, Betty. *Joy in the Morning.* NY. 1963. 1st ed. sgn, dj. ....*$25–$40*

Smith, Clark Ashton. *As It Is Written. . . .* RI. (1982). 1st ed. illus. ltd 1250 cc, sgn by artist, dj. *$20*

Smith, Clark Ashton. *Other Dimensions.* Sauk City. Arkham House. 1970. 1st ed. dj. . . . .*$30–$85*

Smith, Clark Ashton. *Tales of Science and Sorcery.* Arkham House. 1964. 1st ed. dj. . . . .*$75–$125*

Smith, Clark Ashton. *Tales of Science and Sorcery.* Sauk City. 1964. 1st ed. dj. . . . .*$50–$75*

Smith, Daniel. *Company K, First Alabama Regiment. . . ,* Prattville, AL. 1885. . . . .*$900–$1,000*

Smith, F. L. *Wright: A Study in Architectural Content.* 1979. dj. . . . .*$50–$75*

Smith, Gustavus Woodson. *The Battle of Seven Pines.* NY. 1891. 1st ed. wrps. . . . .*$175–$200*

Smith, James Power. *General Lee at Gettysburg.* VA. nd. 1st ed. . . . .*$50–$75*

Smith, Jerome V. C. *Natural History of the Fishes of Massachusetts . . . Essay on Angling.* Bos. 1833. . . . .*$150–$175*

Smith, John. *Hard Times: Suggestions to the Workers, Broad Hint to the Rich.* Chi. Industrial Union Publishing. 1885. . . . .*$40*

Smith, Joseph. *The Book of Mormon.* Liverpool. 1841. 1st Eng ed. . . . .*$1,500–$2,500*

Smith, Martin Cruz. *Gorky Park.* Random House. 1981. 1st ed. dj. . . . .*$20–$30*

Smith, Martin Cruz. *Rose.* NY. Random House. 1996. 1st ed. sgn, dj. *$40*

Smith, Capt. Ross. *Reminiscences of an Old Timer.* np. private ptg. 1930. 1st ed. illus. 86 pp. . . . .*$25–$150*

Smith, Winston O. *The Sharps Rifle.* William Morrow. 1943. 1st ed. *$75*

Smucker, Samuel. *The Life of Col. John Charles Fremont.* NY. 1856. 1st ed. *$65*

Smyth, Henry D. *Atomic Energy for Military Purposes.* Princeton Univ. Press. 1945. 1st ed. dj. . . . .*$90–$95*

Smyth, Henry D. *Atomic Energy for Military Purposes.* 1945. illus. 2nd ed. softcover. . . . .*$35–$55*

Smythe, Frank S. *Kamet Conquered.* Lon. Victor Gollancz. 1933. 2nd imp, photos, maps. . . . .*$14–$20*

Smythe, Frank S. *Kamet Conquered.* Lon. Victor Gollancz. 1932. 1st ed. photos, maps. .... *$45–$60*

Smythe, Sarah M. *Ten Months in the Fiji Islands.* Oxford. John Henry & James Parker. 1864. maps, clr plates. .... *$325–$385*

Snow White. 1978. printed in Czechoslovakia, 6 pop-ups. ...... *$20–$25*

Snowden, R. *The History of North and South America.* Phila. 1813. 2 vols in 1, lea, maps. .... *$75–$100*

Snyder, Gary. *Earth House Hold.* 1969. 1st ed. sgn, dj. .... *$60–$85*

Snyder, Gary. *The Old Ways.* City Lights. 1977. 1st ed. .... *$20–$25*

Snyder, Gary. *Regarding Wave.* Lon. 1970. 1st ed. dj. .... *$35–$45*

Solomon. *Why Smash Atoms?* Camb. 1940. 1st ed. .... *$30–$60*

Solzhenitsyn, Alexandr. *Cancer Ward.* Bodley Head. 1968. 1st Eng ed. dj. .... *$35–$40*

Solzhenitsyn, Aleksandr. *Gulag Archipelago.* NY. 1973. 1st ed. dj. .... *$25–$30*

Solzhenitsyn, Alexandr. *Lenin in Zurich.* Farrar. 1976. 1st U.S. ed. dj. .... *$20–$25*

Solzhenitsyn, Aleksandr. *The Oak and the Calf.* Harper. 1980. 1st U.S. trade ed. dj. *$25*

Solzhenitsyn, Alexandr. *One Day in the Life of Ivan Denisovich.* NY. 1963. 1st ed. 1st U.S. ed. dj. .... *$20–$30*

Solzhenitsyn, Alexandr. *Stories and Prose Poems.* Farrar. 1971. 1st U.S. ed. dj. .... *$15–$30*

Some Accounts ... Soc. of Friends towards Indian Tribes (New Jersey and Pennsylvania). Lon. 1844. fldg map. .... *$200–$350*

Sonneck, Oscar G. T. *"The Star Spangled Banner...."* GPO. 1st ed. illus. .... *$45–$75*

Sontag, Susan. *Illness As Metaphor.* Farrar, Straus & Giroux. 1978. 1st ed. dj. .... *$30–$35*

The Southern Songster. ... Liverpool. 1864. wrps. .... *$175–$225*

Southern, Terry. *Red Dirt Marijuana.* NAL. 1967. dj. *$60*

Southwell, T. *The Seals and Whales of the British Seas.* Lon. 1881. illus. . ... *$175–$300*

Spaeth, Sigmund. *Barber Shop Ballads and How to Sing Them.* NY. 1940. 2nd ptg, 125 pp, drawings. *$17.50*

Spalding's Official Base Ball Guide: Golden Jubilee, 1876–1925. NY. American Sports Publishing. 1925. wrps. illus. .... *$80–$120*

Spark, Muriel. *The Driver's Seat.* Knopf. 1970. 1st U.S. ed. dj. . . . .
. . . . *$25–$30*

Spark, Muriel. *The Girls of Slender Means.* Lon. Macmillan. 1963. 1st ed.
dj. . . . .*$30–$50*

Spark, Muriel. *The Girls of Slender Means.* Knopf. 1963. 1st U.S. ed. dj.
. . . .*$25–$30*

Spark, Muriel. *The Prime of Miss Jean Brodie.* NY. (1962). 1st Amer ed.
dj. . . . .*$30–$40*

Spark, Muriel. *The Prime of Miss Jean Brodie.* Lon. 1961. 1st ed. dj. . . .
. . . .*$30–$35*

Sparks, Jared. *The Life of George Washington.* Bos. 1839. 1st ed. . . . . . .
. . . .*$65–$95*

Sparks, Jared. *The Life of Gouverneur Morris.* Bos. Gray & Bowen.
1832. 3 vols. 1st ed. . . . .*$100–$300*

Spears, John R. *The American Slave-trade.* NY. 1900. illus. . . . .*$45–$67*

Specimen Book of Monotype, Linotype and Foundry Type Faces, Etc.
Bos. 1941. 1st ed. . . . .*$28–$35*

Specimen Book of Type. Chi. Barnhart Bros. & Spindler. 1900. 4to, 879
pp. *$200*

Speck, F. G. *Penobscot Man.* NY. 1970. rprnt, map, illus. . . . . . .*$50–$80*

Speck, Frank G. *The Tutelo Spirit Adoption Ceremony.* Harrisburg. 1942.
illus. photos. . . . .*$25–$50*

Spencer, Ambrose. *A Narrative of Andersonville.* NY. 1866. 1st ed. 272
pp. . . . .*$70–$85*

Spencer, Elizabeth. *The Night Travelers.* NY. 1991. 1st Amer ed. sgn. . .
. . . .*$30–$40*

Spender, Stephen. *Forward from Liberalism.* NY. Random House.
(c 1937). 1st Amer ed. *$50*

Spender, Stephen. *The New Realism: A Discussion.* Lon. The Hogarth
Press. 1939. 1st ed. printed wraps. *$50*

Spender, Stephen. *Poems.* Lon. Faber & Faber. (1933). 2nd ed. dj. . . . . . .
. . . .*$75*

Spender, Stephen. *Poems of Dedication.* Lon. Faber & Faber. (1947). 1st
ed. dj. *$75*

Spender, Stephen. *Trial of a Judge: A Tragedy in Five Acts.* Lon. Faber &
Faber. (1938). 1st ed. inscrb. *$75*

Spengler, Oswald. *The Decline of the West.* NY. Knopf. 1932. 1st 1-vol
ed. charts. . . . .*$35–$45*

Spenser, Edmund. *Prothalamion; Epithalamion.* Bos/NY. 1902. illus. ltd 400 cc, folio, dj. ....*$67–$85*

Sperry, Earle E. *The Jerry Rescue.* NY. 1921. 16 pp. ....*$15–$25*

Spillane, Mickey. *The Deep.* NY. Dutton. 1961. 1st ed. dj. *$65*

Spillane, Mickey. *Kiss Me, Deadly.* NY. 1952. 1st ed. dj. ....
....*$45–$75*

Spiller, Burton L. *Firelight.* Derrydale. 1937. illus by Lynn Bogue Hunt, ltd 950 cc. ....*$180–$350*

Spiller, Burton L. *Grouse Feathers.* NY. 1947. illus by Lynn Bogue Hunt. ....*$50–$60*

Spivak, John L. *Georgia Nigger.* Lon. 1933. 1st ed. ....*$175–$250*

Splan, John. *Life with the Trotters.* 1889. presentation copy. ....
....*$110–$125*

Splawn, A. J. *Ka-Mi-Akin, the Last Hero of the Yakimas.* Portland. 1917. 1st ed. illus. photos, lea. ....*$90–$110*

The Sports of Childhood. New Haven. S. Babcock. nd. wrps. 8 pp, 73 by 45 cm. *$110*

Sprunt, Alexander Jr. *North American Birds of Prey.* Harper & Bros. 1955. 1st ed. dj. ....*$25–$40*

Spyri, Johanna. *Heidi.* Bos. Ginn. (1899). 1st ed thus, 365 pp. *$125*

Spyri, Johanna. *Heidi.* John C. Winston Co. 1927. clr plates. ....
....*$24–$30*

Squier, E. G. *Lecture on the Condition and True Interests of the Working Man in America.* Albany. 1843. 16 pp, wraps. ....*$45–$55*

Squier, E. G. *The States of Central America.* NY. 1858. illus. maps. ......
....*$30–$50*

St. John Roosa, D. B. *A Practical Treatise on the Diseases of the Ear.* NY. 1876. illus. ....*$42–$55*

Stalin, Joseph. *Leninism.* NY. International Publishers. 1928. 1st Amer ed. ....*$60–$75*

Standing Bear, Chief. *My People, the Sioux.* Bos. 1928. 2nd prtg, dj. ....
....*$35–$40*

Stanley, Dean. *Picturesque Palestine.* Lon. 1880–84. 5 vols. plates. ......
....*$275–$350*

Stanley, Henry M. *The Autobiography ... Edited by His Wife.* Bos. Houghton Mifflin. 1909. 1st ed. photogravures, fldg map, teg. ...*$50–$70*

Stanley, Henry M. *The Congo and the Founding of Its Free State.* NY. Harper & Bros. 1885. 2 vols. illus. maps. ....*$150–$180*

Stanley, Henry M. *The Congo and the Founding of Its Free State.* Lon. 1885. 2 vols. 1st ed. 5 fldg maps, pictorial cloth. . . . .*$300–$500*

Stanley, Henry M. *In Darkest Africa.* NY. 1890. 2 vols. illus. 540 pp, fldg maps, decorated cloth. . . . .*$195–$225*

Stanley, Henry M. *In Darkest Africa, or The Quest, Rescue and Retreat of Emin, Governor of Equatoria.* NY. Scribner's. 1891. 2 vols. illus. fldg maps. . . . .*$80–$120*

Stanley, Henry M. *My Early Travels and Adventures in America and Asia.* NY. 1895. 2 vols. . . . .*$265–$295*

Stanley, Henry M. *Slavery and the Slave Trade in Africa.* NY. Harper & Bros. 1893. 1st Amer ed. illus by Frederick Remington. *$50*

Stanley, Henry M. *Through the Dark Continent.* NY. Harper. 1879. 2 vols. maps. *$130*

Stanley, Henry M. *Through the Dark Continent.* NY. 1878. 2 vols. 1st Amer ed. illus. *$170*

Stanley, W. H. *My Kalulu Prince, King and Slave.* NY. Scribner's. 1890. illus. *$150*

Stansbury, Howard. *Exploration and Survey of the Valley of the Great Salt Lake.* Phila. 1852. . . . .*$225–$425*

Stanton, Elizabeth Cady. *Eighty Years and More.* NY. 1898. 1st ed. 474 pp. *$90*

Star Trek. Random House. 1977. 4 fan-folded pop-ups. . . . .*$40–$55*

Star Trek Technical Manual. 1975. 1st ed. . . . .*$20–$25*

Star Trek. *Trillions of Trillings.* Star Trek Concordance. 1976. 1st ed. pop-up. . . . .*$28–$35*

Starkie, Walter. *Scholars and Gypsies.* Berkeley. Univ. of California Press. [1963]. 1st Amer ed. sgn, dj. . . . .*$25–$30*

The Steamboats of Lake George, 1817–1832. Albany. 1932. illus. 174 pp, maps, photos. . . . .*$500–$700*

Stearns, Samuel. *The American Herbal. . . .* Walpole, MA. 1801. 1st Amer ed. lea. . . . .*$500–$800*

Steele, Chester K. *The Gold Course Mystery.* NY. George Sully. (1919). 1st ed. illus. . . . .*$35–$45*

Steele, Matthew Forney. *American Campaigns.* DC. 1909. 2 vols. 1st ed. . . . .*$85–$125*

Stefansson, Vilhjalmur. *The Adventure of Wrangle Island.* NY. 1925. 1st ed. illus. fldg clr map, sgn. . . . .*$75–$100*

Stefansson, Vilhjalmur. *Arctic Manual.* NY. 1944. 1st ed. . . . . .*$28–$65*

Stefansson, Vilhjalmur. *The Fat of the Land.* NY. 1956. 1st ed. sgn. . . . .
. . . .*$35–$45*

Stefansson, Vilhjalmur. *The Friendly Arctic.* Macmillan. 1944. . . . .
. . . .*$20–$25*

Stefansson, Vilhjalmur. *My Life with the Eskimo.* NY. Macmillan. 1921.
maps, inscrb, rprnt. . . . .*$40–$50*

Stefansson, Vilhjalmur. *Not by Bread Alone.* 1946. 1st ed. . . . .
. . . .*$25–$30*

Stegner, Wallace. *All the Little Live Things.* NY. 1967. 1st ed. dj. . . . . . .
. . . .*$35-$45*

Stegner, Wallace. *Crossing to Safety.* Random House. (1987). 1st ed. dj. .
. . . .*$25–$35*

Steichen, Edward. *The Family of Man.* NY. MOMA. 1955. . . . .
. . . .*$15–$20*

Steichen, Edward. *A Life in Photography.* Garden City. 1963. 1st ed. illus.
dj. . . . .*$50–$65*

Stein, Gertrude. *An Elucidation.* np. Transition. 1927. 1st separate ed.
printed wrps. *$100*

Stein, Gertrude. *Four in America.* New Haven. 1947. 1st ed. dj. .*$45–$60*

Stein, Gertrude. *The Gertrude Stein Reader and Three Plays.* Lon.
(1946). dj. . . . .*$50–$65*

Stein, Gertrude. *Lectures in America.* NY. Random House. (1935). 1st ed.
dj. *$150*

Stein, Gertrude. *Wars I Have Seen.* NY. Random House. (1945). 1st ed.
dj. . . . .*$35–$45*

Stein, Gertrude. *The World Is Round.* Lon. 1939. dj. . . . .*$20–$30*

Stein, Leonard. *The Balfour Declaration.* Lon. 1961. dj. . . . .*$18–$25*

Steinbeck, John. *Burning Bright.* NY. 1950. 1st ed. dj. . . . .*$45–$50*

Steinbeck, John. *Cannery Row.* NY. Viking. 1945. 1st ed. 1st issue, blue
wrps. *$750*

Steinbeck, John. *Cup of Gold.* NY. Robert McBride. 1929. 1st ed. 1st
issue, author's first book, yellow cloth, teg, dj, scarce. *$3,500*

Steinbeck, John. *The Grapes of Wrath.* NY. Viking Press. (1939). 1st ed.
619 pp, dj. *$1000*

Steinbeck, John. *The Grapes of Wrath.* Viking. 1939. 1st ed. dj. . . . .
. . . .*$400–$650*

Steinbeck, John. *The Log from the Sea of Cortez.* NY. dj. . . . . .*$50–$100*

Steinbeck, John. *The Moon Is Down.* 1942. 1st ed. dj. *$80*

Steinbeck, John. *The Moon Is Down.* 1942. dj..................$60

Steinbeck, John. *Of Mice and Men: A Play.* (1937). Covici Friede ed. 2nd ptg, dj. $50

Steinbeck, John. *Of Mice and Men: A Play.* Covici Friede. 1937. 1st issue, dj. ....$200–$550

Steinbeck, John. *The Pearl.* NY. 1947. 1st ed. illus. dj. ....$18–$25

Steinbeck, John. *The Red Pony.* NY. (1945). illus. dj. $25

Steinbeck, John. *Sea of Cortez.* 1st ed thus, 7,500 cc. $240

Steinbeck, John. *Sweet Thursday.* NY. Viking. (1954). 1st ed. dj. ....
....$55–$85

Steinbeck, John. *Travels with Charley.* Viking. 1962. 1st ed. dj. ....
....$25–$40

Steinbeck, John. *The Wayward Bus.* NY. Viking. 1947. 1st ed. dj. ......
....$40–$75

Steinbeck, John. *The Winter of Our Discontent.* NY. (1961). 1st ed. dj. ..
....$45

Steinbeck, John. *The Winter of Our Discontent.* Heinemann. 1961. 1st Eng ed. dj. ....$25–$65

Steiner, Jesse Frederick, and Roy M. Brown. *The North Carolina Chain Gang.* .... Chapel Hill. 1927. 1st ed......................$100–$150

Steinmetz, Andrew. *Sunshine and Showers: Their Influence throughout Creation: A Compendium of Popular Meteorology.* Lon. 1867. 432 pp. ...
....$95–$150

Stejneger, L. *The Poisonous Snakes of North America.* DC. 1895. ......
....$20–$27.50

Stellman, Louis J. *Mother Lode.* 1939. photos. ....$28–$37

Stephens, J. *Incidents of Travel in Yucatan.* NY. 1843. 2 vols. 1st ed. foldout plate, ex lib. $85

Stephens, James. *Crock of Gold.* Lon. 1912. 1st ed. presentation copy, sgn. ....$95–$250

Stephens, James. *The Crock of Gold.* Lon. 1912. 1st ed. dj.....$85–$95

Stephens, James. *The Demi-gods.* Lon. 1914. 1st ed. 1st issue. ...$45–$50

Stetson, George R. *The Southern Negro As He Is.* Bos. 1877. 1st ed. ....
....$75–$100

Stevens, Abel. *History of the Methodist Episcopal Church.* NY. 1868. 4 vols..$30–$45

Stevens, Hazard. *The Life of Isaac Ingalls Stevens.* Bos. 1900. 2 vols. 1st ed. illus. ....$50–$85

Stevens, Thomas. *Around the World on a Bicycle, Vol. 1.* NY. 1889. illus.
....*$35–$50*

Stevens, William Oliver. *Nantucket.* NY. 1937–39. ....*$24–$35*

Stevenson, Robert Louis. *Catriona.* Lon. Cassell. 1893. 1st ed. ....
....*$70–$90*

Stevenson, Robert Louis. *David Balfour.* Scribner's. 1924. illus by N. C.
Wyeth. ....*$55–$60*

Stevenson, Robert Louis. *Kidnapped.* Scribner's. 1946. illus by N. C.
Wyeth, rprnt. ....*$30–$45*

Stevenson, Robert Louis. *Kidnapped.* Scribner's Classic. 1913. illus by
N. C. Wyeth. ....*$45–$75*

Stevenson, Robert Louis. *The Strange Case of Dr. Jekyll and Mr. Hyde.*
NY. 1930. illus. 1st thus.................................*$50–$65*

Stevenson, Robert Louis. *Treasure Island.* Phila. 1930. illus by Lyle
Justis, #1 of the Anderson books. ....*$45–$55*

Stevenson, William G. *Thirteen Months in the Rebel Army ... by an
Impressed New Yorker.* Lon. 1862. 1st ed. 1st Eng ed. rbnd. .....*$50–$75*

Stewart, Elinore Pruitt. *Letters of a Woman Homesteader.* Bos. 1914. 1st
ed. illus by N. C. Wyeth.................................*$25–$37*

Stewart, Henry. *The Shepherd's Manual.* NY. 1876. illus. .....*$27–$35*

Stickley, Gustav. *Craftsman Homes.* NY. 1909. 1st ed. ......*$125–$250*

Stiles, Henry Reed, M.D. *Bundling: Its Origin, Progress and Decline in
America.* Albany. 1869. 1st ed. 139 pp. ....*$85–$100*

Still, A. T. *Autobiography of Andrew T. Still.* Kirksville, MO. 1908. illus.
2nd ed. rev, 404 pp......................................*$85–$145*

Stockham, Alice. *Tokology: A Book for Every Woman.* Chi. Sanitary Publishing Co. 1883. 1st ed. seventh thousand, 277 pp. ....*$75–$125*

Stockham, Alice. *Tokology.* Chi. 1907. rprnt. ....*$30–$45*

Stockman, David A. *The Triumph of Politics: Why the Reagan Revolution
Failed.* 422 pp, photos, dj. ....*$30–$45*

Stockton, Frank. *Pomona's Travels.* Scribner's. 1894. illus. *$65*

Stockton, Frank. *The Girl at Cobhurst.* NY. 1898. 1st ed. ......*$45–$50*

Stoddard, John L. *Stoddard's Lectures.* Bos. 1909. 15 vols. lea, mar bds.
....*$30–$50*

Stoker, Bram. *Dracula.* NY. Grosset & Dunlap. (1931). illus. from the
Universal picture, Photoplay ed. dj. ....*$500–$700*

Stoker, Bram. *Dracula's Guest and Other Weird Stories.* Lon. 1914.
rprnt. ....*$35–$45*

Stoker, Bram. *Dracula.* Limited Ed. Club. 1965. illus. sgn by Hoffman, slipcase. . . . .*$35–$45*

Stoker, Bram. *The Jewel of the Seven Stars.* NY. Harper. 1904. 1st Amer ed. . . . .*$70–$85*

Stoker, Bram. *The Mystery of the Sea.* NY. 1902. 1st ed. . . . .*$40–$50*

Stoker, Bram. *Personal Reminiscences of Henry Irving.* NY. 1906. 2 vols. 1st Amer ed. illus. . . . .*$50–$75*

Stone, I. F. *Hidden History of the Korean War.* NY. (1952). 1st ed. . . . .*$25–$35*

Stone, I. F. *The Haunted 50s.* NY. 1963. 1st ed. dj. . . . .*$30–$40*

Stone, William. *Visits to the Saratoga Battle Grounds.* Albany. 1895. 1st ed. . . . .*$35–$40*

Stoney, S. G. *Plantations of the Carolina Low Country.* Charleston. 1938. 1st ed. dj, slipcase. . . . .*$85–$165*

Stories about Indians. Concord, NH. Rufus Merrill. nd. wrps. 24 pp, 155 by 10 cm. *$55*

Stories by American Authors. NY. Scribner's. 1884–85, 10 vols. scarce. *$300*

Stories by Gen. Warren, by a Lady of Boston. 1835. lea. . . . .*$20–$30*

Story, A. T. *The Story of Wireless Telegraphy.* 1904. 1st ed. illus. . . . .*$45–$85*

Story of Dark Plot, or Tyranny on the Frontier. Warren Press. 1903. . . . .*$28–$35*

Story of King Arthur and His Knights. Scribner's. 1903. 1st ed. illus by Howard Pyle. . . . .*$85–$115*

Story of the Fourth of July. NY. Kiggins & Kellogg. nd. wrps. illus by Uncle Ned, 16 pp, 9 by 55 cm. *$40*

The Story of the Irish Citizen Army, by P.O. Cathasaigh. Dublin/Lon. Maunsel & Co. 1919. 1st ed. author's first book, printed wrps. *$200*

Stout, Rex. *And Four to Go.* NY. Viking. 1958. 1st ed. dj. . . . . . .*$25–$35*

Stout, Rex. *Black Orchids.* 1941. 1st ed. dj. *$350*

Stout, Rex. *Death of a Doxy.* Viking. 1966. 1st ed. dj. . . . .*$25–$60*

Stout, Rex. *Death of a Dude.* NY. Viking. 1969. 1st ed. dj. *$75*

Stout, Rex. *Double for Death.* NY. Farrar & Rinehart. 1939. 1st ed. dj. *$950*

Stout, Rex. *A Family Affair.* NY. Viking. 1975. 1st ed. dj. *$45*

Stout, Rex. *Fer-de-Lance.* 1941. 1st ed. dj. *$85*

Stout, Rex. *The Mother Hunt.* NY. Viking. 1963. 1st ed. dj. . . . .
. . . .*$32–$40*

Stout, Rex. *Prisoner's Base.* NY. Viking. 1952. 1st ed. dj. *$125*

Stout, Rex. *The Red Box.* 1936. 1st ed. dj. *$80*

Stout, Rex. *Three at Wolfe's Door.* 1960. 1st ed. dj. *$135*

Stout, Rex. *Too Many Women.* NY. Viking. 1947. 1st ed. dj. *$400*

Stout, Rex. *Triple Jeopardy.* 1952. 1st ed. dj. *$160*

Stowe, Harriet Beecher. *Dred: A Tale of the Great Dismal Swamp.* Bos.
1856. 2 vols. 1st ed. . . . .*$40–$55*

Stowe, Harriet Beecher. *A Key to Uncle Tom's Cabin.* Bos. 1853. 1st ed.
. . . .*$65–$150*

Stowe, Harriet Beecher. *Men of Our Times.* Hartford. Hartford Publishing
Co. 1868. 1st ed. illus. *$65*

Stowe, Harriet Beecher. *Sunny Memories of Foreign Lands.* NY. 1854. 2
vols. 1st Amer ed. 750 pp. . . . .*$60–$75*

Stowe, Harriet Beecher. *Uncle Tom's Cabin, or Life among the Lowly.*
Bos. 1852. 2 vols. 1st ed. with no mention of "thousands" on the title
pages. . . . .*$800–$1,200*

Strachey, Lionel (trans). *Memoirs of an Arabian Princess.* NY. 1907. . . .
. . . .*$95–$115*

Strand, Paul. *Retrospective. 1915–1968.* large folio. . . . .*$90–$110*

Strange, Daniel. *Pioneer History of Eaton County, Michigan,
1833–1866.* . . . 1923. 1st ed. illus. . . . .*$60–$85*

Striker, Fran. *The Lone Ranger and the Gold Robbery.* Grosset & Dunlap.
1939. Lone Ranger #3. . . . .*$40–$60*

Striker, Fran. *The Lone Ranger and the Haunted Gulch.* Grosset &
Dunlap. 1941. 1st ed. Lone Ranger #6, dj. *$47*

Striker, Fran. *The Lone Ranger and the Silver Bullet.* 1948. 1st ed. dj. . . . .
. . . .*$20–$35*

Striker, Fran. *The Lone Ranger and the Mystery Ranch.* 1938. 1st ed. dj.
#2 . . . .*$35*

Striker, Fran. *The Lone Ranger on Powderhorn Trail.* 1949. 1st ed. dj. . . .
. . . .*$20–$35*

Striker, Fran. *The Lone Ranger Traps the Smugglers.* Grosset & Dunlap.
1941. Lone Ranger #7. . . . .*$35–$45*

Strode, Hudson. *Jefferson Davis, Confederate President.* Harcourt. 1959.
wrps. dj. . . . .*$20–$30*

Strong, Chas. J. and L. S. *Strong's Book of Designs.* Chi. Drake & Co. 1917. "new and enlarged" ed. $100

Stuart, James. *Three Years in America.* NY. 1833. 2 vols. 1st Amer ed. .. ..$50–$90

Stuart, Jesse. *Kentucky Is My Land.* 1952. sgn, dj. ....$50–$80

Stuart, Jesse. *Man with a Bull-tongue Plow.* NY. 1934. 1st ed. sgn, dj. ... .$270–$300

Stuart, Jesse. *Taps for Private Tussie.* NY. Dutton. 1943. 1st ed. dj. ....$50–$90

Sturgeon, Theodore. *More Than Human.* NY. 1953. 1st ed. dj. ....$100–$150

Sturgeon, Theodore. *Sturgeon in Orbit.* Lon. 1970. 1st Brit ed. dj. ....$100–$150

Sturgeon, Theodore. *Without Sorcery.* np (Phila). Prime Press. 1948. 355 pp, dj. ....$30–$45

Styron, William. *The Confessions of Nat Turner.* Random House. (1967). 1st ed. sgn, dj. $75

Styron, William. *The Confessions of Nat Turner.* NY. Random House. (1967). 1st ed. dj. $40

Styron, William. *Lie Down in Darkness.* Ind. 1951. 1st ed. dj. ....$90–$155

Styron, William. *Set This House on Fire.* Random House. (1960). 1st ed. dj. ....$40–$50

Styron, William. *Set This House on Fire.* NY. 1960. 1st ed. sgn, dj. ....$55–$85

Styron, William. *Sophie's Choice.* Random House. 1979. 1st ed. sgn, dj. . ...$60–$75

Suckow, Ruth. *The Bonney Family.* NY. 1928. 1st ed. ltd #66/95 cc, sgn, dj. ....$35–$40

Sue, Eugene. *The Wandering Jew.* Lon. 1844–1845. 1st ed. ...$275–$315

Summers, Montague. *The History of Witchcraft and Demonology.* Lon. 1973. rprnt of 1926 ed. dj. ....$8–$12

Summers, Montague. *The Vampire in Europe.* NY. Dutton. 1929. 1st U.S. ed. ....$35–$45

[Sumner, Charles.] *Speech of Hon. Chas. Sumner of Massachusetts on Cession of Russian America t. U.S.* DC. Congressional Globe. 1867. 1st ed. wrps. $85

Sumner, William G. *A History of American Currency.* NY. 1874. 1st ed. . ...$20–$25

Sun Chief. *The Autobiography of a Hopi Indian.* Yale. 1942. 1st ed. illus. 459 pp. . . . . *$28–$35*

Sunday School Almanac. NY. Carlton & Philips. (1854). wrps. illus. 32 pp, 112 by 73 cm. *$40*

Supplement; Wholesale and Retail Catalogue of Military Goods. NY. Francis Bannerman. 1905. pictorial wrps, 42 pp, illus. . . . .
. . . . *$40–$50*

Surtees, R. S. *Hawbuck Grange.* Lon. nd. illus. . . . . *$50–$85*

Surtees, R. S. *Hunts with Jorrocks.* NY. 1908. illus. . . . . *$50–$85*

Susann, Jacqueline. *Every Night, Josephine!* NY. 1963. 1st ed. dj, author's first book. . . . . *$150–$200*

Sutherland, C. H. V. *Gold: Its Beauty, Power, and Allure.* McGraw-Hill. 1969. 2nd ed. dj. . . . . *$25–$35*

Sutton, Margaret. *The Mysterious Half Cat.* Grosset & Dunlap. 1936. Judy Bolton #9, dj. *$20*

Sutton, Margaret. *Seven Strange Clues.* Grosset & Dunlap. 1932. Judy Bolton #4, dj. *$20*

Sutton, Margaret. *The Trail of the Green Doll.* Grosset & Dunlap. 1956. Judy Bolton #21, dj. . . . . *$14–$25*

Sutton, Margaret. *The Vanishing Shadow.* Grosset & Dunlap. rprnt, Judy Bolton #1, dj. . . . . *$10–$15*

Sutton, Richard and Emmy Lou. *An Arctic Safari: With Camera and Rifle.* . . . St. Louis. C. V. Mosby. 1932. 1st ed. sgn & inscrb by author, 100 photos, dj. . . . . *$75–$90*

Swan, Isabella. *Lisette.* Grosse Isle. the author. 1965. 1st ed. wrps. illus. with frontis, lacks dj. . . . . *$45–$58*

Swanson, W. E. *Modern Shipfitter's Handbook.* NY. 1941. illus. 2nd ed. dj. . . . . *$25–$30*

Swanton, John K. *The Indian Tribes of North America.* DC. GPO. 1953. 726 pp, fldg maps. *$65*

Swanton, John R. *Indian Tribes of the Lower Mississippi Valley.* . . . DC. 1911. . . . . *$45–$60*

Swift, Jonathan. *Gulliver's Travels.* NY. Dent/Dutton. 1909. 1st ed. illus by Arthur Rackham, ltd 750 large paper copies, sgn by illustrator. . . . .
. . . . *$650*

Swinburne, Algernon. *Bothwell: A Tragedy.* Lon. Chatto & Windus. 1874. 1st ed. *$50*

Swinburne, Algernon Charles. *A Century of Roundels and Other Poems.* NY. 1883. 1st Amer ed. dj. . . . . *$40–$45*

Swinburne, Algernon. *Chastelard: A Tragedy.* Lon. Edward Moxon. 1865. 1st ed. *$150*

Swinburne, Algernon Charles. *Erechtheus.* Lon. 1876. ....*$40–$55*

Switzerland and the Adjacent Portions of Italy, Savoy and the Tyrol. NY. Scribner's. 1905. map. *$22*

Swope, John. *Camera over Hollywood.* NY. 1939. illus. dj. ....
....*$95–$125*

Symmes, Rev. Frank R. *History of Old Tennent Church.* Freehold, NJ. 1897. illus. 144 pp. ....*$18–$25*

Synge, John M. *Poems and Translations.* Churchtown, Dundrum. Cuala Press. 1909. 1st ed. 1/250 cc. *$250*

Szyk, Arthur. *The Haggadah.* Jerusalem. 1956. 1st ed. mor, boxed. .....
....*$100–$145*

Szyk, Arthur. *The New Order.* NY. 1941. dj. ....*$125–$200*

Taber, Gladys. *Daisy and Dobbin: Two Little Seahorses.* Phila. 1948. illus. ....*$18–$25*

Taber, Gladys. *Especially Spaniels.* Macrae-Smith. 1945. illus. 4th ptg, photos, dj. ....*$10–$15*

Taber, Gladys. *The First Book of Cats.* Franklin Watts. 1950. illus. ......
....*$18–$25*

Taber, Gladys. *The First Book of Dogs.* NY. 1949. dj. ....*$25–$40*

Taber, Gladys. *Harvest of Yesterdays.* 1976. 1st ed. dj. ....*$10–$15*

Taber, Gladys. *Mrs. Daffodil.* Phila. 1957. 1st ed. dj. ....*$45–$55*

Taber, Gladys. *Reveries at Stillmeadow.* 1970. 1st ed. dj. ....
....*$22–$30*

Taber, Gladys. *Stillmeadow Cook Book.* Lippincott. 1985. 1st ed. dj. .....
....*$35*

Taber, Gladys. *A Very Personal Cat.* NY. 1970. 1st ed. dj. ....
....*$20–$30*

Taber, Gladys. *What Cooks at Stillmeadow.* Phila. 1958. lst ed. dj. ......
....*$37–$55*

Tabor, Grace. *The Landscape Gardening Book.* Phila. Winston. 1911. 1st ed. illus. 180 pp, plates. ....*$55–$75*

Taft, J. A. *A Practical Treatise on Operative Dentistry.* Phila. 1868. calf. .
....*$37–$45*

Tait, L. *Diseases of Women.* NY. 1879. ....*$40–$50*

Talbot, Bishop Ethelbert. *My People of the Plains.* NY. 1906. 1st ed. ....
....*$52–$65*

Talbot, F. A. *Aeroplanes and Dirigibles of the War.* Phila. 1915. 1st Amer ed. illus. . . . .*$30–$40*

Tallant, Robert. *Voodoo in New Orleans.* NY. 1946. 1st ed. . . . .
. . . .*$22–$30*

Tan, Amy. *The Joy Luck Club.* NY. (1989). 1st ed. author's first book, dj.
. . . .*$100–$300*

Tan, Amy. *The Kitchen God's Wife.* NY. Putnam. 1991. 1st ed. sgn, dj. . .
. . . .*$50*

Tanner, Z. L. *Deep-sea Exploration.* DC. GPO. 1896. illus. drawings, fldg plates. . . . .*$50–$85*

Tarbell, Ida. *The Business of Being a Woman.* NY. 1919. rprnt. . . . .
. . . .*$25–$35*

Tarbell, Ida M. *In the Footsteps of the Lincolns.* NY. 1924. illus. . . . .
. . . .*$30–$40*

Tarbell, Ida M. *The Life of Abraham Lincoln.* 1924. 4 vols. Sangamon ed.
. . . .*$60–$75*

Tarbell, Ida M. *The Life of Abraham Lincoln.* NY. 1903. 5 vols. . . . .
. . . .*$45–$50*

Targ, W. *Bibliophile in the Nursery.* Cleve. 1957. 1st ed. dj. . . . .*$25–$35*

Tarkington, Booth. *The Fascinating Stranger.* NY. Doubleday, Page. 1923. 1st trade ed. dj. *$85*

Tarr, Judith. *The Hall of the Mountain King.* Tor. (1986). 1st ed. sgn, dj.
. . . .*$20–$25*

Tate, Allen. *The Fathers.* Putnam. (1938). 1st ed. dj. . . . .*$110–$140*

Tatham, Julie. *Clinic Nurse.* Grosset & Dunlap. 1952. Cherry Ames #13, dj. *$25*

Tatham, Julie. *Night Supervisor.* Grosset & Dunlap. 1950. Cherry Ames #11. . . . .*$12*

Taverner. P. A. *Birds of Canada.* 1934. illus. . . . .*$35–$40*

Taverner, P. A. *Birds of Western Canada.* Ottawa. 1926. 1st ed. . . . .
. . . .*$30–$40*

Taylor. *Pondoro, Last of the Ivory Hunters.* NY. 1955. 1st ed. dj. . . . .
. . . .*$25–$35*

Taylor and Munson. *History of Aviation.* NY. (1976). Folio, dj. *$25*

Taylor, Bayard. *Colorado: A Summer Trip.* NY. 1867. 1st ed. . . . .
. . . .*$40–$55*

Taylor, Bayard. *Eldorado.* NY. Putnam. 1859. 2 vols. 1st ed. 1st issue, plates. *$585*

Taylor, Griffith. *With Scott: The Silver Lining.* Lon. 1916. 1st ed. illus. maps. . . . .*$450–$500*

Taylor, Hannis. *Cicero: A Sketch of His Life and Works.* Chi. 1916. 1st ed. illus. . . . .*$25–$35*

Taylor, J. *Lives of Virginia Baptist Ministers.* Richmond. 1838. 2nd ed. lea. . . . .*$35–$45*

Taylor, John. *Man-eaters and Marauders.* Barnes. 1960. 1st ed. dj. *$150*

Taylor, John L. *Memoir of His Honor Samuel Phillips, LL.D.* Bos. 1856. 1st ed. illus. . . . .*$30–$75*

Taylor, Peter. *Happy Families Are All Alike.* NY. McDowell & Obolensky. (1959). 1st ed. dj. *$40*

Taylor, Peter. *In the Tennessee Country.* Lon. Chatto & Windus. (1994). 1st ed. dj. *$45*

Taylor, Peter. *The Old Forest.* NY. 1985. 1st ed. dj. . . . .*$15–$22*

Taylor, Peter. *The Oracle at Stoneleigh Court.* NY. 1933. 1st ed. dj. . . . .*$15–$22*

Taylor, Peter. *A Summons to Memphis.* NY. 1986. dj. . . . .*$15–$25*

Taylor, Rev. William. *Christian Adventures in South America.* NY. 1976. . . . .*$30–$40*

Teasdale, Sara. *Strange Victory.* NY. 1933. 1st ed. dj. . . . .*$15–$40*

Telephone Appeals—1887. 1887. 1st ed. softcover. . . . .*$125–$165*

Telephone Catalogue and Students' Manual for the Practical Instruction of Learners of Telegraphy.... NY. J. H. Bunnell & Co. 1900. illus. printed wrps, 112 pp. . . . .*$40–$50*

The Telescope. Bos. Massachusetts Sabbath School Society. 1843. wrps. 16 pp, 11 by 70 cm. *$30*

Telescopes for Town and Country. Rochester, NY. Bausch & Lomb Optical Co. 1928. pictorial wrps, illus, 16 pp. . . . .*$40–$50*

Tell It All: The Story of a Life's Experience in Mormonism. Hartford. 1874. . . . .*$25–$35*

Teller, Daniel W. *The History of Ridgefield, Connecticut.* Danbury. 1878. illus. three-fourths mor. . . . .*$50–$75*

Tennyson, Alfred. *Harold: A Drama.* Lon. Henry S. King. 1877. 1st ed. inscrb. *$150*

Tennyson, Alfred. *Ode on the Death of Wellington.* Lon. Edward Moxon. 1853. printed wrps. *$100*

Tennyson, Alfred. *The Passing of Arthur.* Lon. Macmillan. 1884. 1st ed. printed wrps. *$300*

Tennyson, Alfred. *Tiresias and Other Poems.* Lon. 1885. 1st ed. 12mo. . .
....$60–$80

Terkel, Studs. *American Dreams Lost and Found.* dj. ....$12–$15

Terkel, Studs. *Division Street: America.* Pantheon. 1967. 1st ed. dj. .....
....$28–$35

Terkel, Studs. *Working.* Pantheon. 1974. 1st ed. dj. ....$25–$30

Terry, Adrian. *Travels in the Equatorial Regions of South America in 1832.* Hartford. 1832. 1st ed. 290 pp. $150

Terry, Ellen. *The Story of My Life.* Lon. 1908. illus. ltd 1,000 cc, plates, teg, sgn. ....$125–$150

Terry, Ellen. *The Story of My Life.* NY. 1908. ....$20–$50

Tesla, Nikola. *Experiments with Alternate Currents of High Potential and High Frequency.* NY. 1896. illus. ....$95–$125

Tesla, Nikola. *Lectures, Patents, Articles Published by Nikola Tesla Museum.* CA. 1973. rprnt, illus, wraps. ....$60–$75

Thacher, J. *The American Revolution.* Hartford. 1861. illus. ....
....$37–$55

Thatcher, B. B. *Indian Biography of Historical Account of Those Individuals . . . Distinguished among North American Natives.* NY. 1832. 2 vols. 1st ed. 324 pp. $50

Thatcher, James. *History of the Town of Plymouth: From Its First Settlement in 1620 to the Present Time.* Bos. 1835. illus. map. .....$175–$200

Thayer, Tiffany. *Doctor Arnold.* (NY). Julian Messner. 1934. 1st ed. ....
....$30–$45

Theory of the Universe. NY. 1868. ....$50–$65

Theroux, Paul. *The Black House.* Houghton. 1974. 1st ed. dj. . . .$30–$35

Theroux, Paul. *The London Embassy.* Bos. 1983. 1st Amer ed. dj. ......
....$25–$32

Theroux, Paul. *The Mosquito Coast.* Houghton Mifflin. 1982. 1st ed. dj. .
....$35–$50

Theroux, Paul. *O Zone.* Lon. Hamish Hamilton (1986). 1st ed. dj. ......
....$50

Theroux, Paul. *Saint Jack.* Bos. 1973. 1st ed. dj, sgn. ....$95–$100

Third Marine Division. DC. 1948. 1st ed. ....$42–$50

Thirkell, Angela. *High Rising and Wild Strawberries.* NY. 1951. 2 vols. 1st ed. djs. ....$25–$40

Thirkell, Angela. *Love at All Ages.* NY. 1959. 1st U.S. ed. ....
....$18–$22.50

This Is Japan. Asahl Shimbun. 1958. illus. slipcase, dj. *$75*

Thomas, Dylan. *The Beach of Falesa.* NY. 1963. 1st ed. dj. . . . .*$35–$45*

Thomas, Dylan. *Adventures in the Skin Trade.* NY. New Directions. 1953. 1st ed. dj. . . . .*$55–$75*

Thomas, Dylan. *Adventures in the Skin Trade.* Lon. Putnam. (1955). 1st ed. dj. *$75*

Thomas, Dylan. *A Child's Christmas in Wales.* 1954. 1st ed. dj. . . . .*$40–$65*

Thomas, Dylan. *Collected Poems, 1934-1952.* Lon. Dent. (1952). 1st ed. dj. *$150*

Thomas, Dylan. *The Doctor and the Devils.* Lon. Dent. (1953). 1st ed. dj. *$75*

Thomas, Dylan. *New Poems.* Norfolk, CT. 1943. 1st ed. dj. . . . .*$30–$50*

Thomas, Dylan. *Portrait of the Artist as a Young Dog.* Lon. 1940. 1st ed. . . . .*$75–$100*

Thomas, Dylan. *Portrait of the Artist as a Young Dog.* Norfolk, CT. New Directions. (c 1940). 1st Amer ed. dj. *$250*

Thomas, Dylan. *Quite Early One Morning.* NY. 1954. 1st ed. dj. *$40*

Thomas, Dylan. *Quite Early One Morning: Broadcasts.* Lon. Dent. (1954). 1st ed. dj. *$75*

Thomas, Dylan. *Under Milk Wood.* NY. 1954. 1st ed. dj. . . . . .*$60–$100*

Thomas, Edward H. *Chinook: A History and Dictionary of N.W. Coast Trade Jargon.* Portland. 1935. . . . .*$35–$50*

Thomas, Fred D. *Darktown's Daily Dozen.* Exposition Press. (1948). illus. sgn. . . . .*$20–$25*

Thomas, Katherine. *Women in Nazi Germany.* Lon. 1943. 1st ed. . . . .*$25–$35*

Thomas, Lowell. *Old Gimlet Eye: The Adventures of Smedley D. Butler.* NY. 1933. 1st ed. sgn by author and Butler. . . . .*$125–$175*

Thomas, Will. *God Is for White Folks.* NY. 1947. 1st ed. dj. . . . .*$15–$20*

Thompson, D. P. *History of the Town of Montpelier.* Montpelier. 1860. . . . .*$30–$50*

Thompson, Henry T. *Ousting the Carpetbagger from South Carolina.* Columbia, SC. 1927. 2nd ed. dj. . . . .*$50–$75*

Thompson, Ruth Plumly. *The Cowardly Lion of Oz.* Reilly & Lee. (1923). 1st ed. illus by J. R. Neill, 12 plates, dj. . . . .*$300–$400*

Thompson, Ruth Plumly. *The Gnome King of Oz.* Reilly & Lee. (1927). 1st ed. illus by J. R. Neill, 12 plates. . . . .*$200–$300*

Thompson, Ruth Plumly. *The Hungry Tiger of Oz.* Reilly & Lee. 1926. illus by J. R. Neill. ....$60–$100

Thompson, Ruth Plumly. *The Lost King of Oz.* Chi. (1925). 1st ed. illus. clr plates. ....$100–$250

Thompson, Ruth Plumly. *The Purple Prince of Oz.* Reilly & Lee. (1932). 1st ed. illus by J. R. Neill, 12 plates. ....$100–$200

Thompson, Ruth Plumly. *The Wishing Horse of Oz.* Reilly & Lee. (1935). 1st ed. illus by J. R. Neill, 12 plates. ....$500–$700

Thompson, Ruth Plumly. *The Yellow Knight of Oz.* Reilly & Lee. illus by J. R. Neill, dj. ....$60–$100

Thompson, W. G. *Training-schools for Nursing.* NY. Putnam. 1883. 1st ed. ....$90–$150

Thompson, Zadock. *Geography and Geology of Vermont . . . State and County Outline Maps.* VT. 1848. illus. maps. ....$50–$85

Thompson, Zadock. *History of Vermont.* Burlington. 1842. illus. engr. .. ..$30–$75

Thomson, A. L. (ed). *A New Dictionary of Birds.* Lon. (1964). ....$30–$40

Thomson, J. J. *Corpuscular Theory of Matter.* Lon. 1907. 1st ed. ....$55–$100

Thoreau, Henry David. *Cape Cod.* Bos. 1865. 1st ed. ....$300–$750

Thoreau, Henry David. *Men of Concord.* Bos. 1936. illus by N. C. Wyeth, dj. ....$45–$55

Thoreau, Henry David. *Walden, or Life in the Woods.* Bos. The Bibliophile Society. 1909. 2 vols. illus. ltd 483 cc, vellum-like paper over brown buckram, slipcases. ....$200–$325

Thoreau, Henry David. *Walden.* Bos. 1854. 1st ed. ....$950–$1,600

Thrasher, Halsey. *The Hunter and Trapper.* 1863. ....$65–$100

The Three Kittens. Lon. nd. wrps. ....$50–$75

Thurber, James. *Fables for Our Time.* NY. 1940. 2nd issue. ....$25–$40

Thurber, James. *Is Sex Necessary?* NY. 1929. author's first book. ....$350–$500

Thurber, James. *The White Deer.* NY. 1945. illus. ....$8–$15

Thurber, James. *The Wonderful O.* NY. Simon & Schuster. (1957). 1st ed. dj. $60

Thurman, Arnold. *The Folklore of Capitalism.* New Haven. 1937. 1st ed. ....$85–$115

Thurston, Robert. *History of the Growth of the Steam-engine.* NY. 1878.
....$45–$60

Thwaites, Reuben, and Louise Kellogg (eds). *Documentary History of Dunmore's War, 1774.* Madison, WI. Wisconsin Historical Society. 1905. 1st ed. illus. 1/1000 cc, 472 pp, maps. ....$100–$225

Tillotson, John. *Palestine, Egypt and Syria with the History of the Jews.* Phila. clr maps, illus. ....$70–$85

Tilman, H. W. *The Ascent of Nanda Devi.* NY. Macmillan. 1937. 1st ed. photos, maps, dj. ....$55–$75

Tjader, Richard. *The Big Game of Africa.* NY. Appleton. 1910. 1 vol. 1st ed. map, plates. $225

Tocqueville, Alexis de. *Démocratie en Amérique.* Paris. 1835. 2 vols. map.
....$1,000–$3,000

Todd, W.E.C. *Birds of the Labrador Penninsula and Adjacent Areas.* Tor. 1963. illus. ....$50–$75

Toffler, Alvin. *Future Shock.* NY. 1970. dj. ....$15–$20

Toklas, Alice B. *The Alice B. Toklas Cook Book.* Lon. 1954. 1st ed. illus. .
....$150–$225

Toler, Ernst. *Man and the Masses.* Garden City. 1924. 1st ed. 109 pp, photos. ....$60–$75

Tolkien, J.R.R. *Father Christmas Letters.* Lon. 1976. 1st ed. ...$50–$65

Tolkien, J.R.R. *The Hobbit.* Bos. 1938. illus by Tolkien, 1st Amer ed. ...
....$250–$500

Tolkien. J.R.R. *The Hobbit.* Houghton Mifflin. 1966. 3rd ptg, boxed. .....
....$32–$45

Tolkien, J.R.R. *The Lord of the Rings.* Bos. Houghton, Mifflin. 1967. 3 vols. 2nd ed. rev, dj. ....$150–$200

Tolkien, J.R.R. *Pictures.* Bos. 1979. 1st Amer ed. slipcase. .....$48–$65

Tolkien, J.R.R. *The Silmarillion.* 1977. 1st ed. dj. ....$45–$100

Tolkien, J.R.R. *Smith of Wooton Major.* Bos. Houghton, Mifflin. 1967. illus by Pauline Baynes, 1st Amer ed. dj. ....$80–$120

Tolkien, J.R.R. *Tree and Leaf.* Bos. Houghton Mifflin. 1965. 1st Amer ed. 112 pp, dj. ....$50–$65

Tolley, Cyril. *The Modern Golfer.* NY. 1924. illus. ....$30–$50

Tolstoi, Alexis. *Vampires: Stories of the Supernatural.* NY. 1969. 1st English-language ed. dj. ....$40–$50

Tomes, Robert. *The Battles of America by Sea and Land.* NY. 1878. 3 vols. illus. ....$145–$175

Tompkins, Peter. *Secrets of the Great Pyramid.* NY. Harper & Row. (1971). 1st ed. illus. dj. .... *$24–$30*

Tooker, William W. *The Indian Place-names on Long Island....* NY. 1911. .... *$35–$40*

Tooley, R. V. *Maps and Map-makers.* Lon. B. T. Batsford. (1949). 1st ed. illus. dj. .... *$25–$35*

Towne, Ezra. *Social Problems.* NY. Macmillan. 1923. .... *$14*

Towne, H. R. *A Treatise on Cranes.* CT. 1883. .... *$40–$50*

Trade Price List; Manufacturers of Parlor, Chamber, and Dining Room Furniture.... NY. Edward W. Baxter & Co. 1871. wrps. ....*$145–$200*

Train, Arthur. *Mortmain.* NY. Appleton. 1907. 1st ed. ....*$30–$40*

Train, Arthur. *Page Mr. Tutt.* NY. Scribner. 1926. 1st ed. dj. ....*$30–$35*

Train, Arthur. *Yankee Lawyer—The Autobiography of Ephraim Tutt.* NY. 1943. 1st ed. illus. dj. .... *$35–$50*

Traver, Robert. *Anatomy of a Fisherman.* McGraw Hill. 1964. 1st ed. dj. *$150*

Travers, P. L. *Mary Poppins.* (1934). dj. *$200*

Travers. P. L. *Mary Poppins Comes Back.* NY. 1935. 1st U.S. ed. dj. .... *$30–$45*

Trevor, William. *Family Sins.* Viking. (1990). 1st Amer ed. dj. .... *$25–$35*

Trevor, William. *The Old Boys.* NY. 1964. 1st ed. dj. ....*$85–$100*

Trial of Andrew Johnson, President of the U.S. DC. GPO. 1868. 3 vols. . ... *$50–$100*

Trilling, Lionel. *The Liberal Imagination.* NY. Viking. 1950. 1st ed. dj. *$35*

Trilling, Lionel. *The Middle of the Journey.* NY. 1947. 1st ed. sgn....... .... *$45–$65*

Trimble, Harvey M. *History of the 93rd Regiment Illinois Volunteer Infantry.* Chi. 1898. illus. fldg map. .... *$125–$150*

Trip around the World in an Automobile. McLoughlin Bros. 1907. wrps. illus. lithos. .... *$50–$80*

Triscott, C. Pette. *Gold in Six Lessons.* Phila. nd. 1st ed. illus. ..*$30–$40*

Trollope, A. *The West Indies and the Spanish Main.* NY. 1860. 1st Amer ed. .... *$70–$90*

Trollope, Anthony. *Can You Forgive Her?* Lon. 1864. 2 vols. 1st ed. illus. *$250*

Trollope, Anthony. *The Last Chronicle of Barset.* Lon. 1867. 2 vols in 1.
. . . .*$110–$125*

Trollope, Anthony. *North America.* Phila. Lippincott. 1862. 2 vols in 1.
"author's edition," 334 pp. . . . .*$90–$100*

Trollope, Anthony. *North America.* Lon. 1862. 2 vols. 3rd ed. . . . .
. . . .*$125–$180*

Trollope, Anthony. *North America.* NY. 1862. 1st Amer ed. . . . .
. . . .*$60–$125*

Trollope, Frances. *The Life and Adventures of Jonathan Jefferson Whitlaw.* Lon. 1836. 3 vols. 15 eng. *$350*

Trotsky, Leon. *Stalin.* NY. Harper & Bros. 1941. 1st Amer ed. *$55*

Trotter, William. *On the Rearing and Management of Poultry.* Lon. 1852. wrps. illus. . . . .*$28–$35*

Trowbridge, J. T. *The South: A Tour of Its Battlefields and Ruined Cities.* . . . CT. 1866. 1st ed. illus. . . . .*$45–$55*

A True Story of Lucknow. (Bos). American Tract Society, nd. wrps. 16 pp, 9 by 57 cm. *$25*

Truman, Harry. *Memoirs by Harry S. Truman.* Garden City. 1955, 1956. 2 vols. 1st ed. sgn, dj. . . . .*$350–$380*

Truman, Margaret. *Harry S. Truman.* NY. 1973. photos. . . . . . .*$35–$45*

Truman, Margaret. *Murder in the CIA.* 1987. 1st ed. dj. *$40*

Truman, Margaret. *Murder in the Smithsonian.* 1983. 1st ed. dj. *$50*

Truman, Margaret. *Murder in the White House* 1980. dj. . . . . . .*$18–$25*

Truman, Margaret. *Murder on Embassy Row.* 1984. 1st ed. dj. *$45*

Trumbull, James Hammond. *Natick Dictionary.* DC. GPO. 1903. 349 pp.
. . . .*$25–$65*

Tuckerman, A. *A Short History of Architecture.* NY. 1887. illus. calf. . . .
. . . .*$75–$95*

Tuckerman, A. *Index to the Literature of Thermodynamics.* DC. 1890. inscrb. . . . .*$50–$75*

Tudor, Tasha. *Tasha Tudor's Favorite Christmas Carols.* McKay. 1978. illus. dj. . . . .*$20–$30*

Tullidge, Edward W. *Life of Brigham Young.* NY. 1876. 1st ed. . . . .
. . . .*$60–$80*

Turner, William. *Transfer Printing on Enamels, Porcelain and Pottery.* Lon. 1907. illus. . . . .*$115–$150*

Tuttle, Charles. *An Illustrated History of the State of Wisconsin.* 1875. . . .
. . . .*$55–$75*

Tuttle, Florence Guertin. *The Awakening of Woman.* NY. Abingdon Press. (1915). 1st ed. dj. . . . .*$60–$75*

Twain, Mark. *Adventures of Huckleberry Finn.* NY. Chas L. Webster & Co. 1885. 1st ed. early state, green pictorial cloth, stamped black and gold, slipcase, illus by E. W. Kemble. *$1,250*

Twain, Mark. *Adventures of Huckleberry Finn.* NY. 1885. 1st Amer ed. late state, rebound. *$250*

Twain, Mark. *Adventures of Huckleberry Finn.* NY. 1885. 1st Amer ed. 173 text illus, deluxe lea, speckled-sheet pale yellow endpapers. . . .*$4,887*

Twain, Mark. *Adventures of Tom Sawyer.* Hartford. 1876. 1st Amer ed. 159 wood engr illus, blue cloth. . . . .*$1,750–$5,175*

Twain, Mark. *Adventures of Tom Sawyer.* 1876. 1st Amer end. 2nd ptg. . . . .*$450–$1,250*

Twain, Mark. *American Claimant.* 1st ed. *$100*

Twain, Mark. *The Curious Republic of Gondour.* NY. Boni & Liveright. 1919. 1st ed. 140 pp, dj. *$950*

Twain, Mark. *A Dog's Tale.* Lon. Anti-National Vivisection Society. 1903. wrps. 1st separate ed, original wrps. *$200*

Twain, Mark. *Europe and Elsewhere.* NY. Harper. (1923). 1st ed. 406 pp, intro by A. B. Paine, dj. *$950*

Twain, Mark. *Extract from Captain Stormfield's Visit to Heaven.* NY. Harper & Bros. 1909. 1st ed. . . . .*$100–$125*

Twain, Mark. *Following the Equator.* Hartford. American Publishing Co. 1897. 1st ed., first state 8vo, 712 pp, blue cloth. *$250*

Twain, Mark. *The Innocents Abroad.* Leipzig. Bernhard Tauchnitz. 1879. 2 vols in 1st. authorized ed. 1st ptg, 16vo, half lea, inscrb. . . .*$800–$1,000*

Twain, Mark. *Life on the Mississippi.* 1883. 1st Amer ed. 1st issue. . . . .*$250–$550*

Twain, Mark. *Life on the Mississippi.* Bos. 1883. 1st ed. 2nd state. . . . .*$125–$150*

Twain, Mark. *Old Times on the Mississippi.* 1st hardbound ed. *$150*

Twain, Mark. *Personal Recollections of Joan of Arc.* Leipzig. 1896. 2 vols. wrps. . . . .*$40–$50*

Twain, Mark. *The Prince and the Pauper.* Bos. 1882. 1st Amer ed. . . . .*$100–$175*

Twain, Mark. *Pudd'nhead Wilson.* . . . Hartford. 1894. 1st Amer ed. . . . .*$100–$185*

Twain, Mark. *A True Story, and the Recent Carnival of Crime.* Bos. 1877. 1st ed. 4 illus, mor slipcase. *$1,150*

Twenty Sixth Annual Catalogue of Fancy Goods and Toys. ... Bos. Cutter, Hyde & Co. 1870s. illus. .... *$65–$75*

The Twenty-third Psalm. Worcester. 1965. St. Onge miniature. ....
.... *$15–$25*

Twiss, Travers. *The Oregon Territory: Its History and Discovery.* ... NY. Appleton. 1846. 1st Amer ed. 264 pp. .... *$180–$225*

Two Soldiers: The Campaign Diaries of Key and Campbell. Chapel Hill. 1938. .... *$20–$27*

Tyler, Anne. *The Accidental Tourist.* Knopf. 1985. dj. *$35*

Tyler, Anne. *Dinner at the Homesick Restaurant.* NY. Knopf. 1982. 1st ed. dj. .... *$45–$60*

Tyler, Anne. *Saint Maybe.* NY. Knopf. 1991. 1st ed. dj. .... *$50–$85*

Ude, Louise Eustache. *The French Cook.* Phila. 1828. rbkd with lea. ....
.... *$295–$375*

Undertakers' Specialities; Catalogue No. XVII. Albany or Rochester, NY. National Casket Co. August 1903. illus. paper-covered cloth wrps, 120 pp. .... *$50–$75*

Underwood, L. H. *With Tommy Tompkins in Korea.* Revell. (1905). ......
.... *$25–$35*

Universal Indian Sign Language. Boy Scouts. 1929. .... *$32–$45*

Updike, Daniel Berkeley. *Printing Types.* Cam. 1927. 2 vols. 1st ptg of 2nd ed, dj. *$100*

Updike, John. *Bech Is Back.* NY. Knopf. 1982. 1/500 cc, sgn, nbr, slip-case. *$125*

Updike, John. *Hoping for a Hoopoe.* Lon. Victor Gollancz. 1959. 1st Eng ed. author's first book, dj. *$120*

Updike, John. *A Month of Sundays.* NY. Knopf. 1975. 1st ed. dj. ....
.... *$20–$25*

Updike, John. *Odd Jobs.* NY. Knopf. 1991. 1st ed. dj. .... *$25–$40*

Updike, John. *Of the Farm.* Knopf. 1965. 1st ed. dj. *$125*

Updike, John. *Pigeon Feathers.* NY. 1962. 1st ed. dj. .... *$75–$125*

Updike, John. *Problems and Other Stories.* NY. Knopf. 1st ed. dj. ......
.... *$30–$40*

Updike, John. *Rabbit at Rest.* NY. Knopf. 1990. 1st ed. dj. ..... *$30–$45*

Updike, John. *Rabbit Is Rich.* NY. Knopf. 1981. 1st ed. sgn, dj. ....
.... *$85–$100*

Updike, John. *Rabbit Redux.* NY. Knopf. 1971. 1st ed. dj, sgn. ....
.... *$40–$50*

Updike, John. *Rabbit, Run.* NY. 1960. 1st ed. dj. . . . .*$250–$400*

Updike, John. *Trust Me.* NY. 1987. 1st ed. dj. . . . .$18.00–$25.00

Updike, John. *The Witches of Eastwick.* Franklin Library. 1984. illus, lea, sgn. . . . .*$65–$85*

Updike, Wilkins. *History of the Narragansett Church.* Bos. 1907. 3 vols. . . . .*$75–$125*

Urban, John W. *In Defense of the Union.* DC. 1887. 1st ed. illus. . . . .*$35–$45*

Uris, Leon. *Exodus.* Franklin Library. sgn, no dj as issued. *$50*

U.S. Camera. 1950. 1st ed. dj. . . . .*$20–$25*

U.S. Camera. 1947. 1st ed. dj. . . . .*$25–$30*

U.S. Camera. 1935. . . . .*$25–$40*

U.S. Camera. NY. 1955. 316 pp, illus. . . . .*$40–$50*

U.S. Camera Magazine. #1. (1938). wrps. illus. 73 pp, spiral bound. . . . .*$30–$40*

U.S. Cartridge Company's Collection of Firearms. U.S. Cartridge Co. nd. cat. . . . .*$50–$85*

The Uses of Elleman's Embrocation. Slough. 1902. 3rd ed. illus, 188 pp. . . . .*$35–$45*

Usher, Leonard (ed). *Fiji.* . . . Suva. 1943. wrps. illus. *$18*

Vale, Robert B. *How to Hunt American Game.* Stackpole. (1936). 3rd ptg. . . . .*$12–$14*

Van Dine, S. S. *The Canary Murder Case.* NY. Scribner's. 1927. 1st ed. dj. *$75*

Van Dine, S. S. *The Dragon Murder Case.* NY. 1933, 1st ed. dj. . . . .*$100–$150*

Van Dine, S. S. *The Dragon Murder Case.* NY. 1933. 1st ed. . . . .*$25–$30*

Van Dine, S. S. *The Gracie Allen Murder Case.* NY. Scribner's. 1938. 1st ed. dj. *$225*

Van Dine, S. S. *Scarab Murder Case.* NY. 1930. 1st ed. dj. . . . .*$90–$150*

Van Dyke, Henry. *Travel Diary of an Angler.* Derrydale Press. 1929. illus. ltd 750 cc. . . . .*$225–$250*

Van Dyke, Theodore S. *Southern California.* NY. 1886. 1st ed. sgn. . . . .*$100–$125*

Van Gulik, Robert. *The Chinese Bell Murders.* Lon. Michael Joseph. 1958. 1st ed. dj. *$200*

Van Gulik, Robert. *The Chinese Lake Murders.* NY. 1960. illus. 1st U.S. ed. . . . .*$45–$65*

Van Gulik, Robert. *The Chinese Nail Murders.* Lon. Michael Joseph. 1961. 1st ed. dj. *$175*

Van Gulik, Robert. *The Haunted Monastery.* Lon. Heinemann. (1963). 1st ed. dj. . . . .*$50–$65*

Van Gulik, Robert. *Judge Dee at Work.* Lon. Heinemann. 1967. 1st ed. dj. *$125*

Van Gulik, Robert. *The Monkey and the Tiger.* Lon. Heinemann. 1965. 1st Eng ed. dj. *$125*

Van Gulik, Robert. *Murder in Canton.* NY/Lon. 1967. 1st Amer ed. dj. . . . .*$30–$75*

Van Gulik, Robert. *Necklace and Calabash.* NY. 1971. 1st ed. dj. . . . .*$35–$45*

Van Gulik, Robert. *The Willow Pattern.* Lon. 1965. illus. 1st Brit ed. dj. . . . .*$25–$35*

Van Nelsen, Andrew G. *Science and Technology.* Pitts. 1961. dj. . . . .*$30–$45*

Van Rensselaer, Stephen. *American Firearms.* Watkins Glen. (1947). illus. . . . .*$25–$35*

Van Ronk, Dave, and Richard Ellington. *The Bosses' Songbook . . . Modern Political Songs of Satire.* NY. 1959. 2nd ed. wraps. . . . . .*$65–$75*

Vance, Wilson J. *Stone's River: The Turning Point of the Civil War.* NY. 1914. 1st ed. . . . .*$45–$75*

Vanderveer, Helen. *Little Slam Bang.* Volland. 1928. . . . .*$30*

Vandiveer, Clarence. A. *The Fur-trade and Early Western Exploration.* Cleve. 1929. 1st ed. . . . .*$95–$145*

Van Loon's Catskill Mountain Guide and Bird's-eye View. . . . NY. 1879. illus. maps. . . . .*$175–$225*

Variety, Inc. *Radio Directory, 1937–1938.* 1937. 1st ed. . . . .*$45–$60*

Varney, Almon. *Our Homes and Their Adornments, or How to Build, Furnish, and Adorn a Home.* Detroit. J. C. Chilton. 1885. illus. 486 pp. . . . .*$50–$85*

Vassall, Henry. *Football: The Rugby Game.* NY. 1890. 1st ed. . .*$65–$95*

Vaughan, B. F. *Life and Writings of Rev. Henry R. Rush, D.D.* . . . Dayton, OH. 1911. 1st ed. . . . .*$55–$75*

Verne, Jules. *In Search of the Castaways.* Phila. 1874. illus. 2nd U.S. ed. . . . .*$50–$85*

Verne, Jules. *A Journey to the Centre of the Earth.* Bos. nd. illus. . . . .
. . . .*$18–$25*

Verne, Jules. *North Against South: a Tale of the American Civil War.* Lon. 1888. illus by L. Benett. *$450*

Verne, Jules. *Their Island Home.* NY. 1924. 1st U.S. ed. . . . .*$40–$50*

Verne, Jules. *The Tour of the World in Eighty Days.* Bos. Osgood. 1873. 1st Amer trade ed. red cloth. . . . .*$150–$250*

Verne, Jules. *A Winter in the Ice.* Bos. 1876. . . . .*$25–$35*

Verne, Jules. *The Wreck of the Chancellor.* Bos. 1875. 1st U.S. ed. . . . . .
. . . .*$20–$30*

Victor, O. *History of the Southern Rebellion.* NY. 4 vols. illus. . . . .
. . . .*$165–$225*

Vidal, Gore. *Kalki.* Random House. 1978. 1st ed. dj. . . . .*$10–$18*

Vidal, Gore. *Myra Breckenridge.* Little Brown. 1968. 1st ed. dj. . . . .
. . . .*$28–$35*

Vidal, Gore. *The Season of Comfort.* NY. 1949. 1st ed. dj. . . . . .*$25–$40*

Vietnam Experience. Boston Public Library. 1981–1985. 12-vol set. . . . . .
. . . .*$285*

Vlerebome, A. *The Life of James Riley, Commonly Called Farmer Riley, One of the World's Greatest Psychics.* [Akron]. published by author. (1911). 296 pp. . . . .*$9–$15*

Vonnegut, Kurt. *Breakfast of Champions.* NY. 1973. . . . .*$20–$25*

Vonnegut, Kurt. *Canary in a Cat House.* NY. 1962. sgn, dj. . . . .
. . . .*$100–$125*

Vonnegut, Kurt. *Cat's Cradle.* NY/Chi/SF. (1963). 1st ed. 1/6,000 cc, dj.
. . . .*$750*

Vonnegut, Kurt. *Galapagos.* PA. The Franklin Press. 1985. 1st ed. aeg, silk ribbon marker, sgn. . . . .*$60–$85*

Vonnegut, Kurt. *God Bless You, Mr. Rosewater.* Holt, Rinehart & Winston. 1965. 1st ed. dj. . . . .*$95–$125*

Vonnegut, Kurt. *Jailbird.* np. 1979. 1st ed. dj. . . . .*$25–$75*

Vonnegut, Kurt. *Palm Sunday.* Delacorte. 1981. 1st ed. dj. . . . . .*$30–$45*

Vonnegut, Kurt. *Player Piano.* NY. Scribner's. 1952. 1st ed. author's first book, dj. . . . .*$300–$450*

Vonnegut, Kurt. *A Precautionary Letter to the Next Generation.* np. 1988.
. . . .*$18–$30*

Vonnegut, Kurt. *Slapstick.* NY. Delacort Press. 1976. 1/250 cc, sgn, slipcase. . . . .*$100–$125*

Vonnegut, Kurt. *Slaughterhouse Five.* NY. 1969. sgn, dj. . . . .*$175–$300*

Vose, George L. *Bridge Disasters in America.* Bos. 1887. 1st ed. . . . .
. . . .*$28–$35*

Voth, H. R. *Oraibi Natal Customs and Ceremonies.* Field Columbian Museum. 1905. illus. vol 6, #2. . . . .*$35–$50*

Voth, H. R. *The Oraibi Oaqol Ceremony.* Field Columbian Museum. 1903. illus. vol 6, #1. . . . .*$85–$130*

Voth, H. R. *The Oraibi Summer Snake Ceremony.* Field Columbian Museum. 1903. illus. vol 3. . . . .*$95–$145*

Vrooman, J. J. *Forts and Firesides of the Mohawk Valley.* Phila. 1943. 1st ed. ltd 106 cc. . . . .*$65–$90*

Wack, Henry Wellington. *The Story of the Congo Free State.* NY. 1905. 1st ed. illus. . . . .*$125–$175*

Wagner, Jack R. *Goldmines of California.* San Diego. (1980). dj. . . .*$25*

Waite, Frederick C. *The Story of a Country Medical College.* Montpelier. Vermont Historical Society 1945. 1st ed. wrps. illus. . . . .*$30–$45*

Wakefield, H. R. *They Return at Evening.* NY. Appleton. 1928. 1st Amer ed. 266 pp, no dj. . . . .*$65–$75*

Wakefield, J. *History of Waupaca County, Wisconsin.* Waupaca, WI. 1890. 1st ed. . . . .*$60–$85*

Wakoski, Diane. *Love the Lizard.* Prov. 1975. sgn. . . . .*$20–$25*

Walcott, Mary Vaus. *Illustrations of North American Pitcherplants.* DC. Smithsonian Inst. 1935. 1st ed. illus. folio, 34 pp, portfolio with ties, 1/500 cc. *$225*

Waley, Arthur. *More Translations from the Chinese.* NY. Knopf. 1919. 1st Amer ed. . . . .*$40–$50*

Walker, Alice. *The Color Purple.* NY. 1982. sgn, dj. . . . .*$325–$450*

Walker, Alice. *The Temple of My Familiar.* Harcourt. 1989. ltd 500 cc, sgn, dj, slipcase. . . . .*$85–$100*

Wall, E. G. *Handbook of the State of Mississippi.* Jackson. 1882. 1st ed. illus. . . . .*$85–$125*

Wallace, Alfred R. *Australia.* Lon. Edward Stanford. 1879, 1st ed. illus, 2 clr maps, pictorial cloth. . . . .*$195–$250*

Wallace, Anthony F. C. *King of the Delawares: Teedyuscung, 1700–1763.* Phila. 1949. 1st ed. dj. . . . .*$40–$60*

Wallace, Dillon. *The Camper's Handbook.* Fleming H. Revell. 1936. . . . .
. . . .*$12–$15*

Wallace, Dillon. *The Long Labrador Trail.* Chi. 1923. illus. sgn. *$22–$30*

Wallace, Dillon. *The Lure of the Labrador Wild.* NY. Fleming H. Revell. [1913]. 11th ed. illus, map. ....*$25–$35*

Wallace, Dillon. *The Lure of the Labrador Wild.* NY. Fleming H. Revell. 1905. ....*$40–$50*

Wallace, Edgar. *Tam o' the Scoots.* Bos. Small, Maynard. (1939). 1st Amer ed. ....*$35–$45*

Wallace, Isabel. *Life and Letters of General W.H.L. Wallace.* Chi. 1909. 1st ed. illus. ....*$95–$125*

Walsh, John Evangelist. *Into My Own.* NY. (1988). 1st ed. dj. ....
....*$15–$22*

Walter Camp's Book of College Sports. NY. 1893. 1st ed. ......*$50–$75*

Walton, Evangeline. *The Cross and the Sword.* NY. Bouregy & Curl. (1956). 1st ed. inscrb, dj. ....*$55–$65*

Walton, Evangeline. *The Virgin and the Swine.* Chi. 1936. 1st ed. ......
....*$40–$50*

Walton, Evangeline. *Witch House.* Sauk City. 1945. 1st ed. ltd, dj. ....
....*$150*

Walton, Evangeline. *Witch House.* Arkham House. 1961. dj. ....
....*$45–$50*

Walton, Izaak. *The Compleat Angler.* illus by Arthur Rackham. ....
....*$125*

Walton, Izaak. *The Compleat Angler.* 1931. illus by Arthur Rackham, #49/775 sgn by Rackham. ....*$550–$650*

Walton, Izaak. *The Compleat Angler.* Lon. J. M. Dent. 1896. illus. ....
....*$45–$55*

Walton, Izaak (and Charles Cotton). *The Compleat Angler.* Oxford Univ. Press. 1958. dj. *$35*

Walton, Izaak (and Charles Cotton). *The Complete Angler, or Contemplative Man's Recreation.* Lon. 1784. illus. 4th ed. slipcase. ....
....*$350–$450*

Walton, Izaak (and Charles Cotton). *The Complete Angler.* NY. 1848. three-fourths lea, bds. ....*$50–$60*

Walton, Izaak. *The Universal Angler.* Lon. Marriott & Brome. 1676. .....
....*$700–$850*

Warbey, William. *Vietnam: The Truth.* Lon. 1965. 1st ed. ......*$25–$30*

Ward, Austin. *Male Life Among the Mormons, or The Husband in Utah.* Phila. 1863. ....*$45–$60*

Warhol, Andy. *"A."* NY. 1968. 1st ed. dj. ....*$35–$45*

Warner, Charles Dudley. *My Winter on the Nile: Among the Mummies and Moslems.* Hartford. American Publishing. 1876. 1st ed. . . . .
. . . .*$80–$120*

Warren, Donald. *My Bongo and A Week of Arctic Daylight.* 1st and only ed. 33 pp, privately printed, photos. *$125*

Warren, John. *The Conchologist.* Bos. 1834. 1st ed. illus. presentation copy, lea, bds. . . . .*$115–$130*

Warren, Lillie E. *Defective Speech and Deafness.* NY. Edgard S. Werner. 1895. 116 pp. . . . .*$50–$75*

Warren Report. GPO. 1964. 26 vols. *$1,500*

Warren, Robert Penn. *Meet Me in the Green Glen.* NY. 1971. 1st ed. presentation copy, sgn. . . . .*$100–$225*

Warren, Robert Penn. *Wilderness.* Random House. 1961. 1st ed. dj. . . . .
. . . .*$30–$50*

Warshburn, Robert Collier. *The Life and Times of Lydia E. Pinkham.* NY. 1931. 1st ed. 221 pp, illus. . . . .*$25–$35*

Washington, Booker T. *Up from Slavery.* NY. Doubleday Page. 1901. 1st ed. *$100*

Washington, Booker T. *Working with the Hands.* Doubleday. 1904. 1st ed. . . . .*$55–$75*

Watanna, Onoto. *The Heart of the Hyacinth.* Harper. 1903. illus. teg. . . .
. . . .*$18–$24*

Watanna, Onoto. *A Japanese Nightingale.* Harper. 1901. 1st ed. illus. . . .
. . . .*$17–$24*

Waterman, Jonathan. *High Alaska: A Historical Guide to Denali.* NY. American Alpine Club. 1988. 1st ed. photos, route photos, maps, dj. . . . . .
. . . .*$40–$50*

Waters, Ethel. *His Eye Is on the Sparrow.* NY. 1951. . . . .*$25–$35*

Watson, Francis Sedgwick. *The Operative Treatment of the Hypertrophied Prostate.* Cupples & Hurd. 1888. 167 pp photogravures. . . . .
. . . .*$100–$140*

Watson, John F. *Historic Tales of Olden Times.* Phila. 1833. 1st ed. illus. lea, 316 pp. . . . .*$50–$85*

Watson, Wilbur J. *Bridge Architecture.* NY. 1927. illus. . . . . . .*$50–$75*

Watson, William. *Adventures of a Blockade Runner.* Lon. 1892. . . . .
. . . .*$100–$155*

Watson-Watt, Sir Robert. *Three Steps to Victory.* 1957. illus. 1st Brit ed.
. . . .*$45–$60*

Watts, Rev. Isaac. *An Arrangement of the Psalms, Hymns and Spiritual Songs of.* . . . Bos. James Loring. 1818. . . . .*$70–$100*

Watts, Rev. Iaac. *Psalms, Hymns, and Spiritual Songs of the Rev. Isaac Watts.* Bos. 1852. . . . .*$10–$15*

Psalms of David, by Isaac Watts. Albany. 1828. lea. . . . .*$22–$30*

Wauchope, R. *Handbook of Middle American Indians, Vol 1.* Austin. 1964. illus. dj. *$35*

Waugh, Evelyn. *Brideshead Revisited.* Bos. Little Brown. 1946. 1st Amer trade ed. dj. *$50*

Waugh, Evelyn. *Edmund Campion.* Lon. Longmans Green. (1935). 1st ed. *$50*

Waugh, Evelyn. *Helena.* Lon. Chapman & Hall. 1950. 1st ed. dj. . . . . . .
. . . .*$300*

Waugh, Evelyn. *Love among the Ruins.* Lon. 1953. 1st ed. dj. . . . .
. . . .*$35–$45*

Waugh, Evelyn. *Mr. Loveday's Little Outing and Other Sad Stories.* Lon. Chapman & Hall. (1936). 1st ed. *$50*

Waugh, Evelyn. *When the Going Was Good.* Lon. Duckworth. 1946. 1st ed. dj. *$125*

Waugh, F. A. *Landscape Gardening.* NY. 1899. 1st ed. . . . .*$32–$45*

Webb, Sydney, and Beatrice Webb. *The State and the Doctor.* Lon. Longmans Green. 1910. 1st ptg. *$27.50*

Webb, Walter Prescott. *The Texas Rangers.* Houghton Mifflin. 1935. 1st ed. illus. . . . .*$52–$60*

Webb, William Seward. *California and Alaska, and over the Canadian Pacific Railway.* NY. 1890. illus. ltd to 500cc. . . . .*$120–$155*

Weber, Carl J. *Fore-edge Painting.* Irvington-on-Hudson. 1966. illus. dj. . . . .*$165–$200*

Weber, Rev. Francis J. *A Bibliography of California Bibliographies.* Ward Ritchie Press. illus. slipcase, 1/500cc. . . . .*$65–$85*

Webster, Noah. *An American Dictionary of the English Language.* NY. 1832. 10th ed. calf. . . . .*$20–$25*

Webster, Noah. *American Spelling Book.* NY. 1804. illus. woodcuts. . . . .
. . . .*$50–$65*

Webster, Noah. *American Spelling Book.* Bos. 1789. 1st ed. . . . .
. . . .*$175–$250*

Webster, Thomas. *An Encyclopedia of Domestic Economy.* NY. 1845. 1st ed. . . . .*$65–$125*

Wee Gee. *Naked City.* NY. 1945. 1st ed. dj. *$150*

Wee Gee. *Weegee's People.* NY. 1946. 1st ed. illus. photos. . . . .*$27–$40*

Weeden, Howard. *Songs of the Old South.* NY. 1901. 1st ed. illus. clr plates. . . . .*$75–$100*

Weeden Toy Steam Engines. New Bedford, MA. Weeden Manufacturing Corp. 1939. pictorial wrps, illus, 19 pp. . . . .*$65–$75*

Weeks, John. *History of Salisbury, Vermont.* Middlebury. 1860. . . . .*$90–$100*

Weing, Juliana Horatia. *Lob-Lie-by-the-Fire.* Lon. illus by Caldecott. . . . .*$18–$20*

Weld, Isaac. *Travels through the States of North America and the Provinces of Upper and Lower Canada during the Years 1795, 1796, and 1797.* Lon. 1799. 1st ed. 464 pp, plates, maps laid in, small folio. . . . .*$320–$400*

Wells, Carolyn. *Folly for the Wise.* Bobbs Merrill. 1904. 170 pp, illus. *$45*

Wells, Carolyn. *Marjorie in Command.* Dodd Mead. 1910. 268 pp, illus. *$25*

Wells, Carolyn. *Merry-Go-Round.* Russell. 1901. 152 pp, illus by Peter Newell. *$120*

Wells, Emma M. *The History of Roane County, Tennessee, 1801–1870.* Chattanooga. 1927. 1st ed. illus. . . . .*$55–$75*

Wells, Frederic P. *History of Newbury, Vermont.* St. Johnsbury, VT. 1902. illus. fldg plans, three-fourths mor. . . . .*$40–$55*

Wells, H. G. *Ann Veronica.* NY. 1909. 1st ed. dj. . . . .*$75–$100*

Wells, H. G. *First and Last Things.* NY. 1908. 1st U.S. ed. . . . .*$40–$50*

Wells, H. G. *The Invisible Man.* Lon. 1897. 1st ed. *$1,000*

Wells, H. G. *The Invisible Man.* NY. Edward Arnold. 1897. 1st Amer ed. 279 pp, orange cloth. . . . .*$1,000–$1,150*

Wells, H. G. *Men Like Gods.* Lon. (1923). 1st ed. dj. *$350*

Wells, H. G. *Tales of Space and Time.* NY. Doubleday & McClure. 1899. 1st Amer ed. . . . .*$45–$65*

Wells, H. G. *The Time Machine.* Lon. 1895. 1st ed. *$250*

Wells, H. G. *The Time Machine.* NY. 1931. illus by Dwiggins. . . . .*$30–$45*

Wells, H. G. *When the Sleeper Wakes.* NY. 1899. 1st ed. *$65*

Wells, Helen. *Island Nurse.* Grosset & Dunlap. 1960. Cherry Ames #21, dj. ....*$14–$17*

Wells, Helen. *Jungle Nurse.* Grosset & Dunlap. 1965. Cherry Ames #25. . ...*$30–$40*

Wells, Helen. *Student Nurse.* Grosset & Dunlap. 1943. Cherry Ames #1, dj. *$12*

Wells, Helen. *Veterans' Nurse.* Grosset & Dunlap. 1946. Cherry Ames, #6, dj. *$8*

Wells, Seth Y. *To the Elders, Deacons, Brethren and Sisters of the Society in Watervliet.* [Watervliet, NY]. 1832. [4] pp. *$950*

Welsh, William. *Report of a Visit to the Sioux and Ponka Indians on the Missouri River.* DC. GPO. 1872. ex lib. *$40*

Welty, Eudora. *The Bride of the Innisfallen and Other Stories.* NY. Harcourt Brace. (c 1955). 1st ed. 2nd issue, dj. *$150*

Welty, Eudora. *A Curtain of Green: A Book of Stories.* Garden City. Doubleday Doran. 1941. 1st ed. author's first book, dj. *$850*

Welty, Eudora. *Delta Wedding.* NY. (1946). 1st ed. dj. ......*$100–$200*

Welty, Eudora. *The Golden Apples.* NY. Harcourt Brace. (1949). 1st ed. 244 pp, water staining to leaves, chipped dj, owned by Welty's editor. *$150*

Welty, Eudora. *The Golden Apples.* NY. Harcourt Brace. (1949). 1st ed. 244 pp, sgn, dj. *$400*

Welty, Eudora. *In Black and White.* Northridge. Lord John Press. 1985. sgn. ....*$165–$250*

Welty, Eudora. *One Writer's Beginnings.* Camb. 1984. dj. ....*$30–$40*

Welty, Eudora. *The Ponder Heart.* Harcourt. (1954). 1st ed. sgn, dj. ....*$75–$125*

Welty, Eudora. *The Robber Bridegroom.* Garden City. Doubleday Doran. 1942. 1st ed. dj. *$375*

Welty, Eudora. *Short Stories.* NY. Harcourt Brace. (c 1949). 1st ed. 1/1500 cc, no glassine dj present. *$100*

Welty, Eudora. *The Wide Net and Other Stories.* NY. 1943. 1st ed. dj. ... .*$350–$500*

Werner, Carl. *A Textbook on Tobacco.* NY. 1914. illus. ....*$25–$35*

West, Anthony. *The Vintage.* Bos. 1950. 1st Amer ed. dj. ......*$25–$30*

West, Benjamin. *The New England Almanack for 1776.* Prov. 1775. ....*$125–$150*

West, James E. *The Lone Scout of the Sky.* NY. 1927. Boy Scout Book. . . . .*$15–$18*

The Westerners Brand Book, Los Angeles Corral, 1948. 1949. 1st ed. illus. two fldg maps, 1/400 cc. *$85*

The Westminster Shorter Catechism Ratified . . . Presbyterian Church in Augusta, Georgia. VA. 1861. wrps. Confederate imprint. . . . . . .*$95–$125*

West, Jerry. *The Happy Hollisters and the Indian Treasure.* Doubleday. 1953. . . . .*$10*

Wetmore, Mrs. Helen C. *Last of the Great Scouts: The Life Story of Buffalo Bill.* Duluth. 1899. 1st ed. illus. plates. . . . .*$75–$175*

Whall, W. B. *Sea Songs and Shanties.* Glasgow. 1920. illus. 4th ed. . . . .*$50–$75*

Wharton, Anne Hollingswroth. *Colonial Days and Dames.* Phila. 1895. 5th ed. . . . .*$20–$25*

Wharton, Edith. *The Children.* NY. 1928. 1st ed. dj. . . . .*$75–$125*

Wharton, Edith. *Crucial Instances.* NY. Scribner's. 1901. 1st ed. *$85*

Wharton, Edith. *The Custom of the Country.* NY. Scribner's. 1913. 1st ed. *$50*

Wharton, Edith. *Ethan Frome.* NY. 1911. 1st issue. . . . .*$150–$165*

Wharton, Edith. *The Fruit of the Tree.* NY. Scribner's. 1907. 1st ed. 633 pp. *$100*

Wharton, Edith. *Italian Villas and Their Gardens.* NY. 1904. 1st ed. illus by Maxfield Parrish. . . . .*$150–$350*

Wharton, Edith. *Old New York, New Year's Day.* NY. Appleton. 1924. 1st ed. illus by E. C. Caswell, dj. *$150*

Wharton, Edith. *Sanctuary.* NY. Scribner's. 1903. 1st ed. illus by Walter Appleton Clark, 184 pp, scarce. *$150*

Wharton, Edith. *Summer.* NY. 1917. 1st ed. dj. . . . .*$65–$95*

Wharton, Edith. *Tale of Men and Ghosts.* Lon. Macmillan. 1910. 1st Eng ed. 438 pp. . . . .*$45–$55*

Wharton, Edith. *The Valley of Decision.* NY. Scribner's. 1902. 2 vols. 1st ed. *$85*

Wharton, Edith. *Xingu and Other Stories.* NY. 1916. 1st ed. . . . .*$60.00–$75.00*

Wheeler, F. G. *Billy Whiskers at the Fair.* Akron. 1909. 1st ed. illus. plates. . . . .*$30–$35*

Where to Hunt American Game. MA. 1898. 1st ed. illus. . . . . . .*$50–$75*

Whistler, James McNeill. *The Paintings of.* . . . New Haven/Lon. 1980. 2 vols. illus. dj. . . . .*$85–$150*

Whitaker, Fess. *History of Corporal Fess Whitaker.* Louisville, KY. 1918. 1st ed. illus. . . . .*$60–$75*

White, Alma. *The Ku Klux Klan in Prophecy.* NJ. 1925. 1st ed. . . . .*$150–$275*

White, Charles A. *On Invertebrate Fossils from the Pacific Coast.* DC. GPO. 1889. . . . .*$15–$25*

White, E. B. *Charlotte's Web.* NY. (1952). 1st ed. illus by Garth Williams, dj. . . . .*$200–$450*

White, E. B. *Charlotte's Web.* NY. 1952. dj. . . . .*$22–$35*

White, E. B. *The Fox of Peapack and Other Poems.* Harper. 1938. 2nd ed. sgn and dated. . . . .*$60–$75*

White, E. B. *Stuart Little.* NY. 1945. dj. . . . .*$50–$175*

White, James. *The Early Life and Later Experiences . . . of Elder Joseph Bates.* Battle Creek. 1877. illus. 320 pp. . . . .*$115–$150*

Whitehead, Alfred North. *Science in the Modern World.* NY. 1925. 1st ed. . . . .*$40–$50*

Whitehead, Don. *The FBI Story.* NY. 1956. sgn by Hoover, dj. . . . .*$45–$50*

Whitman, Walt. *Leaves of Grass.* NY. Random House. 1930. illus. 400 nbr cc, sgn by illustrator, folio, 423 pp. *$2,000*

Whitman, Walt. *November Boughs.* Phila. 1888. 1st ed. . . . .*$90–$325*

Whitney, Ada. *Mother Goose for Grown Folks.* NY. 1859. 1st ed. sgn. . . . .*$125–$250*

Whitted, J. A. *A History of the Negro Baptists of North Carolina.* Raleigh. Edwards & Broughton. 1908. 1st ed. illus. *$225*

Whymper, C. *Egyptian Birds for the Most Part Seen in the Nile Valley.* Lon. 1909. illus. . . . .*$70–$85*

Whymper, Frederick. *Travel and Adventure in the Territory of Alaska.* Harper & Bros. 1871. illus. . . . .*$65–$85*

Wickersham, James. *A Bibliography of Alaskan Literature, 1724–1924.* . . . Cordova. 1927. . . . .*$225–$275*

Wiggin, Kate Douglas. *The Birds' Christmas Carol.* 1912. illus. . . . .*$18–$27*

Wiggin, Kate Douglas. *The Diary of a Goose Girl.* Bos. 1902. 1st ed. . . . .*$20–$30*

Wiggin, Kate Douglas. *The Old Peabody Pew.* Bos/NY. 1907. 1st ed. . . .
. . . .*$35–$50*

Wiggin, Kate Douglas. *Rebecca of Sunnybrook Farm.* Bos. Houghton
Mifflin. 1903. . . . .*$100–$135*

Wight, J. B. *Tobacco: Its Use and Abuse.* Columbia, SC. 1889. . . . .
. . . .*$20–$35*

Wightman, Orrin. *The Diary of an American Physician in the Russian
Revolution. 1917.* Brooklyn. Daily Eagle 1928. 1st ed. photo, 230 pp, sgn
presentation copy. . . . .*$95–$125*

Wilbur, Mary. *Every-day Business for Women.* NY. Houghton Mifflin.
1910. 1st ptg. *$24.50*

Wilcox, Walter Dwight. *The Rockies of Canada.* NY/Lon. 1900. . . . .
. . . .*$75–$100*

Wilde, Oscar. *The Canterville Ghost.* Bos. J. W. Luce. 1906. 1st separate
ed. illus, tri-color slate cloth, teg. . . . .*$100–$125*

Wilde, Oscar. *The Picture of Dorian Gray.* Lon. 1891. 1st ed. ltd,
#177/250, sgn by Wilde, red mor. *$2,875*

Wilde, Oscar. *The Poems of Oscar Wilde.* NY. 1927. illus. . . . . .*$30–$65*

Wilder, Thornton. *The Bridge of San Luis Rey.* NY. 1962. 1500 cc, slip-
case. . . . .*$100–$150*

Wilder, Thornton. *The Cabala.* NY. 1926. 1st ed. . . . .*$100–$360*

Wilder, Thorton. *Theophilus North.* NY. (1973). 1st ed. presentation
copy, sgn, dj. . . . .*$80–$100*

Wildflowers of Palestine. 1895. . . . .*$50–$60*

Wilhelm, Kate. *The Clewiston Test.* NY. (1976). 1st ed. dj. . . . . .*$15–$25*

Willard, Frances E. *How to Win.* NY. 1887. 4th ed. . . . .*$50–$65*

Willard, Frances E. *A Wheel within a Wheel.* Chi. Woman's Temperance
Publishing Co. (1898). 1st ed. *$125*

Willard, Frances E. *Woman in the Pulpit.* Chi. Woman's Temperance
Publishing Co. 1889. 1st ed. *$125*

Williams, Mrs. *The Neutral French.* . . . published by author. 1841. . . . . .
. . . .*$50–$75*

Williams, Garner F. *The Diamond Mines of South Africa.* NY.
Macmillan. 1902. 1st ed. fldg map, plates. . . . .*$125–$200*

Williams, Joseph J. *Hewbrewisms of West Africa: From Nile to Niger
with the Jews.* NY. Dial Press. 1930. 1st ed. maps. . . . .*$50–$80*

Williams, Morris. *Stair Builder's Guide.* NY. David Williams Co. (1914).
illus. 256 pp. . . . .*$55–$75*

Williams, S. Wells. *The Middle Kingdom.* NY. 1883. 2 vols. wrps. rev ed. 2 fldg frontis, pocket map. .... *$150–$225*

Williams, Tennessee. *Cat on a Hot Tin Roof.* Secker. 1956. 1st Eng ed. dj. .... *$75–$90*

Williams, Tennessee. *Cat on a Hot Tin Roof.* NY. 1955, 1st ed. dj. .... *$75–$100*

Williams, Tennessee. *The Glass Menagerie.* NY. Random House. 1945. 1st ed. dj. .... *$65–$80*

Williams, Tennessee. *The Roman Spring of Mrs. Stone.* NY. 1950. 1st ed. dj. .... *$50–$75*

Williams, Tennessee. *The Rose Tattoo.* New Directions. 1951. 1st ed. dj. . ... *$60–$125*

Wiliams, Tennessee. *A Streetcar Named Desire.* [NY]. New Directions. (1947). 1st ed. 171 pp, bds, dj. *$350*

Williams, W. *Appleton's Northern and Eastern Traveller's Guide.* NY. 1855. illus. maps. .... *$85–$130*

Williams, William Carlos. *The Complete Collected Poems, 1906–1938.* Norfolk, CT. New Directions. (c1938). 1st ed. dj. *$150*

Williams, William Carlos. *Life along the Passaic River.* Norfolk, CT. New Directions. 1938. 1st ed. dj. *$200*

Williams, William Carlos. *Patterson (Books One through Five).* New Directions. (1946, 1948, 1949, 1951, 1958). 1st ed. 8vo, each vol is 1/1000 cc except the last, which was 1/3000 cc, djs. *$1,200*

Williams, William Carlos. *White Mule.* Norfolk, CT. New Directions. 1937. 1st ed. dj. *$200*

Williamson, Henry. *Salar the Salmon.* Bos. Little Brown. 1935. 1st ed. dj. .... *$40–$50*

Wilson, Angus. *Hemlock and After.* 1952. 1st ed. first novel, dj. *$45*

Wilson, Colin. *The Philosopher's Stone.* NY. Crown (1971). 1st Amer ed. dj. .... *$35–$40*

Wilson, Edmund. *The Boys in the Back Room: Notes on California Novelists.* SF. Colt Press. 1941. 1st ed. 1/1000 cc, sgn. *$600*

Wilson, Edmund. *Poets, Farewell.* NY. Scribner's. 1929. 1st ed. dj...... .... *$225*

Wilson, Edmund. *Travels in Two Democracies.* NY. Harcourt, Brace. (c 1936). 1st ed. dj. *$275*

Wilson, Rev. Edward F. *Missionary Work among the Ojebway Indians.* Lon. 1886. 1st ed. illus. .... *$75–$150*

Wilson, Elija N. *Among the Shoshones.* Salt Lake City. 1910. 1st ed. . . . .
. . . .*$200–$250*

Wilson, Joseph Thomas. *The Black Phalanx: A History of Negro Soldiers of the U.S.* CT. 1888. 1st ed. illus. . . . .*$175–$250*

Wilson, T. *The Biography of the Principal American Military and Naval Heroes.* NY. 1821. 2 vols. . . . .*$55–$65*

Wilstach, Frank J. *Wild Bill Hickock.* Garden City. 1926. . . . . . .*$15–$22*

Wimsatt, Genevieve. *Chinese Shadow Shows.* Camb. Harvard Univ. Press. 1936. 1st ed. illus. dj. . . . .*$50–$80*

Winchester and Hotchkiss Repeating Fire Arms, Rifled Muskets, Carbines . . . of All Kinds. New Haven, CT. Winchester Repeating Arms Co. 1884. illus. printed wrps, 68 pp. . . . .*$175–$225*

Winkfield, Uncle Eliza. *The Female American.* Vergennes, VT. Jepthah Shedd. 1814. 2nd ed. 12mo, 270 pp, calf, scarce. . . . .*$150–$250*

Winter, William. *The Life of David Belasco.* NY. 1918. 2 vols. 1st ed. illus. . . . .*$40–$50*

Winthrop, Theodore. *The Canoe and the Saddle.* Bos. Ticknor & Fields. 1863. . . . .*$75*

Wirt, Mildred A. *Ghost beyond the Gate.* Cupples & Leon. 1943. Penny Parker # 10, dj. *$13*

Wise, John. *Vindication of the Government of New-England Churches.* Bos. 1772. 2nd ed. . . . .*$100–$150*

Wodehouse, P. G. *Bachelors Anonymous.* Simon & Schuster. 1974. dj. . .
. . . .*$30*

Wodehouse, P. G. *Bill the Conqueror.* NY. 1924. 1st Amer ed. . . . .
. . . .*$50–$75*

Wodehouse, P. G. *Carry On, Jeeves!* NY. 1927. 1st U.S. ed. . . . .*$45–$65*

Wodehouse, P. G. *The Code of the Woosters.* Lon. 1938. 1st ed. .*$35–$50*

Wodehouse, P. G. *Golf without Tears.* NY. 1924. 1st ed. . . . .*$60–$85*

Wodehouse, P. G. *The Head of Kay's.* Lon. 1924 . . . .*$30–$40*

Wodehouse, P. G. *The Inimitable Jeeves.* Lon. 1923. 1st ed. . . . .*$40–$50*

Wodehouse, P.G. *Love among Chickens.* Lon. 1936. . . . .*$35–$40*

Wodehouse, P. G. *Mike at Wrykyn.* 1953. 1st ed. dj. . . . .*$20–$25*

Wodehouse, P. G. *Piccadilly Jim.* Lon. 1924. . . . .*$30–$40*

Wodehouse, P. G. *Plum Pie.* NY. 1967.dj. . . . .*$16–$22*

Wodehouse, P. G. *The Prince and Betty.* 1912. 1st ed. . . . .*$50–$65*

Wodehouse, P. G. *Sunset at Blandings.* Lon. 1977. dj. . . . .*$28–$38*

Wodehouse, P. G. *Thank You, Jeeves.* Lon. 1934. 1st ed. . . . .*$75–$85*

Wodehouse, P. G. *Uncle Fred in the Springtime.* NY. 1939. 1st ed. dj. . . .
. . . .*$40–$55*

Wodehouse, P. G. *Uneasy Money.* Lon. 1934. . . . .*$30–$35*

Wodehouse, P. J. *Very Good, Jeeves.* NY. Doubleday. 1930. 1st U.S. ed.
340 pp. *$65*

Wolf, Simon. *The American Jew as Patriot, Soldier and Citizen.* Phila.
1895. 1st ed. . . . .*$65–$75*

Wolfe, Thomas. *From Death to Morning.* NY. 1935. 1st ed. dj. . . . .
. . . .*$100–$225*

Wolfe, Thomas. *Of Time and the River.* NY. Scribner's. 1935. 1st ed. 512
pp, chipped dj. *$125*

Wolfe, Thomas. *Of Time and the River.* NY. Scribner's. 1935. 1st ed. . . .
. . . .*$45–$65*

Wolfe, Thomas. *The Web and the Rock.* NY. Harper. 1939. 1st ed. 695 pp,
dj. *$125*

Wolfe, Thomas. *The Web and the Rock.* NY. 1939. 1st ed. dj. . . . .
. . . .*$70–$120*

Wolfe, Thomas. *You Can't Go Home Again.* NY. Scribner's. (1940). 1st
ed. 743 pp, dj. *$125*

Wolfe, Thomas. *You Can't Go Home Again.* NY. 1940. 1st ed. dj. . . . . . .
. . . .*$40–$125*

Wolfe, Tom. *Bonfire of the Vanities.* 1987. 1st ed. dj. . . . .*$40–$60*

Wolfe, Tom. *Mauve Gloves and Madmen, Clutter and Vine.* Farrar. 1976.
1st ed. dj. *$40*

Wolfe, Tom. *The Painted Word.* 1975. dj. . . . .*$20–$40*

Wolfe, Tom. *The Right Stuff.* Farrar. 1979. 1st ed. dj. *$40*

Wollstonecraft, Mary. *A Vindication of the Rights of Woman.* Bos. 1792.
1st Boston ed. 340 pp. *$1,250*

Woman's Kingdom. NY. 1869. illus. 1st Amer ed. . . . .*$22–$30*

Wood. *In Heart of Old Canada.* Tor. 1913. . . . .*$18–$20*

Wood, Edward J. *Curiosities of Clocks and Watches from the Earliest
Times.* Lon. 1866. 1st ed. . . . .*$150–$220*

Wood, Edward J. *Giants and Dwarfs.* Lon. 1868. 1st ed. . . . .*58–$75*

Wood, Rev. J. G. *Common Objects of the Microscope.* Lon. nd. illus. . . . .
. . . .*$30–$40*

Wood, Robert W. *Physical Optics.* NY. 1914. illus. rvsd. . . . . . .*$25–$30*

Wood, Wales W. *A History of the Ninety-fifth Regiment Illinois Infantry
Vols.* Chi. 1865. 1st ed. . . . .*$145–$175*

Wood Walter. *Harvesting Machines.* NY. 1882. wrps. ....$30–$40

Woolf, Virginia. *Flush.* Lon. 1933. 1st ed. illus. by Vanessa Bell, dj. ....
....$50–$75

Woolf, Virginia. *Reviewing.* Lon. Hogarth Press. 1939. 1st ed. illus. ......
....$50

Woolf, Virginia. *Three Guineas.* NY. Harcourt, Brace. (c 1938). 1st Amer
ed. dj. $85

Woolf, Virginia. *The Waves.* Lon. 1931. 1st ed. dj. ....$75–$225

Woolf, Virginia. *A Writer's Diary: Being Extracts from the Diary of Virginia Woolf.* Lon. Hogarth Press. 1953. 1st ed. dj. $85

Woolf, Virginia. *The Years.* NY. Harcourt, Brace. 1937. 1st Amer ed. dj. . .
....$100

Woolfe, Virginia. *Contemporary Writers.* NY. 1965. 1st U.S. ed. dj. ....
....$40–$50

Wordsworth, William. *The Prelude.* NY. Appleton. 1850. 1st U.S. ed.. . .
....$250

Wordsworth, William. *The Sonnets of. . . .* Lon. Moxon. 1838. 1 vol. 1st
ed. calf. $425

The World Encompassed: An Exhibition of the History of Maps. Balt.
Walters Art Gallery. 1952. 1st ed. illus. 60 plates, pictorial wrps. ....
....$100–$150

Worthington, T. *Brief History of the 46th Ohio Volunteers.* DC.
1877–1880. wrps. ....$75–$100

Wouk, Herman. *The Caine Mutiny.* Garden City. 1951. 1st ed. dj. ......
....$75–$115

WPA. *Alaska.* 1943. ....$30–$35

WPA. *Anthology of Writers in Federal Writers' Project.* ....$50–$75

WPA. *California.* NY. 1939. 1st ed. map. ....$35–$45

WPA. *Cape Cod.* 2nd ptg. ....$30–$35

WPA. *Cavalcade of the American Negro.* Chi. 1940. ....$50–$75

WPA. *Florida: A Guide to the Southernmost State.* NY. Oxford. (1944).
3rd ptg, 600 pp, photos, maps in rear packet. $17.50

WPA. *Iowa.* NY. 1938. 1st ed. pocket map, dj. ....$30–$40

WPA. *Key West.* NY. 1949. 2nd ed. dj. ....$14–$20

WPA. *Maine.* Bos. 1937. 1st ed. ....$25–$35

WPA. *A Maritime History of New York.* NY. 1941. illus. dj. ....
....$45–$55

WPA. *Maryland.* NY. 1941. 5th ptg. . . . .*$12–$15*

WPA. *Medicine and Its Development in Kentucky.* Louisville. Standard Printing Co. 1940. 373 pp. *$100*

WPA. *Michigan.* Ox. 1941. 1st ed. pocket map, dj. . . . .*$30–$40*

WPA. *Minnesota.* NY. Viking Press. 1938. 1st ed. map, dj. . . . . .*$40–$45*

WPA. *Montana.* 1st ed. map, dj. . . . .*$35–$100*

WPA. *New Hampshire.* 1st ed. . . . .*$20–$40*

WPA. *New Jersey.* 1st ed. map. . . . .*$35–$40*

WPA. *The Negroes of Nebraska.* Lincoln, Nebraska. 1940. 1st ed. . . . . . .
. . . .*$45–$60*

WPA. *New Orleans City Guide.* 1938. map. . . . .*$22–$30*

WPA. *New York City Guide.* Random House. 1940. map, dj. . . . .
. . . .*$28–$35*

WPA. *New York City Guide.* 1939. pocket map. . . . .*$30–$40*

WPA. *North Dakota.* Fargo. 1938. 1st ed. . . . .*$37–$50*

WPA. *South Dakota.* NY. 1952. 2nd ed. maps, dj. . . . .*$40–$50*

WPA. *Texas: A Guide to the Lone Star State.* NY. 1940. 1st ed. illus. dj. .
. . . .*$24–$35*

WPA. *Wyoming.* 1st ed. map, dj. . . . .*$60–$95*

WPA, Anderson, Nels. *Men on the Move.* Univ. of Chicago Press. (1940). photos. *$17.50*

Wright and Ditson's Lawn Tennis Guide for 1895. wrps. . . . .*$*
. . . .*25–$45*

Wright, Frank Lloyd. *An American Architecture.* NY. Horizon. 1955. 1st ed. *$55*

Wright, Frank Lloyd. *Drawings for a Living Architecture.* NY. Horizon Press. 1959. 1st ed. illus. 255 pp. . . . .*$450–$600*

Wright, Frank Lloyd. *The Future of Architecture.* NY. Horizon Press. 1953. 1st ed. dj. . . . .*$95–$125*

Wright, Frank Lloyd. *Genius and the Mobocracy.* Lon. 1949. 1st ed. dj. .
. . . .*$200–$300*

Wright, Frank Lloyd. *The Japanese Print and Interpretation.* NY. 1967. 1st ed. boxed. . . . .*$90–$250*

Wright, Frank Lloyd. *The Living City.* 1958. 1st ed. dj. . . . .*$55–$67*

Wright, Frank Lloyd. *The Natural House.* Horizon Press. 1954. 1st ed. dj.
. . . .*$100–$150.*

Wright, Frank Lloyd. *On Architecture.* NY. 1941. 1st ed. . . . .*$95–$125*

Wright, Frank Lloyd. *An Organic Architecture.* Camb. MIT Press. 1970. 3rd ed. rprnt. . . . .*$50–$75*

Wright, Frank Lloyd. *When Democracy Builds.* Univ. of California Press 1945. . . . .*$75–$125*

Wright, Frank Lloyd. *The Works of. . . .* NY. Bramhall House. 1965. illus. Wendingen ed, 163 pp, dj. . . . .*$100–$155*

Wright, G. Frederick. *The Ice Age in North America.* Appleton. 1889. 1st ed. . . . .*$70–$100*

Wright, G. Frederick. *The Ice Age in North America.* NY. 1890. illus. maps, 622 pp. . . . .*$50–$75*

Wright, H. B. *Long Ago Told Legends of the Papago Indians.* 1st ed. facs dj. *$675*

Wright, H. B. *Shepherd of the Hills.* 1907. 1st ed. . . . .*$45–$70*

Wright, Harold B. *The Uncrowned King.* The Book Supply Co. 1910. . . . .*$30–$40*

Wright, Harold Bell. *Devil's Highway.* NY. 1932. dj. *$150*

Wright Harold Bell. *Mine with the Iron Door.* NY. 1923. 1st ed. dj. . . . .*$25–$65*

Wright, Harold Bell. *Re-creation of Brian Kent.* Chi. 1919. dj. . . . .*$20–$35*

Wright, Harold Bell. *A Son of His Father.* NY. 1925. 1st ed. . . .*$15–$20*

Wright, Henry. *History of the Sixth Iowa Infantry.* Iowa City. 1923. . . . .*$55–$65*

Wright, Richard. *Black Boy.* NY. (1945). 1st ed. dj. . . . .*$65–$90*

Wright, Richard. *Native Son.* NY. 1940. 1st ed. dj. . . . .*$200–$300*

Wright, Robert. *Dodge City—The Cowboy Capital and the Great Southwest.* np. nd. 2nd ed. . . . .*$65–$100*

Wright Thomas. *A History of Domestic Manners and Sentiments in England during the Middle Ages.* Lon. Chapman & Hall. 1862. 1st ed. illus. aeg, bound by Zaehnsdorf. . . . .*$100–$150*

Wright, William. *The Grizzly Bear.* NY. 1913. illus. . . . .*$40–$75*

Wulff, Lee. *The Atlantic Salmon.* Barnes. 1958. 2nd ptg. dj. *$30*

Wyatt, Thomas. *Manual of Conchology.* NY. 1838. 1st ed. illus. lithos. . . . .*$65–$85*

Wyeth, Betsy James. *Christina's World.* Bos. 1982. 1st ed. illus. oblong folio, dj. . . . .*$50–$75*

Wyeth, Betsy James (ed). *The Letters of N. C. Wyeth, 1901–1945.* Bos. 1971. 1st ed. dj. . . . .*$50–$75*

Wylie, Elinor. *Collected Poems.* NY. Knopf. 1932. ed by William Rose Benet, 1st ed. 1/210 cc, sgn. $100

Wylie, Elinor. *Mr. Hodge and Mr. Hazard.* NY. Knopf. 1928. 1st ed. author's first book, sgn, dj. $400

Wylie, Elinor. *Nets to Catch the Wind.* Lon. Knopf. 1928. 1st Brit ed. dj. $50

Wylie, Elinor. *Nets to Catch the Wind.* NY. Harcourt, Brace. 1921. 1st ed. dj, author's first book. $100

Wylie, Eleanor. *The Orphan Angel.* NY. Knopf. 1926. 1st ed. 337 pp, 1/30 cc large paper, sgn. $425

Wylie, Philip. *The Murderer Invisible.* NY. 1931. 1st ed. ....$35–$50

Yadin, Yigael. *Masada.* NY. Random House. (1966). 1st Amer ed. illus, dj. $25

Yeats, William Butler. *The Hour-glass.* NY. Macmillan. 1904. 1st Amer ed. large paper, #73/1000 cc, dj. $150

Yeats, W. B. *In the Seven Woods.* NY. 1903. dj. ....$95–$125

Yeats, William Butler. *Michael Robartes and the Dancer.* Dublin. Cuala Press. 1920. ltd 400 cc. ....$100–$145

Yeats, William Butler. *On the Boiler.* Dublin. Cuala Press. (1939). 2nd ed. wraps. $150

Yeats, W. B. *Per Amica Silentia Lunae.* NY. 1918. 1st Amer ed. ....$35–$45

Yeats, William Butler. *Plays for an Irish Theatre.* Bullen. 1911. 1st ed. . . ..$25–$35

Yeats, William Butler. *Synge and the Ireland of His Time.* Churchtown, Dundrum. Cuala Press. 1911. 1st ed. $275

Yeats, William Butler. *The Words upon the Window Pane: A Play in One Act.* Dublin. Cuala Press. 1934. 1st ed. 1/350 cc. $200

Yolen, Jane. *Dragon's Blood.* Delacorte Press. (1980). 1st ed. dj. ....$20–$25

Yolen, Jane. *Neptune Rising: Songs and Tales of the Undersea Folk.* NY. (1982). 1st ed. sgn, dj. ....$25–$35

Yolen, Jane. *Sister Light, Sister Dark.* NY. 1988. 1st ed. sgn, dj. ....$25–$35

Young, Ann Elizabeth. *Wife Number 19.* Hartford. 1876. 1st ed. illus. 605 pp. ....$70–$85

Young, C. A. *The Sun.* NY. 1898. ....$15–$22

Young, Clarence. *Jack Ranger's School Victories.* Cupples & Leon. 1908. #3, dj. $10

Young, Clarence. *The Motor Boys on the Atlantic.* Cupples & Leon. 1908. #6, dj. ....$40–$60

Young Lady's Friend, by a Lady. Bos. 1837. ....$35–$40

Yount, George C. *George C. Yount and His Chronicles of the West.* Rosenstock. 1966. 1st ed. illus. fldg map. ....$50–$75

Zaharias, Babe Didrikson. *This Life I've Led.* 1955. 1st ed. dj.......$35

Zahm, J. A. *Through South America's Southland.* NY/Lon. 1916. illus. .. ..$18–$25

Zangwill, Israel. *Children of the Ghetto.* Lon. 1892. 3 vols. 1st ed. ....$125–$150

Zeitlin, Ida. *Gessar Khan.* NY. 1927. 1st ed. illus. ....$50–$60

Zelazny, Roger. *Doorways in the Sand.* Harper & Row. (1976). 1st ed. dj. ....$25–$35

Zelazny, Roger. *Lord of Light.* Garden City. Doubleday. 1967. 1st ed. dj. $1,250

Zelazny, Roger. *Sign of the Unicorn.* Garden City. 1975. 1st ed. dj. ....$30–$45

Zelazny, Roger. *Trumps of Doom.* NY. (1985). 1st ed. dj. ......$25–$35

Zhang Ming-tao, et al. *The Roof of the World.* NY/Beijing. Abrams/Foreign Language Press. (1982). 1st Amer ed. illus, dj. ....$30–$45

Ziemann and Gillette. *The White House Cook Book.* Chi. 1903. illus. plates. ....$35–$45

Zinsser, Hans. *Rats, Lice and History.* Bos. 1945. rprnt. ....$35–$45

Zogbaum, Rufus Fairchild. *Horse, Foot, and Dragoons....* NY. Harper & Bros. 1888. 1st ed. illus by the author, 176 pp, pictorial cloth, teg. ....$180–$200

Zolotow, M. *Marilyn Monroe.* NY. 1960. 1st ed. sgn, presentation copy. . ...$45–$75

Zucker, A. E. *The Chinese Theatre.* Bos. 1925. illus. ltd #329/750 cc, slipcase. ....$195–$250

Zwemer, Rev. S. M. *Arabia: The Cradle of Islam.* Revell. (1990). illus. maps, 434 pp. ....$40–$60

BIBLES LISTING

That Book in many's eyes doth share the glory
That in gold clasps locks in the golden story.
—WILLIAM SHAKESPEARE, *ROMEO AND JULIET*

Leif Laudamus, seller of fine and rare books in Leyden, Massachusetts, and one of a rare few dealers in Bibles, offered general guidelines to help sort out the mysteries and misconceptions that confuse most people about Bibles.

Although the Bible has been on the bestseller list since Gutenberg made it readily available, Bibles in general are not collectible. "Nevertheless," Leif says, "current collector interest is high." He hastens to list some caveats for the novice and uninitiated. "For every edition of interest, there are literally hundreds of scant or no interest."

When the publication date of a Bible gets into the nineteenth century, the book is less likely to be collectible. In general, Leif says, American Bibles must be published before 1800 to be of value. European Bibles should be published before 1700. But again, after 1800, ask for counsel from a credible bookseller on whether or not you have a prize; some later editions are interesting, he said, so don't rush to discard your book without checking first.

What else makes a Bible valuable besides its age? Well, you

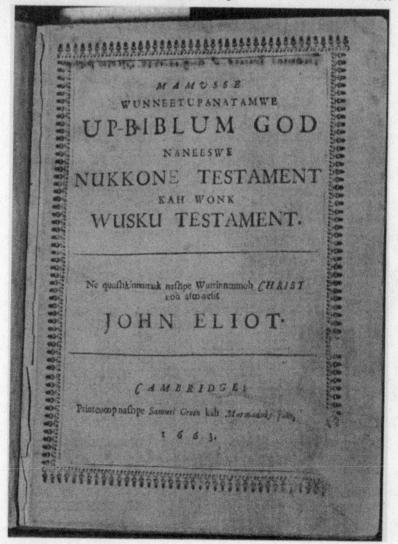

The earliest example in history of an entire Bible translated into a new language. By John Eliot, known as the Eliot Bible or Natick Bible, it was printed for the Natick colony of "praying Indians" west of Boston, Massachusetts, and completed 1663. (Courtesy of the Trustees of the Boston Public Library. Photographed by Marilyn Green.)

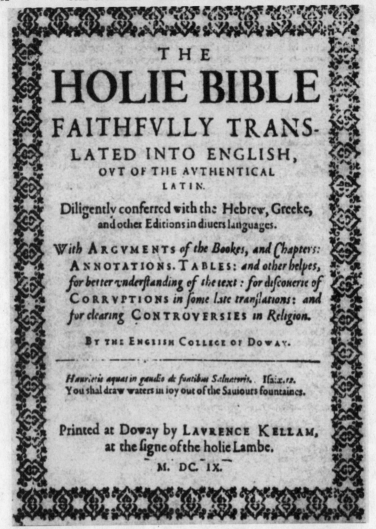

THE
HOLIE BIBLE
FAITHFVLLY TRANS-
LATED INTO ENGLISH,
OVT OF THE AVTHENTICAL
LATIN.

Diligently conferred with the Hebrew, Greeke,
and other Editions in diuers languages.

With ARGVMENTS *of the Bookes, and Chapters:*
ANNOTATIONS. TABLES: *and other helpes,*
for better vnderstanding of the text : for discouerie of
CORRVPTIONS *in some late translations: and*
for clearing CONTROVERSIES *in Religion.*

BY THE ENGLISH COLLEGE OF DOWAY.

Haurietis aquas in gaudio de fontibus Saluatoris. Isaiæ.12.
You shal draw waters in ioy out of the Sauiours fountaines.

Printed at Doway by LAVRENCE KELLAM,
at the signe of the holie Lambe.
M. DC. IX.

Title page of the first edition of the Roman Catholic Old Testament
in English. It was printed at the city of Douai in France, spelled
phonetically "Doway." It was considered unwise to attempt such a
publication in England, where Protestantism had been adopted as
the recognized state religion. The border is composed of repetitive
impressions of a standard design, found in the stock of most
printers of that time.

might one day run across the first Bible printed in a particular place, country, state, or city. Or the first Bible printed in any language, such as the Eliot or Natick Bible printed for the Natick colony of "praying Indians," west of Boston, completed in 1663.

The first Bible printed, translated, or edited by a woman would be a prime example of a significant book even with a later publication date. Also, Bibles owned by famous people, miniature Bibles called "thumb-Bibles," hieroglyphic Bibles, unusual volumes in fine bindings, or those printed for children.

Most people think of the family Bible, old, leather-worn, and bearing the ancient script of a long deceased ancestor, as surely a valuable treasure. Indeed it is, not in dollars, but in the pleasure and fortune of having a precious family heirloom tucked away safely or prominently spotlighted in your home.

Listed below are some Bibles of collectible value.

American Bible. The "Eliot" or "Natick Bible." Cambridge, MA . . . 1663. Indian-language translation, scarce. . . . .*$175,000–$250,000*

American Bible. Phila 1790. 2 vols. 1st Amer ed of the Douai or Roman Catholic Bible . . . .*$6500–$10,000*

American Bible. Trenton. 1791. . . . .*$1000–$1300*

American Bible. Phila. 1794. pocket size. . . . .*$75–$100*

American Bible. Windsor, VT. 1812. . . . .*$800–$1000*

Bible. Edin. 1817. red mor, aeg. . . . .*$25–$35*

Bible. NY. American Bible Society. 1831. lea. . . . .*$24–$35*

Bible. Lon. Edward Whitechurch. 1541. 6th ed. folio, sheepskin binding. . .
. . . .*$1900–$2500*

Bible in English. Oxford. Baskett. 1717. 2 vols. large folio, many errors, called the "Vinegar Bible" for a proofreading error in Luke 20 (word "vinegar" substituted for "vineyard"). . . . .*$600–$900*

Bible in English. The Oxford Lectern Bible. Ox. 1935. designed by Bruce Rogers, large folio. . . . .*$6000–$8000*

Bible, Latin. A leaf from the Gutenberg Bible containing the end of Wisdom and the beginning of Jerome's preface to Ecclesiasticus. folio. . . .
. . . .*$24,150*

Biblia Latina. Paris. 1985. facs of the Gutenberg Bible in 4 vols. . . .*$3450*

Biblia Pauperum. np. 1815 or after. three-quarters morocco, purple moire bds. *$431*

Biblia Sacra Polyglotta. Lon. 2 vols. folio. . . . .*$250–$275*

The Birth of Christ from the Gospel According to St. Luke. Golden Cockerell Press. 1925. half-leather over bds, 370 cc. . . . .*$95–$150*

Gospel of Matthew in the Mpongwe Language. Gabon. West Africa. 1850. . . . .*$145–$250*

The Four Gospels of the Lord Jesus Christ, According to the Authorized Version of King James. Waltham St. Laurence. The Golden Cockerel Press. 1931. illus. with 65 wood engravings by Eric Gill, #20/500 cc, tan cloth, white pigskin spine and corner, teg, by Sangorski and Sutcliffe, slipcase. *$7,500*

The Holy Bible. Bos. 1812. lea. . . . .*$150–$175*

The Holy Bible. Hartford. 1842. lea. *$350*

The Holy Bible. Hartford. 1845. steel engr, 2 maps. *$75*

The Holy Bible. Phila. Berriman & Co. (1796). folio, calf. . . . .
. . . .*$100–$150*

The Holy Bible. Hartford. 1845. steel engr, 2 maps. *$75*

The Holy Bible. Somerset, PA. Goeb, Friederich, printer. 1813. . . . . .*$295*

The Holy Bible. NY. American Bible Society. 1838, 1839. 26th ed. . . . . .
. . . .*$30–$40*

Holy Bible. Lon. 1963. 3 vols. . . . .*$75–$95*

Holy Bible. Oxford. 1817. Clarendon press. 3 vols. lea. . . . . . .*$150–$200*

Holy Bible. Phila. Bible Society of Philadelphia. 1812. lea. stereotype ed. .
. . . .*$125–$225*

Holy Bible Contained in the Old and New Testaments and the Apocrypha. Bos. (1904). 14 vols. illus. full lea. . . . .*$250–$300*

Holy Bible, Containing Old and New with Apocrypha. Isaiah Thomas. 1791. engr, calf. *$1400*

Holy Bible, Containing the Old and New Testaments. Isaiah Thomas. Worcester. 1800. . . . .*$120–$150*

Holy Bible, Containing the Old and New Testaments. Cooperstown, NY. 1839. lea. . . . .*$30–$45*

Holy Bible, Containing the Old and New Testaments. Phila. 1796. illus. large folio, 376 unnumbered leaves, 16 engr plates, 2 maps, full calf, gilt. .
. . . .*$1500–$2000*

Holy Bible, Containing the Old and New Testaments and the Apocrypha. Bos. nd. 14 vols. *$400*

Holy the Great Book, Old Testament and New Testament. Lon. 1861. Cree language, calf. . . . .*$500–$850*

Jerusalem Bible. Garden City. 1970. illus by Salvatore Dali, 32 clr plates.
....*$500*

Magil, Joseph. *Magil's Linear School Bible: The Five Books of Moses.*
NY. 1905. ....*$15–$24*

New Testament. Lon. 1616. 136 pp, mor. ....*$75–$100*

New Testament. Lon. 1816. folio, silver hinges and clasps. .*$1200–$1400*

New Testament, Translated into the Cree Language. Lon. 1876. lea. ...*$*
....*250*

Old and New Testament and Apocrypha. Boston. Hinkley. ltd 488 cc, 14
vols. ....*$175–$250*

Pages from the Gutenberg Bible of 42 Lines. NY. 1940. ltd. 2,000 cc,
folio. ....*$100–$125*

Yates, Elizabeth. *Joseph: The King James Version of a Well-Loved Tale.*
Knopf. 1947. 1st ed. dj. ....*$15–$22*

DEALERS

We wish to thank the dealers listed below who responded to our request for catalogs. Most of them, except where a specialty is noted, are general booksellers covering a broad field of subjects.

Abracadabra Booksearch
International
Alan and Mary Culpin, Booksellers
32 South Broadway
Denver, CO 80209
1-800-545-2665

Abracadabra Booksearch
International
3606 Chalkstone Cove
Austin, TX 78730
512-502-9042

Antiquarian and Collector Books
Rodger and Joan Bassett
P.O. Box 536

Fullerton, NE 68638
308-536-2377

An Uncommon Vision
1425 Greywall Lane
Wynnewood, PA 19096-3811
610-658-0953

Artis Books
201 N. Second Avenue
Alpena, MI 49707
517-354-3401

Barbara B. Harris Books
8 Morgan Way
Gilford, NH 03246
603-524-5405

Barry R. Levin
Science Fiction and Fantasy
720 Santa Monica Boulevard
Santa Monica, CA 90401
310-458-6111

Bev Chaney, Jr., Books
73 Croton Avenue
Ossining, NY 10562

Bibliomania
129 Jay Street
Schenectady, NY 12305
518-393-8069

Bookcell Books
Box 506
Haverford, PA 19041
610-649-4933

Brick House Bookshop
RFD 3 Box 3020
Morrisville, VT 05661
802-888-4300

Cattermole
20th Century Children's Books
9880 Fairmont Road
Newberry, OH 44065
216-338-3253

David M. Lesser
One Bradley Road #302
Woodbridge, CT 06525
203-389-8111

DeWolfe and Wood
P.O. Box 425
Alfred, ME 04002
207-490-5572

Edwin Glaser
P.O. Box 1765
Sausalito, CA 94966
415-332-1194

Emmett Harrington
P.O. Box 27236
San Francisco, CA 94127
415-587-4604

Ethnographic Arts Publication
1040 Erica Road
Mill Valley, CA 94941
415-383-2998, 332-1646

Foundations Antiques
Stephen Smith
148 North Main Street
Fair Haven, VT 05743
802-265-4544

Frances L. Robinson
U.S. Rt. 2, 81 South Street
South Hero, VT 05486
802-372-6622

George Kolbe
Fine Numismatic Books
P.O. Drawer 3100
Crestline, CA 92325-3100
909-338-6527

Heinoldt Books
1325 West Central Avenue
South Egg Harbor, NJ 08215
609-965-2284

J & J House
731 Unionville Road
Route 82, Box 919
Unionville, PA 19375
215-444-0490

James Cummins, Bookseller
699 Madison Avenue
New York, NY 10021
212-688-6441

James W. Beattie Rare Books
105 North Wayne Avenue
Wayne, PA 19087
215-687-3347

Julian J. Nadolny
121 Hickory Hill Road
Kensington, CT 06037
203-225-5353

Just Good Books
P.O. Box 232
Belgrade MT 59714-0232

Ken Andersen
P.O. Box 621
Auburn, MA 01501
508-832-3527

Knollwood Books
P.O. Box 197
Oregon, WI 53575-0197
608-835-8861

L. & T. Resspess Books
P.O. Box 1604
Charlottesville, VA 22902
804-293-3553

L. W. Currey, Inc.
Water Street Box 187
Elizabethtown, NY 12932
518-873-6477

Leif Laudamus
752 Greenfield Road
Leyden, MA 01301-9418
413-774-5722

Lyders Fine Books
P.O. Box 250
Peacham, VT 05862
802-592-3086

Monroe Street Books
Dick and Flanzy Chodkowski
7 Monroe Street
Middlebury, VT 05753
802-388-1622

Mordita Books
P.O. Box 79322
Houston, TX 77279
713-467-4280

Nouveau Rare Books
P.O. Box 12471
5005 Meadows Oak Park Drive
Jackson, MS 39211

Orpheus Books
11522 N.E. 20th Street
Bellevue, WA 98004-3005
360-776-4912

Peninsula Books
451 North Madison
Traverse City, MI 49684-2112
1-800-530-6737

Poor Richard's Books, Ltd.
968 Balmoral Road
Victoria B.C., Canada V8T 1AB
604-384-4411

Richard Adelson Antiquarian
Booksellers
Jane and Richard Adelson
HC 69 Box 23
North Pomfret, VT 05053
802-457-2608

Roy C. Kulp
Handwritten Americana
Box 264
Hatfield, PA 19440
215-362-0732

Rudolph Wm. Sabbat
6821 Babcock Avenue
N. Hollywood, CA 91605
818-982-4911

Ruth Woods
Oriental Books & Art
266 Arch Road
Englewood, NJ 07631
201-567-0149

Second Life Books, Inc.
P.O. Box 242, 55 Quarry Road
Lanesborough, MA 01237
413-447-8010

Stan Clark Military Books
915 Fairview Avenue
Gettysburg, PA 17325
717-337-1728

Steve Finer
Box 758
Greenfield, MA 01302
413-773-5811

The Eloquent Page
Donna and Marilyn Howard
21 Catherine Street
St. Albans, VT 05478
802-527-7243

The Inquisitive Sportsman
Books
Box 1811
Granite Falls, WA 98252
360-691-7540

The Printer's Shop
4546 El Camino Real B10 #207
Los Altos, CA 94022
415-941-0433

The Unique Antique
Jonathan Flaccus
P.O. Box 485 Main Street
Putney, VT 05346
802-387-4488

Thomas Cullen
Rockland Bookman
Box 134
Cattaraugus, NY 14719
716-257-9116

Trotting Hill Park Books
P.O. Box 1324
Springfield, MA 01101
413-567-6466

William L. Parkinson, Books
P.O. Box 40
Hinesburg, VT 05461
802-482-3113

RECOMMENDED PERIODICALS AND RESEARCH SOURCES

AB Bookman's Weekly. P.O. Box AB. Clifton, NJ 07015. This weekly magazine is arguably the most valuable single source of information currently available for the serious bookman. It includes articles and commentary on specialty markets and personalities in the business, as well as an extensive advertising section of want lists and books for sale. May be the most widely disseminated magazine in the trade, seen all over the world by more dealers and collectors than any other current publication in the field.

AB Bookman's Yearbook. P.O. Box AB, Clifton, NJ 07015. This treasure is included in the package when subscribing to the weekly magazine, or it can be bought separately. Its features include: bookseller associations directory, geographical listings of dealers, categorical listings of dealers, dealers' permanent want lists, directories of specialty publishers, remainder houses, bookselling services, directories of auction houses, information about foreign dealers, and advertisements.

Ahearn, Allen. *Book Collecting.*
   A guide to values for the first book by an author.

Ahearn, Allen and Patricia. *Collected Books: The Guide to Value.* This guide offers information identifying first editions of books in hand.

American Book Prices Current. Box 1236, Washington, CT 06793. The annual compilation of realized prices of books sold at auction. It lists sales of $50 or more. While an excellent investment, the volumes are expensive; your best bet is to find a good library that carries this source in the reference department.

Antiquarian Booksellers Association of America (ABAA). *Membership Directory.* 50 Rockefeller Plaza, New York, NY 10020. A comprehensive listing of dealers in the association. This may overlap the directories in the *AB Bookman's Yearbook* somewhat, but it is more complete and well worth the price.

Barlow, Ron, and Ray Reynolds. *The Insider's Guide to Old Books, Magazines, Newspapers and Trade Catalogs.* Windmill Publishing Co., El Cajon, CA 92020.

Baumgarten, Lee E. *Price Guide for Children's and Illustrated Books for the Years 1850–1960.* 718 1/2 W. John Street, Martinsburg, WV 25401.

Book Seminars, Inc. P.O. Box 660, Lodi, NJ 07644-0660. Seminar-Workshops on the Out-of-Print and Antiquarian Book Market. Contact for information and application forms.

Bookman's Price Index. Gale Research Inc., Detroit, MI 48226-4094. A pricing resource.

Broadfoot, Tom. *Civil War Books.* Broadfoot Publishing Company, 1907 Buena Vista Circle, Wilmington, NC 28405.

Howes, Wright, ed. *US-Iana.* R. R. Bowker Co., New York, NY. A bibliography of books on the United States.

Mandeville, Mildred. *The Used Book Price Guide.* P.O. Box 82525, Kenmore, WA 98028. "Mandeville" has been a standard for dealers for decades, offering extensive lists of books and current prices, but subject to the usual cautions as to errors or fluctuations in the markets that pertain to any regularly produced price guides.

Mattson, E. Christian, and Thomas B. Davis. *A Collector's Guide to Hard Cover Boy's Series Books 1872–1993.* Mad Book Co. 273 Pollydrummond Rd., Newark, DE 19711. (302) 738-0532.

McBride, Bill. *Identification of First Editions—A Pocket Guide.* Hartford, CT 06105. Pointers for identifying first editions from various publishers over the years.

Muir, P. H. *Book Collecting As a Hobby.* Out of print, but worth finding.

Seagrave, Ronald R. *Civil War Books, Confederate and Union.* Sgt. Kirkland's Museum and Historical Society, Inc., 912 Lafayette Boulevard, Fredericksburg, VA 22401-5617.

Synsine Press. Box 6422, Rheem Valley, CA 94570. Children's series books.

Zempel, E. and L. A. Verkler (eds). *Book Prices Used and Rare.* Spoon River Press, 2319-C West Rohmann, Peoria, IL, 61604-5072. A price guide.

ABOUT THE AUTHORS

PAT GOUDEY started out thirty years ago to become an English teacher and writer, then switched her college major to psychology. As fate would have it, she became a writer after all. Her first experience in the publishing trade came with a job as an editorial assistant in the college text department of Prentice-Hall, Inc., in Englewood Cliffs, New Jersey, where she learned about editing and publishing up close.

While her children were growing, she worked as a newspaper reporter for the community weekly, *The Sharon Advocate*, in Sharon, Massachusetts, moving up to managing editor before leaving to establish an editorial service, write magazine features, and put together the first edition of *The Official Price Guide to Old Books* with her partner (and mother), Marie Tedford.

After a two-year detour as Assistant to the General Manager of a performing arts center in Foxboro, Massachusetts, where she worked on a broad spectrum of projects including public relations, graphic arts, advertising, audience services, and contract issues, she returned to writing full-time.

Married and the mother of two grown sons, she currently works with her father, editor Ted Tedford, on the community weekly newspaper *The Mountain Villager*, in Underhill, Vermont. She also maintains an office, The Editorial Resource Center, in Warren, Vermont.

Ever since MARIE TEDFORD was old enough to get lost in her local library, she has had a passion for books. She started out as a bookscout for John Westerberger, the Yankee Peddler, in Rochester, NY, twenty-some years ago. One cold day in January, the worse month of the winter, Marie and a small band of intrepid Vermont booksellers negotiated snow-packed roads to the town of Ludlow and began the Vermont Antiquarian Booksellers Association. Learning the book trade is a never-ending journey, Marie says, no plateaus, only heights to soar. When she isn't beating the bushes for books, she writes non-fiction and has written three children's books for an educational publisher. She lives in Underhill Center, Vermont, with her husband, Ted, and their daughter Laurie. Currently another daughter, Paula, and her family, which includes two lively little boys, are sharing the Tedfords' country house. Marie is a general bookseller and her bookroom is open by appointment or chance.